THE
SECRET
OF THE
INCAS

THE SECRET OF THE INCAS

MYTH, ASTRONOMY, AND THE WAR AGAINST TIME

William Sullivan

THREE RIVERS PRESS
New York

Grateful acknowledgment is made to the following for permission to reprint previously published material:

Beacon Press: 10 lines from *The Broken Spears* by Miguel León-Portilla. Copyright © 1962, 1992 by Miguel León-Portilla. Reprinted by permission of Beacon Press.

Blackwell Publishers: excerpt from *The Tiwanaku: Portrait of an Andean Civilization* by Alan Kolata. Used by permission of Blackwell Publishers.

Cambridge University Press: excerpt from *Peruvian Prehistory* by Richard W. Keatinge, editor. Reprinted by permission of Cambridge University Press.

Paulist Press: excerpt from *Native Meso-American Spirituality* by Miguel León-Portilla. Copyright © by Miguel León-Portilla. Reprinted by permission of Paulist Press.

Theosophical University Press: excerpts from *Esotericism of the Popol Vuh: The Sacred History of the Quiche-Maya* by Raphael Girard, translated from the Spanish by Blair A. Moffett (original Spanish title: *Esoterisimo del Popol Vuh*). Published by Theosophical University Press in 1979. Reprinted by permission of Theosophical University Press.

University of Oklahoma Press: excerpt from *Aztec Thought and Culture: A Study of the Ancient Nahuatl Mind* by Miguel León-Portilla, translated by Jack Emory Davis. Copyright © 1963 by the University of Oklahoma Press.

University of Texas Press: excerpts from *The Huarochiri Manuscript: A Testament of Ancient and Colonial Andean Religion*, translated and edited by Frank Salomon and George L. Urioste. Copyright © 1991 by Frank Salomon and George L. Urioste. Excerpt from *At the Crossroads of the Earth and Sky: An Andean Cosmology* by Gary Urton. Copyright © 1981 by Gary Urton. Reprinted by permission of the University of Texas Press.

Published by Three Rivers Press, 201 East 50th Street, New York, New York 10022. Member of the Crown Publishing Group.
Originally published in hardcover by Crown Publishers, Inc., 1996.
First paperback edition printed in 1997.

Random House, Inc. New York, Toronto, London, Sydney, Auckland
http://www.randomhouse.com/

THREE RIVERS PRESS and colophon are trademarks of Crown Publishers, Inc.

Printed in the United States of America

Design by Deborah Kerner

Library of Congress Cataloging-in-Publication Data
Sullivan, Francis, 1946–
The secret of the Incas: myth, astronomy, and the war against
time / William Sullivan.
Includes bibliographical references and index.
1. Inca mythology. 2. Inca astronomy. 3. Inca philosophy.
I. Title
F3429.3.R3S85. 1996
984'.01—dc20   95-34627
ISBN: 0-517-88851-3

3   5   7   9   10   8   6   4

In Memory of
John and Elizabeth Bennett

ACKNOWLEDGMENTS

I MUST THANK the Roothbert Fund and the generosity of Josh Reynolds and Melissa McCleod for financial support of my research.

The late Douglas Gifford, my supervisor at the University of St. Andrews, went out on a limb for me more than once, seeing to it that neither my own shortcomings nor academic skepticism scuttled the investigation. I was equally fortunate in being able to work with Leslie Hoggarth, my Quechua teacher, whose thirty years in Peru had given him not only mastery of the language but a love and respect for those who speak it.

Owen Gingerich of the Harvard-Smithsonian Astrophysical Observatory made it possible for me, a stranger, to use the Hayden Planetarium in Boston, and took the time to observe and comment on the experiments. Edwin Krupp, Claudette Columbus, William Isbell, and Johanna Broda have all chosen to look past perfectly reasonable reservations about this research in order to encourage the spirit of exploration.

While by no means agreeing with everything I have written, Hertha von Dechend and David Kelley have stood by me in good times and bad. The support and friendship of these two people have meant more to me than I can say.

At a time when I had become resigned to the idea of never getting published, the fates put me in touch with a first-class agent, Richard McDonough, who not only walked me through the process of writing a proposal, but then proceeded to produce a book contract so fast it made my head precess. But for his help, this book would have remained an unrealized dream.

My editor, Peter Ginna, believed in this project from the proposal stage onward. As the beneficiary of his consistently intelligent questions and criticisms, I learned early on that having him to work with was an amazing stroke of luck. I am grateful for his help in shaping this book.

More friends than I can possibly mention have helped and encouraged me over the years. Among them are Tony Blake, Kim Jobst, Ladd Bauer, Bill Bleak, Jerry Toporovsky, Bob Machin, John Speed, Terry Reed, Bruce Wilson, the Millers River Morris Men, and their (clearly) better halves.

My wife, Penelope, and my children, Jonathan and Phoebe, as well as my mother and my sisters, Christine and Mary, have all behaved as if it were perfectly normal for a husband, father, son, and brother to spend enormous amounts of time with his eyes closed, trying to imagine the movements of the stars. Without the island of stability they create, I could never have written this book.

My thanks to all.

CONTENTS

THE
SECRET
OF THE
INCAS

CHAPTER 1

THE MYTH OF
PREHISTORY

*Sight, then, in my judgment is the cause of the highest benefits to us in that no word
of our present discourse about the universe could ever have been spoken, had we never
seen stars, Sun, and sky. But as it is, the sight of day and night, of months and the
revolving years, of equinox and solstice, has caused the invention of number, and
bestowed on us the notion of time and the study of the nature of the world; whence we
have derived all philosophy, than which no greater boon has ever come or shall come
to mortal man as a gift from heaven.*

—PLATO
TIMAEUS

I

WHEN I FIRST began to read the history of the Inca Empire, I was surprised
to learn that it had existed for less than a century before being utterly
destroyed by the Spanish Conquistadores. More startling still were the genu-
inely peculiar circumstances surrounding the demise of this South American
kingdom, an empire built by military conquest, which stretched down the
spine of the Andes from modern-day Colombia to southern Chile, and from
the Pacific coast to the eastern foothills of the Andes. Into the midst of this
mighty state, a Spanish expeditionary force of 170 adventurers blundered,
late in the year of 1532, and succeeded in subjugating an empire of some six
million souls.[1]

Were this story fiction, it would be considered the product of a baroque
imagination.[2] Here were the Spanish, led by Francisco Pizarro, by now a
hardened adventurer, who had left behind the cold, arid plateaus of his
native Extremadura in Spain at the age of fourteen, to follow the lure of
gold. Like their leader, these men were impoverished *hidalgos*—of warrior

lineages too proud for manual labor, but too obscure for service with the king—men whose not-so-distant ancestors had been the scourge of the Saracens. These were the Spanish Tercios, the most feared fighters in Europe. Proud, reckless, armored in lightweight steel mesh, astride enormous war-horses, and wielding swords of tempered Toledo steel, they were the Hell's Angels of Europe, fearless, dashing, ruthless—and poor.

Pizarro understood his men. Having at last landed on the northern coast of Peru after several failed expeditions, and after a few weeks of indecisive skirmishes and raids that turned up trinkets of gold and tales of more—in the Empire in the mountains—Pizarro saw that he had no choice but to strike boldly into the heart of the unknown. His men could endure great physical hardship, fear, uncertainty, and danger, but a wavering of purpose would be unsupportable. The great historian William Prescott remarked of the Conquistadores that one could not understand the Spanish role in the Conquest of Peru, unless one understood that the Spanish were not hypocrites. For them the quest for God, gold, and glory was a seamless endeavour.

Thus motivated, 120 horsemen and fifty foot soldiers began their ascent of the Andean massif. What they did not know, as they climbed, was that the climactic battle of a great civil war was being fought above them. For a number of years two brothers, Huascar and Atahuallpa—sons of the last great Inca, Huayna Capac, who died in about 1525 of smallpox, which raged through the native population all the way from the Caribbean—had been engaged in a bitter war of succession. The faction loyal to Huascar was centered in southern Peru in the capital city of Cuzco. Atahuallpa's adherents came from Quito, a city built and much loved by Huayna Capac, who had died there.

The Spaniards' advance had been watched from the moment of their landing on the north coast. Greatly preoccupied with civil war, Atahuallpa dispatched an ambassador to Pizarro's strange contingent only after several weeks. The ambassador invited Pizarro to meet with the Inca at Cajamarca, very near the Spanish line of march. Pizarro agreed. The Spanish climbed an Inca trail so vertiginous that they could have been annihilated at a dozen spots along it, the advantages of horses being nil in such terrain. They ascended unmolested.

In the afternoon of the fifteenth day of November, 1532, Pizarro's men entered the broad, fertile valley of Cajamarca. Nothing in their experience since arriving in the New World could have prepared them for the shock of what they saw. A mile to their right lay the tents of an encamped army of forty thousand men.

Their recourse was bravado. They invested the small walled town, which contained a "convent" of the Virgins of the Sun, and then sent emissaries to the Inca. The first two Europeans to see the Son of the Sun were Hernando De Soto and Pizarro's brother Hernando. They rode boldly into the center of the encamped army, bragged of their military prowess, declined the Inca's offers of hospitality, and invited him to meet Francisco Pizarro on the morrow. Atahuallpa agreed to come the following morning. The two Hernandos wheeled their horses and sped away.

That night, desperate, the Spanish decided that their only hope of salvation lay in capturing the Inca. When he came, they would invite him to dine. If he declined, they would attack. The walled compound of Cajamarca had porticoes on three sides—cover for the horses—a wall with a gate opening onto the plain, and a small blockhouse in the midst of the open plaza. Pizarro ordered the artillery pieces placed within this structure. They would signal an attack, if necessary.

Few men slept that night. Many went to confession. Others wrote last letters home, or wills. Some men gambled; some wept. When the morning finally broke, the tension was extraordinary, yet all through the interminable hours of the forenoon, there was no sign of the Inca. In the early afternoon, the Inca army began to fill the plain. This process took several hours, hours in which the Spanish had time to reckon the odds. At last the Inca emerged, borne on a palanquin. An escort of six thousand unarmed men funneled through the entrance into the plaza. At this point, by prearrangement, a Spanish priest came forward to greet the Inca with the Requirement, the Inquisition's version of Miranda rights, informing the god-king that if he submitted to the king of Spain and the Holy Roman Church, no harm would befall him.

The Inca replied that the Spanish must return all goods stolen and consumed since their landing. The priest responded by offering a Bible. Curious, Atahuallpa examined it, apparently amazed at his inability to rub the print from the page. The Emperor then became furious, perhaps because his royal composure had momentarily been disrupted by this fascination with the priest's book. Atahuallpa hurled the Bible to the ground. The priest proclaimed, "It is the Antichrist." Pizarro signaled the artillery, which fired off two shots.

Then from every portico in the compound at Cajamarca thundered Spanish destriers, war-horses bred for size and nerve, animals whose chests bore down at eye level upon their foes. Rattles had been tied to the horses. The wind keened through the jingling chain mail. The *hidalgos* raised their war cry, "Santiago y a los!" ("St. James and at them!"), and fell upon the astonished and unarmed honor guard, aiming straight for the Inca.

Within five minutes the Inca had been seized. Countless Inca nobles gave their lives trying to shore up his litter, but they were simply dismembered in a flash of steel. When the Inca was seized, so great was the panic among the remaining guard that when they fell upon the lone, narrow exit, their sheer weight knocked down the six-foot-thick adobe wall. The view for the Inca army, out on the plain, was one of pandemonium. Their comrades were fleeing for their lives, pursued by 120 warriors whose mounts clambered over mounds of suffocated dead. The Inca army broke and ran. The Spanish rode out onto the plain at Cajamarca in hot pursuit. They killed until it was too dark to see. It is estimated that they killed about seven thousand men and seriously wounded as many as ten thousand more.

The Inca was held for a ransom of gold. From that point onward, a combination of luck, guile, and determination guided the Spanish star. Within a few years, and with gold-hungry reinforcements pouring in from Panama, all resistance to the Spanish was destroyed. The mightiest empire that the western hemisphere had ever seen had fallen to a force of less than two hundred men.

I remember thinking, when I first read of these events—in Hemming's *Conquest of the Incas*—"How could this happen?" One is accustomed to think of destiny as somehow more subtle. At the time I shrugged inwardly, never expecting an answer. I had other questions on my mind.

II

FROM A VERY young age, I have been drawn to the past. Some of this must have to do with the experience, common to a generation, of being born in the shadow of Hiroshima, an event that colored even the most commonplace of childhood pursuits. The attempt to construct a bow and arrow would become the occasion for an extended reverie on impermanence. How did the Native Americans know what wood to use, how to make the arrowhead, how to fix it on the shaft? As I sat beneath tall oaks, I would picture the gracious lawns of my hometown gone back to forest, back in time to days long ago. Where did they camp? How did they get water? How did they make the tools that made their tools? Because, if you thought about it— seeing this summer-drowsy suburb gone back to the wild—you might just as well be looking at the future as the past. Roads sprouting trees. No factories. No plumbing. It could happen. I wondered if any of the neighbors knew how to work deer sinew into bowstring. I was too young even to laugh at the prospect. Irony is a modern survival skill, and an adult one. The cicadas hummed and the squirrels jabbered high up in the oaks. By comparison, their purchase on the world seemed suddenly secure. They carried all they needed to know in their bodies. It was we people who were out on a limb.

It would be many years before I realized that myth speaks directly to this perception. Human culture is not natural, and the hard-won truths of millennia can of a sudden become as vulnerable as orchids in the snow. What I was aware of, as a child, was a world of artifacts—refrigerators, cars, sprinklers, bulldozers. They made me uneasy. You could use them, but you couldn't make them. So I communed with an imaginary presence, some wise elder who, for all that I dressed him in a superfluity of buckskin fringe and tacky beadwork, nonetheless knew what was essential.

Myth is a vessel designed and fitted for essential cargo. There is no room on board for the coarse, the dross, the chaff, because human memory is finite, and myth is orally transmitted. Myth is an ark, whose builders had one and only one concern, the welfare of future generations. They were the grownups, the ones who recognized what the Chinese call "interesting times" for what they were, and prepared for the flood. They were willing to change, to shed the husk of outworn times before it strangled the inner seed, which was the knowledge of what it takes to remain human. They fashioned the ark of myth to save this knowledge from inundation beneath the floodwaters of Time. They were intimate with risk.

Myths of the end of the world are ubiquitous. The tradition of the creation and destruction of successive "worlds" exists both to tell us something about the past and to validate the intuition that there can be times when the conditions of ordinary existence carry an urgent message. This ancient tradition of successive Ages of the World acknowledges the existence of those rare times, millennial times, when whole ways of life perish and new worlds are born. At such times there is a tension in the air. The familiar and what has yet to be conceived do battle for primacy on the field of the human heart. Hence, lurid images abound, cast up upon the screen of consciousness: Kali, goddess of creation and destruction, the beneficent Earth Mother with a necklace of skulls. You can't make an omelette without breaking some eggs.

At such times, facts may unexpectedly take on a new intensity and, like subatomic rubble in a cloud chamber, collide, releasing energy and creating new events:

- In the United States of America, roughly 80 percent of those who visit a doctor's office are ill because their immune system has been damaged by stress.
- Carl Jung expressed concern at how profoundly unaware North Americans are of the presence in their collective unconscious of the Native American legacy.
- The number of people now alive represent more than the total of all people in all times who have lived and died up to now, and there will be 9 billion of us within forty years.
- Several times in this century people have discovered, independently, that illiterate bards in remote regions continue to sing, virtually verbatim, large sections of mythic poems such as the *Epic of Gilgamesh* and the *Iliad*, a transmission of ideas across five thousand years of time, without the use of writing.
- In the ambit between animal ethology and human psychology, it is now well established that of all the higher organisms, humans manifest the greatest resistance to change, preferring to repeat over and over behaviors that lead to results undesirable from the point of view of the subject.

This book is a product of its time. It could not have been written even thirty years ago; it depends too heavily on recent information and recent information technology. And, as I have tried to indicate, it also depends on a particular emotional perception, one that I now believe is itself the product of interesting times. This feeling includes a sense of loss—bordering on dismay—about the indifference of the contemporary world to the past. There is in this perception a sort of subtle pressure from the past: "Do not lose us, do not forget us, those who have gone before—not because we need you (though we may), but because *you* need *us* now." And implicit in that message is a promise: that somewhere, in some domain that is accessible, the past *must* exist available to the present, simply because those who have gone before us would have willed it so.

This book would never have been written, had not a friend handed me two other books in two weeks in 1974. In those volumes lay information that reawakened in me this long dormant feeling about the past, and transformed it into full-blown curiosity.

The first of these was Alexander Marshack's *The Roots of Civilization*, a study suggesting a completely unsuspected interpretation of a certain class of Ice Age artifacts. The story of the evolution of Marshack's book is, in its own way, as instructive as its discoveries.

A science writer, Marshack had been hired by the National Aeronautics and Space Administration to produce an account of how humankind had come to the threshold of a lunar landing. Marshack found several pages of the first chapter, in which he proposed to trace the origin of humanity's interest in the moon, impossible to write because of, as he put it, all the "suddenlies" concerning the appearance in the archaeological record—from Sumer, Egypt, and India—of sophisticated solar-lunar-stellar calendars related to agriculture. To his way of thinking, these achievements implied millennia of preparation. The only generalization Marshack was able to extract from his survey of the literature was that behind all these calendric systems lay an earlier calendric tradition based on lunar cycles.

Under the pressure of a deadline, and unable to write a satisfactory first chapter, Marshack picked up at random an article from *Scientific American* about a bone with incised scratches from Ishango, at the headwaters of the Nile, dating from about 6500 B.C. The author of the article concluded that the scratches probably represented "an arithmetical game," perhaps having to do with multiplying by two.[3] Finding this explanation unsatisfactory, because it implied no purpose for the markings, Marshack was struck by the thought that these scratches must represent some sort of notation, some sort of "storied meaning." Following this line of thought, he pushed the NASA moon manuscript to one side, and decided to see if the pattern of scratches bore any resemblance to lunar periods. Within fifteen minutes he came to see that it was possible that his hypothesis was correct, and that it was impossible to rule it out.

Years of research in museums all over Europe into incised Ice Age bones were required before Marshack could publish his results, which confirmed his initial flash of insight. *The Roots of Civilization* demonstrates that since the arising of our genotype, *Homo sapiens sapiens*, some forty millennia ago, attention to the measurement of periods of time as manifested by celestial bodies and motions has been an activity as persistently and widely pursued by people as the getting of food or the making of tools.

III

THE SECOND BOOK was *Hamlet's Mill* by Giorgio de Santillana, a professor of the History of Science at MIT and Hertha von Dechend, in the same field at Wolfgang Goethe University in Frankfurt. The thrust of this book was that myth, on one level, represented what they called a "technical language" designed to record and transmit astronomical observations of great complexity, particularly those connected with the precession of the equinoxes. In fact this study—styled by the authors as a "first reconnaissance" into an ancient philosophical system based on a particular kind of astronomical knowledge disseminated throughout all areas of "high culture" around the planet—appeared to describe just that knowledge whose loss, at about the time of Plato, was lamented by Aristotle.

Again, the evolution of this work is worth recounting. The discoveries were Dechend's. As a graduate student in the history of science in Frankfurt, she was interested to learn more about the *deus faber*, the creator, or fabricator god found in so many cultures as the genius of civilized arts. Her particular interest lay in Polynesian myth, and, after making her way through ten thousand pages of primary materials, she reached a single, immutable conclusion: that she understood nothing whatsoever of what she had read.

At this point, astronomy was the last topic on Dechend's mind. In fact, at the time of her graduate work, various scholarly attempts to understand myth in terms of astronomy had already foundered. For example, Max Muller's "solar hypothesis,"[4] which sought to "explain" the Vedas in terms of an overarching schema of solar astronomy, was very popular at first, but soon fell into disrepute when it became obvious that such a structure could not bear the full weight of the rich Vedic texts. Then there was the work of Alfred Jeremias (1929). Although Jeremias had a number of uncanny insights into the astronomical level of myth, his mercurial temperament, combined with a tendency to state as fact hypothetical dates with which archaeology could not concur, led to the eclipse not only of his work, but of the very idea that myth and astronomy had anything to do with each other.

It was in this atmosphere, and with a strict intention to have nothing whatsoever to do with astronomy, that Dechend persevered with the Polynesian material. She immersed herself now in the secondary sources, looking for something—anything—that might provide a way into the Polynesian mind. Then came a day when she was occupied with trying to understand a minor mystery of Polynesian archaeology: why two islands, separated by three thousand miles of open water, should be strewn with dozens of "temples" of a design not found elsewhere. She consulted an atlas and noticed something that had not been noticed before—or rather, not for a very long time. One island lay on the Tropic of Cancer, and the other on the Tropic of Capricorn. It was then that, with the utmost reluctance, she muttered to herself, "Ech, astronomy!" Transmission received.

Her subsequent work would lead her to discover an extraordinarily wide distribution in cultures all over the world of a particular set of verbal conventions designed to encrypt astronomical observations within myth. She found that the central preoccupation of those myths was the phenomenon known as the precession of the equinoxes. The precession is a slow wobble of the earth's axis that causes the earth slowly but continuously to change its orientation within the sphere of fixed stars. This motion is very much like that of a gyroscope, which, after a time, heels over and, spinning all the while, begins slowly to wobble on its axis. A single such precessional wobble of the earth's axis requires 26,000 years to complete.

To get an idea how precession might appear to the naked eye, imagine that some time-traveler had undertaken to photograph the stars rising in the east just before sunrise on spring equinox in Jerusalem, each year from the birth of Christ to the present. If those photos were put together in sequence, one would have a motion picture of the constellation Pisces *setting in the east,* with the constellation Aquarius "descending," that is, also being pulled eastward to replace Pisces as the constellation marking the spring equinox (see figures 1.1a and 1.1b). Thus, "this is the dawning of the age of Aquarius."

Perhaps the most important contribution of *Hamlet's Mill* is its explication of the conventions of the technical language whereby myth transmits information concerning precessional motion. There are three simple rules. First, *animals are stars.* (Our word *zodiac* comes from the Greek meaning "dial of animals.") Second, *gods are planets.* And finally, *topographic references are metaphors for locations—usually of the sun—on the celestial sphere.*

The very "earth" itself, as we shall see in due course, lies in the stars, between the tropics of Cancer and Capricorn. And all the millennia of myths from around the world recounting the destruction of that world by flood, fire, earthquake, and so on—far from representing an ignorance of geological processes—"re-count" the solar year in terms of the "destruction" (via the passage of precessional time) of the old stars marking the solstices and equinoxes and the "creation" of a new "world" whose parameters are determined by the new stars, or "pillars," now upholding the "earth" at the solstices and equinoxes. This "earth," of course, is "flat," again, not as a matter of ignorance, but of *terminology,* a means of describing the ideal plane, the ecliptic, "supported" by the four "pillars." And all the "animals" in Noah's Ark did survive the "flood" when they landed on Ararat, the "highest mountain on earth," itself a term describing a particular position of the sun on the celestial sphere.

IV

THE IDEAS IN *Hamlet's Mill* staggered me. The book stood conventional notions of "prehistory" on their head. For practical purposes, the definition of prehistory as "before recorded events," has always hinged on the presence of a written record. Prehistory means pre-writing. This definition dismisses the possibility of any means other than writing for transmitting important information from the past, and thereby creates the impression that such transmission was not a priority for our forebears. *Hamlet's Mill* was making the startling assertion that the apparent gulf between history and prehistory was a figment of the modern imagination, a failure of faith with those who had gone before, a product of the "deteriorated expectations of our time."[5]

For me this book was a kind of food, nourishing my all-but-forgotten childhood intuitions about the interplay between past and present. More than that, I felt that I was looking—as if through the glass of a museum case —at the comprehensive tool kit, the very nuts and bolts, used by "prehistoric" humanity to fashion a critical component of human consciousness and transmit it unalloyed into the deep future. The implications of *Hamlet's Mill* appeared to me nothing short of revolutionary:

- Embedded within myths were astronomical observations at least as accurate as carbon dates, thus enabling investigators to compare the content of myths so dated with the archaeological record.
- Was it not possible that myth represented the "software" that would show us how to run the "hardware" of ancient astronomical monuments?
- Was it not possible that the term *prehistory* was a misnomer if oral tradition possessed the means to transmit not only the seminal philosophical ideas of the human race, but the precise skies (i.e., time) that inspired these thoughts?
- And, as a consequence, did not a completely unsuspected history of the human race—in the form of the recorded myths of ancient and contemporary "prehistoric" (nonliterate) peoples—lie gathering dust in libraries around the world?

I simply had to know if these ideas were true.

As I cast about for a means of learning more, I was disappointed— though not surprised—to learn that these works, published in 1972 (Marshack) and 1969 (Santillana), had had virtually no impact on the scholarly community. This is not to say that they were belittled. No less an authority than the late Mircea Eliade praised both, but something in the temper of the times was not receptive. Thus, for example, it remains a "fact" for historians of science that Hipparchus discovered the precession of the equinox ca. 125 B.C., working from written records.

An incident that captures something of the modern incomprehension of the uses of myth, and one that particularly amused Dechend, occurred in the late seventies, when Soviet authorities registered heated protests against a proposed American expedition to Mount Ararat—in Turkey, near the sensitive border with Soviet Armenia—to search for Noah's Ark. Assuming that no one could be that stupid, the Soviets reasoned that the expedition must be a cover for establishing an electronic listening post.

One electronic listening post that was established in the seventies was the giant parabolic radio telescope, more than half a mile wide, built into a hillside in Arecibo, Puerto Rico. Designed to monitor radio waves from deep space, the Arecibo antenna has been used, among other purposes, to scan the heavens for signs of intelligent life.

From the present perspective, the ground at Arecibo is fertile with ironies. To begin with, there is the assumption that any source transmission worth spending money on finding must emanate from beyond our solar system. Anyone capable of reaching us by these means must be "advanced." Of course such putative sources must themselves lie in the deep past, thousands of light-years away—just not in *our* past. For all we know, they are signaling *us* for help. This use of the Arecibo antenna reveals the discouraging and seldom questioned contemporary assumption that the past of some group of unknown aliens has got to be of more use to us than our own. According to this view, Wisdom, the angel who danced at the feet of the Lord, has never evinced much interest in planet Earth.

Arecibo, incidentally, was named after the chief of the tribe of indigenous peoples who lived at the site of the present city. Those of his people who were not killed by European diseases were worked to death, along with their chief, by Spaniards anxious to have a road built to connect them with the rest of the island. No one ever asked, nor will we ever know, anything whatsoever about this group of people, other than the general remarks by Columbus that the people of these large islands were the happiest, healthiest, most prosperous, most generous people he had ever encountered.

Later, in 1611, Arecibo was incorporated by the Spanish governor, who named it San Felipe de Arecibo, after the Apostle Philip, whose name is attached to the Gnostic Gospel of the Nag Hammadi texts. Until the discovery of these texts in 1945, the only extant fragment of this Gospel, found in Epiphanus, involved instructions for the souls of the dead: "The Lord revealed to me what the soul must say when she mounts to heaven, and how she must answer each of the powers above." So the hills of Arecibo, where the dish antenna awaits a message from some distant planet, teem with the ghosts of a bygone transmission that we will never receive.

V

THIS BOOK IS the story of an experiment—of the deployment, if you will, of an antenna designed to pick up transmissions from beyond the veil of "prehistory." I chose to try focusing this device on Andean civilization for several reasons. First of all, so far as is known, there was no system of writing in the Andes in, or before, the Inca Empire.[6] Andean civilization was classically "prehistoric," relying on oral tradition for the transmission of knowledge.

Second, this knowledge survived intact until relatively recently. Although the Spanish felt that their civilization was superior, they nonetheless had a great curiosity about every aspect of Inca life. The early priests, soldiers, and administrators of the Spanish Crown, for various reasons both professional and private, wrote down an enormous amount of information about this Bronze Age empire, alive and well into the sixteenth century. Collectively these documents are known as the Spanish Chronicles, and they contain a wealth of myth.

Third, for myself, I just wanted to know if it could be done—making contact with the past by the means suggested in *Hamlet's Mill*. And since that book stipulated that the technical language of myth will be found anywhere in the "band of high culture," the Andes certainly seemed to qualify as an ideal, if somewhat stern, venue for testing all these ideas.

Although the views put forward in this book concerning Andean civilization in general, and the dynamics of the Inca Empire in particular, are not to be found elsewhere, neither do they contradict what is already known. For example, the astronomical identifications employed throughout this work are based not only upon my own ethnoastronomical fieldwork in Peru and Bolivia during the late seventies,[7] but also on the earlier investigations of Pucher, Urton, and Zuidema.[8] The identities of the celestial objects described in the pages that follow are now well established. My findings were substantially the same as those of others. Where this book differs from the standard literature is in suggesting that these objects were employed in making astronomical observations over and above those related to the yearly agricultural and ritual calendar—observations undertaken, rather, to monitor the flow of time on the vast scale of precession.

Nor do the dates of the precessional events encrypted in Andean myth challenge the standard archaeological chronology or interpretation. To the contrary, the insights available from the astronomical level of the myths provide a complementary dimension of interpretation that enriches, and is at the same time supported by, the archaeological record. Still, I think it would be misleading not to make clear that the entire thrust of this book is emphatically distinct from the current overview of Andean and later Inca civilization, simply because it finds—at the very core of Andean social, intellectual, political, and religious sensibility—the influence of a complex astronomical cosmology whose very existence among any people has yet to be conceded by any academic discipline.

Therefore, much of what I have written in this book diverges in focus and emphasis from that of the scholarly literature. The idea that Andean myth recounts significant precessional events (chapter 2), or that the three worlds of Andean cosmology were understood, on one level, as locations on the celestial sphere, united by the Milky Way (chapter 3), though arguably ancient in the Andes, is news to Western scholarship. Similarly, the idea that the Andean peoples not only had names for all the planets visible to the unassisted eye, but associated them with important deities (chapters 4 and 5), runs completely counter to the orthodox view that the Andean peoples had never given names to any planet other than Venus.

In chapters 6 through 8, I have attempted to narrate how the ideas of this unknown Andean cosmology became one of the most important forces in the unfolding of Andean history. One thread that runs through these chapters, again not found in the literature, is how Andean myth records transformations that occurred in the social and celestial spheres simultaneously, and whose synchronous occurrence can be verified by recourse to the archaeological record on one hand, and planetarium and archaeoastronomical computer data on the other. This method of historical "triangulation" enables one to see precisely how the Andean peoples strove for millennia to base the social reality on specific celestial models.

Chapters 9 and 10 chronicle how this system of thought, already ancient when the Incas appeared on the stage of history in the early 1400s, became, in the hands of the Incas, a separate reality in its own right, the foremost justification and defining force in the unfolding of the Inca Empire. The title of this book alludes to the fundamental mission that the Incas felt obliged to execute. For me, these discoveries concerning the esoteric agenda of the Inca Empire were the most riveting—and disquieting—of all. Within the technical language of Andean myth lay the seeds not only of Inca greatness, but also of a vulnerability so comprehensive as to place the fate of a vast empire in the hands of fewer than two hundred interlopers.

This book is, above all, a work of history. It draws upon many disciplines, but always from the point of view of the irreducible historical question "What happened?" Among the assumptions that have allowed for the somewhat radical departure of this book from accepted ways of viewing the "prehistoric" Andean world, by far the most important is the notion that Andean myth was designed to transmit the past to the present. I now believe this assumption to have been valid, and for this reason I have come to believe that our contemporary notion of "prehistory" is obsolete.

The implication of this conclusion is so important that it has dictated the form of this book. I have attempted, in the pages that follow, to describe how I learned what I learned. As the reader will see, this entire process was possible because I eventually understood that the myths were so designed as to answer the questions they provoked. Over and over again, I found that apparently illogical elements in the myths seem to have been placed *specifically for the purpose of arousing further questions*. Each new difficulty of understanding that the myths presented had the uncanny habit of turning into a doorway. My own experience in dealing with these myths is that some very unusual spiritual perception, with deep insight into the operations of the human mind, stands behind their formulation.

It would be a pity if anyone with a love of myth should assume that this book purports to reduce myth to a sub-branch of astronomical observation. That is not my intention. It is my understanding that *some* myths function, on *one* level, to encode complex astronomical observations. The astronomical level of myth appears to me to operate as something like a particular line of music in a polyphonic score. In the chapters that follow, I have attempted to show how Andean myth interweaves celestial, social, political, religious, and spiritual elements into disarmingly simple and charming stories. Nonetheless, it would be disingenuous of me not to add, insofar as Andean myth is concerned, that the astronomical level of meaning appears to play a prominent role, the celestial backdrop being an important element in all the dramatic events of Andean history.

To my knowledge, this book represents the first in-depth monograph focusing on a single New World civilization that tests for the existence of a technical language of myth. There is no rule book that states how this should be done, and any reader has a right to be skeptical of a work that makes claims as sweeping as those of the present volume. After all, why shouldn't one take the resounding, collective silence of the scholarly community on the matter of the technical language of myth as the appropriately definitive statement?

I have addressed this question at some length in chapter 7, where I have tried to describe how and why anthropology and archaeology—the fields primarily concerned with the interpretation of "prehistory"—have, for perfectly innocent reasons, maintained a historic and built-in resistance to the notion of the widespread diffusion of important ideas, unless such ideas can be explained as "universal" or "independently invented." As will become clear, the technical language of myth is simply too idiosyncratic to have been reinvented independently over and over again. Therefore, if one concedes the existence of the technical language of myth, then one must also concede that anthropology and archaeology have systematically underestimated the range and significance of human interaction around the planet for at least the last six thousand years.

VI

RESEARCHING THIS BOOK was an adventure, one that began and ended with a single myth. Of its two extant versions, one, recorded by the Spanish priest Cristóbal de Molina ("el cuzqueño") about the year 1573, goes as follows:

> In the province of Ancasmarca, which is five leagues from Cuzco, in the Anti-suyu division, the Indians have the following fable.
>
> They say that a month before the flood came, their sheep [*llamas*] displayed much sadness, eating no food in the daytime, and watching the stars at night. At last the shepherd who had charge of them asked what ailed them, and they said that the conjunction of stars showed that the world would be destroyed by water. When he heard this, the shepherd consulted with his six children, and they agreed to collect all the food and sheep they could, and go to the top of a very high mountain called Ancasmarca. They say that as the waters rose, the hill grew higher, so that it was never covered by the flood; and when the waters subsided, the hill also grew smaller. Thus the six children of that shepherd returned to people the province. These and other tales are told, which I do not insert, to avoid prolixity. The chief cause of the invention of these fables, was the ignorance of God and the abandonment of these people to idolatries and vices. If they had known the use of writing, they would not have been so dull and blind.[9]

The Western inclination to view myth and oral tradition as a playground for arbitrary imagination has a long history.

Time and again as my research progressed, I returned to this story with renewed understanding. The more questions this story raised, the more

astonishing were the answers it prompted. I came to see that Santillana and
Dechend had written a very clever book indeed, but even as this realization
was sinking in, I was whisked through the looking glass into the indigenous
version of indigenous history, which began with the foundations of Andean
agricultural civilization and ended with the tragic playing out of a prophecy
that had inspired the formation of the Inca Empire even as it foretold its
destruction.

The other version of the myth, somewhat longer, is part of a larger
collection of myths, known today as *Gods and Men of Huarochirí*. This chronicle was initiated by a Spanish priest, Francisco de Avila, who wanted to
collect in Quechua, the original language of the inhabitants, the myths of
the region where he was assigned, with an eye toward using the information
as intelligence, for the purpose of destroying Andean religion. *Gods and Men
of Huarochirí* is the only complete myth cycle of an Andean people ever
recorded. Here is a translation of the version of the great flood as told by
some unknown native peasant to a native scribe, trained by Avila to translit-
erate the Quechua language by means of the Spanish alphabet. By so attenu-
ated a thread hangs the tale.

What they say is as follows: In ancient times this world was in danger
of disappearing. A male llama, who was pastured on a hill with excellent
fodder, knew that the Mother Sea had decided to overflow, to fall
down like a waterfall. This llama became very sad; he kept crying out
"in, in," and didn't eat. The llama's master, very angry, hit him with an
ear of maize. "Eat, dog," he said. "You are lying about on the best
pastures." Then the llama, speaking as if he were a man, told the
shepherd, "Pay very close attention, and remember what I am going to
tell you: Five days from now the great ocean will be here and the whole
world will be flooded." And the shepherd was stricken with fear; he
believed him [the llama]. "We will go somewhere to escape. Let us go
to Mount Vilcacoto; there we must save ourselves; bring food for five
days," he [?] ordered. And so, from that instant, he started walking,
taking his family and the llama. When he was about to reach the top
of Mount Vilcacoto, he found that all the animals were reunited: puma,
fox, huanaco, condor, every species of animal. Hardly had the man
arrived than the water began to fall in rivers; and so there they were,
squeezed together at the top of Huillcacoto, in a tiny space, at the very
peak, where the water couldn't quite reach. But the water did manage
to reach fox's tail and get it wet, which is why fox's tail, to this day, is
black. And after five days, the waters began to recede and dry up. The

dry part began to grow. The sea retreated more, and as it retreated and things dried out, it killed all the men. Only he of the mountain survived, and with him the rest of the people [family?] returned to multiply, and by him exists mankind today.[10]

VII

IN THE END, the key that unlocked for me the meaning of these and other Andean myths was one simple assumption: that myth has the power and intention to speak across vast gulfs of time. The following pages contain a version of the Andean past and of the advent of the Europeans that has never before been put in writing. I believe that this version represents a fair approximation of how the Andean mind perceived the Conquest of the New World. And if the chapters on the Incas represent tragic and unsettling findings, then perhaps they provide a fitting counterpoint to the events in Cajamarca.

The journey to these final chapters is a long one, for it encompasses nothing less than learning to read directly from myth the entire saga of the Andean peoples in their ascent from scattered bands of hunters to masters of one of the earth's most demanding ecosystems. In order that the reader may better appreciate the scope of this journey, rather than be overfaced by it, a few words of orientation are in order.

I have attempted to use the terms *Andean* and *Inca* consistently and in context. There is no general term, other than *Andean*, for the agricultural civilization that, as archaeological research has discovered, constituted the dominant life-way of the Andean highlands from about two centuries before the birth of Christ. The theme of this civilization—as myth confirms—was unity in diversity. Although there were very many tribes, languages, and customs within the Andean ecumene, there was, as I will try to show, a unifying religious view, one founded on a shared, astronomically based, cosmological vision. It is this civilization—for civilization it was, in every sense of the word—to which the word *Andean* refers. The Incas did not become a force in Andean life until early in the 1400s. Nonetheless they were, along with the other tribes of the Andes, direct heirs of Andean tradition. Therefore, there will be times in the book when, in using the term *Inca*, I am referring to evidence from the Spanish Chronicles specifically about the Incas, which is also evidence of the Andean tradition in which the Incas participated.

In the opening sections of chapter 2, I have attempted to give the reader some sense of the time-depth and drama of Andean culture history, beginning with the present and working backwards in time. With this background, it will be possible to appreciate better the significance and antiquity of the myths of the llama and the flood, which form the centerpiece of the chapter. As we shall see, the "world" destroyed in that flood ended nearly a millennium before the first Inca Emperor took the path of conquest. The myth of the llama and the flood describes celestial events that transpired in the seventh century A.D.

In the sequence of discoveries forming the narrative thread of this book, one moment stands out for me. That moment occurred as I pondered why, in the second version of the myth of the great flood, the llama was specified as male.

I remembered, for no apparent reason, that I knew of a Quechua word for the male alpaca, a member of the llama family, prized for its fine wool. This word is paqo. Then there was a moment of confusion, because I had never before noticed that this word and the word for "shaman" are the same. The paqo, or male alpaca, in the myth was a shaman. As the significance of this realization dawned on me, a passage from the Chronicles came to mind that described in detail the behavior of the Andean priest-astronomer:

> His life was a religious one, of great abstinence; he never ate meat, only herbs and roots, along with the customary bread of maize. His house was in the countryside, very rarely in town; he spoke little; his dress was common, plain, of wool, but decent, down to the knees . . . and over this a very long mantle, gray, or black, or purple; he drank no wine, but always only water. The life in the countryside was in order more liberally to contemplate and meditate on the stars, which he held for his gods in the ideas of his religion.[11]

This description of the shaman was virtually the same as that of the behavior of the paqo/alpaca in the myth: living in the countryside, eating sparingly of herbs and water, clothed in wool, and staring all night at the stars. The impact of this realization was, for me, electrifying and unforgettable. I returned to the myth and read again the words, the direct words, of an Andean priest-astronomer, transmitted without interruption across a span of more than 1,300 years: ". . . the llama, speaking as if he were a man, told the shepherd, 'Pay very close attention, and remember what I am going to tell you. . . .'"

PART I

THE TECHNICAL LANGUAGE OF ANDEAN MYTH

CHAPTER 2

WHY FOX'S TAIL IS BLACK

... with you and other peoples again and again life has only lately been enriched with letters and all the other necessaries of civilisation when once more, after the usual period of years, the torrents of heaven sweep down like a pestilence leaving only the rude and unlettered among you. And so you start again like children, knowing nothing of what existed in ancient times, here or in your own country.

—PLATO
TIMAEUS

I

BY DAY, IN the thin, dazzling air of highland Peru and Bolivia there vibrates a song of inconsolable sadness. From the shame of crumbling, gully-washed terraces on endless, abandoned hillsides, to the desolation of square miles of alkali-encrusted altiplano around Lake Titicaca, the injured earth cries out for her lost husbandmen. She is *pachamama*, "our mother in space-time." Four and a half of her six million children lay dead within fifty years of the Conquest. The survivors, the salt of the earth, who have endured through the centuries the degradation, disdain, and suffering of the cataclysm, have never forgotten her.

By night, as black dogs huddle together for warmth, and the visible scars of profane history lie blanketed in oblivion, a firmament of unblemished brilliance blazes forth in fierce affirmation of once and future worlds. Here, on the vault of heaven, are written the sacred thought-forms of Andean civilization. Here the Milky Way, in other climes a brightish band in the night sky, scintillates with such intensity that its great whorls of interstellar dust appear in stunning definition, inky black and fathomless. These black clouds are named: llama, condor, partridge *(lluthu)*, toad *(hanp'atu)*, serpent, fox.¹ Myth is told at night.

These myths speak of a past and a sorrow more ancient than the Spanish Conquest. The Inca Empire, an endeavor conceived in desperation and executed by force of arms, arose to stanch a spreading stain of blood, eight centuries of intertribal war. At stake was a way of life whose ancient origins were still remembered in myth, but that now staggered under the burden of its own successes.

Once a domain capable of supporting only sparse bands of roving hunters and, later, the domesticators of the llama and hunting groups experimenting with horticulture, the high Andes had been transformed, beginning about two centuries before Christ, in one of the most dramatic feats of ecological integration ever undertaken. By A.D. 1400, when the Incas solemnly arrogated destiny's mantle, the Andean peoples, now numbering in the millions, had run out of space and, so the Incas believed, out of time. Once masters of one of the earth's most demanding ecosystems, the Andean peoples were now its prisoners.

The historian John Murra has chronicled the immensity of the Andean achievement. The staple crops of Andean agricultural society, maize, potatoes, and quinoa, are grown at altitudes between ten thousand and thirteen thousand feet. Below ten thousand feet, jungle chokes the vertiginous eastern flanks of the Andes, where rivers roar through boulder-strewn gorges. At about six thousand feet, where the verticality of the Andes gives way to the gentler *montaña*, it is possible to clear land for the cultivation of fruits and coca. Above fourteen thousand feet, on the treeless *puna*, a kind of dune grass called *icchu* supports the flocks of llamas and alpacas.

Agriculture in the high Andes requires a community effort, because broad valleys are rare and the hills must be terraced and irrigated if they are to support stable populations. To work in this environment, human beings require wool for warm clothing, and occasional meat and fat, as well as the dietary supplements of fruits and coca from the *montaña*. Coca, in moderation, is a valuable dietary supplement for those engaged in high-altitude agricultural labor because it enhances stamina and the ability to withstand cold.

It was a classic case of the chicken and the egg. To live solely as a nomadic herdsman on the high *puna*, was a precarious proposition, requiring one to eat one's wealth. To live by hunting and horticulture in the highland valleys was, at best, to survive. A slash-and-burn life in the *montaña*, without the riverine resources of the Amazon basin, meant a solitary, seminomadic life in small, isolated bands.

About 200 B.C., these prospects were radically altered when a creative impulse of enormous power entered into Andean life. There began to be formed, and quite rapidly, what Murra calls "vertical archipelagoes,"[2] that is, the welding of *puna*, high-altitude arable valleys, and *montaña* into single, interdependent systems capable of supporting large communities. These communities, called *ayllus*, controlled all the land in a given valley, from sixteen thousand feet all the way to the *montaña*. Such "vertical archipelagos," often sixty or more kilometers from top to bottom, allowed a critical mass of people to assemble who could undertake the enormous work of terracing and irrigating the Andes.

In this brilliant synthesis, what had been the insurmountable barrier of Andean geography—towering knots of mountains, isolated valleys, scant arable land, and harsh, discrete ecosystems—became an asset, the basis of a new civilization. A topography of separation and scarcity had been transformed, by sheer human will, into a setting of naturally defined homelands, pouring forth plenty and vitiating conflict.

This event is commemorated in Andean myth as the creation of the world by a creator god in human form, Wiraqocha. Tradition places this event at Lake Titicaca, a vast sweetwater lake that lies at 12,500 feet above sea level, set like a great mass of lapis lazuli in the dun-colored expanse of the altiplano. Long, long ago, so the story goes, there was a world without light. Then, above the still, dark waters of Lake Titicaca, Wiraqocha created the sun, moon, and stars, and commanded them to rise above a cliff of black rock looming out of the lake, an island called Titicaca, known today as the Island of the Sun. Then, according to the myth, Wiraqocha created all the tribes of the Andes—each with its distinctive dress, language, customs— and commanded each to emerge from caves, springs, and trunks of trees in the centers of their respective tribal homelands.[3]

In its various versions, this myth constitutes the charter document of Andean civilization. Herein lay the social compact that held Andean civilization together. Although, it was recognized, the tribes had differing languages, customs, and dress, each was nonetheless related to the other as creations of a common god, Wiraqocha. Each tribe possessed a statue, or lineage *waka*, commemorating—as described in the myth—the creation by Wiraqocha of the tribal ancestor, an entity conceived of as androgynous and nonhuman. The deed of possession of tribal lands was sealed by each group's reference to its particular place of emergence—the caves, fountains, and so on—called *pacarina*, literally "place of dawning." The very diversity of the tribes was thus portrayed as springing from an underlying principle of unity. This is why, in so many versions of the myth, Wiraqocha is portrayed as speaking to the people "with much gentleness, admonishing them that they should do good, and no evil or injury to one another, and that they should be loving and charitable to all."[4]

After the Spanish Conquest, a Jesuit priest, Pablo José de Arriaga, charged with destroying Andean religion, root and branch, wrote a training manual for Jesuit missionaries called *The Extirpation of Idolatry*. This text impressed upon its students that their very first duty, upon entering a village, was to get their hands on the lineage *waka* and destroy it. If the *pacarina* could be located and destroyed or defaced, so much the better.[5]

Archaeological research has only recently confirmed the special position occupied by the Lake Titicaca region in the development of Andean civilization. The rapid expansion of the "vertical archipelago" system of ecological integration that began about 200 B.C. was preceded by about four centuries of agricultural experimentation in the Titicaca basin. Beginning no earlier than 600 B.C.,[6] experiments in irrigation on the broad expanse of altiplano around Lake Titicaca produced a distinctive system of raised mounds, recently discovered in satellite photos.

In this system, water, let in from the lake, was kept permanently in the ditches between mounds. In dry times, crops planted on the mounds could wick up the water, and on cold nights the water would give back the heat of the day's sun, preventing frost damage to the plants. Fish were raised in the ditches, providing a source of dietary protein as well as fertilizer for the crops. It is estimated that in the years between 200 B.C. and A.D. 600, as much as three hundred square miles of land were under this form of cultivation. Today this method of agriculture is being reintroduced, because it produces higher yields than do plots treated with chemical fertilizer.[7]

These communal works were connected to what is called the Tiahuanacan civilization. The city of Tiahuanaco, which reached the height of its political and architectural greatness about A.D. 600, is the Andes' sacred center. Now in ruins, it is to South America what Teotihuacán is to Mexico, or Stonehenge to England: the seat of legend, a talisman, a touchstone. It was here, according to myth, that the world, in the sense of the integrating principles of Andean agricultural civilization as laid out by Wiraqocha, was created. The ruins lie some twelve miles from the shores of Lake Titicaca, a shimmer on the northwest horizon. Facing the rising sun is the most famous archaeological monument in South America, the Gateway of the Sun, above which is carved the visage of Wiraqocha.

At its apogee, the cultural influence of Tiahuanaco reached far to the

north, well into the central Andes and beyond. The myths of the people of
Huarochirí in the central Andes, from which one of the llama myths comes,
affirm that in "the most ancient times" accessible to memory, it was Wiraqocha who came and showed the people how to terrace the land and build
irrigation systems.[8]

But beginning in the seventh century A.D., with the rise of the military
state of Wari in the central Andes, near present-day Ayacucho, organized
warfare first entered Andean life. By A.D. 1000, Tiahuanaco would lie abandoned as a long, dark age descended upon the Andean peasantry. The Incas,
nothing if not politically astute, understood the importance of this heritage
when they reworked the Andean creation myth to include their own special
creation by Wiraqocha at Titicaca, and built an exquisite shrine on the
Island of the Sun.

Throughout all these centuries, the teaching of Wiraqocha remained the
essential cultural tool for mastering the complexity of the physical environment of the Andes. Down to the present day and impermeable to time, there
endures among the Andean peasantry the fundamental religious principle of
Andean agricultural society, taught by Wiraqocha. This is the principle
of reciprocity—reciprocity between man and the environmental Powers,
reciprocity between the living and the dead, and reciprocity among people.
And since the dawning of the Age of Wiraqocha at about 200 B.C., the
fundamental theme of Andean history has been the peasantry's nearly superhuman effort to keep this principle alive despite successive hammerblows on
the anvil of fate. Beginning with the advent of warfare in the seventh century, through the abandonment of the spiritual heart of the Andes at Tiahuanaco about A.D. 1000 and the accompanying fracturing of Andean life into
a mosaic of warring tribes, through successive conquests by the Incas and
the Spanish, and present-day exploitation and neglect, the native peoples of
the Andes have tuned their collective soul to this ancient vibration. Reciprocity, rather than hatred, was and remains the price of cultural survival,
impeccably paid.

I know of no clearer statement of the fierce spark of dignity still alive in
the banked fires of the native Andean heart than that uttered in 1953 in
Puquio by an old man who had lived his entire life under the cruel boot of
the Spanish hacienda system—as a serf on his own ancestral lands:

We [the indigenous people] wish only that the government would
order that the *mistis* [Europeans] and the Indians should live apart, and
that we not seek help from one another. Then it would be known who
is of more value here in Puquio. We, poor as we are, are able to live an

honest life; they would come crying to us for help; because they do not
know how to till the land, nor how to irrigate, nor harvest, nor how to
tend livestock. Nothing. They know nothing, except how to get on a
horse and give orders. They would die of hunger if they were obliged
to live apart. . . .[9]

II

IT IS FROM the limitations of human memory that myth derives its authority,
since there is no room for chitchat aboard the vessel of oral transmission.
Space is limited to that information on whose safe transport into the future
the welfare of unborn generations depends. Myth, by definition, is important. This chapter is the story of why Fox's tail is black. The flood which
nearly overtook poor Fox on the mountaintop really happened, and the
soaking of Fox's tail was a historical event. It is, in fact, possible to understand precisely why Fox's tail is black, why the event was important, and
exactly which world was destroyed in the flood. The reason it is possible is
that the creators of the myth were working with a precise medium of transmission, the technical language of myth. Events like this from the Andean
past *are* available to the present because the Andean mythographers willed
it so.

To understand how the astronomical level of Andean myth worked, it is
necesary to know something about its great overarching schema, the tradition of five Ages of the World, culminating with a Fifth Age, unilaterally
declared, as it were, by the Incas.[10]

One chronicler who discussed the five Ages of the World was Felipe
Guamán Poma de Ayala ("Guamán Poma" means "Hawk-Puma"), an indigenous nobleman from Huamanga, near present-day Ayacucho in northwest
quarter of the Empire. His work (1584), styled as a "Letter to the King," was
an attempt to motivate King Philip II of Spain to establish a more moderate
rule over Peru by demonstrating that its people lived by principles more
Christian than the Christians.

According to Guamán Poma, the people of the First Age lived in caves,
contended with wild animals and "wandered lost in an unknown land, leading a nomadic life." Those of the Second Age lived in crude round houses,
wore animal skins, broke "virgin earth," and lived in fixed settlements. The
people of the Third Age multiplied "like the sands of the sea," knew weaving,
built houses like those built to this day, had marriage customs, lived by
agriculture, had weights and measures, shared a tradition of emergence from

caves, springs, and so on, and lived harmoniously together. War was un-known throughout the first three Ages. The Fourth Age, *"auca pacha runa,"* or the "Age of Warriors," began with "internal conflicts" that spread rapidly, giving way to the distinctive house type of the age, the hill fortress. Warriors left field and family behind; bridges were cut and human sacrifice under-taken. The Fifth Age was that of the Incas.[11] Guamán Poma's description of the Five Ages is, generally speaking, in remarkable concordance with the findings of archaeology concerning the sequence and nature of cultural changes in the Andes.

A second source attesting to a tradition of Five Worlds was the chroni-cler Martín de Murúa, a Spanish priest whose sympathy with native Andeans and curiosity about their world gave him access to information not readily volunteered.

> . . . since the creation of the world until this time, there have passed four suns without [counting] the one which presently illumines us. The first was lost by water, the second by the falling of the sky on the earth . . . the third sun they say failed by fire. The fourth by air: they take this fifth sun greatly into account and have it painted and symbolized in the temple Curicancha [the Inca Temple of the Sun in Cuzco] and placed in their *quipus* [knotted cords used for counting and record-keeping] until the year 1554.[12]

The use of the term "Sun" as the chronometric equivalent of "world-age" was a practice common to the Incas and the Aztecs,[13] and at this point it is not necessary to elaborate on the specific reasons for this usage. The indige-nous term for "world-age" that had pan-Andean usage was the word *pacha*, as for example in Guamán Poma's usage, *auca pacha runa*, Age of the Warriors. Another chronicler, Juan de Santacruz Pachakuti Yamqui Salcamaygua, an indigenous nobleman from the Lake Titicaca region, referred to this same era of warfare before the advent of the Incas as *purunpacha*, *ccallacpacha*, and *tutayacpacha*, alternatively "the age of barabarism," "the age of wall-breaking," or "the dark age."[14]

The precise meaning of the word *pacha* is critical for understanding Andean mythical thought. In an age such as ours, where it is customary to crunch data, digest sound bites, process words, and regurgitate information, we are likely to encapsulate mythical tales of the Ages of the World (in order to make them easier to swallow) as stories of "disaster" and "cataclysm," without ever pausing over the words we use, or considering what meaning they might convey. We do not, for example, notice that these words come from the boiler room of our own mythic heritage, whose life still pulses beneath the thin skin of language: "dis-aster" being a literal "sundering of the stars" and "cataclysm" from the Greek *kataklysmos*, meaning "deluge." Because terms of Andean myth existed, as did terms which have found their way into Western languages, to transmit information precisely, it is worthwhile to be precise about their meaning.

The Spanish invaders understood the word *pacha* to mean "world" (*mundo*) or "the earth" (*tierra*). The most cursory inventory of one's understanding of the word *world* reveals that it is a slippery term. The English word *world* has sixteen separate definitions in the *American Heritage Dictionary*. It may mean the planet Earth; the universe; a particular habitat, as in "the marine world"; a historical period such as "the Elizabethan world"; the domain of qualities, such as "the world of letters"; a means of livelihood, such as "the boxing world"; humanity at large, as in "world opinion"; and so on. It is, therefore, important to note that in the authoritative Quechua lexicon of Gonzalez Holguín (1608), there is only one entry for the word *pacha*: "*tiempo suelo lugar*," or "time ground place."[15]

Whereas in Western thought, the sense of the word *world* has been rendered so elastic as to mean something like "flavor," taking on significance only by means of the nearest adjective, the Quechua word *pacha* means one, and only one, thing: place and time *simultaneously*. If I tell you I will meet you at the same *pacha* tomorrow, it is up to the context of our conversation to establish whether we are talking about the same place, the same time, or both. In Andean thought, "this place" today is not the same "place" tomorrow. Time is a defining condition of space, and the particularities of space are the ground from which time arises.

English is a language with few words that speak directly to that dimension of human experience called being, which can be simply defined as what one can assimilate and bear. The "world" in which we contemporary people live is kaleidoscopic, fragmented, the product of fluctuating states. We are encouraged to take things as they come, to cultivate a degree of existential panache in the face of future shock. We think of contemporary life as somehow at the cutting edge of an as yet unrealized future, and we live life accordingly: cutting through, sloughing off, being razor-sharp, traveling light.

By contrast, the Quechua "world"—*pacha*—requires, by an act of sheer linguistic programming, that its inhabitants bear without flinching the weight of history. To do otherwise is to snap the diaphanous elasticity of space-time, abandon identity, forget the past, and betray the suffering and labors of those who have gone before. It is not a coincidence that Quechua children from the age of four or five are given a burden to bear, a piece of textile in which to place provisions or a few trade goods whenever they set off from home. The physical burden they are obliged to shoulder foreshadows the weightier burden of culture these children will one day carry. And because this whole cultural "package"—language, dress, custom, myth—is preeminently a means of reaching the future through the living, it is a burden that every true human bears with pride. The indigenous name for the Quechua language is *runa simi*, "the language of humans."

To understand the word *pacha*, then, is to understand the eternal burden of impermanence, the mythical dimension of all presents, the extreme poignancy of life, the pain of loss, and the price of endurance. The Quechua term *pacha*, recognizable to us in its mythical sense of "world-age," is the irreducible matrix of Andean myth and culture. Hereby Andean culture enlists nothing less than the faculty of feeling to serve as the organizing field for memory. One feels myth first, and understands it later.

The magnetic nodes around which Andean myths cluster are events called *pachakuti*. The verb *kutiy* means "to turn over" or "to turn back."[16] *Pachakuti* is the name given to the millennial moment when one "world" perishes and the next begins. It means, quite literally, "the overturning of space-time."[17] At the time of the Spanish Conquest, there existed specific terms for different modes of destruction: *lloclaunu pachakuti*, or "an overturning of space-time by inundation of water," *nina pachakuti*, the same by fire, and so on.[18] This terminology places the concept of *pachakuti* squarely within the framework of the various world-ages described above by Murúa, involving successive "destructions" of the "space-time world." (And if the reader begins to experience the shock of recognition, wondering if a *pachakuti* differs so very much from other traditions where "worlds" are destroyed and new ones created—as, for example, Deucalion's Flood, or the Norse Twilight of the Gods—it is perhaps equally curious to note how one is accustomed to explain away each such similarity as some sort of generalized activity of the primitive human mind, found now here, now there around the world.)

The Andean sources make clear that a *pachakuti* was a very rare occurrence because the Ages themselves lasted for a very long time. Guamán Poma, for example, assigns numerical values to the Ages, the shortest period being eight hundred years, the longest well over a thousand. Pachakuti Yamqui mentions that a "very great number of years transpired" (*"muchissimos años passaron"*) during the age of warfare. In turning now to the myths of the llamas and the flood and an inquiry into the matter of Fox's tail, we come to a mythical description of a flood, one that has destroyed the whole world.

The weight of contemporary scholarship encourages one to believe that

mythic terminology concerning rhythmic creations and destructions of the
"world in space-time," whether from Greek, Nordic, or Native American
tradition, represents a sort of fuzzy "mythopoeic" vision of the past, created
by the savage imagination in lieu of records. The idea that the language and,
indeed, the entire structure of such tales *are* the records themselves, has
entirely eluded the contemporary imagination. Although, according to the
prevailing view, such mythical terminology can have nothing to do with
astronomy—much less history—reference to common sense suggests otherwise.

The two Andean myths recounted in chapter 1 describe a *lloclaunu pachakuti*, "an overturning of space-time by inundation of water," that is, an event
marking the end of a long, long age and the beginning of the next. In
matters chronometric, humankind—as with the *paqo*—has always turned its
gaze to the heavens, whence come all the measures of time.

III

IT IS NOT that these myths yielded their message easily. After two years of
work on a master's degree, including some ethnoastronomical fieldwork in
Peru and Bolivia, production of a master's thesis called "Quechua Star
Names," and an additional eighteen months of research, I hadn't gotten very
far. In fact I was stuck. I couldn't understand these myths. By the same token,
I couldn't get around them. They became for me a litmus test, a barrier, a
source of frustration and of hope, because if any myths from the pre-
Columbian Andes made clear that astronomy was afoot, it was these.

Take, for example, the words of the informant in Molina's version: "At
last the shepherd who had charge of them [the llamas] asked what ailed
them, and they said that the conjunction of stars showed that the world
would be destroyed by water." The myth itself makes the connection between space and time by relating an imminent *lloclaunu pachakuti*—that is, a
world-destroying flood—to a "conjunction of stars." Molina, of course, was
free to editorialize ("If they had known the use of writing, they would not
have been so dull and blind"), but this curious excerpt, understood as the
product of minds anything but dull, appeared to me as only the most obvious
of a number of elements in both versions that refer the whole matter of an
imminent *pachakuti* directly to the Andean heavens.

In Avila's version, the llama "knew that the sea [Quechua *mamaqocha*,
meaning "mother sea"] had decided to overflow, to fall down like a waterfall."
Were one to assume the narrator was "dull and blind," one might then

comfortably assume that the placement *overhead* of the "sea" in question was a good example of his stupidity. It is, however, unnecessary to repeal the law of gravity in order to make sense of the statement. In hymns to Wiraqocha, recorded by Pachakuti Yamqui, one finds the term *hananqocha*, literally "the sea above,"[19] in direct reference to the starry heavens.[20] Whatever else the myth might mean, the sources of the impending flood lay somewhere out there, on the celestial sphere. But that was as far as I could get—until I came up with a decent question.

The question seemed innocent enough, and hardly potent: Why were these stories told from the point of view of the llama? In fact it was a trick of language—the play between the figurative and literal meanings of the phrase "point of view"—that opened up the world this book seeks to explore. I had meant, in asking the question, simply to ask why it should be these animals, these llamas, that were given the role of seeing the future. Why was *their* point of view so important?

It may strike the reader as unbelievable to hear that in the year and a half during which I had struggled to understand the astronomy of these myths—and despite having first seen the "celestial Llama," an enormous and beautiful cloud of interstellar dust, black against the background glow of the Milky Way, three years earlier during fieldwork in Bolivia—it had never occurred to me that the llamas in the myths might refer to the llama in the sky. It took a year and a half for the thought to cross my mind that all the animals in the myths might be celestial objects whose identity I already knew. All I'd needed all along was to consider the llamas' "point of view."

This experience produced in me a peculiar mix of feelings: elation that my research might finally be getting somewhere; incredulity—embarrassment, really—that, although Santillana and Dechend had mentioned that "stars are animals," I had been blind to the "obvious" for such a long time; an eerie sense of communication with another time and place; and the very clear realization that, until that moment, I had not fully believed that what I was looking for might exist.

Now the myths "reconstellated" themselves into a coherent pattern. I saw a picture in my mind's eye: a single mental image of the celestial Llama setting in the west, "watching" some object rise in the east. It was an image from the llama's "point of view," and with it I experienced a concatenation of no less than five separate realizations within the span of a few heartbeats. Taken together, these realizations created a coherent and testable interpretation of myths that had proved so elusive for so long.

First came the "obvious" connection between the llama in the myth and the celestial Llama. The myth was describing a configuration of the night

sky. The identity of the celestial Llama is well established in both contempo-
rary[21] and Conquest-period literature. The "black cloud" celestial Llama runs
from the star epsilon Scorpius, in the "tail" of the Western constellation
Scorpius, south to the stars alpha and beta of the Western constellation
Centaurus (see figure 2.1). These two first-magnitude stars, called alpha
Centauri and Hadar in Western astronomy, are known in the Andes as *llamaq
ñawin*, "the eyes of the llama." At the time of the Conquest, the natives of
Huarochirí described this magnificent object to Avila:

> They say that Yacana, as we call it, is like the shadow of a llama, a
> double of this animal which walks down the center of the sky, as it
> were a darkness in the sky. That's how we men see it coming, yes, dark.
> They say that this Yacana (when it reaches the earth) walks beneath
> the rivers. It is very large indeed; blacker than the night sky, it ad-
> vances; with its long neck and two eyes, it comes.[22]

Garcilaso de la Vega likewise recorded:

> In the milky way of astronomers, upon some dark spots which spread
> over part of it, they fancied there was the shape of a sheep [llama] with
> the body complete, and giving suck to a lamb.[23]

The "baby llama" is a small black cloud at the hind flanks of its mother
(see figure 2.1).

The second realization implicit in the mental image of the celestial
Llama setting in the west, looking east, was that the myth was probably
describing some object rising at the same moment in the east, shortly before
dawn. I realized that there was a rightness to this image. This sense of
rightness was based on an understanding of the importance in Andean astronomy of what are known as "heliacal rise" phenomena.[24]

At most latitudes, including the southern Andes, there are stars that,
because they are too close to the sun (as viewed from the earth), are not
visible at night for a certain portion of the year. After "clearing" the reach of
the sun's brilliance, each such star will make its first reappearance for a brief
instant before sunrise just as the gathering light of dawn extinguishes its
visibility. On successive mornings such a star will rise earlier, and linger
longer in the predawn skies. The first day of reappearance of such a star is
called its date of heliacal rise.

The use of the technique of heliacal rise is a powerful tool in fine-tuning
a solar calendar. For example, determining the day of a solstice by observa-

tion of the sun's movement alone is not easy. The word *solstice* literally means "the sun sits," and that is precisely the problem for the naked-eye observer —the sun just sits there. On the June solstice, for example, when the sun rises as far north of due east as it will all year, there is a "window" of several days either side of the event when the sun's motion at its rising point along the horizon is difficult to detect. Thus, if over a period of years an observer charged with keeping the calendar has been able to determine that a particular star rises heliacally, say, four days before the June solstice, he will have relieved himself of considerable anxiety by establishing a reliable benchmark.[25]

Now, a somewhat baroque example of the uses to which heliacal-rise observations were put in ancient Peru is provided by the so-called *seque* system of Imperial Cuzco. Although this example is complex, it demonstrates the importance to the Andean astronomers not only of heliacal-rise phenomena in general, but also of the Pleiades in particular, a group of stars that, as it turned out, played a key role in the myths of the llama and the flood.

From the gold-encrusted epicenter of the Inca Empire, the Temple of the Sun in Cuzco, there emanated a system of between forty and forty-two imaginary lines in all directions to the horizon. These lines, called *seques*, meaning "rays," functioned, among other uses, as a calendar. Each *seque*, conceptualized as running over hill and dale in an unswervingly straight line to the horizon, passed through or near a number of shrines along the way. Those shrines—called *wakas*, either natural or man-made, but each connected to Inca lore and religion—numbered on average between seven and nine per *seque*, and there were a total of 328 in all. Zuidema and Urton have pointed out that, according to the Spanish Chronicles, each *waka* of the *seque* system was allotted its own day for special propitiation, accounting for 328 days out of the 365 in the year. What about the "missing" thirty-seven days? Zuidema and Urton argue persuasively that these are accounted for by the thirty-seven days of invisibility of the Pleiades (owing to their proximity to the sun) at the latitude of Cuzco.[26]

So the idea that the myth was recounting the heliacal rise of some object "witnessed" by the celestial Llama, setting in the west, gave rise to a third, virtually simultaneous, realization. I had read about just such an observational practice, undertaken in the present day by Quechua-speaking peasants. This decisive clue in unraveling the sense of the llama/flood myths came from a reference to the contemporary Quechua observation of the Pleiades, recorded in fieldwork near Ayacucho in the central Andes, by John Earls. Earls noted that in June the local people would go into the mountains before dawn to watch the rise of the Pleiades and the simultaneous set of a constellation known locally as *cruz calvario*, the Cross of Calvary.[27]

Cruz calvario is a large, elegant, perfectly rectilinear cross of stars whose last star, epsilon Scorpius, lies at the hind flank of the celestial Llama and beside her suckling calf, the small dark cloud mentioned above by Garcilaso.[28] (See figures 2.2 and 2.3.)

Several points of clarification will demonstrate that the observation recorded by Earls is the same as the one described in the myths of the llama and the flood. To begin with, the reader may well wonder what a constellation called the Cross of Calvary is doing in the Quechua heavens. The implacable determination of the Spanish missionaries to destroy native religious beliefs soon led them to the realization that a process of what might be called "guerrilla syncretism" was going on right under their noses. Because these churchmen meted out severe punishment, up to and including death, for unrepentant adherence to the old ways, the Andean peoples quickly learned to take on the appearance of piety while continuing, to the extent possible, exactly as they had done before.

One such example transpired on the Eve of All Souls' Day (Halloween). In Inca times the ancestors were thought to return annually to earth, and this festival was celebrated at the December solstice. The custom was to provide food and drink, thus maintaining the correct relationship with the ancestors. The peasantry, recognizing the pagan roots of a Christian custom, had taken to propitiating the ancestors on the day allotted to the ancestors in the Christian liturgical calendar. To this day, in Mexico and Peru, native peoples bring a picnic dinner to the cemetery on All Hallows' Eve, waiting for the dawn, and the return of the dead. Arriaga forbade this practice, and made sure that he could enforce the ban by forcing the peasantry to bury their dead in the churchyard, where he could keep an eye on them.[29]

The Cross of Calvary is another example of Quechua guerrilla syncretism, because the brightest star in its crosspiece, epsilon Scorpius, marks precisely the same cosmologically important point in the heavens occupied by the Llama and her calf. *Cruz calvario* and the celestial Llama interpenetrate one another. This location, in terms of Western astronomy, marks the crossing of the ecliptic, that is, the sun's apparent annual path through those stars we call the zodiac, and the Milky Way. This location, in native Andean belief, marked the crossroads of the land of the living and the land of the dead, the "bridge" across which the dead annually returned to earth. By creating the constellation *cruz calvario*, the peasantry accomplished two things. First, they identified a cosmologically important celestial location with the Christian term most likely to evoke its significance. The Cross of

Calvary stands for the idea of death and resurrection. Second, by using the Christian term, they hoped to be able to keep indigenous notions (as well as themselves) alive through the appearance of Christian piety.

Awareness of this pattern of guerrilla syncretism, characteristic of Andean thought since the Conquest, therefore suggested that here, in Earl's information, lay a contemporary replication of the observation encoded in the llama/flood myths. In other words, the myths recounted the heliacal rise of the Pleiades, simultaneously "viewed" by the Llama, setting in the west.

This realization triggered the fourth insight. Since it had never crossed my mind to look for the Pleiades in the myths, I had never found them. The moment I realized they might be there, they appeared instantaneously, encoded as the *name* of the mountain in Avila's version, "Vilcacoto."

The word *vilca* is from the Aymara language and means "sun." The word *coto* is found in both Quechua and Aymara and means "pile." Translated literally, *vilcacoto* means "sun-pile," and this is how I had thought of it until now. The word *coto* has, however, a second meaning, well established in the ethnographic literature: the Pleiades.[30] This usage of the word for "pile" in relation to the Pleiades has to do with the use of the Pleiades in divination of crop-planting times. The Pleiades are likened to a small pile of seeds in need of planting.[31] Observation of the relative clarity in the stars of the western or eastern edge of the rising Pleiades determines the timing for planting.[32]

After literally years of difficulty, I saw a door open. Vilcacoto—"Sun-Pleiades Mountain"—referred not just to the Pleiades, but to the Pleiades *in relation to the sun*, as clear a reference to the *heliacal rise* of the Pleiades as one might hope to find—if, of course, Andean myth had anything to do with astronomy. Either the relation between the anxious llamas scanning the skies above Mount Vilcacoto was meant to convey nothing in particular, or here was a myth from pre-Columbian tradition describing, with utter precision and almost offhanded ease, the simultaneous heliacal rise of the Pleiades and heliacal set of the celestial Llama.

Promising as these possibilities appeared, they were dwarfed by the fifth element implicit in their unveiling. If it was really true that the myths had been constructed to record, among other things, particular night skies, then the mythographers had also left behind the date of their endeavors. The myths, I now realized, contained within them reference to the era of their creation.

IV

IN THE SAME way that men today in rural New England lean on the sides of pickup trucks, feet in slushy snow, and trade opinions on whether the time has come to tap the maples, contemporary Quechua peasants confer about the clarity of the Pleiades and the proper time to plant. It is a timeless practice. But these Andean myths of an impending deluge are not talking about ordinary times. The shamans are nervous. A world is about to end. An event is in progress.

I realized that, since the stars slip slowly eastward in relation to the solar year, as a result of the precessional wobble of the earth's axis, one could date the time frame of these myths, *if one could establish a solar benchmark.* In other words, the Pleiades have risen, and always will rise, heliacally on *some* day of the year. But if the myth specified *which* day in the solar year the Pleiades were observed rising heliacally, then one could work out when the myth was formulated.

I now realized that the myths appeared to contain this information. According to the hypothesis of Santillana and Dechend, it is the astronomical function of topographic references in myth to represent by analogy *the position of the sun on the celestial sphere.* Their suggestion that animals in myth refer to stars had proved reliable. I had also learned from their work that attention to the literal meaning of particular words—such as *vilcacoto*—could yield important results. What, then, might be gained by paying attention to the topographic clues, namely the "very high mountain" mentioned in each story?

The image of the towering mountain is associated both in Andean and Mesoamerican tradition with the June solstice. Each year at June solstice during the Inca reign, as Urton has described, the Inca priests would walk upstream along the Vilcamayu, literally "River of the Sun," to its headwaters at the foot of the towering mountain Vilcanota—"Place of the Sun." The Incas considered Vilcanota "the highest mountain in the world."[33]

The association of the June solstice with "the highest mountain in the world" suggests that in Andean thought *the sun's northernmost location in the stars —the June solstice—was likened to a position atop the highest mountain in the world.* Johanna Broda's work reveals exactly the same pattern of thought in Mexico.[34]

Reference to the famous cosmological diagram (drawn about 1613) of the indigenous nobleman Pachakuti Yamqui, shows, in another way, the association between the mountain and June solstice (see figure 2.4). Here the Andean cosmos is conceptualized as divided between male and female elements. The left side is connected with men, the sun, day, and the dry season; the right with women, night, the moon, and the season of rains. The heart of the Andean dry season is at the time of the June solstice, and on that side of the diagram appears a drawing of a high mountain. Its spatial opposite, a spring or lake, is depicted on the opposite side in the heart of the rainy season, which occurs around the December solstice.

Furthermore, the *name* of the mountain in Molina's version of the myth, Ancasmarca, recapitulates this same reasoning in an *architectural* metaphor. The Quechua word *marca* means "the highest part of a house, up under the roof," and *ancas* means "sky blue."[35] Guamán Poma, in describing the Ages of the World, made drawings featuring the distinctive house type of each age (figure 2.5), and Pachakuti Yamqui's diagram depicts the entire "world" as "housed" within a structure with a pitched roof (figure 2.4). Further, the term *ancas*, "sky blue," resonates with Pachakuti Yamqui's diagram, which conceptually aligns the cloudless dry season, around the June solstice, with the sun and day, as opposed to rain, moon, and night.

Another cosmologically significant use of the word *ancas* is found in the name Ancasmayu, literally "sky-blue river," given by the Incas to the river marking the *northern boundary* of the Empire. Surprisingly, "north," in Andean thought, is considered "higher" than "south," as evinced for example by the division of Cuzco into upper (*hanan*) and lower (*hurin*) halves, "Upper Cuzco" lying to the north of the east-west line, and "Lower Cuzco" to the south.[36] Thus the term *ancasmarca*, aside from its function as the name of "a very high mountain," literally means "the highest part of the sky-blue house," suggesting the northernmost position of the sun (the dominant luminary of the blue sky), at the northern tropic on June solstice.

Thus, through both the topographical imagery of the high mountain and the architectural imagery implicit in its name, the myths provided the solar benchmark necessary to locate them in time—again, if they had anything to do with astronomy. The "flood" in question occurred at "the highest mountain in the world," that is, on the June solstice.

Next, and equally important, both myths make clear that the heliacal rise of the Pleiades is *not* the deluge itself, but its harbinger, because in both versions the llamas, watching the Pleiades rise, predict a flood some days hence. Molina's version has it that this prediction occurred "a month before the flood." (For a discussion of the significance of the figure of "five days" lead-time before the Flood, mentioned in Avila's version, see note.[37]) The Quechua word for both month and moon, *killa*, denotes the month of phases, the so-called synodic month, the period of time from full moon to full moon —that is, a month of twenty-nine or thirty days.[38]

Therefore, were one to look at the myth *as if it were an intentional transmission of a complex astronomical observation,* one would have to interpret Molina's version as making the following particular statement: During that era when the Pleiades rose heliacally ("Vilcacoto") one month before the June solstice (the "mountain"), some precessional event (a "flood") transpired at the solstice of sufficient cosmological import to merit the designation of *unu pachakuti,* literally "space-time turns over by inundation of water." At the very least, there now existed a testable hypothesis. The myth carried within itself all the information necessary either to confirm or disprove my suspicions.

V

I KNEW THEN that I needed access to a planetarium. Computers and astronomical software weren't even in my consciousness in 1982. Besides, I wanted to "see" this myth on a broad canvas and with experienced observers present. Here I got lucky. Although he did not know me at all, or anything about my work beyond the briefest of descriptions, Professor Owen Gingerich of the Harvard-Smithsonian Astrophysical Observatory not only graciously arranged for me to use the planetarium in Boston, but went so far as to come and observe the experiment in person. Besides having a distinguished career in astrophysics, as well as expertise in the history of astronomy, Professor Gingerich had given planetarium shows during his days as a graduate student.

The scene that ensued at the Hayden Planetarium in Boston's Museum of Science remains unique in my memory for being experienced like an exceptionally vivid dream. I was very nervous, not only because the list of questions I had with me had the potential—if they could not elicit sensible answers—to terminate the research there and then, but also because Professor Gingerich was an extremely busy man and I wanted the experiment not to be a waste of his time. He arrived late, bringing with him two colleagues he had just picked up at Logan Airport. These two men, my friend Eric Mandel, and a couple of curious staffers, sat in the planetarium's movie-theater chairs and looked on.

In preparation, I had gone over the calculations of both Aveni and Hartner concerning the means for determining the date of heliacal rise of a star.[39] These numbers were very important because they would dictate the distance in degrees between the Pleiades and the sun, and thereby determine the year in which the event occurred. Although it is possible to predict mathematically the location of a star in relation to a particular horizon at any given time, it is another matter to determine what the human eye can see in the gathering dawn. Atmospheric distortion, altitude, the magnitude of the star to be observed, and the distance of the sun beneath the horizon all play a part in determining the date of its heliacal rise.

The rule of thumb is that the brighter the star, the closer to dawn it will remain visible. Very bright objects, such as planets brighter than first magnitude, may be visible with the sun depressed as little as nine degrees beneath the horizon, that is, thirty-six minutes before dawn.[40] Dimmer stars cannot be seen at heliacal rise unless the sun is further depressed.

Astronomers usually call it "absolute darkness" when the sun is depressed twenty degrees, an hour and twenty minutes before dawn. At this point dim stars can be observed at heliacal rise. The individual stars of the Pleiades are relatively dim—third magnitude. But because they are a dense clustering, they are more easily visible than an individual star of third magnitude. Aveni says that, in the absence of haze, the Pleiades can be seen at heliacal rise with the sun depressed seventeen degrees.[41] Hartner prefers twenty degrees, asserting that atmospheric haze is always a factor.[42]

Based on my own experience in the Andes, and after discussing these considerations with Professor Gingerich, we decided to split the difference. It was agreed that, in the conditions of the Andean dry season, and allowing two degrees leeway for a combination of haze and the undulation of topography at the horizon, the Pleiades, a dense cluster of third-magnitude stars, should be visible two degrees above an ideal (zero degrees) horizon, with the sun "depressed" eighteen degrees.

Having determined the basic relationship between sun and star necessary for observing the heliacal rise of the Pleiades in any era, we now went looking for the *year* specified by the myth. The planetarium instrument was set for the latitude of Cuzco and "precessed" back in time until the heliacal rise of the Pleiades occurred *thirty days before June solstice*, just as the myth specified. The planetarium stopped precessing at A.D. 650. Figure 2.6a shows the heliacal rise of the Pleiades on Julian date May 20, 650, thirty days before the June solstice, which, in that era, occurred on Julian date June 19.[43] This year was not only well within the time frame of Andean agricultural history—when one might expect such an observation to have been made—but also marks an important historical moment, when, according to the archaeological record, organized warfare first appeared in the Andes with the appearance of the military state of Wari. This was a good start.

The next step was to look west in order to watch the setting of the celestial Llama. Just as the myth had appeared to indicate, the Llama was in the process of setting (see figure 2.6b). Again, this was a good result. If the myth was not intended to convey astronomical information, then there was no reason that the relationship of "llamas" watching the stars rise over "Sun-Pleiades" mountain should bear any relationship to the heavens and be corroborated in the planetarium.

The main reason for examining the western sky sprang, however, not from any doubt of Earls's report of the contemporary observation of this phenomenon, but from another concern. How could the Andean astronomers have observed the setting of the Llama, when it was a "black cloud" object setting in the gathering dawn? In other words, with the sun depressed eighteen degrees in the east, it was unlikely that the Llama, visible only as a dark "hole" against the background glow of the Milky Way, would be visible at all both near the horizon and with dawn approaching. If the astronomers couldn't see it, how did they know where it was?

Before going to the planetarium, I had anticipated this problem. Initially I had assumed that the astronomers must have "spotted" the Llama by means of some star. At first, the most logical candidate appeared to be epsilon Scorpius, the brightest (third-magnitude) star near both the hind flanks of the Llama and the ecliptic (see figures 2.3 and 2.6b).[44] On further investigation, however, it was unclear whether the naked eye could pick up a third-magnitude star so near the western horizon with dawn approaching. Professor Gingerich also expressed doubt as to its visibility under such conditions, even in the Andes.[45]

I had thought long and hard about this problem. One could, of course, go with the Lawrence of Arabia gambit—"they had better eyesight than ours"—but there were already too many anomalies as yet unexplained in these stories to start papering over them. One such anomaly the reader may already have noticed: in Avila's version, the llama who speaks is specified as being male, while it is the female, or celestial Llama, with her suckling calf who appears the center of astronomical focus.

This discrepancy had also concerned me. On further consideration, however, it dawned on me that the discrepancy might prove the *solution* to my other problem: how the Andean astronomers kept track of the setting (female) Llama. As various of the Spanish chroniclers, among them Cobo and Polo de Ondegardo, had noted, native Andean people identified the constellation known to Western astronomy as Lyra—deep in the northern sky and far from the female, dark-cloud celestial Llama—as "the male llama," *urcuchillay*. This Andean constellation contains the first-magnitude star Vega.

At first the presence of the male llama seemed an unnecessary complication or, worse, an indication that the animals were not intended to evoke their astronomical counterparts at all. It seemed a feckless endeavor to "cherry pick" these stories for what astronomy one might find, while discarding any number of apparently inexplicable elements because they didn't "fit." Either these stories were meant to be understood on an astronomical level or they were not. But what had Vega to do with the astronomical situation described in the myth?

In casting about for a solution, I reread Gary Urton's discussion of the celestial Llama and its relationship to another black-cloud constellation, the celestial Fox. The Fox extends eastward into Sagittarius from the hindquarters of the Llama (see figure 2.7). As a contemporary Aymara-speaker from Bolivia said in commenting on a folktale about Fox, "The fox is in the sky, in the river, he always follows the llama."[46] Urton, whose landmark studies of Andean ethnoastronomy maintain a consistent awareness of the relationship between earthly realities and their cultural projection into the heavens, has noted that the positional relation between the celestial Llama and Fox mirrors the behavior of these animals in life. The fox will attack the young of cameloids, and the mature animals will fight back. The celestial Fox's head is close to the celestial Llama's calf, coming in from the side. Urton cites the chronicler Cobo's description of the vicuña, a wild subspecies of llama:

> There are usually a large number of foxes where vicuñas live; and the foxes chase and eat the young of the vicuñas. The vicuñas defend their young in the following way. Many vicuñas rush together to attack the fox, striking it until it falls to the ground. They then run over it many times without giving it a chance to get up until they kill it by their blows.[47]

This description brought to my mind a photograph I had seen in *National Geographic* showing a male vicuña standing alone on a hillock. The caption had described the male's behavior, namely that it stands alone, apart from the females and young, keeping guard, and only joining the group to mate or defend. The nagging problem of the relative invisibility of epsilon Scorpius, Urton's insight, and the memory of this photo conspired to dredge into my consciousness the word *paranatellon*.

This word refers to a technique, at least as old as Babylonian astronomy, of employing the rising or setting of a very bright star to monitor the simultaneous rising or setting of another, dimmer star in which one is interested, but has trouble seeing. Was it possible that the behavioral relationship of the male cameloid to the females—aloof but connected—had been projected into the Andean heavens by some ancient priest-astronomer, the *paqo* himself?

This was the question now at issue in the planetarium. I explained briefly to Professor Gingerich that some lore suggested that Vega might have been used as a paranatellon for the setting (female) Llama. As the night sky of A.D. 650 rolled toward the setting of the celestial Llama, Vega, far to the north along the horizon, also was setting. He nodded, seemingly interested for the first time. It is, of course, not possible to state scientifically that this coincidence was noticed by the Andean astronomers, but this thought was very far from my mind at the time. I was just busy trying to take everything in, watching Vega—alpha *urcuchillay*, the celestial analogue of the Andean male alpaca/*paqo*/shaman—occupying as clever a position in the planetarium as it appeared to occupy in the myth. I felt a tingle of awe.

Here were observations being re-created in the planetarium—the simultaneous heliacal rise of the Pleiades and heliacal set of the celestial Llama with further reference to its paranatellon Vega, or *urcuchillay*—that had, so it seemed, been made and recorded without aid of written language by an allegedly "primitive" people at a historical moment somewhere between the death of Mohammed and the first Moorish invasion of Spain. As Vega began to set, one of Professor Gingerich's colleagues said to his companion in a voice loud enough to hear, "He seems to have done his homework." When the session was over, and, curious, I asked Professor Gingerich who the man was that had made the comment, he replied, "The Vatican Astronomer."

VI

SEVERAL SURPRISES REMAINED in store. The most important question had yet to be asked: What was going on at heliacal rise on the June solstice A.D. 650 —that is, at the moment of the "flood" as specified by the myth? But before turning to this most critical observation, I wanted to see what the *December* solstice sunrise would have looked like in this year. I wasn't sure where, or if, such information might fit in, but it was a question that the myth apparently demanded be asked, since the celestial Llama, Fox, and Puma[48] all were located in the general area of sky rising heliacally around December solstice.

Initially, this fact had both confused and concerned me. If, as a preponderance of Andean and Mesoamerican ritual suggested, the very high mountain had a cosmological connection with the June solstice, what were these "December solstice animals" doing "on top of the mountain," scrabbling to survive the "flood"? Had my desire to find a solar benchmark in the myths led to a distortion of the sense of the stories?

As I began to ponder this problem, I recalled that Santillana and Dechend had drawn attention to a convention of Old World myth whereby the stars rising heliacally either at both equinoxes or at both solstices were often paired *simultaneously* in myth. The purpose of this convention was the better to establish the era or age under consideration in a given myth by reference not just to one, but to two heliacal-rise events.

The way this was done was by reference to the equinoctial or solstitial "colures," that is, either of two imaginary great circles connecting either the stars marking the equinoxes or else the solstices through the poles. It was when I remembered this reference to the mythic convention of simultaneously noting two events separated by half a year that I realized there was ample evidence in the Andes of a similar mode of thought. And it was here that Urton's astronomical field research concerning the situation "on the ground" proved once again invaluable.

Between 1976 and 1980, Urton conducted ethnoastronomical fieldwork in a single community, Misminay, in the Department of Cuzco. Among his findings was the fact that the village itself was divided into four quarters by two intersecting footpaths. The footpaths ran intercardinally, that is, one ran northeast-southwest, while the other ran southeast-northwest. These paths crossed in the middle of the village. Noting reports of similar quadri-partitions of villages in contemporary Ecuador and the Ayacucho region of Peru, as well as evidence of similar arrangements by the Incas, Urton concluded that, ideally, *the footpaths were thought to run to the four rising and setting points of the solstice suns on the horizon* (see figure 2.8).[49]

Urton's explanation of the importance of the intercardinal, solstitial cross in connecting terrestrial and celestial space at the horizon underscores the Andean habit of thought—the notion of *pacha*—which seeks to unite space and time into a single conceptual whole. Each intercardinal axis serves this function, the one by uniting the June solstice sunrise point on the horizon (northeast) to December solstice sunset (southwest), the other by uniting December solstice sunrise (southeast) to June solstice sunset (northwest). This convention offers the practical means of keeping track of the stars involved in both solstices simultaneously.

This important convention is mirrored in Pachakuti Yamqui's diagram (figure 2.4), uniting as it does both halves of the year, dry season and rainy season, in complementary union, sexually imagined. Urton shows how this conceptual linkage is maintained in Misminay by various kinds of lore.

Thus, for example, when the December-solstice sun rises in the black-cloud celestial Fox (southeast), terrestrial foxes are said to be born at the foot of the mountain marking the horizon point connected to the June solstice sunset (northwest).[50] Conversely, along the other axis—in a variation of the relationship expressed in Earls's observations, and in the llama/flood myths —the Pleiades and the tail of the Western Scorpius (a.k.a. *cruz calvario* and the hindquarters of the Llama) are given the *same name, collca,* meaning "granary."[51] Finally, as will be discussed at greater length in chapter 5, Andean myths of the mythical "trajectory" of the god Wiraqocha, also stressed one of these intercardinal axes. Wiraqocha first appears at Titicaca (southeast), thence to travel the Andes in a northwesterly direction, finally leaving this world at Manta in Ecuador.

For these reasons, the anxiety I had initially felt about finding "December solstice animals" on "June solstice mountain" abated considerably. If the Andean priest-astronomers *were* aware of the phenomenon of precessional motion, they would also have been aware that a change in the heliacal-rise date of *any* star or object—as, for example, the Pleiades—meant a change in that of *every* other star or object. Moreover, they had the conceptual means at hand—the solstice cross—to make such simultaneous observations. This was a perfectly decent working hypothesis. Nonetheless, I had no idea what to expect when we turned the planetarium to the moment of heliacal rise at the December solstice.

What, then, did the planetarium indicate? The planetarium was not, of course, set up to display Quechua "black-cloud" objects. But I knew how Fox lay among the stars. What we found, by making the necessary adjustments to accommodate the visibility of a dark cloud against the background glow of the Milky Way at heliacal rise,[52] is illustrated in figure 2.9a. An observer watching the black-cloud objects rising in the Milky Way at December solstice in A.D. 650 would have seen Fox *almost* completely risen above the horizon, with the exception of his tail, sunk now—owing to precessional motion—beneath the horizon, soaked, bedraggled, and blackened in the rising waters of the celestial sea. Unexpectedly I had discovered why Fox's tail is black: it just took time.

VII

I HAD STOOD eyeball-to-eyeball with these myths for nearly two years. Now Fox had blinked. It may have been of some marginal interest that an astronomical observation carried on by present-day Andean natives (the

Llama/Pleiades axis) may have been described in an Andean myth. Such examples of cultural continuity are legion. It was quite another matter to find that the myth was *constructed to describe the skies of a particular era*. The relationship of the rising Pleiades to the setting Llama is a given, something that happens at some hour of most nights of the year. To understand the myth as designed to describe a particular heliacal-rise event (the Pleiades) in relation to precessional change at June solstice was unheard of in Andean studies, and I could not have faulted anyone for suggesting that this interpretation was a stretch. I had doubts myself. But now, thanks to Fox, things had changed. The myths had generated the date of ca. A.D. 650 not just once (via the Pleiades rising a "month" before June solstice), but *twice*.

In addition, not only did the myths evince an internal consistency, they also operated within a context of indigenous concepts of spatial organization demonstrated independently in the research of others. The heliacal rise of Fox at December solstice, mentioned in relation to events at June solstice, and the axis expressed by the Pleiades/Llama observation, appeared not just to corroborate the importance of the intercardinal cross among Conquest-period natives of the Andes, but to suggest as well a whole new dimension of its utility.

Nonetheless, the most important observation had yet to be made, the moment of the "flood" itself, June solstice, in the era of A.D. 650. I did not yet know why—or even if—this moment in time should, from the astronomical and cosmological viewpoint, have been considered worthy of memorialization in such finely crafted tales. In fact, if some explanation were not forthcoming, the very idea that the tales *did* function to record a moment in precessional time would have to be viewed with renewed suspicion. Therefore this final observation was in many ways the most crucial. Either I would find that some *significant* precessional event, some "flood," had occurred at June solstice, or else the whole thrust of the research would appear to have no point at all.

Accordingly, the machine was turned to the predawn moments of June solstice in A.D. 650, to find out what was visible.[53] The result of this experiment was to reveal that a *pachakuti*—an "overturning of space-time"—had in fact occurred, not because of what was visible, but because of what was no longer there. The experiment showed that in the southern Andes at about A.D. 650 *the Milky Way had ceased to rise heliacally at June solstice* (Julian date June 19[54]), *for the first time in more than eight hundred years* (see figure 2.10a). In other words, an observer waiting to see the Milky Way's reappearance at June solstice, along the horizon at the point where the June solstice sun rises, would have seen . . . nothing. Now the myths had generated a *third* means of establishing their date, because they revealed that a celestial locus of great cosmological import—the junction of the solstice sun in the Milky Way—had been "destroyed" by the passage of time.

The next chapter discusses the supreme significance of the Milky Way in pre-Columbian Andean thought, and how the cessation of its rise at June solstice implied the end of an era. For now, perhaps the best and quickest way to express the cosmological importance of this event to the Andean astronomers is to relate the final surprise that these myths held in store.

In the Huarochirí version of the myth, it was the priest-astronomer himself, the *paqo*, in the mythic guise of the male llama, who raised his eyes to the heavens and cried out in dismay at the signs of the gathering flood. It is from his "point of view" that the flood is foreseen. Figure 2.10b[55] shows the position of the celestial *paqo*, i.e., the first-magnitude star Vega, at the moment of the "flood," that is, during the predawn moments of June solstice in A.D. 650, when it became clear to any observer looking east (figure 2.10a) that the solstice sun and the Milky Way had parted company forever. As we shall see in the next chapter, the *paqo* had his eye on no less an important event than the destruction of the entrance to the land of the gods. What other celestial object in the Quechua heavens was in a better position to "observe" the event than the *paqo*, alpha *urcuchillay*/Vega. And what villager of the ancient Andes was better qualified to make the observation than the priest-astromoner, known as *paqo*?

In the celestial relationship of the distraught *paqo* to the events unfolding in the east, I had found yet a fourth means by which the myths made clear the era of their creation. With so much internally consistent evidence, I was, in my own mind, free for the first time to accept that the astronomy of myth was among the most potent intellectual pursuits of the pre-Columbian Andes. The existence of this way of thinking had become for me a reality, and no matter how much I had left to learn, I would never again see the Andean material in quite the same way.

The cessation of the heliacal rise of the Milky Way at the solstice constituted a "dis-aster." The discovery of this event and its implications constituted for me a doorway into an unexpected world, the beginning of the unfolding of a saga of gain and loss, the history of the advent, erosion, and transformation of sacred influences in Andean history. As the Andean *paqo* stood anxiously scanning the horizon through the cold, thin air of the high *puna*, an ululation of dismay rang out, announcing the end of a world, as simultaneous events in both the celestial and terrestrial spheres outstripped the power of human agency to control them.

CHAPTER 3

THE THREE
WORLDS

It is above that you and I shall go;
Along the Milky Way you and I shall go;
Along the flower trail you and I shall go;
Picking flowers on our way, you and I shall go:[1]

—WINTU

I am the child of the Earth and the starry
Heavens, but my origin is of heaven alone.[2]

—ORPHIC GRAVE TABLET

In this world we are exiled from our homeland in the world
above.[3]

—QUECHUA

Yonder comes the dawn,
The universe grows green
The road to the Underworld
Is open! yet now we live,
Upward going, upward going![4]

—TEWA

I

THE HISTORIAN OF science A. G. E. Blake has observed:

> One of the most important features of any era is the way in which it
> attempts to bring the knowledge and experience of mankind into a
> whole. To say this is to suppose a *synergic action* which operates beyond
> the current boundaries of recognized human cognition.
>
> This action is reflected in the history of what Toynbee and others
> have called "civilization." . . . Every civilization has at its core a pool of
> creativity aligned with a set of values. This is to say that they have all
> been bridges between the known and the unknown.[5]

The core value of Andean civilization was reciprocity. It remains to the
present day the operative principle of indigenous life in the Andean village.
Groups of men work together, now preparing one another's fields for planting, now working together to make adobes for a newly married couple's first
house. Young children tend the flocks. While the women spin and weave,
the men collect llama dung on the high slopes for use in the agricultural
fields. When it is time to plant, men open the earth with a foot plow, the
chaclla, while women place the seed in the earth. Everyone in the village
participates in the annual cleaning of the irrigation ditches. One hand
washes the other.

The ideal of reciprocity has deep roots in Andean civilization, which
sought from its inception to build bridges between the world of the living
and the unseen worlds, the worlds of the gods and of the ancestors. It was
to the ancestors that the gods had revealed their plan for humanity. It was
from the ancestors that the living had received the body of traditions and
skills that made agricultural civilization in the Andes possible. To forget the
ancestors was to sever the ties of reciprocal obligation that ensured the
welfare of both the living and the dead in their separate modes of existence.
And thus to dishonor the ancestors was to reject the ancient legacy vouchsafed them from the realm of the divine. Without its bridges to the gods
and the ancestors, Andean civilization could neither have commenced nor
endured.

These ideas were objectified in the sky. The teaching of Andean religion
was that the reality of humanity's reciprocal obligations was laid out with
rigorous exactitude on the vault of heaven. The Great Divide between the

world of the living and the unknown worlds was visible in the plane of our galaxy, the Milky Way. Across this boundary lay the bridges to the supernatural worlds.

"They say that a great river crosses the middle of the sky, which they call that great white belt we see from below here, called the Milky Way."[6] So wrote the chronicler-priest Bernabé Cobo of the testimony of native informants. In the pre-Columbian Andes, the Milky Way was styled a river (*mayu*) or, less frequently, a road (*ñan*).[7] It was the route traveled by both the gods and the spirits of the dead in order to reach the world of the living. Both Cobo and Molina, in recording a myth from the Cañaris of the Ecuadorian Andes, also mention a mountain, called Huacayñan,[8] literally "llama road." And we have seen, from Avila's description of the celestial Llama, how she is said to "walk down the middle of the sky beneath the rivers."

The idea that the Milky Way functioned as the frontier between worlds was at one time a notion as widespread among the earth's people as the idea that it was possible to throw a bridge across the divide. The Bushmen call the Milky Way "the ashen path" or, more properly, a trail of glowing coals.[9] Behind this "belief" lies a mythical convention of very wide distribution that memorializes an era when, as the result of precession, the sun "entered" the Milky Way, "naturally" setting it afire, but, more to the point, opening up "new ways" of contact between the living and other worlds. The "ashen path" is but a cryptic version of the myth of Phaethon, whose Andean elaborations may be found in the next chapter. Likewise the seminomadic Naskapi of Labrador, whose culture horizon has been termed mesolithic, speak of the possibility of contact between worlds along the Milky Way, which they call "ghost trail," or "dead person's path." The souls of the living originated in the sky where they "rest in the firmament until they become reincarnated."[10]

From the point of view of Western scholarship, it is axiomatic—in trying to understand something about the astronomical thought of the pre-Columbian Andes—to view the Milky Way in terms of its *function*. That is to say, it is of special interest to students to analyze how the Milky Way moves through the night sky and the seasons, and how its kinetic "behavior" is perceived by the culture that has incorporated its motions into calendar and ritual. This approach is wholly useful. Zuidema and Urton, for example, have shown how the Incas created an entire calendar—specifically geared to the annual tasks and accompanying rituals having to do with the management of llama flocks—based on the seasonal positions of the branch of the Milky Way containing the celestial Llama.[11]

Yet the lingering implication of this approach—which dominates the Western social sciences—is that spiritual "belief" is something of an afterthought, a codification in ritual of economically useful information derived from observation of the natural world. Variations on this theme—from *The Naked Ape* to *The Astonishing Hypothesis*—are legion, and share in a view of the human race as an aggregation of exceptionally clever animals. Ironically, in reducing the validity of religious experience to a sophisticated form of autosuggestion, Western social science has—without pang of curiosity— relegated to the dustbin labeled "belief" that specific dimension of the human experience which lies at the foundations of the human tradition of scientific inquiry.

It was here, then, in confronting the peculiar syntax of the technical language of myth—where scientific fact and spiritual value lie in synergic equipose, the one energizing the other—that I felt bound to regard with skepticism the influential convention of Western ethnography that refers to those mythical propositions positing order and meaning in the heavens as "beliefs," that is, ideas not susceptible to rigorous proof. This convention, I had begun to see for myself, has served as a sort of classificatory sinkhole into which have disappeared millennia of the most carefully crafted records of complex astronomical observation.

It seemed to me simply erroneous to assume of people who have not experienced "the awful art of separation" between heart and intellect that their "beliefs" about the natural order must skew their ability to make careful empirical observations. The whole purpose of studying the phenomenology of the natural world lay in establishing a dialogue with the world of spiritual value. The basis of this dialogue lay in trusting that the underlying principles of the natural order carried a message for humanity. This assumption lay very close to the heart of the efforts of Newton and Kepler.

For the early mythographers, lacking writing or complex mathematics, the language of this interchange had to span the gulf between the worlds of spirit and matter they sought to bridge. Impeccable observation was an offering of work to the powers of enlightenment. Myth, in recording the numinous import of astronomical patterns, had no business putting hatchmarks on the continuum between fact and belief. Astrology presupposed astronomy.

It was with such thoughts that I approached the Andean lore concerning the Milky Way. My conceptual vantage point lay less with the conventions of social scientific inquiry than with what I had already seen for myself. I now knew that the "flood" of A.D. 650, that is, the cessation of the heliacal rise of the Milky Way at June solstice, was an event of exceptional importance to the priest-astronomers of the Andes. I also knew that they were aware of precessional motion, that they were concerned about the impact of this phenomenon on the world of the living, and that they were especially interested in the Milky Way. I had assumed that "stars were animals" and that topographic references were meant to encrypt locations of the sun on the celestial sphere. The myths had responded. Now, with Andean notions about the Milky Way, I found myself following the turns of a celestial river possessed of a number of mysterious bridges and fords, mythical loci familiar to any student of the Old World myth. Had I found in the Andes a teaching that had once girdled the globe?

From the outset, I found one pregnant fact particularly hard to ignore. To the Andean astronomers, north was "up." For those of us who live in the temperate latitudes of the northern hemisphere, north is "up" because the pole star is high up in the northern sky and because the winter sun is low in the southern sky. In the southern Andes, the northern pole star is permanently invisible beneath the northern horizon. Conversely, the earth's south celestial pole lies above the horizon, and, while not as high in the sky as in temperate latitudes, this pole would at least suggest a better candidate for "up" than north. More to the point, the December-solstice sun lies only ten degrees south of the zenith at noon at the latitude of Cuzco (thirteen degrees south latitude), whereas the June solstice sun is noticeably lower, some thirty-six degrees down from (and north of) the zenith at noon. At this latitude there are about four hours a day more sunlight at December solstice than at June solstice. Nonetheless, in Andean thought, north was "higher" than south. "Upper Cuzco" was the northern half of the city. The "highest" mountain stood for June solstice. The Inca Empire's northern boundary was marked by a river called "the highest part of the sky-blue house."

At first I had attempted to ignore these kinds of data. I could find no explanation in the secondary literature for why, in the southern Andes, north should be so styled, and I kept thinking I must be missing something. I was operating on a sort of vague hypothesis that the ideas embodied in the technical language of myth might have filtered down to the Andes, where they gestated for an unknown length of time, eventually to issue forth reinvented for southern latitudes. Only after seeing for myself in the planetarium the results of assuming that north was "up" (the "highest" mountain being the northernmost position of the sun on the celestial sphere), did I begin to entertain the notion that the astronomical system of the Andes might have arrived somehow more directly.

North being "up," then something else was "up" as well: the possibility that Andean civilization had been fundamentally influenced by a teaching of staggering antiquity. And if such a teaching was alive and thriving in the

New World at the time of the Conquest; this meant that Andean civilization had preserved, right up to the very threshold of the modern era,[12] a portion of the human legacy thought only to exist in fragmentary form among various shards of the record of Old World antiquity. Therefore, as I turned to the Andean lore about the Milky Way—information recorded in abundance and in pristine ignorance by Spanish Conquistadores—I held my mind open to the possibility that I might well be looking at a stratum of human thought that lay at bedrock, whence had arisen not only the great religious traditions of the planet, but the practice of precise scientific observation as well. We begin on the "scientific" side, with the Andean understanding of the complex geometry of the Milky Way.

II

THERE ARE A number of serious "barriers to entry" to an understanding of the astronomical level of myth. Some have to do with the grip of preconceptions about what the ancients may or could have known, and to what extent they were capable of, or interested in, spreading their knowledge through seaborne adventure. But for sheer difficulty no barrier is more formidable than that of visualizing the complexities of naked-eye astronomy and then imagining the ensuing problems of recording observations without benefit either of mathematics or of writing. Without such an ability, "this dog don't hunt." In my opinion, this barrier, more than any other, explains why the wide distribution of a technical language in myth has escaped general recognition ever since Aristotle's lament that Plato was the last man who truly understood the significance of myth. Investigators predisposed neither toward an interest in naked-eye astronomy nor toward the suspicion that astronomy is particularly important in the culture under study can hardly be expected to sort out the important issues, much less ask the right questions.

One relevant exception is the ethnoastronomical fieldwork of Gary Urton. His discovery of the contemporary usage of the intercardinal solstice cross in organizing terrestrial space in an Andean village has already been discussed. Of interest now is his further discovery that the present-day Quechua practice of dividing space into quarters does not end at the horizon, but extends to the vault of heaven itself. Whereas terrestrial space is organized by the location of the rising and setting points of the solstice suns on the horizon, *celestial space is organized by means of the seasonal axes of the Milky Way.*[13]

To understand this formulation requires an effort of visualization. Our solar system lies within a galaxy that we call the Milky Way. Our galaxy is shaped something like a flying saucer: that is a disk with a slight bulge toward the center. Our position in the galaxy is about two thirds of the way toward its outer edge. Because we live *within* the galaxy, with its 100 billion stars, we experience the Milky Way as a continuous band of light in the sky. But because we live on a planet, which at all times blocks our vision of the sky beneath us, we cannot see the whole Milky Way all at once. From our perspective, it has, as it were, its *seasonal rhythms*. If one were out in space, free-floating, one could see the entire great circle of the galaxy. Because we are *within* the galaxy, it appears as a band on the celestial sphere that surrounds us.

The next point to understand is the orientation in the night sky of the Milky Way from the vantage point of the earth. Anyone who has observed the sweep of a "branch" of the Milky Way in the night sky may have noticed that it cuts across the heavens diagonally; that is to say, it is tilted about twenty-six degrees from the poles. For example, one branch of the Milky Way runs northeast-southwest, the branch visible in the night sky around *June* solstice (see figure 3.1a). The background glow of stars in this branch is exceptionally vivid because one is looking toward the center of the galaxy and the densest clustering of stars, the bulge in the "flying saucer." Within this branch lie the constellations we know as Scorpius and Sagittarius as well as the Andean black-cloud objects known as the celestial Llama and Fox. When this northeast/southwest branch is visible above, the other branch, or other half, of the great circle of the Milky Way lies in the skies beneath the earth—daytime in Tibet.

Now comes the tricky part. In *December*, when the other "branch" of the Milky Way (passing through the ecliptic in Gemini and Taurus) is visible in the night sky, *it runs along the opposite diagonal*, that is, northwest-southeast (see figure 3.1b). How does a continuous band of stars produce a seasonal pattern of alternating diagonals? I found this idea very difficult to visualize until I took an orange and drew a circle around it with a pen, making the circle pass diagonally by the "poles" of the orange about a third of the way toward the orange's "equator." I looked at the face with the northeast-southwest diagonal and then turned the orange 180 degrees around its "axis." *Voila!* Now the other half of my little galactic circle was running northwest-southeast.

One additional point is probably worth emphasizing here. The two seasonal branches of the Milky Way are visible in the night sky in the season *opposite* their time of heliacal rise. I have shown in figures 3.1a and 3.1b the position of the Milky Way for the era of the "flood" of A.D. 650. As we saw in chapter 2, the branch passing through Gemini and Taurus was just ceasing to rise heliacally at June solstice. At this time of year it would pass through the zenith at about midday, invisible. To follow this branch of the Milky Way throughout the night, one would have to wait six months until late December, when it rose at *sunset*. Conversely, if one wished to watch the harbinger of December solstice, Fox, disport himself in the night sky, the ideal time to do so would be late June and July.

Now, to return to Urton's research, what his informants told him was that it was their practice to *link* terrestrial and celestial space together *at the four solstice points on the horizon* by utilizing the fact that the sun is also "in" the two branches of the Milky Way. That is, when the sun rises on a solstice, it is in one or the other of the branches of the Milky Way. In a given twenty-four-hour period at, say, June solstice, the rising sun will "carry" the northwest-southeast branch of the Milky Way through the sky. At noon this branch will run (invisible) through the zenith. At midnight that night, the other—northeast-southwest—branch will run through the zenith. *The imagined "crossing"* of these two branches, visible overhead at night in alternating seasons, provides the conceptual framework for the quadripartition of *celestial* space (see figure 3.2[14]). This division is thereby linked to the quadripartition of *terrestrial* space by the sun's presence both "in" the Milky Way and "at" the horizon points of the solstitial cross.[15]

One particularly fascinating aspect of this present-day practice discovered by Urton is that it is, strictly speaking, *a historical relic*. In the present era, *neither* branch of the Milky Way any longer rises heliacally at a solstice. While Urton is quite right in saying that the sun is "in" the Milky Way, this sort of observation is one made by Western science, which can calculate the position of the sun in the stars. But it is not the indigenous Andean practice, which is to observe (visible) heliacal-rise events. One simply cannot see the stars through which the sun is passing. This point in no way detracts from Urton's findings, which were, after all, based on the input of native informants. Rather, it testifies to the durability in the Andean imagination of the ideal configuration of solstice heliacal-rise events "nested," as it were, in the rising branches of the Milky Way (see figure 3.3). This complete phenomenon was last visible to the unassisted eye some 1,350 years ago. The myths of the llama and the flood announce the moment of demise of this ideal configuration. Urton's conclusions are certainly correct, and are therefore the more interesting because of their depth and durability in time.

A second major discovery of Urton's was that in the present-day indigenous mind, the Milky Way is considered to be *two* rivers. In other words, in the same way that it is convenient for us to conceptutalize the Milky Way as having two "branches," it is also native Andean practice to employ this metaphor. According to one of Urton's informants,

> The Milky Way . . . is actually made up of two rivers, not one. The two Mayus [rivers] originate at a common point in the north, flow in opposite directions from north to south, and collide head-on in the southern Milky Way. The bright stellar clouds in this part of the Milky Way represent the "foam" (posoqu) resulting from the celestial collision. These data indicate that the celestial River has a second center, a "center of origin," in the north.[16]

Figure 3.4a shows the "headwaters" of the Milky Way at heliacal rise on June solstice, A.D. 650. At this moment, looking to the northern horizon one would have seen the northernmost reaches of the Milky Way stretching across the northern sky and bending southward at both the eastern and western horizons toward the direction of the June and December solstice points in the stars, as Figures 3.4b and 3.4c help to show. (These last two illustrations, incidentally, represent nothing more than a more panoramic view of the aspects shown in Figures 2.10a and 2.10b). Thus did the waters of the celestial river(s) pour forth, crossing the path of the sun (ecliptic) en route to their terminus at the Southern Cross.

The great value of Urton's work is how it shows beyond quibble that the native peoples of the Andes possess a complete mastery of the seasonal rhythms of the Milky Way, a mastery with demonstrable roots in the past. Moreover, in his discussion of the relationship between the intercardinal solstitial cross that organizes terrestrial space, and its celestial counterpart in the imagined crossing of the zenith axes of the Milky Way, Urton's work fully corroborates the enduring importance in the indigenous mind of the linkage of the Milky Way and solstice suns. Finally, Urton's work offers yet another example of how, even to this day, the indigenous Andean mind conceives of north as "up." This is shown by the simple fact that rivers always flow downhill. As the headwaters of the two branches of the celestial river lie in the north, and debouch in the south, in the vicinity of the Southern Cross, then north must be "higher" than south. And, since rivers rise in the mountains, the cosmic mountain must also lie in the northern heavens.

III

THE STUDENT OF Amerindian oral literature John Bierhorst has remarked on the "geometrical bias" of Native American myth.[17] Nowhere is this insight better illustrated than in the Andean integration of the solstice and Milky Way crosses, and the appearance of this substructure as the organizing reference system of the myths of the llama and the flood. The Milky Way is the only "natural" plane in the heavens. Others, such as the ecliptic—the apparent annual path of the sun through the stars—are mental abstractions, the product of accumulated observations seen in the mind's eye, not by the physical eye. The Milky Way's visibility to the naked eye, and its consequent usefulness as a means of organizing celestial space, may in part explain its prominent place in cosmological myths the world over.

But this is only half the story, the "left brain" side of the cosmological equation that gripped the Andean imagination. For the Milky Way was more than simply a celestial thing, a chronometric tool for the organization of calendars or politically useful rituals. In its incandescent presence the peoples of the Andes saw the visible manifestation of mankind's connection to supramundane worlds. In order to understand how the seasonal axes of the Milky Way related to the spiritual consciousness of Andean civilization, it is necessary to begin by noting that the supernatural worlds had names.

According to the indigenous view at the time of the Conquest, the cosmos was composed of three domains: *hanaq pacha,* literally "the world above"; *kay pacha,* "this world"; and *ukhu pacha,* "the world below."[18] Likewise the same notions were held by Aymara-speakers of the Lake Titicaca region, who also distinguished among three worlds, also called *pacha*(s): *alakh pacha, aca pacha,* and *mancca pacha,*[19] again literally meaning "the world above," "this world," and "the world below."

The Spanish blithely assimilated these "worlds" to the Christian concepts of "heaven," "earth," and "hell." An exception to this practice is found in the writings of the Spanish chronicler Santillán, who apparently listened a bit more carefully, noting that the dead returned whence they had come, "which was beneath the earth [read *ukhu pacha*]; and that someone who died as a result of just punishment for theft or other sins went to hell [infierno]."[20]

In other words, he found, in the indigenous view, a distinction between a fate of damnation to "hell" and an ordinary fate for ordinary people, who went to *ukhu pacha,* "the world below." To this day, many native Andean people hold the same view, with the additional clarification that "hell" refers to a fate of wandering the earth as a *condenado*, "a condemned one," neither of this world or the next.[21]

I eventually came to see that the Spanish descriptions of the indigenous view of the afterlife were thoroughly booby-trapped. For example, the lexicographer Holguín, who interpreted the indigenous lore about three worlds according to Christian preconception, recorded the Andean folk notion that appears as an epigraph to this chapter: "In this world we are exiled from our homeland in the world above." ("*Caypachapim hanacpacha llactanchicmanta hahuanchananchic.*") If ordinary people went to *ukhu pacha*, the "world below," when they died, what did they mean by claiming that their ultimate abode lay "up there," in the sky? Who was confused?

Other chroniclers assimilated this aspect of the native viewpoint about *hanaq pacha*, the "world above," to the Christian notion of "heaven." Cobo, for example, said that "those whom God had made outstanding people and given happy and prosperous circumstances in this life, without any doubt went to Heaven."[22] It is probable that one source of confusion for the Spanish arose from the fact that, in the time of the Incas, only those of noble lineage were thought to go to *hanaq pacha*, "the world above." Cobo's observation that only "prosperous" folk go to *hanaq pacha* is logical, since, in the tightly controlled economy of the Inca world, only those of noble lineage were allowed significant wealth. Still, the fact that the vast bulk of perfectly innocent Andean humanity journeyed at death to *ukhu pacha*, "the world below," apparently didn't stop them from referring to the sky when asked about the ultimate abode of the dead.

So in fact there are, in the Spanish chronicles, two sets of misunderstandings running in parallel: the Christian-influenced preconceptions of the Spanish, compounded by an overlay of class consciousness manufactured by the Andean nobility, which sought to differentiate the final resting place of the nobility and the peasantry into worlds "above" and "below," so that the nobility could rest "above" with the gods.[23] And yet, to repeat, this latter practice did nothing to prevent Andean peasants from pointing directly to the sky when asked about their destination in the afterlife.

My own introduction to these apparent contradictions about the location of the afterworld came during fieldwork in Peru. I spent several hours one evening sitting by a hearth conversing with a fifteen-year-old boy and his grandfather. After translating into Spanish a near-death experience related in Quechua by his grandfather—an experience replete with spirit-dogs, a passage across the "River Jordan," and an encounter with "gates"— this young man from the village of Amparaes escorted me to the door. As we stood looking at the sky, I asked him where the River Jordan was. In the

discreet manner of the native Andean peasantry, he pointed with his elbow
—to the Milky Way of the July night sky, that is the branch associated even
now in the native mind with December solstice, the branch containing the
celestial Llama and Fox.[24]

It would be many years before I understood with my mind what I felt at
that moment—a tremendous wallop of realization that a mode of knowing
millennia-old, and requiring the participation of both hemispheres of the
brain, still operated actively in the psyches of living people. The boy's
grandfather, when he hovered between life and death, had entered the
spiritual dimension of myth and found himself seeking passage across the
mayu.

I would learn that Andean myth and its allied cultural expressions such
as ritual, geomancy, and architecture are constructed along the lines of a
hologram. Their parts literally cannot be seen in isolation from the whole.
In highly simplified terms, a hologram is created by exposing photographic
film to "coherent light," as from a laser, beamed upon an object. This procedure produces a three-dimensional image. If one has a hologram of, say,
an elephant and is interested in tusks, breaking off the bit with the tusks
merely reproduces the whole elephant once again, only more faintly. Any
part of the image contains the whole, and the larger the image, the sharper
its definition. Likewise, one cannot "break off" the astronomical level of a
myth or ritual without importing its spiritual matrix in the process, and,
conversely, one cannot understand Andean spiritual life apart from its astronomical context. (An example of how a single Inca ritual recapitulates the
entirety of Andean cosmological thought has been placed in Appendix 1.)

I would come to appreciate how the strict geometrical consciousness—
the "coherent light"—of the Andean mastery of the motions of the Milky
Way, had the power effortlessly to sort out the apparent contradictions in
the Spanish chronicles and illuminate the underlying meaning of the three
"worlds" of Andean spiritual life. I would find that, in the same way that
north was "up" and south "down," the way to the "world above," *banaq pacba*,
lay in the direction of the branch of the Milky Way associated with north
and the June solstice; and the way to the "world below" led—not "down"
into the earth—but into the sky, across the branch of the Milky Way
associated with the direction south and the December solstice, down the
great river of time, in the train of the stately celestial Llama.

IV

THE NOTION THAT the Milky Way is connected to the ultimate abode of
the dead is very widespread among native American peoples. In a little-read
tour de force of Victorian-era comparative ethnography, Daniel Brinton,[25]
referring among others to Algonkin, Creek, and Iroquois ideas about the
location of the abode of the dead, noted that "the milky way which nightly
spans the arch of heaven was in their opinion the road that led thither and
was called the path of souls."[26]

The Creek Indians of the southeast United States called the Milky Way
"the spirit road."[27] The Yuman and Luiseño of California called it the "ghost
road."[28] The Mocoví of Bolivia's Gran Chaco state that it is a river abounding
in fish, where the spirits of the dead go fishing.[29] The North American Fox
Indians called it "Wâpisipow . . . the river of the stars yonder in the sky.
Along its shore dwell manitous, people who once lived on earth."[30]

In the present-day Andes, Quechua-speaking natives hold that the spirits
of those who have died must travel a long road leading to a turbulent river.
There the spirit must enlist the spirit of a black dog to carry it to a village
on the far banks of the river, where the ancestors dwell. Only those who
have been extremely abusive to dogs in life fail to make the passage. Other
variations include a difficult passage through a gate.[31] Often the name of the
river is Jordan[32] (another example of guerrilla syncretism), which, in Old
World thought, was also identified with the Milky Way.[33]

These same notions appear unalloyed in the Spanish chronicles of the
Conquest period. The extirpator Arriaga attests to the presence, among "all
the peoples of the sierra which we have visited," of ideas about a land to
which the souls of the dead must journey, including passage across "a great
river, which they have to cross by means of a very narrow bridge made of
hair; others say they have to cross by means of black dogs."[34]

The importance in indigenous thought of black dogs, serving in the
manner of canine psychopomps, to help the dead across the "river" is underscored by the large number of pre-Columbian burials containing mummified
dog remains.[35] Arriaga labored to eradicate the practice of raising black dogs
to be slaughtered specifically for funerary purposes.[36]

Brinton speaks for a wide range of native American comparative material:

How strange at first sight does it seem that the Hurons and Iroquois
should have told the earliest missionaries that after death the soul must

cross a deep and swift river on a bridge formed by a single slender tree
most lightly supported, where it had to defend itself against the attacks
of a dog? If only they had expressed this belief, it might have passed
for a coincidence merely. But the Athapascas [sic] (Chippewayans) also
told of a great water which the soul must cross in a stone canoe; the
Algonkins and Dakotas, of a stream bridged by an enormous snake, or
a narrow and precipitous rock. . . . With the Aztecs this water was
called Chicunoapa, the Nine Rivers. It was guarded by a dog and a
green dragon, to conciliate which the dead were furnished with slips of
paper by way of toll. The Greenland Eskimos thought that the waters
roared through an unfathomable abyss over which there was no other
bridge than a wheel slippery with ice, forever revolving with fearful
rapidity. . . .[37]

Where, then, is this underworld and the entrance to it, and how can it
be called "the world below," and at the same time lie in the sky, in the
vicinity of the Milky Way? Explicit information, particularly from the modern era, is scant. Urton, citing Fock, has noted that in the Ecuadorian Andes,
kay pacha ("the earth") and *ukhu pacha* are considered mirror images.[38] We do
know this mirroring extends to the sky, from such ethnographic clues as
"When it is dawning for us, night is falling in the world of the *ukhu
pacha* . . ."[39]

During fieldwork in Bolivia, one informant was particularly keen that I
should see the celestial Llama clearly. He took great pains to mimic its exact
posture, and added that when one looks up into the sky, one is seeing the
animal's *back*, and that it is "right side up" when it is under the earth. This
was important information, not only because it gave clues to how "under the
earth" was visualized, but also because the skies were obviously included in
the visualization.

Other bits of data, such as the contemporary notion that the toad
(Quechua *hanp'atu*), along with men and dogs, is the only being who possesses a spirit that survives death, lead persistently back to the sky, particularly the southern sky, where dwelt Toad, a small black cloud near the
Southern Cross (see figure 3.5). In contemporary folklore, Toad is said to
live in *ukhu pacha*, the extraterrestrial "world below."[40]

Then there is the curious tale, recorded by the chronicler Avila, of a
meeting between the god Wiraqocha and the last Inca, Huayna Capac.
Wiraqocha invites Huayna Capac to journey with him to Titicaca, thence
to dispatch emissaries to the "lower regions," to seek a gift from the ancestors. Huayna Capac obliges, sending shamans of the condor, falcon, and

swift, all eager to serve. The swift-shaman wins the race and carries out his orders. Two points are of interest for the present context: first, obviously, the use of *birds* to get to the land of the dead implies that this topos lay in the sky; second, the three "birds" described elsewhere in Avila as "three stars in a straight line" near the celestial Llama, are the same three that formed the crosspiece of the post-Conquest constellation *cruz calvario*. That is, they lay in the tail of Scorpius,[41] where the ecliptic crosses the Milky Way. This area certainly began to look like a candidate for the entrance to the land of the dead, especially if one assumed that the *location* of these "bird-stars" had something to do with their *role* as emissaries to the underworld.

Now it was just this area of the sky—where Fox, the celestial Llama, and *cruz calvario* converge—that was visible rising at *December solstice* during the reign of the Incas (see figure 3.6). *The Inca festival of the dead, Capac Raymi, culminated at the December solstice.*[42] At this time each year, according to indigenous religious custom, *the dead were said to return to earth* in order to reanimate the power of tradition by communing awhile with the living. The centerpiece of the Inca ritual was a kind of carousing with the ancestors, four days of eating and drinking with them "as if they were alive."[43] These feasts took place during the "solstice window," that is, during the four days, beginning two days before the solstice and continuing until one day after the solstice, when the sun appeared to "sit" immobile at its southernmost point of rise on the eastern horizon.[44]

On the last day of the feeding of the ancestors, according to Molina, the newly knighted warriors broke their fast in order to feast with the ancestors. The mummified remains of the Inca kings and "all the *wakas*" were brought from various shrines into the main plaza.[45] These *wakas* were the lineage *wakas* of all the tribes of the Empire. It will be recalled that these were the representations of the lineage ancestors created by Wiraqocha, and hence the ancestry of the entire Andean people was represented as present at the ceremony. The celebrants then offered libations and food to these mummies and *wakas* of the ancestors. According to Cobo, "The reason they brought out the bodies of the dead was so their descendants could drink with them as if they were alive; and particularly on this occasion, since the knights had been initiated, they wished to ask that the ancestors make them as brave and adventurous as they had been."[46]

As the sun "rested" upon the southern tropic, appearing to rise at the same point on the horizon over successive days, the people of Cuzco also rested, taking part in a riotous saturnalia celebrating the annual opening of the land of the dead to the land of the living. The way was open because the great celestial River, which each mortal must cross to reach the land of the dead, lay accessible on the horizon, rising with the solstice sun. The importance of *dawn*—actually the moment of heliacal rise—in this equation is preserved in both Conquest-period and present-day sources. Avila, for example, noted that, at the time of the Conquest, the same idea—that the souls of the dead ancestors return at dawn—was held in Huarochirí.[47]

There was, then, in the pre-Columbian Andes, a breathless moment out of time when the barriers between this world and the next could be bridged. This moment came at dawn on the December solstice, when time itself seemed suspended with the brief arresting of the sun's motion along the horizon. At this moment the Milky Way lay in visible contact with the horizon in the gathering dawn. The earth was for a moment "connected" to the great River by whose banks lay the celestial homeland of the Andean peoples. And if the entrance to this otherworldly realm lay open at the moment the sun achieved its southermost position on the celestial sphere, this world would be called *ukhu pacha*, "the world below," confirming once again the great conceptual structuring of the night sky in terms of north and south, of up and down.

One final aspect of Capac Raymi, the ritual use of the conch trumpet, recapitulates in yet another way the importance of the relationship between the December solstice sun and the Milky Way in keeping open the routes between this world and the land of the dead.

Up and down the Andes, the opening of the entrance to the land of the dead was heralded by the sonorous boom of the *huallay qepa*, or conch-shell trumpet, sounded on the very eve of the December solstice. This signal also marked the commencement of rites for the augmentation and care of the llamas.[48] The two events were interrelated. A substantial number of Andean tribes claimed descent from the celestial Llama.[49] It was, in a sense, the prototype for all lineage *wakas*. As figure 3.6 shows, the Llama was rising at dawn on December solstice in the era of the Incas. According to folk knowledge so widespread as to attract the malign notice of Arriaga, "the souls of the dead go to where their lineage *waka* lies."[50] This meant that when the ancestors returned to earth, they were returning from the abode of their lineage *waka*, in this case from the celestial Llama. No doubt, the dead, upon returning, might also be pleased to observe rites concerning the augmentation of "the flock."

The idea that the conch trumpet had a special significance at December solstice is not a guess, and its symbolic meaning was not arbitrary. Rather there exists a persistent pattern of extraordinarily wide distribution in which the conch stands both for the December solstice and, in those ages in which the Milky Way rises there, the entrance to the land of the dead as well. The reason for this is that the conch is a ritual "term" of the language of archaic astronomy.

In the classical Greek myth of Deucalion, for example, "the devastating waves of the flood were ordered back by Triton's blowing the conch: the conch had been invented by Aigokeros, i.e., Capricornus, who ruled the winter solstice in the world-age when Aries 'carried' the sun."[51] Foerstmann's investigations led him to the conclusion that the Mayas connected the conch with the December solstice and the turtle shell with June solstice.[52] Dechend has pointed out that the Maya glyph for "zero" was the conch, standing for the completion of one cycle and the beginning of the next.[53] Eliade notes that in North America and in Asia, shamans occasionally use the shell trumpet instead of the drum at the outset of journeys to the underworld.[54] In the Aztec myth of Quetzalcoatl, the hero gains entry into the land of the dead by managing to sound the conch trumpet of the Lord of the Dead Land.[55]

It must be that the conch stands for December solstice by the same reasoning that the mountain stands for June solstice. The conch comes from the sea floor (the spatial opposite of "the highest mountain in the world"), representing the earth's lowest or southernmost extreme, just as the December solstice represents the southerly extreme of the sun's yearly round. Reference to Pachakuti Yamqui's diagram (figure 2.4) demonstrates that such logic was operative in the Andes. The terrestrial opposite of the "June Solstice Mountain," is a body of water labeled *mamaqocha*, "mother sea (or lake)," connected to a *puquio*, or "spring," found on the rainy-season, December-solstice side of the drawing. As we have already seen, Andean myth may style any entrance into the earth, such as caves, springs, and hollow trees, as an entrance to *ukhu pacha*, and this is why, as we have already seen, contemporary Quechua-speakers say that toads, which hibernate in the earth, live in the underworld, and why, in the Conquest period, all the ancestors were said to have emerged from such terrrestrial orifices.

The greatest such "emergence" site in all the Andes was Lake Titicaca. The Quechua and Aymara words for "lake" and "sea" are the same, *qocha*. The present line of reasoning explains Arriaga's advice to his priests to be aware that in many villages they would find a bit of local topography called "Titicaca," and that this area would be associated with the ancestor cult. In contemporary Chincheru, an informant told me that the low plain beneath the towering, Inca-period terraces was called Titicaca.

And this interpretation of the sense of the marine symbolism of the conch—that, as an artifact from the seafloor, it stands for the sun's "lowest" position on the celestial sphere at December solstice—also explains why the Huacaypata, the plaza where the Inca rites of December solstice were staged, was covered to a depth of two feet with sand laboriously hauled ten thousand feet up into the Andes from the shores of the Pacific Ocean.[56]

The association of the conch with both December solstice and the entrance to the land of the dead, implicit in the Incas rites of Capac Raymi, is explicitly linked in several Mesoamerican examples. Linda Schele has written about two Maya monuments at Palenque: the Temple of Inscriptions, containing the sarcophagus lid of Lord Shield-Pacal, and the accession monument of Lord Chan Bahlum—including depictions of his dead father—in the Temple of the Cross (see figures 3.7 and 3.8.).[57] Each of these monuments depicts a three-tiered cosmos representing the celestial, terrestrial, and underworlds, a scheme already familiar from the Andean example. In each temple the sun is depicted as sinking into "the jaws of the underworld." The symbol representing the point of interface between the world of the living and the underworld in each temple is the conch shell. At each temple in turn, a solar hierophany—an architectural "special effect," here using light and shadow cast by the setting sun—lights first the center of the temple depicting Lord Pacal descending in the "jaws of the underworld," and then the site of Lord Bahlum's accession and his father's demise. At the latter site, the last light of day shines upon God L, the Lord of the Underworld. Both hierophanies take place on the same day and during the same event, *sunset on December solstice.*[58] Here we find evidence marvelously complementary to the notion that the souls of the ancestors return at sunrise on December solstice: that is, the newly dead "depart" at sunset on December solstice.

We find the jaws of the underworld, again, in a Zapotec genealogical register (see figure 3.9). According to Marcus's analysis, "Above the couple are the 'Jaws of the Sky,' flanked by stylized conch shells. Descending from the 'Jaws of the Sky' is a personage perhaps ancestral, perhaps mythical, holding in one hand a strand of beads."[59]

What this register demonstrates, as clearly as iconography can, is that the entrance to the underworld, marked by conch shells, *lies in the sky.*[60] Now, as neither Schele's nor Marcus's articles was particularly interested in matters of the topography of the afterlife, there is no mention of the Milky Way. But it was most definitely "there," at the December solstice during the era of Palenque's greatness. In Marcus's article, moreover, there is reproduced a Conquest-period map of a Zapotec village and associated toponyms on the horizon, with cosmologically pregnant names such as "Burning Mountain" and "Distaff Hill." In the southwest quadrant is located the toponym "*Suigox-anaya/Rio debajo de la tierra,*" that is, "River Beneath the Earth."[61]

If the conch shell stood for the position of the solstice sun "at bottom" upon the southern tropic at the entrance to the underworld, might one not surmise, on the basis of the "geometrical bias" of Andean thought, that the entrance land of the gods lay upon the other tropic, at the top of the cosmic mountain?

V

THE LAST TIME the Incas celebrated the December rite of Capac Raymi in its full, uninhibited splendor was in December of 1533, this time in conjunction with a victory celebration of "liberation" from the hated occupying army of Quito and its now-deceased renegade Emperor, Atahuallpa. The Spanish, just then "allies," witnessed the saturnalian spectacle, and were particularly impressed by the unending rivers of urine that poured through the city's gutters from the tens of thousands of inebriated celebrants. Among the wonders they recounted was the parade of the mummified remains of the Inca kings, including the remains of Huayna Capac, who had died in Quito, probably of smallpox. They marveled at his state of preservation, noting that only the tip of his nose was missing.[62]

These eyewitness accounts are of particular interest in light of a persistent apocryphal tradition that Huayna Capac was buried in the Ancasmayu, the river marking the northern boundary of the Empire. According to this tradition, the river was temporarily diverted from its bed to allow for the construction of a tomb for the dead Emperor.[63] After the intentions of the Spaniards came clear, the Incas of Cuzco hid the mummies, but Viceroy Toledo found them—in 1571—and, before burning them all, identified that of Huayna Capac yet again.[64] What, then, was the point of maintaining the fiction that Huayna Capac was buried in the bed of the Ancasmayu River?

The Ancasmayu rises on the western side of the Andean watershed, between Quito and Pasto, and flows northwest into the Pacific Ocean.[65] As already noted, the Quechua word *ancas* means "sky blue," and can be connected with the ideal position of the sun at June solstice. This reading is further supported by the meaning and symbolism of the Quechua cognate *anca*, meaning "eagle."[66] We have already seen how various bird-shamans vied for the honor of carrying the Inca's message to the underworld, but how only the smallest managed to carry out the task. Large, high-soaring birds, on the other hand, are equipped for flights to the "world above."

Among Siberian shamans, the eagle is "father of the First Shaman of the sun, messenger of the celestial god, intercessor between god and mankind."[67] In contemporary Aymara folklore, the eagle is always classified as belonging to the "world above,"[68] which, in turn, as we have seen, is connected with the June solstice. Garcilaso, speaking of a series of terrible omens portending the end of the Empire, describes how an *anca* fell dead to earth in Cuzco during Inti Raymi ceremony (held at June solstice) during the reign of Huayna Capac.[69] The etymological link between *ancas* and *anca* reflects the symbolic association between the solar bird, high in the blue sky of the dry season, and the position of the June-solstice sun. It therefore appears not to be a coincidence that the legend of Huayna Capac's burial should be associated with "Sky-blue River," which flowed northwest—the direction of the June-solstice sunset—into the sea. Ancasmayu represented more than a terrestrial border, for it also carried the soul of Huayna Capac to the land of the gods.

The same southeast-northwest axis also dominated the Inca rites of June solstice. Urton has reasoned that, since the myths of Wiraqocha have the god traveling northwest, and leaving the earth at Manta in Ecuador, the ritual of the Inca priests, who followed the course of the Vilcamayu—the terrestrial analogue of the Milky Way—to its headwaters at Mount Vilcanota, thence to return northwest to Cuzco, represented a re-creation of Wiraqocha's final journey. In support of this reading, Urton has drawn attention to a further aspect of this ritual: according to the Inca priests, the headwaters of the Vilcamayu at Vilcanota represented the "birthplace of the sun." Noting that contemporary Quechua-speakers refer to the Milky Way as two rivers originating in the north, Urton further reasoned that this explains the notion that the sun was "born" at June solstice, at the "headwaters" of the Milky Way.[70] Strictly speaking, the headwaters of the Milky Way lay at its northern terminus (figure 3.4a). The Inca priests apparently assimilated this position of the Milky Way to the simultaneous rise of the Milky Way at June solstice (figure 3.4b)—last occurring ca. A.D. 650—and termed the sun "born" at the headwaters of the Milky Way.

In turn, these observations illuminate further information that has heretofore been impossible to place within a coherent context. First, there is the title of Wiraqocha found in a series of hymns recorded by Pachakuti Yamqui: *vilca ulcaapu*. This title literally means "lord fountainhead of the sun,"[71] a recasting of the general notion that Wiraqocha was the creator of the heavenly array within the specific imagery—"the birth of the sun"—employed by the Inca priests at Vilcanota.

In drawing attention to the topography around the towering mountain Vilcanota, Juan Larrea has described the terrestrial analogue of this configuration, imprinted in the landscape. A small lake at the foot of this mountain lies at the headwaters of not only the Vilcamayu, flowing northwest, but also of the Pucara River, which flows south into Lake Titicaca. Thus the topography of Vilcanota mirrors exactly the cosmological notion that at "June solstice mountain" the sun is "born" at the headwaters of the two celestial branches of the Milky Way, the one branch flowing northwest toward the land of the gods, the other flowing southeast toward Titicaca, associated with the underworld. Larrea has reproduced a drawing of a Conquest-era drinking cup (figure 3.10), depicting this entire symbolic complex of ideas as seen in the indigenous mind.

Finally, the great importance attached to this image by the Incas is most clearly manifest in the magnificent Inca shrine on the Island of the Sun in Lake Titicaca. On the east side of the island, the Incas fashioned a long stairway leading from the water's edge upward to a fountain gushing forth from the very cliffside where Wiraqocha was said to have created the sun, the moon, and the stars. The water from this fountain, which is faced in flawless Inca masonry, pours into a large, equally perfect stone basin, thence to flow back into the lake via two channels flanking the stairway. Here, at the spiritual epicenter of the Andes, the Incas embossed the cosmogram of the two-branched Milky Way pouring from the north (the cliff, or mountain) all the way to the underworld (the lake). This is the same imagery— the opposition of mountain to lakes and springs—as found in Pachakuti Yamqui's drawing (figure 2.4).

If the Inca rites of dawn on June solstice tell us something about the "fountainhead" of sacred influences in the Andes, the chronicler Pachakuti Yamqui tells the tale of the last days on earth of *vilca ulcaapu*, "Lord Fountainhead of the Sun," the god Wiraqocha. Old now, with a gray beard, and carrying a wooden staff, Wiraqocha moves through an Andean twilight of the gods. Treated with disrespect by all but the father of the mythical head of the Inca lineage, the old man returns to the ancient sacred center, Tiahuanaco, where it all began. Various versions recording the god's ascent to "heaven"[72] have him walking northwest and out to sea, disappearing forever. Pachakuti Yamqui's version includes one other bit of information concerning the god's route: "They say that Tunapa [Wiraqocha] followed the river Chacamarca until he reached the sea. I understand that he went by these straits to the other sea."[73]

The name of the river Chacamarca literally means "the bridge at the highest part of the house." The use of the term *marca*—the same architectural image for June solstice encrypted in the name of the mountain, Ancasmarca, in Molina's version of the flood myth—in association with the term "bridge," *chaca*, establishes once again a sense of complementary balance among cosmological elements. Just as the souls of deceased *mortals* must cross a bridge over the celestial river at sunset on *December* solstice, so must Wiraqocha, a *god*—old, tired, in the "twilight" of his years—leave the earth by means of a bridge over a river, flowing northwest to the sea, which is to say he crossed the Milky Way at sunset on *June* solstice. Nor had the god any choice; the floodwaters of time were already seething about the bridge (figure 2.10a). And so also, in ritual memory of this moment, the Incas threw into their own, man-made floodwaters from the bridge at Ollantaytambo a "final offering" of coca to Wiraqocha, said to dwell in the "northern sea" (see Appendix 1).

The sense of finality transmitted in this tale snapped me out of a long reverie. So lulled had I become by the symmetry of Andean thought that I had lost track of my original question. Why was the "flood" of A.D. 650 so important to the Andean priest-astronomers? I now realized that I had unconsciously formed a mental image of the "bridges" across the Milky Way, an image that was not up to the task of answering this question. I had begun to think of those "bridges" as simply the track of the sun (ecliptic) across the two branches of the Milky Way. But this tale of Wiraqocha could not be reconciled to my "solution." The god was gone, and "forever." But if the "world above," *hanaq pacha,* lay simply "across" the bridge spanning the June-solstice branch of the celestial river, then surely the "bridge" would be open some other time, just not on the solstice proper.

To put the matter in Western terms, the branches of the Milky Way will always be visible rising at some time of the year at the horizon point where the sun will rise. There are, in other words, *always* two crossing areas of ecliptic plane (sun) and Milky Way. Moreover, these two "bridges" will *always* lie in Scorpius and Sagittarius on the one hand, and Gemini and Taurus on the other.[74] If these two areas constituted the "bridges" between worlds, as I had unconsciously assumed, why had Wiraqocha departed for the land of the gods, and forever?

I sensed that the answer must have something to do with the fact that the Milky Way no longer rose at *June solstice.* But it was not until I realized what a miserable student of *Hamlet's Mill* I had been that I grasped the full significance of the pattern I was trying to understand.

I had yet to realize the precision with which the terms *hanaq pacha, kay pacha,* and *ukhu pacha* were meant to be understood. For, on one level, they represented pure celestial analogues for the supernatural realms. The "other worlds" were not some vague northerly and southerly regions of the sky. The land of the gods and the land of the dead had very specific boundaries. What good was a bridge, if it couldn't take you where you wanted to go?

VI

AS IT WAS, I tried to clarify what the mythical term "bridge" was meant to convey. In Western classical antiquity, according to Macrobius, reincarnating souls, who had left the earth at the lower "Gate," in Sagittarius, returned by way of Gemini, the "Gate . . . where the Zodiac and the Milky Way intersect."[75] This formulation would not have puzzled the Norsemen. Their dead had to traverse a great rushing water to enter the hereafter through the gate called *Helgrind*, known on occasion to lie open, but only "when the dead return to visit the earth." As in the Andes, the road to the underworld was a two-way street. As for the gods, they passed by a bridge "fragile and steeply poised above the abyss, as thin as a needle or a sword-edge." The *Bifrost* bridge, across which the gods thundered on horseback, was said by Snorri Sturluson to span the Milky Way. It was reduced to splinters at *Ragnarok*, the twilight of the gods, when Midgard, the "middle realm" of living people, and Asgard, the realm of the gods, were laid waste.[76] It seemed that Snorri Sturluson might have understood the urgency of Wiraqocha's final journey.

Brinton, too, was aware of the proliferation of bridges spanning traditional literatures:

> We everywhere hear of a water which the soul must cross, and an opponent, either a dog or an evil spirit, which it has to contend with. We are all familiar with the dog Cerberus (called by Homer simply "the dog"), which disputed the passage of the river Styx, over which the souls must cross. . . . Relics of this belief are found in the Koran, which describes the bridge el Sirat, thin as a hair and sharp as a scimitar, stretched in a single span from heaven to earth; in the bridge Bifrost, which, according to the Edda, stretches from earth to heaven; in the Persian legend where the rainbow arch Chinevad is flung across the gloomy depths between this world and the home of the happy; and even in the current Christian allegory which represents the waters of the mythical Jordan rolling between us and the Celestial City.[77]

The word *chaca*—meaning "bridge" in both Quechua and Aymara—was frequently used, in astronomical contexts, to describe locations on the celestial sphere of inherent geometrical interest. Holguín also lists *puncuchaca*, where *puncu* means "door" and *chaca* then refers either to a threshold or a lintel. Another, related word—again found in both languages—is *chacana*,

meaning "ladder" or "stairway."[78] These words—styling important astronomical junctures "bridges," "doorways," and "stairways"—functioned in mythical
usage to identify boundaries that were, at the same time, astronomical and
lay between differing modes of existence, or states of consciousness.

The only celestial object clearly identified in the Conquest-period literature by one of these names—chacana—is the three stars of Orion's Belt,
known to the Spanish as "the Three Marias."[79] These three stars lie along
the celestial equator, that is, the great circle of stars passing through the
zenith as viewed from the earth's equator. Urton has suggested that the name
chacana indicates the indigenous notion that these three stars connected, as
might a ladder, two distinct zones of the celestial sphere, north and south
of the celestial equator.[80] Again, the specific use of the term "ladder" to
denote the division between the northern and southern celestial hemispheres
suggests the notion of verticality, of ascent and descent, of "up" and "down"
between north and south.

In Andean culture, then, the concept of a "bridge" (or "stairway") had
uses as a cosmological metaphor: in myth it stood for a point of contact
between this world and the supernatural worlds, while in purely astronomical
uses it referred to abstract "junctions" on the celestial sphere, that is, to
locations whose significance lay in marking areas of the sky critical for
grasping the essential geometry of the fixed sphere of stars.

Thus, for example, the Incas reiterated the importance of the concept
of a celestial equator, chacana, by establishing the east-west baseline as a
fundamental organizing principle in the layout of Cuzco. This line was
determined by observation of the rising of the equinox suns[81] over a mountain which they named Pachatusan,[82] literally "support pillar of space-time."

To the north of this fundamental baseline, in hanan (Upper) Cuzco,
lived the prestige moiety, or half, of the population, associated with warfare
and Empire, and to the south of this line lay hurin (Lower) Cuzco, inhabited
by the moiety associated with religion and agriculture. (Similarly, the dead
of Upper Cuzco were destined for eternal rest to the north with the gods,
accessible through the June solstice, while the deceased of Lower Cuzco
would traffic across the December-solstice bridge to the south.) Thus the
architectural subtext of Andean thought, found in important place names
such as Ancasmarca and Chacamarca, as well as in the "house," framing
Pachakuti Yamqui's drawing, stated insights into the structure or geometry
of the celestial sphere. Its reappearance in the toponym "Pachatusan" underscores the importance to the Incas of the celestial equator as a conceptual
element in the structure of the "world house," as well as the pervasive

geomantic thrust of Inca thought, which sought to mirror the principles of organization of the celestial sphere in both the social and civic spheres.

Urton and Zuidema have written exhaustively on the topic of the word *chaca*, and how, at the time of the Conquest, this term, meaning "bridge," was dropped from usage in favor of the Christian term *cruz*, "cross."[83] For example, the present-day Quechua name for the Southern Cross is *huch'uy cruz* ("little cross") or *lluthu cruz* ("tinamou [the Andean partridge] cross"). The identification of the Southern Cross with a partridge, *lluthu*, is undoubtedly of pre-Columbian origin. Avila's informants identified *lluthu* as "a black spot which goes a little bit in front of" the celestial Llama.[84] *Lluthu* remains to this day the Andean name for the Western Coalsack, a black cloud nestled in the southeast quadrant of the Southern Cross, which rises, as Avila described, "a little bit ahead of" alpha and beta Centaurus, "the eyes of the llama" (see figure 3.5). The reason why the *lluthu cruz* should merit the title of a *chaca* is, aside from its appearance, that it marks a notable juncture in the Quechua heavens. As Urton has pointed out, the Southern Cross lies where the two branches of the Milky Way, with "headwaters" in the north, "collide" in the southern skies.[85] This location constitutes a *chaca* in its purely astronomical sense of "important juncture."

Another such *chaca*, dressed up in post-Conquest verbiage, was *cruz calvario*, or the Cross of Calvary, which we have already seen (see chapter 2, pages 34–35 and figures 2.2 and 2.3). These stars, marking the area of the sky where the Milky Way crosses the ecliptic, were, up through Inca times, visible rising at December solstice. The position of these stars demands that they be styled as a cross, or *chaca*, because they identify the location of the mythical bridge across the Milky Way, leading to the land of the dead. It is unknown whether these precise stars were considered a single constellation in the pre-Columbian Andes, but the three stars of its crosspiece represented the three "bird-stars" in a straight line that sped toward the underworld.

In the post-Conquest era, then, this locus was masked under the Christian notion of the death and resurrection of Christ, as symbolized by the Cross of Calvary. Here again is an example of how Spanish repression during the Conquest period drove the indigenous people of the Andes to acts of "guerrilla syncretism." The essence of this practice was to identify and adopt those elements of the technical language of myth that seemed also to be present in the tradition of their oppressors. During the three days between His death on Mount Calvary and His resurrection, according to Christian tradition, Jesus descended into the underworld to free the souls of the dead.

At this point I started to make some drawings, as an aid to visualization. Figure 3.11a depicts a viewpoint *outside* the fixed sphere of stars, looking in, with the earth an infinitesimal point in the center of the circle. The diagonal circle represents the ecliptic plane, the pathway of the earth's orbit around the sun; the sun's positions—as seen against the background of fixed stars— at the June and December solstices are marked accordingly. North is marked in terms of Polaris.

To help clarify my thinking I also drew in the northern and southern tropics—that is, the celestial tropics of Cancer and Capricorn (figure 3.11b). On the globe of the earth, these circles mark the northernmost and south- ernmost latitudes at which the sun passes through the zenith. These events occur on the June and December solstices respectively. Projected onto the celestial sphere, as is the custom in celestial navigation, these circles indicate the northernmost and southernmost celestial latitudes that the sun can reach; taken as a whole, they mark the circle of stars that will pass through the zenith when viewed from the latitude of the tropics on earth, at twenty-three and a half degrees north and south latitudes respectively.

After I looked at this sketch for a while, I began to understand how all the Andean material about the entrances to *hanaq pacha* and *ukhu pacha* could be reconciled to the anxiety of the priest-astronomers observing the "flood" of A.D. 650. For a second time I had occasion to wonder about my own stubborn obtuseness. As with my first attempts to understand the myths of the "flood"—when I had wasted months oblivious of the fact that the animals in the myths referred to their counterparts in the sky—I had once again failed to apply what I already knew to the situation at hand. Once again I had come up against some aspect in my thinking that resolutely balked at really believing the ideas of Santillana and Dechend. The answer I was looking for was there for the having. The key lay in understanding that the greatest of all the topographical metaphors in the technical language of myth was that of the "earth" itself:

> ... "earth," in the most general sense, meant the ideal plane laid
> through the ecliptic ... "earth" is the ideal plane going through the
> four points of the year, the equinoxes and solstices. Since the four
> constellations rising heliacally at the two equinoxes and two solstices
> determine and define an "earth," it is *termed* quadrangular (and by no
> means "believed" to be quadrangular by "primitive" Chinese, and so on).
> And since constellations rule the four corners of the quadrangular earth
> only temporarily [because of precession], such an "earth" can rightly be

said to perish, and a new earth to rise from the waters, with four new constellations rising at the four points of the year.[86]

Now I reworked my first drawing to include the equinox points along the ecliptic (figure 3.12a), and shaded in the "quadrangular earth." Then, as shown in figure 3.12b, I sketched the "World House," that is, the metaphoric alternative to the topographical metaphors of "mountains," "sea," and so on. I drew the "pillars" at the solstices and equinoxes (whose locations in the stars were viewed in Cuzco over a mountain named "support pillar of space-time") from tropic to tropic, in order to conceptualize the "top and bottom" of the structure. Figure 3.12c gathers these steps into sequence.

Finally I drew the "celestial earth" from the point of view of the Andean terminology (figure 3.13). At the June solstice point I placed "the highest mountain in the world," and at the December solstice I laid the conch shell on the floor of the "sea," the lowest topos of the celestial earth.

I now realized that, from the mythical standpoint, the middle "world" of the three Andean *pachas*, that is *kay pacha*—translated by the Spanish as "the earth," but literally "this space-time"—*must refer to the zone of the celestial sphere between the tropics.* The interpretation conflicted with none of the information I had found and illuminated it all.

The idea of a "celestial earth" laid out with utter clarity the astronomical basis of the theory of world-ages. During a *pachakuti* ("space-time turns over"), when, according to the myth, "the whole world" is destroyed, it is the "earth" as defined by the stars rising heliacally at the solstices and equinoxes (the four "pillars" holding up the "world") that is "destroyed," i.e., displaced by precessional motion. As we have seen, this phenomenon constituted the central focus of the Andean myths of the flood. On the surface they said that the "whole world" was destroyed by a flood, while the astronomical subtext was about nothing other than the fate of the solstice points in the stars. Earth and "earth"—these were the two levels upon which the myths of the llama and the flood operated. One told a story about events on earth (*kay pacha*, "this world"), while the other spoke of time and motion, of the demise of *this* space-time (again, *kay pacha*) and the creation of a new "this space-time," all owing to the predations of time and motion on the scale of precession.

The logic of these ideas was as relentless as it was supple. The limits of the "celestial earth" were identical with the limits of the ecliptic plane. Hence the metaphorical associations flowed without effort. Just as the highest point on earth is a mountain, the highest—meaning northernmost—point on the "celestial earth," that determined by the location of the sun in the stars on the June solstice, must be *termed* "mountain." The same logic demands that the conch be blown on the December solstice. Further, and wholly logically, *if there were three "worlds," and the boundaries of the middle world,* kay pacha, *were known to extend to the tropics, then the exact location of the "world above,"* hanaq pacha, *and the "world below,"* ukhu pacha, *was also knowable. The land of the gods was the entire section of the celestial sphere north of the northern tropic, and the land of the dead was the entire section of the celestial sphere south of the southern tropic.*[87] This idea is depicted in figure 3.14.

And now I knew why the flood of A.D. 650 was so important to the Andean priest-astronomers: the "bridge" to the land of the gods had been destroyed—not because the sun no longer crossed paths with the galactic plane, *but because this crossing no longer led to the land of the gods.* This is why Wiraqocha left, and left "forever." This bridge had a name—*chacamarca,* "the bridge at the highest point of the house"—and this name meant the northern tropic, the highest point of the "world house." But the bridge was going under—under the northern tropic, to be precise—"pulled down" by precessional motion. The Milky Way would no longer rise where and when the sun touched the northern tropic. This was, as we have seen, *precisely* the astronomical focus of the myths of the "flood." The celestial analogue of "access to the gods"—that is, the "bridge" to *hanaq pacha*—had been destroyed. For the first time since the Milky Way had "come to earth" in 200 B.C., this connection—the visible manifestation of the foundations of Andean spiritual life, the great seal of reciprocal harmony stamped upon the heavens by the Creator himself—was gone.

VII

ALL THE INFORMATION I had collected about the Milky Way and the routes to the supernatural world was consistent with this understanding. And much of this information took on deeper meaning in light of it. For example, once I realized that *ukhu pacha,* "the world below," had precise boundaries, I noticed something new about the black-cloud objects—Fox, Toad, Partridge, and Serpent.[88] I already knew that these animals were associated with the underworld, and that this was true not only of modern classificatory schemes, such as those of the Aymara,[89] but is also found on a case-by-case basis in the Conquest-period literature. The only exception is the Llama, who is only sometimes associated with the underworld (probably because she represents, as it were, "the mother of all ancestors"), and sometimes with the earth.

Therefore it was startling to realize that *all the dark-cloud constellations authoritatively identified either from the Conquest period or from contemporary investigation—that is, Llama, Toad, Fox, Partridge, and Serpent—all lie south of the southern tropic.* Furthermore, I came to realize that, again with the exception of the Llama, the behavior of the earthly counterparts of these objects shared a single common feature: *all of these animals live in holes in the ground, which in mythic parlance represent entrances to the underworld.* Toad hibernates in the ground. Fox lives in a den. Partridge, or *lluthu,* lays its eggs in a depression in the ground. Serpent dwells beneath the earth. *Ukhu pacha* lay beneath the southern tropic.

Other insights followed. I realized that Fox, an inky black canine[90] athwart the Milky Way, probably represented the mythical black dog whose job it was to carry (in lieu of a bridge) the souls of the dead to their final resting place on the "other side" of the celestial River. Among contemporary Aymara speakers, terrestrial foxes are commonly referred to as "the dog of the mountains," and are classified in folk tales, along with the toad and other animals who live "inside the earth," as being associated with the underworld.[91] Moreover, Fox faced the right direction to get the job done. His snout rose first, his tail last, meaning that, as the sun set on December solstice, he was "headed west," ready to carry the souls of the departing dead across the great River to the land of the dead.[92]

It was no different to the north. In Andean thought, stars north of the northern tropic "belong," to "the world above." The only celestial object known from the Conquest period to occupy this locale is the male Llama, Urcuchillay/Lyra, who, like the shaman, keeps to himself high in the mountains.

Besides his nickname of *paqo* (shaman), the male Llama had another important sobriquet: *llaca,* meaning "war lance with plumes."[93] That the lance was connected both to shamanism and the star Vega, a.k.a. *urcuchillay,* the male Llama, is suggested by the fact that a salt effigy of this same lance was awarded to the victorious runners at Ollantaytambo during rites coinciding with the heliacal rise of Vega in Lyra (see Appendix 1 and figure 3.15). In the same way that the dark-cloud constellations are associated with the underworld, it is the *paqo/llaca/shaman* who belongs to the "world above." In the hierarchy of shamanism in the environs of contemporary Cuzco, the most exalted title, held by only one man, is *hanaq waqayoq,* "he who is able to see the world above."[94] The symbolic importance of the lance in such shamanic transactions is found in both present-day and Inca custom.

Zuidema and Quispe's investigations, for example, reveal that this lance is the central symbol of complex, present-day rituals concerned with the augmentation of the flocks, and conducted during the Feast of San Juan, on June 24, in Inca times the final day of the June-solstice festival of Inti Raymi. In today's ceremonies, a shaman, the master of livestock, carries the *llaca* (lance) high into the mountains in order to communicate with the mountain gods; the *wamani*, on behalf of the flocks.[95] The *llaca*, the llamas, the mountain peaks, and June solstice—this Andean thought-form has proved impervious to time.

Zuidema has also shown that the symbolism of the lance has deep roots in the pre-Columbian Andes. Here he speaks of the Andean *ushñu*, a five-stepped pyramidal structure whose flat top represented the summit of the cosmic mountain:

> The chronicler Cabello Valboa mentions as another name for ushñu: "chuqui pillaca." Chuqui is lance and as to pillaca Holguín (1608) says: "Pillaca llayta, llautu (ribbon) of two colors woven in counter fashion, purple and black." Now in his book *Tihuanacu* Posnansky reproduces the design on an Inca k'ero [a wooden tumbler] of an ushñu in colors and of an Inca with all his royal insignia. The pyramid has six levels. Placed on the uppermost level is a lance adorned with two ribbons, one purple and one black.[96]

Remember those two ribbons. They will prove later to be of extraordinary significance. For now the point is that, as the Inca sat atop the man-made mountain, or *ushñu*, he carried a staff named *llaca*, which stood for the power of shamanic dominance, a power whose guiding star was Vega in Lyra, the male Llama also called *llaca*, whose seat lay in the land of the gods, above the northern tropic. As a living demigod, Son of the Sun, both the Inca's authority, symbolized by the *llaca*, as well as his final destiny, like that of the staff-bearing Wiraqocha, lay in the "world above."

If elegance was an indication of sound theory, I had reason to be encouraged by what I had found so far. The leanest explanation for the importance of the mythical "flood" of A.D. 650 lay in understanding that the Andean supernatural worlds had celestial analogues with precise locations in the heavens. I felt that this frame of reference could withstand Occam's razor. It shed "coherent light" on countless shards of apparently disparate information, such that each individual datum appeared to project an image of the whole. And, when tested, this image lit up the planetarium like a pinball machine.

On the other hand there was, quite literally, a gaping hole in this picture of how the Andean priest-astronomers imagined the heavens. If you look at figure 3.13, you will see that it represents the limits of the "celestial earth" in terms of parallel tropics. This conceptualization implies that the Andean priest-astronomers were thinking in terms of *polar and equatorial coordinates*. Such a system begins with a concept of a celestial sphere, and organizes this fixed sphere of stars by means of projecting the earth's axis of rotation out onto a pole star. The pole of this sphere runs through the celestial equator at right angles. All other reference points on this sphere, so conceptualized, can be found on imaginary bands through the stars parallel to the celestial equator, bands that we call latitude. The celestial tropics represent two such bands. The conceptual basis of the astronomical system described in *Hamlet's Mill* rests on polar and equatorial coordinates.

The problem was that this system is not supposed to have existed in the Andes, and to say that it did constituted a flat contradiction of the most influential model of how Native American peoples living in tropical latitudes, from Mexico to Bolivia, conceptualized celestial motions. This paradigm, developed by Anthony Aveni,[97] is based on the assumption that, since at tropical latitudes the angle of rise and set of heavenly bodies is less acute, the people living there will use, as their fundamental reference system for observation, the circle of the horizon and the vertical axis formed by the sun's passage through the zenith, a phenomenon that occurs only in tropical latitudes (see Appendix 2).

But what bothered me was not so much how the evidence seemed to call this scheme into question. If you look again at figure 3.13, you can see the problem. There is no pole in the picture. I really had no idea if the Andean astronomers worked with the concept of an axis of the celestial sphere, and I hadn't a clue where to look for such information. In fact, as far as I could tell, the information wasn't there. How discomfiting: no celestial pole, no tropics; no celestial tropics, no sense to the myths of the "flood."

I looked over all the steps that had led me to this impasse. In the end I decided that this was no time for an anxiety attack. It was time to learn to trust the tradition I was studying. The priest-astronomers who constructed the myths of A.D. 650 were serious people. I knew enough of the archaeological record to know that the years immediately around A.D. 650 were among the most tumultuous in all of Andean history, for it was then that institutionalized warfare first took hold of Andean society. Consequently, the introduction of force into the midst of Andean life could not have been other than a heavy blow to the great foundation of reciprocal obligations upon which the Andean sense of justice rested. In this sense, the spirit of Wiraqocha must most certainly have seemed to "leave the earth." And if the great celestial thought-form, which embodied the god's teaching, had indeed undergone its own, parallel catastrophe, with the obliteration of the "bridge" between the worlds of the living and the Powers Above, I was not prepared to gainsay the wisdom of remembering that moment through all time.

For my part, I had a lot of catching up to do on the subject of the *axis mundi*. I envisaged a long and arduous process. As it turned out, it didn't take long at all—just enough time to look up a single word in a very old dictionary.

CHAPTER 4

WIRAQOCHA

... The miseries of men
I will recount you, how, mere babes before,
With reason I endowed them and with mind;
And not in their disparagement I speak,
But of my gifts to memorize the love:
Who, firstly, seeing, knew not what they saw,
And hearing did not hear; confusedly passed
Their life-days lingeringly like shapes in dreams,
Without an aim; and neither sunward homes,
Brickwoven, nor skill of carpentry, they knew;
But lived, like small ants shaken with a breath,
In sunless caves a burrowing buried life:
Of winter's coming, no sure sign had they,
Nor of the advent of the flowery spring,
Of fruitful summer none: so fared through each,
And took no thought, till that the hidden lore
Of rising stars and setting I unveiled.

—AESCHYLUS
PROMETHEUS BOUND

The Gods of earth and sea
Sought through nature to find this Tree;
But their search was all in vain:
There grows one in the Human brain.

—WILLIAM BLAKE

I

THE LATE HISTORIAN of religion Mircea Eliade has shown how the imagery of three interconnecting worlds is detailed with gorgeous elaboration in the symbolism of North and Central Asian shamanism. Among these cultures, "the universe is conceived as having three levels—sky, earth, underworld— connected by a central axis."[1] This axis is symbolically conceptualized as the central support pillar of buildings or, where architectural styles differ, by the smokehole in the roof. The cosmic pillar is also sometimes represented as the notched trunk of a tree, ascended as a ladder by the shaman in trance. This "world tree" runs through the "navel of the earth" and provides the shaman access to the three worlds by means of ecstatic ascents and descents. A third image, the cosmic mountain, serves the same purpose. Both the world tree, with branches spread into the starry heavens and roots in the underworld, and the cosmic mountain "are merely more developed mythical formulations of the Cosmic Axis (World Pillar, etc.)."[2]

Here, as with the Incas, the direction north is assimilated to the vertical, as for example in the case of the cosmic mountain. For the Yakut shaman who ascends a seven-story mountain, the summit is "the navel of the sky," synonymous with the Pole Star. For the Hindus, the sacred Mount Meru represented the center of the world, above which hung the Pole Star. The Buryat shamans have it that the Pole Star is fastened to the summit of the World Mountain.[3] With utter fluidity this imagery transfers to architecture:

> The Turko-Altaians conceive the Pole Star as a pillar; it is the "Golden Pillar" of the Mongols, the Kalmyk, the Buryat, the "Iron Pillar" of the Kirgiz, the Bashkir, the Siberian Tatars, the "Solar Pillar" of the Teleut, and so on. . . . The Tatars of the Altai, the Buryat, and the Soyot assimilate the tent pole to the Sky Pillar. Among the Soyot the pole rises *above the top of the yurt and its end is decorated with blue, white, and yellow cloths, representing the colors of the celestial regions.*[4] [Emphasis added.]

Likewise the Inca *llaca*, festooned with ribbons, fluttered atop the stylized mountain called *ushñu*, and was represented in the sky *above the northern tropic* by *urcuchillay*, the male Llama in Lyra.

The imagery of the central pillar provides for the representation of various "holes" punched between worlds, allowing access for the shaman in trance. These can lead to the underworld as well as to the world above. The costume of the Yakut shaman bears a symbol of the "Opening into the Earth," called "Hole of the Spirits," and he is accompanied into the spirit world not by any burrowing mammal, but by a bird, the grebe, which can both fly and dive into the sea. Among the Altaians, descent into the under-world is achieved through the "smokehole of the earth,"[5] suggesting a stacked model of cosmic levels, one atop the other.

This model was operative among the Maya, where the floor of the ball court rested upon the roof of the house of the underworld Lords of Xibalbá,[6] just as it was operative among the Goldi of Siberia, who reckoned with three cosmic trees, one for each world, and among other Siberian peoples where the tree of the world of the living reaches the palace of the upper world, Bai Ulgan.[7] Among the Hopi, whose myths subsume the ideas of Ages of the World, the ceremonial *kiva*, with its entrance by ladder through a hole in the roof, also has a hole in the floor called *sipápuni*. *Sipápuni* stands for the navel and the point of emergence of the ancestors from the previous world, just as the hole in the roof looks out, both to the world above and to the future.[8]

Santillana and Dechend have explored a particular aspect of this pattern, namely the reason why the near circumpolar stars of the northern sky should have been termed by the Arabs "the hole of the mill peg," or why Cleomedes (ca. A.D. 150) should say of these same celestial regions, "The heavens there turn around in the way a millstone does."[9] In other words, the axial imagery of the pillar-mountain-tree is found in yet another conceit, pregnant with its own particular set of valences. For it is the function of the image of the celestial mill to speak of time and motion. The world pillar rising to the Pole Star becomes the axis of a stupendous mill, forged by the gods. The mill-stone itself—that is, the celestial equator—"hafted" on the precessing polar axis, grinds out the ages of the world through the zodiac. In Norse mythol-ogy this was the Mill of Amlethus/Amlodhi, also known as Hamlet. In the Prose Edda of Snorri Sturluson, it was called Grotte, "the crusher," owned by Frodhi and grinding out gold, peace, and plenty. But Frodhi's greed drove the two giant maidens who ran the mill to curse him. Then the sea god Mysingr rose up, slew Frodhi, and took the mill aboard his ship. The ship sank somewhere in the North Atlantic:

> the huge props flew off the bin
> the iron rivets burst,
> the shaft tree shivered,
> the bin shot down,
> the massy mill-stone rent in twain[10]

From that time onward—and it is of time the story speaks—a whirlpool sucked through the hole in the millstone, grinding out salt at the bottom of the sea.

With an erudition that, for both breadth and depth, is unusual in our time, Santillana and Dechend go on to trace the ubiquity of "Hamlet's mill" in India, Persia, Scandinavia, and so on. *The mill had an owner, whose celestial manifestation was the planet Saturn.* For our purposes the Grotte, literally "axle-block," is sufficient to make the point: here was an image that "organized" the celestial sphere of fixed stars into a single conceit, the same polar-equatorial system used to this day in celestial navigation. Moreover, when the "shaft tree" or "world pillar," fixed at the pole star, broke free from its socket and the "whirlpool" began, we find the unmistakable imagery of precession, the mill that grinds out time. Because the orientation of the earth's axis of rotation shifts within the sphere of fixed stars (see figure 4.1), the pole stars change over time. The Great Pyramid was oriented to the star Thuban (alpha Draco) some five thousand years ago, a fact so often over-looked by scholars as to provoke, so Santillana and Dechend note, Dr. Alexander Pogo of the Palomar Observatory to remark, "I give up quoting further examples of the obstinate belief of our Egyptologists in the immobil-ity of the heavenly pole."[11] In other words, according to Santillana and Dechend, the verbal conceit "whirlpool" stands, at least in one application, for an area of about forty-seven degrees of arc in diameter—twice the 23.5-degree radius formed by the tilt of the earth's equator to the ecliptic—in the northern heavens where the earth's axis of rotation swirls around the pole of our solar system, the axis of rotation of the sun.

The "whirlpool" was also known as the "navel of the sea," which, like the Hopi umbilicus, *sipápuni*, stands at the "center" of the vertically arranged cosmos. Again, the fluidity with which such images exchange their meanings is expressed by Eliade:

> . . . because of its situation at the center of the cosmos, the temple or the sacred city is always the meeting point of three cosmic regions: heaven, earth, hell. *Dur-an-ki*, "the bond of heaven and earth," was the name given to the sanctuaries of Nippur and Larsa . . . it is always Babylon that is the scene of the connection between the earth and the lower regions, for the city had been built upon the *bab-apsi*, the "Gate of the Apsu"—*apsu* designating the waters of chaos before the Creation [as well as the swampy marshes at the head of the Persian Gulf]. The rock of Jerusalem reached down into the subterranean waters (*tehoum*). . . . The summit of the cosmic mountain is not only the highest

point of the earth; it is also the earth's navel, the point at which the Creation began. . . . "The Holy One created the world like an embryo. As the embryo proceeds from the navel onwards, so God began to create the world from the navel onwards and from there it was spread out in different directions." . . . In the Rig-Veda . . . the universe is conceived as spreading from a central point. . . . According to Mesopotamian tradition, man was formed at the "navel of the earth," in *uzu* (flesh), *sar* (bond), *ki* (place, earth), where *Dur-an-ki*, the "bond of heaven and earth," is also situated.[12]

The distinctiveness of these conceptions brings us before a historical problem. Eliade is clear that these ideas do not "belong" to shamanism:

Although the shamanic experience proper could be evaluated as a mystical experience by virtue of the cosmological concept of the three communicating zones, this cosmological concept does not belong exclusively to the ideology of Siberian and Central Asian shamanism, nor, in fact, of any other shamanism. It is a *universally disseminated idea* connected with the belief in the possibility of direct communication with the sky.[13] [Emphasis added.]

Elsewhere Eliade makes clear that, in his opinion, the "dissemination" of these ideas resulted from direct cultural influence rather than any psychic mechanism involving "universal" or "natural" ideas. Thus he notes the impact on the development of shamanism of "influences from the south . . . which altered both cosmology and the mythology and techniques of ecstasy. Among these southern influences we must reckon . . . in the last analysis, Mesopotamian influences. . . ."[14] Santillana and Dechend make clear their own, similar understanding that this same "most ancient" Near East is the source of notions concerning the three domains, the seven or nine heavens, a "world pillar," and so on.[15]

Under the current "rules of engagement" of scholarship, this view poses a distinct difficulty. A liberal view of what constituted the "most ancient" Near East would be seven thousand years B.P., pre-Ubaid Mesopotamia. The Bering land bridge went under about eleven thousand years B.P., and with it, according to the weight of orthodox scholarship, also disappeared any but the most incidental of contact between New World and Old. On the other hand, the three domains of Andean cosmology and the multiple heavens of the Maya and Aztecs—not to mention the Andean *axis mundi*, which is the centerpiece of this chapter—suggest either that another, earlier source must be sought for the origin of distinctive ideas thought to have arisen in the ancient Near East, or else that such ideas reached the Americas through channels of diffusion not yet sufficiently credited. And make no mistake, we are confronting the outlines of a "meta-language," transposable as between different ecosystems and latitudes, but in no sense "obvious." Why else, for example, should the Incas, with their capital city at 13 degrees south latitude, style the direction north as "high" and assimilate it to "up," "roof," and "mountain"?

The use of comparative material from beyond the Americas in the foregoing chapters has not been critical in making this case; the Andean material thus far presented stands on its own. Information from beyond the Americas has been included not primarily to suggest the ubiquity of the pattern—though it does—but rather to suggest to the reader that something is amiss in how we have been taught to perceive the history of human life on earth. From the stepped pyramids of Babylon to those of Palenque, and from the Dendera zodiac to the celestial Llama, one finds evidence not of some feeble set of "beliefs" about the beyond, but of a ubiquitous and highly structured language mirroring an equally sophisticated grasp of celestial mechanics, all in aid of probing the nature of humankind's ultimate destiny. The best minds and the public treasure of the archaic world were lavished on this pursuit. Should it come, then, as such as a shock that people—serious people—might be willing to risk journeys to "the edge of the known world" in search of kindred spirits? Anyone who has studied Polynesian navigation knows that archaic technology was equal to the task, and Polynesian mariners equal to the adventure. The history of such transactions has yet to be written, nor will it ever be written so long as we contemporary people remain unaware that the quest has a history, which is myth.

Ironically, I now found myself awash in such gloomy ruminations as the direct result of the provisional success of the research outlined in the foregoing chapters. Like the "sky, earth, and underworld" of Asian shamanism, the three *pachas* of Andean cosmology gave every indication of a conceptual orientation to the vertical, understood as north, along the polar axis of the celestial sphere. This axis was integral to the overarching scheme of three "worlds." I just didn't happen to know of any indigenous reference to it.

But this was only part of the problem—the left-brained, technical side of the problem. I began to be aware that I had lost control of the right-brained half of the equation as well. If I looked coldbloodedly at the myths of the llama and the flood, the only thing I could say with any certainty about them was that they described a particular astronomical event. With the exception of a single guess that the bridge trod by Wiraqocha was

connected with the flood predicted by the *paqo*, I knew of no explicit connection between everyday Andean religious beliefs and the apparent preoccupation of Andean myth with telling time on the scale of precessional
change. To say that these myths were connected to Andean spiritual and
religious thought because they drew attention to the cessation of the heliacal
rise of the Milky Way at June solstice was a tautology. I—rather than the
myths themselves—had supplied the "missing" dimensions of the myth by
exploring material that *appeared* to be related.

On the other hand, it seemed beyond question that the llama/flood
myths were important. Why else trouble to fashion and remember them? To
me, it appeared absurd on its face to hold that such myths as that of the
llama and the flood did not lie very close to the heart of Andean spiritual
thought. The alternative was to contemplate the ludicrous spectacle of a
cosmology in search of a religion.

At this point, I thought I had two separate problems: the one "technical,"
dealing with the "missing" axis of the celestial sphere, the other "right-
brained," dealing with the "missing" connections between the Andean tradition of astronomical observation and Andean religion. I had yet to realize
that the solution to both problems was hidden in plain sight. Wiraqocha,
you see, carried a staff.

I had reached a turning point in my research. I had followed the suggestion of Santillana and Dechend that in certain mythic applications "animals
are stars," and "toponyms are metaphors for locations on the celestial
sphere." The results produced by this method spoke for themselves. I now
realized that the question I was asking of the material—"What was the
relationship between Andean 'gods' and the astronomy of Andean myth?"—
had also been anticipated in *Hamlet's Mill*. The "third rule" of Santillana and
Dechend's research—"gods are planets"—lay squarely in my path. I had
either to go forward or to stop.

I hesitated for three reasons. First of all, I had never fully grasped the
role of "planetary deities" in the archaic cosmology described by Santillana
and Dechend. In fact, I was not sure I could ever understand this part of
their work. Second, I found myself once again bumping up against my own
credulity threshold. I had simply never considered it a serious possibility
that technical terminology as arcane and convoluted as the Old World
planetary lore cited in *Hamlet's Mill* could conceivably have existed in the
Andes as well. Besides, the unanimous verdict of contemporary scholarship
was clear: the only planet with which the Andean peoples had been sufficiently familiar to have given it a name was Venus. Period.

Third, it seemed to me that to explore the possibility that the Andean gods may have had planetary manifestions would lead inevitably to a kind of methodological meltdown. With nothing but silence in the scholarly literature, I would be forced to make a case based on the comparative characteristics of Old World and Andean deities. At the time I never dreamed that purely Andean material might provide the means for testing and proof.

In retrospect, it is sobering to realize just how close I came to abandoning this avenue of inquiry. I had yet to test for myself whether the literal meanings of the names of the Andean gods might contain astronomical information. At most, a day's poking around in the early dictionaries for etymologies of the various names of the god Wiraqocha was all that was required. If there was even the glimmer of some connection between the literal meaning of these names and the technical language of myth, then it might be worth looking further. But I had read the secondary literature, and there was little there—other than the cruel and unusual punishment of the phonemes of certain of the names of Andean gods[16]—to suggest that any systematic themes or logic undergirded Andean religious "beliefs."

For example, the empty interpretation of the name of the god Wiraqocha as meaning "foam of the sea" had been established in print as early as 1551, and nothing written since has replaced this reading as standard. This same ground had been gone over numerous times already. The idea, then, of searching the dictionaries appeared at the outset merely an exercise in futility. Conditioned as I was by the literature, I assumed that finding a meaning for the name Wiraqocha was hopeless.

What tipped the balance in favor of going forward—however tentatively—was the thought that I could at least look up one or two of Wiraqocha's other titles, just to be sure there was nothing there. I began with the name "Tunapa," found throughout the Chronicles as a title of Wiraqocha, but used especially often (more than twenty times) by Pachakuti Yamqui, the indigenous nobleman from the Lake Titicaca region. Quechua and Aymara abound in compound words. I knew that in both languages the verb apa-y means "to carry." Then I looked up tuna. It means "millstone." Tunapa Wiraqocha was the "bearer of the mill." This process had taken about ninety seconds.

Meaningless coincidence aside, there is no currently acceptable historical explanation why this conceit should appear in the southern Andes. Dechend's interest all along had been to reach a more complete understanding of the deus faber, the "fabricator" god, whose trail led through the myths of high culture from Oceania to Scandinavia and, finally, to the understanding that this god, who owned a mill, was the planet Saturn. With one long-ignored exception, explicit information on Andean ideas about planets is almost entirely lacking in the early sources, as well as in contemporary ethnographies. Moreover, the Eurasian "mill" was decidedly constructed of polar-equatorial coordinates, whereas, according the currently accepted paradigm,[17] Andean astronomy was a horizon-based, mid-latitude system, employing the circle of the horizon and the zenith axis of the sun as the primary —indeed the only—means of orientation. It is difficult now to recapture the shock I experienced upon reading this single dictionary entry. It had opened up a vast can of worms.

II

IT SEEMED I needed to look a little deeper into the whole question of what the Andean peoples did and did not know about planets. The planet Venus was the logical place to start, since it was the only planet identified with an indigenous name—*chasca coyllur*—in more than one Spanish chronicle.[18] *Coyllur* means "star" in Quechua, while *chasca* means "tangled or disheveled hair,"[19] nomenclature directly comparable to the Aztec Venus *tzonte mocque*, meaning "mane."[20]

The English word *planet* comes from the Greek *planêtai*, meaning "wanderer," which describes the distinctive "behavioral" characteristic of planets: whereas the fixed stars do not move in relation to each other, the planets "wander" the ecliptic with a bewildering variety of periodicities and orbital quirks. Since planetary magnitudes are as bright as, or brighter than, the brightest of stars, it is difficult to imagine a situation in which celestial observers as diligent as the Andean peoples would have failed to distinguish among the planets, already unusual for their "wandering." Yet just such a state of affairs is what the literature written by outside observers of Andean civilization—beginning with the Spanish Chroniclers and up to the present day—would lead one to believe.[21]

Still, but for the imposition of a scholarly "paper curtain" barring the possibility of significant contact between New World and Old, the case of *chasca coyllur* might long ago have suggested to students of Andean civilization another avenue of approach. The Babylonian (and later Arab) Ishtar/Venus was "one with hair," or a "mane." Pliny commented that "sometimes there are hairs attached to the planets."[22] The Semitic *juba*, meaning "mane," and *jubar*—"a beaming light, radiance"—usually refer to Venus, although sometimes they are used in the more general sense as "morning star."[23] That the "one with hair" is preeminently Venus is also clear in the case of Pliny from his reference to rutilated smoky quartz—that is, quartz containing thin needles of translucent titanium dioxide—as *veneris crinis*, "the hair of Venus."[24]

For those who care to remember, the mnemonic dance never ends. In the Andes, the modern lexicographer Lara has noted a Quechua neologism, *ch'askachau*—literally "the day of disheveled hair"[25]—meaning *viernes*, the Spanish word for Venus's day. The Quechua-speaking people themselves remain one of the few sources to evince any interest in this "taboo" vein of comparative ethnography.

If, therefore, one depended solely on the stone wall of modern secondary sources, it might come as a surprise to learn that, in a document written by the Anonymous Chronicler[26] (ca. 1585), and valued by scholars as one of the more reliable chronicles, *there appears a list of all five visible planets* (Venus, Jupiter, Saturn, Mercury, and Mars) *offering their indigenous Inca names and attributes.* According to this source, these planets were among the primary deities of the Incas, who "worshiped only the luminaries of the sky and the stars."[27]

He begins his list of planetary deities with Venus, *chasca*, the morning star who "casts dewdrops upon the earth when she shakes her hair." Jupiter is called *pirua*, literally "granary," and identified as the planetary guardian both of the Inca Empire and of the fruitfulness of the fields. According to the Anonymous Chronicler, the very name "Peru" is derived from the god *pirua*. Mars is *aucayoc*, literally "he with enemies," the god of war. Mercury, *catu illa*, is the protector of merchants, travelers, and messengers. Saturn is *haucha*, a word meaning "fierce" in both Quechua and Aymara. *Haucha* is the keeper of celestial fire, bearer of a staff, and the god of justice and retribution.[28]

A passing acquaintance with the gods of classical antiquity qualifies one to understand the impulse behind ignoring this information. It simply defies orthodox scholarship. And so, although modern scholars frequently cite the work of the Anonymous Chronicler as authoritative, they nonetheless feel justified in ignoring these pages, particularly inasmuch as they are aware of no other source that corroborates the information.[29] No sense opening a can of worms.

But one other source from the Conquest period *did* allude to a tradition of five planetary deities, although I know of no recognition of this reference in the scholarly literature. Avila's informants in Huarochirí, speaking in Quechua, affirmed not only the general proposition that they worshiped celestial objects, but that they venerated five "stars" in particular. The Quechua word used in the text for "star" is *coyllur*, the same word used in the name of Venus, *chasca coyllur*. It is therefore of some interest to note that the "stars" mentioned in the Huarochirí text are said to "move" as they circle, a redundant description—unless "they" are planets, wandering the ecliptic against the backround of fixed stars. "They call the stars that shine, moving about as they circle [Quechua *muyo muyolla*] 'Pichcaconqui.' But the ones that appear biggest, the really big ones, they call 'Pocochorac' [who sets the ripening], Huillcahuarac [who causes the sun to rise], 'Canchohuarac' [who causes brilliance to appear]."[30]

The above translation into English utilizes the translation of Arguedas from Quechua into Spanish for the meaning of the three named "stars." The characteristics of those three "stars," specified as the "biggest" of the *pichcaconqui*, conform to the characteristics of the three brightest planets—Jupiter, Venus, and Saturn—named as Inca gods by the Anonymous Chronicler: Jupiter *(Pirua)* as guardian of crops, Venus *(Chaska)* as morning star, and Saturn *(Haucha)* as the god of celestial fire.

The only word not translated by Arguedas is *pichcaconqui*. Its meaning is illuminating. *Pichca* is the Quechua word for "five."[31] So these "very bright stars" (the three brightest of which are named) are five "somethings." *Con* is an ancient epithet for the god Wiraqocha, "Con Ticce Wiraqocha." According to Quechua lexicons both early and recent, the word *con* refers literally to thunder and, by metonymy, to the sound made by spherical grindstones—rolling thunder.[32] The closest cognates of *con* are the Quechua and Aymara words for "grindstone," spelled variously *qhona* and *ccuna*.[33] Here we find reference to five of them, five spherical grindstones. Reenter the mill.

As the name given to five "stars," *con* is probably therefore best understood as sufficiently numinous to be translated as "sacred entity." Used in the context of planets—that is, "stars" with the peculiar characteristic of "moving while they circle"—the word *con* represents, to my knowledge, the first time we have ever identified an indigenous Andean term corresponding to the true mythical sense of the word "god." The Quechua ending -qui, found in the term *pichca/con/qui*, is written today *qe* and represents what the Quechuist Antonio Cusihuaman calls an "adoptive," that is, a particle used to lend the sense of metaphorical patrimony to the word so modified.[34] Therefore the word *pichca-con-qui* literally means something like "Our Five Gods"—the same five, it appears, as described by the Anonymous Chronicler, and a far cry from the notion that the native Andeans had never bothered to discriminate the celestial "wanderers."

This was beginning to get interesting. The one planet universally acknowledged as an Andean cultural fixture, Venus, conformed in her attributes with Old World models, and these attributes could readily be explained by the appearance and orbital "behavior" of the planet.[35] Furthermore, there did appear to be a second source, beyond the long-ignored planetary list of the Anonymous Chronicler, which mentioned the same five planetary deities, and described three of them in terms very similar to the Anonymous Chronicler. I reckoned that as long as I was stuck with a can of worms, I ought to make the best of it and go fishing.

I knew it wouldn't do simply to compile a dry list of comparative characteristics between New and Old World gods: "All you gods of fire, please line up in column A; anyone considering him/herself androgynous in column B," and so on. What I needed to do was to understand the logic behind any given list of characteristics; that is to say, I had to understand how any grouping of characteristics attributed to a particular planet participated in the technical language of myth, and what precise astronomical information such characteristics were meant to convey. If similarities existed at this deeper level of coherence—as integral elements of the technical language of myth—I felt that the methodological risks might be outweighed by the potential historical gains.

In order to proceed, I knew that I would have to return to *Hamlet's Mill*, the only modern source which has attempted to elucidate such connections. What follows now is background, a discussion of how Santillana and Dechend came to perceive the inner logic of the manifold characteristics of the fabricator god—the *deus faber*, whose planetary manifestation was Saturn, and whose presence they discerned in mythical traditions around the world.

First, however, let me clear up a point that may already have perplexed the reader. The title of Wiraqocha—Tunapa or "mill-bearer"—suggests he may be a Saturnine figure, yet the Anonymous Chronicler states that the Quechua name for the planet Saturn is *haucha*. The differentiation of the "god" from his planetary manifestation was a practice familiar both to the Greeks (Chronos/Kronos) and the Hindus (Kala/Yama).[36] Such a differentiation deserves emphasis in the context of Andean thought because it would constitute gross oversimplification to imply that Wiraqocha "is," simply, Saturn. Just as in Greek and Vedic myth, knowledge of the physical "behavior" of the planet Saturn led to the imagery of a "god" who imparted motion and the measures of time to the cosmos, so also in the Andes Wiraqocha occupies this level of abstraction. *Haucha* is discernible in the night sky, but Wiraqocha is everywhere.

III

FATHER TIME IS the image of Saturn that has survived into our day. He is the old man, bearded, carrying a staff, weighed down by the burden of years. In his fearsome aspect he is the Grim Reaper, genitor of the ineluctable laws of time. In his beneficent aspect, as the Orphic Hymns tell us, he is Prometheus,[37] the benefactor of mankind, selfless bearer of the priceless gift of "fire," that is, the creative spark that allows mankind to transcend the limits of time by becoming privy to the secrets of its measurement. Therefore Saturn is the old, old god, the King of the Golden Age—before warfare, before class, before the codification of human laws. The latter are matters for Jupiter/ Zeus, the King, but "before the reign of Zeus, Kronos ruled on this very earth."[38] Saturn rules by force of moral suasion. Saturn wishes mankind well —he stole "fire" on our behalf—but woe unto him who breaks the norms, for Saturn is above all the god of measure, the giver of the measures of the cosmos; he remains the " 'Star of Law and Justice' in Babylon, also the 'Star of Nemesis' in Egypt, the Ruler of Necessity and Retribution—in brief, the Emperor."[39]

Undergirding the feeling-tone of the god stands the muscular structure of scientific observation expressed with the means at hand. Take, for example, how it is that "fire" came to earth. There was a time when Saturn was King. It was a time when the "ways" were open between heaven, earth, and the underworld. This time was when the Milky Way stood "on the earth," that is, when it rose heliacally, visibly in touch with the horizon, one branch at spring equinox in Gemini, the other at autumnal equinox in Sagittarius. This was the Golden Age, the Reign of Saturn, when the equinoctial colure —that is, the great circle connecting the equinox points through the poles —and the Milky Way were approximately identical.

This era, when the god Saturn brought the "fire" of direct insight to the hearth of human consciousness, was forever fixed in memory as the moment when *the sun touched the Milky Way and set the entire galactic band of the heavens afire.*[40] In other words, a *terminology*, predating the advent of mathematics, was established to memorialize the era when the equinox suns "entered" the Milky Way. "Naturally" the heat of the sun caused the river to catch fire, and the fire spread throughout the great circle of the galaxy. The Milky Way was thus styled (i.e., not "believed" literally to be) the old "track" of the sun, the smoldering remains of some obsolete, former ecliptic plane. This notion is stated in the myth of Phaethon—the self-willed son of Helios, who set the galaxy ablaze by recklessly driving his father's chariot, the sun, into the precincts of the galactic band. This is the "ashen path" of the Bushmen, where once the fire burned. And, of course, this terminolgy, simply because it existed, *embodied* the gift of creativity vouchsafed to humankind—"fire" itself.

Nowhere is the triumph of these early mythographers over the difficulty of stating formal propositions without recourse either to writing or mathematics more apparent than in the formulation "gods are planets." Planets are "gods" because, unlike the fixed stars, they possess the power of *motion*, understood as the signature of Will. Planets are the "movers and shakers," what Plato called "the instruments of time."[41] Through patient study, one might determine the "habits" of the individual planets, but the complexity of the interplay of motions among sun, moon, and five visible planets against the background of fixed stars presented the spectacle of an endless dance. To find pattern in the dance—to enter the mind of the Choreographer— this was the challenge, and the passion, that fired the archaic imagination.

But, lacking writing and mathematics, how might one express a shattering encounter with the Lord of the Dance? In Greek myth, Kronos/ Saturn, son of Gaia (earth) and Ouranos (the sky), emasculated his father and threw his private part into the sea, whence arose Venus, a tale that led Macrobius into what, at first glance, appears to be a stupendous non sequitur: "From this they conclude that, when there was chaos, no time existed, insofar as time is a fixed measure derived from the revolution of the sky. Time begins there, and of this is believed to have been born Kronos [Saturn] who is Chronos [Time]. . . ."[42]

How could Macrobius possibly conclude from *this* tale that "Time begins here"? Santillana and Dechend gather up the shards of information required for reconstruction. They compare the Orphic Hymn to Kronos—"you who hold the indestructible bond according to the *apeirona* (unlimited) order of Aiôn [eon]"—to the attributes of the Assyrian Saturn figure, Ninurta, who holds "the bond of heaven and earth."[43] We have already seen this bond, the *dur-an-ki*, described by Eliade as the world pillar linking together the three worlds. So it is Kronos who has his hand upon the axis of the celestial sphere—the erstwhile penis of Ouranus cast into the star-sea, memorializing the first wrenching realization that the whole apparatus was in motion—but what of the millstone itself, the celestial equator, grinding out time through the ecliptic? And, more baffling still, how might a planetary wanderer of the ecliptic plane possibly "control" the polar axis? Santillana and Dechend cut the Gordian knot by refocusing attention on the peculiar circumstances of the birth of Kronos/Saturn in Greek myth.

In this tale, Saturn in fact creates, as it were, his own parents. Until the emasculation of his "father," Ouranus—an act that isolated the concept of a fixed sphere of stars, rotating around an axis—"earth" (Gaia) and "sky" (Ouranus), were an undifferentiated totality. And from what was Ouranus-the-fixed-sphere-of-stars separated? This was the ecliptic plane—the domain of Gaia as "celestial earth"—the apparent annual path of the sun, the same path through which moved the moon and all the planets as well. Thus, at the moment of separation, Venus—the morning-star-harbinger of the sun, standing for the entire ecliptic, embracing both day and night—is born.

The ecliptic had a name—the zodiac. This zodiac, or "dial of animals," formed the theatrical backdrop, a set of familiar, earthly analogues[44] against which the celestial dance was performed. And when the celestial players, the luminaries of the ecliptic, began to dance within this theater—with settings ranging from "sea" to "mountaintop"—truly the whole world became a stage: the original proscenium arch, also known as the "world house" (see figures 3.12b, 3.13).

The conceptual shorthand for expressing these relationships would later be the Greek letter *chi*—X—standing for the crossing of the celestial equator and the ecliptic plane. X marks the "separation of the world parents" into two planes: the one standing for the principle of the starry realm with all the stars fixed in relation to each other, revolving like a great mill; the other standing for the ecliptic, where beings different from the stars—sun, moon, and planets—wove their patterns (see figure 3.11a).

And what of the peculiar fact that Kronos/Saturn was obliged to create his own parents in order to create himself, Chronos/Time itself? Santillana and Dechend say,

> The fact is that "the separation of the parents of the world," accomplished by means of the emasculation of Ouranos, stands for the establishing of the obliquity of the ecliptic: the beginning of measurable time. . . . And Saturn has been "appointed" to be the one who established it because he is the outermost planet [a deduction based on the fact that Saturn has the longest orbital period, about thirty years], nearest to the sphere of the fixed stars. "This planet was taken for the one who communicated motion to the Universe, who was, so to speak, its king"; this is what Schlegel reports of China.[45]

By "the beginning of measurable time," Santillana and Dechend are referring to the seminal moment of the discovery of the precession. This perception was encrypted as the "separation of the world parents," because it was only then, when the "grinding," to be blunt, of this celestial pair first became apparent, that Time itself appeared.

To state matters another way, were the earth's axis not tilted in relation to that of the sun, the dynamic field in which the earth's gyroscopic wobble is set in motion would not exist. Hence, as the earth orbited the sun, not only would there be no seasons (a function of the tilt of the earth's axis); there would be no difference from year to year, from eon to eon, in the regular progression of the rise and set of the stars in relation to solar dates. Celestial equator and ecliptic would be one, *and all time eternally circular.* Hence there could be no means of marking the "beginning of measurable time," any more than one can designate the "beginning" of a circle.

Here, with the fact that one's vantage point upon the heavens happens to be a planet oriented by its *spin* to one frame of reference—the sphere of stars—and by *the path of its orbit* around the sun to a second frame of reference —roughly speaking, an orbit around the *sun's* equator (the ecliptic)—we approach the epicenter of a very difficult visualization. The tension of a spinning earth, so tilted to its orbital path, creates dynamics that manifest as precessional wobble. Our viewing platform, the earth, is "heeled over" (23.5 degrees) in relation to its orbital path like a gyroscope spinning around its axis while the axis itself is heeled over in relation to the tabletop, whose surface is roughly analogous to the ecliptic. Although the gyroscope may maintain the same angle to the tabletop as it "precesses," its axis nonetheless continuously changes its reference to the walls of the room (the fixed sphere of stars). Perhaps the most difficult thing to visualize is that, although the earth precesses, *this wobble has nothing whatsoever to do with determining the dates and horizon locations of the solstices and equinoxes.* With minor variations, the earth's inclination to the ecliptic remains a constant 23.5 degrees, even though it is precessing. What precession does affect is the stars' rising heliacally on these dates. Any reader troubled by this visualization may turn to the notes to this chapter for a further exercise.[46]

The result of this motion over time is that stars which once rose helia-cally at a given solar date—such as a solstice—will rise "late." Because this precessional shift is so slow—one degree (= about one day of "lateness") in seventy-two years—historians of science have assumed that it could only have been noticed by reference to written records. On the other hand, as Phillip Morrison of MIT has noted, all that is really required to discover precession is an old tree (a solar gnomon) and faith in the veracity of one's grandfather (an oral record).

How, then, did it come to pass, as the result of coming to this awesome realization concerning the "separation of the world parents," that *Saturn* should emerge with the title "author of time"? Although there is a very precise reason for this nomenclature, it is sufficient, for the present purposes, only to say that Saturn was given this title because this planet, with its assiduous pace, requiring thirty years to return to the same location in the stars, possessed the longest periodicity of any single visible celestial object, and hence was useful in keeping track of time on the scale of precession. Mythically speaking, Saturn "communicated motion to the Universe" (read "sphere of fixed star") or, alternatively, he "controlled" the axial wobble of the mill *because he gave the mythographers themselves a "handle" on tracking vast periods of time.*

The enormous shock delivered by the discovery of precession was fully mirrored in the equally shocking imagery (emasculation) designed to memorialize the moment. For unknowable eons, humankind had lived within the great seasonal round of the year, cradled in an Eden-like innocence. With the realization that the past must have transpired under different skies came the inevitable conclusion that the "present," heretofore understood as an eternally repeating cycle, would also pass away. It was here that Time began. Henceforth, and forever, the clock would run. The circle *did* have a beginning after all, for now there was a hatchmark on the vault of heaven, laid upon the ecliptic at its juncture with the celestial equator. Now distinct entities, the world parents—Ouranos and Gaia in equinoctial coition, belly to belly, equator to ecliptic, grinding out the Ages of the World—came into being (were conceptualized) at precisely the instant of the appearance of their own offspring, Time ("Chronos who is Kronos").

It requires no feats of research to find the tale in the Americas as well. Bierhorst recounts a North American version:

> In the great myth cycle of the Iroquois, for example, the preculture state is supposed to have existed in a world above, said to be the first bride sexually enticed by a dragon. As a result of her temptation, the sky opens and she finds her feet "hanging down into the chasm"; as she slips into the real world of society and culture, the serpent himself hands over the requisite corn and homemaking utensils . . . the Iroquois composer of the Ritual of Condolence, contemplating a serious breach of the social ethic, harks back to the origin of the myth and warns of a future time when "the feet of the people," like the feet of the first bride, "will hang over the abyss of the sundered earth. . . ."[47]

As with the Greek myth of Ouranos and Gaia, the fall from precultural innocence ("chaos") transpires at the moment of the separation of sky and earth. Time begins with culture, agriculture to be precise, and its attendant tools, preeminent among which is the calendar. The "earth" so separated from the sky is, of course, the "celestial earth," a creation of time itself, whose parameters are delineated by the stars rising heliacally as solstices and equinoxes. And like all created things, this "earth" is frangible over time, as the Iroquois myth warns, and as the Andean *paqo* also predicted.

Because the separation of "earth" and sky was styled as transpiring sexually—Ouranos and Gaia rent apart, or the seduction of the Iroquois maiden, falling from the sky to the "sundered earth"—the "prime mover," Saturn, is often depicted as androgynous, as befits the creator of his own parents, of two from one. He is the "man-woman" of the "Oracle of Kronos" from the Great Magical Papyrus of Egypt, a document that, not coincidentally, recommends invoking the god with the turnings of a mill.[48]

The mill looms always in the background,[49] the definitive signature of a meta-language. The astronomical sense of the mill's imagery has already been described, but why this mill's owner, maker, and operator should be identified with a planet requires further explanation. How is it that a planet, confined to the precincts of the ecliptic, could possibly "move" the axis of the celestial sphere through time?

One might begin by noting that the "Seven Rishis" of Vedic tradition are identified sometimes as the seven luminaries of the ecliptic—sun, moon, and five visible planets—and sometimes as the seven stars of the Great Bear, our Big Dipper, sedulously revolving around the Pole Star. Such a formulation can only be understood in one of two ways: either the makers of such tales were hopelessly confused, or we are before *terms*—that is, components of a meta-language that allows its users the means of stating relationships that are not *kinetic* in nature, but rather are concerned with the *measurement of time.*

Saturn "controls" the mill—the image against which precessional time may be reckoned—because, as the planet closest to the fixed stars, and the one with the longest orbital period, *he offers the mythographers the means of controlling their own data.* Saturn's gift to mankind is the measure of time. Thus an Orphic fragment collected by Proclus flatly states that Saturn provides "all the measures of the whole creation."[50] As the celestial object assigned the primordial role of "giver of the measures," Saturn is understood to be a creator-god, a divine Emperor, the fountainhead of surpassing wisdom. In China he is the Yellow Emperor, Shih Huang-ti, who "established everywhere the order for the sun, the moon and the stars,"[51] a formulation so congruent with Andean notions concerning Wiraqocha as to require no further elaboration.

There is, to repeat, a very specific means by which Saturn provides "all the measures" of time, one that justifies Macrobius's title "the originator of time," and that will be discussed in its proper place, in the next chapter. The point at present is to outline how the work of Santillana and Dechend has revealed myths of very wide distribution across Eurasia, where the mythical god Saturn "controls" the mill, and with it the magisterial pace of precessional time. This sense of "control" is vividly portrayed in William Blake's famous etching *The Ancient of Days*, which depicts the old, bearded Yahweh with a pair of calipers, laying out the measures from above. And one suspects that, in assigning to Saturn the "pivotal" role in determining the locus of the Pole Star through the ages, the mythographers shared in the same vertiginous perspective of omnipotence depicted by Blake, as they looked, in the mind's eye, down upon the whole creation through the eyes of the Lord of Measures.

These aspects of Saturn by no means exhaust the list of "diagnostic characteristics," but they do speak to the heart of the matter. Others appear arcane at first, but always lead back to the holographic vision. Plutarch, for example, spoke of the Egyptian lament for the departed Chronos, ruler of the Golden Age, who was born in the south but "suffers dissolution" in the north,[52] a trajectory reminiscent of Wiraqocha's advent at Tiahuanaco and departure from the earth in Ecuador. Coincidence? Elsewhere Plutarch notes that the "servants of Kronos" may visit their departed Lord, at his home in celestial exile on the isle of Ogygia, only every thirty years (thirty years being the time required for Saturn to return to the same place in the stars), when Saturn is in Taurus. The western half of the Milky Way, where Gemini gives way to Taurus, is, as we have seen, also spanned by a "bridge" called *chacamarca*, and trod by a god called Wiraqocha as he left the earth for his celestial home in the "world above."

One final characteristic bears watching. Outside the Americas, planets are often associated with metals: Saturn with lead, Venus with copper, and so on. Saturn's association with lead is connected to his function as measurer, and his specific mode of measuring accomplished with the plumb bob (Latin *plumbum* = "lead").

We find the plumb bob in the tool kit of the Egyptian astronomers—the *merkhet* and *bay* used to measure the transit of stars[53]—as well as among the Chinese.[54] As for Saturn, it is the task of the legitimate ruler of a given world-age to "measure the depths of the sea," that is, to establish the framework—from pole to pole—of a new "mill" or coordinate system of a world-age: ". . . it is literally the 'fundamental' task of the ruler to 'dive' to the topos where times begin and end, to get hold of a new 'first day.' "[55] The means of accomplishing this measurement, for Saturn, was to plumb.

This method of measurement, moreover, implies the deep southern skies, that is to say the plumb bob hangs "down." Santillana and Dechend have suggested that the "weight" on the plumb line is the star Canopus, called "the weight" by Arab astronomers and "ponderosus" in the later *Alfonsine Tablets*. The star Canopus has the distinction of residing very close to the point in the sky marking the southern axis of rotation of the sun. Therefore, as the earth's axis of rotation circles about this fixed point in the passage of precessional time, and as the times and azimuths of rise of all other stars change, Canopus appears "immobile" as regards precession. As the "precession-proof" star, it merits the title of the unerring plumb bob, marking "absolute down."[56] So Saturn is associated with lead, a notion connected to the god's function and manner of measuring. Saturn plumbs, but Jupiter hurls.[57] Enough for the Old World.

IV

ACCORDING TO ANDEAN myth, the god Wiraqocha was an old man, a graybeard,[58] who wore a long robe and carried a staff.[59] He is, as we have seen, considered the oldest god, credited with creating the sun, the moon, and the stars, and with providing humankind with the arts of civilization—agriculture, weaving, and the rest—the Andean *deus faber*. Therefore he was addressed as "Ticci Viracocha." *Ticci* is Quechua for "source, beginning, foundation, prime cause,"[60] a phrase also redolent of the Old World formulation of Saturn as "the originator of time." Among Wiraqocha's manifold titles is *pachayachachi*,[61] literally "world teacher," and there is concordance among the sources that his mode of teaching was one of loving kindness, delivered with great solicitude.[62] But Wiraqocha was not a god to be crossed. Sarmiento de Gamboa was one of a number of sources who recorded the myth of Wiraqocha's vengeance at a place called Cacha:

> Besides this they tell of a strange event, how that Viracocha, after he had created all people, went on his road and came to a place where many men of his creation had congregated. This place is now called Cacha. When Viracocha arrived there, the inhabitants were estranged owing to his dress and bearing. They murmured at it and proposed to kill him from a hill that was near. They took their weapons there, and gathered together with evil intentions against Viracocha. He, falling on his knees on some plain ground, with his hands clasped, fire from above came down on those on the hill, and covered all the place, burning up

the earth and stones like straw. Those bad men were terrified at the fearful fire. They came down from the hill, and sought pardon from Viracocha for their sin. Viracocha was moved by compassion. He went to the flames and put them out with his staff. But the hill remained quite parched up, the stones being rendered so light by burning that a very large stone which could not have been carried on a cart, could be raised easily by one man. This may be seen at this day, and it is a wonderful sight to behold this hill, which is a quarter of a league in extent, all burnt up.[63]

The scorched earth around Cacha was the site of an Inca temple dedicated to Wiraqocha, later destroyed by the Spanish.[64] This huge temple, described by Garcilaso, has been identified with the ruins at modern-day Rajchi,[65] ten miles on the Cuzco side of the high pass of La Raya, marking the ancient, traditional dividing line between the Titicaca Basin and the southern Andes. It was also a stop near the end of the pilgrimage trail followed at June solstice by the Inca priests,[66] and is therefore called by some authorities the Temple of Vilcanota,[67] after the mountain where the "sun was born" in the two branches of the Milky Way. Given that Cieza de León described the temple at Cacha as the third most important shrine in the Empire (the Temple of the Sun and Mount Huanacauri in Cuzco ranking ahead), it is likely that the major rites celebrating the "birth of the sun" at June solstice were staged here by the Inca priests. The momumental ruins had only one line of sight—to the east.[68]

After a time, one learns to trust the geomantic instincts of the Incas; so it comes as no surprise to find—besides the towering mountain, giving birth to two rivers, hard by the volcanic tuff where Wiraqocha invoked cosmic fire—another peculiar geologic phenomenon, right at the headwaters of the "River of the Sun," (the Vilcamayu, a.k.a. the Urubamba) as described by the Spanish priest Acosta: "This spring, when it rises at the cliff at Vilcanota of which I have spoken, is like lye-water, *ashen colored, and everywhere steaming with smoke like something burning,* and so it runs for a long stretch until the multitude of other waters which enter into it *put out the fire and smoke* which it has at its source."[69] (Emphasis added.)

Acosta was not the only one to make the connection with ashes, for the natives of this area, at precisely the same time as the Incas,[70] also threw the ashes of their yearly sacrifices to Wiraqocha in the "northern sea" into the turbulent headwaters of the Vilcamayu, born in smoke and fire.[71] So the old god of fire is implicated, as he is in the Old World, with the origin of the river of fire in the sky.

The chronicler Guamán Poma, no friend of the Incas, restates the matter in yet another way. Relishing the period of death, disease, famine, and pestilence that befell the reign of the first truly historical Inca, Pachakuti Inca Yupanqui, Guamán Poma compares this manifestation of the wrath of god to the destruction of Sodom, "which burned with llamas from heaven."[72] It is really quite an image: a host of llamas—doubtless dispatched from "the herd of male llamas," Lyra/*urcuchillay*—hot-footing it to earth, from the River of Fire in the sky, in order to torch Sodom and Gomorrah.

Among the titles for Wiraqocha found in the hymns collected by the chronicler Molina is *huallpayhuana*.[73] Holguín lists "*Haullpayhuana* or *ninanina*. The diligent worker, ardent and animated like fire."[74] (The synonym *ninanina* comes from the Quechua word for fire, *nina*.) It is not easy to combine the characteristics of "fieriness," and diligence, but this has always been understood as the function of Saturn, bringer of fire, but also a god systematically sweeping through the ecliptic plane every thirty years, meting out the arts of civilization—or castigation—as the situation merits.

Wiraqocha was also androgynous. Molina was told that neither the creator nor his "children"—that is, the nonhuman lineage *wakas* he created for each tribe—were "born of woman," but rather were "immutable" and "without end." Two different prayers to Wiraqocha, transcribed by Pachakuti Yamqui, posed a question to the god: "Are you male; are you female? [*Cay cari cachun/Cay huarmi cachun?*]"[75] The question is repeated a third time in the notations on Pachakuti Yamqui's cosmological drawing (figure 2.4). Here the chronicler describes the central oval as the "symbol" [*unancha*] of Wiraqocha, which is placed, as it were, androgynously between and at the head of the sexual division of the cosmos into male and female elements.[76]

The theme of androgyny appears again in the visage of the so-called "Gateway God" of Tiahuanaco (figure 4.2), representing the figure of Wiraqocha. Here the creator's androgyny is expressed in the fact that the head is a composite of sun and moon, which in the Andes were conceived as being male and female.[77]

The purely astronomical valencies of Wiraqocha's androgyny are also elucidated in Pachakuti Yamqui's diagram by the placement of crosses above and below the central oval. The upper cross is called *orcorara*, an Aymara word, literally "great herd, crowd of men, or male animals."[78] The lower cross, called *chacana en general*, "cross or ladder in general," is further labeled with the words *saramanca* and *cocamanca*, meaning "olla (large ceramic pot) of maize and olla of coca," terms discussed at length by Zuidema and Urton in connection with lakes, fountains, and subterranean waters, that is, the "female" elements of the cosmos.[79]

I considered these references to Wiraqocha's androgyny the heart of the matter. The question they raised was whether or not the god's androgynous nature was part of the formal terminology of the "separation of the world parents," standing for the discovery of the obliquity of the ecliptic plane to the celestial equator. Perhaps it really was simply "natural" to look upon the creator as a benign old man with a bit of fire in him (to ensure that the rules are obeyed), who, as creator, must, as a simple matter of ontological consistency, be androgynous. On the other hand, there was nothing apparently "natural" in the fact that Wiraqocha possessed yet another Saturnine characteristic: he is the mill-bearer, a technology that in the Andes was also sexually imagined.

V

HOLGUÍN'S 1608 LEXICON carries the following entries for the Andean mill:

> *Cutana* or *tuna*. Grindstone, the upper one. *Maray*. The lower stone.[80]

And under *maray* he records,

> *Maray* or *maran*. The grindstone which is below, the upper one [is called] *urcun* or *tuna*.[81]

The technology described here is that of the "rocker mill" distinctive to the Andes, in that the upper stone, *tuna*, is shaped like a half moon, or half a wheel of cheese. It is probably the most efficient hand mill ever devised. The lower, passive stone, *maran*, is a "flat quadrangular stone for grinding grain."[82] The *maran* is found on the floors of peasant homes throughout the Andes.

At the outset of my research into the nature of the Andean rocker mill, *tuna*, I was more than a little concerned by the fact that this particular artifact was not a rotary mill. Santillana and Dechend were, however, emphatic on the point that the imagery of the mill—along a spectrum from true rotary mills to "deteriorated" versions as simple as a wooden mortar—can be found in the most far-flung of traditions in impeccable cosmological context. They recount, by way of example, a Cherokee myth about the people of the South who had a corn mill (a simple mortar) from which meal was constantly being stolen: ". . . the owners discovered the thief, a dog, who 'ran off howling to his home in the North, with the meal dropping from his mouth as he ran, and leaving behind a white trail where now we see the Milky Way, which the Cherokee call to this day, "Where the dog ran." ' . . ."[83]

It was when I looked further into the early Quechua and Aymara dictionaries that I began to find, in the synonyms and cognates related to the technology of milling, extremely persistent notions about the power of sexual complementarity, or androgyny. For example, in the above-cited definition of the upper, active grindstone, *tuna*, Holguín lists as a synonym the word *urcun*. In both Quechua and Aymara the first meaning of the word *urco* is the male of any species of animals.[84] We have seen the use of the word *urco* in the constellation of the male Llama, Urcuchillay, and in the upper cross of Pachakuti Yamqui's diagram, *orcorara*, or "group of men or male animals." And just as, in Quechua, *urcun* means the "upper grindstone," the same definition applies to the Aymara word *urcoña*.[85] At a minimum, this aspect of the Andean rocker mill, then, conformed to the requirement of mill as cosmic machine, insofar as it belonged within the "male" domain. Did this imply that the upper, "male" grindstone had something to do with "father sky," a.k.a Ouranos, the sphere of the fixed stars?

To me, the "maleness" ascribed to the upper grindstone certainly *appeared* to suggest an intentional projection of axial imagery. Again, the dictionaries confirmed the suspicion. For example, *orco*, a synonym for *tuna*, is also the the Quechua word for "mountain." By the same token, Tunapa Wiraqocha is always described as carrying a staff. Further, Ludovico Bertonio, the author of the 1611 Aymara dictionary cited throughout this study, sometimes wrote Wiraqocha's title as "Tunuupa."[86] Herein lies a clue to the origin of the word *tuna* as rocker mill, an invention that appears on the archaeological horizon about 200 B.C.,[87] when the Aymara-speaking civilization around Lake Titicaca—the seat of Wiraqocha—began its florescence. The word *tunu* is found both in Aymara and Quechua. Bertonio lists:

Tunu. The top of a large tree.[88]

Holguín records the Quechua meaning:

Tunu. The central support pillar of a round house.[89]

As quickly as that, examination of both the cognates and synonyms for the upper grindstone reveals the words for "mountain," "tree," "central pillar," and "mill," *all the fundamental mythical terms listed both by Eliade and by Santillana and Dechend as images of the axis of the celestial sphere.*

In the Andean context, we have already seen the mythical uses of the cosmic mountain as well as the consistent use of architectural terms as astronomical metaphors. As for the "world tree," Valcárcel noticed that the "behavior" of the mountains in the Andean llama/flood story very much resembled the behavior of a mythical tree in the tales of Amazon forest tribes, where, of course, mountains were not available for refuge: "Among some forest tribes there is the legend of the Flood of red waters from which a very few men were saved in the top of a tree which, like the two mythical mountains [i.e., as found in the two myths of the llama and the flood], had the virtue of rising with greater rapidity than the waters."[90]

Now, as already mentioned, the imagery of the Old World mill, as a variant of mountain/world-tree/pillar, affords the means for describing time and motion. These associations also inhere in the Andean rocker mill. Among synonyms listed for *tuna* (above) by Holguín is *cutana*. This word, literally "for grinding," derives from the Quechua verb *cutay*, "to grind."[91] *Cutay* (in modern orthography *kutay*) shares the root *kut-* with another Quechua verb already discussed, *kutiy*, "to turn over or turn back," the same verb used in the terminology of the succession of world-ages, namely *pachakuti*. In a stone-old fragment of myth, recorded by Avila, time and motion are objectified as the mountains grinding against each other at the moment the "sun dies," that is, at the end of a long world-age.[92]

These linguistic indicators pointed me directly back to the cosmological drawing of Pachakuti Yamqui (figure 2.4), where the *tuna*, the "pillar/tree/ mill" carried by Tunapa Wiraqocha, reappears as the central organizing principle of the diagram. The notations around the central oval—said on the diagram to represent Wiraqocha—repeatedly refer to it as an *unancha*. This word means "any sign, standard, insignia, or escutcheon," and also "branding iron."[93] A "standard" (*estandarte*) is an emblematic figure raised on a pole. If you look to the top left corner of Pachakuti Yamqui's drawing, you will see the *unancha* of Wiraqocha redrawn on its own. Notice that there is a star at the bottom of the oval, just as there is one at the bottom of the oval in the main drawing. In other words, this cross, which Pachakuti Yamqui labeled "male" (*orcorara*) has a long vertical upon which is hoisted the symbol for Wiraqocha, the oval.

Further, you can see that he defined the horizontal portion of this "male" cross as *tres estrellas todas yguales*, that is, "three stars all the same," which suggests the three stars of Orion's Belt, "the Three Marias" in Spanish lore. Zuidema, for one, has identifed those three stars in the drawing with Orion's Belt.[94] As we have already seen, Orion's Belt lies on the celestial equator, whose relationship to the horizon of Cuzco was marked by a mountain named "support pillar of the world-age." It is wholly logical, then, that the "standard" of Wiraqocha should be supported by a cross of stars, *orcorara*, specified as "male" and containing, via Orion's belt, reference to polar and equatorial coordinates. Like the *tuna* carried by Wiraqocha, the star-studded "male cross" of Pachakuti Yamqui's diagram—the structural support of Wiraqocha's *unancha*/standard—is an ideogram of the earth's orientation within the sphere of fixed stars, the world of "father sky."

"Mother earth," on the other hand, was, in the formal terminology of ancient myth, the domain of the ecliptic, ranging from tropic to tropic. The structural "pillars" of this "quadrangular earth" (figure 3.13a) were defined as the stars rising heliacally at the solstices and equinoxes. Likewise, the Andean lower grindstone, *maray*, specified (as shown above) in the early lexicons as being "female," is not just any old shape, but quadrangular. Interestingly, there are no Quechua words that might suggest a derivation. The cognate is found, as is so very often the case with critical cosmological terms, in the Aymara language of the Titicaca region. The word *mara* means "year,"[95] which is an objective unit of measure based on *the sun's annual path through the stars along the ecliptic, the domain of the "celestial earth."*

Now, as we have seen in Andean tradition, the limits of the "celestial earth" are expressed in terrestrial space by means of the intercardinal cross laid out in villages, and running to the rise and set points of the solstice suns. Beneath the oval of Wiraqocha there is an intercardinal cross, called "cross in general," and specified as "female." This starry "female" cross is the ideogram expressing the astronomical concept of the "celestial earth," that is, the limits of the ecliptic as observed by following the sun's yearly (= Aymara *mara*) journey to the solstitial limits of its domain against the backdrop of fixed stars. In the metaphorical terminology of myth, the figure of the intercardinal cross represented "mother earth," *pachamama*, "our mother in space-time."

The relationship of an "upper" male cross to a "lower" female cross is the same relationship as the upper "male" grindstone (*tuna*), to the lower "female" grindstone (*maras*). Thus, above and below the "standard" of Wiraqocha stand the two fundamental principles of cosmic organization, sexually imagined. Further, by specifying Orion's Belt as the star group specifically diagnostic of the principle of polar-equatorial coordinates, the diagram equally specifically alludes to the relationship of the celestial equator to the domain of the ecliptic as laid out by the intercardinal cross. Here, then, arrayed about the central symbol of Wiraqocha—an oval on a stave—are the world parents, separated above and below. Here also the ultimate, cosmic origin of Wiraqocha's androgyny is fully expressed. As the creator of the starry and ecliptic realms, Wiraqocha was also their offspring. The great god and his teaching arose with the separation of the world parents.

As I began, provisionally, to reach these conclusions, I was still unsure about the significance of the symbolism of the central oval, hoisted upon Wiraqocha's *unancha*. I was also concerned by what, at the time, I thought was a separate problem. To associate the "female cross" in the diagram with the ecliptic plane, although logically consistent, left open the whole question of how—or even whether—this plane was conceptualized in the sky. There is nothing in the secondary literature to suggest that there existed an Andean notion for "ecliptic."

Two pieces of information, heretofore overlooked, would resolve both of these problems by demonstrating that the oval in the diagram stands for the ecliptic plane. Before looking at this information, let me put the silence of the sources concerning the existence of an indigenous notion of the ecliptic plane into context.

Despite lack of information from Conquest-period sources, it is difficult to imagine a scenario wherein the Andean peoples would have been ignorant of the band of stars along the ecliptic which we call the zodiac, because such ignorance implies that the Andean peoples had no *lunar* zodiac. It is, in fact, much easier to familiarize oneself with the stars through which the ecliptic plane passes by reference to the moon than by reference to the sun. Like the earth and all the planets, which circle the sun on a plane roughly equivalent to the sun's equator (ecliptic), the moon likewise circles the earth on the same plane, plus or minus five degrees. In other words, as with the planets and the apparent motion of the sun, *the moon travels along the ecliptic plane, through the zodiac*. In the period of a single month, one can, if one wishes, follow the moon through the entire zodiac. If one wishes to use the sun to determine the ecliptic plane, the difficulties are greatly compounded. Unlike the moon, one cannot see the stars through which the sun passes. Therefore, to identify the stars of the ecliptic, one would be required to identify and remember the stars rising just before sunrise at the point on the horizon where the sun is about to come up. This more difficult observation would take twelve times as long—a year—as the same observation utilizing the moon.

It is no coincidence that the earliest calendars in the Americas—and elsewhere—were divided into between twenty and twenty-eight "stations" of the moon on its monthly progress through the stars of the ecliptic, and this is probably one source of the base-twenty number system in Mesoamerica.[96] It should also be noted that the integration of a solar calendar with an earlier lunar calendar takes place almost universally with the advent of agriculture. Such a sequence makes utter sense, since one needs to be sedentary, to have "control" of one's horizon, in order to calibrate a solar calendar by means of the heliacal rise of stars. In an era before agriculture, when people followed the game, camps would shift many times in the year. The horizon might change, but the track of the moon through the stars was consistent, and required no reference to the horizon.

The Incas ran two calendars simultaneously, one solar and one lunar, and the Inca Empress, as Daughter of the Moon, presided over an array of women's rites. Urton noted that when working with a woman informant using star maps, she was unable to orient herself until he showed her where the moon was in the stars at the moment. This led Urton to suggest that a whole lore of woman's lunar-based astronomy might await the arrival of a woman anthropologist interested in ethnoastronomy.[97] Lunar matters were, and remain, in the domain of women, and so it is not surprising that the Conquistadores are silent on the matter.

Be that as it may, there are two sources that speak to the existence of the concept of the ecliptic plane. The first is found, again, in Pachakuti Yamqui's drawing, and for a very long time I did not notice it. This lapse resulted in part from my having accepted the standard translation of one of the diagram's marginal notes, the one describing the central oval hoisted upon Wiraqocha's standard. Toward the end of this long notation, which includes a recapitulation of many of the god's titles, there is an epithet for the god that is found nowhere else in the Spanish chronicles: *Intipintin ticci-muyo camac.* This has been translated as meaning "the sun of the sun, creator of the fundamental circle."[98] This translation gives no information at all about the significance of the oval. The term "the sun of the sun," doesn't mean anything. Offered as a synonym for "the creator of the fundamental circle," it is no help in determining what this circle might be.

In studying a photocopy of the original diagram, I realized that there is a very serious problem with this translation, in that it requires a correction of Pachakuti Yamqui's Quechua. A phrase meaning "the sun of the sun" would normally have been written *intip intin*, and not run together as *intipintin*. Taken at face value, that is "uncorrected," the phrase means something radically different. The Quechua particle *-ntin* gives the sense of "taken-altogether,"[99] as in the Inca name for the Inca Empire, *tawa/ntin/suyu*, literally "the four/taken-altogether/zones."

The phrase *inti/p/intin ticci/muyo camac* literally means "the sun/'s/taken-altogether fundamental/circle creator," a rendering utterly unlike the (uncritically) accepted translation, "the sun of the sun, creator of the fundamental circle." If one's child were to come home from a basic astronomy class in school and—rather than parrot the textbook definition for the ecliptic ("the apparent annual path of the sun")—were instead to define the ecliptic as "the sun's taken-altogether basic circle," one could rest assured that the child had grasped the essence of the matter. The words say that Wiraqocha created the ecliptic plane.

At this point I hesitated to trust my own faculties. I was well aware that I was looking for a reference to the ecliptic. Although my training qualified me to parse Quechua, it did not relieve me from the responsibility of applying skepticism to evidence. Still, the grandiose—and also empty— rendering for *intipintin*, "sun of the sun," bothered me far more than my own reading. But if there was another reference anywhere in the early sources to the ecliptic, I had missed it.

At about this point I was reminded of another phrase, whose universal translation in the literature I also classified as "empty": the meaning of "Wiraqocha" as "foam of the sea." Throughout my whole investigation of the god Wiraqocha, I had continued to consider it impossible that one could turn up anything new by looking for this particular etymology in the old dictionaries. Surely, scholars must have investigated this word exhaustively. More to satisfy my pessimism than anything else, I picked up Bertonio's Aymara dictionary. Moments later I was staring in utter amazement at an absolutely clean etymology identifying Wiraqocha with the ecliptic plane, an etymology that had been simply disregarded for almost five hundred years.

The name "Wiraqocha" posed a genuine riddle to the Conquistadores, for they were addressed by this title when first they advanced to Cuzco. They wanted to know what the word meant, and expressed puzzlement and dissatisfaction with what they learned. According to the Spanish chronicles, the only known meaning for the word "Wiraqocha" was "foam of the sea." While accepting with diffidence this definition, Cieza de León sought to debunk the story that the Spanish were called Wiraqocha because they came from across the water like "the foam of the sea." The real reason, so the nobles of Cuzco told Cieza, was that the Spanish appearance at Cuzco marked the end of the tyranny of the forces of the victorious usurper Atahuallpa (as the Cuzco faction of the civil war saw him). So, when the Spanish arrived, the inhabitants of Cuzco hailed them as "Wiraqochas," reasoning "that they must be sent by the intervention of their great God Ticiviracocha."[100]

This solution, while carrying the ring of authenticity, has obscured the fact that the meaning of the word as "foam of the sea," dutifully recounted down to our time, remains an absurd etymology. The Quechua word *wira*, written *uira* by the Spanish, means the grease or fat of animals.[101] On what aesthetic basis would poetic fancy attempt to generate "foam" from lard cast upon the cold waters of Andean lakes, or in the frigid waters of the Humboldt current of the Peruvian coast? Moreover, the Quechua language already had a perfectly serviceable word for "foam," *posoqo*.[102] Like Cieza de León, Garcilaso expressed complete skepticism of the etymology, but mentioned no alternative.[103]

By far the clearest statement of how preposterous this meaning was to the native ear was expressed by the so-called *quipucamayocs* of Vaca de Castro, native specialists in Inca history who discussed various aspects of the Conquest. They were terribly amused at how the Spanish "Wiraqochas" understood their new-found title to mean "grease of the sea." It made them laugh. With stoic irony, they dismissed out of hand the notion that their supreme god would be called—and these are *their* words—"garbage from the sea" (horruras de la mar),[104] all the while doubtless enjoying such a definition as applied to the Spanish. But if Wiraqocha had a meaning, they weren't talking.

I was therefore amazed to find the word *wira*, written in the Spanish convention of the day as *uira*, in Bertonio's Aymara dictionary. Omission of any mention of this source in the secondary literature is perplexing.[105] Aymara either shares with Quechua, or else outright provides the loan-words for, most of the important religious terms used by the Incas. Aymara is a language of the Lake Titicaca region, of the homeland of the god Wiraqocha and of the fabled empire of Tiahuanaco. Nonetheless, investigators for half a millennium have been satisfied to seek the meaning of the god's name in a foreign language, Quechua. It seemed to me, as I stared at this entry, almost as if there were an unwritten rule to expect *not* to find evidence of intelligent transmission of important information through language. Though this may be true of our time—perhaps due to the influence of advertising—it does not appear to have been true in the pre-Columbian Andes. Here is what Bertonio has to say on the matter:

Uira vel [i.e., "see also"] *huaa huaa.* The ground, or anything whatever which goes downhill. (*El suelo, o qualquiera cosa que va cuesta abajo.*)[106]

Under the synonym *huaa huaa*, he adds:

Huaa huaa, Uira. Ground or roof where one part is higher than another, or goes downhill (*Suelo o texado que es mas alto de una parte, o cuesta abajo.*)[107]

So *wira* was an abstract term standing for the concept of obliquity. It is probably best translated as "tilted plane." In the language of Wiraqocha's homeland, his name meant "tilted plane of the (celestial) sea." And, when linked by Bertonio to concrete examples, the references for *wira* are tectonic (ground) and architectonic (roof), just as in myth the formal terminology for the parameters of "celestial earth"—the ecliptic—is either tectonic or architectonic. Mythical terms, such as "the height of mountains" and "the depths of the sea," designed to describe the sun's northernmost and southernmost positions on the celestial sphere, make clear the "up and down" of the matter, that is to say the "inclination" of the celestial "earth," the obliquity of the ecliptic.

Equally important to grasp is that implicit in the notion of "obliquity" is some other referent that establishes the concept of "level." "Tiltedness" cannot exist without reference to a second plane. Therefore the meaning, in Aymara, of the name of the Aymara god Wiraqocha denotes *the relationship of two abstract planes.* In the very act of naming their androgynous god, the ancient priest-astronomers of Tiahuanaco expressed their understanding of the notion of the separation of the world parents, the obliquity of the ecliptic to the celestial equator.

It is also important to recognize that the Incas were quite well aware of the meaning of the Aymara word *wira.* The precise spot mentioned by Molina as a pilgrimage stop of the Inca priests,[108] and identified by Larrea as the *divortium aquaram,*[109] or continental divide, sloughing the two rivers at Vilcanota in opposite directions, was called *uirauma.* In Quechua this would mean "fathead." In Aymara, where *uma* means "water,"[110] it might be translated literally as "tilted plane of waters" or, better, "the roof of waters" or, best of all, "watershed."

And so I returned to Pachakuti Yamqui's diagram (figure 2.4). It was now clear to me that the reason Wiraqocha—literally "the tilted plane of the (celestial) sea"—was represented by the oval in Pachakuti Yamqui's drawing was that, as the notation states outright, the oval represents "the sun's taken-altogether fundamental circle," the ecliptic plane. Wiraqocha's name stated the "obliquity" of this plane to the celestial equator, represented by the three stars of Orion's Belt in the drawing. Finally, the god's title, Tunapa, stood for his "control" of the axis of the celestial sphere, and was represented in Pachakuti Yamqui's drawing at right angles to the celestial equator, running through the oval/ecliptic plane. Since these two fundamental planes of orientation were presented with sexual imagery—an androgynous god depicted by male and female crosses, by male and female grindstones, by ecliptic and celestial equator—the tradition of the "separation of the world parents" appeared to have been present, by whatever historical process, in the pre-Columbian Andes.

VI

TWO FURTHER EXAMPLES, one geomantic, the other mythic, demonstrate how the symbolism of the separation of the world parents can be detected in other manifestations of Andean thought. First, the entire symbolism of the *unancha* of Wiraqocha was replicated in the layout of both the imperial city of Cuzco, and the Empire as a whole. The primary division of the Empire into quarters was accomplished by means of the cardinal directions, that is, the "male cross." First came the east-west baseline, running from Mount Pachatusan through the Temple of the Sun and so westward. The two northern quarters were separated by a north-south line emanating from the Temple of the Sun. This line did not, however, continue due south to divide the southern quarters, but, as Urton has shown, was skewed to the southeast, to the azimuth of rise of the Southern Cross.[111]

This anomaly serves to underscore the importance of polar and equatorial coordinates in the layout of the Empire. There are no bright objects near the earth's south pole of rotation. Instead, a number of objects—Toad, Partridge (both dark clouds), *huch'uy cruz* (the Southern Cross), and *llamaq ñawin* (alpha and beta Centaurus, "the eyes of the llama") rise in succession at virtually the same point on the horizon and rotate in a tight band around the "empty" pole (figure 3.5). So the Incas incorporated into the formal layout of the Empire this means of locating the pole.

Also emanating from the Temple of the Sun were the four roads to the four quarters, laid out intercardinally—the "female cross"—toward the heart of the four major provinces, or *suyus*, of the Empire and, ideally, to the four solstice points on the horizon. These are the same two crosses as found on Pachakuti Yamqui's drawing. Likewise the oval, that is the ecliptic plane, was represented in this schema by means of the Temple of the Sun, which in Quechua was called Coricancha, literally "corral of gold." The allied verb *canchay* means "to encircle."[112] The imagery of the "golden circle of the sun" thus suggests, in another manner, the ecliptic plane. At the Coricancha—with sections devoted to Venus, the Pleiades, and the moon (all "denizens" of the ecliptic plane)—one finds another masterpiece of Inca masonry, the great elliptical wall, reminiscent of the oval in Pachakuti Yamqui's diagram, with its balcony looking southwest.

The second example, from a myth recorded in the original Quechua in the Huarochirí document, demonstrates the mythical uses of these same "male" and "female" elements in telling tales of time and motion.

In this story, a young Everyman seeks to better his lot in life by offering to cure the baffling disease of a nobleman. In return, the hero demands the hand of the lord's daughter in marriage. Desperate, the lord agrees, and Everyman reveals that the man is ill because of the various sacrilegious acts of his adulterous wife.

Now, in order for the nobleman to be healed, his house must be torn down. This lord, moreover, is described as a "false god," a notion already discussed in regard to mythic terminology of "legitimacy" (see page 97). The "legitimacy" of a "god" is determined by his ability to provide the measures of a new world-age by plumbing, or otherwise measuring, the "depth of waters," that is by establishing "absolute down" at the southern pole. Because he is a "false god," the lord and his house are, by definition, on shaky "ground."

The house in this tale is, of course, no ordinary house. The roof is thatched with feathers, suggesting the role of the solar bird "flying" to the northern tropic. Further, when the "house" is pulled down, there is found, under the nether grindstone (*maray ukhupi*), a "two-headed toad." The Quechua celestial Toad, *hanp'atu*, lies along that band of stars used by the Incas to locate the southern pole of rotation, the same band toward whose rising point the southern portion of the north/south baseline of the *seque* system was skewed (figure 3.5). In the myth, Toad "hops" away, and disappears into a spring at the bottom of a deep ravine.[113]

In the context of the Huarochirí document, whence also comes the tale of Fox's tail, this episode takes place after the "flood" of A.D. 650. In the centuries preceding the "flood," when Fox's tail was still "dry," the Southern Cross, at heliacal rise on December solstice, stood at the vertical (superior conjunction), pointing straight down to the empty region of sky marking the earth's south pole of rotation. In the centuries following the "flood," as the Southern Cross was pulled farther and farther east at heliacal rise on December solstice by precessional motion, the dark-cloud constellation *hanp'atu*, the Toad, just to the southwest, replaced the Southern Cross at superior conjunction, thus marking the pole. So when the nether, quadrangular grindstone, *maray* (standing for the four-cornered "celestial earth"), was "turned over," after the flood of A.D. 650, the Toad quite "naturally" jumped to the "lowest" topos available—that is, an astronomical position marking the earth's southern pole of rotation. The era of this new configuration was about A.D. 850, and is depicted in figure 4.3. It is for this reason that Toad is termed "two-headed," for it is he, and no longer the Southern Cross, that marks the confluence of the two celestial rivers. Contemporary Quechua-speakers have a nickname for the little Andean toad; they call him *pachakuti*.[114]

The overturning of the *maray*, the "female" grindstone in the center of the floor of the house, and symbol of the four-cornered "celestial earth," represents a faithful kinetic rendition of a *pachakuti*, literally "space/time turns over." The other "earthly" artifact destroyed in the tale is the house of the "false god," that is, the architectural analogue of the *maras*, the world house, running from tropic to tropic.[115] The "result" of all this activity is that Toad takes up a new "location," thus establishing the location of the earth's axis of rotation—the new frame of the fixed stars—in the ensuing era.

Finally, the mythic use of the *maray* in this story merits comparison with certain Old World motifs, as when Zeus "tilts" a table (at a place called Trapezous), causing the flood of Deucalion,[116] or when Christ-militant overturns the tables of the moneylenders, announcing a New World, and bearing, like Arthur, not peace, but an unabashedly axial "sword."

VII

THE ABOVE, THEN, represents a partial inventory of the "can of worms" upended by the Andean rocker mill. A similar investigation could be carried out for Mesoamerica, as for example with the Aztec deity Ometéotl, the "old god," who was invoked thus:

> *The God of Duality is at work,*
> *Creator of men*
> *mirror which illumines things.*
> *Mother of the gods, father of the gods, the old god*
> *spread out on the navel of the earth*
> *within the circle of turquoise.*
> *He who dwells in the waters the color of the bluebird,*
> *he who dwells in the clouds*
> *The old god, he who inhabits the shadows of the land of*
> *the dead*
> *The lord of fire and time.*[117]

The question of where the Andean "navel" was located will be addressed in the next chapter. Here it is enough to point to the broader outlines. The Aztec king Nezahualcoyotl built a temple to the androgynous Ometéotl, "lord of fire and time," who was often addressed as Tloque Nahuaque, "Lord of the Near and Close." [118] In hymns to Wiraqocha collected by the chronicler Molina, we find yet another epithet for the god, *caylla*, meaning "ubiquitous" or "ever present." [119] The Aztec temple to Ometéotl depicted the god abstractly, as the tenth and highest level, above the nine heavens. This tenth level was built entirely of black stone. [120] Likewise, at the Temple of Wiraqocha at Cacha, "The floor of the upper story was composed of very brightly polished black flagstones, looking like jet, which were brought from very distant lands." [121] Like the sacred black cliff of the Aymara at Titicaca, where Wiraqocha created heaven and earth, the sacred stone of the Ka'aba is black, and rested, during pre-Islamic days, beside the statue of the god Hubal—that is, Saturn. [122] The very name for the Vedic Saturn, Kala, meant "blue-black." [123] For although Saturn may have retired to Ogygia in the highest heaven, he was also understood, in his aspect as the Grim Reaper, to be the Lord of the Underworld. His color was as black as the blackest night.

Incidentally, the black cliff Titicaca, from which the lake takes its name, means, literally, in Aymara, "rock of lead." [124] Doubtless there are those who, in plumbing the meaning of this situation, will find further evidence of the pervasive reach of meaningless coincidence.

Such black humor was about all I could muster in the face of this evidence. Personally, I was satisfied that in Andean thought Saturn probably represented the planetary manifestation of Tunapa Wiraqocha. But I didn't relish the prospect of presenting this evidence in public. True, I had done more than simply compile a list of comparative similarities; I had found reasons to believe that the characteristics of Wiraqocha as Saturn conformed to the inner logic of the technical language of myth. He was an old graybeard who carried a staff. His name, Tunapa, meant "mill-bearer." He was androgynous, and this androgyny had numerous demonstrable astronomical valences.

Nonetheless, inasmuch as no scholarly discipline had ever embraced the notion that the technical language of myth even existed, I knew that I lacked sufficient evidence to risk suggesting a paradigm shift. Too bad. There was, to my knowledge, no direct proof, no Andean testimony to the integration of planetary observation into their mythic thought. In a situation like this, one needed a smoking gun. If I tried to argue from this evidence, I would get beaten black and blue. Just like Saturn.

Black and blue. Black and purple. I thought about the two ribbons—one black and one purple—displayed atop the ceremonial lance held by the Inca as he sat enthroned upon the pyramidal *ushñu*. If the black one stood for

Saturn, what did the purple one represent? I had the whimsical thought that the other ribbon must represent the imperial purple of Jupiter the King. But of course that had to be impossible. And yet . . . Could something as simple as two ribbons fluttering in the breeze indicate a conjunction of events so stunning as to spell the end of the world? Perhaps there *was* direct proof in the Andean record. I wasn't sure, but now I realized that I knew exactly how to find out.

CHAPTER 5

PASSING THE STANDARD

Ah Wiraqocha, ticci capac . . .
The sun, the moon,
The day, the night,
The seasons of ripening and rain,
They are not free;
From Thee they take their order.
Thee they obey.
Where, and upon whom,
Hast Thou bestowed
Thy tupa yauri?

—PRAYER OF MANCO CAPAC[1]

I

I HAD, I thought, seen a relationship among three facts, facts that now arranged themselves into a sort of equipotential triangle. To me it had the look of a treasure map. The first information came from the planetary list of the Anonymous Chronicler. According to him, it was the testimony of native informants that the mythical head of the Inca lineage, known as Manco Capac, was the regent of the planet Jupiter on earth:

They called Jupiter *Pirua,* stating, first of all, that the great *Illa Tecce* [Wiraqocha] had ordained that this planet be the lord and guardian of the empire and provinces of Peru and of its republic and lands; and therefore they sacrificed to this planet. . . . They entrusted to this god their granaries, treasure, and stores. . . . Second of all, they said that the great *Pirua Pacaric Manco Inca,* the first inhabitant of these lands, when he died, was taken to heaven to the house and place of this god called *Pirua*, and that there he was ensconced and feasted by that same god.[2]

I had read this before, without being able to see how the information was meant to be taken. As I have said, I was, at the time, in need of reviewing what Santillana and Dechend had to say about the precise role of the planetary deities in archaic astronomy.

As a result of that review, I came upon a second fact. According to Santillana and Dechend, the Orphic hymns describe how Kronos/Saturn gives to Zeus/Jupiter "all the measures of time," a reference to a very particular kind of knowledge concerning the conjunctions of Saturn and Jupiter. Again, at that time, I had no inkling that such thinking might also be operative in the Andes. Nonetheless, when a whimsical question about two fluttering ribbons drifted through my thoughts, a third piece of information locked with ringing finality into the pattern. According to a myth recorded by Pachakuti Yamqui, the god Wiraqocha, just before leaving the "earth" via the river Chacamarca, met with the father of the yet-unborn Manco Capac *and left for the child his "staff."*

Here was an Andean myth that appeared to describe a conjunction of Saturn and Jupiter. Moreover, as will be explained, the myth appears to make clear that the event occurred on a particular day of a particular year, and under conditions so rare that such an event cannot happen more than once in a millennium. In other words, there lay at hand extremely stringent means for testing the planetary identifications of the gods Wiraqocha and Manco Capac in their planetary manifestations as Saturn and Jupiter.

A positive result would represent more than just a smoking gun. If it was true that the priest-astronomers of the Andes were recording the flow of precessional time by reference to conjunctions of Saturn and Jupiter and, moreover, recording their observations in a technical language of myth whose mode of transmission can only have been effected through human contact, then this would suggest that we contemporary people have yet to be introduced to the true dimensions of our own, human past. If this "prediction" of the astronomical significance of the myth was verifiable, it would raise profound questions about the aims, means, and extent of human contact over great distances and across great spans of time.

As the child is father to the man, I found myself, once again, in a peculiar state of tension caused by the hope that the past was not lost to the present. During the planetarium experiment, I had experienced an overpowering impression of the connection between our time and the events of A.D. 650. This impression was not simply connected with the similarities between that time and our own. More eerie was the realization that without the advanced state of scientific technology represented by the planetarium, it would have been, as a purely technical problem, nearly impossible to construct questions or receive answers with anything like the precision that the planetarium offered.

The first planetarium was conceived in 1913 and built in 1923 by the firm of Carl Zeiss, and could render the night sky only at the latitude of Munich. It was not until after the Second World War that the era of modern planetarium construction came into its own. Likewise, computing machines were not available, outside of national security applications, until that time. Until quite recently, hundreds of hours of mathematical calculation with pencil and paper would have been required to render what a planetarium can reveal in a few minutes, or a computer program in a few seconds. In other words, the kinds of questions raised by investigating the technical language of myth could not, as a practical matter, have been answered, and, as a curious matter of historical fact, have not been asked, until the last twenty-five years.

Now, once again, I was in a situation where I needed certain tools— tools representative of the triumph of Western scientific materialism—in order to seek understanding of a realm of human endeavor whose very existence this same contemporary culture has systematically denied along a spectrum ranging from disinterest to derision. For me, the strangeness of this exercise resonated on a level deeper than irony. Was it coincidence that this lost Atlantis of human thought might emerge—and could emerge—from the waters of oblivion only in our time?

With the question of planetary conjunctions and their relationship to precessional time, we enter the precincts of pure measurement, the most important function of the planetary gods. For it is from such information that "control" of the "mill," in the sense of understanding how to measure precessional time, arises. We have just seen information suggesting that the mythical head of the Inca lineage, Manco Capac, represented the planet Jupiter on earth. Before turning to the two further critical pieces of informa- tion—the Old World use of conjunctions of Saturn and Jupiter, and the Andean myth that appears to memorialize just such an event—it is first necessary to pick up the trail where we left it, in order to describe the ultimate Saturnine characteristic of the god Wiraqocha, his role as the lord of measures.

⁘⁙⁘ II ⁘⁙⁘

IN HYMNS TO Wiraqocha recorded by the indigenous chronicler Pachakuti
Yamqui, there exists yet another title for the god, *cuzco capac*. The early
chroniclers did not explore the literal significance of this term, nor have
scholars in the modern era. One of the hymns to Wiraqocha begins, "*Cam
cuzco capaca*," that is, "You are the king of Cuzco,"[3] according to Urteaga's
translation, a reading that is standard in the literature. If one takes this
translation at face value, it implies an intimate connection between the god
Wiraqocha and the foundation of Cuzco in the early 1400s, whereas the
Chronicles paint a different picture—a deep and bitter dispute between the
founder of Inca greatness, Pachakuti Inca, and his father, the legendary
Wiraqocha Inca, advocate for the old religion of the Andean creator. This
translation of *cuzco capaca* illustrates a principle for avoiding many of the
historical problems raised by the Andean material: if you're going to skate
on thin ice, don't bring along anything heavy—like a dictionary—lest you
find yourself all at once in deep waters.

To begin with, *cuzco* means "navel."[4] As Eliade's research has shown (see
page 80), the "navel of the earth" in Old World shamanism stands at the top
of the cosmic mountain, and it is from this point that the measures of the
"earth" are laid out. Because of the nature of the symbolism of the Center—
which involves maintaining connection among all three worlds—"palaces,
royal cities, and even simple houses were believed to stand at the 'Center of
the World,' on the summit of the cosmic mountain."[5]

But the navel—be it mountain, temple, city, or a simple *omphalos*
(= Greek "navel") stone—must ultimately rest upon the waters of the deep.
These are the waters of the great sweet-water ocean beneath the salt seas of
the "earth," which "saltwater" extends only so far as the southern tropic (see
figures 3.13, 3.14). In Babylon, this sweet-water sea was called *apsu*, whence
comes our word *abyss*. It is therefore in the nature of the navel at the Center
to provide access not only to the "world above," but to that "below."

> In Jewish legends it is told that "since the ark disappeared there was a
> stone in its place . . . which was called foundation stone [of the Tem-
> ple]." It was called foundation stone "because from it the world was
> founded." And it is said to lie above the Waters that are below the
> Holy of Holies.[6]

This is the same point occupied by the quadrangular, "female" grinding stone, the *maray*, in the "house of the false god." And when that stone is overturned, and the "hole" looking over the deep southern sky is revealed, "all underworld" breaks loose, and the times change.

According to Inca myth, Cuzco was "founded" at the location of "an uncovered navel stone" (*cuzco cara urumi*),[7] distinguishable as such because it emerged from a (sweet-water) marsh. But it was not the Incas who, among Andean peoples, originated these ideas or this terminology. "The King of Cuzco," in its technical sense, is a concept vastly predating the Incas or the foundation of their capital. The ancient Aymara name for the Holy of Holies, Tiahuanaco, was *taypicala*,[8] literally "the rock in the center."[9] And, in the fundamental Andean myth of the creation of the universe by Wiraqocha, the symbolism is also present, for it is at Titicaca, a cliff of black rock rising out of the waters of a sweet-water lake, that the sun, the moon, and the stars were created, and the tribal organization of the Andes laid out from this navel of the world. Here, Wiraqocha plumbed the depths of waters, at a place named "rock of lead."

In the situation at the Center, everything depends upon the King, the Lord of Measure. If he creates heaven on earth—outwardly by rendering terrestrial space sacred through replication on the physical earth of the order of the heavens, inwardly by establishing the norms of social behavior, particularly the virtues of tolerance, hospitality, and orientation toward the common good—then the welfare of the people is assured. Forthwith emerges a Golden Age. This sacramental action takes place at and from the navel—where heaven, earth, and the land of the dead meet—and the legitimacy of all terrestrial kings, their right to "rule"—meaning "to measure," as we also say in English—derives ultimately from the sanction and example of the Lord of Measure, who is Saturn.

These observations concerning the "navel" lead to the second word of Wiraqocha's title, *capaca*. Pachakuti Yamqui usually wrote this word *capac*, understood in the colonial Quechua lexicons as "king."[10] In the phrase *cuzco capaca* (with an extra *a*), Pachakuti Yamqui gives us the Aymara word, also understood to mean "king." Reference to Bertonio's dictionary, however, contributes an unexpected dimension to the term:

> *Ccapaca:* King, or Lord. This is an ancient word which now no longer is used in this sense.[11]

The word for "king" among the Aymara was so ancient as to represent an anachronism of speech. One might expect this information to be of

sufficient interest to have aroused curiosity among scholars. Why did the
Incas name *their* institution, the imperial kingship, after a foreign idea already
obsolete before the first stone of Cuzco was laid? Exploration of this point
might have explained other data, as for instance the reason Betanzos heard
such a long and tedious account of how Pachakuti Inca personally laid out
and measured the new city of Cuzco.[12] Nonetheless, the literature on the
Incas reveals the assumption that the words *capaca* and *capac* always and only
meant "king."

But this is not the case. In Quechua, the particle for agency (which
in English is provided by *-er* added to the stem of the verb), was written
as *-c* by the Spanish. Its use is found, for example, in the name of the
coastal deity Pacha*camac,* "world maker," from the Quechua verb *camay,* "to
make."

The Quechua verb *capay* refers to a means of measurement:

Kapay. To measure by palms (*Medir a palmos*).
Kapa. Palm. The hand extended and the measure (*Palmo. La mano estendida y la
    medida*).[13]

Aymara shares the term:

Capatha. To measure by palms (*Medir a palmos*).
Capa. Palm (*El palmo*).[14]

So the word for "king," *capac,* literally means "he who measures by
palms," while the title for Wiraqocha—*cuzco capaca,* or *cuzco capac,* rendered
in the scholarly literature as "the king of Cuzco"—literally means "the one
who measures the navel of the earth by palms."[15]

The palm measure, that is, the distance between thumb and forefinger
extended at arm's length, has historically provided "archaic" peoples with a
useful means for *measuring time on the celestial sphere.* For example, David Lewis
found the palm measure, called *naf,* used by the contemporary Polynesian
navigators of the Caroline Islands, still using traditional methods. Lewis
surmises that this measurement, described as "the forefinger to thumb distance at arm's length, or about 10 degrees . . . may well reflect an ancient
technique."[16]

The Aztec astronomers also "used their hands in the manner of sextants
to measure the movements of the stars," according to León-Portilla, who
translates an Aztec title for their astronomers, *i-ne-ma-taca-choliz:*

". . . he measures with his hand the flight or crossing of the stars." That the Nahuatl astronomers not only observed, but also measured the stars and plotted their courses is proved by the exact mathematical calculations involved in the calendar, and by the even more obvious fact that the *maitl* or hand measure was a Nahuatl unit of measure.[17]

Unaware of the dimensions of the game that was afoot, no chronicler of the Conquest of Peru experienced the slightest curiosity about a particular aspect of the only statue of Wiraqocha ever seen by European eyes:

> Capac Yupanqui [the Inca Pachakuti] was the first who ordered built the houses of Quisuarcancha, where he placed a statue of the Creator [Wiraqocha], who, in their language is called Pachayachachi ["World Teacher"], and which statue was [made] of gold the size of a boy of ten, and was in the figure of a man standing up, *the right arm high, with the hand almost closed, except for the thumb and forefinger [held] high, like a person who is commanding.* [Emphasis added.][18]

The ancient "kings" of the Aymara, the *capaca*, were priest-astronomers.

III

I HAD STUMBLED upon the above information as a result of tracing the etymology of the titles of Wiraqocha, in order to determine whether they fit the "profile" of Saturnine characteristics. Nonetheless, this information remained in its own watertight compartment, separated from connection with other information. I still did not grasp the full implications of the title *cuzco capac*. I had yet to find the answer to some basic questions. If measurement was the crucial aspect of the "ruler's" legitimacy, what is it that is measured, and how is this function accomplished? It still exceeded my credulity threshold to consider seriously that a particularly abstruse (to me) section of *Hamlet's Mill*, dealing with Orphic Greek fragments, might hold the answers to my questions. Convinced though I already was that *Hamlet's Mill* was an important book, I still somehow balked at the idea of a comprehensive sharing of astronomical information between Old World and New.

I was willing to accept that the answer to the first part of my question might be found in Old World sources. This was the general idea that the legitimate planetary ruler of an age was obliged to measure time on the scale of Ages of the World, and imprint upon the earth, from the "navel" outward, the boundaries of this new creation in the stars. To be the master of time, one must first be master of space, space laid out from the navel of the earth. Thus the layout of the Inca Empire, reconciling the relation of the ecliptic to the fixed sphere of stars, imprints on terrestrial space the image of the sacred marriage of the heavenly elements, and provides the conceptual framework within which the "temper of the times" may be brought to fruition in the affairs of men. This seemed a broad enough general proposition to be susceptible of wide dissemination.

As for the second part of the question—how precisely was the measurement made—I have come to regard this technique as one of the great scientific triumphs of the archaic world. And the reclamation of this information from the scrap heap of history is, perhaps, the single greatest accomplishment of *Hamlet's Mill*. The technique in question involves the pattern formed by the very regular conjunctions of Saturn and Jupiter as they move through the ecliptic plane. Just slightly less than every twenty years, these two planets come into conjunction. The next conjunction occurs a third of the way around the ecliptic plane against the background of fixed stars, the stars familiar in the West as the zodiac. The next conjunction transpires, again, a third of the way around the zodiac, and so on, passing by the original location in the stars by about nine degrees, so that the figure created in time by the pattern of these conjunctions is much like a moving equilateral triangle whose vertices turn slowly through the ecliptic plane.

Figure 5.1 shows Kepler's drawing of (and interest in) this phenomenon. After eight hundred years (794$\frac{1}{3}$ years to be precise), that is, after forty such conjunctions, the triangle has turned through one third of the ecliptic, thus replicating its "original" position in the stars.

> This Trigon of Great Conjunctions presented itself as the instrument by which one could "narrow down" the almost imperceptible tempo of the Precession. To move through the whole zodiac, one of the angles of the Trigon needs approximately 3 × 794$\frac{1}{3}$ = 2,383 years. That comes tolerably near to one double hour of the greatest "day" of the precession of 25,900 years. . . . A new zodiacal sign was termed to "rule" starting from the day of a great conjunction at the place of the "passage" [of the conjunction into the zodiacal sign].[19]

The evidence for an understanding of this phenomenon and its usefulness in ancient times was found by Santillana and Dechend in an Orphic fragment preserved by Proclus in his commentary on Plato's *Cratylus*:

The greatest Kronos [Saturn] is giving from above the principles of intelligibility to the Demiurge [Zeus/Jupiter] and he presides over the whole "creation" [demiourgia]. That is why Zeus calls him "Demon" according to Orpheus, saying, "Set in motion our excellent genus Demon." And Kronos seems to have with him the highest causes of junctions and separations. . . .[20]

This commentary ends with Proclus stating that Kronos [Saturn] "prophesies" to Zeus [Jupiter] "continuously," and that *he gives him all the measures of the whole creation."*[21]

Here, then, is the ultimate source of Saturn's "power" as the Lord of Measures. By giving "continuously" to Jupiter the "principles of intelligibility," he gave to mankind the chronometric means of reading the history of the Ages of the World, written in the stars.

IV

WHEN IT FINALLY dawned on me that knowledge of this astronomical technique might really have existed in the Andes, I forced myself to proceed systematically. If the Anonymous Chronicler's assertion (cited at the beginning of this chapter) of an association between the mythical head of the Inca lineage, Manco Capac, and the planet Jupiter was in fact true, then there ought to be evidence in Inca myth that Manco Capac manifested characteristics of the planet Jupiter concordant with the technical language of myth. In other words, in the same way that I had explored the significance of the names and "behavior" of Wiraqocha, I now felt constrained to do the same with Manco Capac. To draw a direct connection between the Anonymous Chronicler's information and Pachakuti Yamqui's myth of Wiraqocha passing his "staff" to Manco Capac without taking this step would constitute a weak link in the chain of evidence. Besides, if what I now suspected really was true, then such information about Manco Capac would be there.

In the same way that the Caesars commissioned Virgil to create the *Aeneid* as a means of establishing the family's pedigree as descendants of Venus, the Incas strove to establish their claim as legitimate rulers by asserting a special relationship with the planetary gods through the founder of their dynasty, Manco Capac. At least that is what the Anonymous Chronicler reported. The mythical head of the Inca lineage derived his authority from the planet Pirua/Jupiter, which in turn was "ordained" by the creator, Wiraqocha, to be the tutelary deity of the Empire and its rulers. If this formulation sounds familiar—"The greatest Kronos is giving from above the principles of intelligibility to the Demiurge [Zeus] and he presides over the whole 'creation'"—what might be learned from other sources about the identity and nature of Manco Capac?

Manco Capac was the name of the "first" Inca. According to Inca tradition, which was taken literally for centuries after the Conquest, there had been eleven Inca kings, ending with Huayna Capac. Zuidema has shown why this account cannot be taken at face value. First, Cuzco was divided into moieties, or social "halves," and the kingship may have alternated between the two moieties or, more likely, there may have been a diarchy, that is, two simultaneous kings: one from the lower moiety (living in the southern half of the city called *urin* [i.e.,"lower"] Cuzco), more concerned with matters of religion, the other, from "upper" Cuzco, who was more the military leader.[22] Furthermore, according to Zuidema, the record of five generations of eleven kings is not historical in the sense that we understand the word, but represents what might be called a structural representation of the past:

> The consequence must be that the mummies of the former first kings in both moieties were taken out of the Temple and that they lost in fact all social and *historical* importance to the living. Not so much the mummies were of importance to the living but their positions in the system. These were kept constant, only in each succeeding generation the positions were occupied by other mummies.[23]

The way the Incas represented their past, no more than eleven kings would be remembered, no matter how many there might have been.

The name of Manco Capac, therefore, is not meant to evoke the traceable lineage of a historical king. Manco Capac is a purely mythical character, that is to say, not less than real, but more than human. Zuidema has pointed out that the chronicler Guamán Poma places Manco Capac far back, in the Fourth Age—that is, the Age of Warriors[24]—when the dominion of the states of Wari and Tiahuanaco began to wane. Zuidema has also shown how the Incas took not only their claim to be the legitimate emperors of the Andes from this period, but many of the administrative techniques of Empire as well.[25] Although it is true to say that the Incas traced their "lineage" as inheritors of the right to "rule" the Andes from such distant and mythical events as the time when Wiraqocha "left the earth," there is far more at work in this formulation than a blunt political claim of precedence. That is why the information of the Anonymous Chronicler is so important.

If we pause for a moment to consider, for example, the literal meaning

.of the Quechua word *pirua*, after which the planet Jupiter was named, we at once find ourselves within the familiar topos of our original hologram. *Pirua*, and its Aymara variant *piura*, refers to a kind of building, a round storehouse for grain.[26] These structures relied for their stability, as did the Ages of the World, on four sturdy pillars, around which were worked wattle and daub into a round shape.[27] Holguín distinguishes the wattle-and-daub *pirua* from the *collca*,[28] a square storehouse of imperial construction, made from adobe, according to Cobo.[29] The *pirua* was the ancient granary of the peasantry. Arriaga and Acosta both noted the ceremonies of the peasantry concerned with guarding their crops in the *pirua*.[30] To have named the guardian deity of one's empire after the traditional structure that protects abundance and projects stability was doubtless a valuable asset in the portfolio of imperial persuasion.

If, then, the Empire of the Sun was the House that Jove built, then it should not be surprising that the god's attributes are displayed with utter authority by Manco Capac in various versions of the myth of the foundation of Cuzco. As just discussed above, the mythical site of the foundation of Cuzco was the *cuzco cara urumi*, or "uncovered navel stone." Various sources specify that this site was located at a swampy area with a sweet-water spring.[31] The storyline of the myth is that Manco Capac, along with his brothers and sisters,[32] went off in search of a suitable location to found a great city. Manco Capac carried with him a scepter of gold, called *tupayauri* by Pachakuti Yamqui, the same wooden staff, now miraculously transformed, that was given to Manco's father by Wiraqocha before the child's birth. As they traveled, Manco probed the ground with the staff, testing for arable lands. At the *cuzco cara urumi* he hurled the *tupayauri* into the marshy ground, and it disappeared, signifying the end of the search.[33]

By this action, Manco Capac performed the godlike task of establishing "the depth of waters," the irreducible task of any god who would claim the legitimate right to "rule" a new age. He did so by probing at the interface between this world and the "world below," at a spring open all the way down to the sweet-water ocean of the underworld abyss beneath the "celestial earth." In doing so, he replicated the foundation of the world at Titicaca, and at Tiahuanaco/Taypicala—"the rock in the center"—by the god Ticci Wiraqocha. But unlike Wiraqocha, whose characteristic mode of measurement involved the use of a "rock of lead," Manco Capac established the *axis mundi* of a new age by driving the *tupayauri* into the earth. Saturn plumbs, but Jupiter hurls.

That this reading of the myth is no mere fanciful "spin" placed on a perfectly innocent tale is evinced by the literal meaning of Manco Capac's

name. Again, it is the Aymara language, and not Quechua, where the cosmological weight of the words is lodged.[34] In Quechua the possible cognates
for *manco* comprise "a pot," "a dolt," or "a woodcutter."[35] In Aymara, Bertonio
lists, as noted in chapter 3, that the word *mancca* means "below," and was
used, in the formal Aymara terminology describing the three worlds, to
designate the underworld, *mancca pacha*.[36] And elsewhere he spells the term
manqhue pacha, where *manqhue* means "depth, or depth of waters."[37] Manco
Capac's name, then, means "he who measures by palms the depths of waters,"
which is to say that his name describes precisely what he was required to do
in order to establish a new world at the navel of the earth, Cuzco. By hurling
the *axis mundi* to the very bottom of the abyss, Manco Capac had staked his
claim, as the rightful heir of Wiraqocha, to the stewardship of the mill.

V

PACHAKUTI YAMQUI TRACES for us all the steps by which the staff of Wiraqocha came into the possession of the Incas.

> They say that this man [Wiraqocha] came to the village of a chief called
> Apo-tampu very tired. It was at a time when they were celebrating a
> marriage feast. His doctrines were listened to by the chief with friendly
> feelings, but his vassals heard them unwillingly. From that day the
> wanderer was a guest of Apo-tampu, to whom it is said that he gave a
> stick from his own staff, and through this Apo-tampu, the people lis-
> tened with attention to the words of the stranger, receiving the stick
> from his hands. Thus they received what he preached in a stick, mark-
> ing and scoring on it each chapter of his precepts. . . . Tonapa [Wiraqo-
> cha] then followed the course of the river Chacamarca until he came
> to the sea.
>   They say that the staff which Tonapa delivered into the hands of
> Apo-tampu was turned into fine gold on the birth of his son named
> Manco Ccapac Ynca, who had seven brothers and sisters. Their names
> were Ayar-cachi, Ayar-uchu, Aya-raeca, etc. The said Apo Manco Cca-
> pac, after the death of his father and mother, named Apu Tampu Pacha
> and Mama Achi, being now an orphan, but grown to man's estate,
> assembled his people to see what power he had to prosecute the new
> conquests which he meditated. Finding some difficulties, he agreed
> with his brothers and sisters to seek new lands, taking his rich clothes
> and arms, and the staff which had been left by Tonapa. This staff was

called *Tupayauri*. . . . Thence he went to Collcapampa with the *tupayauri* in his hand, and with a sister named Ypa mama huaco, and with another sister and a brother. They arrived at Collcapampa where they were for some days. Thence they went to Huamantiana [i.e., *waman tiana*, "seat of the hawk," or Sacsayhuaman fortress], where they remained for some time, and thence they marched to Coricancha where they found a place suitable for a settlement. There was good water from Hurinchacan and Hananchacan . . . which are two springs. A rock was called by the natives (who are the Allcayriesas, the Cullinchinas, and the Cayaucachis) by the name of *cuzco-cara-urumi*, whence the place came to be called Cuzco-pampa and Cuzco-llacta; and the Yncas were afterwards called Cuzco-Capac and Cuzco-Ynca.[38]

The *tupayauri*, defined by Holguín as "the royal sceptre, staff, royal insignia of the Inca,"[39] was the symbol of Imperial authority among the historical Incas. *Tupa* means "royal"[40] in Quechua, while *yauri* is the Aymara word for copper.[41] When drawing royal personages, Guamán Poma depicted them with this staff of office. Figure 5.2 is his drawing of Manco Capac holding the *tupayauri*, a wooden pole with a copper knife affixed to the top. It was this lance, or one like it, that the Inca carried with him atop the *ushñu*, and from which fluttered ribbons of purple and black.

The magical properties of the *tupayauri*, as the talisman of Inca invincibility, are apparent in the Inca myth concerning the pivotal battle between the Incas, led by the Inca Pachakuti, and their archenemies the Chancas. In the heat of battle, as the story goes, Pachakauti Inca is knocked unconscious, and a voice from heaven asks him why he does not have the *tupayauri*. Rousing himself, he takes the scepter in hand and rallies his men. The Chancas are defeated and the course of empire set.[42] As long as the Incas possessed this talisman of legitimacy, their destiny would be assured.

The etymology of the word *tupa* makes clear the source of the *tupayauri*'s magical powers. Comparison with the Quechua word *capac* demonstrates that the standards for determining royalty are invariant. The Quechua verbs sharing the root *tup-*, the verbs *tupay* and *tupuy*, mean "to grind, or rasp" and "to measure with a staff" respectively,[43] and the same cognates are to be found in Aymara.[44] A number of Inca emperors, such as the great Tupac Inca Yupanqui, incorporated the word into their names. *Tupac* means "the one who mills," a title as inseparable from the criteria for "rulership" as is *capac*, "the one who measures."

These, then, were the individual pieces of the puzzle. It remained only to test their fit—on the basis of purely Andean material. I was about to find out whether the image formed from these pieces represented a mirage or a picture of historical reality not seen since the Conquest of Peru.

VI

SO I PICKED up the telephone and called Professor Gingerich, who had helped me at the planetarium a year and a half earlier. At that time he had mentioned in passing that the planetarium did not lend itself to looking at past planetary conjunctions, because this involved turning the machine backwards through every year to the desired point in the past, rather than merely tilting the machine to a given year, thus ignoring proper planetary positions. To get to A.D. 650 would have tied the instrument up for an enormous number of hours. This bit of arcana hadn't seemed important then, as I had no expectation of getting involved with Andean planetary lore.

"You need to consult the planetary tables," he said.

"Planetary tables?"

"Yes."

"You mean it's in a book? You just have to look in a book?"

"Yes." He seemed to have a lot of patience. Then he told me what to look for, and rang off.

So . . . it was that simple. The abruptness of the transition from myth time to "real" time had caught me unprepared. As I drove to the library to find the book of planetary tables, my state swung between the poles of hope and gloom. The question, or test, that I had formulated left virtually no wiggle room. Either I understood the myth of Wiraqocha and Manco Capac in a manner that would confirm their identity as planets and confirm that in the Andes the technical language of myth was operating at the heart of Inca thought right up until the Conquest, or I understood nothing. If the planetary tables failed to confirm the myth of Pachakuti Yamqui, I would be back at square one, unable to explain how a cosmology, such as expressed in the llama-flood myth, could exist in a religious vacuum. But more than anything else I wanted it to be true that, in the past, people had taken pains to communicate to the future.

The test, or "prediction," of the astronomical situation described in Pachakuti Yamqui's myth was almost monstrously precise. Pachakuti Yamqui's statement that Wiraqocha had "left the earth" via the river Chacamarca had for a long time appeared to me to be susceptible to one, and only one, astronomical interpretation, namely that the event occurred during the "flood" of ca. A.D. 650. This conclusion was based not simply on the available historical information connecting the "departure" of the god Wiraqocha with the onset of an era of endemic warfare; it also seemed to follow logically from my presumed understanding of the technical language in Andean myth. Wiraqocha *must* have left "by a bridge across a river" at about A.D. 650, *if* the Andean peoples indeed possessed a knowledge terming access to the land of the gods a function of the relationship between the June solstice sun and the Milky Way, waning, coincidentally, with the era of peace now being replaced by warfare. The bridge was "going under" then, and if Wiraqocha was successfully to exit this mortal coil, he had to leave then.

Because of my foray into planetary identifications, it was now necessary to make additional stipulations. First, of course, I now had to consider that the myth referred to Wiraqocha in his planetary manifestation as Saturn. Further, there must have been a *conjunction* of Saturn and Jupiter (the "meeting" of Wiraqocha and Manco Capac) during this event. In itself, this would not constitute an unusual occurrence. Saturn and Jupiter come into conjunction every twenty years. Therefore, in the window of time—A.D. 650 plus or minus fifty years—generated by the planetarium experiment, there was no question that one would find such an event. If, however, my reading of the cosmological drama was correct, the conjunction of Saturn and Jupiter that I sought must have occurred *at a particular place in the stars*, namely on the eastern edge of the Milky Way in Gemini, where lay the entrance to the "bridge" to the land of the gods. This is an event that, owing to the geometry of the trigon of conjunctions of Saturn and Jupiter, can occur *only once in eight hundred years.*

But this was just the beginning of the list of constraints. Next, the event must have taken place not just sometime in the year, but *on a particular calendar date*—that is, at June solstice, or more probably on the eve of June solstice—as one age ended and the next began. In other words, if part of the significance of the "flood" of A.D. 650 was that Wiraqocha "left the earth," then the conjunction of Saturn and Jupiter must have occurred at June solstice, as the "bridge" was going under.

Next, this event must have been visible *at sunset* on the eve of the solstice, because, according to the concordance of Andean myth, Wiraqocha "left the earth" in the northwest. This condition was also mandated by the strict mythical convention of the technical language, noted in chapter 3, that *access to the supernatural worlds from the earth occurred at sunset.* And *north*west represented the direction of access to the land of the gods.

Finally, if this pattern for understanding the myths was correct, then there existed the further stipulation that the conjunction must have been visible not just anywhere in the sky at the time of sunset—but *at the northwest-*

ern horizon as close as possible to the celestial river in order to replicate clearly the departure of Wiraqocha even as he surrendered to Manco Capac the rulership of a new age.

So there it was. If the myths I sought to understand really did conform to a strict technical language, then all of the above conditions had to be met. Violation of any one of them would make the entire reading of the event suspect. I was looking for a conjunction of Saturn and Jupiter, which occurred on the eastern edge of the Milky Way in Gemini, at the horizon, at sunset, on the eve of June solstice, ca. A.D. 650. A conjunction of Saturn and Jupiter at a particular location in the stars was a rare enough event (eight hundred years). To add the stipulations that it must occur on a particular calendar date in the solar year (June solstice) and be visible at a particular hour in relation to the horizon (sunset) meant that I was looking for an event so rare as to be virtually unique.

After five years of research, everything I thought I understood about Andean cosmology, as described in the preceding chapters, was on the line —on one line, to be precise, of a book of numbers the size of the Yellow Pages, *Planetary, Lunar, and Solar Positions A.D. 2 to A.D. 1649 at Five-Day and Ten-Day Intervals*, known as the Tuckerman Tables.

When I found the Tuckerman Tables on the library shelf, I made myself leave the stacks and go to a table. I looked at the title page. The tables had been printed in 1964. Tuckerman had produced the tables for IBM, and the project had been undertaken to demonstrate the usefulness of digital computers to historians and other practitioners of the humanities. I was holding a tool not quite twenty years old. Would it reveal, as the planetarium had, another odd conjunction of past and present?

I opened the book to A.D. 650, prepared to search ten years on either side of this date for the nearest conjunction of Saturn and Jupiter. This proved unnecessary. There was a conjunction of Saturn and Jupiter in A.D. 650 (see figure 5.3).

In order to read these tables, it is first necessary to take into account that they are presented with the Julian dates for use by historians of Western culture. To determine the Julian date of a solstice, it is not, however, necessary to consult a table of interpolations, because this information is provided by the sun's longitude. Point zero is the vernal equinox, and every solar longitude thereafter moves eastward; the higher the number, the farther east it is.

The June solstice takes place at solar longitude 90 degrees, that is, a quarter of the year around from the equinox. According to the Tuckerman Tables, the June solstice, A.D. 650, occurred at Julian date June 19. If you look to the left of the "Sun" column, you will see that on the eve of this date, Saturn and Jupiter are in conjunction within one degree of each other, having been in exact conjunction several days earlier. (First Wiraqocha gave his staff to Manco Capac; then he left the "earth.") Finally, note that Saturn and Jupiter were in conjunction at about 101 and 102 degrees respectively, that is, between eleven and twelve degrees east of the sun, meaning that Saturn, in the evocative language of modern astronomy, was nearing the point of "extinction" in the setting sun on the eve of June solstice A.D. 650 (see figure 5.4). Within three nights—that is, by the end of the solstice period—Saturn had disappeared into the sun, not to be seen again for three weeks. After studying these tables for a time, I saw that *the event met every every single constraint that the myths had appeared to stipulate.* As "ordained" by Wiraqocha, the standard had been passed to a new generation of gods, foremost among whom was Pirua Manco Capac.

VII

THE MAYA WARRIOR king Bonampak went to war by the phases of Venus.[45] In the ancient Near East, the Persian Magi saw, in the return of the conjunction of Saturn and Jupiter to Pisces, the dawn of a new age, and hence set forth, following the "star in the east," to find its King.

To the early Maya, conjunctions of Saturn and Jupiter and particular positions of Saturn were important and may prove a means of sorting out certain calendric anomalies as yet unresolved.[46] Among the Maya, the most ancient deity, god of fire and supreme being, was Hunab Ku, literally "one palm measure house," or "the giver of unified measure."[47]

There is little question that, as between New World and Old, there was a concordance of opinion concerning the numinous import of the wanderings of the various planetary powers: "freedom" of motion was the signature of Will, and number its music. In the Andes the number forty represented wholeness. After forty conjunctions of Saturn and Jupiter, the trigon replicates itself in the stars. There were forty *seques*, or rays, emanating from the Temple of the Sun in all directions to the horizon, an idealized number of forty chieftains representing all the peoples of the Empire, a census unit of forty thousand, forty dances danced at the Inca Temple of the Sun at Lake Titicaca at the time of June solstice.[48] Why did the number forty represent wholeness? As we shall presently find among the Incas, the end of a yet another world-age transpired exactly forty conjunctions of Saturn and Jupiter after the *paqo* had raised his eyes to the heavens and declared, according to Molina's version, "that the conjunction of stars showed that the world would be destroyed by water."

With the "smoking gun" of the events of A.D. 650, I had, I believed, discovered the broad outlines of the technical language of myth, fully operative in the Andes. Like some megalithic stela looming out of the fog, it stands as an artifact of immense proportions, organizing by its cunning design the entire sacred history of the Andean experience. A tool of extraordinary promise for unlocking the "prehistoric" record did indeed exist. I thought that I had done enough, but I was mistaken. But for a single loose end, I might never have understood how to use this tool. As soon as I tried to grasp this last loose end, it turned into the tail of a tiger—or, to be precise, a jaguar. At this point the research literally took on a life of its own, and I simply followed the symbol of the jaguar where it led—deep into the native Andean past, to the dawning of the Age of Wiraqocha, and beyond. By the time I returned from this mythical journey, I saw not only the Andean experience, but particularly the Inca Empire, through utterly transformed eyes.

PART II

THE DESCENT
OF HISTORY

CHAPTER 6

THE SEARCH
FOR FATHER

Whoso boleth my kyne,
Ewere calf is mine.

—OLD ENGLISH PROVERB

I

SOMETHING HAPPENED IN the Andes for which myth offers a benchmark of A.D. 650, the moment when Wiraqocha "left the earth." That something was the advent of organized warfare, previously unknown in the Andes, and caused in large part, according to mythic sources, by pressure on the land from population growth. In the social and political upheaval that ensued, the Andean ecumene was shaken to its foundations and emerged forever altered, the institution of warfare now permanently woven into the social fabric. Although, for reasons including political expediency, the Incas projected their own ancestry back into the thick of the events of A.D. 650, the fact remains that what had begun there was the Age of the Warriors. As Jupiter stands between the cool detachment of Saturn and the red heat of Mars, Andean society would have to endure bitter centuries of bloodshed before the institution of the Imperial Inca would intervene in an attempt to balance the needs of the peasantry with those of the warrior nobility.

Although this view of the importance of the "flood" of A.D. 650 may sound sensible, none of it was obvious to me from the research described thus far. Nor had I grasped the extent to which this "flood" lay at the heart of the Incas' own view of themselves as a people with a mission—a mission involving the redress of perceived cosmic imbalances accumulated since the catastrophe of A.D. 650, and manifest in the failure of the military state of Wari and the subsequent collapse of the fabled civilization of Tiahuanaco.

Without knowing it, I was about to embark on research that led inevitably to these conclusions. I would learn that in order to understand the forces that led to the formation of the Inca Empire and the peculiar vision that animated it, it was first necessary to understand the profound transformation in Andean society that commenced about A.D. 650. In turn, an understanding of this event depended upon a clear grasp of what was lost, or at least badly damaged—namely the old principles of social organization of Andean society as ordained by Wiraqocha—in the mythical cataclysm that marked his "departure."

None of the rest of this book would have been conceived or written had I not become somewhat stubbornly fixated upon a single question: Why was the face of the Andean creator god Wiraqocha depicted as feline? As I sought a comprehensive answer to this question, I began to cast my net farther and farther afield, all the while telling myself that this fishing expedition was "off the record," the indulgence of a personal whim: experts in iconography said that Wiraqocha's face was feline, and I wanted to know why it was feline. It seemed to me I should be able to figure this out. The more I dug into this question, the more puzzled I became by its apparent intractability. I began to see that I understood much less about Andean religion than I thought I did.

It took me a long time to realize that I was barking up the family tree. This chapter, and the two that follow, describe the indigenous perspective on the uses and abuses of different kinds of descent systems, as expressed in the mythical record. If the previous chapters have traced the great celestial thought-form into which the Andean peoples poured their spiritual perceptions, these next chapters attempt to describe how these same perceptions were brought to earth and incorporated as the social structures distinctive to Andean agricultural civilization. I would learn that this mode of thought—linking as it did the origins and destiny of humankind to the stars—would generate first the foundations, and later, as it became increasingly politicized, the scourge, the resurrection, and, in the end, the apocalyptic annihilation of Andean civilization.

The centerpiece of this chapter is the origin of the most durable of all these structures, the distinctive double-descent system of the Andean peasantry, the ancient practice of tracing one's lineage through both the male and the female line. It was this system that was ordained by Wiraqocha at the very outset of Andean civilization; it was this system, stressing balanced equality between the sexes, that constituted the structural heart of Pachakuti Yamqui's Conquest-period drawing; and it is this system that continues to the present day as the fundamental organizing principle of Andean village life. What I did not know, as I grasped after the ever-disappearing tail of the Andean feline, was that it would lead me back in time through the mythical accounts of the formation of the Andean agricultural *ayllu* to a world and a time when the very concept of "father," as we know it, did not exist. The entire story begins and ends with the otherworldly visage of the creator of the sun, the moon, and the stars.

About A.D. 600 the face of Tunapa Wiraqocha,[1] literally the Andean god-head, was carved upon a ten-ton block of andesite that today forms the lintel of the Gateway of the Sun at Tiahuanaco (figure 4.2). As with the classic art of any civilization, this carving represents the summation of centuries of cultural heritage. The rays emanating from the head are solar, described in the chronicles as standard in (later) Inca iconography for the sun.[2] The face is feline,[3] an interpretation corroborated by the "tear element" running down the face. George Bankes has identified these "tears" as hail and as always present in representations of the Gateway God.[4] These same hail-tears are visible emanating from the eyes of the feline on the female, lunar side of Pachakuti Yamqui's drawing (figure 2.4) and are labeled "granisso."[5]

I was drawn to this face because, having concluded that Wiraqocha represented on one level the Lord of Measure/Saturn, I hoped it might be possible to find evidence of such thinking in the carving at Tiahuanaco. As I studied this face, however, I began to realize that there were a number of apparent contradictions that I had no clue how to reconcile. For example, in the Andes, Sun and Moon were conceived as being male and female. Therefore, given the scrupulous attention to the balance of opposite forces sexually imagined in the Andean cosmos, and given that experts in iconography identify the rays of the head as solar, it ought to follow that the feline face itself is lunar. But this logic is not carried through into Pachakuti Yamqui's diagram, where the hail-cat, called *choqquechinchay*, although placed on the side of the moon, is located several levels below, opposite lightning.

An additional source of confusion lies in the ethnographic record, where there is no clear indication how to reconcile the idea of lunar associations with a feline, which, in Inca times, was most visible as a symbol of the male warriors of the sun. Zuidema, for example, has traced how the Inca Pachakuti was said to have donned a lion (puma) skin in the war against the Chancas, and those same skins appeared during the rites of passage of the young warriors. On the other hand, as Zuidema also notes, there is ample evidence that at the time of the Conquest the feline as an animal was considered to be the guardian of both flocks and of crops in rites associated with the lunar calendar.[6] Were these latter felines meant to be thought of as female? At times the feline seemed male, and at other times female, sometimes lunar, possibly solar at other times, and at still other times a meteorological phenomenon. It was clear that I lacked some crucial element of perspective needed to reconcile these contradictions.

I decided provisionally that the feline face of the Tiahuanacan Gateway God must represent the moon, although, at the time, I had no way of accounting for the anomalies mentioned above, and no explicit verification of the Andean identity of moon and feline. My reasons for making this provisonal identification were based on five kinds of information. First of all, solar eclipses[7] were thought of at the time of the Conquest as a jaguar devouring the sun, a "fact" that makes perfect sense if the moon "is" a jaguar. For another thing, given the androgynous nature of Wiraqocha, it was only logical that the solar rays of his head would be balanced by a lunar reference —that is, the feline face.

Third, it appeared likely that the Gateway God's visage represented the integration of the solar and lunar calendars in service of full-scale agriculture. Recent ethnographic studies have revealed the existence of extensive lunar planting lore among Quechua-speaking peasants. This lore involves planting by the phases of the moon to ensure maximum germination—tubers at full moon, grains and beans in the waxing moon.[8]

From the point of view of a people whose primary means of sustenance is agriculture, the problem with lunar calendars is that twelve lunar cycles total about 355 days, so that every third year a thirteenth lunar month must be added to keep approximate time with the sun. In the Andes this adjustment is particularly critical for maize, whose growing season just squeezes between killing frosts. In Inca times the decision whether or not to add an intercalary month was taken in September, at the beginning of the rains and the planting season, in the lunar month of Coya Raymi, the "Festival of the Queen," the Inca's wife and terrestrial representative of the moon.[9] Finally, as already noted, for practical purposes, the accuracy of solar calendars is largely a function of the observation of the heliacal rise of stars. In this sense, the soli-lunar visage of the Creator is emblematic of the "creation of the sun, moon, and stars," in the sense of the integration of the solar and lunar calendars in the service of agriculture.

A fourth reason for suspecting that the feline face of the Gateway God represented the moon has to do with the hail-tears running from the feline's eyes. As mentioned, Pachakuti Yamqui's drawing also calls attention to the importance of this meteorological phenomenon. Lightning and hail—intense meteorological phenomena depicted on the same level as male and female components of weather in Pachakuti Yamqui's drawing—while a nuisance to a hunter, can spell disaster for an agricultural people. The face of the Gateway God states not only the dependence of the people on their deity to restrain the devastating effects of intense weather, particularly hail, but also an association between the feline and precipitation. This connection is of interest given the widespread association between the moon and rain in the Americas, and the further linkage in Pachakuti Yamqui's drawing between the hail-cat and the spring from which it rises, as well as between the rainy season and the moon. To the present day, Andean peasants consider the hail-cat, ccoa—"seen with hail running out of his eyes"—a beast to be reckoned with.[10]

My final reason for making a provisional identification of the feline face of the Gateway God with the moon has to do with the celestial location of the Inca constellation choqquechinchay, bearing the same name as the hail-cat in Pachakuti Yamqui's drawing. This constellation was said to mean "golden jaguar."[11] In modern-day Cuzco, chinchay means "small mountain cat," while to the north chinchay is used to name "a small 'tiger' with black spots on a white background."[12] At the time of the Conquest, Pachakuti Yamqui described a choqquechinchay brought to Cuzco by the chiefs of Carabaya as "quite dappled in many colors, they say he was the lord of the jaguars."[13] Among the contemporary Aymara, it is held that the constellation Scorpius is a "jaguar,"[14] while among Urton's Quechua-speaking informants, the tail of Scorpius is called choqquechinchay.[15] And in Avila's myth of the flood, among the animals crowding upon the mountaintop were the llama, fox, and puma, suggesting the proximity of the puma to the other animals in the December-solstice branch of the celestial river.

The weight of evidence, then, suggests that the constellation choqquechinchay lay in the Milky Way, somewhere between Scorpius and Sagittarius. It may seem an act of gratuitous cruelty to throw a feline into the celestial river, but unlike almost every other species of feline, the jaguar is quite accustomed to swimming.[16] So the celestial jaguar lay in the realm of the December solstice in the stars, the same realm as specified in Pachakuti Yamqui's diagram as the ideal position of the moon. December solstice, night, the rainy season, the moon, the jaguar, the celestial river—all converge in the lore of choqquechinchay, the hail-cat.

Yet—and this was the problem—it was still unclear to me, in any organic sense, why the moon should be associated with a jaguar in the first place. Still considering this question "off the record," I turned without hesitation to Raphael Girard's classic study of the myth cycle of the Quiché-Maya of Guatemala, the *Popol Vuh*.

II

I HAD TWO reasons for making this abrupt segue out of the Andes and into the Maya heartland. First of all, insofar as the origins of lunar symbolism is concerned the Andean mythic record was, to my mind, fragmentary and difficult to interpret. It wasn't simply that the Andean record seemed to lack any explicit links between the moon and the jaguar; it was as if—aside from a few opaque references to the moon—all memory of events preceding the dawn of the Age of Wiraqocha at Titicaca had been left behind. Unless I wanted to entertain the notion that Andean civilization represented a singular exception to the well-nigh-universal pattern of lunar calendars preceding solar calendars, I needed to find some way into the fragmentary Andean material. By contrast, the *Popol Vuh* made clear references to the jaguar in the context of the moon in the cultural era immediately preceding the advent of agriculture. So it was there I went, looking for a key.

In my own mind, it was becoming increasingly clear that the same system of astronomical thought that underlay Andean myth was also operative in Mesoamerica. For this reason, I suspected that if I could catch hold of the sense of the jaguar's association with the moon in Mesoamerica, I might unearth a similar way of thinking in the Andes. Some of the material upon which I based such an approach has already been discussed. One example is the three-tiered, vertically arranged cosmos at Palenque, where the dying lord sinks, at sunset on December solstice, into the "jaws of the underworld," symbolized by the conch shell. Another is the strikingly similar notion shared by the Maya and the Incas concerning the astronomical imagery of a "race along the Milky Way." (See Appendix 1.)

Then, too, like the Andean peoples, the Quiché-Maya reckoned with Ages of the World. According to the *Popol Vuh*, the development of the Quiché way of life spanned four Ages, beginning with the most primitive era of nomadic hunters and culminating with the Fourth and final Age of agricultural village life. In the similar Andean scheme, there were five Ages, the Third Age ushering in the agricultural era, while the Fourth and Fifth Ages were set aside for the advent of the Warriors, and then of the Incas.

In the *Popol Vuh*, the commencement of agriculture coincided with the birth of the Twin culture heroes of the Quiché-Maya, Sun (Hunahpú) and Moon (Ixbalamqué). The appearance of this formulation at the inception of the agricultural era again conformed to my understanding of the Andean model, memorialized in the soli-lunar face of the Gateway God, the integration of solar and lunar calendars being an absolute necessity once a people made the full-scale commitment to agriculture. And this reading was further confirmed by the fact that the *Popol Vuh* specifies that the *stars* were "created" at the beginning of the Fourth (agricultural) Age,[17] just as, in the Andes, Wiraqocha, in one stupendous creative stroke, created the sun, the moon, the stars, and the agricultural *ayllu*. As I have already tried to indicate, the stars "come alive" at that precise moment when a people begins to employ the heliacal rise of stars in aid of a precise soli-lunar calendar, and this event is inseparable from the advent of agriculture.

In turn, as soon as the stars are "created," there also appears at the same moment the singular consequence of having to take precession into account. Solar calendars calibrated by reference to the heliacal rise of stars will inevitably fall into disrepair within a few generations, owing to precession. Although I was, for the moment, being drawn away from my central question concerning the relationship of the jaguar to the moon, I felt I had no choice but to stay in touch with the internal logic of Quiché thought, or else risk losing my way. And in pursuing this aspect of Quiché-Maya thinking, I quickly became convinced (aside from the implicit evidence of reckoning in World Ages) that the same technical language employed in Andean myth to describe and conceptualize precession existed also among the Maya.

This information is placed in the *Popol Vuh* by reference to the *ancestry* of the Twin heroes of the agricultural age, Sun and Moon. The Quiché-Maya trace this pair back to an *androgynous* godhead, the primordial pair, Grandfather (Ixpiyacoc) and Grandmother (Ixmucané). Grandfather/Ixpiyacoc remained aloof, hence to be associated with the remoteness of the god of the sky, while Grandmother stood as the goddess of both the earth and the moon. This formulation of Grandfather-sky and Grandmother-earth certainly appeared to partake in the formal terminology of the separation of the world parents, that is, a (male) fixed sphere of stars and a (female) celestial "earth" laid out through the ecliptic by reference to the moon. I found this reading fully corroborated in further information about the generations descendant from this primordial pair.

The generation standing between Grandfather and Grandmother and their grandchildren Sun and Moon was represented, on the female side by Ixquic, daughter of Grandmother, and the mother of Sun and Moon. Like her mother Ixmucané, Ixquic is a lunar-earth goddess,[18] who, according to the *Popol Vuh*, was magically impregnated by another, nonhuman being of the same "generation." This being, known as the Seven Ahpu, was (were) the Quiché god of sevenfoldness, the "son(s)" of Grandfather/Ixpiyacoc. They appeared to Ixquic in the form of seven magical fruits hanging from a tree. Longing to try them, Ixquic is made pregnant by the saliva of the God-Seven. These seven "sons" of Grandfather-sky fulfilled the obligations of their patrimony by representing the seven fundamental directions standing for the knowledge of polar and equatorial coordinates—the four cardinal directions (north, east, south, and west) to the horizon, plus zenith, nadir, and center.[19]

One further fact about the Seven Ahpu leaves little room for debate over whether the Quiché notion of a "male sky," oriented by reference to the cardinal directions, refers to a system of polar and equatorial coordinates: the glyphic emblem of the Seven Ahpu was Ursa Major and Orion.[20] Ursa Major, or the Big Dipper, revolves around (and hence marks) the Pole Star, while Orion's belt lies upon the celestial equator. Not coincidentally, the *Popol Vuh* states that the cosmos was created through the superimposition of *two* cosmic planes—heaven and earth—the former represented in Quiché iconography by the cardinal directions, the latter by the solstitial cross.[21] This relationship of the world parents—the marriage of heaven and earth— is further reiterated by a glyph depicting the (polar-equatorial) God-Seven, laid upon the navel of the Earth (goddess).[22]

And this same thinking is carried down into the generation of the Twins. The *nahual*, or spirit-world alter ego of Sun/Hunahpú was Hunrakán, the "one-legged god."[23] This god was none other than the constellation Ursa Major, the male valence of the fixed sphere of stars as represented by the pole, "inherited," as it were, from the Twins' nonhuman father, the God-Seven. The "female" line comes down through Moon/Ixbalamqué. As with Hunahpú on the male side, Ixbalamqué inherited the *nahual* of the lunar-earth goddesses (Grandmother/Ixmucané and Mother/Ixquic). *This nahual was the jaguar.* And the association of Ixbalamqué/Moon with the jaguar is further confirmed by the incorporation of the Maya word for jaguar—*balam* —within Ixbalamque's very name.[24]

As I looked at this material, it seemed to me that I could discern a description of the successive stages in the development of astronomical knowledge among the Quiché-Maya, *expressed in a metaphor of descent.* From the androgynous nature of the creation emerged first Grandfather-sky and Grandmother-earth. Grandfather-sky was a remote deity because, at that early era, the relationship of the fixed sphere of stars to keeping time by means of the heliacal rise of stars had yet to be developed. By contrast, Grandmother, the lunar-earth goddess, was a more accessible figure. This reality corresponds to the historic precedence of lunar calendars and lunar zodiacs in the deep past, whose origins in the Upper Paleolithic were discovered by Marshack. (See chapter 1, pages 6–7.)

In the next generation the "male" side, represented by the Seven Ahpu, reveals a further development in astronomical knowledge, because the god stands for the awareness of cardinal directions derived from the observation of the Pole Star and celestial equator (Ursa Major and Orion). Yet this knowledge has yet to be integrated with the more familiar ecliptic (the lunar-earth goddess) whose stars are known by means of tracing the moon's monthly passage through the plane of the "celestial earth." For this reason the Seven Ahpu, according to the *Popol Vuh*, remain wrapped "in a kind of foggy cloud,"[25] a reference to the era of "darkness" before the stars "awoke," that is, the era before the integration of the soli-lunar calendar employing the heliacal rise of stars. The light bursts forth with the birth of the Twins, Sun and Moon, standing for this last stage of astronomical integration ushering in the agricultural era.

Now, according to Girard, this genealogy was meant to represent a *historical* description of the *social* worlds leading up to the agricultural era, or Fourth Age. In other words, I was, as it were, "cross-ruffing" astronomical "aces" out of material that Girard regarded primarily as history. For the sake of clarity, I must say that I now believe *both* interpretations to be correct. But at that time I understood the genealogical information to be functioning as pure metaphor. I had yet to understand that this metaphor was a two-way street—that is, the successive stages in astronomical development, as described in the *Popol Vuh*, could also be read as a metaphor for the social transformations undergone by the Quiché-Maya en route to a society based on agriculture.

The reason I balked at entertaining Girard's ideas more fully was his consistent misuse of a critical term. According to Girard, the Third Age of the Quiché, immediately preceding the advent of agriculture, was an Age whose economic hallmark was a strategy of mixed horticulture and hunting, and whose defining social arrangement was *matriarchy*.[26] As will be discussed at greater length presently, the idea that there were ever societies ruled by women has no demonstrable basis in fact anywhere in the world. For this reason I was unable to digest the critical information that Girard offered: that the Twins were born without benefit of any earthly "father." They were, rather, conceived immaculately in the womb of Ixquic, represented as a flesh-and-blood woman. The crucial information was that the principle of

fatherhood commenced only with the agricultural era. I had yet to understand either what this idea meant, or that it described a genuine historic
reality.

And so I had gotten as much from Girard's work as I was capable of
absorbing at the time. Three things were clear at that point. The association
of the moon with felines was a fact insofar as the Maya material was concerned. Second, there were far too many precise correspondences between
Mayan and Andean astronomical conceptions to be explained away by "coincidence." In turn, this concordance suggested the existence of a historic
interaction between the Andes and Mesoamerica, commencing at a very
early era. But if the feline face of the Gateway God appeared to resonate
with a cultural experience wider than the Andes, I still remained clueless
about the reasoning that connected the jaguar to the moon.

III

I WAS BY now fully in the grip of my own stubbornness. I was aware that
among peoples inhabiting the eastern slopes of the Andes there are numerous myths that bear a remarkable similarity to the *Popol Vuh*. These tales are
about the miraculous birth of Twins—Sun and Moon—and their perilous
adventures as they seek to escape the predations of the Jaguar people. To
repeat, no such myths from the Andean highlands themselves found their
way into the colonial record. Stories about the moon in connection with the
era preceding agriculture, though they do exist in the Andean material, are
few and fragmentary. Unwilling to give up, I wondered if I might be able to
find an answer to my central question: *Why* was the moon associated in
Andean thought with a feline—there, on the eastern slopes of the Andes?

Girard himself had commented on the apparent cultural continuity between Mesoamerica and South America. It is Girard's position that the Four
Ages of Quiché myth refer to four cultural cycles, beginning with the most
primitive and ending with agriculture. In his view, it is possible, through the
exercise of comparative ethnology, to trace the path of migrations[27] from
the Maya heartland both north and south all the way into the forests and
jungles east of the Andes. Those tribes that expanded into new lands, as
Maya culture developed through successive culture horizons, demonstrate
characteristics of the earlier culture cycles of Quiché history, because these
peoples had long since ceased to live in contiguity with the seminal influence
of the Maya homelands, even as their own odysseys took them farther and
farther afield.

So, as I turned to myths from the eastern slopes of the Andes, I did so hoping to find in them the connection between the jaguar and the moon "missing" from the Quiché-Maya material. I chose three myths, collected by the Peruvian archaeologist Julius Tello,[28] from among three tribes: the proto-Arawakan Amuesha,[29] the Jívaro of the eastern forests, and the Guarani, who, in the years immediately before the Conquest, had crossed the Chaco desert to raid tribes along the Inca frontier.[30]

This effort was doomed to failure, because I proceeded to analyze these myths in the same manner as I had approached Girard's discussion of the *Popol Vuh*. What I did was to analyze these myths from the perspective of astronomy. (The interested reader will find this analysis in Appendix 3.) I found that these myths, too, contained all the indicators of a participation in the technical language of myth, but I was once again unable to grasp that the interplay between astronomy and genealogy was a two-way street. I was still spinning my wheels. I discerned, through this exercise, a pattern whose significance would later come clear. And this pattern, similar in all respects to the *Popol Vuh*, is as follows:

A young woman is pregnant with Twins—Sun and Moon. She has been impregnated magically by a nonhuman father. She is killed by a jaguar, but the Twins in her womb survive. The jaguar is specified as Grandmother, and is important enough a personage to be given a proper name: "Patonille" in the Amuesha tale, "Lari" in the Guarani version. This Grandmother, who is associated with the moon, undertakes to raise the Twins in her home. Her home is a "small hut" with a garden outside, where she grows food, and keeps house for the jaguar men who are away hunting. When they return, they smell the Twins and try to eat them. The twins escape, and survive by setting fire either to the roof thatch of the house, or to a bridge across which they escape and that spans a river at the top of a towering cliff—both references (architectonic and tectonic) to the entry of the June-solstice sun into the Milky Way.

But this approach got me nowhere. Because I was so determined to hold on to the Ariadne's thread of astronomy, as I worked my way through this mythic labyrinth, I continued to ignore what turned out to be the most important thematic element in the stories collected by Tello: they all transpired in the shadow of a quest—the quest for the "true father" of the Twins. It was not that there was anything wrong with maintaining an astronomical perspective; it simply wasn't wide enough. I did not understand the significance of the "absent" father. With history staring me in the face, I continued looking up at the stars.

Although it was clear that the moon was associated with the jaguar also on the eastern slopes of the Andes, I *still* had no idea why. I no longer had serious qualms about considering the feline face of the Gateway God as having lunar associations. Nonetheless, it was annoying—a point of pride, really—not to be able to tie up a minor loose end, but then again, one couldn't live one's life worrying about the loose-end police. I had a dissertation to write. I'd had enough. I gave up.

IV

IT IS OFTEN the case, at the outset of a big project, that one suddenly finds a dozen other things that need doing first. In my case, instead of starting to write, I was overcome by a sudden, inexplicable, and utterly pointless urge to find an obscure reference to the zoological *nahual* of the Talamancas (a lizard), buried somewhere inside Girard's study of the *Popol Vuh*. As I leafed through that book, I was drawn back to his discussion of how the Four Ages of Maya myth represented authentic historic testimony concerning progressive culture cycles of the Maya:

> To emphasize the beginning of their cultural era, the Mayas have it begin with the latest creation, *which is also the creation of the great luminaries and of the stars.* All that came before the Fourth Creation has as little importance as if it had not existed, since in the Mayan conception the world begins with the coming of their historic era. The Chumayel document confirms the Quiché text, declaring that, *"then the stars awoke and from that moment the world began."* [Emphasis added.][31]

Once again I marveled at the concordance between Andean and Mayan thought. According to the *Popol Vuh*, the situation immediately preceding the dawn of the agricultural age was that at that time, "only very little light was found on the earth, because the sun did not exist. The faces of the sun and moon were covered."[32] Likewise, in the Andes, the era preceding the creation of the agricultural *ayllu* by Wiraqocha was one of darkness. "They say," Betanzos recorded, "that in ancient times Peru lay in darkness, and that there was neither light nor day."[33] But simultaneous with the creation of the various agricultural tribes, "at that same hour he [Wiraqocha] came forth . . . and they say that he created the sun and day, and the moon and the stars."[34]

Sarmiento de Gamboa heard the same tale, which included reference to an age of "darkness" preceding the creation of the agricultural world at Titicaca:

Viracocha determined to people it [the world] a second time, and, to make it more perfect he decided upon creating luminaries to give it light. With this object he went, with his servants, to a great lake in the Collao, in which there is an island called Titicaca, the meaning being "rock of lead," . . . Viracocha went to this island, and presently ordered that the sun, moon and stars should come forth and be set in the heavens to give light to the world, and it was so.[35]

And so began agricultural civilization. For the Quiché, it was the culture heroes Hunahpú and Ixbalamqué who first showed men how to work the milpa[36] and provide for their families. Thus we find Hunahpú's ringing declaration to his grandmother: "We remain so as to feed you."[37]

To this commitment by the male husbandman to engage in agricultural labor, Girard contrasts the picture of the earlier, Third Age humanity, as found in the Popol Vuh and other documents. Here the picture presented is one in which women do all the hard work of growing food, aside from an initial clearing of the fields, while the men are free to hunt, fish, lie about in hammocks, pursue random amorous conquests, and take drugs,[38] behaviors characteristic of such present-day tribes as the Talamanca and Sumo, who, in numerous ethnographic details, replicate the descriptions of Third Age humanity found in the Popol Vuh:[39]

The texts of Mayan and Quiché sources mutually confirm and complete each other. They agree that during the Third Age or Third Katún, humanity was imperfect from the point of view of Mayan ethics, and the vices of that epoch . . . caused its ruin. Among those characteristics stand out cruelty, envy, and indolence in the men as seen in the invention of the hammock, which is regarded even now as a symbol of idleness. . . . The hammock began to lose its importance in the era of Maya culture from the time of the change of the social arrangement . . . that reflected new concepts about work and condemned the vice of slothfulness.[40]

This age of male indolence was the Age ruled by Grandmother, Ixmucané, the lunar-water goddess of what Girard calls the Horticultural Cycle, our lady of the jaguar nahual. Her daughters did all the work; and the dominant celestial referent of the epoch was the moon. Girard cites the definitive explanation of this situation, found in the Chilam Balam of Chumayel, the mythical annals of the Yucatán Maya:

When anciently the world had not awakened [allusion to the precultural epoch according to the Mayan conception] the Month [moon]
was born *and began to walk alone.* . . . After the Month [Deity] was born,
it created the one called Day [young sun], and this one walked with
the mother of his father and with his aunt and with the mother of his
mother and with his sister-in-law.[41] [Brackets and emphasis in original.]

Girard comments, "This is authentic testimony to the existence of the
lunar before the solar calendar, since a mother precedes her son. The relationship according to the female line, mentioned above, also points to the
existence of a matrilineal state contemporaneous with the computation of
time by lunations."[42]

The *Popol Vuh* further explains that the reason for tracing descent
through the female line, that is matrilineally, in the Third Age was a direct
function of the primary economic strategy, namely mixed horticulture and
hunting: "In effect, the teachings in the *Popol Vuh*, confirmed by the ethnographic reality, established the fact that masculine or feminine dominance
in the structure of the family invariably derives from the economic factor,
since the ones who assure the group's subsistence are those who predominate
in the social order."[43]

Fascinated as I was by Girard's ability to find windows into the history
of the lunar goddess, I was once again disturbed by his frequent use of such
terms as female "dominance" (above) and "matriarchal" in describing the
social reality of the Third Age. As the anthropologist Robert Lowie wrote
many years ago: "Matrilineal descent was at one time interpreted to mean
that women governed not merely the family, but also the primitive equivalent of the state. Probably there is not a single theoretical problem on which
modern anthropologists are so thoroughly in accord as with respect to the
utter worthlessness of that inference."[44]

The passage of time has done nothing to alter this verdict.[45]

At this point I made a decision to look into the anthropological literature
concerning the institution of matriliny. I needed to clarify for myself why
the issue of tracing descent through the female line was of such importance
in the *Popol Vuh*. I was confused, and also concerned, that Girard's otherwise
insightful work should contain the blatant red flag called *matriarchy*.
Strangely, this decision, while prompted largely by Girard's mistaken use of
that word, would turn out to be the single most critical step I would take in
unraveling the mystery of the jaguar and the moon.

As I understood the *Popol Vuh*, there appeared to be no mention of a
matriarchal state, but clear reference to matriliny. In reading about the

anthropology of matriliny, I came to the conclusion that Girard had not so much misinterpreted the *Popol Vuh* as simply misused the word *matriarchy*. In fact, the *Popol Vuh*, as elucidated by Girard, corresponds with really dramatic precision to contemporary anthropological findings concerning matrilineal households, and how men dominate such situations.

To begin with, anthropological research has revealed that the practice of tracing descent through the female line arises directly from the kind of household *mandated by the particular economic strategy* embraced by a people. In other words, one does not begin with an *idea* of matrilineal descent, thence to form a household arrangement supportive of this idea.[46] Rather, the household arrangement, precisely as Girard notes of the *Popol Vuh*, is determined by the economic strategy employed.

The economic strategy described in both the *Popol Vuh* and the myths from the eastern slopes of the Andes is one of mixed horticulture and hunting. The crucial difference between this strategy and agriculture is one of *scale*. *Horticulture* means "garden culture," and is usually performed by women whose men are off hunting. *Agriculture*, on the other hand, means "field culture," and generally requires a massive input of male labor. Agriculture also subsumes the relative ascendance of a plant-based diet over a meat-based one.

The economic strategy of mixed horticulture and hunting required the proximity of game in sufficient abundance to rule out the necessity of frequent, nomadic changes of campsites. Otherwise gardens could not be maintained. The luxuriant jungles of Mesoamerica and the eastern slopes of the Andes provide such conditions; not coincidentally, these locales constitute the most favored habitat of the jaguar.[47]

From this economic strategy flows a household arrangement conducive to the formation of matrilineal descent systems. Where horticulture, performed by women and supplemented by the hunting of males, is the dominant economic strategy, then the household, with its gardens and hearth, logically falls—given the extended absence of the hunting males—under the control of the senior woman, grandmother. In other words, *women own the property*. In the *Popol Vuh*, Grandmother Ixmucané's dwelling is a small house with a garden where she cooks for the men. Likewise in Andean myth, the Second Age house type (that is, the one preceding the Age of Agriculture) is specified, according to Guamán Poma, as *pucullo*, meaning a "tiny hut" (see figure 6.1). This word is cognate with the Mayan root *puc*, "hill." Such dwellings are found on hillocks on the altiplano, among the preagricultural peoples of the Andes. And in the versions of the jaguar myth from east of the Andes, the scene is that of a small hut in a forest clearing, owned by

Grandmother Jaguar and visited occasionally by hungry, returning hunters, that is the jaguar males. The Jívaro version specifies Grandmother's garden as the site of a ruse by the Twins.

In turn, this household arrangement leads inexorably toward the institution of matrilineal descent, *not* because the women have taken power—this would be matriarchy—but for precisely the opposite reason: *in order to control the property, the men must control the women.*

It is the dominant role of the males in this situation which the anthropological literature particularly addresses. The male is defined by two relationships. First, he is grandmother's son, establishing his relationship to the senior woman, or property holder. But even more important is his role as *mother's brother*, because the source of his real power is his relationship with his sister, whose children and property he controls. He is a man whose household is inhabited by women to whom he is related by blood, and who has authority over children not his own. A man's defining relationship in matriliny, according to anthropologist I. M. Lewis, is that of mother's brother:

> Where descent is traced matrilineally, through women, the men nevertheless monopolize all the positions of power; a man's closest relative is his sister, and his most immediate heir and successor (after his brother) is her son. In such circumstances men must seek control of their sisters and their sisters' children. A sister's marriage is of crucial concern to her brother, for the marital relationship which ensures the perpetuation of the matrilineage may compromise the sanctity of the bonds between brother and sister, and between mother's brother and sister's son. Husbands must not come between siblings except within well defined limits. Matrimony must not jeopardize matriliny. Ideally marriage should always give way before the overriding interest of matrilineal kinship. Now the closer a brother lives to his sister and her husband, the more easily he can keep a watchful eye on their relationship and ensure that marriage is kept in its proper place. Hence where the married couple lives is always a crucial issue in matrilineal kinship systems. *The simplest way to safeguard the sibling bond is for brothers and sisters to live together in the same place and to allow men in from outside to impregnate the women at convenient intervals.* [Emphasis added.][48]

It is important here to grasp just how alien such an arrangement is to modern sensibility. In this situation the very concept of "fatherhood" is anathema. The father of a child of a matriline is persona non grata, a

biological necessity, but a social nonentity. In the words of anthropologist
Robin Fox, matrilineage

> reduces the role of "husband" to sexual companion. The husbands,
> in fact, merely impregnate the women on behalf of the men of the
> matrilineage. They do not live with the women or acquire any of their
> domestic services; the reproductive services of the women are still
> under the control of the matrilineage men—the "brothers" and "uncles."
> These men will of course have sexual relations with women of other
> groups, but they will remain attached to their own group. *Paternity is
> unimportant here,* and it really does not matter how many "husbands" a
> woman has. Only problems of sexual jealousy, or notions of propriety,
> might limit and order the mating relationships. [Emphasis added.][49]

In the *Popol Vuh,* the matrilineal kinsmen of Ixquic, who is magically
pregnant with Twins, are outraged—as a matter of propriety—when she
stubbornly (and truthfully) insists that "never had she known the face of any
man." An incensed council orders her to be sacrificed in the fork of a tree.[50]
Likewise, in the myths from the eastern slopes of the Andes, the young
heroine/mother of the Twins is accused of every form of impropriety because
the "true father" of the Twins is, as was the case with Ixquic, a nonhuman,
supernatural entity. The mothers in these myths are "devoured" by Grandmother Jaguar, dramatically portraying the norms of cruelty and inferior
status allotted to women under the matrilineal regime.

This situation is further elucidated in the *Popol Vuh,* where the Lords of
Xibalba, the underworld lords representing the Third Age male prototypes,
rage to destroy Hunahpú and Ixbalamqué, who, as representatives of the
ideal husbandmen of the dawning Age of Agriculture, spell the end of these
cruel lords' dominion. Hunahpú fully intends to assume the role of husband
and father, and therefore must die. Thus, as Girard explains, the *Chilam Balam
of Chumayel* characterizes the Third Age as a time when *"sons had no fathers and
mothers no husbands"* [emphasis added],[51] and the people of the epoch as *"those
creatures" who "had no fathers, lived a life of misery, and were living beings but had no
hearts."* [Emphasis added.][52]

Again, in the myths examined from east of the Andes, the same laser-like
anthropological perception is found in the truly scary presence of the heartless male jaguars who return from the hunt ready to tear the little hut apart
to get at those two delicious morsels, the Twins. Again we find the portrayal
of Third Age humanity—the jaguar people—as persons without hearts. The
men are beasts. The mother of the children is literally devoured. And the

children, whose mother had originally set out to find their true father, are now left fatherless, dominated and threatened by their heartless male "uncles."

And it was just about here that the light bulb went on. At last I understood why the moon was a jaguar: in the Third Age of Maya myth, when the dominant economic strategy was horticulture performed by women, when the dominant luminary was the moon, when descent was traced through the female line, *the dominant social reality could be compared to the social organization and behavior of jaguars in nature*. I was certain that if I looked up a zoologist's description of the jaguar, I would find an analogue of the social world of hunter-horticulturalists.

Like the people of the matrilineal-horticultural cycle, "generally jaguars stay within defined territories. In areas with a rich food supply, the territory can measure from five to twenty-five kilometers in diameter. . . . "[53] As we have seen, it is just such a strategy of exploiting a circumscribed, tropical territory (hence eliminating nomadism) that gives rise to the matrilineal household arrangement.

Further, in tropical areas the jaguar may breed at any time, but this is the only time when the male will aproach the female. The male jaguar, like the males of the horticultural world, did not live with his mate. At other times, she—like the women of the horticultural compound—is left alone, to fend for herself and her cubs. Male jaguars, like matrilineage men, play no part in rearing their own offspring.[54] Having no interchange with his own young, the male jaguar, like other great cats, will murder cubs, including his own, without warning. This is the situation in the myths of the eastern slopes, where the returning male hunters/jaguars set about trying to eat the Twins. The children of the matrilineage have no father to protect them.

The South American jaguar myths transpire in the shadow of the question, "Where is Father?" Father Jaguar, of course, is nowhere to be found, just as male jaguars in nature know no paternal role. To the contrary, the "family structure" of jaguars is one characterized by the freedom and indifference of the males relative to the isolation, and disproportionate responsibility, of the females. The *Popol Vuh* emphasizes the ethical bankruptcy of such Third Age male prerogatives, symbolized by the hammock, where—like great cats—the men doze on in blissful disregard of the women's unending round of responsibilities.

From the Maya point of view, then, the situation in the matrilineal-horticultural cycle was like living with a pack of jaguars. The males were free to express any and all excesses of indifference without reciprocal obligation or responsibility. The females and "cubs" were theirs to do with as they pleased. And like the Mayan depiction of Third Age humanity, the single most important characteristic of the American jaguar is its utter lack of mercy. The people of the horticultural cycle, through no real fault of their own, were a people without heart, a people without fathers, the jaguar people.

Henceforth, as the Fourth Age of Maya civilization dawned, the bond of marriage between man and woman would become a sacred bond. A man might have to eschew the juvenile joys of the extended hunt and of the indolence of the men's house in order to engage the sober realities of agricultural labor, but in so doing he would create the conditions for the emergence of his own humanity, his own heart, in the company of his wife and his children. The search for Father was over.

The ultimate mystical moment of transition, according to the *Popol Vuh*, arrives when the Lords of Xibalba have apparently succeeded in beheading Hunahpú—only to set the stage for his miraculous resurrection as the sprouting maize plant. It is during this interminable night of waiting that

Ixbalamqué, alone in the midst of the infernal beings, exemplifies the functions of the Lunar goddess who unaided defends humanity against the monsters of the night when sun has disappeared below the horizon. From that time on the jaguars (*balam*), nahuals or alter egos of the female deity, watch over the Indian's village and his roads and lands during the night.[55]

The miracle of the transformation of the dead god into maize is fully mirrored by the miracle of the social transformation from the horticultural cycle to that of agriculture. The jaguar, to this day a terrifying demon to those peoples whose culture conforms to the Third Age of the *Popol Vuh*, had become for the Maya a protector, an ally of the night. It is certainly noteworthy, and hardly coincidental, that this process is in all aspects identical to that described in depth in psychology, where repressed elements of the psyche constellate as demons until brought to consciousness, where they may be redirected, and enlisted as allies. This saga of the transformation of cruelty into love—the once-terrifying jaguar now marshaling all its fierceness to protect the sleeping children of the Maya villages—is one of the most beautiful stories in the annals of the world's literature. It is authentic testimony not to the pious hope, but rather to the living reality of the relative perfectibility of human nature. It comes straight from the heart of the Americas, where truth and beauty, like Sun and Moon, are twin aspects of the same reality.

V

THIS UNDERSTANDING OF the jaguar's relation to the moon had the power to cut through the whole Gordian knot of confusions I had encountered about the significance of the feline icon in Andean thought. For example, its appearance in the Andes—now as demon, now as protector of crops and flocks—seemed fully to mirror the transformation of the significance of the jaguar described in the *Popol Vub*. Other problems, as for example why the jaguar should sometimes be associated with males, evaporated with the understanding that, whatever its sex, the "jaguar" was a member of a matrilineal household, with all the mercilessness that situation embodied. So the Inca warriors donned the skins of felines when it came time to protect the people. This was the good news.

The bad news, of course, was that these "solutions" were valid only insofar as the Andean peoples themselves understood the jaguar as referring in part to a matrilineal age of horticulture. In other words, a huge question had been raised: If the leitmotif of the lunar jaguar was sufficiently useful in Andean thought to merit incorporation into the visage of the creator god, did its inclusion imply a statement concerning the existence of a historic matriliny in the Andes before the advent of Wiraqocha? A "minor" loose end was taking on the dimensions of a hawser.

A number of possibilities swarmed to mind. To follow them, it is important first to understand the distinctive nature of the descent system of the Andean peasantry. The organizing principle of the Andean double-descent system was the practice of tracing one's descent through both the male and female lines simultaneously. Irene Silverblatt has termed the double-descent system "one of the principal rules of prehispanic Andean kinship."[56] This system—known to have vastly predated the Incas[57]—represents the social foundation of the Andean *ayllu*, an unequivocal statement of the Andean position on the value equality of men and women.

Whereas, for example, among the Maya (who trace descent patrilineally), it is the man who must plant the seed, while the woman remains behind in the village, it is, to this day, the Andean custom that men and women work side by side in the fields. The man opens the earth with the foot-plow, and the woman plants the seed. I have seen, on more than one occasion during drunken fiestas, husbands and wives stand toe-to-toe and "duke it out." What was remarkable to me—even more than the fact that the women usually won—was that it was considered normal behavior by other native onlookers.

I stress this point at the outset to emphasize that the equality of native men and women of the Andes is a living reality, not a sham honored in the breach. This equality is a sincerely held sentiment, elaborated in its cosmic ramifications in Pachakuti Yamqui's drawing, as well as in the androgynous nature of the Andean godhead. It was therefore of some interest, as I began to explore the possibility of a historic matrilineal age in the Andes, to find the ghost of a paradox haunting the system. Although Wiraqocha was indubitably androgynous, he was always referred to as "he." Or what does one make of the fact that among the Aymara, who reckon descent through both lines, the word *ayllu*, or "agricultural community," also means "penis."[58] In the end I came to understand this apparent "tilt" toward the masculine not as a violation of the spirit of the Andean double-descent system, but as a vestige of time when principles of patrilineal descent on an equal footing with descent through the female line were first introduced. In other words, there was a moment when something had to give.

This ethnohistorical reality reappears as a thematic element in Andean myth, where we find, for example, the moon equated with a savage age. Ossio has noted the widespread Andean tradition that (as with the Maya) "conceives of a first epoch in which everything was dark and the Moon was thus the dominant luminary,"[59] in connection with present-day tales he collected from Andamarca concerning the moon. This situation corresponds to the "darkness" preceding Wiraqocha's creation of sun, moon, and stars. In one story a naked wild man was taken into the village to be "civilized." When asked the name of his mother, he replied, "The moon." In another version, a woman called Quillas, literally "Moon," whose lineage was among the most ancient in the community, managed originally to escape to the village "after the *nina para*, or rain of fire, which put an end to the era of the wild people."[60]

These themes are associated with the exploits of Wiraqocha as well. For example, Pachakuti Yamqui tells the tale that Wiraqocha found a "female idol" upon the hill of Cachapucara and was so wroth that he burnt the idol and destroyed the hill.[61] This hill is, of course, at the same fire-blasted site of Cacha already discussed in its mythical association with fire and the Milky Way. So, in Ossio's tale, as well as in Pachakuti Yamqui, we find reference to the destruction by fire of life-ways deemed savage and where the dominant luminary was the moon, or where the primary god(dess) was female, and where descent was mentioned in terms of women and the moon. Furthermore, the consistent reference to cosmic fire suggests the time frame when the June-solstice sun first "ignited" the Milky Way—that is, ca. 200 B.C. (see figure 6.2). This is the same date assigned by archaeology to the beginnings of full-scale agriculture in the Andes, known as the Early Intermediate Period.[62]

In Sarmiento's version of the creation of the world by Wiraqocha, we find these themes once again. Here, there is a sticky moment as Wiraqocha creates sun, moon, and stars, a moment contemporaneous with the creation of the *ayllu*. The moon is too bright, brighter in fact than the sun, which, enraged, takes up a handful of ashes and throws it in the face of the moon, forever dulling its relative brilliance.[63]

This vignette is a classic example of the powers of compression of information in Andean myth. Here it is suggested that, at the outset of Andean agricultural civilization, the brightness of the moon threatened the function of the sun, and swift action was taken. At this moment, with the advent of the power of the androgynous godhead, a new relationship between sun and moon is struck, a relationship specifying the relative "demotion" of the moon. The time frame of this event is, again, through the ineluctable rules of the technical language of myth, fixed at about 200 B.C. by the presence of ashes, which can only be found in proximity to fire (figure 6.2). We have already seen, in the Inca rite of the intentional flooding of Cuzco, variations on the theme of a connection between ashes and the Milky Way. (See Appendix 1.)

Again, corroborative reference to the *Popol Vuh* demonstrates the operation of these notions within Maya myth. Here, the Twins' ordeals continue at the hands of the Lords of Xibalba, who this time attempt to cremate the pair, but they are miraculously resurrected when their ashes are thrown into a "river" and, in the same manner as the Amuesha Twins, sink for protection to the "bottom of the river."

The advent of fire simultaneous with the relative demotion of the moon is further associated in Andean myth (just as in the *Popol Vuh*) with the advent of agriculture. Here we find the notion that, at the critical moment of the advent of agriculture, the god of the new epoch shows mankind the proper methods of agricultural labor, yet does so "magically," as it is not proper for a god to do the work of men. In the *Popol Vuh*, Hunahpú and Ixbalamqué demonstrate all the procedures for planting the milpa, but do so in a moment's time, magically.[64] The Andean analogue of this event is found in *Gods and Men of Huarochirí*, when Wiraqocha, "in the most ancient of times," showed the people how to build irrigation ditches and agricultural terraces "simply by speaking."[65]

Now, whereas in the *Popol Vuh* the advent of agriculture was correlated with the Fourth Age, in the Andes this event corresponds to the Third Age, when, as Guamán Poma describes it, we find for the first time a long list of characteristics diagnostic of the *ayllu*, among them the creation of the institution of marriage and the first building of agricultural terraces. These events, of course, must be connected if, as with the *Popol Vuh*, the commencement of agricultural civilization was contemporaneous with the institution of marriage, when men gave up easier ways in order to assume the roles of husband, father, and agricultural worker. Hunahpú's paradigmatic statement had been "we will remain so as to feed you." The Quechua word for "husband" was *yana*—literally "servant."[66]

The motif of Wiraqocha's magical intervention in showing mankind the art of agricultural terracing is interesting not simply for its similarity to notions in the *Popol Vuh*. It also refers to a *specific historical event*, that moment when a massive input of male labor was required in order to build the terraces and irrigation systems required for agriculture. *And the time when this occurred can be determined by reference to archaeology.* We are now looking at the historic moment of the formation of the "vertical archipelagos" that transformed Andean civilization. According to the archaeological record, evidence of terracing and irrigation first began to appear in the Titicaca basin about 500 B.C.[67] and then began rapidly to spread throughout the Andean highlands in general at the onset of the Early Intermediate Period, that is about 200 B.C.[68]

This date is, of course, the same as suggested by the myths through the imagery of the destruction of a lunar-oriented age by fire. To repeat, the myths specify this date by reference to the "fire" struck in the Milky Way by the advent of the June-solstice sun into its precincts (figure 6.2). It is also worth repeating, in this context, the fact that the Andean rocker mill, the *tuna*, was not invented—and hence not named—until this same time, ca. 200 B.C.

As I looked over this material, I did so with a combination of elation and unease. The anthropologically sophisticated perceptions expounded by the *Popol Vuh* seemed to be replicated in the Andean material: a savage lunar age, destroyed by fire, and followed by the undertaking of full-scale agriculture, an endeavor in turn enabled by social transformations involving marriage. Although I suspected from this evidence that something very similar to the social transformation described in the *Popol Vuh* had transpired in the Andes, I had not found any direct evidence of Andean thinking on the matter of matriliny or its place in historic time. In my gut I suspected what the feline must represent in Andean thought, but I had no way to prove it. On the crucial matter of an Andean opinion on the matrilineal customs of the "jaguar people," I had come up empty.

VI

HAVING EXHAUSTED THE material with which I was familiar, and being
caught up once again by "the question that would not die," I returned to
Tello's massive work on Andean ethnography and archaeology, where I
came upon the following passage:

> In the folklore of the Collao [the Aymara-speaking Titicaca basin], Lari
> is a phantasm, a monstrous feline. . . . Lari or Wari is the same person-
> age which until today plays an important role in the rich folklore of
> the Andes. . . . Wari is the monster invoked from the lake or shrine by
> the magician or curer . . . which presents itself in the form of a feline
> from whose eyes and skin issue forth bursts of fire.[69]

I had never seen either of these terms in relation to felines before,
although I was aware of the contemporary name for the hail-cat as *ccoa*, a
phantasm issuing from springs, as with Tello's description and Pachakuti
Yamqui's drawing. I had never thought of *wari* as other than a proper name,
referring to the central Andean state of Wari, but, on the off chance, I
looked it up. It turned out to be an Aymara word meaning "untamed."

> *Huari vicuña: Animal salvaje.* ("Wild animal.")[70]

Here again was the suggestion that the lunar feline—like the "wild" man
who was "civilized" by villagers and who said that his mother was the moon
—belonged to a savage culture horizon. Yet, also again, there was no explicit
evidence to link this notion of "wildness" specifically with the institution of
matriliny.

Equally tantalizing was a second usage of the Aymara word *wari*:

> *huari: Liquido no espesso: Dizese de macamorras y cossas assi.* ("A liquid which
> is not thick: said of soups and similar things.")[71]

Reference to this mode of cooking, associating soup with "wildness,"
also appears in the *Popol Vuh*:

> The *Popol Vuh* specifies that the first kind of food made from
> maize took the form of a drink—the nine drinks of Ixmucané

[Grandmother]. . . . The nine drinks of Ixmucané become the sacred food par excellence reserved exclusively for offering to the agrarian gods. . . . This custom, whose origin goes back to the episode described in the *Popol Vuh*, would seem to confirm that maize as food was first employed in a liquid or paste form. . . . Another piece of evidence supporting this postulate lies in the fact that the peoples separated from the common cultural trunk at an early stage—such as the Andes culture —still consume maize preferentially in liquid or paste form. . . .[72]

In the Andes, where to this day soups and stews are staples of the diet, there nonetheless remained formal nomenclature identifying the antiquity of the custom.

Again, there *seemed* to be good reasons to associate the jaguar icon in the Andes with a matrilineal situation, but everything had to be run through the *Popol Vuh* first. It was like trying to nail Jell-O to a tree. I was so frustrated by the failure of this fresh clue to lead any further that I almost missed what was staring me in the face. The other name specified by Tello for the feline was "Lari." I had seen that word somewhere before, also written with a capital *L*, that is, as a proper name. I finally remembered where. Lari was the name of Grandmother Jaguar in the Guarani Twin myth.

I looked over at Bertonio's seventeenth-century Aymara dictionary, and weighed the odds. If it was in there at all, *lari* would probably mean "feline deity" or some such notion, another dead end. I went ahead and looked up *lari*, and found the following astonishing entry:

> *Lari*: Uncle, mother's brother, and almost all the male relatives on the side of the mother are called Lari.[73]

When I saw what *lari* meant in Aymara, I knew once and for all that the Andean people were accustomed to transmit on the same wavelength of anthropological consciousness as was evident in Mesoamerica. The nightmare feline of the Bolivian altiplano was one's mother's brother, that specific relationship underscored by the anthropological literature as the pivotal relationship in matriliny, and identified in the *Popol Vuh* as the epicenter of heartlessness of Third Age humanity. For the historic Aymara, who had lived for more than a millennium before Bertonio's dictionary was compiled under a double-descent system honoring the male husbandman and the rights of the biological father, the memory of the menace of mother's brother lay locked in the matrix of language and myth.

A second entry listed by Bertonio involving *lari* demonstrates further that, just as in Mesoamerica, the people of the Andean agricultural epoch considered barbarity inextricably tied to the power of mother's brother.

Larilari: People of the high *puna* who do not recognize [the authority of] the village headman; wildmen.[74]

In Aymara, where redoubling of a word denotes "essence of," "mother's-brother-mother's-brother" is a savage, incapable of following the norms of *ayllu* existence.

The use of the word *lari* as an Aymara kinship term means the Aymara "owned" the problem, a problem solved by the creation of the double-descent system. That the Aymara principle of descent through the female line was understood to have roots in a historic matriline is further demonstrated by another term found in Bertonio:

Tunu lari: The lineage on the side of the women.[75]

The Aymara word *tunu,* as we have already seen, literally means "the top of a tree." If you look at Pachakuti Yamqui's drawing, you will find this same family tree at the base of the female side of the picture. The phrase *tunu lari,* "the treetop of mother's brother," therefore points directly to that other prominent mythic figure of the matriline, Grandmother, the archetypal *dueña* of the matrilineal household. The lineage head in the matriline of my mother's brother is his mother, my grandmother. There are no "fathers" or "grandfathers" about, just *lari.*

Finally, a situation where mother's brother may be terrifying to me, a child, is impossible in the home of my own true father. Therefore, if Lari, the monstrous feline of the altiplano, is so scary, then the principle of descent through the female line must historically have preceded the inclusion of patrilineal descent in the social world of the *ayllu.*

The establishment of the double-descent system, the social foundation of the Andean agricultural *ayllu,* cannot have occurred without considerable trauma. One can imagine how difficult this transition must have been particularly for the male husbands, or "servants," whose brethren of matrilineal bent must have scorned their engaging in the "women's work" of growing field crops. It is not, however, necessary to rely solely on the faculty of imagination in reconstructing this situation. The psychological reality of the scornful attitude of the men of the matriline toward those of the new agricultural community is preserved in its entirety in the *Popol Vuh,* where the vainglorious half brothers of Hunahpú and Ixbalamqué consider the Twins beneath contempt—virtual slaves—because of their insistence on growing food.

In my opinion it is precisely this dynamic that resolves the apparent paradox introduced above—namely that Andean social norms assume the absolute value equality of men and women, yet the myths appear to "tilt" toward the men, toward the "maleness" of Wiraqocha. In the transition from horticulture to agriculture, what was under attack by the *ayllu* was not women but the culture of matriliny, with all its thoughtless cruelty, indolence, and lack of ethical focus. What was at issue was not a tilt toward men but a tilt toward the establishment of the principle of patriliny on a par with matriliny. From this wedding would emerge an entirely new civilization.

One can also imagine the women of the *ayllu*—now relieved of slavelike status, empowered to live in matrimony with their lovers, and in a position to see their children, particularly their daughters, raised by men who loved them—rejecting matriliny and embracing the social transformation enabling and enabled by agriculture. Perhaps it was the women who first conceived the possibility of change. And perhaps it was the women—shouting across the social ramparts separating them from their sisters in matrilineal bondage —who most joyfully taunted their outraged brothers with the double meaning of the word *ayllu*—"community" and "penis."

In the Age of the *ayllu*, the jaguar would become a favored helper of the god Wiraqocha and, as with the Maya, the guardian of flock and field. Henceforth also, in the subconscious mind of every man, woman, and child, would be lain, like a sort of submarine mine, the stricture against ever again considering *lari*—that is mother's brother—as a relationship to be cultivated; for *lari lari* was a throwback, a misfit, a wild man, a monster. Mother's brother must henceforth find his own identity, not through her, but on his own, as husband, father, provider. *Lari* was no longer an organizing principle for respectable manhood. The jaguar was allowed to return to the wild, where it belonged.

VII

THE MAGNITUDE OF symbolic power emanating from the visage of the Andean Gateway God stands in forlorn contrast to its present-day surroundings. The great irrigation systems are gone, their remains all but invisible. From its purchase on a cracked lintel, the image of the god stares impassively to the east as, below, legions of the curious come and go in unending pilgrimage. Few places on earth evoke so comprehensively the desolation of loss.

The face is too otherworldly to betray sadness. That would be human projection. But it does speak with utter authority of a better time and place, and of an event that changed the world. Or so it now seemed to me as, having come full circle, I once again contemplated the face of the god. The face was, beyond question, soli-lunar. This fusion of male and female elements speaks to the god's androgynous nature, a being of balance and justice. Specified as a feline, the lunar aspect of the god's face makes allusion to the historical evolution of the double-descent system out of matriliny. Hereby —that is, through the replication of the god's androgyny within the social reality—the god's face bears witness to the paradigmatic action of Andean civilization: the creation of a human world designed to harmonize with cosmic reality. As above, so below.

If one assumes that the lunar aspect of the god's face is meant to represent a *full* moon, then every further significant aspect of the dawn of the Age of Wiraqocha is manifested by the visage of the Gateway God. First, the opposition of sun to full moon represents the "conceptual calipers" needed to lay out the solstitial cross, because a full moon lies, by definition, 180 degrees around the ecliptic from the sun. If, for example, there is a full moon on the eve of June solstice, then, as the sun sets in the northwest, the full moon rises in the southeast, where the sun will rise on December solstice. The following morning, as the moon sets at that horizon point where the December-solstice sun will set, the rising sun completes the layout along the horizon of the solstice cross. Hereby, as the possibilities of Pachakuti Yam-qui's diagram makes clear, the ideal layout of the year's agricultural calendar appears within a single night.

Moreover, by understanding the power of the sun and full moon at a solstice to refer to the stars rising heliacally at *both* solstices, the face of the Gateway God explicates the most important tenets of religion by reference to the "opening of ways" accomplished by the heliacal rise of the Milky Way at opposing solstices. The symbol thereby alludes to those fundamental characteristics of Andean religion—ancestor "worship" enabled by the opening of the land of the dead at December solstice, and access to the teaching of the god via the opening of the "bridge" at June solstice—which contributed to the creation of an agricultural society.

Finally, the god's visage bespeaks a civilization in control of its own history, for just as the sun and full moon at a solstice lay out the parameters of the agricultural year, so also do they define the limits of the world-age— the solstice suns "nested" in both branches of the Milky Way. Thus, historically speaking, the face expresses conscious understanding of every important facet of Andean civilization: the *who*, that is, the people of the double-descent system; the *what*, the advent of agriculture expressed by the emphasis on meteorological phenomenon; the *how*, the agricultural calendar; the *where*, Titicaca; the *when*, ca. 200 B.C.; and the *why*, the advent of a teaching at once practical and transcendent, in which the same means used to control the agricultural calendar also contained the potency to make manifest the drama of human life played against the backdrop of successive Ages of the World.

There remained only one odd gap in the record. So far as I knew, there was no direct statement from the Conquest period that there existed an Andean technique of employing the sun-to-full-moon relationship for marking out seasonal oppositions. This concept is, of course, implicit in such oppositions as those of Pachakuti Yamqui's diagram or myths juxtaposing the caves of jaguars with the tops of mountains. (See Appendix 3.) The only moon on a June solstice that can occupy the place held by the sun at December solstice is a full moon. Yet the fact that the sun–full moon opposition was, if not a figment of my imagination, at base an assumption made me uncomfortable. It is in the nature of "holographic" systems of thought that they be self-referential—that is, that they work by setting up a series of interacting resonances through which any part consistently replicates the whole. If I was introducing an alien element into the equation, then I was distorting the entire picture.

As I pondered the problem, I came to the conclusion that, written records aside, the only other possible way that the sun–full moon opposition could have been expressed would be through prominent reference to the number nineteen, representing what is known in the West as the Metonic cycle. The number nineteen represents the number of years it takes for a particular lunar phase to recur on a given solar date. In other words, if there is a full moon on your birthday, this will not happen again for nineteen years. But, again, I knew of no such references in the literature.[76]

My original impulse to chuck this whole long digression into the significance of the feline, and get on with writing a dissertation, now returned. The implications of the jaguar material simply compounded the number of possible controversies the project could be expected to generate. If only there was some information, somewhere, stating Andean awareness of the Metonic cycle—nineteen years, nineteen solar cycles before a full moon can fall again on a solstice—then the game might be worth the candle. Well, if only frogs had hip pockets, they could carry a pistol to shoot snakes.

Unless—could it possibly be so simple?—could one just count the number of solar rays around the lunar face of the Gateway God (figure 4.2)?

CHAPTER 7

A BOLT
FROM THE BLUE

The Word is for everyone in this world; it must come and go and be interchanged, for it is good to give and receive the forces of life.

—DOGON PROVERB[1]

I

AS FAR AS I could discern, the veil of prehistory had fallen. And the reason for this, again so far as I could see, had nothing to do with forcing a clever "interpretation" on the mythical, linguistic, and artistic heritage of the Andes. Rather, it appeared to me that the Andean peoples possessed both a historical consciousness and the means to transmit it. I had gotten my wish—to connect with a "prehistoric" past intentionally transmitted to the future—and now I was in deep galoshes.

It was one thing to make a case for the existence of the technical language of myth within Andean tradition. It was quite another to take this conclusion as a given, and proceed to "read" Andean history from its mythic record.

But that was precisely what I now thought was possible. As the result of tracing the pedigree of the Andean feline, it was now clear to me that the Andean mythical database contained far more information than simple dates, astronomically encrypted. Andean myth now appeared something like a meditation on the significance of transformations that occurred *simultaneously* in the social and celestial spheres. For this reason, the face of the Gateway God could be read like a book—a history book.

On the other hand, I was well aware that the very existence of the means of transmitting this information—the technical language of myth— had not yet been conceded by any academic discipline, not by anthropology or archaeology, by history, by the history of science or the history of religion, by the humanities, by comparative literature, or even by archaeoas- tronomy. And, more to the point, I was aware that just those disciplines *most* resistant to the implications of such research would assume "jurisdiction" over judging its results. If I went on to treat a hypothesized level of myth as a real force in Andean history, I would be challenging some of the fundamen- tal assumptions of these disciplines.

The major theoretical objections to the sort of research I was conducting come from archaeology and anthropology, the disciplines charged with the examination of prehistory. Archaeology examines the physical traces left by human societies, while anthropology emphasizes the study of peoples whose cultures are "prehistoric"—that is to say pre-literate. Between the two disci- plines has arisen the aim of attempting to develop theories, and ultimately laws, of human cultural development. Many factors, especially the elegance of linguistic models, led to the idea that the study of early humankind could become a science.

The single most important methodological principle in furthering this endeavor has been what is called "the comparative method," the practice of looking at discrete cultures as if they developed in isolation, in order later to develop laws of culture development.

Historical considerations, referred to as "the problem of diffusion," nec- essarily muddy these waters. Diffusion means the transmission of cultural elements—technologies, ideas, techniques—from one culture to another. Evidence of significant contact between cultures has the unfortunate prop- erty of contaminating the integrity of this comparative base, thereby making it harder to develop the laws of cultural development. For this reason those archaeologists and anthropologists who do find evidence of significant cul- tural contact, especially over long distances and where long-standing tradi- tion says otherwise, are given the title of "diffusionists." The subtext of "diffusionist" is "subversive" because diffusionist studies look at the raw data of anthropology and archaeology from a historical perspective. By its very nature, this approach undercuts the reliability of such data as a basis for discerning laws of culture development.

This is not to say that anthropologists and archaeologists are not interested in historical questions. Still, the emphasis here is, again, more on
theoretical perspective than on the particularity of events. Anthropology
seeks to establish "diachronic models" of culture change, models drawn
from the data in the archaeological and ethnographic record depicting how
cultures change through time. The purpose of this procedure is to isolate
the variables and dynamics involved, all in order one day to formulate the
"laws" of cultural change.

Such models will include evidence of diffusion, if it can be found "on the
ground"—that is, in the archaeological record. Archaeologists are entirely
pragmatic about all theory. If a new find demands a new theory, then
archaeologists adapt and go on: "No blame," as the *I Ching* puts it. It is also
true, however, that the more fundamentally important and geographically
distant the evidence of a possible diffusionary element may be, the less likely
it is to be accepted by archaeology. Furthermore, it has proved an empirical
truth that the more significant a long-range diffusionary claim, the less
evidence for its support will be found "on the ground." This makes sense,
since travel over very long distances will more likely involve trading ideas
than artifacts. Nonetheless, orthodox archaeology interprets the lack of
physical evidence on the ground as prima facie proof of lack of contact.

On the other hand, David Kelley has pointed out the subtle pitfalls
involved in measuring the probability of significant long-range contact between cultures with this particular yardstick: "A major problem of any attempt to show long-range transmission of objects or ideas from one culture
to another lies in the fact that the best proof of such transmission is normally
to be found in those cultural elements which are of *least* importance in the
receiving culture."[2]

By way of example, Kelley points to the apparently authentic find of a
Roman figurine at Calixtlahuaca in Mexico (at a believable stratum, i.e., later
than its manufacture), and notes that all the find can prove is "that a Roman
figurine head could, somehow, have reached Mexico."[3]

Conversely, as Kelley notes, "Certain classes of systematically arranged
data having common components," such as the Mesoamerican, Oceanian,
and Eurasian calendar systems, evince a high probability of contact,[4] although there will be nothing "on the ground" to prove it. Rather, such
elements can *appear* to have been locally generated. It is precisely this appearance which makes possible the practice of the comparative method and the
marginalization of history.

For me, matters came to a head when, out of a sense of logical balance,
I felt drawn to investigating Andean ideas about the other half of the double-

descent system, that is, the cosmological basis of the principle of descent through the male line. From my reading, I knew that this material contained an extensive lore involving the symbolic use of lightning to stand for the male generative principle. Further, this symbolism was couched in terms of a cult of Twins, associated in turn with fire, the Milky Way, and the planet Saturn. These ideas were so inextricably bound to the technical language of myth, and their distribution around the world in space and time so extensive, that they forced the issue.

I was, I believed, dealing with a system of thought that, because of its distinctive manner of formulating astronomical observations—stars are animals; topography is uranography; planets are gods; the frame is a "mill"; and so on—could not have been reinvented over and over again. Here was a classic case of a diffusionary element of such immense scope that it could be hidden in plain sight. Nothing would be found "on the ground." Nonetheless, so far as I could see, Andean agricultural civilization issued from the matrix of this system of thought. I was on the verge of thinking and writing things about the civilizations of the Americas that were heretical, even possibly irresponsible.

As long as the modern study of human prehistory has existed, it has been founded on the bedrock assumption that the intricate, repeating pattern of the world's early civilizations—with their temple-mountains, their navel-stones, their underworlds, their strange "pillars" and "millers"—arose out of human nature, and not from the disseminated results of individual human insight. In this view, the early history of the world's peoples represents nothing less than the unconscious manifestation of the structures of the human mind.

My own research was leading me toward a different conclusion. Civilizations based upon the authority of myth were engaged in an active quest to shed the limitations of ordinary human consciousness by courting the precincts of a greater Consciousness, written in the sky. In this enterprise, the one indubitably disposable commodity was outworn manifestations of human nature—the "heartlessness," for example, of the jaguar people. This endeavor was anything but "natural" and "unconscious." Myth, it seemed, sought to establish a dialogue with the celestial pattern in order to ask the Big Questions about the nature and extent of human responsibility. Myth was conscious.

The first appearance of the apparatus of this quest, the great holographic thought-form wedding heaven to earth, was more than a historical event; for millennia it remained *the* historical event, the moment when Time itself began. Its appearance in the Andes, apparently sometime in the first millennium B.C., raised, as far as I could tell, basic questions about the range, daring, and motivation of long-distance travelers in the distant past. To walk the earth apprised of this hologram was to carry in one's consciousness the seeds of civilization. All that was required was to find fertile ground.

I knew I was before a unique opportunity: to study how the seminal ideas that spawned Old World civilization—ideas older than Babylon—had played out within a civilization fully committed to their implications at the very beginning of the modern era. Viewed in this light, the Spanish Chronicles took on a dimension approaching science fiction, with the Conquistadores destined to rendezvous with the sacred origin of their own civilization —and lay it waste. To say the least, I was curious. The question was, how much trouble did I want?

On impulse, I looked up the word *curious*. The first two meanings were "1. desirous of learning or knowing; inquisitive 2. prying, meddlesome."[5]

I had to laugh. The value of curiosity, like the existence of the technical language of myth, was, it appeared, in the eye of the beholder. Seeking a little guidance out of my quandary, I had gotten a mirror of it instead.

By now my research had reached a point where I was no longer "thinking" in the ordinary sense of the word. Patterns simply began to present themselves. I no longer "controlled" the direction of the research, and I was not at all sure where it was leading. For example, I now thought that I could discern something in the myths of Huarochirí—something concerning the astronomically based claims of descent of the Warriors (see chapter 8)— that was at once so strange and so ominous, as to cast new light on virtually every aspect of Andean history. In a sense I was no longer working on the myths; they were working on me.

About here, it occurred to me that it was time to stop worrying about being wrong and consider what the responsibilities of being right might be. How much of a high wire was I ready to walk? It would be stupid to overreach, to jeopardize what I'd learned so far. In a sense, that would be tinkering with the future of the past. On the other hand, at what point did exercising care degenerate into gormlessness? In the end I just decided the hell with it—I wasn't prepared to stop.

Save for the final chapter, then, this book is based on material I originally presented as a doctoral dissertation. Ironically, I had so grossly exceeded the word limit that my committee directed me to end the dissertation with the chapter on the jaguar and the moon anyway. Once I had submitted the dissertation, however, I also sent copies of the "uncut" version to several academic publishing houses. In each case it was returned with the same review—anonymous, as is the academic protocol. This review outdid my worst nightmares. Whom the gods would rough up, they apparently first render curious.

> The methodology dogmatically adheres to the extreme determinism of *Hamlet's Mill*, in which precession is assumed to be a universally recognized phenomenon of supreme importance, with respect to which civilizations not only marked their world ages but as a result also underwent cataclysmic transformations.

Although I had read *Hamlet's Mill* four times, I could not remember encountering so much as a word of "extreme determinism" suggesting that civilizations "underwent cataclysmic transformations" as a result of precession. That would make Santillana and Dechend look kind of loony. Unfortunately, the reviewer was just getting warmed up.

> The method consists of a single-minded quest for Andean mythic elements that can be contorted to suit the world age–precession dogma. The orientation is purely West European ethnocentric. The so-called astronomical level of myth is defined in western terms and taken to be universal. Coordinates are polar-equatorial, planes are ecliptic and equatorial. . . . Worst of all, the planetarium, symbolic of modern technology of the twentieth century, is the final arbiter, the "decoder," of the truth. . . .
>
> The work is too self-centered, too progressive, too much like Us. . . . Confidence of the order expressed in this manuscript is indeed a rare and precious possession. Fortunately, it is beyond the possession of most scholars. There is a lack of skepticism here that seems to be shared by many of those who picture themselves as decoders of secret, hidden knowledge. Indeed, many of them, Marshack included (his name is consistently misspelled throughout), appear as the author's heroes.
>
> The work is a misguided piece of dogmatic scholarship, written by a very learned person, who might have turned his knowledge and skills to a more productive task.

The world had been protected from yet another self-absorbed wacko. In the dreadful hush that ensued, the only sound to be heard was editors scattering. I felt bad about misspelling Marshack's name.

The point of this chapter is twofold. On the one hand it aims to demonstrate that the origin of the Andean symbolic equation "lightning = principle of male generation" cannot be separated from the technical language of myth. On the other hand, in order not to insulate the reader from just how controversial such ideas are, this chapter employs the issue of the paternity of lightning as a backdrop for contrast with the more traditional perspective of archaeology.

As I will try to show, the well from which the Andean mythographers drew the symbolism of lightning was the oldest stratum of Andean culture, that of nomadic huntsmen and herders, people who, historically, traced descent through the male line. These were the people of the First Age, who, like the "jaguar people," or horticulturalists, of the Second Age, were found ethically wanting by the members of the Third Age, the agriculturalists of the double-descent system.

As discussed in chapter 2, the great synthesis that gave rise to Andean agricultural civilization involved the creation of a society capable of integrating and exploiting vertical archipelagoes ranging from high-altitude pastures through arable highland valleys to the temperate fruit and coca-growing areas of the eastern slopes. In the Andean view, the social harmonization of patrilineal and matrilineal traditions—the one holding the knowledge of food plants, the other the arts of animal husbandry—was an inescapable precondition for the economic integration of vertical archipelagoes.

It is this integration that the Andean myth of creation describes. According to the myth, the people who performed this feat—the various tribes of the Andes—were created at Titicaca by Wiraqocha. In other words, Andean tradition assigns to the Lake Titicaca region the origin of the seminal ideas that made agricultural civilization possible, ideas that transformed the Andean social order into integrated tribal-territorial units. Further, as we have seen, there is a concordance between the Andean archaeological record (the appearance of terracing and irrigation systems) and the Andean mythic record (a lunar age destroyed by "fire") that these ideas spread rapidly throughout the Andes about 200 B.C.

However these ideas reached the Andes, and whoever the priest-astronomers—the *capacas*—were who created the hologram for an entire civilization, its advent must have arrived like a bolt from the blue. Once the Andean peoples recognized the integrative potential of this teaching, they would forever remember the events that had transpired at Titicaca, events first written in the Andean sky along the River of Fire when Time began.

Because of the peculiar power of the Andean myth of creation at Titicaca to cast these historical events within the framework of the very teaching that made these events possible, it was, and remained, authoritative. At that moment—when both the myth and the new "world" enabled by it arose together from the waters of Titicaca—there commenced not only Andean history, but the historical consciousness of the Andean peoples as well. And from that moment—as the final chapters of this book will attempt to show —this newly awakened historical consciousness would henceforth become a dominant force in the unfolding of Andean history.

This is because, for good or ill, a people with a "past" is a people for whom the journey through time has already become significant, and for whom the future becomes the measure by which the present will be judged. By contrast, a people for whom the only temporal dimension of myth is "dream time" is a people for whom the nature of man is an ontological given, rather than a historical problem. Partaking of the fruit of the tree of the knowledge of good and evil spells the end of such innocence. Once myth achieves the means and will to weave the past into a pattern of significance, ethical considerations take center stage in the theater of history: "We will remain so as to feed you." Once the great clock is turned on, there is no going back; the gates to Eden slam shut, and Prometheus is laid out for carrion on a rock, for the sin of stealing fire from the gods.

II

AS ONE MIGHT expect from a glance opposite the golden jaguar of Pachakuti Yamqui's diagram (figure 2.4), Andean notions concerning descent through the male line involve the symbolism of lightning. The researches of Zuidema and of Irene Silverblatt have made clear the ubiquity in the Andes at the time of the Conquest of the indigenous practice—operative long before the advent of the Incas—of tracing ancestry through the male line in terms of the generative power of lightning.[6]

> The most important celestial deity in local cosmology was the mascu-
> line god of thunder and lightning—Illapa. . . . Lightning is one of the
> principal cults noted by Hernandez Principe in the three communities
> of Ancash. . . . Each family dedicated a chapel to it in a mountain
> outside the village where the cult was carried on. These chapels were
> attended by the head of the family, churi. . . . Each head of a family was
> considered the offspring of lightning, whether by direct contact or
> through his mythical ancestors, male sons of lightning.[7]

Both Silverblatt and Zuidema discuss this material in relation to "conquest hierarchies," that is, the class systems established in the Andes during the Age of Warfare, which commenced about A.D. 650, when lightning became a symbol of martial dominance. Yet the notion of the generative power of lightning is demonstrably older than the advent of war in the Andes. For example, the Gateway God (ca. A.D. 600), Tunapa Wiraqocha, holds lightning bolts in his hands: the right one stylized, according to Bankes, as "a spear thrower [that] has an eagle head at the upper end to represent the hook,"[8] and the lightning in the god's left hand representing a sling.[9]

The theme of the hurled weapon reappears with the Inca lightning god, Illapa, imagined carrying a sling whose characteristic "crack" of release was the thunder.[10]

Since the reason for this emphasis cannot originally have been martial, as the iconography of lightning predated the advent of war, the logical alternative is that the imagery of the hurled weapon as *meteorological* phenomenon represents a statement of the transformation of hunters and herdsmen into agriculturalists. Just such a parallel transformation from a matrilineal/horticultural era to agriculture is evinced in the transformation of the jaguar into the hail-cat.

The further implication that the hunters of the high Andes traced descent patrilineally is confirmed not only by the male valence of lightning-weapons in Andean iconography, but by anthropological evidence as well. In the same way that the economic strategy of mixed horticulture and hunting created a matrilineal household arrangement, a strategy of nomadic hunting and/or herding has been found to generate patterns of patrilineal descent. Groups of male hunters on the move, whose women move with them, must—owing to the universality of the incest taboo—"export" sisters and daughters and "import" wives.[11] In such a situation, a woman is identified by reference to either her father's or her husband's group. The anthropologist Robin Fox has termed such bands "perhaps the most primeval of truly human groups" and "probably the social unit of our paleolithic hunting and foraging ancestors."[12]

The archaeological record confirms a cultural continuity between the earliest Andean hunters and later pastoral nomads who domesticated what had previously been a primary game animal, the guanaco, the wild forebear of the llama. For example, at a recently excavated complex of villages dating from about 1200–800 B.C. and known as Wankarani, about one hundred miles south of Lake Titicaca, archaeologists have found a culture with rudimentary high-altitude plant cultivation, but a sophisticated pattern of llama breeding and interregional trade. The Wankarani pastoralists traveled as far as the Pacific coast of Chile, exchanging, besides goods, "information, ideologies, and most likely marriage partners."[13] Wankarani displays an early attempt to integrate agriculture into a tradition of pastoral nomadism based on patrilineal principles. One reason that the agricultural component of this culture remained at a subsistence level must have been that the men, pursuing the ancient logic of the patrilineal group, were primarily involved in herding and long-distance trade.

Another aspect of the cultural continuity between hunters and nomadic herders is illuminated in the work of David Browman, who has drawn attention to the practice of "carnivorous pastoralism," that is, raising camelids for meat: "In hunting societies, and to a lesser extent in carnivorous pastoralism, the highest value is on sharing the kill. Men are motivated to produce by an ideal of generosity, and status is achieved through the prestige associated with generosity."[14]

Kolata has found evidence of this ethos in the enormous number of llama bones, disarticulated and cracked for their marrow, throughout the urban sprawl of Tiahuanaco, among richer and poorer alike.[15]

The Andean herders of llamas shared a further characteristic of the early hunters: the use of the hurled weapon, especially the bola. The bola is mentioned in the myths of Huarochirí as the weapon used to "trap" game in an annual hunt conducted by local *ayllu* men in concert with a band of hunters who still pursued this ancient life-way at the margins of Andean society in the relatively late era after A.D. 650.[16] For herdsmen, the bola was a useful tool for rounding up strays and culling a flock, because it could immobilize an animal without harming it. Significantly, the bola, like the atlatl, or spear-thrower, and sling grasped by the Gateway God, was also associated with lightning. In the Huarochirí myths we learn how a group of villagers, "playing with hunting bolas," precipitated an enormous electrical storm.[17] In the Andes north of Cuzco, the name for the god of lightning was Libiac,[18] from the Quechua word *livi*, meaning "bola."[19]

Finally, as the pioneering work of Jorge Flores Ochoa and David Browman has shown,[20] Andean pastoralism is an "ancient and independent subsistence tradition,"[21] whose distinctive life-ways have endured to the present day. The contribution of the nomadic pastoralists was critical to the success of "vertical archipelago" formation. While members of the agricultural *ayllus* kept some animals for wool, it was the pastoralists who kept huge flocks on the otherwise desolate *puna* and bartered agricultural foodstuffs for meat. Moreover, the pastoralists had maintained trade networks for centuries before the formation of the *ayllus*.[22] When the *ayllus* began to produce surpluses

—the fruits of terracing and irrigation—the importance of the pastoralists' cargo-carrying skills became critical in the moving of goods between resource zones. Llama caravans were the bloodstream of the vertical-archipelago system. In this way the pastoralists were drawn, as honored partners, into the ambit of the world created by Wiraqocha.

Many such groups apparently adopted the double-descent system, increasing their commitment to agriculture on the somewhat marginal high-altitude lands they inhabited, while continuing to manage large flocks. In a myth analyzed more fully below, the Cañari of Ecuador, agriculturalists who reckoned descent through both the male and female lines, describe the acceptance by their male pastoral ancestors of aid from supernatural female helpers sent by Wiraqocha to offer the arts of agriculture.

It is important to grasp that, although the double-descent system of the agricultural *ayllus* drew upon models of male descent taken from the world of the pastoralists, this pastoral tradition, unlike the world of the matrilineal hunter/horticulturalists, never fully disappeared. As the next chapter indicates, the continuity, or perhaps renaissance,[23] of this independent pastoral tradition would have profound consequences for the future unfolding of Andean history. Nonetheless, it was the synthesis of the economic and social strategies of horticulturalists and pastoralists that would give rise to the classic pattern of *ayllu* existence. As the archaeological record indicates, this synthesis first occurred in the Andes in the Titicaca basin.[24]

Just how the patrilineal tradition of hunters and herdsmen became transformed by the agricultural *ayllus* into participation in the double-descent system is recorded in the Andean symbolism of lightning. The heart of this symbolism lay in its emphasis on the bolt itself, that is, the object hurled. The ancient Quechua- and Aymara-speaking highlanders distinguished among three phenomena: lightning (*illapa/illapu*), thunder (*cunununu/kakcha*), and objects hurled to earth by the god. The word for the concept of the bolt—sometimes also called "thunderstone" in English—was *illa*,[25] from which the word for lightning derives. Thus the sling of the storm god was the lightning, its characteristic crack the thunder, and the stone hurled was the bolt or thunderstone. Cobo tells us that any strange stone uncovered by the rain was considered sacred (*sagrado*) because "thunder sent it."[26]

The reason for this symbolic emphasis on the lightning bolt lay in connecting the male principle of generation straight back to the male side of the androgynous godhead. The origin of all thunderstones lay with Wiraqocha in his role as "father sky," the celestial god of fire. This relationship is expressed in two of the god's most frequently used titles, Illa Ticce and Con Ticce. As already noted, *ticce* means "origin, foundation, beginning." "Illa

Ticce" therefore literally means "primeval thunderstone." As for the word *con*, or *cun*, it also means "thunderstone," and is found in the root of the Quechua word for thunder, *cununu*, and in both the Aymara and Quechua roots for "grindstone."[27] The word's celestial resonances, discussed earlier, are also delineated in Avila's document, where the "five *con*" probably refer to planets.[28] Thunderstones came from the sky, from the very gods—*con*—themselves.

In his role as extirpator, Avila well understood the problems presented by the concept *con*. Here he speaks of the *con churi*, literally "firstborn son of thunder," a kind of stone:

> In all the said villages there were greater and lesser idols, and there was not an Indian family, even if but a single person remains of it, which lacks its particular *penate* god in the house, in such manner that, if they came from one, eight, or ten persons, these have an idol left to them by the person who preceded them. The most important person of each family guards this and he is the person who has the right of succession to the goods and the rest, in such a way, that to guard this idol is like having right of *padronazgo* [hereditary patronage] among us, passing with the inheritance, and when, by law of blood kinship, there is no one to whom it may be transmitted, the one who possesses it usually entrusts it to the person who seems to him most appropriate by reason of affinity, or his best friend, and when he has no one to leave it to, he takes it with him, if he can, to where his progenitor is buried, which would usually be a cave, because he was a prehispanic mummy, and there he leaves the said idol, and if he cannot take it there, he buries it in his house. This sort of idol has the general name of *cun churi* or *chanca*.[29]

Where *illa*, the root for lightning and the refulgent qualities of light, conjures the spark of flint, the explosion of the "bolt," in short the whole celestial litany of star-sparks, the word *con*, the thunderstone handed down through the generations as primeval proof of legitimate descent, speaks to the durability of the stone-old god.

Arriaga, too, set out in hot pursuit of the thunderstone, because, as he soon learned, each family had a shrine to lightning in the mountains, and there the thunderstones were hidden, guarded as proof of the male line's descent from the sky. These stones, called by Arriaga *conopas* and *chancas* (apparently a classification by function, as opposed to origin[30]), represented for the extirpator a crucial artifact in the system of worship he intended to destroy, because the men of the peasantry "guarded them as the most precious thing left them by their father, nor have they [the thunderstones] been relinquished up until the present visit."[31]

Nor was the generative power of the thunderstone confined to the human realm. Arriaga listed a whole class of crystals—*lacas*—placed in the fields, with specific types for the augmentation of maize, potatoes, and livestock.[32] Eliade has found the same mystique at work in Old World shamanism concerning "the virtues of meteorites and thunderstones. Fallen from the sky, they are impregnated with a magico-religious virtue that can be used, communicated, disseminated; they form, as it were, a new center of uranian sacrality on earth."[33]

Wiraqocha's identification as "primeval thunderstone"—the *con* or *illa*— bears comparison as well to the supreme Quiché-Maya deity Cabahuil, or "Heart of Heaven,"[34] who materialized from the void the "Great Stone of Grace":

> [The] one that is the Divinity and the Power, brought into being the Great Stone of Grace, there, where before was not heaven, and from it were born the Seven sacred stones, Seven Warriors suspended in the spirit of the wind, Seven elected flames, and then seven times were lit the seven measures of the night. . . .[35]

The Great Stone of Grace represents the concept of the sacred Center, whence arises "heaven." "Heaven," or the fixed sphere of stars, is "created," that is first conceptualized, through the sevenfold apprehension of space— "the seven measures of the night"—which, as we have already seen, was associated both in Maya and Aymara (Titicaca region) thought with the polar-equatorial organization of "father sky."

This reading is confirmed by the fact that the deity Cabahuil, the creator of the Great Stone of Grace, is itself associated with Hunrakán—Ursa Major —the constellation whose circumpolar rotation delineates the location of the Pole Star.[36] As with the sacred Babylonian temple-mountain, the *dur-an-ki*, where the invisible polar axis unites three worlds through the sacred center, Cabahuil/Ursa Major brings forth the Great Stone of Grace in the Center.

Thus, as with the Andean view—where Illa Ticce Wiraqocha created the world at the *titicaca*, or "rock of lead" arising from the primeval waters of the lake, or, alternatively, at Taypicala/Tiahuanaco, the "stone in the center" —the Maya concept of the moment that the stars "awoke" involves a primordial "Great Stone of Grace," manifesting as seven stones, or seven flames illuminating the primeval "darkness" (= lack of understanding).

In this context it is instructive to look at the lower left corner of Pachakuti Yamqui's drawing (figure 2.4), opposite the "tree" on the female side. Here is found a group of seven circles, labeled "eyes of every kind." Among both the Andean peoples, who are accustomed to thinking of celestial luminaries as "eyes,"[37] and the Maya, who assimilate the notion "heaven, solar eye, God,"[38] the notion of celestial luminaries as the eyes of deity is common coinage. Comparison with the stars depicted on an Inca drinking cup (figure 3.10) also suggests that the seven "eyes" follow an iconographic convention for depicting stars.[39]

Until now, the lateral—that is the male-female—axis of Pachakuti Yamqui's drawing has drawn particular emphasis. Here the importance of the vertical dimension comes to the fore. The placement of the seven "eyes" on the male side of the drawing, opposite the tree on the female side, bespeaks the principles of descent through the male and female lines respectively. The seven "eyes" and the "tree" opposite lie at the *bottom* of the drawing, beneath the depictions of both the earth (mountains and springs) and of man and woman. As we have seen, that world that lies "below" the world of the living, or *kay pacha*, is the domain of the ancestors *ukhu pacha*. Thus the placement of the seven eyes and of the tree suggests a symbolism of origin or descent.

This interpretation is corroborated by the fact that the tree on the female side is given its Quechua name *mallqui*. This word means both "tree" and, as Arriaga quickly discovered, "mummified ancestor."[40] Likewise, we have already seen precisely the same image of the tree as a symbol for descent through the female line in the Aymara term *tunu lari*, where *tunu* means both "tree" and "head of a female lineage."

Here then, in the unerring syntax of "father heaven" and "mother earth," we find expression for the principles of descent through the male and female lines, running, as it were, in parallel. Whereas the descent of the children of "mother earth" is expressed in the symbolism of the spreading branches of the tree of life, the principle of male generation avails itself of the idiom of sevenfoldness—the signature for expressing polar-equatorial orientation within the starry realm, also known as "father sky." Whereas matrilines descend through the branches of the family tree, patrilines are sevenfold chips off the old block, the "great primeval lightning stone" Illa Ticce Wiraqocha.

III

WITH THE POSSIBLE exception of the interpretation of the seven eyes in Pachakuti Yamqui's drawing, there is little in the above description that would trouble a professional ethnographer. It has long been understood that, in Andean thought, lightning represents the male generative principle, and that the god Wiraqocha is implicated in the mix. The only problem with this description is that it manages to evade virtually every historical question raised by Andean notions concerning the symbolism of lightning.

The center of gravity of this problem is the concordance between Old World and New concerning a complex thought-form involving lightning and fire, the planet Saturn, Twins, and the Milky Way. These correspondences are not a simple matter of coincidental similarities, but rather are products of the logic of the technical language of myth. The relationship of the sun to the Milky Way in Gemini (seat of the Twins, Castor and Pollux —the one mortal, the other spawned by lightning) was expressed in terms of the ignition of celestial fire along the whole track of the Milky Way. The "god" from whom originated the creative insight required to make such observations is the old god Saturn, keeper of celestial fire.

The number of instances in which Native American thought links these elements could fill another volume. Aside from the examples already cited, Métraux's survey of Twin myths in South America notes that even among remote peoples, such as the Yaghan of Patagonia, the Twins acquire fire for mankind, as do the Twins of Bakairí myth. Among the Tamanak, Twins "sought to arrange the Orinoco [River] in such a way that it would flow simultaneously up and down,"[41] (a reference to the two-branched Milky Way), while among the neighboring Ayrico of the Amazon basin, electrical storms were said to represent brawls between the Brothers.

The extirpators Avila and Arriaga were concerned about the very complex rites performed by the Andean peasantry whenever male twins were born, because therein was affirmed the blasphemous notion that "one of the twins is a son of lightning."[42] Both sources describe how the parents of the male twins had to undergo a long ordeal of expiatory suffering before the twin children could safely be allowed into the community.[43] According to Arriaga, the peasantry took twin birth as "something sacrilegious and abominable and . . . they [the parents] made great penances, as if they had committed a great sin." In his study of the world-wide phenomenology of twin taboos, Rendel Harris pinpoints the nature of this sin: "It became more and more clear that this initial application of reason which started from the observation that the mother had either done or suffered something dreadful, resulted in the hypothesis of a double paternity. . . ."[44]

In other words, for the members of the *ayllu*, twin birth raised the specter of either adultery or rape. Either act represented the threat of chaos —social dynamite—in a large, interdependent agricultural community. Whereas in a matrilineal society, the identity of the biological father is of relatively minor import, the *ayllu* depended upon the sanctity of the marital bond to cement the new rights and responsibilities of the men. From the male perspective, the trade-off had been hard labor in exchange for a fulfilling ritual and family life. The fact that both husband and wife were required to undergo penitential suffering suggests that the aim of the twin-rites, rather than blaming the woman for an act of adultery, was to bring before the entire village the whole issue of the management of sexuality within the community.

Therefore, both the mother and father were obligated to undergo considerable suffering, lying on one side upon the the floor of their house for five days, and then five days lying on their other side, fasting all the while.[45] A variation on this practice, noted by Arriaga, was to require the parents of the twins to assume the positions of animals, that is on the ground on all fours, for a period of ten days.[46]

The centerpiece of the expiatory ritual that followed involved *the hunting of a deer* by the relatives of the couple, the breaking of the fast by eating its flesh, and then a procession in which the father of the twins had to wear the skin and horns of the deer. Throughout the entire rite, which took about twenty days, a bonfire was kept burning throughout the nights.[47] Following the bathing of the infant twins in frigid water—a further test of legitimacy by ordeal—a male lineage figure called Con Churi, after the thunderstone he possessed, formally asked what faults of the parents had led to the twin birth. Those in the community who had been born twins replied that the extra baby represented restitution by the deity of lightning for the death of an ancestor killed by lightning.[48]

Thus, as regards the "extra" child, it was established that lightning— and not some adulterous male—was the father, thereby establishing the "legitimacy" of the second twin. But even so, the couple was further enjoined from indulging in sexual intercourse for a full year.

The underlying theme of the ritual was that acts involving sexual misconduct were dangerous to the norms of *ayllu* existence. The central place of the deer sacrifice in this ritual suggests that the deer in some way represented sexual guilt. The deer, apparently, stood for the "rapist" or "adulterer" whose specter the twin birth had raised. This specter had to be exorcised.

In the Huarochirí document, the relatives of the couple, having captured the required deer alive, bring the animal to the house where the couple has been confined for ten days, and force it to walk there while stating their accusation: "This is the one who has confused you, Who has outraged you!"[49] The "confusion" introduced by the deer was one of sexual excess.

This same relation between deer, the power of lightning, guilt, and expiation is expressed in the Maya *Cuceb*, a late-sixteenth-century book of omens, where "the deer stands for the human surrogate, either as sacrificial victim pure and simple . . . or as the embodiment of sin."[50] Here the natural calamity of drought, understood as an offended god of lightning withholding the rain, is considered punishment for sin. Thus:

> . . . thunder and/or lightning presaging rain and fruitfulness [was] . . . a sign that the god has been appeased. The idea is clearly set forth by the commentator of Codex Vaticanus 3738: ". . . they would placate him [the god] with these sacrifices [i.e., of deer] . . . after they had performed these penances for a long time there would appear above the earth a loud ripping [thunder] . . . giving them to understand that the punishment of heaven had ceased and that the earth would gladden and fructify . . . they depicted the sinner as a deer."[51]

The role of the deer, as representative of sin, specifically the sin of lasciviousness or excess sexual activity, is objectified in nature by the deer's reproductive pattern, namely routine twin birth, raising the possibility of multiple paternity. Both the Andean *taruka* (*Hippocamelus antisiensus*) and the tiny brocket deer, called *lluychu*, routinely give birth to twins.

The logic behind the association of the deer with sexual sin is clarified by reference to language. As a primary game animal of the early Andean upland hunters, the deer stands for the people and lifeways of that era. Thus the Aymara had the term *tarukha haque*, literally "deer-man," defined as "a savage, heartless man, who does not know how to treat with anyone, a yahoo."[52] As with the "heartless" men of the Quiché Third Age, and the similarly pejorative Andean description of the *larilari*, it appears that, again, there is at work here a mythical convention identifying the people of an earlier cultural cycle with a species of animal, whose habits in nature objectify a lack of specific civilized norms important to the *ayllu*. Thus, for example, the "deer-men," besides lacking sexual restraint, had no concept of how to grow food, as expressed in the the term *taruka sillu*, literally "utterly unskilled deer-man," meaning, "to plant potatoes or maize either too close or too far apart."[53] Any man who rutted like a stag among the females and who mismanaged seed-stock was a throwback, with no place in the *ayllu*.

The "deer-men," then, belong to the earliest culture horizon, that of hunting and gathering preceding the advent even of plant experimentation. Guamán Poma, in his description of Andean First Age humanity, specified that these people lived in caves, wore clothes of twigs and bark, and routinely gave birth to twins,[54] a remarkable allegation in light of the extreme anxiety produced by this event in the life of the *ayllu*.

Further reference to language confirms the identity of the sacrificial deer with the First Age of Andean myth. The word *illa*, besides meaning "thunderstone," also means "male twin" and "bezoar stone," that is, the gastric calculus of deer and other ruminants.[55] Arriaga noted that *conopas*—the thunderstones guarded as proof of descent from lightning by male heirs—were often bezoar stones.[56] Thus, notions of a primeval generation of mankind, possessed with a superabundance of generative male energy, symbolized by lightning and intertwined with the zoological lore concerning the primary game animals of these same hunters, represent the nexus of Andean associations concerning the origin of patrilines. For the *ayllu* to exist, the "deer" had to be sacrificed.

The Andean peoples, then, understood the origins of each branch of the double-descent system. From the "deer-men" and the "jaguar people" came both the tradition and attendant problems of tracing descent through a single line, either male or female. This information, placed in language, lore, and ritual, located the myth of the Dawn of the Age of Wiraqocha at Titicaca squarely upon the hinge of history. What came before, though recognized as contributing rudimentary models of descent, is dismissed as ethically inferior because lacking "heart."

The Andean myth of creation directly expresses the essence of these historical realities. At the same moment that Wiraqocha created the celestial luminaries, he also created the agricultural tribes of the Andes.[57] Through emphasis on this doubly creative act, the myth itself confirms the historicity of the event, not simply because the myth says so, but because the entire story is framed in the very language of the cosmological knowledge that empowered the Andean peoples to embrace the promise of agricultural civilization. The myth is itself the teaching.

It is important to be clear on this point. As discussed in Appendix 3, the jaguar myths from east of the Andes establish the location of the solstice suns in the stars by reference to "caves" and "mountains." As with Pachakuti

Yamqui's diagram, in which moon, December solstice, and springs (holes to the underworld) reside on the female side of the diagram, and as with the notion cited above that the ancestors of the Andean tribes emerged from caves (= holes to underworld = domain of ancestors), these jaguar myths place the home of the lunar jaguars in caves. Conversely, the twins escape by climbing the mountain, crossing a bridge over a "river."

This same symbolism, associated with the advent of agriculture—involving control of the calendar, and knowledge of the religious teaching implied in the opening of ways to the gods and the ancestors—appears in dazzling shorthand in Mexico as well. In Nahuatl (Aztec), the term for the basic social unit of life, the agricultural village, is *alteptl*, literally "mountain full of water." Johanna Broda has observed that the glyphic representation for this word is *a mountain with fangs and a cave at its base.* This symbolism encompasses within a single concept the socio-political category which is the village and its ideological foundations in cosmovision.[58] [Emphasis added.]

The "cosmovision" of which she speaks includes the notion that mountains are hollow vessels filled with water from subterranean sources, a vision in which "caves were the entrance to this subterranean realm immersed in water. At the same time they were considered places of origin. . . ."[59]

Those familiar with Andean civilization will recognize another ringing concordance. Although the chroniclers usually defined the word *Titicaca* as "rock, or cliff of lead," the word *titi* has, in both Quechua and Aymara, a second meaning: the puma, or Andean mountain lion, whose dull gray coat may explain its association with lead. So Titicaca also means "cliff of the lion," recapitulating by verbal formulation the Mexican glyph (of a mountain with fangs and a cave at its base) "mountain full of water," standing for the agricultural village. At "lion-cliff," on the east side of the Island of the Sun where Wiraqocha created the "world," and where the the Incas constructed a shrine, water gushes forth from the black cliff wall.

The myth of creation at Titicaca is ground zero, because here time began. With awe-inspiring symbolic economy, the very word *Titicaca* tells the entire tale. As with the Mexican *alteptl*, the "lion-cliff" of Titicaca, rising from the waters of the lake, expresses the birth of a new world, for from these images might a people fashion the solstice cross, and with it become masters of society, of the calendar, of the land, and of the meaning of human history itself.

Just as surely as the awakening of the stars would transform the world, so also would this event change forever the meaning of the past, because, with the advent of the measures of time, the past itself began. Insofar as the past represented a significant field for the exercise of human imagination, it was transformed in its essence by the events at Lake Titicaca. The reality of this unexpected perspective is expressed in the fact that the past is now recast in the lingua franca of the new creation, that is the technical language of myth.

Whether we hear of the "jaguar people" ranging upon the mountain, or the "deer-men" throwing twins[60] and slingstones, and whether we choose or not to conjecture which stars once were called "jaguar" and "deer" (Appendix 3), the exploits of these bygone folk, their ethical shortcomings against which the present could now take its own measure, all are expressed in terms of a vast holographic thought-form of which these earlier people lived in utter ignorance. Or so the Andean creation myth tells us. If it is to be believed, the last time the world had witnessed such an illumination was some six millennia earlier, in the Old World, when the equinox suns "entered" the Milky Way.

IV

IN THE OLD World, the celestial identity of the Twins with the stars alpha and beta Geminorum was virtually ubiquitous: the Asvins of the Vedas, Castor and Pollux of the Romans, Hebrew "Brethren" (Teomim), Arabic "Twins" (Jauza), Aborigine "Young Men" (Turree and Wanjil), Babylonian "Great Twins," Phoenecian "Pair of Kids," Egyptian "Pair of Gazelles," and so on.[61] Often, one or the other of the Twins is said to be the son of lightning. In regard to the Andes, that region of the sky associated with the Western Gemini at its intersection with the Milky Way is associated in Andean myth with the locus of origin of celestial fire.

It is therefore of more than passing interest to note the prevalence of Old World associations between the twin stars alpha and beta Geminorum and the elements of fire and lightning. In classical antiquity the celestial Twins were the particular friends of mariners, protecting them from electrical storms, and ruling over electrical phenomena, from lightning to St. Elmo's fire. The sign of Gemini, according to the Acts of the Apostles, was emblazoned on the figurehead of Saint Paul's ship as he set forth to proselytize the Mediterranean.[62]

The martial associations so easily brought to mind by wild electrical phenomena probably explain why the Spartans carried the banner of Gemini to war. "The Gemini were invoked by the Greeks and Romans in war as well as in storm."[63] The Vedic Twin-stars, imagined as horsemen, were thought to provide protection to warriors and merchants.[64] It is likely that the vulnerability of the Aryan horsemen of the treeless steppes to lightning strikes, as with the vulnerability of mariners on the open sea, played a role in this association.

It should be noted in passing that the same "cult of good luck" for merchants associated with the celestial twins in Old World lore inheres to the concept of *illa* in the Andes, where, besides meaning "thunderstone" and "twin," and forming the root of the word for lightning, *illa* also bears the following definition:

Illayoc runa [literally "a man who has *illa*"]. A rich and lucky man, one who has and protects a treasure.
Illayoc. One who gets rich quickly and has great luck.[65]

Part of the vast archaic taspestry within which lore concerning alpha and beta Geminorum was woven has been described by David Kelley. In his article "Calendar Animals and Deities," Kelley discusses the similarities between calendar lists from Eurasia, Polynesia, and Mesoamerica, based on various versions of named day sequences derived from the system of twenty-eight lunar mansions connected with the sidereal lunar month. Recognizing that the antiquity and hermetic nature of much of the material makes definitive interpretation of all its interrelationships hazardous, Kelley nonetheless concludes that the similarities are sufficiently consistent to rule out independent invention.

> Some of the relationships between the Mayan and Polynesian sequences decidedly illuminate relationships in the other lists. Thus the Mayan day name Chicchan corresponds to Proto-Polynesian *Filo, and Mayan Eb corresponds to Polynesian Hua. Chic means "twist" and Chicchan means "twisted serpent"; eb also means "twist," as does the equivalent Aztec day malinalli. The Hindu lunar stations which I have equated with malinalli are ruled by the Sarpas, or serpents, and the Hindu equivalent of the Maya Chicchan, the "twisted serpent" is ruled by the Asvins, or twins, divine physicians. *Filo, which means "twist, thread," is the name of the Polynesian god of thieves, and Maori mythology makes him the twin brother of Hua. In Samoa, Filo is a name given to Castor (one of the stars of the constellation of the Twins or Gemini) and among the Maoris Whiro (from *Filo) was the name applied to the planet Mercury. The Greeks applied the name Apollo both to the planet Mercury and to the star Castor, while the Roman Mercurius, god of thieves, was also god of the planet Mercury. Al-

Beruni gives the meaning of the sixth lunar station of the Arabs, two stars in Gemini, as "to wind and twine one thing around another."[66]

In the above passage, Kelley calls to attention a group of ideas that cluster around the word *Filo, standing in varying connections for "twisted," Castor (i.e., alpha Geminorum), intertwined serpents, the planet Mercury, and "thread." Consider, then, the following Quechua and Aymara words formed from the root *illa-*:

Illa. Male twin.[67]

Illahua. The threads with which the warp is fastened, and by which it is raised and lowered while weaving.[68]

Illawa. Comb for the threads in weaving.[69]

Illawi. Domesticated snake with a black back and white abdomen.[70]

Catu illa. To [the planet] Mercury—*Catu illa*—is given responsibility over matters pertaining to merchants, travelers, and messengers.[71]

Leaving aside the suggestion that the word *illa* could (as with the Spanish word for thread, *hilo*, and the English "filament") be cognate with *Filo (Quechua and Aymara lacking a sound for *f*), the motif of "twisted threads" figures prominently in the logic of Andean notions about twins. First of all, the birth of *male and female* twins was considered good luck. Apparently, this idea was based on the notion that twins of the opposite sex were considered to be manifestations of a single entity.[72] Male twins, on the other hand, bespeak double paternity. The suggestion is that twins of distinct sex represent an "unraveled" being, with all the stupendous potential of androgyny. For this reason the female of such twins was called *ahua*, which also forms the root of the verb "to weave," and her brother *illa*, a root, as noted above, also associated with weaving.

The motif of twisted thread appears in Avila's record of the twin rites, where the parents are obligated to wear "twisted chokers" (*collares torcidos*) fashioned of black and white thread. (Note above that *illahua* means both thread used in weaving and a black and white serpent.) In agricultural rites for fertility of the crops, potatoes or special ears of maize were chosen as fertility symbols. Double-eared maize, or maize in which the grains spiraled (twisted) around the cob were especially favored. A dance called *ayrihuaysara* (*sara* means maize) was performed.[73] According to Holguín, *ayrihua sara* means "two grains of maize sprouting joined, or a stalk of maize with both black and white ears."[74] Any sport of nature miming the principles of cosmic, androgynous balance was thought an especially fortunate phenomenon.

If it requires an effort of will to separate the intertwined snakes on at least one Inca escutcheon[75] from the twisted threads of this knot of associations, then it may not be entirely surprising to hear the hint of the caduceus of Mercury (*illawa* being a black and white serpent) in the Inca Temple of the Sun, worshiped as *catu illa*, Mercury, patron of merchants, messengers, travelers, and healers. In the Old World the planet Mercury reached its exaltation, or greatest power, in the House of Gemini, while in the faint echo of a south Andean twin myth we learn that Wiraqocha had two itinerant sons, one a specialist in medicinal herbs.[76] As Kelley forewarns, the possibility of falling into some systematic error of interpretation is high. But that is not the point. Whatever the significance of discrete linkages between the elements, the pattern of associations, full-blown in venues around the world, speaks to a common origin. The alternative is to declare this huge tapestry an unconscious expression of the structures of the human mind.

To complete the picture of Old World associations, it remains to note the connection between the celestial twins alpha and beta Geminorum and Saturn, the ancient god of fire. This can be expressed succinctly by reference to Greek myth. That Prometheus stole fire from the gods is expressed in the Sanskrit root of his name, *pra-mantha*, meaning the churning firestick of a firedrill (considered male). As an Orphic hymn bluntly informs us, Prometheus is Kronos/Saturn.[77] By means of this firedrill, assimilated to the precessing (= churning) axis of the celestial sphere (the mill shaft "owned" by Saturn) was fire struck around the whole band of the Milky Way when the vernal equinox reached the Milky Way. At this time the galaxy came very close to being a true equinoctial colure, a great circle of the celestial sphere connecting the equinoxes through the poles.[78]

The armies of Sparta marched forth under the sign of Gemini. According to Richard Hinckley Allen "The sign's symbol—II—has generally been considered the Etrusco-Roman numeral, but Seyfert thinks it is a copy of the Spartans' emblem of their Twin Gods, carried with them into battle."[79] Whatever the exact configuration of the symbol, the fact remains that, for the Spartans, alpha and beta Geminorum "were represented by a strange symbol called the *dokana*, two wooden beams joined by a crossbeam, which has been explained as a primitive apparatus for kindling fire."[80]

In Mexico, according to the monumental chronicle of Sahagún, the Aztecs watched of an evening for the rise of three stars which they hoped would bring good fortune. Two of these stars are identified as "Castor and Pollux," i.e., alpha and beta Geminorum. The name of this constellation was *mamalhuaztli*, meaning "firedrill."[81] Some modern commentators have decided that Sahagún must have been mistaken, based on the assumption that the

celestial firedrill must look just like the real item.[82] Anyone who has struggled
with trying to see the "crab" in Cancer or the "maiden" in Virgo may long
since have suspected either that the ancients were endowed with an imagination far more vivid than the modern one, or else that some imperative
other than exact verisimilitude may have played a part in the naming of
constellations. In the present case, suffice it to ask where better for the Aztec
firedrill to operate than hard by the River of Fire where the lightning Twins
dwelt? (For a further discussion of the origin and logic of constellation-
naming, see Appendix 5.)

As is often the case with Twins in both New World and Old, the Aztec
Castor and Pollux were given assonant names, Yoaltecutli and Yacauitztli,[83]
meaning "Lord, Grandfather of the Night," and "Hummingbird Guide" respectively. Among the Aztecs, hummingbirds were considered the reincarna-
tion of fallen warriors. Cognate to these names is the patron deity of the
Aztec merchants, Yacatecutli[84]—"Lord Who Guides"—worshiped in the
form of fire itself: "[D]uring the night before the departure of a caravan . . .
they would sacrifice birds, burn incense, and throw magic figures cut out of
paper into the flames. On their return they would give the fire its share
of the feast with which they celebrated the fortunate outcome of their
voyage."[85]

Finally, lest the reader suspect that the relationship between the Aztec
words for their Twin stars and the name for the Old God of fire, Yacatecutli,
is a mere phonetic sport, it is necessary to point out that Yacatecutli was
also the Aztec name for the planet Saturn.[86]

The merchant guild, the *pochteca*, whose appeals were sent to the "Lord
who Guides"/Saturn through the medium of fire, were indeed in need of
protection, for theirs was a perilous undertaking. They traveled, often in the
dead of night, deep into the heart of enemy territory not only to trade but
also to spy.[87] Because of the intelligence they provided to the Aztec Emperor, they were granted status as honorary warriors. Thus, in approaching
their deity of fire they sought good luck both as merchants and as warriors,
a function that can be traced in the Old World, as noted, all the way back
to the Vedic Twin stars alpha and beta Geminorum, under which same pair,
styled as the *dokana*, or firedrill, the Spartans would later march into war.

V

THERE IS A story that a man once asked Picasso why he didn't paint things
objectively, the way they actually look. Picasso said he didn't understand, so

the man pulled a picture of his wife out of his wallet. "See," the man said, "this is my wife, and this is how she looks." Picasso is said to have replied, "She's rather small, isn't she? And flat."[88]

One of the few Andean Twin myths to come down through the Spanish chronicles, that of the Cañari of Ecuador, provides the opportunity for an exercise in historical depth perception. This story was recorded by Molina, Cobo, and Sarmiento de Gamboa.[89] Here, two young men, brothers named Ataorupagui and Cusicayo, survive a flood, an *uno pachakuti*, by climbing a very high mountain that, rising above the waters, provides safe refuge. When the floodwaters clear, they return to a "little hut" (*choza*), where they try to keep from starving to death. They forage for roots and herbs or, in Sarmiento's version, make an ineffectual attempt to plant seeds. One day, returning to their hut from a day of foraging, the brothers find an abundant spread of food and *chicha* (maize beer) laid out for them. After this goes on for "ten or twelve days," the brothers resolve to take turns hiding in order to try to get a glimpse of their benefactors.

Two macaws, called *guacamayas*, richly dressed, enter the hut and set about preparing the food. When they remove their *mantas*, they are seen to be two beautiful women, or macaws with the heads of women. They wear the hairstyle and weavings distinctive to the Cañari woman down to this day. When sexually assaulted by the brothers, they fly off, not to return for several days. When at last they do return to feed the famished brothers, the lads entrap them, quiet them with loving words, and persuade them (according to the versions of Cobo and Sarmiento) to explain the reason for their largesse. The women affirm that "Ticciviracocha had instructed them to perform this mystery, giving succor to them in their hour of need, so that they would not die of hunger."[90] The brothers marry the *guacamayas*, and from this union proceeds the Cañari people.

The myth provides an astronomical framework, first by specifying that an *uno pachakuti*, or "space-time overturning by water," is at issue. The presence of the mountain draws attention to June solstice and, as is traditional in Andean myth, the entire solstitial colure is identified, here by the mountain's name, "Huacayñan," in the versions of Molina and Cobo. The word *huacay*, or sometimes *huacaybua*, means "cargo llama,"[91] while *ñan*, the word for "road," is, as noted earlier, another name for the Milky Way. So the name "llama-road-mountain," places the time frame of the story within the precincts of the Milky Way, a phenomenon commencing about 200 B.C. Further, the specificity of the term "cargo llama" refers to an era when the llama had not only been domesticated, but was being used in the transport of goods.

This usage suggests that the brothers were, like the Wankarani people discussed above, seminomadic herdsmen, lineal descendants of the first hunters. The archaeology of Wankarani showed a people highly skilled at llama caravan trade but possessing only rudimentary agricultural skills. This reading of the Cañari myth is supported by the fact that the brothers are portrayed as inept at planting seeds. As noted, the Quechua idiom for such men is *taruka sillu*, "utterly unskilled deer-man," meaning "ignorant of how to plant potatoes or maize."

As for the June solstice branch of the celestial array, this information is carried in the person of the *guacamayas* themselves. Although Molina says that *guacamaya* is a Spanish word, it is in fact Arawak. The Arawak word *guaca*(= *waka*)*maya* in turn is cognate with the Maya *wok, guok,* or *guoc,* the word used in the *Popol Vuh* to name the macaw, which, as the zoological *nahual* of the solar deity, descends from the zenith to watch the ball game.[92] The word *wok* is among the most ancient and widespread terms for divinity in the Americas, found in North America as the name of the Great Spirit or supreme deity Wakantanka; as the six macaws—*guoc*—flanking the ball court at Copan; and in the Andes as *waka,* the term for sacred entities, including the mythical lineage ancestors created at Titicaca by Wiraqocha. Cobo noted that he himself had seen the lineage *waka* of the Cañaris in Lima, "a small column of copper with two macaws at the top."[93]

Similarly, the name of the flood-withstanding mountain in Sarmiento's version relates the sacred macaw messengers of Wiraqocha to the June-solstice branch of the Milky Way. The name of the mountain given by Sarmiento is "Guasano," although no Quechua words start with the sound *gua-*. To generate the sound *gua-*, as written by Sarmiento, Quechua-speakers must prefix a short *a*, thus *agua* or *akwa*. *Akwa*,[94] spelled *agua* by Molina,[95] is the Quechua word for "macaw."

Now, as has been demonstrated, in Andean myth the formal terminology describing the possibility of interchange between the gods and humanity relates the June-solstice sun to the Milky Way. The name "Macaw Mountain" suggests that the June-solstice sun, as well as its December-solstice counterpart in the "cargo-llama road," lies within the precincts of the Milky Way. This is not only because, as messengers of Wiraqocha, they are associated with the seat of deity in *hanaq pacha* accessible via the Milky Way, but also because, as birds, the macaws fly, or "descend," from above, offering the starving brothers hope of succor from the realm of the divine. It may also be that the reference to the "ten or twelve days" of consecutive arrival of the macaw-women-messengers of Wiraqocha is a reference to the fact that, on about twelve consecutive days, one can observe the heliacal rise of the June-solstice branch of the Milky Way in contact with the earth.[96]

The drama and nature of the divine help sent by Wiraqocha is played out in the interaction between the brothers and the macaw-women. The brothers are anxious to learn the source of their new and marvelous (plant) foods.

> So one day they hid themselves, to spy on the bringers of their food. While they were watching they saw two Cañari women preparing the victuals and putting them in their accustomed place. When about to depart the men tried to seize them, but they evaded their would-be captors and escaped. The Cañaris seeing the mistake they had made in molesting those who had done them so much good, became sad and prayed to Viraqocha for pardon for their sins. . . . Then there was friendship between the women and the Cañari brothers and one of them had connexion with one of the women. . . . From these all the Cañaris that now exist are descended.[97]

Likewise, in the versions of Molina and Cobo, the Cañari brothers accost the macaw women, who flee in outrage.

Herein is portrayed the social gulf that the teaching of Wiraqocha had to span. The men, living in the high mountains in the mode of herdsmen, are alone in their small hut. When they see women, even women who have come to their aid, they are unable to behave with respect. They are portrayed as having a sexual appetite uninhibited by any set of conventions. Such behavior toward women of the *ayllu* would, in the present day, bring down upon the perpetrator an inevitable beating at the hands of the woman's male relatives. But this is the story of how the Cañari *ayllus* came into being.

The women are portrayed as having mastered plant domestication, as evinced by the rich spread of food that they offer. Further, in the name of the mountain in Sarmiento's version—Guasano—we learn that the women are versed in the arts of pottery, *sañu* meaning "earthenware." Nonetheless the women, too, are alone in their own world. They do not wish to be seen, implying that the question of sexual availability is absolutely out of the question. It is not right for them even to be seen in the house of men to whom they are not related by blood.

Eventually the brothers, ashamed of their earlier behavior, manage, during a protracted period of courtship, to persuade the women to remain with them. Thus the myth elucidates the critical components of the vertical archipelago—animal husbandry and plant domestication—assigns a sexual valence to each skill, thereby objectifying systems of patrilineal and matrilineal descent in terms of the economic strategy associated with each, demonstrates the incompatibility of these life-ways, and finally reconciles the conflict in the name of Wiraqocha, by bringing these men and women together in matrimony. Couched in the framework of the astronomical knowledge that generated both the agricultural calendar and the religious cosmology of the *ayllus*, the myth concludes by identifying itself as the story of how the *ayllu* form of civilization came to the Cañari people. To use the words of the archaeologist Alan Kolata in reference to the genius of Tiahuanacan civilization, in the name of whose god, Wiraqocha, the *guacamayas* appeared, "The social and physical ecologies of agriculture and pastoralism, although in and of themselves potentially antagonistic, were made to mesh by formulation of the ritual calendar: the rhythms of rite, crop, and herd were brought into productive synchrony."[98]

Finally, in the Cañari myth, the prestige of the contribution of women —plant domesticators—to Cañari life is a given. The brothers were in dire straits without them. Nonetheless, these women are willing to throw in their lot with the brothers, suggesting, in the balanced syntax of Andean thought, that the men had something to offer as well. But if the arts of animal husbandry were at least somewhat less important than the plant foods, suggesting the primary role of the Andean male as agricultural husband (= *yana* = "servant"), what did these brothers bring to the situation that could level the "prestige playing field" in preparation for the seeds of the double-descent system?

The answer to this question is found in the meaning of the names of the brothers. The younger brother's name, Cusicayo, is noncommittal enough, meaning "happiness" or "well-being." But the name of the elder brother, Ataorupaqui, is another matter. The Quechua root *rupa* means "burning hot."[99] The word *atau* means "good luck in war, honors, games, or finances."[100]

Here, then, is a myth about two brothers whose exploits transpire at the precessional moment of the commencement of the heliacal rise of the Milky Way at June solstice, a point marked in the sky by the Western constellation Gemini, the Twins.[101] In the Old World these Twins are associated with celestial fire, good luck in war and finances, and the planet Saturn, just as among the Aztecs they are associated with the firedrill, good luck for merchants and warriors, and the planet Saturn. In Cañari lore, the brothers, one of whom is named "burning hot good luck in war and finances," are rescued through the agency of the god Wiraqocha, the keeper of celestial fire, the "primeval thunderbolt," the planet Saturn.

According to Cañari myth, the lightning bolt of this colossal, internally coherent thought-form came to earth at the moment of conception of Cañari agricultural civilization. And it was dispatched toward these herdsmen by Wiraqocha, from his throne in Tiahuanaco. The Cañari brothers possessed all the credentials needed for full and honorable participation in the Andean double-descent system.

VI

ACCORDING TO JOHN Howland Rowe, one of the deans of Andean archaeology, such an interpretation of the Cañari origin myth would have to be classed as utterly naive. In Rowe's view, the pan-Andean creation myth— Wiraqocha at Titicaca—was a late invention of the Incas, "an ingenious explanation for all of these local origin myths,"[102] a myth concocted by the Incas as a convenient theological rationalization for asserting imperial dominion. As the final chapters of this book will show, I am among the last people who would dispute that the Incas "massaged" the mythological heritage of the Andes for political purposes. But Rowe's account of how the Andean creation myth came into being cannot be justified by the fact that the Incas were demonstrably clever. Rather, Rowe's perspective betrays a consistent methodological bias against the possibility of a dynamic set of ideas working within a large cultural sphere. For example, in "The Origins of Creator Worship Among the Incas," Rowe states,

> Almost every village in the Andean area had its own origin story of the same sort as the one the Incas told, describing how the ancestors of the people living there had emerged from some hill, cave, rock, or spring. The places of origin named in these stories were called generically *pacarina* (literally, "means of origin") and became important local shrines.[103]

Nowhere in this article does Rowe attempt to account for how it came about that "almost every village in the Andes" had a similar origin myth. The unanimity of local origin myths—that each tribe had a nonhuman, androgynous mythical lineage head, the *waka*, which appeared at a *pacarina*, and which *pacarina* established for each tribe the "deed" of primeval possession of land—makes it plain that, long before the Incas, there existed a concordance of opinion among the tribes about how an agricultural society could best be established. Does such precise agreement over so enormous and rugged a terrain as the Andes from Ecuador to Chile require no source? If not from Titicaca, as the Andean peoples said, then where did these ideas come from? Or are they to be explained as "natural"?

Rowe goes on to argue that the Andean creation myth must have been a late formulation by asserting that *Wiraqocha* is a Quechua word, and, crucial to his argument, that Tiahuanaco was "unknown to the Incas before the reign of Pachakuti Inka Yupanki,"[104] that is, before about 1436. Perhaps he means that the Incas, owing to the endemic state of enmity between tribes at the time, could only visit Tiahuanaco as conquerors. This is quite possibly true. It is, however, another matter entirely to assume that inhabitants of the southern Andes, such as the Incas, lived in absolute ignorance of a legendary Tiahuanaco (unlike Europeans of the nineteenth century, who knew about the as-yet-unexcavated Babylon), unless the whole tale was a late creation, and peoples lived, as it were, hermetically sealed in the concerns of their own valleys.

Of course, such a situation would represent an ideal laboratory for the exercise of comparative method, and Rowe makes no bones about it. He has stated that theories of diffusion constitute an impediment to "the development of general and comparative studies in archaeology. . . . The assumptions of the diffusionists undermine the very foundations of comparative study."[105]

Patricia Lyon has written of Rowe,

It is too easy for all Peruvianists to forget how much we owe to the fine relative chronology we have, and to the fact that without it we would be in the same boat as most other archaeologists in the New World, wallowing around in time spans of 500 years or longer. This relative chronology exists because of the work of a relatively small number of people, above all the work of Dorothy Menzel, John H. Rowe, and Lawrence Dawson. . . ."[106]

This chronology is the product of archaeological virtuosity harnessed to comparative method; without it, the dramatic concordance between the dates embedded in the technical language of myth with the archaeological record would not be demonstrable. This situation is more than ironic, and deserves further clarification. The comparative method is a two-edged sword, in that it can both generate and suppress insights into the past. In order to understand how this paradoxical situation has arisen, it is necessary to understand how and why the comparative method came into being.[107]

When first the fabled cities of the biblical and heroic past began to appear beneath the spades of nineteenth-century archaeologists, all manner of historical theories—some of them quite mad—were poured into the void. Meanwhile, even as the decipherment of ancient writing systems began to flesh out the Old World archaeological record, the whole field of anthropology exploded in significance as untold numbers of "pre-literate" peoples around the world were threatened by destruction and/or assimilation into the industrializing world. Because nature abhors a vacuum, all manner of speculation arose concerning real and imagined patterns of cultural similarities among widely dispersed peoples—for example, the notion of the Hopis as a Lost Tribe of Israel. As the clock ticked, it became apparent to professional students of the past that there wasn't time to do anything but get the goods. No theories need apply. This was common sense, and formed part of the rationale that led to the establishment of the comparative method.

The "walling off" of the Americas began innocently enough in the late nineteenth and early twentieth centuries, among ethnologists who simply wanted to get on with studying native peoples without staggering about under a load of preconceived notions and theories about the significance of apparently similar cultural and technological traits from the Old World. The theoretical catalyst for this approach was provided by the German scholar Adolph Bastian, who developed the idea of the "psychic unity" of mankind. His argument was that, at bottom, the human psyche is the same everywhere and will therefore produce the same "elementary ideas" (*Elementargedanken*).

This idea cut the Gordian knot. The tension inherent in trying to understand the similarity of long lists of culture traits in Old and New World societies was gone. They arose from the psychic unity of mankind, not from the diffusion of ideas and techniques. Difficult matters such as metallurgy—how probable, for example, the repeated independent invention of bronze might be, when any admixture of tin deviating slightly from the required eleven percent renders a lump of useless copper alloy—were put in a shoebox on a closet shelf. Carl Jung, to whom the West owes its best description of the nature and extent of the psychic unity of mankind, never represented himself as a historian of technology.

It was Franz Boas (1858–1942) who was to wield decisive influence on the future of American ethnological studies. Trained in Germany, in association with Bastian, Boas, from his chair at Columbia University, trained several generations of American ethnologists to do the hard work of making meticulous studies of individual tribes, without indulging in grand theoretical schemata. Otherwise too much information was likely to go unrecorded as a result of theoretical "filters." The rich ethnographic literature on native North Americans, snatched from a rapidly disappearing frontier, is a tribute to Boas's integrity in insisting on modest goals. The raw material needed to be gathered; matters of diffusion could come later.

But later never came, because nature abhors a vacuum. The requirement to maintain an icy distance from speculative interpretation, while heroically salvaging rapidly disappearing information, opened the way for the distinctive form of "meta-interpretation" that defines anthropological study today. Various schools of thought coalesced to produce the era of the "comparative study." The idea behind this method was that by comparing ethnographic descriptions of various groups, laws explaining how cultures come into being and change could be developed. Comparative study of course produced numerous schools of thought—evolutionist, Marxist, materialist, and so on. But while all this was going on, nobody seemed to notice that the theoretical underpinning that made the whole enterprise possible—the notion of the "psychic unity" of mankind—had gone unquestioned for so long as to ascend to the Olympus of orthodoxy. The agenda for anthropology had been set. The "study of mankind" (anthropos logos) was, quite suddenly, cut adrift from history. What had begun as a temporary hiatus from the historical interpretation of preliterate cultures had become something entirely different, a discipline with an inbuilt resistance, bordering on hostility, to historical perspective.

The complex ironies implicit in this situation stem from the fact that comparative method has produced a number of incalculably important insights into human nature while preventing other, equally valuable ones from being recognized. The point is not that there is anything intrinsically wrong with cross-cultural comparison. Anthropological theory, for example, vindicates, and is vindicated by, indigenous testimony concerning the origins of patrilines and matrilines in both Central and South America. And if Western social science has proved one fact beyond question, it is that all of us are conditioned by the culture in which we live, a fact that any historian ignores to his peril. The outcome of our whole contemporary drama, suspended between the vision of a global village and the nightmare of a terminally pillaged earth, in large measure hinges on how well this fact is grasped.

On the other hand, as guardians of the interpretation of "prehistory," anthropology and archaeology have had a chilling effect on the modern grasp of human nature as expressed in human history. Archaeologists must work by inference from physical remains, and hence are limited to describing a range of activities whose traces are left behind in physical objects. Evidence of human activity—economic, social, political, religious—is viewed from the perspective of the site, and tied to the web of necessity that the site itself expresses, namely, the maintenance of physical existence. Insofar as archaeology is limited to the interpetation of material—as opposed to conceptual—artifacts, it tends to portray "pre-literate" man as preeminently materialistic. Travel was preeminently for trade, and so on.

Anthropology, influenced by the detached precision of archaeology, resists "value judgments" about the intellectual contents of a given culture. That is a problem for historians. Rather, the ideas of a particular culture become reified into "psychic potsherds," and rearranged to reconstruct the cultural vessel under study. And where archaeology is site-bound, anthropology is "peoples-bound," focusing on a particular group and moving to a more inclusive view only when moving toward a greater level of abstraction, in the search for laws of culture genesis.

Under this approach, few forms of human adventure, outside of war, qualify for consideration. As the psychic unity of mankind will generate over and over again the same "elementary" ideas, there is no need to address the impact of search, exploration, adventure, nonmaterial interchange at a distance, long pilgrimage, personal quest, or the simple dissemination of information. In fact, were the importance of such human activities taken seriously, they would constitute another of the famous "threats" to comparative method.

Therefore, as these disciplines see it, any cultural interchange at moderate distance is trade. Interchange at great distance, beyond the feasibility of trade, leaving as it does no physical evidence on the ground, will not have occurred, except by such accidents as the landfall of storm-tossed seagoing craft.[108] In short, for theoretical reasons, the "inertial predisposition" of anthropology and archaeology, inaugurated with the inception of comparative method, cannot and will not treat with certain of the higher impulses of human nature. Yet these remain the disciplines that tell us where, "historically," our human nature comes from. This is a pity.

In the whole tedious debate between diffusionists and their more conservative brethren, the subtext of the interchange is always about this question. Having expelled from the frame the quixotic traveler, the romantic, the mystic, the exile, the seeker, the giver—because such characters by definition travel light, trading in ideas only, thereby presenting the ever-present danger of contamination to the "sterile field" of comparative study—site-bound archaeology and peoples-bound anthropology will always call the diffusionists themselves the romantics. They hold that the diffusionists have projected their own romantic delusions upon the past.

The diffusionists, caught in the trap of professional standards, have found it difficult to call this bluff. Their opponents on the one hand artfully decline from an obligation to prove the negative (that significant, long-distance, intercivilizational contact did not exist), while categorizing evidence suggesting conceptual exchange as a fantasy spawned in ignorance of the equally famous "psychic unity" of humankind. (Yet, to repeat, Jung never claimed to be a historian of science.) Diffusionists, recognizing that it is professional death to be labeled "irrational and emotional," refrain from emphasizing the importance of those very qualities as an engine of diffusion. Trade is rational. Quest is not.

Starting from the most mundane of facts, one must quickly conclude that even if the disciplines responsible for the study of our ancient forebears have succeeded in purging such "irrational" characteristics from the past, we, the living, have not. For example, there are only three basic movie plots, one of which is "a stranger comes to town." In a similar vein, the reading public has always had a keen interest in archaeological books about diffusion and the reach of ancient wisdom. The issue is not whether any particular such book is "true" or not, but whether such interest tells us something fundamental about human nature. If the love of quest, exploration, and all the rest is so deeply ingrained in human nature as to constitute a reliable market for the entertainment industry, why does evidence of this activity so seldom appear in the "ethnographic record"? Is it really not there, and interest in it a mere contemporary aberration? Or could it be that professional prehistorians not only do not seek, but in fact rather actively avoid, examining evidence of these qualities?

Which brings us back to the Cañari of Ecuador. The Cañari origin myth puts two questions on the table. The first question, to be addressed presently, is whether it is unforgivably speculative to see in this Cañari myth ties to the Twin cult of Old World mythology. Second, in regard to Rowe's assertion that the pan-Andean myth of Wiraqocha was a late invention, what can the Cañari myth contribute to the matter?

The Cañari myth states that it was the emissaries of Ticce Wiraqocha, in the form of two macaws, who brought the arts of agriculture and the institution of marriage to the Cañari. Here we find, as Rowe would have it, evidence of a late Inca superimposition of the Titicaca myth on the local origin myth of the Cañari. All other considerations aside, there is one very simple historical reason why Rowe's conclusion is improbable: the Cañari Indians hated the Incas with an implacable and quite terrifying intensity. The Cañari were among the most unlikely people in all the Andes to have adopted—much less *maintained* after the Conquest—a "late Inca fiction," concocted out of imperial motivations, concerning their own origins.

In the brief century of Inca ascendancy, Inca armies had twice massacred the flower of Cañari manhood. The first time, some fifty years before the

Spanish Conquest, the Inca Tupac Yupanqui, in extending the Inca domains into Ecuador, had ordered the slaughter of thousands of Cañari warriors captured in a pitched battle after having refused to surrender. Their mutilated bodies were hurled into a lake which to this day is called *yawar qocha,* "Lake of Blood."

When, just before the advent of the Conquistadores, civil war broke out between the Quito and Cuzco factions of the royal family, the Cañari once again took up arms, this time against Atahuallpa, who ruled from Quito. Once Atahuallpa had succeeded in securing his position, he unleashed his generals, and for a second time the Cañari men were massacred without mercy. Atahuallpa ordered the death of *every man* of an age to bear arms. The Spanish learned of these events when, as was their custom, they ordered local inhabitants to carry their baggage. They were surprised when Cañari women and children came forth to do the job. Where were the men? The women explained that there were few men alive, and that they were too precious to carry baggage.

But when the possibility arose of revenge against the Incas, the Cañari men were not too precious to go to war in the service of the Spanish. Three thousand Cañari warriors joined the Spanish when, in 1534, they turned their attention toward the sack of Quito. Later, in 1572, when the last remaining threat to the control of Peru lay in the person of a fugitive Inca Emperor, Tupac Amaru, Cañari warriors once more accompanied the Spanish, and relentlessly ran the Emperor to ground.

The Viceroy Toledo, having decided that the institution of the puppet Inca had become less a benefit than a threat to the Crown, made up his mind to execute Tupac Amaru. The indigenous and Spanish populations, alike stunned and saddened by the viceroy's ruthless resolve, watched in silent anguish the execution of Tupac Amaru:

> The Inca then received consolation from the fathers who were at his side, and taking leave of all, he placed his head on the block like a lamb. The executioner . . . then came forward. He bound his eyes, held him on the dais, and, taking the hair in his left hand, severed the head with a cutlass at one blow, and held it high for all to see. As the head was severed the bells of the cathedral began to toll. . . .[109]

Amid the sorrow and tears that then poured forth from the transfixed throng of witnesses, at least one man remained unmoved: a Cañari Indian, the executioner who held aloft the head of the last Emperor.[110]

VII

IF THE CAÑARI story, viewed as a myth of origin, nibbles away at "the very foundations of comparative study," its implication as a Twin myth displays a heartier appetite. On the one hand this tale implies that as far north as Ecuador, Andean peoples were inclined to acknowledge the significance in their own lives of events that had transpired in Bolivia upwards of two millennia earlier. On the other, it appears to carry echoes of a Twin cult whose emblem was meant to project a nimbus of protection alike around the ship of Saint Paul, the Spartan hoplites, and the horsemen of the Eurasian steppes.

The authoritative and decisive voice in this matter is that of the native peoples of the Andes themselves. This material is found among Arriaga's instructions to the extirpators, and beside it all theoretical argument pales. After describing the twin rites with their associated deer ritual, Arriaga goes on to express, in a tone of bewildered exasperation, why it had now become necessary to prohibit any Indian child from being baptized Santiago or Diego:

As regards the name of Santiago [Saint James], they [the native peasantry] also have a superstition, and they are in the habit of giving this name to one of male twins, which they understand as the sons of Lightning, a title they liked to apply to Santiago. I do not understand what might be meant by the name Boanerges, which Our Lord Christ gave to the Apostle Santiago and his brother Juan [Saint John] when he named them the Thunderbolts (Rayos) which means "sons of thunder" according to the Hebrew phrase; nor do I understand either why this usage should have spread here, or why the old wives' tale exists among boys in Spain that when it thunders, it is the horse of Santiago galloping, or why the Spanish, in the wars they fought, should, when they wanted to discharge their arquebuses —which the Indians call Illapa, or lightning,—have seen fit to call out beforehand, "Santiago! Santiago!" Whatever the case may be, the Indians, with great superstition, helped themselves to the name Santiago, and so among the instructions left behind by all Visiting Priests at the end of their Visit is one stating that no one [i.e., no Indian] is to be named Santiago or Diego [James].[111]

Uninhibited by the constraints of the comparative method, the indigenous peoples of the Andes performed their own analysis of the Old World Twin cult, as expressed in the Holy Bible, and, finding it entirely congruent with their own views on the matter, poured into this waiting vessel the entirety of their own beliefs. It was this vessel that the priests of the Inquisition in Peru resolved to destroy.

Christ named James and John—brothers who were the sons of a man called Zebedee—"Boanerges." This name comes from the Hebrew *bene regesh*, literally "the sons of thunder."[112] If, in his exasperation at the eruption of yet another dangerous cult, Arriaga neglected one further datum—one of which he was surely aware and that should dispel any lingering doubts concerning the authentic participation of the biblical "sons of thunder" in a "lost" mnemonic system of the archaic past—he can certainly be forgiven. In any case, the datum in question is one familiar to every Spanish schoolboy then and now. The road down which Saint James's steed thunders is the Milky Way, known in Spain as the Camino de Santiago.[113]

As clearly as any document can, this passage reveals the paralysis of anthropological method in the face of inconvenient material. For nearly a century now, professional students of humankind's past have, for reasons of methodology, been instructed to stand in relation to material such as this in much the same stance as Arriaga, which is to say in a position of deliberate ignore-ance, with an associated impulse toward suppression. If the designation of James and John (who happen to have been brothers) as "the sons of thunder," and the allocation of the Milky Way as a precinct where they might disport themselves, represents, in relation to Andean culture, an example of the "psychic unity of mankind"—one of those "elementary ideas" that will "naturally" pop up here and there—then the works of innumerable conscientious scholars will continue to languish unread by yet another generation of "trainees." One such work is that of Rendel Harris, whose 1913 study of the phenomenology of Twin lore qualified him to make a few observations about Arriaga's strange account:

> [It] is interesting to note that when the Peruvians of whom Arriaga speaks, became Christians, they replaced the name of the Son of Thunder, given to one of the twins, by the name Santiago, having learnt from their Spanish teachers that St. James and St. John had been called Sons of Thunder by our Lord, a phrase which these Peruvian Indians seem to have understood where the great commentators of the Christian Church had missed the meaning. . . . Another curious and somewhat similar transfer of language of the Marcan [i.e., Gospel of St.

Mark] story in the folk-lore of a people, distant in both time and place . . . will be found even at the present day amongst the Danes. . . . Besides the conventional flint axes and celts, which commonly pass as thunder missiles all over the world, the Danes regard the fossil sea urchin as a thunderstone and give it a peculiar name. Such stones are named in Salling, *sebedaei*-stones or *s'beadaei*, in North Salling they are called sepadeje-stones. In Norbaek, in the district of Viborg the peasantry call them Zebedee-stones! . . . The name that is given to these thunderstones is therefore very well established, and it seems certain that it is derived from the reference to the Sons of Zebedee in the Gospel as sons of thunder. The Danish peasant, like the Peruvian savage, recognised at once what was meant by Boanerges, and called his thunderstone after its patron saint.[114]

The Andean cult of the Twins, relating ideas about Twins to fire, the Milky Way, thunderstones and their origin with Illa Ticce Wiraqocha/Saturn, makes evasion of one further aspect of the presence of the technical language of myth in the Andes impossible: this meta-language must have been introduced from elsewhere and it must have been introduced whole cloth. The Andean myth of the creation represents this break-point in Andean history, by consigning all previous ages to the status of relative ignorance, of prelude.

The mythic record of both the Andes and Mesoamerica takes great pains to underscore the fundamental importance of men undertaking agricultural labor in the formation of agricultural civilization. On its own, archaeology cannot definitively state that the appearance of evidence of a massive input of male labor in aid of agriculture—such as occurred rather generally in the Andes about 200 B.C.—represents the breaching of an age-old psychological barrier restraining men from participation in plant cultivation. On the other hand, given statements in the mythical record of the existence of the barrier, of its breaching, and of the *time* of its breaching (ca. 200 B.C.), which time the archaeological record confirms, one must ask if the Andean mythical record is not, among other things, rather reliable history.

This question is important, not simply for what might be learned about the Andean past were the Andean myth of creation to be "trusted." The question must also be viewed from the indigenous perspective, where there is every reason to assert that the Andean creation myth was understood as *authoritative*. It seems to me that one of the reasons for this situation must be connected with the nature of the advent of the system of thought embodied in the myth. If it came from without, it must have come like a bolt from the blue, reorganizing and reconstellating all modes of thought into a new and stunning picture of the nature of human reality. Until this moment, as the myth itself states, all was "darkness."

The credibility of this system of thought lay in its ability to objectify brilliantly new norms of social order by reference to the order of the heavens. This order, heretofore imperfectly perceived, could be taught, so that individual men and women could see for themselves the higher order of intelligence contained within the teaching. One striking proof of this assertion is that to this day, as Urton's work in the Andes has demonstrated beyond quibble, Andean peasants—men and women alike—carry within their consciousness an extensive and practical knowledge of the sky in its agricultural applications.

This system of thought spread, according to myth, from southeast to northwest, carried by the god Wiraqocha, and in some versions by his helpers. Not every archaeologist takes Rowe's hard line concerning the (in)significance of the myth. In the words of William Isbell, "There are many hints of sustained contacts between Tiahuanaco and Peru's north highlands in sculpture, architecture, and perhaps iconography, through the Early Horizon and Early Intermediate Periods."[115]

The paradigmatic account of this spread throughout the Andes is expressed in the creation myth by Wiraqocha's encounter with hostile villagers at Cacha—the traditional dividing line between the southern Andes and the Titicaca basin. Here Wiraqocha, backed only by moral authority, seeks to spread the word of the new way of life founded to the south. When threatened, Wiraqocha invokes "fire from heaven," which is to say the power of the heavens—the very system of ideas which he seeks to spread—and the people are won over, awed by the majesty of what has transpired. And if current archaeological thought is correct in assigning ecological crises a role in events leading to the creation of the *ayllus*,[116] then the self-evident wisdom of adopting a dynamic new system of food-getting must be viewed as a central element in Wiraqocha's "authority," an unprecedented wedding of the practical with the numinous.

In these ways, both myth and archaeology draw attention to the Titicaca basin in the years immediately preceding 200 B.C. It was at this time and in this place that an event of tremendous creative power transpired, an event that would transform forever the face of the Andean highlands. Because the indigenous record of the event—the creation of the sun, moon, and stars by Wiraqocha at "Lion Cliff"—was couched in the very terminology whose advent it was meant to memorialize, the myth's authority was incontrovertible. Without the ideas expressed in this story, Andean agricultural society

was not only inconceivable, but would have remained quite literally uncon-
ceived.

Perhaps most important of all, beyond its many levels of intellectual
virtuosity, the myth addresses the deep human yearning to found human
society upon objective—which is to say sacred—norms. The unprecedented
economic success of the vertical archipelagoes, which followed the illumination at Titicaca in 200 B.C., could only serve to enhance the myth's powerful
grip on the imagination of the people. For these reasons the Andean myth
of creation was, and would remain, authoritative. As we shall now see, it was
from this myth, and the cosmological teaching it contained, that all future
pretenders to "rulership" in the Andes would seek to derive their own claims
to legitimacy.

CHAPTER 8

THE AGE
OF THE WARRIORS

Turning and turning in the widening gyre
The falcon cannot hear the falconer;
Things fall apart; the centre cannot hold;
Mere anarchy is loosed upon the world,
The blood-dimmed tide is loosed, and everywhere
The ceremony of innocence is drowned;
The best lack all conviction, while the worst
Are full of passionate intensity. . . .

—WILLIAM BUTLER YEATS
THE SECOND COMING

I

SOME THINGS DON'T have a linear explanation. According to the best available archaeological information, large-scale, organized warfare first appeared in the Andes in about A.D. 650 with the arising of the central Andean state known as Wari. Also in A.D. 650, two simultaneous and extremely rare astronomical phenomena, the one planetary, the other precessional, conspired to leave an indelible imprint on the Andean mind. As the *pax wiraqocha* was coming to an end on earth, confirmation of this dire truth was played out in the sky. Andean myth specifies a year—and even the hours, between dusk and dawn leading to June-solstice sunrise—when the whole world was destroyed by a "flood." Wiraqocha, in the twilight of his reign, would leave the earth for his celestial throne in the Milky Way—its entrance, as viewed in the cold light of the following dawn, now slammed irrevocably shut. Meanwhile, on earth, the Andean sierra fell under the sway of a proud, secular, and brutal state.

Never having been one for astrology, I personally had no idea what to make of these peculiar coincidences. This sense of impasse contributed to my thinking (described at the end of chapter 5) that my research was finished. I had found statements in Andean myth making a connection between a major event, evident also in the archaeological record, and an astronomical event of cosmological significance. So the Andean peoples were into astrology—enough to remember the flood across nine hundred years, until the Conquest. What else was there to say?

But, having emerged from a long digression into the lore of descent— the jaguar and lightning—I was soon to experience a decidedly nonlinear "bump" in my thinking. Having long suspected that the myths of the flood were somehow connected to the fundamental realignment of Andean society distinguishing between peasant and "warrior" classes—evident in the eth- nohistorical record from the time of the Conquest—I began to explore the best available source, the myths of Huarochirí, looking for some clue to the origins of this class differentiation in the Andes. I thought I might learn something about the arising of the warriors—who, in distinguishing them- selves from the peasantry, must have had some notions concerning their own ancestry—that could explain more precisely why the "flood" of 650 was so important in Andean thought. Here I stumbled across a single new idea, whose significance I did not at once grasp: the mythical ancestor of the authors of the Huarochirí myths appeared to be the planet Mars. When at last I came to an understanding of this formulation, it immediately stood out as one of the most significant facts I had yet learned about Andean thought.

The importance of this realization did not involve any new insight about Andean astronomy. Nor did it stem primarily from the logically consistent appearance of the planet implicated in both Old World and New with warfare. Rather, its impact had to do with understanding that some of the greatest violence done in those times was to the nature of myth itself. The Age of Warfare, ushered in by events commencing about A.D. 650, would change Andean society forever, and the spearhead of this change would be myth.

The purpose of this chapter is to explore the nature of the "flood" of the year 650, and its indelible impact on Andean cosmological thought. Ten years have elapsed since I wrote the first version of this chapter. Since that time an abundance of new archaeological material has been published concerning the rise of the Wari state. This material, summarized in the next section, leaves little doubt why, from the point of view of the Andean peasantry, the abrupt arising of Wari was remembered as a cataclysm.

What the archaeological record cannot explain, however, is the role played by *ideas* in this change. As the archaeologist William Isbell has observed, ". . . while archaeology is well equipped to deal with vast time differences it is poorly equipped to deal with human ideas—the level at which structural patterns exist. Unlike history, which consists primarily of the ideas people recorded about their times, archaeology recovers only the remains of actual behaviour."[1]

Although there is now little question that Wari represented an exercise in unabashedly aggressive behavior, it has, until now, been impossible to trace fully the changes that occurred in Andean thought as the result of the Wari experiment.

The remainder of this chapter is therefore devoted to an analysis of the changes in cosmological thought expressed in the myths of Huarochirí. This analysis bears a synergic relationship to the archaeological record in that it both illuminates and is illuminated by recently published results concerning the rise and decline of the Wari state.

Finally, because it is now possible to derive precise dates from the myths themselves, it is also possible to state that the myths of Huarochirí are, in one important respect, unique. They represent, to my knowledge, the only extant document in the world's literature chronicling the entire psychological process undergone by a society confronted for the first time by the advent of institutionalized warfare. As I will try to show, this experience changed not only the social order in the Andes, but also the relationship between the people and their myths. It was this latter change, fully expressed in the myths of Huarochirí, that would continue to reverberate down through all succeeding centuries of Andean experience, and contribute decisively to the formation of the Inca Empire. The story begins, then, with the archaeology of the "flood."

II

THE ARCHAEOLOGICAL SITE of Wari lies in the central Andes, near present-day Ayacucho in the high intramontane valleys between the eastern and western Andean cordillera and between the Rio Pampas and Mantaro River drainage systems. Wari is situated about one hundred air miles from the Huarochirí heartland.

For many years, archaeologists had assumed that excavation of Wari sites would unearth evidence of earlier state institutions, evidence of a sort of developmental prelude to the Wari state. Isbell has noted, however, that, although it may sound "improbable," virtually *no* archaeological evidence exists at Wari to indicate the beginnings of a centralized state. Until a series of events that began about A.D. 600,[2] there is no evidence of social class, of government storehouses for feeding tribute-paying laborers, of bureaucratic buildings, of centralized ceremonial centers, of a system of recordkeeping, or of defensive structures.[3]

To the contrary, the archaeological record at Wari reveals the

> pre-state antecedent of vertical archipelago economics which Murra has identified as a uniquely Andean pattern of organization and resource exploitation. . . . The principal feature of the system was the existence of an ethnic capital with exclusive resources in its immediate area, whose members also employed more distant resource zones. . . . Somehow the products of the various resource zones were pooled and redistributed within each ethnic group without the territorial organization or compulsory powers of a state administration.[4]

Here, then, archaeology appears to support myth. The Age of Wiraqocha—commencing with the advent of the "river of fire" in 200 B.C. and ending with the "flood" of A.D. 650—was based on the principle of stateless, classless cooperation between distinct ethnic groups. At the end of the Early Intermediate Period[5] (ca. A.D. 600), the Ayacucho valley appears still to have lain within the temporal and ethical boundaries of the Age of Wiraqocha.

The interchange between the Ayacucho valley and its "more distant resource zones" centered upon long-standing contact with the Nazca-Ica-Paracas area on the south coast of Peru.[6] The people of the Ayacucho region had become particularly adept at terracing steep, marginal lands.[7] In the style of stateless, vertical-archipelago economics, colonists from Ayacucho used this technology to create farmlands in the unused hillsides above the coastal settlements of the Ica valley, and developed a resource network with the coastal people.

Then, about A.D. 600, the colonists from Ayacucho came into armed conflict with altiplano colonists, participating in the resource network of Tiahuanaco in the adjacent Moquegua Valley. It is probable that the preconditions for conflict had been laid during an era of prolonged drought. Ice cores sampled at the Quelcaya glacier (located about halfway between the Cuzco basin and Tiahuanaco) indicate that between A.D. 562 and 594, severe drought enveloped the entire Andean highlands.[8] By about the year 600, this drought, combined with a jump in population levels, created, according to William Isbell, an atmosphere where "conflict would have increased, threatening the old, nonhierarchical system of management with disastrous collapse."[9] Men from Wari, reacting apparently to a perceived threat to their lands and traditional resource network in the Ica-Nazca-Paracas area,[10] sacked and razed virtually every Tiahuanacan structure in the Moquegua valley and quickly secured their position by building an impregnable fortress on the commanding eminence of a mesa known as Cerro Baul.[11]

The consequences of this event are found in the archaeological record of both Tiahuanaco and Wari. By A.D. 600 the leadership of Tiahuanaco had been engaged for centuries in expanding its influence across resource networks far distant from the Titicaca basin. Since about A.D. 400, the bulk of this activity had been directed to the west, south, and east. It appears that Tiahuanacan political control never extended northward much beyond the limits of the Titicaca basin, although strong cultural influence at least as far north as the valley of Cuzco existed right up until the Wari incursion there.[12] Tiahuanaco's influence was not achieved by means of warfare, but rather by its prestige. According to the archaeologist Alan Kolata, Tiahuanaco's leaders "were sensitive to the need to establish alliances with the local populations, and to inculcate a sense of loyalty and identification with the prestige and power of the state."[13]

The most magnetic aspect of Tiahuanaco's prestige was the great complex of architectural monuments in its civic center, and it was this complex that underwent a radical change in about A.D. 600. The centerpiece of the sacred city of Tiahuanaco was the Akapana, a stepped, flat-topped pyramid, from which water cascaded. It was a "mountain full of water," a man-made replication of the sacred cliff at Titicaca. (See figure 8.5 and Appendix 4).

In about A.D. 600, contemporary with the debacle at Moquegua, this preeminent agricultural shrine was "decommissioned" and turned over to a newly arisen warrior class. The drainage system, allowing for water to flow down and through the seven levels of the temple-mountain, was blocked off. Contemporary with this event,[14] twenty-one bodies, the majority being those of males between the ages of seventeen and thirty-nine, were buried at the base of the Akapana. Eighteen were headless. Several were also armless and/or legless.[15] Finally, this whole assemblage appears to have been buried at the same time as the placement of "a tremendous offering of . . . hundreds of fine polychrome vessels . . . shattered into thousands of fragments," sharing "a consistent, standardized motif: *painted bands of stylized human trophy heads.*"[16] [Emphasis added.] These same motifs, which also included zoomorphic entities, are found on the smashed pottery offerings from the same era at Wari sites.[17]

Although Kolata sees in these events evidence of an important episode of "military conquest . . . a transforming event in Tiwanaku history,"[18] in which a new kind of warrior elite took power, there is another possible interpretation that, to my mind, seems more plausible. All evidence indicates that the theocrats—priest-astronomers whose title, *capaca,* defined their function—never relinquished their power at Tiahuanaco. As Kolata himself emphasizes, Tiahuanaco never kept a standing army, and never used military force as a primary means of furthering its influence.[19]

I would suggest that by A.D. 600 the *capacas* of Tiahuanaco faced an unprecedented situation. Accustomed for centuries to an ever-expanding sphere of influence based on the attractiveness of their ideology, they had now, and for the first time, to contemplate the limits of expansion. I would suggest that the prodigious and atypical bloodletting at the Akapana in about A.D. 600 is indicative of the military *defeat* at Moquegua, and that the decapitated, legless corpses at the Akapana were Wari prisoners taken back to Tiahuanaco by the forces retreating from the smoking ruins of Moquegua. The ceding of the Akapana to a new class of warriors by the priest-astronomers reflected a single simple fact: for the first time, *Tiahuanaco had a border to defend.* Those who would defend it attained a new status consistent with this new responsibility.

Before examining the clues concerning the identity of this warrior class, it is first necessary to refer to simultaneous events unfolding in Wari. Following the victory at Moquegua, Wari began an ambitious building program within its own civic center. Before this time, the Ayacucho basin had had no tradition of expert stonemasonry, and no large civic-ceremonial centers. Yet in about A.D. 600,[20] a semisubterranean temple, similar in design and identical in technique to the stonework of Tiahuanaco, was constructed at Wari.[21] William Isbell surmises that this temple was built either by altiplano prisoners captured at Moquegua or by stonemasons dispatched directly from Tiahuanaco as tribute.[22] This construction began a phase of intense interchange between the Ayacucho region and Tiahuanaco, manifest in the simultaneous appearance of a new pottery style in both locales. According to Isbell, the iconographic motifs of this shared style represent "new ideas about cosmic structure and human organization."[23] And what were these motifs? Images in profile of a "sacrificer," trophy heads, and disarticulated arm and leg bones.[24]

The enigmatic interchange between Wari and Tiahuanaco lasted about fifty years. For its part, Wari appears to have hungered for all things Tiahuanacan, for the "trade secrets" of state-building. On its side, Tiahuanaco may have been trying to work with the emerging leadership in Wari, perhaps with the hopes of grooming an ally who would throw the entire northern sierra open to the llama caravans of Tiahuanaco. On the other hand, it is also possible that the theocratic leadership of Tiahuanaco had little control over this interchange. Emblazoned on the new ceramics were images of a new "religion," running, as it were, in parallel with the traditions of Tiahuanaco: a cult of intimidation based on the threat of decapitation and dismemberment. In other words, it is also possible that the shared ceramic styles of Tiahuanaco and Wari at this time were warning shots fired from each side across the bows of each area's newly arisen warrior class.

Whatever the case, within a scant fifty years, Wari struck out on a completely independent course. In about A.D. 650 the semisubterranean temple at Wari was filled in and a new structure, in a new style that would henceforth distinguish the architecture of Wari, was erected over it.[25] Simultaneously, "at around A.D. 650,"[26] Wari erected a huge building complex, covering twenty-five hectares, in the same style some 150 miles to the south, at the southern end of the valley of Cuzco. This site, called Pikillacta, was heavily garrisoned, and all five entrances to the valley accessible from the *altiplano* to the south were fortified.[27]

At the same time, Wari also constructed an equally imposing complex, 450 miles to the north at Wiracochapampa, dominating the trade routes north all the way to Ecuador.[28] In all, Wari constructed at least eleven building complexes between the valley of Cuzco and the valley of Cajamarca, far to the north. While the two southernmost complexes—Pikillacta and Cerro Baul—were heavily defended against Tiahuanaco, sites to the north were less overtly military. Specialists disagree over the nature of Wari's northern outposts. Some consider Wari's northward expansion an example of interregional cooperation and adaptive evolution (willing acceptance of new ideas, i.e., high-altitude terracing of steep hillsides),[29] while others judge Wari to have used force, or, at a minimum intimidation, in carving out control of Peru's major north-south roadways.[30]

At the same time that Wari began to chart its own independent course, as evinced by its ambitious construction of outposts, another equally independent and highly significant divergence from Tiahuanacan influence appeared in the realm of ceramic iconography. Anita Cook has shown that, whereas Tiahuanaco continued to represent its religious ideas by portraying supernatural entities on its ceramics, those of Wari differed by *depicting actual individual members of a newly created ruling class.*[31] This style, diagnostic of Wari influence, portrayed individual lords, with the Tiahuanacoid icons, including the Gateway God and the "sacrificer," displayed about their persons. (See figure 8.1.) For the first time outside the Titicaca basin, and in a manner radically different from the style of Tiahuanaco's theocracy,[32] Wari had established a highland ruling class, separate from the ordinary run of people.

The expansion of Wari was a studied exercise in control. Insofar as Wari attempted to emulate the mystique of spiritual authority inhering to the *capacas* of Tiahuanaco, this effort was grounded in a cult of intimidation based upon the taking of trophy heads. It was as if the leaders of Wari knew, and acknowledged from the beginning, that there was—and always would be—only one Tiahuanaco. Their path to power lay along a route different from the priest-astronomers of the altiplano. In fact, Wari, as numerous investigators have concluded, was, by the standards of its time, a shockingly secular state, concerned with the control of resource networks without apparent interest in commensurate reciprocal obligation.[33] The rulers of Wari were primarily interested in the acquisition of luxury goods, and employed displays of naked power to achieve that end. They sought to establish new criteria for leadership, based upon the creation of a social class whose primary "spiritual" merit was a willingness to use force.

Consistent with this outlook, Wari created another new institution, taxation of labor.

> Huari administrators transformed a system of vertical archipelago economics based on reciprocal exchange among comparable units into revenue collection by the state. The essence of the new system involved the collection of labor rather than goods, and the disguise of compulsory labor for the state with all the trappings of traditional, reciprocal exchange of labor.[34]

Throughout its domain, Wari took the labor of its subjects for a variety of purposes. One activity was a massive effort to create state lands by using local, uncompensated labor to build agricultural terraces for the production of maize in support of its own herdsmen moving into previously unexploited pastures.[35] In a number of cases, whole villages were rebuilt at lower altitudes, specifically to force local inhabitants to conform to Wari's preferred pattern of resource exploitation.[36] Wari also used the labor tax in setting up centers for the *production* of luxury goods[37] from metals, gemstones, textiles, shell, and clay.

Wari's interest in expanding the trade of luxury goods was integral to the institution of social class. The northward trade undertaken by Wari brought "obsidian, ceramics, and possibly lapis lazuli" north, "while goods from the north included Cajamarca pottery and *Spondylus* shell from Ecuador."[38] The importance of those goods to the new ruling class of Wari is reflected in the appearance for the first time, beginning about A.D. 650, of elite burials, associated with a profusion of luxury items.[39] Also, a large number of subfloor cists for guarding precious objects have been unearthed in the elite housing of Wari.

The ceramic representations of the new ruling class at Wari (figure 8.1) demonstrate the essential contradiction at the heart of Wari's expansion: the attempt by the lords of Wari to surround themselves with the iconography —and hence the mystique—of the religion of Wiraqocha while changing its essential message. No longer were the ethnic, tribal units of the Andes equal partners in reciprocal exchange. A new, superior class of men would preside over the organization not only of resources, but of labor as well.

The nature and identity of this new class, promoting an iconography of force, further clarifies the dynamics of Wari expansion. Anita Cook has recently shown that the new ceramic motifs, which appeared simultaneously in Tiahuanaco and Wari, and which included depictions of trophy heads, of a "sacrificer"[40] leading a tethered llama, and of disarticulated arm and leg bones, represent the *revival* of an older style associated with the northern Titicaca-basin city of Pucara.[41]

Pucara, which flourished from about 200 B.C. until about A.D. 200, constituted a rival polity to Tiahuanaco. The relationship between these two cities appears to have ranged from intense competition to open hostility. The famous Thunderbolt Stela found at Tiahuanaco has been shown, thanks to the research of Sergio Chavéz, to have been broken from its base in Arapa (then under the control of Pucara) and transported ninety miles by raft across Lake Titicaca to Tiahuanaco.[42] Until its complete disappearance in the fourth century, Pucara appears to have been the main rival—perhaps the only serious rival—of Tiahuanaco in the Titicaca basin.

The ceramic iconography of Pucara, particularly the "sacrificer" (figure 8.2), clarifies the nature of its culture. Early Pucaran depictions of this figure show him leading a llama by a tether held in his left hand, with a staff in his right. This figure sometimes wears a collar depicting tiny trophy heads. In other words, as Cook maintains, the people of Pucara identified themselves as *nomadic pastoralists*.[43] Unlike their counterparts among the Cañari of Ecuador, who, by their own accounts, gratefully accepted the emissaries of Wiraqocha (= influence of Tiahuanaco), the pastoralists of Pucara apparently had no intention of relinquishing their old ways. The source of conflict between Pucara and Tiahuanaco must have lain in the latter's commitment to fostering the spread of agricultural civilization, in which pastoralism would necessarily play a secondary, supporting role. As Kolata has observed, the leaders of Tiahuanaco "in effect harmonized the potentially disruptive

competition between farmer and herder by formally synchronizing productive strategies, adjudicating territorial disputes, and redistributing the very
different work products of these two occupational pursuits."[44] At Tiahuanaco, pastoralists were told where and when to graze their animals.[45]

The resurgence in the early seventh century of Pucaran iconographic
motifs indicates not only renewed prestige for the practice of warfare, but
the identity of the warriors themselves. The practice of llama sacrifice by
pastoralists for divinatory as well as propitiatory purposes is extremely well
documented in the Andean literature. The warrior class came from the
tradition of nomadic pastoralists, who *likened the taking of trophy heads to the
ritual sacrifice of llamas.* Further, the pastoralists' mastery of weapons (the bola
and sling), their intimacy with blood through eons of animal slaughter, and
their tradition of long-distance travel—mobility—preeminently suited them
to the practice of warfare.

It also follows that, since the expansion of Wari was directed by a
leadership intent on the production and trade of luxury goods, those who
would most directly benefit from this trade would be the *masters of llama
caravans,* that is nomadic pastoralists. Therefore, in my opinion, the critical
leverage point in Wari's ascent to power lay in utilizing the culture of
nomadic pastoralism to create a secular state favoring an elite class, which
in return strove to revive and re-empower an ancient pastoral ethos by
promoting a new "religion" based upon the projection of terror and intimidation.

Evidence of the trophy-head cult is found not only in Wari itelf, but at
the extremes of its control, from the skulls and long bones of Pikillacta
to the obsidian-strewn ground at the Wari "temple" of Cerro Amaru near
Wiracochapampa, the gateway to the northern trade.[46] The message was
simple: those who stood against Wari in battle risked being captured and
then ritually slaughtered, dressed out with an obsidian blade in precisely the
same manner as a sacrificial llama.[47] Figure 8.3 shows Guamán Poma's depiction of one phase of the traditional llama sacrifice. In a very real sense, Wari
represented the shadow side of Tiahuanaco, the resurrection of its ancient
foe, Pucara. By A.D. 650 and on a scale previously unknown, something quite
ugly had gotten out of the bottle.

Nowhere is this frightening aspect of Wari culture more evident than in
its distinctive architecture. So different from that of Tiahuanaco was this
style that "the two seem almost to be reactions to one another."[48] The
architecture of Tiahuanaco was open, majestic, given to carving out volumet-
ric space.[49] It was meant to be seen, and above all to be entered. By the
seventh century, the most distinctive feature of Tiahuanacan architecture

was the development of architraves[50]—carved portals opening between great architectural spaces—through which the witnesses of ritual, ordinary people, might enter. Tiahuanacan architecture emphasized the horizontal, aligning the planes of earth, horizon, and sky for the contemplation and edification of those entering its ceremonial spaces.[51] Tiahuanacan architecture was open, unwalled,[52] separated from the profane world only by its moat, which formed a conceptual barrier, rather than a visual one, between the sacred and the ordinary. Tiahuanaco was an invitation to participation.

By contrast, the architectural style of Wari was secular, manifesting an obsession with power, wealth, control, elitism, and intimidation. William Isbell has described the architectural style of Huari as "orthogonal," that is, based upon the repetitive use of right angles. The structures erected by the administrators of Wari, whether in Wari itself or in outlying regions such as Pikillacta, were constructed on a vast scale—sort of instant, walled cities. These structures exuded exclusion and control. From the outside, one had no idea what was going on inside. Access was restricted to extremely narrow gates, themselves framed by walled roadways. Once inside, one found oneself within a rigidly geometric warren of intersecting narrow "streets" formed by the walls of innumerable interior compounds. Periodically, along such streets, were placed narrower gates, even further restricting movement within.[53]

Unlike Tiahuanaco, these cities were built without reference to the site. They were imposed upon the land as if from above, forcing an orthogonal grid upon the natural undulations of the land.[54] Archaeologists are still unsure how anyone inside could move from one area to another without getting lost.[55] The interior walls were devoid of architectural detailing and iconographic representations. Moving through these streets, one had no idea of how the space upon which one trod related to the topography outside. Everything looked the same. Each compound had a narrow entrance off the "street." Each compound was itself a warren of rectangular rooms, with interior access between spaces also severely limited. Wari architectural creations were monuments to control.

Furthermore, in this system of building, all reference to the horizon was obliterated. There were no monumental portals, and few doors.[56] There were no views.[57] It was as if the administrators of Wari, who imposed these grids at site after site, were intent upon severing the ancient Andean relationship between earth and sky. It was as if the buildings themselves were designed to announce to the agricultural peoples of the Andes that the authority once vested by them in the religious teaching of Wiraqocha had passed to living demigods, the lords of Wari. Henceforth the peasantry was obliged to look down, rather than to the heavens, for its instructions.

For archaeologists, the most surprising aspect of these administrative centers was that their endless interior rooms were *not* used for storage. Until recently it had been assumed that such spaces were inherently uninhabitable and must have been used for the storage of goods to be transshipped elsewhere. This assumption was natural, for we know that, later, the Incas kept vast storehouses of food throughout their Empire. The purpose of such Inca storehouses was to see that no region of the Empire, no matter how remote, would ever be threatened by famine. The Incas, in other words, understood their reciprocal obligations.

But that was not the purpose of the honeycomb of rooms in Wari compounds. Aside from the quarters of the administrative upper class, the rooms at Wari sites were occupied by three kinds of people: soldiers, laborers engaged in the construction of the sites themselves, and artisans. Uninterested in the administrative burden involved in moving enormous amounts of foodstuffs, the rulers of Wari were intent on the production, distribution, and trade of luxury goods.[58] These sites were a combination of garrison, factory, construction project, and dormitory for those enjoined under the labor tax to participate. The nightmarish interior bottlenecks suggest the presence of Wari administrators, intent on accounting for the movement and location of each and every laborer impressed for service.

[R]eports . . . that the highly repetitive cellular room-like forms found in Huari [Wari] town plans were not used for storage comes as something of a shock. Such incredibly regimented planning and construction is not otherwise known in the world history of human environments. If these spaces were not for product storage but rather for people, then it is important for us to reconstruct not only the plans of the site but also, so far as we can, the human environmental conditions. In order to identify the conditions in the most densely occupied sectors, we must consider (1) the apparent lack of adequate drainage, (2) the lack of in-compound gardens, (3) the lack of in-compound water supply, (4) the lack of any seeming intercellular communication, (5) the strictly controlled access, and (6) the inevitable containment of human excretion.

The mood of jail or concentration camp hangs eerily over the repetitive cellular portions of these Huari empire site plans.[59]

III

BY A.D. 850 the city of Wari lay abandoned, its dominance shattered. At numerous sites, including Wiracochapampa, Pikillacta, and Wari itself, ambitious building projects were never finished. The legacy of this precipitous collapse was a vacuum, and, consistent with the universal laws of physics, the Andean highlands imploded. The result was a jagged mosaic of warring tribal alliances, setting valley against valley in a sort of grotesque caricature of the situation before the "flood." Where unity in diversity had been the keystone of the Age of Wiraqocha, all that survived the rule of Wari was a fiercely defended sense of local independence.

Traces of this event are found in the archaeological and ethnohistorical records alike. From the Titicaca basin to the north-central sierra, settlement patterns shifted toward defensible ridgetop hamlets.[60] Many of these settlements were divided into halves, suggesting the establishment of what in anthropology are called moiety divisions,[61] or groups divided along class lines. The appearance at this time of elite burials in the Titicaca basin further suggests the arising of class differences.[62] By about A.D. 1,000 Tiahuanaco itself was abandoned, probably as the result of prolonged drought, which, being associated with the El Niño wind pattern, affected the entire sierra.[63] Another jump in population appears to have contributed further to the perpetuation of conflict.[64] With the collapse of Wari and the withering of Tiahuanaco, no cities would be built in the highlands until the establishment of Cuzco.[65] By the end of this period (known to archaeology as the Late Intermediate), according to Edward Lanning, "we get a picture of numerous small tribal groups engaged in constant feuds, shifting their alliances as the occasion dictated."[66] Guamán Poma referred to this era as an age of warfare, whose distinctive building type was the hilltop fortress. (See figure 8.4.)

The ethnohistorical record adds an important dimension to this picture. Numerous sources from the Spanish colonial period attest to the existence of a division of highland communities into conceptual halves. Further, the sources make clear that these moiety divisions were based on principles greatly antedating the Inca expansion. Two kinds of evidence from the Spanish colonial record make reference to this universal Andean pattern. One source involves a surge of land claims made by different ethnic populations based on the situation before the establishment of the recently destroyed Inca Empire. The other came from the "extirpation" trials held throughout the sierra by clerics trained by the likes of Avila and Arriaga.

Both Arriaga and Hernández Príncipe, for example, recorded the names for these moieties.[67] The lower, or southern, moiety was called *llacta*, while the upper, or northern, moiety was know as *llacua*, or *llachua*. The term *llacta* or *llactayoc*, meaning "village" or "villager," referred to that portion of the community that was "native to that village, as were all their ancestors, *with no memory of having come from outside*, and they call *llacuas* those who, although born in that village, both their ancestors and progenitors *came from other parts*. And thus is preserved in the *ayllus* in many places this distinction. . . ."[68] [Emphasis added.]

Likewise, in his examination of the material recorded by Hernández Príncipe, Zuidema has shown that the root of these moiety divisions derived from the fact of conquest, at some remote date, by outsiders over the ancient holders of the land, the *llactas*.[69]

Moreover, Irene Silverblatt has shown that Inca symbolic representations of the relationship between men and women derived from a "hierarchy of conquest" established long before the rise to power of the Incas. The essence of this hierarchical ordering lay in distinguishing between conqueror and conquered in terms of gender. In this scheme the "lower class," or *llactas*, the original inhabitants of the land, were termed "feminine," and the conquerors, from elsewhere, were called "masculine."[70]

Silverblatt's analysis brings us, for the first time, before the central theme of this chapter, the profound changes in Andean cosmological thought wrought by the advent of warfare. Here, four points require emphasis. First, the self-styled identity of the conquerors as "masculine" suggests that they were nomadic pastoralists, accustomed to tracing descent through the male line.

This deduction is corroborated by a second datum, the literal meaning of the name adopted by the upper moiety: *llachua*. *This is the Quechua word for the ritual sacrifice of llamas*. The upper, warrior moieties were "sacrificers of llamas," and the "llamas," in this situation, were the original inhabitants, the peasants themselves. The "common people," or *llactas*, in the region described by Hernández Príncipe, traced—as has been noted elsewhere of other groups—common ancestry back to a mythical llama. "Low class people . . . because of common origin were identified with llamas and the upper class people as conquerors with sacrificers of llamas."[71] Here, then, the ethnohistorical record makes clear that the ethos of warfare—whose essential characteristic was the likening of sacrificing of captured warriors to the ritual slaughter (*llachuar*) of llamas—did not die out with Wari, but rather became institutionalized throughout the Andes in the fundamental structures of local village life.

Third, it is important to recognize that the ethnohistorical record offers, in one sense, a picture of the *result* of the collapse of Wari, and this result comes into clearer focus the closer one gets to the years immediately preceding the rise of the Incas. One important aspect of this has been described by Irene Silverblatt, who makes clear that established moiety systems represented a kind of equilibrium. Even though the relationship between moieties is expressed as a hierarchy of conquest, consistent with the historical reality of conquest at some remote date, the resulting system was one in which peasant and warrior classes lived in relative harmony and stability within their own, shared lands:

> It bears emphasis that the hierarchy of conquest as applied on the local level, was in the first place a hierarchy of prestige, of classification. . . . Within the local political organization, the *ayllu* [called] *llacuas,* by its position, had no prerogatives over the work or the resources of production of the *llactas.* Each *ayllu* was autonomous as regards religious functionaries and the cult of the ancestors.[72]

What is far less clear is how this peculiar equilibrium of heavily defended (and threatened) locally autonomous regions evolved out of the collapse of Wari. The first intimations of a generalized pattern of fortifications and moiety divisions appear in the archaeological record at about A.D. 1000, the benchmark date for the commencement of the Late Intermediate Period. One of the most obscure eras in the Andean archaeological record lies between the collapse of Wari at about A.D. 850 and the emergence, a century and a half later, of patterns on the ground suggesting the commencement of the establishment of moiety divisions.[73] Interestingly, as we shall presently see, it is this "lost" period that is the focus of the main body of Huarochirí myths.

Finally, implicit in these ubiquitous accounts of an ancient era of conquest up and down the Andean sierra is *the existence of a kind of historical tradition.* As we have already seen, native chroniclers such as Guamán Poma and Pachakuti Yamqui used the mythical terminology of world-ages to distinguish an era of warfare that supplanted an earlier, peaceful era. When native peoples came forth to assert land claims, or when the extirpators probed for ways to breach native "cults," the same information was repeated over and over again. In some places the aboriginal holders of the land, the *llactas,* offered another term for identifying themselves and their ancient rights in the land: *huari*.[74] As discussed in chapter 6, *huari* is the Aymara word for the mode of food preparation distinguishing the advent of the agricultural *ayllu*.

Furthermore, as the work of Lorenzo Huertas Vallejos demonstrates, this historical tradition also included a record of events going back to the very origins of the autocthonous peoples, *long before the advent of the warriors*. Particularly important is information from Cuzco, Ayacucho, Cajatambo, the Callejón de Huaylas, and elsewhere linking the aboriginal (agricultural) people *directly back to Lake Titicaca*. According to these traditions the "Huari" were a race of white, bearded giants who had been created at Lake Titicaca, whence they had set forth to civilize the Andes. It was these beings who, according to documents from Cajatambo (remarkably similar to the Huarochirí myths), "laid up dry-stone walls" and taught the people how to construct irrigation canals. These emissaries from Titicaca were credited with creating the order of Andean society. Those who absorbed this teaching took the name Huari.[75] In this way, scraps of information from Spanish legal and extirpation records point to the existence of a pan-Andean, pre-Columbian historical tradition, an idea that scholars have only recently begun to evaluate.[76]

Significantly, the record of this tradition accords with the archaeological record, which indicates some sort of interchange, on the level of ideas rather than trade, between the Titicaca basin and the Andean sierra as far north as Ecuador dating back perhaps five centuries before Christ.[77] The myths of the Cañari tell the same story. Nowhere is this tradition more fully expressed than in the most complete of Andean mythical records, the Huarochirí corpus.

The opening four chapters of these tales deal with events from very ancient times, before the advent of warfare.[78] The first chapter, like the Titicaca origin myth, begins with an era of darkness when "Black Ñamca and Night Ñamca" were the ruling *wakas*. The main point of the chapter, however, is to establish the difficult conditions under which the ancestral deity of the warriors came to power during an era of cruelty and famine. Events farther in the past are presented as a jumbled memory. Although Wiraqocha is mentioned, the tellers are not sure whether he came before or after Pariacaca, the ancestral deity of the warriors. Nevertheless, later in the text the teller returns to clarify this point,[79] stating that Wiraqocha was the father of—that is, antedated—Pariacaca.

In the second chapter of *Huarochirí*, the tellers recount the traditions concerning the era "a long, long time ago," before the advent of their god Pariacaca. This chapter deals with the exploits of Wiraqocha, who is cred-

ited with two seminal acts. First he "fashioned all the villages. Just by speaking he made all the fields and finished the terraces with walls of fine masonry.
As for the irrigation canals, he channeled them out from their sources just
by tossing down a flower of a reed called *pupuna*."[80]

In other words, the text contains a *llacta/huari* tradition connecting the
arising of autocthonous agriculturalists to the creator deity of Titicaca. Further, as mentioned in chapter 6 of the present volume, this description of
the god's activities shares with Mayan myth the characteristic of the agricultural god's ability to do work magically, without effort.

The second exploit of Wiraqocha described in chapter two of the
Huarochirí myths also has direct analogues in Mesoamerica. Here Wiraqo-
cha becomes enamored of a beautiful virgin, a "female *waka*" known as Caui
Llaca, and impregnates her by means of a fruit which he has inseminated.
Likewise in the *Popol Vuh* the virgin Ixquic is impregnated with Sun and
Moon after being inseminated by a strange fruit representing the heads of
the Seven Ahpu, the masculine, sky principle. (See chapter 6 of this book.)
Both stories spell the end of the horticultural era, whose paradigmatic situation is the suffering of a virgin of the matrilineal cycle in giving birth to the
new, agricultural world.

In the tale from Huarochirí the virgin Caui Llaca flees Wiraqocha,
heading westward (the direction of death), eventually to become petrified
with her daughter as two guano-bearing islands—sources of fertility for the
land—in the Pacific Ocean near the shrine of Pachacamac. Pursuing her all
the while, Wiraqocha asks each animal he meets along the way where his
beloved has gone. Helpful animals are rewarded; the unhelpful are punished.
These rewards and punishments create the characteristic behaviors of each
species, viewed from the perspective of their relative helpfulness or harm-
fulness to agriculture. Thus the second chapter of the Huarochirí myths
states that both the end of the matrilineal world and the commencement of
agriculture were the results of the intervention of Wiraqocha. (Conversely,
in other mythological traditions, where the old customs of pastoral nomadism give way to the teaching of Tiahuanaco—as with the destitute
Cañari brothers at "Cargo-Llama Mountain"—it is through the female aspect
of the godhead, represented by the *guacamayas*, that the transformation
occurs.)

The last tales from this "very ancient" time in Huarochirí are the third
and fourth chapters, which describe the cataclysm that ended the Age of
Wiraqocha. Chapter three—recounting the myth of the llama, the fox, and
the flood, and dating to A.D. 650—alludes in several ways both to the
traditional religion of Wiraqocha and to the weakening of this tradition at

the time of the "flood." First, the shepherd, exasperated by the diffidence of his animals, beats one of them with an ear of maize, demonstrating his access not only to pastoral resources but to the kind of prime agricultural land in highland valley bottoms where maize is grown. Further, the sense of times gone awry is vividly captured in this same image of the peasant beating his animals with the maize cob and calling them "dogs." By this action—using the sacred plant maize as a weapon—the peasant violates fundamental norms of behavior through which he may relate to the divine. Equally ominous, he beats the llama, thereby endangering the primordial compact between man and beast, acknowledged throughout the Andean highlands, wherein the llamas agreed to serve man only so long as they were not mistreated.[81] Nonetheless, despite these errors, the peasant comes to his senses in the end, heeds the *paqo*/shaman, and takes those measures necessary for survival. This last action also speaks to the Age of Wiraqocha, in which leadership was not based on force or deception, but belonged to the priest-astronomer, who by merit of superior insight alone was able to command respect.

Likewise, Molina's version of the flood, as told in Ancasmarca, also makes clear that the myth's protagonists are peasants. Here the man is said to have six children. Among the Quiché-Maya, where patrilineal descent was the norm, it was six *sons* who represented the ideal.[82] In Molina, the ideal is "six sons and daughters,"[83] a pretty detail evincing in yet another manner the sincerity of the Andean view concerning the value-equality of men and women, and the adherence of the tellers of this tale to the double-descent system.

With a different set of conceits, the very brief fourth chapter of the Huarochirí stories reprises one last time the cataclysm which enveloped the Andean peasantry:

> In ancient times the sun died.
> Because of his death it was night for five days.
> Rocks banged against each other.
> Mortars and grinding stones began to eat people.
> Buck llamas began to drive men.[84]

The "death of the sun" (a term whose logic within the technical language of myth will be discussed at length in the next chapter) was the Inca term for a *pachakuti*, that is, an event marking the end of a world-age. Here the literal sense of *pachakuti*—"the overturning of space-time"—finds its rhetorical analogue in the upending of the fundamental components of *ayllu* existence. This tale, too, has its counterpart in Maya myth.[85] The very tools for the preparation of agricultural foodstuffs, as well as the domesticated animals linking resource networks, have risen up to devour a way of life. The great mill, time itself, imagined as the very mountains grinding, had run out on the Andean peasantry.[86]

With the narration of these four chapters, the tales of "very ancient times" are complete. Now the narrators turn to their own heritage and the birth of their ancestral deity, Pariacaca, the god of war. In order to understand the fundamental changes in Andean cosmological thought described in the ensuing chapters of the Huarochirí manuscript, it is first necessary to understand how these chapters also relate the context in which these changes transpired. As we shall now see, the myths of Huarochirí provide the clearest and most complete indigenous account of the effects on one people of the expansion, collapse, and aftermath of the Wari experiment.

IV

THE MEN OF Huarochirí who spoke of their past to the priest Avila were the descendants of nomadic pastoralists. Their story, commencing with the fifth chapter, is the record of how they swept down from their mountain fastness to drive out what they saw as a corrupt regime and claim for themselves, rather than these foreign interlopers, a share of prime agricultural lands occupied for untold centuries by a local peasantry either too weak or too gullible to drive off this recently arrived outside threat.

The first words of the Huarochirí corpus, uttered as preface to the myths that would follow, were:

> I set forth here the lives of the ancestors of the Huaro Cheri people, who all descended from one forefather. . . . Village by village it will be written down how they lived from their dawning age onward.[87]

Consistent with this claim of patrilineal descent was the title that the tellers gave to their priesthood: *llacuas*, or "sacrificers of llamas."[88]

Thanks in large part to the work of María Rostworowski de Canseco[89] the ethnic identity of the tellers of the Huarochirí myths has been determined. They were the Yauyo, originally pastoralists who once occupied "the high tundras at the Cañete River headwaters,"[90] and later established, by means of conquest, control of agricultural resources in the heartland described in the Huarochirí text.

This area lies on the western, seaward slopes of the Andean cordillera. Access to this entire region—draining the Cañete, Mala, Lurin, and Rimac rivers, each flowing west to the Pacific—came through a single high pass. In both Inca and Spanish colonial times, the main route from the southern and south central Andes to the central Pacific coast lay through this pass, where the Incas carved steps into living rock on the flanks of a towering volcanic mountain called Pariacaca.[91] Pariacaca was also the name of the war deity and the patrilineal, supernatural ancestor of the Yauyos.

This same pass was an important avenue in the success of Wari's expansion. Not only was the pass at Pariacaca the gateway to the prestigious coastal shrine of Pachacamac, but also to the most prized coca-growing regions in the Andes. These coca lands lay along the lower reaches of the Huarochirí region's river basins, at altitudes between one thousand and three thousand feet in elevation, known as the *chaupi-yunga,* or "half tropics." Very little is known of the archaeology of the Huarochirí region, although it does not appear that Wari ever built a major center there. Nonetheless, it is known that Wari carried on an extensive trade in luxury goods with Pachacamac. Opinions differ on whether Pachacamac was dominated by Wari or achieved a measure of independence, but in either case the interchange between the two, while it lasted, was intense.[92]

The llama trains of Wari, then, passed beneath the split volcanic peak of Pariacaca, virtually under the nose of the relatively impoverished Yauyo, and through the finest coca plantations in Peru, on their way to Pachacamac. It is hard to imagine the acquisitive lords of Wari failing to take an interest in this priceless crop, particularly since every other people of whom there is a record took lands here at the first available opportunity. Coca had been grown on the Pacific slopes of the central Andes for thousands of years. The cultigen peculiar to this area was famous for its superior drought resistance and leaf flavor.[93] According to the research of Rostworowski, intense conflict between the Yauyo in the highlands and the coca producers in the *chaupiyungas* was one of the primary factors in warfare during the period described by the Huarochirí myths.[94] Later the Incas seized the best of such lands for themselves.[95]

Before turning to the famous fifth chapter of the Huarochirí myths, which lays out the circumstances surrounding the "birth" of the war god Pariacaca, one further aspect of the opening four chapters is worth mentioning. The speakers, descendants of the once-pastoral Yauyos, consistently interject into descriptions of life before the flood an implied criticism of the aboriginal agricultural peoples. This criticism is found, for example, in the myth of the flood, where the peasant is characterized as forgetful of sacred norms when he berates and beats his animals.

Likewise, according to the Yauyo tellers, it was the peasantry's insistence on worshiping their ancestors that led up to the "flood."[96] The problem was that peasants put too much pressure on the land by producing too many children, and the reason they were so prolific was that the dead, when they returned, expected to be given food and drink in the presence of living family members. What made the dead especially "happy" was to see a great number of relatives present at these ceremonies.

> And so, at that time, people swiftly increased in number. They lived in
> great suffering, miserably gathering their food, terracing both cliffs and
> ledges for their fields.[97]

Besides being an apparent allusion to the demographic and ecological crisis implicated in the rise of Wari, this statement constitutes a direct attack upon the religious sensibilities of the peasantry. Up until the "flood," the cosmological imperative that energized the spiritual life of the highland tribes had been the responsibility of maintaining right relations between the three worlds, including *ukhu pacha*, the land of the dead. An important part of honoring the ancestors lay in fulfilling the obligation (common to early agricultural peoples everywhere) to be fruitful and multiply.

If, then, the criticism leveled by the Yauyo pastoralists at the agriculturalists of their region reveals the sort of tensions implicit in the creation of a moiety system based upon a "hierarchy of conquest," it is important also to understand that the Yauyos did not claim that the peasantry were *directly* responsible for the chaos that the Yauyos themselves felt obliged to put right. Rather, according to the first chapter of the myths, there appeared from *outside* an evil *waka*, known as Huallallo Caruincho—the principal enemy of the ancestral *waka* of the Yauyos, Pariacaca—who "ordered the people to bear two children and no more."[98] Worse, Huallallo Caruincho was said to devour one of the children himself. In other words, some foreign power[99] had entered the Huarochirí region, and had commenced to outrage the religious sensibilities of everyone there, including the Yauyos, not only by mandating population control, but by employing "cannibalism" (read "intimidation") as a tool of policy.

What this strange tale illuminates is the process of the Yauyos' developing from the very outset of their stories a *casus belli* whereby they may portray themselves *as the protectors of ancient ways against foreign intruders.* (Centuries later the Incas would make precisely the same allegation of rampant cannibalism as part of their justification for taking control of the Andes.) This stance explains the dynamics behind Silverblatt's observation that, while the moiety divisions of the Andes were expressed in terms of conquest, there nonetheless existed, in reality, a situation of autonomy between the moieties. The origin of this ancient compact begins here, with the agreement by the warriors (despite grumblings about the peasantry's habit of "overbreeding") that the old ways were worth defending. If, in return, the warriors expected land, such was their due only insofar as they respected the religion of Wiraqocha. This juggling act—justification of conquest in the name of a spiritual tradition founded upon mutual acceptance and reciprocal obligation—constitutes the great underlying theme of the Huarochirí myths.

As a result of this constraint, a sort of ninth-century Newspeak often emerges out of the text. For example, while taking the peasantry to task for religious beliefs that led to overpopulation, members of the warrior class deemed themelves powerful because they had "so many brothers."[100] Thus, an old priest of the warrior class, considered heroic for resisting the Spaniards, was said to have had six sons.[101] And while the tellers praise this same exemplary warrior-priest as "the wisest, the one who best guarded memory," they nonetheless assert that the critical moment when the war god Pariacaca became the new supreme deity is the same moment when the virtues of memory became entirely dispensable: "And so, those of whom we speak conquered the warm valleys . . . and therefore, forgetting their old gods, they all began to worship Pariacaca."[102] Back and forth, back and forth.

It is within this field of conflicting forces and systemic tension that the fifth chapter begins,

> In the four preceding chapters we have already recounted the lives lived in ancient times.
>
> Nevertheless, we don't know the origins of the people of those days, nor where it was they emerged from.
>
> These people, the ones who lived in that era, used to spend their lives warring on each other and conquering each other. For their leaders, they recognized only the strong and the rich.
>
> We speak of them as the Purum Runa, "people of desolation."[103]

Having dealt with events up until the flood, the tellers begin by expressing a sense of confusion, conflict, and chaos surrounding its aftermath.

Although the text is littered with reference to the "emergence" places (*pacari-nas*) of peoples native to the Huarochirí area, the origin of the "strong and rich . . . people of desolation" is not known. Since the "flood" occurred in A.D. 650, the same time as Wari's explosive expansion, and since the archae-ology of that period stresses the creation by Wari, for the first time in the highlands, of class differentiations based on wealth, backed by intimidation and warfare, it appears that the period described at the beginning of the fifth chapter—when the "strong and rich" were "warring"—refers to the expan-sion of Wari into the Huarochirí area.

Now the narrators speak of their own origins, that is, how their own entry onto the stage of these myths took place after a period of time domi-nated by the "strong and rich." "It was at this time," the text continues, "that the one called Paria Caca was born in the form of five eggs on Condor Coto mountain." [104] Then the tellers introduce the chapter's main protagonist, a young Yauyo lad called Huatya Curi, "the first to see and know" the birth of the war god, Pariacaca. From the outset the narrators seek to establish the moral rectitude and essential worthiness of Huatya Curi. Therefore, in the same way that, in the second chapter, they describe Wiraqocha as accus-tomed to "go around posing as a miserably poor and friendless man," [105] Huatya Curi is cast as "poor and friendless." [106] Huatya Curi, while holding within him the awesome knowledge of the birth of Pariacaca, has the out-ward appearance of a nobody.

The conceit of the outwardly materially poor, yet inwardly shamanically gifted hero is one of the favored themes in all Andean myth, originating with the myths of Wiraqocha. For example, as noted, in chapter 4 of the present volume, Wiraqocha—a poor man, carrying within him the seeds of a new world—comes to Cacha and, when attacked by the heedless villagers, brings down a rain of fire. Above all, this conceit has to do with *justice,* with the relationship which ought to exist between merit and power. By underscoring the essential incompatibility between outward displays of wealth and the inward husbanding of spiritual strength, the narrators of the Huarochirí tales establish their identity as champions of the old religious values associated with the god of justice, Wiraqocha. [107]

The opening lines of the fifth chapter, then, are designed to tap immedi-ately into a simmering aquifer of rage, for Huatya Curi is about to confront a rich and decadent lord. Traveling upcountry from the Pacific, probably returning home from Pachacamac, [108] Huatya Curi falls asleep on the slopes of a mountain. Because of his shamanic powers, Huatya Curi is able to understand the gossip of two foxes, who have stopped to chat. He learns that a lord with vast estates of lands and llamas in the *chaupi-yungas* (coca country) has fallen ill owing to the sexual trangressions of his wife. One fox relates how the lord's wife, while roasting maize one day, has had a kernel of maize pop into her vagina, and has proceeded to feed it to another man. Because of this act (understood as adulterous), her husband, the lord, is dying; the structure of his house is being devoured by a "serpent"; and a two-headed toad dwells beneath the grindstone.

This part of the story was discussed in chapter 4 of the present work, in its astronomical context. The astronomy of the myth, devolving upon the significance of the "two-headed toad" (*hanp'atu*) beneath the grindstone (*maras*) yields an astronomical date of ca. A.D. 850, that is, the same date proposed by archaeology for the collapse of Wari. Therefore the two hundred years between the "flood" and the collapse of the house of the decadent lord appears to represent the period of chaos and warfare brought on by an "unknown" (foreign) people, who "recognized only the strong and the rich." In other words, the fifth chapter apparently begins with a description of the collapse of Wari influence in the Huarochirí region in A.D. 850. It was at this time, according to the stories, that the war god was born. This interpretation is amply supported by the rest of the myth.

Next, the fox mentions that no healer has been able to cure the man, and Huatyacuri sees in the situation an opportunity to better his lot. When he goes to the house of the lord, he proposes to cure the lord in exchange for the hand of his daughter in marriage. Desperate, the lord agrees. When Huatya Curi reveals how the lord has been cuckolded and, worse, that the only cure is to pull down his beautiful house, the lord opts to save his own life and complies.

Now a new character enters the story: the son-in-law of the hapless lord. When he realizes that his father-in-law actually intends to keep his promise and give away the promised daughter in marriage, the son-in-law flies into a towering rage. "You," he screams, "who are a wretch, have taken my sister-in-law as wife, she who is rich and powerful!" This is an unequivocal assertion of class privilege, as the bedrock of any class system lies in establishing what is called an exogamous marriage restriction, that is, a situation in which men of the lower class cannot marry women of the upper class. This situation also means that the lord and his rich son-in-law are following rules of patrilineal descent. Therefore they cannot be aboriginal agricultural people, following a double-descent system.

Next, the outraged and arrogant son-in-law challenges Huatya Curi to prove his worth in a series of tests including dancing, singing, music, building, and drinking. Despite all the son-in-law's access to superior costumes, instruments, building materials, and so on—in short, every material thing wealth and power can provide—he is bested in all these endeavors. Huatya Curi displays the superiority of the inner world, as he receives help every step of the way from the wild animals. This episode is the mirror of *Huarochirí's* second chapter, in which Wiraqocha consults with the animals. Huatya Curi's dominance is a triumph of the old ways over the new. After winning all the contests, Huatya Curi is so disgusted and angered that he turns his opponent's wife to stone and drives the man away. The lord's son-in-law turns into a deer—revealing his uncivilized nature—and he is driven up-mountain, off to the east.[109] So, at the same time (A.D. 850) that the lord's house collapses, his son-in-law—the most vociferous in support of class privilege—is sent packing up and east, back across the pass at Mount Pariacaca, in the direction of Wari.

Besides his excessive displays of wealth, and the aura of decadence emanating from his house, the lord of the manor displays two further characteristics diagnostic of Wari influence. First we learn the origin of the lord's claim to the superior social status so jealously guarded by his son-in-law: the lord has claimed that he is a god. When the fox first speaks to Huatya Curi, he says that the powerful lord "acts as if he were a god" and "pretends to be a god."[110] According to the story, it was the lord's dazzling and calculated displays of wealth that "fooled" the common people into "considering him a god."[111]

Here, then, one finds the mythic analogue of the archaeological record of Wari: a form of rule based upon intimidation clothed in the guise of a new religion. The "false god" of Huarochirí, the decadent lord, therefore bears a remarkable resemblance to the Lords of Wari. In fact, it may be instructive here to look again at figure 8.1—representative of that distinctive pottery tradition of Wari which replaced images of supernatural entities with portraits of actual elite rulers—in order to form a clearer picture of the "false god" of Huarochirí myth. The most telling detail of all is the use to which this character puts his power:

This man, seeing that his life was luxurious, had the people from the villages of all parts come, and *he counted them*, and then posing as a wise man he lived, fooling many men despite his limited intelligence.[112] [Emphasis added.]

The presence in the Quechua text of the word "to count"—*yupay*—provides, in my opinion, the single clearest reference in any Andean source to the intrusion of Wari. As already mentioned, archaeologists are of the opinion that it was the state of Wari that invented the labor tax, and deployed this system of wealth-making between A.D. 650 and 850. The essential precondition to raising labor for taxation is the power to call for a census, precisely the activity that the lord-who-would-be-a-god has undertaken.[113] In this description of a "count" made by a "house" that, too decadent to stand, is "pulled down" in A.D. 850, lies the clearest account of Wari's collapse, and the reasons for it, that we are ever likely to find.

Therefore, anyone with an interest in the origins of warfare might find it profitable to read the indigenous description, from the concluding portion of the fifth chapter, of the birth of the god of war. This account is arguably the single most pristine explanation for the causes of warfare to be found in any historical source, anywhere.

> [F]rom the five eggs which Pariacaca had placed on the mountain, there flew forth five falcons. These five falcons turned into men and set forth walking. And because they had heard enough of the deeds of these men—their forcing others to worship them and their utterances, such as "I am god,"—these five were so enraged by these and other sins that they rose up, turned themselves into the rain, and washed every house and every llama into the sea, sparing not a single hamlet.[114]

The lord and his retinue are driven "into the sea": back toward the Pacific coast and Pachacamac, the client state of Wari, for whom this "false god" likely served as provincial governor. *Sic semper tyrannis.*

The rest of the myths of Huarochirí describe the aftermath of the collapse of the house of the lord. These stories describe two successive phases. First, some time passes. The opening lines of the sixth chapter begin,

> Once Pariacaca had become human and was full grown, he began to search for his enemy.
> His enemy's name was Huallallo Caruincho. . . .[115]

After the collapse of the house of the "false god," the war god "matures" and, now grown, has an enemy to face. As his name implies,[116] this enemy is also foreign to the region. This situation implies that some outside polity attempted to fill the vacuum left by Wari's collapse, a reading that accords well with what the Huarochirí myths go on to describe, because now the god Pariacaca, in a series of epic battles with this evil *waka*, pursues Huallallo high up into the mountains and succeeds in driving him over the pass at Pariacaca mountain. Once Huallallo is driven out, Pariacaca's brother (one of the five falcon-men born from the five eggs) is forever after stationed at this spot, "lest Huallallo Caruincho return."[117]

The most likely identification for Huallallo Caruincho is that he represents a tribal confederation known as the Huancas, also traditional pastoralists, who lived in the lands to the east of the pass at Pariacaca. This is the region of Juaja, which controlled access to the ancient road where it turned west, toward the pass at Pariacaca, the gateway to the central Pacific coast. As he drove Huallallo over this pass, Pariacaca's parting curse upon his enemy was "because he fed on people, let him now eat dogs, and let the Huanca people worship him."[118] As Salomon and Urioste have recognized, this passage represents an "implied claim" by the Yauyos of having liberated the west Andean peoples from the "dog-eating" Huanca.[119]

Here, then, is a specific account of an event universally implicit in the "lost years" of the Andean archaeological record: a period of turmoil after the collapse of Wari in A.D. 850. The Yauyos, rising to the status of warriors, drive off the Huancas, foreign pastoralists with links to Wari,[120] who have attempted to fill the power vacuum left by Wari's demise.

And now, finally, the narrators describe how, in the final phase of the chain of events leading to the establishment of the moiety system in their region, they moved into the agricultural villages of the aboriginal peoples and took for themselves a portion of prime agricultural lands. These stories make up the lion's share of the manuscript, and it is not necessary to follow them in detail. From the present perspective, the important point about them is how doggedly they adhere to the theme of justice and justification. It is clear from reading these myths that the Yauyos took great pains to establish their bona fides as legitimate participants in the tradition of Wiraqocha.

A single example from the sixth chapter of the text will make clear the oxymoronic nature of forcing one's way into a system of voluntary reciprocity. Here Pariacaca himself, pretending to be "just like a friendless stranger,"[121] visits a yunca (= aboriginal, warm-valley) village where the inhabitants are carousing at a festival. In violation of the ancient norms of hospitality, no one there offers Pariacaca refreshment, until one woman realizes the breach of decorum and serves up a large portion of maize beer. Then Pariacaca warns her to take flight because "these people have made me damn mad."[122] He warns her to tell no one else. Five days later he returns as a torrential rainstorm and annihilates the entire village, washing it into the sea.

Here again in this story, Pariacaca is cast in the paradigmatic mythical mold of the friendless stranger. But unlike the myths of Wiraqocha, where the god travels afar with the sole aim of spreading a teaching of loving-kindness, Pariacaca has already entered the village with a chip on his shoulder. Unlike Wiraqocha, who immediately ceases punishing the villagers at Cacha as soon as the threat to his person has passed, Pariacaca has come looking for trouble, hoping to be offended.[123]

Exactly here lies the center of gravity of the Huarochirí myths. The Yauyos no doubt felt entitled to take lands: they had rid the area of a bane. They had defended an already ancient constellation of spiritual ideas against an unregenerately secular and duplicitous state. But if they were to maintain justly their claims to more land, how could they do so without disrupting the divinely ordained partition of lands—the doctrine of the *wakas* and *pacarinas*—which they claimed to defend? Thus painted into a cosmological corner, the warrior moieties would respond with a gambit that would change the Andes forever.

V

THERE IS AN element approaching the comical in the way the Yauyos labored to place their ancestral deity, Pariacaca, within the greater framework of Andean thought. At the beginning of the manuscript after promising to tell the story of Pariacaca, the tellers throw in an aside:

> At that time there was another *waka* called Cuniraya who existed then, but we don't really know if Cuniraya came before or after Pariacaca, or if this Cuniraya existed at the same time as Wiraqocha, who created mankind; because in prayer people said, "Cuniraya Wiraqocha, creator of mankind, creator of the world, you possess all there is to possess; yours are the fields, yours the people."[124]

The second chapter begins with a similar disclaimer, but by the fourteenth chapter the narrators seem to be giving ground:

> They say that Cuni Raya Viracocha did exist from very ancient times. Paria Caca and all the other *huacas* used to revere him exceedingly.
> In fact, some people even say Paria Caca is Cuni Raya's son.[125]

They return to the question again in the next chapter:

> Cuni Raya Vira Cocha is said to have existed from very ancient times.

Before he was, there was nothing at all in the world. It was he who first gave shape and force to the mountains, the forests, the rivers, and all sorts of animals, and to the fields for humankind's subsistence as well.

It's for this reason that people in fact say of Cuni Raya, "He's called Paria Caca's father."

"It was he who made and empowered Paria Caca."

"If Paria Caca weren't his son, he probably would have humbled him," all the people say.[126]

With that grudging "probably," the matter is ended. Cuniraya Wiraqocha came first. Pariacaca was "empowered" by him, and in fact would have been "humbled," were he not the "son" of Wiraqocha. It's all a bit like pulling teeth, but the Yauyo tellers, in the end, acknowledge the traditional Andean order of things. In the same way that they grumbled about the ancestor worship of the peasantry, one can almost hear them grousing, "All right, already! Wiraqocha came first. *He* created the world. Pariacaca is his son." This was the tradition that the warriors of Huarochirí had to acknowledge in order to appear its defenders.

Yet it was here, precisely in the midst of all this bluster, that the narrators had planted an unprecedented claim concerning their lineage *waka*, a claim as simple as it was bold. And it was here that all my efforts to sort out the significance of the "flood" of A.D. 650 coalesced around a single realization. If Pariacaca was Wiraqocha's "son"—at first glance an embarrassing if necessary admission of warrior "juniority" to the peasantry—then a single simple fact followed inevitably: *Pariacaca was a planetary god.* If the Huarochirí war god was a "son," then he must be of the same "species" as his "father." *Cuni* Raya Wiraqocha, cognate with *Con* Ticce Wiraqocha, makes clear the view from Huarochirí—where the *pichca-con-qui* ("our five planetary deities") were worshiped—concerning the pedigree of Wiraqocha. The war god and lineage *waka* of the Yauyo—the "son" of Wiraqocha/Saturn—was a planet.

When I first realized the meaning of Pariacaca's genealogy, I went blank. I didn't know if I knew more, less, or the same as before. The information didn't seem inclined to occupy a mental category in my repertoire. I had to jump-start my brain by analyzing my assumptions about the closest analogous information in my possession: the Inca claim that their mythical ancestor, Manco Capac, was, if not the "son," then at least the favorite, of Jupiter. I quickly realized that I had assumed the Incas had projected this claim back into the remote past as a means of establishing the legitimacy of their imperial rule. The Huarochirí case didn't fit this mold. In fact, if it made one thing clear, it was that the "birth" of Pariacaca took place about A.D. 850. So

much for "projecting back." Did this mean that the Incas, too, had an ongoing tradition of planetary "affiliation" from an equally remote date? Did the
fact that *two* important tribal regions—Huarochirí and the valley of Cuzco
—supported mythical traditions of planetary involvement with their warrior
caste have anything to do with the formation of the moiety systems? If the
Yauyos did assert a claim of planetary descent in A.D. 850, then what was
it *for?*

But this was putting the cart before the horse.

I realized I was obliged to proceed methodically. First I had to find out
—in the same way that I had investigated the mythical nature of Manco
Capac—if the Huarochirí text really supported the view that Pariacaca was
a planetery deity.

In chapter sixteen of the Huarochirí myths, Pariacaca does battle with
his enemy, the fire-wielding Huallallo Caruincho. Under relentless attack
from the thunderbolts of Pariacaca, Huallallo Caruincho unleashes a gigantic
two-headed serpent, *amaru*, which attacks Pariacaca. Suddenly, Pariacaca is
armed with a new and different weapon, "a staff of pure gold," with which
he spears the serpent, pinning it so that it "freezes" (*chiray*), and is henceforth
harmless, turned into stone. Avila's scribes recorded the Quechua word for
this staff, *tauna*, a dialectical variant of *tuna*, the staff of Tunapa Wiraqocha:[127]

Tauna. Staff, pillar, post, architectural pier.[128]

Here also we encounter for the first time an image of the great serpent.
Salomon and Urioste have commented on this passage, "Amaru is the great
mythic water serpent, virtually omnipresent in Andean myths, and usually
symbolic of disorder erupting in the transition to a new order."[129]

Hocquenghem has likewise noted of the mythical serpent, "The *Amaru*
arises at the moment of natural and social catastrophes resulting from a
relationship of unequal forces, because of a disequilibrium. The appearance
of the *Amaru*, sudden and violent, is a sign of change, of alternation, of
pachacuti."[130]

On the level of astronomy, the connection of the *amaru* with catastrophes,[131] or *pachakutis*, is clarified in a number of sources. As has already been
shown from Iroquois myth, the sundering of earth and sky transpired under
the auspices of a serpent, which first seduced a maiden and then, when she
had plummeted into the new world of agriculture, gave her the seeds and
utensils of the new way of life. In another transforming moment, the Andean
"house of the false god" was tottering because a "serpent" was eating away at
its joints.

Tellingly, in the same way that Andean myth uses both architectural and topographical metaphors to describe the "structure" of the cosmos at a given moment in precessional time, the serpent appears as a de-structive force not only in an architectural context (as above), but also in topographic imagery. A colonial document from extirpators of the Archbishopric of Lima records a myth concerning a giant serpent called *"guayarera"*:

> These are some giant serpents which move beneath the earth and have a habit of making mountains fall, and when the said mountains topple and fall, they say that it is this *guayarera* which demolished them.[132]

Here the serpent, like the S-curve of a seismic shock, is identified with tectonic upheavals. On the astronomical level, this metaphor identifies the serpent with those forces that bring down "mountains" (or "houses"), that is to say, those structural elements determinant of the four corners of the "celestial earth," namely the relationship of the heliacal rise of stars to given solar dates, the parameters of a world-age. On the level of astronomy, the giant serpent causes upheavals on the "celestial earth." Thus Pariacaca, as with Manco Capac, establishes his right to rulership of a new age—the Age of the Warriors—by properly wielding the axis of the celestial sphere inherited from his "father," Wiraqocha. But whereas Wiraqocha plumbs, and Jupiter hurls, Pariacaca impales.[133]

Thus, Pariacaca "freezes the snake," that is, "fixes" a new relationship of stars and solar dates, thereby demonstrating his ableness to establish and rule the age. Power will restore equilibrium. And by establishing his power to create and maintain stability in the face of the most destabilizing of forces, Pariacaca once again projects the image of warrior as champion of the agricultural peasantry.

If possession and proper utilization of the *axis mundi* identifies Pariacaca as a legitimate planetary heir to Wiraqocha, it is his peculiar use of lightning that clarifies his precise identity. In his assaults on Huallallo Caruincho, Pariacaca unleashes devastating waves of lightning bolts. These bolts are so powerful that they change the landscape, leveling mountains. In the Inca myths of the foundation of Cuzco, one of Manco Capac's brothers, Ayar Cachi, was said to level mountains by means of mighty slingstones.[134] As already noted, the notion of the lightning bolt as a hurled weapon, was a pan-Andean conceit, associated with pastoralist/warrior metaphors of patrilineal descent. Ayar Cachi was, however, so fierce and warlike that his brothers and sisters felt compelled to resort to a ruse, inducing him to return to their cave of origin in search of some forgotten items. There they entomb him, in an attempt to contain his ferocity.

This apparent reference to the retrograde motion of Mars (see chapter 5, note 32) also describes a sophisticated political lesson, perhaps learned by the Incas in contemplation of the mythical record of Wari, that the ethos of war must be "contained"—that is, tempered—if true empire is successfully to be established. Nonetheless, the siblings regret the loss of their fierce brother, who could have helped them in time of war.[135] Then Ayar Cachi reappears and, far from seeking vengeance, declares:

> Do not fear . . . for I only come that the empire of the Incas may begin to be known. . . . I will remain in the form and fashion that you will see on a hill not distant from here . . . Guanacauri. And in return for the good things that you will have received from me, I pray that you will always adore me as [a] God, and set up altars in that place. . . . If you do this, you shall receive help from me in war. . . .[136]

The hill on the horizon of Cuzco, Guanacauri, where this brother henceforth resided, was the second most important shrine in the Inca Empire, after the Temple of the Sun and before the Temple of Wiraqocha at Cacha. It was here that the young warriors were initiated. Thanks to the Anonymous Chronicler, we know that the planetary identity of the Inca war god was the red planet, Mars, known as Aucayoc, "he with enemies." As for Pariacaca, who, like Ayar Cachi, leveled mountains when in a martial rage, his name means "stone of red cinnabar."[137]

So there it was. The Yauyos claimed descent from Mars.

But why? What did this claim signify? Why did this idea, like Pariacaca himself, make its appearance in about A.D. 850? No peasant of Huarochirí, or, so far as is known, the *capacas* of Tiahuanaco, or even the Incas, who merely traced their ancestry through a man (Manco Capac) beloved of Jupiter, had ever made a claim so lofty as direct planetary descent. The lineage *wakas* of the common people were entirely different in nature— subcreations, as it were, of Wiraqocha, representing the mythical lineage sources of the double-descent system. Presented with the problem of creating a balance between the intention of taking land and the necessity of not appearing to violate ancient norms of the social order, how did the warriors ever conceive it useful to claim a *planet* as their lineage *waka*, when everyone knew that a lineage *waka* was a . . . was . . . what?

That is when I realized: *the lineage* wakas *of the peasantry represented stars.*

The longer I thought about this idea, the more certain I was that it was true. Grasping now for the first time the true magnitude of the "creation" at Titicaca, I also began to understand the cunning involved in the claim of planetary descent by the warriors. This idea had not simply sealed the fate of the secular state of Wari. Once accepted by the peasantry, it would irrevocably transform the spiritual tradition of the Andes.

<h1 style="text-align:center">VI</h1>

ONTOLOGY IS ONE of those formidable terms of Greek derivation that one unlimbers only in cases of extreme emergency. Defined as "the branch of metaphysics which studies the nature of existence or being as such,"[138] this is not a concept that comes trippingly to the mind of Westerners. Politely inquiring, "Who is he?" one expects the sort of reply—"Oh, he's a distributor for a major pharmaceutical firm"—that lets ontological dogs lie. English is a language with such a firm grasp on the functional that it has trouble express-ing the "being-dimension" of experience.

As described briefly (and functionally) in chapter 2, the notion of the lineage *wakas* promoted the principles of peaceful unity-in-diversity among the various highland tribes by virtue of each tribe's descent from a common class of objects created by Wiraqocha. Likewise the doctrine of the *pacarina*, or place of "dawning," whence emerged each tribal lineage *waka*, established the right of each ethnic group to its tribal lands. Finally, because the *wakas* were not human and were single objects of indeterminate sex, they provided the etiological basis for the origins of the double-descent system, so crucial in the formulation of Andean agricultural communities.

Now I reread Molina's description of the creation at Titicaca:

[T]he creator began to raise up the people and nations that are in that region [Titicaca], making one of each nation of clay, and painting the dresses that each one was to wear . . . and to each nation was given the language that was to be spoken, and the songs to be sung, and the food that they were to sow. When the Creator had finished painting and making the said nations and figures of clay, he gave life and soul to each one, as well men as women, and ordered that they should pass under the earth. Thence each nation came up in the places to which he ordered them to go. They say that some came out of caves, others issued from hills, others from fountains, others from the trunks of trees . . . and they say that the first that was born from that place was there turned into stones, others say that the first of their lineages were turned into falcons, condors, and other animals and birds. Hence the *huacas* they use and worship are in different shapes.[139]

This time my attention was drawn to what the *wakas* actually *were*. Insofar as the images created by Wiraqocha had form, *they were animals*. This aspect of Molina's version is repeated in numerous other sources. Various chroniclers described the lineage *wakas* of various tribes as statues, usually of stone— though sometimes of wood or even copper, as in the case of the Cañari— some with no discernible biomorphic form, some in the form of birds or animals.[140] I had been so long accustomed to relating the formulation "stars are animals" to the behavior of animals in myths, that I had never thought to apply it to the lineage *wakas*. As soon as this idea came into my head, it brought to mind a mountain of information.

The notion that each species of animal had a celestial prototype respon-sible for the welfare of that species is a well-established fact of Andean ethnography. As noted, Urton has shown how, in present-day Misminay, the birth of terrestrial foxes is related to the seasonal rhythms of the celestial Fox.[141] Likewise Zuidema and Urton have demonstrated that Inca rituals for the augmentation of the llama flocks were timed according to various posi-tions of the celestial Llama.[142] These notions were familiar also to the Span-ish chroniclers. Acosta wrote,

They [the Indians] attributed differing responsibilities to different stars, and those who had need of their favor worshipped them, . . . And, generally, they believed that for every [species of] animal and bird that there is on earth, its likeness is in the sky, whose responsibility was its [i.e., each species] procreation and augmentation.[143]

Cobo, likewise, says, "In short, for each species of animals they knew a star in the sky, and so there are many [stars] which they worshipped and they had set names and assigned sacrifices."[144]

The Anonymous Chronicler gave the most complete description of this phenomenon:

To other stars, like the various signs of the zodiac, they gave various duties to care for, guard, and sustain; some in relation to the flocks, others for the lions, others for the serpents, other for plants, and so on for all things.

Then some groups said that in each one of these gods, or stars, there existed the ideals and models of those living beings whose welfare was their responsibility; and so they said that such and such a star had the shape of a lamb [i.e., llama], because it was its duty to protect and conserve sheep [llamas]; such and such a star [had the] figure of a lion; such and such a star [had the] figure of a serpent. And that it came about that here on earth were fashioned statues or images of those ideas or things, according to the responsibility each one had. And in this way began idols of stone, wood, gold, silver, etc., and that they said those represent the gods that were in the sky.[145]

The Chronicler's description of these statues is virtually identical with descriptions by others of the statues of the lineage *wakas*. According to the Anonymous Chronicler, statuary represented the celestial prototype and guardian of earthly life-forms. Cobo, likewise, suggests a similar possibility when he speaks of the responsibility of the lineage *wakas* toward the *ayllus* in *exactly* the same way that Acosta and the Anonymous Chronicler talk about the responsibility of the guardian stars to their respective animal species:

> Among them [the Indians] there arose very many places of worship and *guacas*, each province having its own . . . and these *wakas* were the founders and head of each nation. The reason they had this worship was *for the conservation and propagation of the people of the given province.*[146] [Emphasis added.]

The Huarochirí manuscript provides clear reference to this same concept of the lineage *waka* as "creator-sustainer." Here the the *wakas* are addressed in terms of their responsibility to "the people which you created, which you made."[147] Likewise, Arriaga recorded the prayer of a supplicant to the *waka*: "I come here and bring these things [offerings] which your children, your creatures [criaturas] offer you; receive them and do not be angry, and give them life, and health, and good fields. . . ."[148] Arriaga also recorded a pregnant title of the lineage *wakas*: runapcamac, literally "the people's maker."

Salomon and Urioste, in commenting on the use of the second part of this word, *camac*, in the Huarochirí myths, reveal the immensity of the concept:

> [The verb] *camay* escapes the seemingly handy glosses "to create" (because "create" connotes an *ex nihilo* act, while *camay* connotes the energizing of extant matter) and "to fashion" (because "fashion" suggests only an initial shaping of inert matter, whereas *camay* is a continuous

act that works upon a being as long as it exists). But what does *camay* mean? The astronomical or astrological chapter 29 [of the Huarochirí myths] gives a crucial clue: it labels a llama-shaped constellation [i.e., the black-cloud celestial Llama] the *camac* (agentive form, "*camay*-er") of llamas. On descending to earth, this constellation infuses a powerful generative essence of llama vitality, which causes earthly llamas to flourish. All things have their vitalizing prototypes or *camac*, including human groups; the *camac* of a human group is usually its *huaca* [*waka*] of origin.[149]

Further, the notion of "star-guardians" of animal species in the Andes has demonstrable links to a worldwide tradition stretching back all the way to Upper Paleolithic times. (See Appendix 5.) There are numerous reasons for seeing in the notion of lineage *wakas*—the guardian spirits of individual ethnic groups—an extension of this same, ancient logic. The first such line of evidence is etymological.

As noted in the previous chapter, the word *waka* is connected with the proto-Maya word for macaw, *wok*, known in Quechua as *akwa*. First, it should be pointed out that all these words—*waka*, *akwa*, and macaw (from the Tupi-Guaran *macaú*)—are all metatheses of each other, indicative in linguistic theory of a genetic link. As with the Mayan "*wok, guok,* or *guoc*, which designates the mythical bird which descends from the sky,"[150] the mythical descent of the *guacamaya/akwa*/macaw marked the appearance of the lineage *waka* of the Cañari.

The symbolism of the macaw played an important part in the worship of the lineage *wakas*. In ceremonies in Huarochirí in anticipation of the return of the dead, the wing of a macaw was placed on a rock in the center of the village.[151] The Inca Vilahoma, or high priest, wore a macaw-feather headdress.[152] In Aymara, the word for the macaw-feather display used in ritual was *huarampa*. The word *huara*, forming the root of this Aymara word, means "macaw" in the Lenca branch of the Maya language family. Andean peoples prayed to the *wakas* in a supplicating manner, expressed in wailing and nonhuman vocalizations.[153] The Quechua word for this performance contains the root *waka*, while the Aymara word for the same act contains the root *huara*:

Huaccanni—To wail.

Huaccan—The singing of birds, the croaking howling roaring, or squawking of all kinds of animals.[154]

Huararitha—To wail.[155]

Because the members of the Andean *ayllus* considered themselves descended from *wakas* created by Wiraqocha, they prayed to the *wakas* as *intercessors* between themselves and the divine realm. It seems inevitable that the reason for the persistence of the symbolism of the macaw in this function has to do with the simple fact that macaws, large parrots, speak two different languages—human speech, and the language of the animal world. Thus, when addressing the *wakas*, the people transposed the usual order of things, crying out from the heart with sound but not words, in the hope that the *waka* would "translate" their message to Wiraqocha. So charming a concept was not lost on Dr. Doolittle.

The celestial origin of the lineage *wakas*, like that of the *guacamayas* and the Mayan *wok*, is further suggested by the fact that throughout South America words with roots formed from Mayan words for "macaw"—*waka* and *buara*—are the names of important star animals. Among the Chiriguano, for example, the abode of *ahuara tunpa*, literally "fox god," lies in the stars of the tail of the Western Scorpius.[156] Among Quechua-speakers the word *ahuara* means "tapir" or "big animal,"[157] while among the Chiriguano, the Milky Way was identified as "the way of the tapir."[158] Among the Mocoví of the Gran Chaco desert, belonging to the Guaicuru language group, the word for "star" is *avaccani* (= *a-waká-ni*). Finally, among the Aymara—where, as we have seen with the case of *lari* and *lari lari*, reduplication of a word gives the sense of "essence of,"—*buara-buara*, cognate with the Lenca root for "macaw," is the word for "star."

This linguistic evidence in turn resonates with the ethnohistoric material presented in chapter 3 of this book concerning the abode of the dead in or near the Milky Way. The Quechua saying, "In this world we are exiled from our home in the world above," makes clear the destination of departed souls. As for the true abode of the lineage *wakas*, Arriaga learned that "the spirits of the dead go where their *wakas* are."[159] Q.E.D. With this datum we return full circle to the point of departure, the concept of the "creator-sustainer" of species, *camac*, discussed by Salomon and Urioste in relation to the figure of the celestial Llama. As previously noted, the celestial Llama was said to have been claimed as a lineage *waka* by a number of *ayllus*.

Understanding the place of the lineage *waka* within the greater framework of the technical language of Andean myth opened for me a wholly new and dramatic perspective on the entire doctrine of the creation of the *wakas* and *pacarinas* by Wiraqocha. I now saw how those ideas were anchored deep within the cosmology that lit up the skies above Titicaca at the dawn of the agricultural era. For here we learn that the creation of the stars (the calendar, or order of time) and the creation of the lineage *wakas* (the social order) were two aspects of the same process. By associating the lineage *wakas* with the various luminaries and dark-cloud constellations of the fixed sphere of stars, the creators of this Andean myth succeeded brilliantly in objectifying the new social order, one based on a unity—forged from a galaxy of languages, dress, custom, and so on—among the various ethnic groups up and down the Andes.

Just as each *ayllu* descended from a star, the people of each *ayllu* would live in harmony with all others, in the same manner that each star or constellation lived in fixed harmony with all the other stars. And just as each star or constellation possesses its own unique identity among other unique identities, the various ethnic units descended from unique *wakas* would maintain their ethnic identities while participating in a greater unity.

Moreover, just as each star had a unique *celestial location*, each *ayllu* would have a unique *terrestrial location* determined by the *pacarina*, the mythical point of emergence of the lineage *wakas* at the outset of the agricultural age. That this analogy was intended is shown by the fact that *pacarina* means, literally, "place of dawning," suggesting that the arising of the lineage *wakas* mirrored the heliacal rise of stars at the dawn of the Age of Wiraqocha.

In the doctrine of the *pacarinas* I found fully expressed the breathtaking scope of the cosmological notions that transformed the Andean civilization when both branches of the Milky Way "came to earth," about 200 B.C. Wiraqocha made the lineage *wakas*. He told them to go beneath the "earth." Then, at specific points up and down the Andes, these *wakas*, representing stars and constellations, were commanded to *rise* at locations called "places of dawning."

All this transpired during the era when the Milky Way first began to rise with solstice suns. As we saw in chapter 3, the locations of the various lineage *wakas* were specified as lying on the "banks" of the Milky Way. In marking the terrestrial "sister-villages" of the celestial homeland of the various lineage *wakas*, the *pacarinas* of the aboriginal peoples therefore, by analogy, fashioned from the entire spine of the Andes the terrestrial counterpart of the Milky Way. Each *pacarina* was, in a very real sense, its own "star gate." These facts are further expressed in myth by the "trajectory" of Wiraqocha's journey along the terrestrial analogue of the Milky Way—from Titicaca to Manta in Ecuador—and would later be replicated by the Inca priests in their peregrinations to and from Vilcanota.

In this way the makers of Andean myth, in an act of pure creative genius, forged from a pattern of celestial relationships the guiding principles of an entire civilization. The socioreligious bonds of the Age of Wiraqocha—humility, hospitality to strangers, and pride in one's community—were sacred bonds, the living manifestation of the cosmic order. The unparalleled brilliance of these ideas—offering as they did a level of prosperity, social harmony, and spiritual nourishment utterly without precedent—explains their durability throughout the centuries that would follow. This truly was a religious perspective conducive to awe, to harmony, and to peace.

In my opinion, these ideas represent what Isbell referred to as the "unknown mechanism" of peaceful Andean economic integration, one that has surprised many archaeologists who, for theoretical reasons, have expected to find in the archaeological record of Wari more evidence of "state-building" in the years preceding the advent of war. The doctrine of the lineage *wakas* and *pacarinas* explains why states were neither desirable nor necessary until extreme pressure on the land brought matters to a head. Until it was broken, there was no need to fix it. Perhaps, in the fullness of time, the radical, secular intervention of Wari was inevitable. Or perhaps not. In any case we will never know what, if anything, the *capacas* of Tiahuanaco might have done in response to the ecological and demographic crisis that overcame the Andes in the late sixth century. Such activity, apparently, was not in the stars. What Wiraqocha had wrought—a fruitful marriage of heaven and earth—the warriors would put asunder.

VII

IT WAS WITHIN this tradition—where all the land was owned by the children of the stars—that the warriors had perforce to find a means of legitimizing their own claims to land. In a world where a body of myth, rather than of written law, constituted the foundation of the social, economic, and religious order, the warriors had little choice but to promulgate their own agenda by reference to existing cosmology. Wari had apparently not bothered to pay sufficient attention to peasant sensibilities in asserting its secular domain. The warriors—pastoralists who now felt entitled to a share of the agricultural wealth they had defended from Wari—could not afford to make the same mistake. Since rights to arable land inhered to those born there, the taking of some of those lands by outsiders involved an apparent breach of the original, divinely ordained partition. Thus, in order to lay claim to land, the warriors had to find a way to justify their claims by reference to those same principles of celestial order expressed by the technical language of myth.

For this reason the warriors, like the peasantry, claimed descent from a celestial deity. In the case of the Huarochirí area, this deity was Pariacaca/

Mars, the staff-wielding "son" of Wiraqocha. In the case of the Incas, according to the myth of Pachakuti Yamqui (in which Manco Capac's father was specified as a warlord), Pirua Manco Capac, Jupiter's regent on earth, was the one designated to inherit Wiraqocha's staff. Furthermore, not only did the Incas recognize the cosmological ideas of the peasantry as regards descent from a celestial body; they also copied notions of the ultimate destination of the dead in the homeland of the lineage *waka*: "[W]hen he [Manco Capac] died, he was taken up to the sky, to the house and place of this god called Pirua [Jupiter]. . . ."[160]

So the first step in establishing legitimacy for the warriors was to create for themselves, *ex nihilo*, a descent system that, like that of the peasantry, connected them to divinely created prototypes in the sky. The next problem that had to be surmounted was to create a *cosmological justification* for breaking the exclusive hold on the land of the *ayllus*, whose right of possession was based on celestial analogy, namely that the Andean highlands were the terrestrial analogue of the Milky Way. Simply to take land would be to threaten a Wari-like restoration, a denial of the most deeply held religious sentiments of the entire peasantry. No. The peasantry would have to consent —grudgingly perhaps, but consent they must—to a new kind of order if stability was ever to be reestablished.

It was probably impossible for either the peasants or the pastoralists to remain indefinitely high-minded on an empty stomach. Still, when at last it dawned on me how this sleight of hand had been accomplished, I found the solution unsettling. I was looking at the debasement—perhaps unavoidable, but debasement nonetheless—of an ancient system of thought that for centuries had relied for its efficacy upon the intrinsic beauty of its ideas. I now understood how, by declaring themselves descended from planets, the warriors had managed to break into this system.

Planets are differentiated from stars by their power of *movement*. "Objectively" planets, and hence their terrestrial descendants, could not be expected to be bound by the same "positional imperative" as the descendants of the stars. It was simply in the "natural" order of things that the warriors had the right to "move into" any and all territories they chose, just as the planets were free to wander through the stars. Planets, after all, were the "pastoral nomads" of the sky, shepherds of the stars.

The reality of this conception is mirrored in the ethnographic record. Unlike the peasantry, which possessed a very large number of lineage *wakas*, one for each *ayllu*, there were relatively few lineage *wakas* for the warrior caste. The warriors of Pariacaca, for example, occupied lands throughout two entire provinces—Huarochirí and Chaclla Mama, although they claimed descent from a single ancestral deity.[161] Arriaga found this same pattern prevalent throughout the central Andes: ". . . the Llacuazes ["slayers of llamas"], being outsiders, have fewer Huacas. . . ."[162] In conquering large areas and settling some families within each community, the warriors maintained kinship ties across large territories based on descent from a single planetary deity. Descendants of the planetary deities claimed rights in the land by recourse to celestial analogy. They "moved in" on the aboriginal homelands in precisely the same way that a planet will "move into" a given constellation.

The consequence of this strategy was that the warriors were obliged to behave as if they were of a different "species" from the members of the peasantry. In other words, origin of descent from planets formed the basis for the creation of separate classes of people in the Andes. Thus, as the ethnohistorical record makes clear, a male peasant was prohibited from marrying a daughter of the warrior caste. This strategy assured that descent would continue to be traced through the male line only, hence preserving the lands and power won by the warriors through conquest. Intermarriage with the peasantry could only lead to the ultimate dissolution of the warrior caste. Although Wari was gone, class remained.

This manipulation of Andean cosmology, in accommodation to the advent of warfare, contained one element, as yet unemphasized, which was entirely without precedent and would change forever the nature of Andean life. The introduction of military force into the common life was accompanied by an analogous and equally violent introduction of force into the traditional avenues of cosmological discourse.

So delicate is the nature of the territory upon which this violence trod that it is difficult in our own age, where the debasement of language is a commonplace, to recapture the dimensions of the damage. Until the advent of warfare, Andean cosmological knowledge was a form of spiritual food. With the dawning of the Age of Wiraqocha about 200 B.C. there entered into Andean life not only an unprecedented level of astronomical knowledge, but the systematic cultivation of a Great Idea: that in the macrocosmic model of the heavens, humankind might, through patient observation and reverent contemplation, conceive the nature of those laws whose institution upon earth could guide human society into harmony with the will of deity.

So profound is the human intuition of the material world as a dance encoding the Will of God that it informs all the great religious traditions of our planet. Whether one turns to the Buddhists and the endeavor to escape the great wheel of death and rebirth (the ecliptic plane), or to Noah's Ark above Mount Ararat, or to Christ's overturning of the tables of the moneylenders, or to the Islamic worship of the Creator/Saturn at the Kaaba, the roots of all our traditions lie, with those of the Great Tree of Life, in the starry heavens. Before this inexhaustible source of wonder many of the greatest spirits of humanity have opened heart and mind in a profound spirit of reverence.

Into this interior mansion of the human heart the warriors introduced the spore of Ruin. This was not done merely by the use of force. There are times when force becomes inevitable. Nor was this accomplished simply because the warriors drew upon celestial analogy to establish a kinship network. All of this could have been accepted as the inevitable outcome of pressure on the land, and a sensible means of redistribution to the landless. But the warriors went beyond the need to express pragmatic reality with the means at hand, the technical language of myth. They did violence to the language itself, and they did so in the following way.

The Andean mythographers had established a series of verbal conceits that allowed them to transmit the fruits of astronomical observation to future generations. Among these mnemonic techniques was that which designated planets as "measuring instruments." As discussed in chapter 5, for example, the regularity of conjunctions of Saturn and Jupiter were understood as a useful means for keeping track of the passage of time on the scale of precessional motion. Thus, to both Saturn, as "Ticci Capac," and to Jupiter's regent Manco Capac were given the title of "measurer," the literal meaning of the word *capac*. This word was used by Inca times to mean "king," that is, it had become a term of political dominion. Furthermore, as noted in chapter 5, we know from Bertonio's lexicon that the original title in Aymara, *capaca*, did not designate political control, but was given to those who, following the divine example of Wiraqocha, sought to "measure" the flight of the stars with the palm of the hand. In other words, *capaca* designated, in ancient times, the shaman-astronomer, whose authority was defined by his contribution to the common good.

What this transformation of meaning tells us is that at some point in time, an individual or group of individuals conceived of the idea of disengaging entirely from its natural context the technical language of myth and, by twisting its literal meaning, establishing the basis for political control. The word *capac*, originally assigned to the planet Saturn as the supreme measurer of the passage of time, was quite suddenly ripped from context and applied in an entirely deceptive manner. The heart of this deception lay in the betrayal of language itself. "To measure" was made to mean "to control" in exactly the same manner that the English verb "to rule"—originally meaning "to measure"—came to designate the right of kings to control the populace.

Henceforth, in the Andes, the warriors would claim as divine right their power to "rule" the peasantry based on the following proposition: since the lineage *wakas* of the warriors, namely planets, "ruled" the stars—that is, the lineage *wakas* of the peasantry—then cosmic law mandated that the warriors themselves should "rule" the peasantry. The damage done to Andean civilization by the introduction of this Great Lie is beyond calculation. By treating the technical language of myth as if it were *literally* true, the warriors tainted the seminal ideas of Andean civilization. Henceforth language itself, rather than the celestial realities it was designed to describe, would provide the template for interpreting the sacred.

To be fair, this process may well have begun with Wari. The disturbingly arrogant images on Wari fineware (figure 8.1) and the mythical reference to a Wari governor's claim to be a "god" [163] may indicate that the Lords of Wari were intent on scaring the hell out of local populations by a claim of godlike descent, perhaps directly from Wiraqocha. In naming their capital Wari, they may in fact have claimed to be direct descendants of the Huari, the white, bearded giants—sons of Wiraqocha?—who issued from the Titicaca basin in remote antiquity to civilize the world. In any case, we know from the Huarochirí myths that duplicity in matters of cosmological discourse was an activity that was "in the air" as part of the legacy of Wari.

With the corruption of mythical language, then, came the reversal of all traditional forms of intercourse with the numinous. Where celestial motions had once been studied for clues to the proper order of human life on earth, disorder in the human realm was now projected upon the heavens. The "stars" were in need of a "ruler." The result of such "semanticizing" was to trivialize the dialogue between microcosm and macrocosm, and open the door to the hermetic imprecations of the black magician.

This fracturing of the harmonious legacy created a millennium earlier by the priest-astronomers of Tiahuanaco manifested as the shattering of Andean life into a mosaic of warring polities. Valley by valley, as the reaction to Wari grew, new warrior nobilities arose. The ancient and previously peaceful assertion of pride in ethnic diversity and the unquestioned right to local autonomy now became the source of a bitter and endemic hostility between tribes. The priceless intellectual coinage of the Age of Wiraqocha had been debased by the introduction of a brazen falsehood supported by force. The great cosmological schema that had first breathed life into the Andean *ayllus,* and that was woven into every facet of its life, from language to rite, and from textile design to place names, had been cast adrift from its moorings in the heart. And it was here, in the heart of the Andean experience

—where celestial analogy had been food and drink to those with the hunger and thirst for righteousness—that a great wound would now be opened.

It cannot be said that the events beginning with the *pachakuti* of A.D. 650 destroyed Andean religion. Rather it was, along with humanity, divided into two streams. The religion of the peasantry continued to flow, but to flow, as it were, underground. Henceforth, as each valley system armed itself against all comers, each aboriginal ethnic polity would show a martial face to all others, the face of the warrior moiety of its region. Hemmed in by geography and the aspirations of local warrior nobilities to appear as local heroes, the Andean *ayllus* became self-contained universes. The great cities crumbled, first Wari and then, by A.D. 1000, Tiahuanaco. The bridges were cut. A long, dark age settled over the Andean highlands.

Throughout those dark centuries, the warriors maintained the secret of making bronze. So long as warfare endured and this technical advantage remained theirs, the warriors would continue to "rule." They did not rule by domination of the lower moieties with whom they now shared land. Rather they controlled the Zeitgeist of their time, projecting threat outward and offering defense to their local area. This reality remains as a phenomenon of language, where, in Quechua, the word for "to found bronze," *llacsay*, was taken from the verb "to intimidate,"[164] and in Aymara, where the word *pachakuti* was reduced to a single definition, "time of warfare."[165]

As best they could, the Andean peasantry would maintain the old ways, but no longer would the Andean people address their god with a single voice. In this sense, the myths of the llama and the flood represent the last direct transmission from the age before warfare. The death of an age of innocence has all the air of fable to the contemporary ear. Yet, millennia ago, Lao-tze, in witnessing such a spectacle, spoke as well the epitaph for the Age of Wiraqocha:

> [O]ne loses Reason and then virtue appears.
> One loses virtue and then benevolence appears. One loses benevolence
> and then justice appears. One loses justice and then propriety appears.
> The rules of propriety are the semblance of loyalty and faith and the
> beginning of disorder. Traditionalism is the flower of reason, but of
> ignorance the beginning.[166]

In this same way, the Andean mythical tradition, once a language of sacred revelation grounded in empirical observation, became, in the hands of the warriors, a tool of policy. By asserting that the technical language of

Andean myth was literally true, the warriors took the first step in mystifying an ancient tradition and changing forever the cultural heritage of the Andes. Now cut loose from its original function as a mnemonic powerhouse, the technical language of myth would serve the warriors as a means of intimidation, and neither heaven nor earth would ever be the same. The primordial maxim "as above, so below" ceased to be an invitation to participation in a greater harmony. Now it signaled doom, for suddenly, the principles of war and dominance had been discovered in the sky.

PART III

The War
Against Time

CHAPTER 9

THE INCA PROPHECY

[T]hey made use of these [constellations] for their astrology. . . . They did not make ordinary prognostications from signs in the sun, moon, or comets; but only prophecies of very rare import, such as the death of kings and the fall of empires.[1]

—GARCILASO DE LA VEGA,
"EL INCA"

I

THERE EXISTED IN Peru at the time of the Spanish Conquest a tradition that the Inca Empire was born under the shadow of prophecy. About the year 1432, according to this tradition, Wiraqocha Inca foretold the cataclysmic destruction of Andean civilization within five generations. This prophecy was uttered at a time when Cuzco was under the threat of attack by the Inca's most feared—and hated—foe, the Chancas. Unwilling to accept the fatalistic attitude of his father, the great warrior king Pachakuti Inca proposed a different vision, an Empire of the Sun. Henceforth the sons of the Sun and the daughters of the Moon, as the Incas now styled themselves, would embark upon a sacred mission: to rescue Andean civilization from the brink of extinction. It mattered not that the old father, Wiraqocha Inca, was a learned priest; nor did it matter that omens abounded, that enemies were approaching, that the legacy of eight centuries of intertribal warfare had left land and people exhausted. Where others saw stalemate, or worse, Pachakuti Inca discerned the path to greatness.

If ever a people had a rendezvous with destiny, it was the Incas. The brevity of their moment in the sun belies centuries of unique preparation. More intensely than any other highland region, the valley of Cuzco was steeped in the traditions of both Wari and Tiahuanaco. Despite the fact that Tiahuanaco lay another three hundred miles to the south, the lords of Wari heavily fortified all access to their outpost at Pikillacta in the valley of Cuzco. Though never within anything like a sphere of Tiahuanacan "control," the Cuzco region nonetheless owed its primary cultural orientation to the influence of Tiahuanaco.[2] Since Tiahuanaco was not itself in the habit of sending armies so far afield, the construction, garrisoning and fortification of Pikillacta in A.D. 650 suggests that Wari was not the only power in the immediate vicinity to consider this valley a prize.

Cuzco would become the "navel" of the world, erected at the geographical center of two overlapping and fundamentally opposed worldviews whose stark contrasts have led the architectural historian William Conklin to ask,

> What then does this Huari evidence of spatial containment imply about Huari's relationship with Tiahuanaco? If one were to read this architectural evidence bluntly, it would appear that the Huari architects had radically different purposes for their town planning; perhaps they were actually engaging in some form of ritually stated antithesis of the doorway cult of Tiahuanaco and all of its movement and ritual association.[3]

If imitation is the sincerest form of flattery, then these contrasts imply a spirit rather more malign. This spirit, in active contention with that of Tiahuanaco in the valley of Cuzco, was nowhere more baldly expressed than in a set of spectacular archaeological finds in the Wari complex at Pikillacta. On two different occasions during the 1920s, investigators unearthed separate subfloor caches in elite compounds. In each case, a set of forty figures, each about three inches high, and carved either from turquoise or sodalite, was unearthed. Writing in 1933, Luis Valcárcel described and analyzed one of these caches.[4] Each figure was a male human, carved in such a way as to emphasize its tribal dress. No two figures were alike, meaning that forty ethnically different tribes were represented. All the figures were set in sea sand, and *knocked over*, that is, placed in a position of submission, reminiscent, as Valcárcel points out, of the later Inca practice of treading on the bodies of conquered tribal leaders.

Furthermore, these effigies were set in a *circle* around a central set of objects: a bronze rod, a conch shell and some *Spondylus* shell. When I read Valcárcel's article, the hair stood up on the back of my neck. The bronze rod had a slightly conical taper, which moved Valcárcel, probably correctly, to call the object both a "scepter" and a *makana* or "war club." Although Valcárcel interpreted the conch shell in its usage as a war trumpet, this shell, according to his description, did not have the end cut off to make it a trumpet. The significance of the *Spondylus* shell, an important trade item of Wari, is made clear in the Huarochirí myths, where it is the favored food of war deities.[5] They liked to crunch it.

The axis of Wari's policy, then, was "intimidation," or bronze. The idealized number of forty subject nations, arranged in a circle, at once brings to mind the *seque* system of Cuzco with its forty (or forty-two, depending on how they were counted) rays to the horizon. The significance of the number forty, the number of conjunctions of Saturn and Jupiter required for the trigon to replicate itself in the stars, suggests that the Lords of Wari intended to establish their dominion over the coming Age. That the tribal effigies were arranged in a posture of submission around this bronze axis, in association with the food of the war god and with the conch, suggests that the rulers of Wari intended to "send these people to hell," i.e., back to the underworld, where underlings born from the stars (forty positions of the conjunction of Saturn and Jupiter through the stars of the ecliptic) belonged.

The most unsettling aspect of all this is Valcárcel's detailed analysis of the tribal identity of the figures. At the time Valcárcel wrote, it was believed that Pikillacta was an Inca site. Therefore it did not strike him as odd that one of the figures, whom he undoubtedly identified correctly, was a representative of Tiahuanaco. With the exception of a single skirmish at Moquegua, the forces of Tiahuanaco and Wari never met. Pikillacta—three hundred miles from Tiahuanaco—was as close as Wari ever came to "dominion" over the Titicaca basin. What this means is that the subfloor caches at Pikillacta—placed in the private, indoor recesses of elite compounds—represent *black magic*, that is, the intention of doing harm at a distance. The black magicians of Wari aspired to be stealers of souls. There are good reasons for looking to metaphors like "light and shadow" in describing the contrast between Tiahuanaco and Wari.

While the original inhabitants of the valley of Cuzco marinated in this dialectic, Wari walled off the valley. Among the pastoralists in the mountains above were the Incas. Inca myth tells us where their allegiance lay. (See chapter 5, pages 126–27.) While the Lords of Wari invested the exquisitely beautiful valley of the Vilcamayu, Inca myth says that a warrior-chief named Apotambo, father to Manco Capac, accepted from Wiraqocha the staff with which his son would found Cuzco. His people were a rough and ready lot ("vassals"), not interested in being under anyone's thumb—including Tiahuanaco's—but Apotambo saw the wisdom in siding with the light. As Wiraqocha left the earth, the spirit of his rule was passed to the Incas. And, if one's choice of enemies is an indication of one's convictions, then, truly, the Incas were determined to stand by the legacy of Tiahuanaco. At the critical moment in their history, their mortal enemies would be none other than the Chancas, the lineal descendants of the Lords of Wari.

As if in foreshadowing of their future, the Incas would be the only highland people to inhabit an island of relative tranquillity during the centuries before the establishment of empire. The settlements in the central part of the valley were not defended, suggesting that the Incas, having moved into the valley after the collapse of Wari, were already at work experimenting with some unique form of polity.[6]

Partly through blind chance of geography, partly by historical contingency, and partly owing to the remarkable qualities of a single man— Pachakuti Inca, "Lord Overturner of Space-Time"—the Incas were a people destined for greatness. At the same time, they were human, with all the flaws and contradictions that implies. If their instincts were heliotropic, leading them toward an affinity with Tiahuanaco, they were nonetheless too practical to ignore the *realpolitik* of their time. They knew both the shadow and the light, and the uses thereof. What would set the Incas apart was their willingness to risk *everything*. This is a quality that commands respect even as it makes for tragedy. What follows is an attempt to chart the scope of that tragedy and how I came to learn of it.

My interest in the Inca prophecy grew out of its apparent connection to the changes in Andean cosmological thought precipitated by the rule of Wari and the ensuing damage done to Andean society. The creation of a cosmological justification for warfare had unleashed the darker angels of human nature upon the firmament. What else but a sense of doom could be the fruit of such an exercise? To my mind, the Inca prophecy embodied such perceptions, but if I was being drawn in its direction, it was reluctantly. Historians of the Incas have long regarded the prophecy of Wiraqocha Inca as a sort of litmus test for gullibility.

The Inca prophecy was allegedly uttered at the pivotal moment in Andean history when, by most accounts, the young visionary warrior Pachakuti rejected a curious passivity on the part of his father. Historians have dismissed the tale as the royal family's justification in hindsight for the Spanish success. The source most often quoted concerning the prophecy of Wiraqocha Inca is Garcilaso de la Vega, "El Inca." Garcilaso was the son of a Spanish captain and his concubine, the Inca noblewoman Chimpu Ocllo, niece of Huayna Capac. Though educated as a Spanish gentleman, Garcilaso was ignored by his father, who later married a Spanish woman. He grew to manhood with the family of his mother. At the age of twenty, upon the death of his father, Garcilaso left Peru for Spain, never to return.[7] Much later in life he recorded his memories of the Incas in the massive *Comentarios reales de los Incas,* completed shortly before his death at the age of seventy-six. According to Garcilaso, who was descended on his mother's side from the *panaca,* or patriline, of Wiraqocha Inca, this ancestor, when an old man, prophesied

> that after a certain number of Yncas had reigned, there would come to that land a people never before seen who would destroy the religion and empire of the natives. . . . He ordered that it should be regarded as a tradition among the royal princes, and that it should not be divulged to the common people because it was not right to profane that which came through divine revelation, nor was it wise to allow it to be known that hereafter the Yncas would lose their religion and their empire, and would fall from high estate. For this reason nothing more was said of this prophecy until the Ynca Huayna Capac openly referred to it a little before his death. . . . The Indians gave the name of Wiraqocha to the Spaniards because they caused the fulfillment of this prophecy. . . .[8]

Later, Garcilaso would note that Huayna Capac—the last Inca to reign before the appearance of the Spanish at Cajamarca—died with the prophecy of Wiraqocha Inca on his lips. The prophecy had been handed down through five generations, a closely guarded secret of the royal family. As he lay dying of smallpox, Huayna Capac is said to have revealed to those around him the terrible message of the prophecy: he would be the last Inca before the cataclysm. Such was the prophecy of Wiraqocha Inca.[9] Something of this tradition remains in the accounts of Cieza de León and Murúa, in which Huayna Capac foresaw disaster in association with the reports of a Spanish landing on the coast.[10]

With an uncharacteristic lack of generosity toward the Incas, the great historian William Prescott was among the first to dismiss Garcilaso's account categorically as fantasy. Prescott accepted that Huayna Capac was shrewd enough to see in the reports of white men landing on the north coast of Peru a sign of great danger.

But other accounts which have obtained a popular currency, not content with this, connect the first tidings of the white men with predic-
tions long extant in the country, and with supernatural appearances,
which filled the hearts of the whole nation with dismay. Comets were
seen flaming athwart the heavens. Earthquakes shook the land; the
moon was girdled with rings of fire of many colors; a thunderbolt fell
on one of the royal palaces and consumed it to ashes; and an eagle,
chased by several hawks, was seen, screaming in the air, to hover
above the great square of Cuzco, when, pierced by the talons of his
tormentors, the king of birds fell lifeless in the presence of many of the
Inca nobles, who read in this an augury of their own destructions. . . .

Such is the report of the impressions made by the appearance of
the Spaniards in the country, reminding one of the similar feelings of
superstitious terror occasioned by their appearance in Mexico. But the
traditions of the latter land rest on much higher authority than those
of the Peruvians, which, unsupported by contemporary testimony, rest
almost wholly on the naked assertion of one of their own nation [Garci-
laso], who thought to find, doubtless, in the inevitable decrees of
Heaven, the best apology for the supineness of his countrymen.[11]

Since the time of Prescott, the question of the Inca prophecy has remained
a wraith at the periphery of historical vision.

Nonetheless, Prescott's dismissal of the existence of an Inca prophecy
has left a significant void in the historical understanding of the Spanish
Conquest of Peru. Though he allows a measure of "superstitious terror" a
role in the equally baffling collapse of the Aztecs, he allotted the Incas no
motivation beyond inertia for contributing to their own downfall. Surely
Prescott did not fully intend this slight. It appears rather that in his determination not to succumb on such a critical matter to Garcilaso's undoubted
tendency toward embellishment, Prescott was led to reject what was, 140
years ago, the only source available regarding a prophetic Inca vision.

Whatever its apparent weaknesses, Garcilaso's account of an Inca prophecy at least has the merit of offering some sort of explanation for the utter
annihilation of a great empire by a mere handful of adventurers. The domain
into which Pizarro's 175 men so coolly rode spanned a distance of some
2,500 miles from north to south—the distance from Hudson's Bay to Ha-
vana, or from London to Tashkent—and encompassed a land area equal to
the entire portion of the United States from Maine to Florida east of the
Appalachians. The essence of Garcilaso's argument—and the point on which
he insisted his relatives were adamant—was that the Spanish only succeeded

in gaining a foothold because Huayna Capac, following the prophetic utterance of his ancestor Wiraqocha Inca, had enjoined the Incas "to obey and serve" the newcomers.[12]

Another, explicit version of the Inca prophecy does exist, independent of Garcilaso's tale. First published in 1898, it was not available to Prescott. This account, by the so-called *quipucamayocs* of Vaca de Castro, was taken down in 1542, a scant ten years after the Conquest. The *quipucamayocs*, four elderly record-keepers of the Inca court in Cuzco, told Vaca de Castro a story very similar to Garcilaso's: Huayna Capac, dying of smallpox, called his son Atahuallpa before him and told him that the rumored interlopers were *viracochas*, by which he meant that they were "more than human." He further warned Atahuallpa that he faced great travails. According to the *quipucamayocs*, Huayna Capac called the Spanish *viracochas* because they brought to mind the person of Wiraqocha Inca.[13] In other words, these native informants linked, as did Garcilaso, Huayna Capac's apocalyptic vision back to the Inca Wiraqocha.

Although it is therefore no longer strictly true to characterize Garcilaso's account as "unsupported by contemporary testimony," to use Prescott's words, the account of the *quipucamayocs* is nonetheless open to the same criticism of "naked assertion" as those of Garcilaso. An incident described by Garcilaso underscores the futility of judging the authenticity of the prophecy on the basis of what anyone might have said. Garcilaso recounts how, while a child in Cuzco, he once asked an old *orejone* ("big-ear," a reference to the golden ear-spools worn by Inca nobility), related to his mother, how the Incas, with such numerical and geographical advantage, could have been conquered by a handful of Spaniards. The old man stated that Huayna Capac had ordered his people to serve the Spanish and repeated the prophecy.

> Having said this he turned to me somewhat angrily, as if I had accused his people of cowardice and weakness, and answered my question, saying, "These words which our Ynca uttered were the last he spoke to us, and were more powerful to subjugate us and deprive us of our empire than the arms which your father and his companions brought into this land. . . ."[14]

The old man got angry either because the criticism implicit in the child's question was merited, or because it was not merited. One might as well reach for a fistful of smoke.

And yet . . . There were certain indications, here a rite, there a toponym, bits and pieces of information scattered throughout the chronicles, which niggled at me like ill-remembered dreams at the threshold of memory. Where once the antics of Fox and the stately march of the celestial Llama had filled the Andean sky with the legacy of Tiahuanaco, the Incas perceived fell objects—"the one who eats his parents"—while distant, subject tribes spoke also tales of dis-asters looming. A myth from Huarochirí appears among the Aztecs, identical but reworked in the idiom of doom, only to resurface among the Incas. In time the pattern presented itself to my waking mind.

In that moment I had, I believed, touched for an instant the terrible burden and tragic urgency of the Inca vision. The manifestation of this vision, the Inca Empire, had been destroyed in a manner to this day so unbelievable that few schoolchildren are ever told the tale of its demise. What I had glimpsed was so odd that it appeared, paradoxically, to corroborate and therefore jeopardize the credibility of everything I thought I had learned. The Spanish Conquistadores had ridden into the heart of an experiment without known precedent in human history, an experiment by which the contemporary imagination might take the measure of its own impoverishment.

It was also an experiment that defies conventional historical analysis. The scale of the enterprise, quite literally superhuman, dealt in theories of cause and effect utterly discredited in our day. Moreover, the Incas would maintain to the end that the imperial endeavor was a divinely mandated public service. In our time historical inquiry weighs heavily in favor of the practical—political, economic, and social variables. From such a perspective, religion, understood as the stalking horse of special interest, becomes a phenomenon of secondary import, a function of other agendas, rather than a motivating force in its own right. And if such an approach projects a contemporary fascination with power, wealth, and prestige onto the screen of the past, it is only because that is how it has always been for human beings, or so we are told. To stray very far from this truth is to betray flawed powers of judgment, a lack of sophistication as regards the immutability of human nature.

To a certainty, I would never have dared to write the final chapters of this book, had I not come upon a particular myth recorded in the chronicle written by the priest Martín de Murúa. Until that moment I simply had had no means to substantiate what I suspected to be, quite literally, the secret of the Incas. This tale, as preserved by Murúa, constitutes the Inca prophecy in its purest form. Constructed out of the technical language of myth, it represents, in my opinion, the single most important document concerning the origins of the Inca Empire which has survived to the present.

The pages that follow begin with an examination, from the perspective of conventional history, of the great tensions, both inner and outer, under which Inca society labored in the early 1400s. Those conditions constitute the context within which the Inca prophecy was uttered. They also represent the nexus of forces that propelled the Incas to greatness. The remainder of the chapter seeks to demonstrate how just those forces that augured the disintegration of Andean life in the social sphere were perceived as operating simultaneously on the celestial sphere. It was this perception that gave birth to the Inca prophecy. The reaction to it, known to history as the Inca Empire, is the subject of chapter 10, which describes the measures taken by the Incas, beginning with Pachakuti Inca, in an all-out effort to forestall what the Inca Wiraqocha had perceived as inevitable.

II

GARCILASO'S ACCOUNT OF the prophecy of Wiraqocha Inca specifies three elements: the return of Wiraqocha, the destruction of Andean religion, and a time frame of five generations within which the events would unfold. The conditions with which Andean society struggled in the era of Wiraqocha Inca provide in every way a believable context for such an utterance. Wiraqocha, the god of the peasantry, was, in his fiercest aspect, the god of just retribution. The dangerously disintegrative forces abroad in Andean society at the beginning of the fifteenth century, to which we now turn, not only justified the fear of terrible consequences, but formed a framework in which such a catastrophe might be expected. A state of vicious, endemic, and escalating warfare—the antithesis of the teaching of Wiraqocha—was, by all accounts, the predominant reality within and around the Inca heartland in the early 1400s.

There are a number of stories concerning prophecies, omens, secrets, and portents preserved about the Incas which described the period from the end of the reign of Wiraqocha Inca to the accession and consolidation of power by his son Pachakuti Inca Yupanqui. Accounts of the transition of power between those two reigns constitute the most intensely ambiguous and contradictory material in all the Spanish Chronicles. According to all accounts, this transition transpired under the threat of imminent attack by the Chancas, a fierce warrior confederation from the very heart of the old Wari state, two weeks' march to the west. Drawing on the chronicles, Loren McIntyre paints a vivid picture of the Chancas, who

> considered the Incas mere upstarts. . . . The Chancas considered them-
> selves to be descended from the puma, and wore feline heads on top of
> their own, wrote Garcilaso. They plaited their long hair in many tiny
> braids, and used fierce war paint made of vermillion [paria] from the
> mercury mines of Huancavelica. For years the Chanca chieftains—one
> called himself Lord of All the Earth—edged ever closer to the Inca
> capital, swallowing up the Quechua nation en route. Finally a Chanca
> general demanded Cuzco's capitulation, lest he dye his lance in Inca
> blood.[15]

In most versions this war was waged and won by Pachakuti Inca, paving the way for the establishment of the Empire of the Sun.

The fundamental issue aired in the various versions of this tale was the character of the two Incas. According to Garcilaso, Murúa, Cieza de León, and Montesinos, Wiraqocha Inca was a great man.[16] Garcilaso, unlike most others, has Wiraqocha Inca defeating the Chancas. Cieza simply says that he was too old to fight when the Chanca threat emerged. Pachakuti Yamqui and Sarmiento de Gamboa, on the other hand, portray Wiraqocha Inca as weak, cowardly, and vacillating in the face of impending invasion.[17] The quipucamayocs, informants to Vaca de Castro, flatly state that Wiraqocha Inca was the greatest soldier, statesman, and leader ever to rule the Incas,[18] while the Anonymous Chronicler records that under Wiraqocha Inca the priesthood, which he favored, was guilty of treason by fomenting rebellion.[19] In Betanzos's version, the son Pachakuti, fresh from his victory over the Chancas, completely humiliated his father, forcing him to drink from filthy vessels and calling him a woman.[20] Pachakuti Yamqui recalled tales of another such humiliation of the old Inca, when his son Pachakuti Inca withheld proper burial rights from his own father.[21]

The origin of this bitter controversy must be sought in the dynamics of the social divisions of the pre-imperial Incas. This class division was the legacy of the Age of the Warriors. As was the pattern throughout the Andean highlands as the result of the institutionalization of war, the Incas were divided into upper and lower (hanan and hurin) moieties. Wiraqocha Inca belonged to the lower moiety,[22] associated with the "conquered" group, the aboriginal inhabitants of the Valley of Cuzco. According to Zuidema, "From other data on the prelude to the war against the Chancas it appears that the relationship between the moieties was also expressed as a kinship relationship [between Pachakuti Inca and Wiraqocha Inca] which in addition symbolized the opposition of worldly authority (the upper moiety) to spiritual authority (the lower moiety)."[23] Demarest has succinctly summarized Zuidema's views by saying, "Zuidema argues that [the god] Viraqocha as culture hero was patron of the non-Inca conquered peoples and the lower moiety of Cuzco."[24]

Finally, Zuidema has shown that the Inca Empire functioned as a diarchy; that is to say, each moiety had its own king,[25] apparently a reflection of the pre-imperial situation in which each moiety possessed its own institutions of leadership. The upper moiety was more secular, military, and administratively oriented, while the lower moiety was more traditional, agricultural, and religiously oriented[26]—shades of Wari and Tiahuanaco. Thus the conflicting reports on Wiraqocha Inca and Pachakuti Inca may be understood as the conflicting viewpoints of the warrior and peasant classes in pre-imperial Cuzco. Sarmiento de Gamboa was well aware of the necessity of taking into account the moiety or, as he said, "party" of an informant in trying to understand contradictory information:

> By examining the oldest and most prudent among them, in all ranks of life, who had most credit, I collected and compiled the present history, referring the sayings and declarations of one party to their antagonists of another party, for they are divided into parties, and seeking from each one a memorial of its lineage and that of the opposing party.[27]

Although the moiety divisions of Cuzco provide a framework for understanding the conflicting opinions about Wiraqocha Inca and Pachakuti Inca, the reason for the depth and bitterness of their disagreement is not at once evident. The causes for that disagreement lie with the state of endemic warfare under which the whole of Andean society labored in the early 1400s. The restructuring of Andean society undertaken during the Age of the Warriors, and justified by the warriors' promise to protect the local peasantry from predatory attack, had failed to produce the desired result. The peasantry, restive now, longed for the return of Wiraqocha.

The first point to get clear is that Wiraqocha Inca's name is meant most definitely to associate him with the god Wiraqocha, and hence with the views of the peasantry. Garcilaso and Sarmiento both tender accounts of how this king received his name because of seeing a vision of the god.[28] Murúa, moreover, makes the point that Wiraqocha Inca was particularly responsible for the prestige of the priesthood of Wiraqocha, and even took pains to see that they dressed in the manner of the mythical god.[29] In addition, most accounts of the Inca Wiraqocha ascribe to him the characteristics of the god Wiraqocha, as for example that this Inca was bearded.[30] Guamán Poma states that this Inca worshiped Wiraqocha *"con vehemencia."*[31] Cieza's long description of Wiraqocha Inca's exploits contain many parallels with those of the god, including a predisposition toward mercy, and the ability to conquer by hurling fire.[32]

Because of this handling of the life of Wiraqocha Inca in the early accounts, most authorities prefer to assign to his successor, Pachakuti Inca, the distinction of being the first truly historical personage from the Inca king list. Having taken the name of "Overturner of Space-Time," and having by all accounts created the imperial solar cult with its attendant political organization, Pachakuti is clearly historical because he represents a break with the past and the beginning of empire. By contrast, the life of Wiraqocha tends to blur into legend, although witnesses saw what was claimed to be his mummy—which was burned by the Spanish—and stated that it had snow-white hair, squaring with all accounts that have it that Wiraqocha Inca lived to a very old age.[33] So even if Wiraqocha Inca never lived (although he probably did), the legendary figure of that name is meant to stand for the power of the religion of Wiraqocha as practiced by the peasantry or lower moieties, not only of Cuzco, but of highland communities in general. This power was vested in a priesthood, which Wiraqocha Inca patronized. The views of this group are almost always presented in Inca myth in contrast, favorable or unfavorable, to those of the reform-minded Pachakuti Inca.

The contradictory information concerning the transition between the reign of Wiraqocha Inca and Pachakuti therefore suggests a breakdown in the social compact established centuries earlier between peasants and warriors. As the representative of the ancient ways of the peasantry, Wiraqocha Inca must in some way have taken a position in opposition to the warrior moiety sufficiently dangerous as to threaten the social fabric of Cuzco. The picture of the brutal and abject humiliation of Wiraqocha Inca by his son suggests a society on the brink of civil war. But such a conflict would have been suicidal for both parties because, as with all the tribes of the Andes, the Incas were surrounded by enemies both actual and potential.

To understand the threat posed by Wiraqocha Inca to the warrior moiety, and the fatalistic implications of the prophesied return of an angry Wiraqocha, it is necessary to grasp only one simple fact: as a class—irrespective of tribal affiliation—the warriors shared a common interest in seeing that war did not die out. The existence of warfare justified the existence of the warriors, ensured the forbearance of the peasantry, and justified the claims to lands and privilege made by the warriors. The Inquisitors of the Spanish Viceroy Francisco Toledo, who investigated the nature of Andean government before the rise of the Incas, found that the warriors were plainly powerless without a war to prosecute:

> There was no other government than the gallant captains called sinchis, who commanded and governed when they made war on each other, entering one another's territory to steal fodder, wood, and other things. The war once over, these captains were no more important than the rest of the Indians. They were not looked up to and had no power of commandment over the people.[34]

Since, on the other hand, warfare appears to have been endemic before the rise of the Incas, the peasantry was accustomed to the exercise of power by military overlords. Cieza de León, for example, records a common lament of the peasantry that, before the Incas, "they had no Lords, only captains,"[35] suggesting a systemic and increasingly irreconcilable tension between the peasantry and the military class in Cuzco. Such conditions were everywhere apparent. Both the archaeological and ethnohistorical record confirm this picture of warring polities up and down the Andes in the years preceding the Inca expansion.[36]

The people, it appears, were tired of warfare. But, even more, they were tired of the warriors. Only by strength of numbers across traditional tribal divisions could the peasantry hope to change this situation. On the other hand, the warriors had no choice but to oppose the arising of any civil or religious authority across tribal boundaries, since that might lead to a state of peace and hence powerlessness. What confederations did exist before the Inca expansion were confederations of warriors.[37] These were the "intimidators," hereditary groupings holding the monopoly on bronze weaponry.

According to the Anonymous Chronicler, the threat posed by the Chanca confederacy forced the issue in Cuzco. What made the Chanca menace unusual was that it represented part of a *popular uprising*. The account of the Anonymous Chronicler is distressingly opaque regarding the role of Wiraqocha Inca in this uprising, but one thing is clear: it was a war started by the priesthood of the peasantry. And it would bring Cuzco to the brink of civil war.

> Moreover, in the time of Wiraqocha Inca, many of these ministers were the principal reason why the people rose up and rebelled and particularly *Hanta buaylla* [Andahuailas] with the Chinchas, whence came

about great wars and the [Inca] kingdom was almost lost; for this reason
. . . [Pachakuti Inca] conquered his enemies and seized a great number
of priests and idols [wakas] and brought them to Cuzco, and in triumph
deprived them of their offices forever. And now that he had become
absolute king he created a new order of priests and ministers, commanding that henceforth and forever they should come from the class
of the common and poor, and that in the event of treason or rebellion
they would be subjected to the pain of law, namely to suffer a cruel
death.[38]

The essential point in the above account is that an uprising by the
"people" [el pueblo] signifies that the equipoise of forces that had kept the
warriors at the pinnacle of Andean society was being disrupted. According
to the Anonymous Chronicler, in "ancient times"—by which he means the
era before the humiliation of the priesthood by Pachakuti Inca—the high
priest held jurisdiccion over the king,[39] or military leadership, implying some
sort of check on the military aspirations of the upper moiety by the lower
moiety. Now, it appears, the priesthood wished to take on a further preroga-
tive: leadership in war. A successful attempt by the leader/priests of the
lower moieties to take an active military position would have spelled chaos
—class warfare across tribal lines.

The position of the warriors in this tumultuous situation is expressed in
the second part of Wiraqocha Inca's prophecy: the imminent destruction of
the religion of the peasantry. As we shall now see, the whole system of
peasant ancestor worship, with its mandate to be fruitful and multiply, was
once again under attack by the warrior moiety, just as it had been, according
to the Huarochirí myths, in the cataclysm of A.D. 650. And once again the
reasons were the same: pressure on the land from population increase.

The "official" version of Inca history, as recorded for instance by Garcilaso and Cieza de León,[40] emphasizes a sense of urgency and of mission on
the part of the Incas which grew out of the desperate conditions created by
an endemic state of war. Pillage, rapine, and even cannibalism were said to
be the norm.[41] A number of sources recount a time of great famine, drought,
and pestilence at the outset of the reign of Pachakuti Inca.[42] Although these
events are recorded as part of the ominous, turbulent atmosphere attending
the accession and policies of this architect of the Inca Empire, there are a
number of reasons for supposing that they actually took place. For example,
it is said that one of the first actions undertaken by Pachakuti Inca upon
assuming the royal fringe was to increase arable land through a program of
terrace building.[43] Moreover, one of the chief aims of the Empire was to

create an effective redistributive scheme, by building and maintaining sufficient stores of food and clothing to assure that no group in the Empire
should undergo the privations of famine. Such an immense undertaking must
have taken place in response to a real need.

Another illuminating datum, cited earlier, was recorded by Toledo's
Inquisitors: fodder and firewood were so scarce as to become the object of
military raids. Deforestation is always a sign of pressure on the land from
growing population, and wherever deforestation begins to occur on a large
scale, as we are now learning, ecological repercussions, especially in the
form of drought, inevitably follow.

In Cieza's version of the Inca war with the Chancas, the faction loyal to
Wiraqocha Inca wanted to withdraw in the face of the Chanca menace, and
return when the attack was over. It was this passivity, also evident in Wiraqocha Inca's prophecy, which so enraged his son. Yet Wiraqocha's response
underscores that the nature of warfare was for looting and possibly extraction of tribute, but not for conquest or occupation. As Mason puts it, "The
victor in inter-tribal or inter-city wars looted the vanquished, and possibly
imposed a tribute on them, and then let them alone until, possibly, they
again acquired enough power to become a menace."[44] The *orejones*, or military
nobility of the upper moiety, in contrast to the followers of Wiraqocha Inca,
having made Pachakuti Inca leader, wished to drive off the Chancas, but
could not raise enough conscripts to defend the city. According to Cieza de
León, the *orejones* resolved this difficulty by offering land to volunteers. An
army was quickly raised.[45]

The above examples point to the grim dynamic of the time. Warfare
involved staging raids on neighbors to acquire commodities scarce in one's
own area. In the case of Cuzco, capitulation before the Chancas meant that
already scarce resources would be siphoned away as booty and tribute to the
west. On the other hand, simply to dominate the Chancas would mean
ensuring future discord by "exporting" famine. In a world of shrinking resources owing to severe pressure on the land, the temptation must have
arisen to make war more deadly, in the sense of pushing one's advantage to
the maximum, seeking to annihilate the enemy's soldiers so as to avoid future
retribution and assure future tribute. Yet just this state of constant enmity
made it impossible to contemplate the kind of integration of resource use
that might surmount the problem of shortages.

Thus the followers of Wiraqocha Inca, many apparently with no lands
to defend from foraging raiders, had no interest in engaging the Chancas.
When land was offered, they were willing to fight. In wars close to home, as
between the mythical [i.e., before Wiraqocha Inca] Inca Mayta Capac and

the Allcaviquiza, annihilation and arrogation of land was practiced.[46] Distrust, hatred, and fear were common among tribes once united by another kind of feeling. At least two sources mention that, at the time of the accession of Pachakuti Inca, all the bridges in Peru had been cut.[47]

In the midst of these dangerous times, according to various sources, the ancestor cult once again became a scapegoat. According to Guamán Poma, even Wiraqocha Inca proposed to do away with the worship of the *wakas*, but was dissuaded by his wife, who said "that he shouldn't pronounce such a sentence because he would find himself in danger of death if he forgot the law of his ancestors. . . ."[48] Likewise, there is Pachakuti Yamqui's account of the humiliation of Wiraqocha Inca by his son Pachakuti Inca. By withholding customary funeral observances from his dead father, Pachakuti triggered an outpouring of civil disobedience on the part of the women of Cuzco, who supported traditional ancestor worship.[49] Most ominous of all was the apparently growing physical threat to the *wakas* and the *pacarinas*. As the Anonymous Chronicler pointed out, Pachakuti Inca seized the *wakas* of the Chancas in his victory over them. All the old rules, including those of warfare, appear to have been breaking down. With a surfeit of landless and desperate folk willing to soldier for land in other areas, anything might happen. If such a process were to gather momentum, more and more *llacta* populations might be massacred for their lands, their *pacarinas* forgotten and their *wakas* bereft of a people to nurture. The long shadow of Wiraqocha lay across the land. The moment of reckoning—put on hold during the Age of the Warriors—had come back full circle. Once again the ancient ways were under attack, and this time there seemed no way out.

III

IT DOES NOT appear that the Incas, at the outset of Pachakuti Inca's reign, had formulated a coherent plan for forging an empire. Rather it appears that the path to their destiny opened before them little by little, beginning with Pachakuti Inca's decision to confront the Chancas. By most accounts, the first phase of Pachakuti Inca's reign involved trying to stabilize the immediate environs of Cuzco strictly by tough military means. J. Alden Mason summarizes this phase as follows:

Apparently, Pachakuti assembled the Inca forces with intent to bring all neighboring peoples under his control. Those that did not submit at once and pay homage to him were attacked. The first victims were

groups within about twenty miles of Cuzco. These old hereditary enemies were apparently not treated with the leniency that attended later
conquests at greater distances; apparently there were old scores to
settle.[50]

But an empire could not be built and sustained on the basis of force
alone. It took some time, apparently, for this lesson to come home to
Pachakuti Inca. We have seen, for example, that Pachakuti Inca, in resurrect-
ing the ancient position of the warriors, which sought to lay blame on the
religion of the peasantry for demographic pressures, thought initially to ride
roughshod over the sensibilities of the peasant class. Silverblatt[51] has brought
attention to a good deal of such evidence, including a very interesting
passage from Polo de Ondegardo, wherein the mother of Pachakuti criticizes
his emphasis on the worship of the Sun, and states that his troubles with the
Chancas are the result of his having ignored the worship of Wiraqocha.

> [H]is mother told him that she had dreamed that the reason for the
> Chanca victory had been that more worship of the Sun than of the
> Universal Creator [i.e., Wiraqocha] had taken place in Cuzco and that
> henceforth it was expected that they would make more sacrifices to
> him and those statues [i.e., the *wakas*] and more regularly, and that later
> against the Chancas, he would give him the victory and send him
> people from heaven who would help him.[52]

Slowly the Incas came to see that the way to dominance was not, as had
been the Andean pattern for centuries, by trying to smash all opposition on
the battlefield, but by exploiting the yearning for peace and order, not
merely in the lower moiety of Cuzco, but among Andean peasants in general. The way of military domination led to stalemate among powerful
confederations of warriors. The way to empire led through the god Wiraqocha. By exploiting the hostility latent in moiety divisions up and down the
Andes, the Incas—now differentiating themselves from the warriors by the
claim of descent from Sun and Moon—would break the psychological grip
of the warrior aristocracy on the fears of the peasantry by offering peace
instead of war, food instead of famine, and religious toleration instead of
enmity toward the ancestor cult.

Pachakuti Inca displayed markedly more merciful behavior after the first
round of conquests to secure the perimeter of Cuzco.[53] It appears that the
Incas had begun to grasp that really immense power could be theirs if they
could convince the peasantry not to be "cannon fodder" for their local

warrior overlords. Thus a liberal dose of mercy to the conquered, spiced with occasional ruthless treatment of a particularly recalcitrant enemy, soon made clear that the Incas were of a different mold from the old-style warriors. The Incas moved quickly to back conquest with all the administrative techniques necessary to ensure adequate food supplies in every province. They delivered what the warriors no longer could provide, and perhaps no longer cared to: food and immunity from attack.

Further, only rarely did the Incas threaten the religion of the peasantry. Mason has observed that as a general policy, "no coercion was practiced on the native population to compel them to abandon their old language and religion." The Quechua language was pressed only on the military and administrative classes.[54] On the other hand, if a group behaved in what the Incas considered a particularly devious or rebellious manner, its members could expect a fate worse than death in the form of being taken from their native soil, the site of the *pacarina,* and transplanted to some distant land.[55] From the religious point of view, this Inca practice was tantamount to the extinction of the identity of the group.

The account of events leading to the foundation of the Inca Empire suggests that a vise was closing on the Andean tribes, among them the Incas. In a time of scarcity, with intense and unrelenting military pressure from without, and discontent bordering on treason from the priestly spokesmen of the peasant class within, the warrior class was running out of options. They could not seize land in other areas without inviting inevitable retaliation. They could not defend the homelands without conscripts, but the conscripts demanded land. With enemies at the borders, neither moiety could afford an all-out civil war, but the warriors nonetheless laid blame for the situation on the common people's propensity to "overbreed." The peasant moiety simmered on the brink of rebellion. In the midst of this mounting chaos, the Inca priest-king Wiraqocha uttered—for the consumption of his immediate family—his terrible prophecy.

Had this prophecy been simply a recapitulation of the forces delineated above, it would have been no prophecy at all, but simply an indication that Wiraqocha Inca had a firm grasp on the obvious. Although the forces of disintegration at work in Andean society in the early fifteenth century were formidable, none so far described could or would have been the subject of prophecy. To be sure, the times were fertile ground for visions of doom, but the finality of prophecy does not begin or end in current events. If there was a prophecy, neither its existence nor its galvanizing effect upon Pachakuti Inca can be understood in terms of conventional history.

IV

ALTHOUGH THE GREAT bulk of information we have about pre-Columbian Andean life concerns the Incas, many Andean myths speak of earlier times and events. With the exception of a few stories, as for example the fateful meeting of Wiraqocha with Manco Capac's father, few Inca myths belong to these earlier times. Moreover, as with the Aztecs, the Incas were renowned for "rewriting" history, or at least the mythical record of the past, for political purposes. Nowhere is this penchant more clear than in certain versions of the Andean creation myth where Wiraqocha dutifully singles out the Incas, from among all other tribes, as the group destined for hegemony over the Andes.

In this sense the Inca mythical record is entirely untrustworthy. In the same way that the Aztecs cast their roots backwards to the mythical tenth-century Tula of the Toltec god-king Quetzalcoatl in order to conjure the aura of legitimacy, the Incas positioned themselves as the true heirs of Tiahuanaco's legacy, handed over to Manco Capac. The lengths to which the Incas went in exploiting the mythic "database" for political purposes demonstrates the authoritative hold of the mythical heritage on the Andean mind.

For me, the Inca prophecy had raised the question of the extent to which the Incas really were in "control" of the mythic heritage of the Andes. Of course, if the prophecy was a hoax, this was a pointless question. But if there really had been a secret prophecy, guarded by the royal family, this meant that the Incas thought they knew something too dangerous for general consumption. Following this logic, I suspected that the Incas had seen —or, more properly, *foreseen*—something in the sky. As with other Andean peoples, they had been schooled for centuries in the intellectual discipline of understanding history in terms of synchronous terrestrial and celestial events. Now, with the principles of war and dominance projected into the sky, and with the Chancas approaching Cuzco, an Inca Emperor had allegedly uttered a prophecy of doom. If this had really happened, did it not indicate that the Incas were as much adherents of astrological prediction as they were manipulators of celestial metaphor? This view certainly did not contradict Guamán Poma, who specified the development of astrological thought as a characteristic of the Age of Warfare: "They knew by looking at the stars and comets what was going to happen." [56]

I found my way into these issues by investigating the nature of a single celestial object that, though known by another name elswewhere in the Andes, had been given a suggestive and extremely peculiar title by the Incas.

This was the Inca "constellation" known to the chroniclers as *mama mircuc*,[57] which literally means "the one who devours his mother and father." If the damage done to the technical language of myth during the Age of the Warriors had been to project malign forces into the very fabric of the cosmos, then surely the Incas' renaming of this object must have been connected with such a process.

The lexicographer Holguín defined this object as "some stars near the Southern Cross [*cruzero*],[58] and elaborated concerning the meaning of the verb *mircunni*: "To eat one's father or mother, which, because it is such a stupendous sin, they gave it its own term, and pretend that in the sky there is a star opposed to this sin, which influences adversely those who commit it, which they call *Maman mircu cuyllur*, which means Star of those who eat their father or mother."[59]

I was originally drawn to investigating this object because its nomenclature was redolent of the "official" Inca justifications for the creation of the Empire. As noted above, the Incas maintained that a murderous chaos had descended upon the Andes. Among the abominations they listed was cannibalism. The ritual practice of anthropophagy, the consumption of the bones of the ancestors, was a common practice at the time among tribes of the Amazon. In Inca thought, these tribes were always equated with uncivilized savagery. In fact, they created havoc on the eastern frontiers of the Empire throughout the Inca reign. Moreover, by positing the existence of a *mama mircuc* on the vault of heaven—that is, a cosmic force that threatened the devouring of the ancestors—the Incas appeared to be projecting precisely that portion of the Inca prophecy which was the most devastating: the destruction of Andean religion. The religion of the Andean peasantry was founded on the bedrock of *feeding* the ancestors. Here was a force, elevated to the level of a cosmic reality, that boded the absolute reversal of everything sacred, the *eating* of the ancestors. It got my attention.

Zuidema has identified *mama mircuc* (without comment) as the Southern Coalsack,[60] the dark-cloud constellation known from the Huarochirí myths as the *lluthu*, or Andean tinamou, a partridge-like bird. This object lies in the southeast quadrant of the Southern Cross (figure 3.5). Holguín, too, placed *mama mircuc* "near the Southern Cross," but said it was composed of stars. On the other hand, Holguín was unaware of the existence of the Andean system of black-cloud constellations.

Similarly, the modern lexicographer Father Jorge Lira commented in a study on Quechua healing about a celestial object known as *mal ladrón*, the "bad thief," observed by diviners when they wish to catch a thief. The diviner looks to see if the "bad thief" is "near or far from the [Southern] cross."[61] Like Holguín, Lira did not know about black-cloud objects. Since no object in the deep southern skies "moves" in relation to its neighbors, Lira's recording of lore placing the "bad thief" now near, now far from the Southern Cross is probably a reference to a well-known Andean observational practice. Both Urton's and my own field research have shown a pervasive pattern among contemporary native Andeans of divination of stars by observing their appearance in relation to atmospheric moisture.[62] When the moisture level in the atmosphere is sufficient to form ice crystals, light is scattered and the observed object is somewhat obscured. In the case of a dark cloud, the object would appear to shrink or expand, depending on atmospheric ice, thus moving it farther from or nearer to an adjacent star.

Finally, during field research in the Department of Cuzco in 1978, I heard from an informant a long tale about the Southern Cross, which he called *lluthu cruz*, or "tinamou cross." The four bright stars were "good" brothers, while the fifth brother, the Coalsack, was "bad" (*locu*), showing "no respect for his father or mother, or even the local authorities."[63] As with Lira's "bad thief" and the Inca *mama mircuc*, the "bad" brother *lluthu*, the Southern Coalsack, was a sociopathic character whose "behavior" represented the subversion of customary norms.

I was now attempting to grasp the significance in Inca thought of renaming an object, once known by the innocent name of *lluthu*, as "the one who devours his parents." In an attempt to calibrate the shift in mythic perception implied by this change, I turned to a myth from the Age of the Warriors, to my knowledge the only Andean myth of pre-Columbian origin in which the partridge, *lluthu*, plays a significant role. This myth, found in the Huarochirí corpus, involves yet another misadventure of Fox, this time as he heads the party of workers who gather together for the annual cleaning of the irrigation ditches. The party includes "pumas, foxes, serpents, birds of every kind." As the party ascends the mountain (*urcun*) toward the head of the canal,

> all of a sudden a partridge [*lluthu*] flew up. It launched into the air crying "pisc! pisc!" Fox was befuddled, and yelling "Huac!" he fell and rolled down the hill. The other animals got upset and had the serpent take over. They say if Fox hadn't fallen, the irrigation canal would have come from a route higher up; now it flows from a bit lower down.[64]

This lovely bit of whimsy is found in chapter 6 of *Huarochirí*, the chapter immediately following the tale of the fall of the house of the "false god."

The main structural conceit of the story, one by now familiar, is the establishment of the solstitial colure, the great circle connecting the solstice
points in the stars through the pole. As leader of the party of workers, Fox,
rising at December solstice, attempts to "climb the mountain," that is, to
achieve the proper connection with the June solstice point in the stars. As
the myth's outcome makes clear, Fox fails. The headwaters of the irrigation
ditch were meant to rise much "higher" on the mountain, but Fox has
"slipped," and hence the waters come from lower down (figure 9.1). In other
words, in the era after the flood of 650, the celestial source of waters, the
Milky Way, no longer rose at the peak of the mountain, that is to say June
solstice. The myth concedes this point by saying that Fox's party wished to
achieve a spot a bit higher up, not the peak. But Fox has "slipped" even
more, meaning that now not only Fox's tail, but part of his body as well, has
"slipped off the mountain." (Compare figure 9.2 with the situation some two
centuries earlier, figure 2.9a.) And inevitably as well, the source of the
"irrigation canal," that is, the Milky Way, now rises "lower" than hoped on
the mountainside. (See figure 9.1 and compare with figure 2.10a, representing the June solstice of A.D. 650.) Thus the myth states the effect of precessional motion upon both solstice points in the stars simultaneously.

Note also that figure 9.2 depicts the same moment as figure 4.3—when
Toad "hopped" and the house of the "false god" fell. The myth of the fall of
Fox follows immediately after this tale, forming a sort of companion piece.
Toad having taken over the function of marking the south celestial pole of
rotation at heliacal rise on December solstice, lluthu, has, as a necessary
consequence, also "moved." This event is represented in the myth by lluthu's
sudden "flight," which so surprises Fox that he "quails." Thus this myth
appears, as with the myth of the "false god," to represent the time frame of
the fall of Wari and the onset of the age of Pariacaca and the warriors, that
is, somewhere in the ninth century A.D.

In trying to understand the significance of the renaming of lluthu as mama
mircuc, I was aware of several contrasts. First of all, the Huarochirí myth is
funny. The humor, in fact, serves as an aide memoire, a kind of kinetic slapstick
rendering memorable the sense of connectedness of the "events" of the myth.
One of the most interesting aspects of this story is in fact the craftsmanship
used to project this sense of connectedness of the motion of the fixed stars.
If one moves, all move. Lluthu flies, causing Fox to fall, causing all the other
animals to get in an uproar, unleashing "serpent"—that is, the "tectonic"
force that "moves" the celestial earth.

The sense of the unified motion of the fixed stars is further emphasized
by the activity of the animals. In the Andes, to this day, everyone is required

to participate in the annual cleaning of the irrigation ditches. If a person is too sick, or too well-to-do, to perform physical labor, he is nonetheless obligated to hire a worker from another village to take his place. Cleaning the irrigation ditches is the Andean communal activity *par excellence*. In cleaning the irrigation ditches, it is all for one and one for all. If Fox falls, all fall, and the result is inevitable: the "irrigation ditch" flows from a little lower down now.

Archaeological evidence also supports this reading of the myth. As already noted, the fundamental cosmological schema by which the Inca Empire, the *tawanstinsuyu*, was laid out was influenced by the azimuth of rise of the Southern Cross. Where all the other lines in this cruciform division ran to the cardinal points, the line that "should" have run south from the center (the Temple of the Sun) was skewed to the southeast, to the point on the horizon where the Southern Cross—and *lluthu*—rose.

In light of the above tale, it seems evident that the reason for this procedure was an interest in the relationship between precessional motion and *lluthu cruz*. The reason for this focus is simply that the azimuth of rise of stars (their rising points along the horizon) shifts faster along the horizon, owing to precession, in the deep southern sky than do stars nearer the east-west line. The myth makes this statement by noting that it was *lluthu* that initiated the movement of all the other stars. This is not a question of "blaming" the *lluthu* for its precipitous flight; it is just how objects "down there" behave. They represent, as it were, an "early warning system" of precessional motion.[65] Further, the reason why the myth specifies the *lluthu*, rather than the Southern Cross or some other star, is to avoid mixing apples and oranges. The focus of the story is Fox's antics. Fox is a black-cloud object. As a matter of observational necessity—where black-cloud objects begin to fade from view about two hours before sunrise—Fox's position must be compared with the position of another black-cloud object.

I had learned something from this comparison of the mythical *lluthu* with the Inca *mama mircuc*. In the Huarochirí myth, the relationship of the fixed stars to each other is expressed as a homely metaphor—the cleaning of the irrigation ditches—wrapped in the kinetic imagery of a Roadrunner cartoon. The flight of the *lluthu*, which precipitates the action, is not couched in the language of blame, but is a "natural" occurrence on whatever level the story might be understood. On the other hand, the Incas saw in this same object the seat of a truly malignant action. Something had changed in the intervening centuries, some perception having to do with the very nature of heavenly bodies. The Southern Coalsack now threatened to "devour" the ancestors. The only clue I could glean was a general one: as an object rising in the southern skies, *mama mircuc* was a handy indicator of precessional motion. Something about the earth's shifting orientation within the celestial sphere seemed to be bothering the Incas. Meanwhile, a faint memory stirred: I had heard this story somewhere before.

V

VERSIONS OF THE Aztec myths of Quetzalcoatl are scattered through a dozen texts. Of the five extant fragments preserved in the original Nahuatl (Aztec),[66] one deals with the beginning of the Fifth Age, or Sun, of Aztec cosmogony, and the role played by the god Quetzalcoatl in the creation of Fifth Age humanity. This event, recorded in the so-called *Legends of the Sun*,[67] was said to have transpired during the semimythical Toltec period (ca. A.D. 600–1100[68]), which began after a great flood had destroyed the Fourth World. In the Aztec schema, the Fifth Age was still ongoing at the time of the Conquest.

The story begins with the concern of the assembled gods that some new humanity be created that will worship them. It is Quetzalcoatl who undertakes the journey to Mictlan, the land of the dead, in order to retrieve the ancestral bones of humanity. He will bring them back to the land of the gods, that a new incarnation of the race might ensue. At the entrance to the underworld, Quetzalcoatl meets the god of the land of the dead, the dual-aspected Lord and Lady of Mictlan. When he explains his mission, the Lord and Lady consent to his wishes, instructing him first to blow their conch-shell trumpet. But the deity of Mictlan is duplicitous and the horn is stuffed up. Nonetheless, Quetzalcoatl surmounts the obstacle and manages to sound the trumpet. Appearing now to concede Quetzalcoatl his wish, the Lord and Lady of Mictlan tell him to take the bones.

But they have set a trap. They order their "subjects" to demand the release of the bones. Quetzalcoatl objects, attempting a ruse of his own by appearing to agree, even as he flees. At once the Lord and Lady of the Dead Land address their "subjects":

"Holy ones, Quetzalcoatl is truly removing the precious bones, Holy ones make him a crypt!" Then they made it for him. He was startled by quail moreover, and so fell into the crypt, he stumbled, he fell unconscious. And the the precious bones were therefore immediately scattered. Then the quail bit into them and nibbled them. And when Quetzalcoatl regained his senses, he wept. Then he said to his nahual [spirit-world alter ego], "My nahual!/How will it be?" And at once he was answered, "How will it be? It will be undone. But let it be as it will."[69]

Bierhorst comments, "This unhappy episode evidently explains the origin of human mortality."[70]

Perhaps I was about to embark on an "unhappy episode" of my own. As far as I could see, this myth was virtually identical to the myth of Fox and the irrigation ditch. The problem was that the level of interchange between Mexico and Peru implied by this identity is not supposed to have occurred.

The focus of both myths is the December-solstice point in the stars. This fact is expressed in the Aztec version not only by Quetzalcoatl's journey to the entrance to the land of the dead, but also by the fact that the test for entrance is the ability to blow the conch shell, symbolic of the sun's position in the stars at the December solstice. Likewise, the focus of interest in the Huarochirí myth of "Fox and the Irrigation Party," is the heliacal rise of the celestial Fox at December solstice. Next, like Fox, Quetzalcoatl attempts to "ascend." In Fox's case the ascent is on a mountain. In the case of Quetzalcoatl, it involves an attempt to return to the land of the gods. For the Aztecs, as with the Olympuses of countless other peoples, the supreme deity dwelt "on the summit of Omeyocan," in the thirteenth and highest heaven.[71]

Thus, in both tales, the imagery involves the "attempt" to establish the solstitial colure, linking the entrance to the land of the dead with the land of the gods, and these attempts end in "failure." Quetzalcoatl's failure to ascend with the precious bones means that the linkages between the land of the gods and the land of the dead have been ruptured. Therefore the time frame that the myth describes appears identical with that of the Huarochirí tale, namely after the "flood," when Fox had "fallen" and the bridge to the land of the gods via the Milky Way at June solstice had been destroyed. We are spared a long digression to establish the question of dates, thanks to the presence of written records in Mesoamerica. According to Bierhorst, "The Quetzalcoatl story embraces the years 1 Reed (A.D. 850) through 1 Reed (A.D. 902). . . ."[72] This is the same date generated by the Andean version. (See figures 9.1 and 9.2.)

At about this point the "morphological" similarities of the myths end, yielding to an identity of idiosyncratic, idiomatic expression. While it is true to say that tales partaking of the technical language of myth will often take pains to describe the solstitial colure in a certain era, they do so within the idiomatic variations of the local version of this language. In the case at hand, 4,500 miles of distance and a supposed lack of contact between the Incas and the Aztecs is not sufficient to prevent the quail/*lluthu* from breaking cover.

Like Fox, Quetzalcoatl falls when startled by the flushing of a quail. Here, Bierhorst weighs in with a decisive observation concerning the identity of the "subjects" of the Lord and Lady of Mictlan, that is, the "Holy Ones" who are instructed to make a "crypt" for Quetzalcoatl: "The crypt is a motif borrowed from uranic myths, where it is typically associated with the jealous stars who attempt to trap the sun or the morning star in order to prevent it from rising."[73]

It is the activity of all the stars—the "Holy Ones"—taken in concert, and led by the flight of the quail, which ensures the failure of Quetzalcoatl's attempt to establish a celestial colure linking the three worlds. Likewise in the Huarochirí version, it is the puma, the serpents, and "birds of every kind" —that is, all the stars—which "get in an uproar" after the *lluthu* flies off. Yet, in the Aztec case, the stars are now "jealous," malign. And what they prevent from rising is not the physical sun, but the Sun of the Fourth Age, when both branches of the Milky Way rose with the solstice suns.

As for the astronomical identity of the Aztec quail, it is at least certain that the quail, like the Andean *lluthu*, was understood in Mesoamerica as a means of expressing shifts owing to precession in the position of the Milky Way. This information is found in the Maya Cuceb, a murky book of apocalyptic prophecy produced in the colonial period: ". . . perching in swarms, the quail will cry out from the branch of the ceiba [tree]. . . ."[74] Bierhorst paraphrases this passage thus: "Swarming like the numberless souls of the underworld, the evil birds of death come to weigh down the ceiba, i.e., the tree of life. . . ."[75] Thanks to the work of Linda Schele, it is now well understood that the image of the ceiba tree, earthly manifestation of the tree of life, refers, on the level of astronomy, to the Milky Way.[76] The image of the quail in the tree of life is one of destabilization, as anyone who has watched the ungainly behavior of quail in flight, and attempting to land.

Both myths project the notion of the "destabilization" of the Milky Way through the imagery of the quail's ungainly flight. But whereas the Andean version capitalizes on the comic potential of the *lluthu*, the Aztec version is relentless in its projection of the aura of doom. To understand the significance of this difference, it is necessary to understand when the Aztec myth was created.

The Aztecs were notorious for the burning of ancient codices. At the time when the Toltecs reached the height of their greatness, about the tenth century A.D., the Aztecs were numbered among tribes known as Chichimecs, i.e., "barbarians," roving hunters of the arid regions of northern Mexico and southern Texas. When the Toltecs reigned in Tula, the Chichimecs were more concerned with avoiding scorpions and rattlesnakes than with the fine points of mythic tone. When, beginning in about the thirteenth century, these tribes began to migrate into the Mexican heartland, they first came into contact with high civilization. The Aztec versions of the myths of Quetzalcoatl represent *reworkings* of ancient sources whose written versions they destroyed. The Aztecs destroyed codices so that their own version of the mythical database could not be challenged. Part of this endeavor involved the projection of a fatalistic vision that would justify the practices of the Aztec Empire. Although I had yet to grasp the enormity of this vision, I knew enough at the time to spot the uses of doom.

Rereading the Aztec myth of the fall of Quetzalcoatl had rocked me, and not simply because the tale was functionally identical to the Andean myth of Fox and Quail. It was unconventional enough to suggest that as early as the ninth or tenth century some sort of interchange between the Andes and Mexico had occurred. More bracing was the fact that both the Incas and the Aztecs appeared to have commenced, virtually simultaneously, to cultivate the "idiom of doom." The Aztec myth, composed sometime in the 1400s, must have drawn on earlier sources. Quail is now an evil animal, associated elsewhere by the Aztecs with sexual filth.[77] The fate of Quetzalcoatl's venture is sealed when the quail "nibbles" the bones of the ancestors. And there, at the same time, in the fifteenth century in Cuzco, out of the blue, the constellation *lluthu* is given a second name, "the one who eats the ancestors."

I didn't know what was going on. All I could discern was that, since the time of the Huarochirí mythmakers, a radical shift in the perception of the heavens had transpired on the part of the Incas, and that it involved a process of projecting a sense of blame into the stars. I sensed that the root of this idea lay with the cuffing given the technical language of myth by the warriors after the fall of Wari. It was open season on the political uses of sacred tradition. As for why this whole process seemed to be unfolding in Mexico as well, I was at a loss. All I could grasp was that the Incas and the Aztecs seemed to be blaming something on the stars. In the Huarochirí myths, the star-animals were "responsible" for events on the celestial sphere, but there had been nothing like this. Among the Incas an infectious sense of doom was in the air. In Cuzco, prophecies were uttered. Out there in the heavens, something was nibbling away at the bones of the ancestors.

VI

I STUCK WITH what I could see: the issue of responsibility versus blame as projected upon the stars. I tried to think of myths in which stars *participated* in some activity that might merit blame. In the myths of 200 B.C., the stars had been passive. Wiraqocha created them. In the myths of the flood of A.D. 650, the star-animals had reacted to a situation, running up the mountain to save themselves. In the Huarochirí myths they worked together, as peasants do. This was understandable, since these same star-animals were the celestial generators/protectors of the various tribes. Furthermore, the myths of Huarochirí were not myths of the Incas. Perhaps only the Incas were privy to this new secret in the heavens. This made some sense. It was they who had the prophecy, and they who had guarded its secret.

The only other story that seemed remotely to fit the bill was another one from Huarochirí, a fragment concerning the celestial Llama, known there as Yacana:

> They say the Yacana, which is the animator [*camac*] of the llamas moves through the middle of the sky. We native people can see it standing out as a black spot.
>
> The Yacana moves inside the Milky Way. It's big, really big. It becomes blacker as it approaches through the sky, with two eyes and a very large neck. . . .
>
> In the middle of the night, when nobody notices, the Yacana drinks all the water out of the ocean. If the Yacana failed to drink it, the waters would quickly drown the whole world.
>
> A small dark spot goes before the Yacana, and, as we know, people call it the Tinamou.[78]

Here was an object on the fixed sphere of stars with a decidedly major responsibility.

This portrayal of the celestial Llama bore no hint of evil, yet there was something odd about this story, something I did not at once grasp. It seemed to say the celestial Llama was holding back a flood, that this was its "role." This was certainly participatory, and, as with the other myths from Huarochirí, there was no hint of blame. Nonetheless, there was something strangely ominous here. Eventually I realized that this story was the only myth in the Spanish chronicles *told in the present tense*. Was a "flood"—a significant precessional event—*impending*, or was I reading too much into the story? I looked at the Quechua word for the impending flood, translated as "drowning," or by Arguedas as, "buried" (*sepultado*). In the first place, the word was pure Aymara in origin, *pampahuahhuan*. *Pampa* means "a flat plain." *Huahhuan* I had seen before. It was the Aymara synonym for *wira*, the concept of the tilted plane. This term had nothing to do with water and everything to do with astronomy. In other words, "If the llama failed to drink all the water, the plane of the whole world would tilt."

Told in the present tense, this myth meant that a tradition existed in Huarochirí at the time of the Conquest, a tradition of an *impending* precessional event. It was, in a sense, a little prophecy unto itself. Whatever it meant, the celestial Llama was somehow involved. After it hit me what was going on, it all seemed very obvious.

The bridge to the land of the dead was going under.

Like Fox before her, the Llama was slipping. The merciless passage of time was about to terminate intercourse between the lands of the dead and of the living. Her time was at hand. This was why Wiraqocha Inca had predicted the destruction of Andean religion. This was why the Incas renamed the Southern Coalsack "the one who eats his father and mother." As the azimuth of rise of the Southern Cross skittered ever southward, the Llama slipped ever closer to "extinction" at heliacal rise on December solstice: "If the llama failed to drink all the water, the plane of the whole world would tilt."

Figure 9.3a shows the moment of heliacal rise for the Milky Way at December solstice in Cuzco in 1432, the approximate date of the prophecy of Wiraqocha Inca. Here the conditions are precisely the same as for the viewing of heliacal rise in the events of A.D. 650. The sun is depressed twenty-four degrees to allow for the faint glow of the Milky Way to be visible. The portion of the Milky Way along the ecliptic, that is, at the December-solstice point on the horizon, is just barely visible. Just to the south, epsilon Scorpius is just visible, marking the hind flanks of the Llama and her adjacent suckling, the baby llama. As had happened in A.D. 650, the floodwaters of time were rising. In 650 the June-solstice "bridge" to the land of the gods had been destroyed. Now, some eight hundred years later, the "bridge" at December solstice, connecting the people to their ancestors, their past, and their traditions, was about to undergo a similar catastrophe.

The celestial prototype of all the lineage *wakas* was the celestial Llama. Soon her "birth canal," whence came her suckling and, as well, all the generations of man, would no longer shower the earth with the amniotic waters of abundance. The interface between the *waka* homelands and the earth was going under. How, then, henceforth, were the spirits of the dead to return to instruct the living; and worse, how would the people reincarnate when once again ready to be born from the uterus of the great celestial mother?

Figure 9.3b demonstrates the terrible force of Wiraqocha Inca's prophecy. A hundred years later, with the commencement of the Spanish Conquest, epsilon Scorpius, the suckling, and the last vestiges of the Milky Way anywhere near the ecliptic were all gone. As the Spanish probed the coast of Ecuador, and Huayna Capac lay dying, the great emblem of the people's unbroken devotion to their ancestors was sinking into the vast sea of collective memory. Of course Wiraqocha Inca knew the end would come after five kings. It was little more than a shrewd approximation of actuarial realities.

As I thought about these matters, I began to sense the terrible burden under which the Incas must have suffered. If a historian were to see a sense of historical causality in the fact that every major significant event in Andean history coincided, with precision, in relation to the Milky Way at the solstices, he would be considered quite dotty. But the Incas were concerned with pattern, not peer review. And they knew the myths. The wondrous unfolding of Tiahuanacan civilization had begun when the solstice suns entered the Milky Way. This golden age had ended, and ended exactly, when, simultaneously, the Milky Way ceased to rise at the June solstice, and war broke out on earth. Wiraqocha left the earth. The people and their gods would never again be so close. Now, with tribal enmity approaching unprecedented levels of danger, with shortages and hungry mouths to feed, with land in short supply, and a murderous suggestion abroad to stop the peasants from "overbreeding" by whatever means necessary, everything appeared in peril. And there in the skies, once again exactly on time, was the ominous cosmic mirror of events on earth. Who indeed could escape astrological emotion?

For eight centuries the people of the Andes had grappled with the legacy of Wari and of warfare. The sacred teachings of the ancestors, while preserved, had also been transformed. It was a teaching now touted by some as literally true. As the centuries drifted by, the convention of viewing the body of sacred teaching as a separate reality, rather than as a mnemonic tool, became ossified into tradition. Astrology could not but flower. The chickens had come home to roost. The tinkering of the warriors with the subtle nature of the technical language of myth had led inevitably to the astrological perspective. Given the right circumstances, the wages of astrology is the certainty of doom. And then there is the power of the pattern itself. For a span of nearly two millennia, the rhythms of the

Milky Way bear an uncanny relationship to the Period dates of Andean archaeology.

Is it so surprising, then, that Wiraqocha Inca predicted the end of everything? It was written clearly in the stars. Was this, then, the terrible weakness of the Incas, and perhaps of the Mexicans too, the certain knowledge that some cosmic catastrophe of incalculable consequence loomed imminent in the December skies? As far as I could see, there had to be some merit to the idea, simply because it sorted out such an enormous amount of information. All the same, the gap between theory and any means of proof seemed quite unbridgeable. Perhaps some intuitions were meant to be kept under lock and key. And besides, if the Incas really had believed any of this, they weren't talking. Or so I thought.

VII

THERE IS A saying in the East, "If you have no problems, buy a goat." Having bought into the Inca prophecy, I'd bought the flock. It made sense and it didn't make sense. If, as by all acounts was the case, the Inca Empire was born out of a fierce denial of the views of Wiraqocha Inca, was not his prophecy a discredited doctrine from its inception? Yet tradition also had it that the Incas passed this prophecy down through all the generations, until Huayna Capac declared from his deathbed the end of everything. The Incas rejected the prophecy. The Incas preserved the prophecy. The might of the Inca Empire was the measure of its determination not to live by a fatalistic vision. The Empire disintegrated because the Spanish presence meant the fulfillment of that vision. Prescott's position was beginning to look downright enviable. But sweeping an entire llama under the rug would leave a big lump on the living-room floor.

This looked like a splendid opportunity for me to read the chronicle of the Spanish priest Martín de Murúa, an important source because "he consistently viewed events from the Indian side." [79] This was a task I'd put off numerous times because Murúa was a master of the long sentence. Amid a glittering array of subordinate clauses cast in every shade of the subjunctive mood lay a gold mine of archaic subordinate conjunctions running to three, four, and even five words, which served as clues in a scavenger hunt to an excited pack of verbs in search of a subject. It was as if Murúa, bored out of his mind in some ghastly Spanish seminary, had absorbed the Latin syntax of every third-rate Cicero imitator in the abbot's library. Well, I knew how he felt: anything to avoid chasing goats.

If the Incas stopped short of explaining to Murúa the meaning of what they told him, they must nonetheless have trusted him. Morúa was taking down information in an atmosphere where both sides of Inca society encouraged every Spaniard who could write to take down their moiety's point of view, often little more than slander. As Urton has recently shown, some curried favor with the Spanish even as they concocted mythical origin tales to bolster land claims under the new regime.[80] Nonetheless, while a host of Inca "spin doctors" moved among the scribes of Castille, there appear to have been some among the Incas with a wider perspective. Amid this fiddling of the Inca historical legacy, another kind of contact was being cultivated.

Some group of Incas, almost certainly shaman-astronomers, sought out a certain sort of man, a man whom they could trust not to bowdlerize what he was told. Such a man would have to be relatively free from vanity. He was being asked to record faithfully something he did not understand. And such a man must already in his life have faced down the lion of pride. Otherwise he might well ridicule or, worse, "explain" out of existence what he was being asked to preserve. Above all, the task required a man with self-knowledge, one who could surmount the prejudices of his time and, by reference to some inner compass, grasp the gravity of the moment. Martín de Murúa must have been such a man. Here is what the Incas told him concerning the pivotal moment in their history when Pachakuti Inca took command of the destiny of his people:

> The powerful and valorous Inca Yupanqui, who was also called by another name, Pachacuti Inca Yupanqui, was a prince, a son of the great Manco Capac, the first king there was in this kingdom, and likewise, this great Pachakuti was the first warrior prince and conqueror that there was in this kingdom, who conquered all the environs of the great city of Cuzco; he made himself feared and had himself called Lord; they say he was not so brave as he was cruel, because he was of very harsh temperament, and he was the first who ordered that the wakas be adored, and [the first who] gave orders about how they had to sacrifice to them, and he divided them [the *wakas*] up and ordered that they be worshipped throughout the empire; and there are those who say, although mythically [*fabulosamente*], that the reason for this was that in the time of this great captain and prince Pachacuti, above the city in a place called Chatacaca, or Sapi, a person dressed in red, like the one in the picture[?], with a trumpet in one hand and a staff in the other [appeared], and that before he appeared, it had rained heavily for a month, pouring down day and night without surcease, and that they

feared that the world would turn over, what they call a pachacuti, and that this person had come on the water and that he began four leagues from Cuzco; the prince went out to meet him where they had agreed, and he pleaded [with the apparition] that he not play his trumpet, because they feared that if he did blow it, the whole world would turn over, and [further he pleaded] that they be brothers and that [in fact] he did not blow it, and after a certain number of days he [the apparition?] turned into stone and for this reason he called himself Pachakuti which means to turn the earth over, or in another sense abandoned and disinherited by one's own; this prince and captain had great wars and clashes with his enemies, and he emerged with victory like a brave and powerful captain; and later he ordered great feasts and many sacrifices; and he arranged that the year begin in December, which is when the sun arrives at the extreme of its course, because before this prince governed, the year began in January.[81]

Murúa's informant(s) began with the accomplishments of Pachakuti Inca: conquest and religious reform through the reorganization of the worship of the *wakas*. Then they explain why Pachakuti took these steps. To do so, they shift into the language of myth. Or, perhaps more accurately, they explain that Pachakuti was acting and thinking in mythical terms.

The tale opens with portents of disaster. For thirty days and thirty nights it had rained an unearthly rain. Was the world about to be destroyed? From other sources we know that there existed a tradition concerning the first years of Pachakuti Inca's reign. They were extraordinarily difficult. Both Pachakuti Yamqui and Guamán Poma speak of devastating drought.

In those days there was a great famine which lasted for seven years, and during that time the seed produced no fruit. Many died of hunger, and it is even said that some ate their own children.[82]

Expressing with something approaching glee what befell the hated Incas in the reign of Pachakuti Inca, Guamán Poma records:

In that time, there existed great loss of life among the Indians from hunger, thirst and pestilence, because, as punishment, God withheld the rain for seven years, some say for ten years. There were cataclysms, earthquakes, and many storms, it being now the occupation of all to weep and bury the dead.[83]

It appears likely, then, that there was a historical drought at the beginning of the reign of Pachakuti Inca. This could not have helped the new king. He was angry at his father, Wiraqocha Inca. He did not wish to submit to a fatalistic vision. His own mother was lecturing him about his duties to the religion of Wiraqocha. Yet he could not decide what to do. He wished to conquer all threats on the battlefield, but the peasantry within and without the valley of Cuzco had dug in its heels. As the forces of history swirled about him, he was racked by frustration and indecision. According to Betanzos, Pachakuti Inca had a vision of victory before the climactic battle with the Chancas. At first he thought that the figure in his vision was Wiraqocha, but then later, when planning the erection of a temple, he changed his mind and decided the figure in his vision must have been the Sun.[84] It was as if the angels of war and compassion—the shadow of Wari and the light of Tiahuanaco—sat upon either shoulder of the king, whispering now in one ear, now in the other. And the very forces of nature seemed to conspire against him with drought, death, and pestilence—the slings and "arrows" of *Aucha*, the planetary manifestation of Wiraqocha, god of Justice. The specter of Wiraqocha loomed above Cuzco.

And this is precisely what Murúa's tale recounts. Clad in the same red robe with which Wiraqocha Inca dressed the priesthood, an apparition stood above the city. And it carried a staff. Pachakuti Inca went forth to meet it at a place called Sapi. Sapi was the name of the place above Cuzco where, each January, the Incas released the floodwaters that would carry the ashes of the year's sacrifices to Wiraqocha.[85] (See Appendix 1.) And now another sort of flood threatened, one with all the terrible force of the inevitable. Pachakuti Inca was brought to his knees. He went forth to beg Wiraqocha to withhold the waters of doom.

The myth makes categorically clear the nature of that flood. Wiraqocha carried the conch-shell trumpet in his other hand. Here, I realized, was confirmation of my intuitions. The flood that threatened would occur at December solstice. The entrance to the land of the dead was about to be washed away. It appeared that the moment of realization of Wiraqocha Inca's terrible prophecy of the utter destruction of Andean religion was at hand. The conch was the emblem of the entrance to the land of the dead. Wiraqocha had returned in his aspect of the Lord of the Underworld.

The same symbolism appeared in the Aztec myth of Quetzalcoatl. The Lord and Lady of Mictlan had given the conch to Quetzalcoatl as a test of entrance, and this pair was the "mask of Ometéotl,"[86] the androgynous Aztec Saturn, "mother of the gods, father of the gods, the old god / spread out on the navel of the earth / . . . the Lord of fire and of time."[87] Likewise, among the Maya, we have met this aspect of the god. At Palenque, as the dead king sank into the jaws of the underworld, flanked by conch shells, the setting sun of December solstice cast its light upon Lord L, identified by Kelley as the planet Saturn in its manifestation as Lord of the Underworld.[88] Finally, this reading of the significance of Wiraqocha's conch is entirely corroborated by the fact that, at the end of the tale, Pachakuti Inca decides to reorganize the calendar so that the year begins precisely on the December solstice. The story makes no bones about it; the focus of every ominous portent is the December solstice.

If Murúa's tale provided confirmation of the validity of my suspicions concerning the astronomical basis of the Inca prophecy, it failed to resolve —and even seemed to exacerbate—the central paradox already encountered. Once again the status of the prophecy is entirely unclear. Pachakuti begs Wiraqocha not to blow the trumpet because, he says, he wants to *prevent* a *pachakuti*. In the next breath he declares a *pachakuti*, even takes the name as his own. A moment's reference to figures 9.3a and 9.3b makes clear the hopelessness of this maneuver. Yet, by all accounts, Pachakuti Inca declared the commencement of the Fifth Sun even as he took his new name. Did he believe the prophecy, or did he reject it? It was back to square one.

Meanwhile, I was fighting a brushfire. Although this initial reading of the myth seemed to hold extraordinary promise, I was troubled by the fact that Murúa had referred to Pachakuti Inca as the "son" of Manco Capac. If Murúa believed this, then his information had to be suspect, but from other parts of his writings, it was clear that he understood the Inca king list as well as anyone of his time. Why, then, did he call Pachakuti—the ninth Inca— the son of the first Inca? After some thought, it occurred to me that perhaps Murúa had copied down this formulation for Pachakuti Inca's genealogy because his informants wished to stress that Pachakuti had inherited, from the source, the legitimacy of being the regent on earth of the planet Jupiter.

Did this mean that Murúa's myth was talking about a conjunction of Saturn and Jupiter, Wiraqocha and the "son" of Manco Capac? The accepted date for the accession of Pachakuti Inca is 1438.[89] Both Guamán Poma and Pachakuti Yamqui had specified a period of seven years of troubles. In Guamán Poma's case, this may have been a biblical allusion. In the case of Pachakuti Yamqui, that possibility is less likely. Moreover, the Andean number usually associated with a mystical passage of time is the number five— five days for the germination of seed and five days for the passage of the souls of the dead. If the critical moment for Pachakuti Inca did fall seven years after his succession, then this would have occurred in 1445, or 1444 if one counted 1438 as year one.

There was a conjunction of Saturn and Jupiter in 1444. (See figure 9.4.) Again this is not so unusual, as there is a conjunction every twenty years. But here another, electrifying surprise lay in store. This was no ordinary conjunction. It was *the conjunction*, the replication of the trigon after eight hundred years, or 794 to be precise. *Saturn and Jupiter, for the first time since A.D. 650, had come back into conjunction at the same area in the stars where, centuries before, Wiraqocha had "left the earth."* (Compare figure 9.4 with figure 5.4.) Pachakuti Inca had indeed ascended to meet the apparition, all the way to the pinnacle of the cosmic mountain at the entrance of the land of the gods. This is why he refers to the apparition as "brother," a bit cheeky, perhaps, but Pachakuti was a proud man, and, as Jupiter's regent, of the same kind—planetary—as the apparition.

It was clear now why Pachakuti Inca had no option but to declare the commencement of the Fifth Sun. Just as in A.D. 650, when Saturn passed the staff of planetary, and hence earthly, rulership to Manco Capac even as the bridge to the land of the gods was breaking up, so now, in 1444, the old god had returned, as the entrance to the land of the dead approached "extinction," once more to affirm the Inca's right to rule. I had misjudged Pachakuti. He had not gone to beg, but to bargain. He had met Wiraqocha at Sapi, also called *chatacaca*, literally "stone where one pleads one's case." Perhaps the turning of the apparition to stone, as mentioned by Murúa, was the turning of this event into memory above Cuzco. It was indeed an event worth remembering. The history of earth and heaven seemed once more in alignment. How strange, and yet how utterly in accord with the sacred teaching of the Andes, were the times.

So Pachakuti Inca had struck a deal with Wiraqocha. The Lord of the Underworld forebore from blowing his trumpet. Yet once again the aura of paradox shrouds this event. Wiraqocha had come with the conch. Beyond question, the bridge to the land of the dead was doomed . . . but not yet. There still remained one fragile century, five generations before the final end. What had Pachakuti said to the apparition? What could he say? What would all the power and all the glory of empire mean if it was destined to perish in the blinking of an eye? Yet Pachakuti's head remained unbowed. He accepted the prophecy, and he rejected it. At long last he had accepted all the pregnant power of the old god of the peasantry, even as he declared the dawning of the Fifth Sun.

My mind swarmed with the elements of this paradox. As above, so below. War was everywhere. There were too many people, too many of these worshipers of *wakas*. Their religion was at fault. They made too many babies. They were a threat to themselves. Their religion was doomed,

doomed on earth and doomed in the heavens. Yet Pachakuti, *because* he understood this, declared the Incas' role as saviors of Andean life beneath the banner of the Fifth Sun.

And yet again, the Incas, better than anyone, knew the parameters of the inevitable. It was they who carried in secret the prophecy, they who had identified the enemy *mama mircu*, and structured their entire conceptualization of space so as to draw a bead, to the southeast, on this loathsome object. They viewed the cataclysmic severance of man from his ancestors with a steady gaze. And they acted. They made war, war caused by the troublesome peasantry, descendants of the stars. *Pachakuti ordered the reorganization of the wakas. Wakas,* stars. The stars drifting ever closer to catastrophe. A new Sun. Inevitable loss. Indomitable will. Yes, the prophecy is true. No the prophecy is not true.

When the resolution of this paradox presented itself, I could barely take it in. Pachakuti Inca intended to change the course of history by changing the course of the stars.

THE SECRET

In the month of December, called Capac Inti Raymi, [the Incas] celebrated the feast of the powerful Sun King, in the form of a great and solemn festival, because they considered that the Sun was the all-powerful king of the sky, of the planets, and of the stars. . . . In this month they performed great sacrifices to the Sun, offering it great quantities of gold and silver vessels, which they buried. They also sacrificed five hundred unblemished boys and girls, whom they buried alive. . . . [1]

—FELIPE GUAMÁN POMA DE AYALA

I

THERE IS NO clearer proof that the Incas guarded secrets than Murúa's account of the fateful meeting between Pachakuti Inca and Wiraqocha above Cuzco. Had this version of the Inca prophecy been a mere sop to wounded pride, concocted in hindsight for the delectation of posterity, there would have been no point to its hermetic language. This is a tale by priests, and for priests. If it also constitutes a message in a bottle, cast upon the waters of time toward some unimaginable future shore, then the transmission of this tale represents a measure of the desperation of its senders. But there was nothing else for it. No priest of Rome, no matter how decent, could be trusted with the secret of its meaning. Such a gesture could only have been suicidal, raw meat for the dogs of the Inquisition. Yet, given the tale undiluted, Murúa might just propel it toward safe haven at the breakwaters of history. After all, there was nothing left to lose.

Secrecy was a principle of the Inca priesthood, one established long before the advent of the Conquistadores. Garcilaso, much maligned for his "gullibility" before the Inca prophecy, recorded other tales as well, including the words of Inca Rocca, the fifth successor to Manco Capac: "He ordered that the children of the common people should not learn the sciences, which should be known only by the nobles, lest the lower classes should become proud and endanger the commonwealth."[2]

This sentiment reappears in many times and venues. Copernicus, for one, stood his ground: "I care nothing for those, even Church doctors, who repeat current prejudices. Mathematics is meant for mathematicians. . . . As to those who try to impart these doctrines in the wrong order and without preparation, they are like people who would pour pure water into a muddy cistern."[3] In the same way, the tribal elders of the African Dogon people, before revealing their uncanny astronomical cosmology, let Marcel Griaule and Germaine Dieterlen "ripen" for sixteen years. Dieterlen wrote:

> [A]mong groups where tradition is still vigorous, this knowledge, which is expressly characterized as esoteric, is only secret in the following sense. It is in fact open to all who show a will to understand so long as, by their social position and moral conduct, they are judged worthy of it. Thus every family head, every priest, every grown-up person responsible for some small fraction of social life can, as part of the social group, acquire knowledge, on the condition that he has the patience and, as the African phrase has it, "he comes to sit by the side of the competent elders" over the period and in the state of mind necessary.[4]

Among the Andean peoples, a sign might mark the candidate for shaman-priest. Surviving a lightning strike was a good sign, as was the survival of an infant male twin upon the immersion into frigid water that was his lot. Absent a sign, other qualities—aptitude, persistence, physical or moral courage—would, as with the Dogon, open the doors to the elders' house. The esoteric was held tightly, because it was precious, but it was not hidden with cabalistic zeal. The survival to the present era of a practical astronomical knowledge among the Andean peasantry makes clear that the invitation to further knowledge was freely offered. For the same stars and dark clouds consulted by the peasantry at planting time also moved through their myths. If one sensed a secret therein, one was free to pursue it. Attitude, patience, a kind of tempered longing—these were the qualifications of the apprentice shaman-priest.

And so, if the Inca prophecy was the secret of the royal family alone, its astronomical basis was not hidden from the Andean priesthood. This much, at least, we know from the Huarochirí myth of the "llama holding back the flood." The circle of esoteric knowledge was wider than the court of Cuzco. The priest-astronomers of the Andean tribes—the cultural heirs of the *capacas* of the Titicaca basin and the natural leaders of the peasant moieties— they also had eyes to see. The Fifth Sun, if there was to be one, would not preside over the dismantling of the ancient ways.

Time and again, in the paradigmatic conflict between the splenetic Pachakuti Inca and the forces of tradition—represented variously by Wiraqocha, Wiraqocha Inca, the priesthood, and the traditionalism of the women —one encounters the relentless determination of the peasantry to channel the fierce implacability of the new Emperor toward more magnanimous behavior. It was they, as much as Pachakuti, who created the persona of the Andean Emperor, the beneficent conqueror. This was a dynamic inherent both in the structure and the historic unfolding of the Empire, and its playing-out lasted until the end. Garcilaso records how Huayna Capac, enraged by a rebellion of the Chachapoyas in Ecuador and contemplating bloody revenge, was dissuaded by a legation of women led by an old woman who had been one of his father's wives. So impressed was he by her pleas for mercy that he empowered her to administer the reintegration of her people back into the Empire.[5]

Notwithstanding the power of the Andean lower moieties to modify the behavior of the Emperor, Pachakuti could never have attempted anything so simple as a "restoration" of the Age of Wiraqocha. Such a position would have galvanized the entire Andean warrior class into a single force of opposition to the Incas, simply because a world run along the old lines had no room for warriors. An Inca drive to "liberate" the peasantry, even presuming such a wellspring of altruism, would have unified and hence rendered invulnerable the warrior class. Paradoxically, therefore, the continuation of warfare was as necessary to the Incas' success as the establishment of peace. Nothing short of an expanding Empire would provide the sort of dynamic equipoise demanded by the situation. Negotiating between the Scylla and Charybdis of these opposing forces was the burden of Pachakuti Inca. As we have seen from Betanzos's example, his vision of victory was, he thought at first, Wiraqocha. Later he would understand it to be the Sun. He inhabited a crucible. If the path to power led through the god Wiraqocha, the way around the warriors was lit by the imagery of the Sun.

Through the symbolism of the Sun, the Incas announced a strategy of rulership that sent one message to the warriors and another to the peasantry. Herein the warriors could recognize and understand the affirmation of the commanding masculine presence. The Sun dominated. Its light obscured "stars" and "planets" alike. The Sun controlled. By means of a solar calendar, the Incas would centralize authority through regulation of the yearly calendar of ritual over a large area. The Sun was a warrior. The very brazenness of the Inca claim to descent from Sun and Moon—what Guamán Poma called "a great lie!"—proclaimed that the Incas were one of them. Had not the warriors themselves taken lands through an unprecedented claim of planetary descent? The first step in making peace with an enemy was to gain his respect.

To the peasantry, the Inca claim of descent implied something entirely different. This claim would place the Incas beyond the reach of the warriors and firmly within the hearts of the peasantry. The Incas asserted that they were born from Sun *and* Moon. In doing so they affirmed, in the strongest terms, the fondest hopes of the peasantry: *to find rulers who respected the cosmic validity of the double-descent system, grounded in the teaching of Wiraqocha.* The Inca was the king of the men, while his wife, the Coya, was the queen of the women. For the peasantry this symbolism represented a validation of all the cosmological rightness of the Andean tradition of Wiraqocha. In it lay a recognition of the double-descent system, of the value equality of men and women—in short, of all the hopes of the peasantry for better days ahead.

At the same time, it was an idea that the warriors could not attack on its merits, since it would inevitably call into question their own cosmological assertions about descent from the planets. It appears that the Incas themselves never made a direct claim of planetary descent. According to the sources, their relationship with the planet Jupiter was one of affinity rather than consanguinity. The Anonymous Chronicler refers to Manco Capac as Jupiter's "regent," while Pachakuti Yamqui's tale of Wiraqocha handing over his staff makes clear that Manco Capac's father was a human who had found favor in the eyes of deity. It is of course possible that the Incas simply changed their story when it suited them, but the early sources do make reference to the contempt in which the Chancas held the Incas for their claim of descent from Sun and Moon (see above). Since this opinion refers to the period *before* the Inca imperial expansion, it is possible that the Incas had been experimenting with these ideas, and that these same ideas—a means to amalgamate the spirit of Tiahuanaco with some of the less onerous of Wari's administrative techniques—had something to do with the relative tranquillity of the valley of Cuzco up until the Chanca onslaught.

In either case, the Incas had conceived the means to take a very powerful position by declaring their unique right to rule as direct descendants of the unique celestial *wakas*, Sun and Moon, and by limiting the arena of debate over this claim to the battlefield, an area where they were particularly adept. The message projected by the armies of the Inca Sun King was the restoration of order. To a peasantry tired of living in fortified hamlets under constant threat of attack, the symbolism of Sun and Moon, the primary regulators of the agricultural year, showed respect for their concerns. To the extent that the peasantry might be willing to accept such regulation, the warriors would have to look to their own backs.

The Incas held their position impeccably by acting out all the necessary ramifications of their claims, as for example the practice of royal incest between brother and sister to preserve the divine inheritance through a double-descent system from Sun and Moon. Where the peasantry would see ancient ideals recast in symbolism appropriate to the Fifth Sun, the warriors would see masters of the game of power at work.

Perhaps the most important consequence of the Inca claim to solar descent as regards the warriors was that it provided the warriors with a way to accept defeat without shame. The Incas made it clear early on that they had no intention of trying to eradicate the warrior class, but rather sought to work with it to extend the Empire, leaving local control in the hands of the existing warrior nobility. Therefore a given warrior group, having acceded to, or been defeated by, the Incas, suffered no diminution of its status in relation to local peoples, but on the contrary was showered with imperial goods. At the same time the warriors had room to assert the rightness of capitulation to a superior power, the Sun. Insofar as they accepted and promoted the Inca idea of the "natural" superiority of the Sun, the warriors could sidestep shame. Moreover, there remained for the warriors ample opportunity to continue practicing warfare, now under the banner of the Incas. The Incas actually provided the warrior class with incentives to lose. The Andes were bedazzled by the Sun.

While some elements of the foregoing analysis may be novel, they are nonetheless cast in the mold of conventional historical perspective. The analysis stresses the contending demands of various power bases set within a context of crisis due to ecologic and demographic pressure.

The problem with this view is that it leaves an impression that the formation of the Inca Empire was a sort of reptilian insinuation into the interstices of power, the survival of the cleverest. Banished from this picture are other elements, no less real for being intangible. There was a recognition of the deep sorrow abroad in the land, as well as a sense of beauty, a joy in risk, and the attendant possibility of tragedy that interpenetrated every mundane Inca undertaking. In some manner, which only such words as *charisma* can approach, the Andean people were drawn to the orbit of Cuzco.

All the lesser expediencies that had conspired to produce the fractured prism of Andean life during the Age of the Warriors yielded to a greater aim. If the Incas cast something like a spell over the Andean cordillera, it was composed of elements of the cultural heritage familiar to the widest possible circle of Andean humanity, elements that only increased in refinement and power as they approached the inner, esoteric circle whose center was now Cuzco. For good or ill, the destiny of the Andean people would henceforth be bound to the destiny of the Sun. But if the survival of the Sun now depended on the success of a very particular kind of war, the secrets of its efficacy would not be cast indiscriminately before the common people.

II

SOMETIME IN THE 1400s, a new term entered the technical language of myth in the Andes, and, as it happens, in Mexico as well. This was the term "Sun," and it stood as a synonym for the idea of "world," or "world-age." Just why this term should have appeared at this time, what precisely it was meant to convey, and the purposes for which it was introduced into myth have been misunderstood since the time of the Conquest.

Both Guamán Poma and Murúa discussed the five Ages of Andean tradition at some length. (See chapter 2, pages 26–27). Murúa, as well as Garcilaso,[6] uses the term "Sun" to refer to the concept of world-age. Further, the mythical formulation "Death of the Sun" refers to the same event as the word *pachakuti*, namely the moment of destruction of one Age or Sun, and the commencement of the next. We have, for instance, already seen reference to this term in a myth from Huarochirí. (See chapter 8, page 221). Besides his discussion of the doctrine of the five Suns, Murúa referred to these ideas a second time, apparently in relation to the commencement of the Fifth Sun:

> They say that in that time there was a very great flood, and they believed it was the end of the world, but that they would first suffer a very great drought, and the Sun and Moon which they worship would be lost, and for this reason were the Indians accustomed to cry and give out great shouts and lamentations when there was an eclipse, especially of the Sun.[7]

Among the interesting insights found in this passage is the notion that among the Incas it was not just the "Death of the Sun" which was to be avoided, but the "Death" as well of its consort, the Moon. This formulation corresponds exactly to ideas already examined, namely that the soli-lunar visage of the Gateway God, standing for the sun and full moon at opposing solstitial points, was intended, among other things, to convey the means of expressing the parameters of an entire world-age, laid out in the stars. Here we find the culmination of this view in the Inca arrogation of the symbolism into language itself, an actual synonym for the idea of the world-age. But students of the Incas, beginning with the Spanish and continuing down to the present, have failed to grasp the significance of Inca "solar" symbolism, particularly the relationship of the notion of a world-age Sun to the welfare of the Empire. The importance of the term "Sun" as world-age has either been discounted or else considered a fancy adjunct to Inca "worship" of the physical sun. The whole lore concerning the Five Ages, or Five Suns, has, at best, been understood as a "mythopoeic" imagining of the past, and, at worst, dismissed as woolly thinking.

Such unquestioned assumptions have created a sort of aphasia in front of certain kinds of information. For example, although Murúa makes clear that eclipses were regarded as possible *omens* regarding a *pachakuti*, or "Death of the Sun," students of the Andes are, to this day, taught that the native peoples were terrified of eclipses because they thought that the physical sun or moon might die. Likewise, in the case of the Aztecs, where the "Death of the Sun" meant exactly the same thing as in Peru, we find the persistent notion that the Aztecs were so afraid concerning the fragility of the "Sun" that they feared every morning that the sun might not rise. Perhaps esoteric knowledge is supposed to work by promoting smokescreens such as these. If so, it has succeeded brilliantly in diverting the curious, and even deadening curiosity itself, for going on five centuries.

It is important, then, to be absolutely clear. In its esoteric sense, the word "Sun" stood for any long number of years between significant precessional events. In the case of the Andes, significance attached to the gain or loss of "access" to the Milky Way at heliacal rise on either solstice. In the older terminology of *pachas* and *pachakutis*, the "world" that was destroyed consisted of an imaginary plane through the ecliptic, the "celestial earth" supported by "four pillars," that is, the stars rising at the solstices and equinoxes. These worlds were "destroyed" when, in the course of precessional time, their "pillars" "sank into the sea," giving way to the next "world." The word "Sun" used in the sense of world-age is merely another way of looking at the same phenomenon. There was, let us say, a "Sun" that rose in a particular era in a particular set of stars marking the equinoxes and solstices. But when these four "pillars" sank, then the "Sun" that rose with them also disappeared. Now appears a new "Sun," one that consorts with a different array of celestial players.

This interpretation is not conjecture. Although the esoteric meaning of the word "Sun" may have been tightly controlled by the Incas in the furthering of their aims, at least one tribe on the fringes of the Empire, the Mocoví, understood and preserved, into the first half of the eighteenth century, the sense of the terminology.

One time [the sun] fell out of the sky, and this so touched the heart of a Mocobí [sic] that he managed to put it back up and tie it in place [amarrar] so that it wouldn't fall back down. The same thing happened to the sky, but the ingenious and robust Mocobís hoisted it back up on the ends of poles and reattached it to its axes [ejes].

The sun fell a second time, either because its moorings [ataduras] were not sturdy enough or because time had weakened its strength. And so the time came when inundations of fire and llamas covered everywhere, and burned everything, and consumed trees, plants, animals, and men. A few Mocoví, to save themselves, plunged to the bottom of the rivers and lakes and turned themselves into capiguaras [capybaras] (Hydrochoerus) and caimans. But two of them, husband and wife, sought asylum in the top of a very high tree, from where they watched flow rivers of fire which flooded the surface of the earth.[8]

Here, in a less anxiety-ridden idiom than the Inca conception of the "Death of the Sun," the Mocoví describe their encounters with a sun possessed of the klutzy habit of falling down every so often. Being by nature helpful, the Mocoví tie the sun back in place. "Naturally" the sky falls at the same time and they hoist that back up as well, on poles—one might conjecture four poles. Human beings are the only ones who can perform this function, because only humans possess the powers of perception necessary to notice the phenonemon (precession) in the first place and hence "fashion" new "poles," that is designate the new stars upon which a subsequent "world" might rest. In any event, later, the sun falls again, "either because its moorings were not sturdy enough, or because time had weakened its strength," the latter being about as explicit a statement on the reasons for the sun's strange behavior as one might hope to find anywhere. If the sun coming loose from its "moorings" recalls another ritual of Inca "sun worship"—

the "tying of the sun"—perhaps it is possible to withhold the verdict of "superstition" at least long enough to take a closer look.

III

WHEN HIRAM BINGHAM discovered Macchu Picchu in 1911, he found the only remaining example of a class of objects systematically destroyed by the Spanish, known as the *intihuatana*. The *intihuatana* of Macchu Picchu is a pillar, or gnomon, rising from a block of granite about the size of a grand piano. It is known from the nubs of similar ruined monuments at Cuzco, Pisac, and elsewhere that the *intihuatana* played an important part in Inca ritual. Krupp has described one theory that the *intihuatana* may have served some calendric function, utilizing shadows cast by the sun over the gnomon.[9] *Intihuatana* literally means "for tying the sun,"[10] although it is most often translated to mean "hitching post of the sun."

This latter image gives the impression of the sun "tethered" to the gnomon. The wide distribution of myths of "the binding of the sun," found throughout the Americas and Oceania, and with less frequency in Europe and Asia,[11] may be the source of this interpretation. In such myths, the "binding" of the sun is regularly associated with the solstices.[12] Of great antiquity, this idea has often been interpreted as a description of the sun's annual path. The emphasis on the solstice, further, is thought to represent the primitive notion that, were the people not to "bind" the sun, it might just keep on going past the solstice point, and onward to oblivion. The Mocoví tale cited above demonstrates, however, that—at least at the time of the Incas—matters were not so simple. Every time the sun "fell," the sky "fell" as well, suggesting a disjunction involving both sun and stars.

With this thought in mind, one might fruitfully reexamine the meaning of the word *intihuatana*, "for tying the sun," by asking, "To what must the sun be tied?" The *intihuatana* at Macchu Picchu in fact appears to stand for the sun itself. Not only does the *intihuatana* cast shadows at the behest of the sun, and no shadows at all when the sun, like the gnomon itself, stands at the vertical on the day of zenith passage, but it also, like the sun, occupies the central position in ritual. As mentioned earlier (see chapter 7, note 39), the investigations of Dr. Ray White have demonstrated that around the base of the *intihuatana* are arrayed representations of the four constellations symbolizing the *suyus*, or quarters, of the Inca Empire. The same pecked glyphs are found at long distances from the gnomon, on four stones that form the pattern of an intercardinal (solstitial) cross. If the gnomon itself represents the sun, and the "lines" emanating from it are for "mooring" the sun, then it appears that the *intihuatana* was "for tying the sun to the stars."

It is precisely this symbolism that dominated the geomantic configuration of Cuzco. As discussed at some length in chapter 2, the Temple of the Sun in Cuzco was the center of emanation of forty "rays" or *seques* to all points around the horizon.[13] Four of these represented the four (intercardinal) roads to the four quarters of the Empire. Another ran due east to the "equinox mountain," Pachatusan, the "support pillar of space-time." Another, as we have seen, pointed directly to the azimuth of rise of the Southern Cross, known as *lluthu cruz*, a.k.a. *mama mircuc*. With forty *seque* lines extending in all directions to the horizon, there existed, from the point of view of the Sun (Temple), the practical means of observing the azimuth of rise of stars all around the horizon.

Further, as noted in chapter 5, the number forty corresponds to the number of conjunctions of Saturn and Jupiter composing a world-age.[14] We know, thanks to Murúa, the very great importance attached to the "return" in 1444 of the conjunction of Saturn and Jupiter of A.D. 650, during the reign of Pachakuti. Here, with Pachakuti's creation—the *seque* system—we get a first inkling of what was meant by Pachakuti's "reorganization of the *wakas*," mentioned by Murúa. In the 328 *wakas* strung out along various *seques* in a straight line to the horizon, we find the representation of the lineage *wakas* of the conquered tribes. The similarities between this arrangement and that of the forty "turquoises" of Pikillacta indicate that the importance of the number forty was not as an idealized number of tribes—there were 328 tribal *wakas* represented at Cuzco—but lay rather in its astronomical significance. Since these *wakas* were effigies representing different celestial objects on the fixed sphere of stars, and since they were arrayed toward the horizon, we find, on one level, that the *seque* system symbolized the totality of an entire world-age, that is, the forty conjunctions of Saturn and Jupiter through the stars.[15] On the practical level, the *seques*, I suggest, offered the Incas an unparalleled apparatus for monitoring the flow of precessional time.

The Incas had every reason to do just this. The Fifth Sun had been born under a prophecy of doom. It could live only so long as the celestial Llama could "live," just as the viability of the gateway to the land of the dead was inextricably bound to the movement of all the stars taken in concert.

Understood in this way, the similarities between the *intihuatana* at Macchu Picchu and the *seque* of Cuzco become of more than passing interest. Did the Incas construct the *seque* system in order to watch helplessly as the inevitable unfolded? One might draw this conclusion if one assumed that the *seque* system, like the *intihuatana*, was designed for "tying down the sun."

In this view, the Temple of the Sun, with its forty "moorings" to the horizon, would resemble Gulliver waking from a bad dream to find himself lashed into immobility by a mass of Lilliputians, the stars. This image brings us back to the ground of the Inca prophecy, the foretaste of doom.

Or, is it not possible to find here some flicker of defiance on the part of the Incas? Unquestionably, it was not the Inca position that the Sun was subject to the stars. The Sun was the Emperor, king, and victorious warrior.[16] The arrangement of the *seque* system projected the image of the Sun triumphant, seated in the center, master of all it surveyed. One might well ask what the point of such optimism could be, if the Sun was doomed to perish in less than a century? While pursuing other avenues that display a similar confidence, the reader is invited to entertain a gestalt shift. The Temple of the Sun, as with the *intihuatana*, was indeed designed "for tying the Sun"—in its esoteric sense as world-age—and tying it tight, both to the stars in the heavens and to their pesky earthly descendants, the tribal populations of the Andes. For, thus "moored," how could the Sun possibly come crashing down? After all, Pachakuti Inca, as he set out on the path of conquest, fully intended to bind the destiny of the Andean peoples to the destiny of the Sun.

IV

INCA GEOMANTIC PRACTICES grew from roots as deep as Andean tradition itself. If the array of Andean tribes and the mythical route of Wiraqocha represented the imprint of the celestial river along the spine of the Andes, the Inca priests would recapitulate this trajectory in the rites of the June solstice at Vilcanota. If the three worlds were constantly revivified by the waters from the deep, recirculated by the celestial river, then the Incas would replicate this thought-form in a fountain of magical beauty on the Island of the Sun in the sacred waters of Titicaca. And when the last Emperor died, it must be said that he was buried in the riverbed leading to the land of the gods.

As the Fifth Sun commenced, and the immense task of redeeming Andean civilization from the jaws of death fell upon the shoulders of the Incas, the survival of this Sun became the overriding issue of public policy. In this situation the concept of boundaries became a focus of geomantic thought. The Inca Emperors were required to be warrior-kings. If the Andean tribes labored under the scourge of endemic warfare, then through conquest must the forces of disorder be hurled back, away from the center. In the heavens as well, the Sun was required constantly to risk all, ever to labor at the

frontiers of its domain to hold fast the borders of the Fifth Sun—the fragile
Fifth Celestial Earth—against the concerted motion of the "star tribes." The
borders defended by the Sun ran from tropic to tropic. Only the celestial
Llama held back the flood.

Wave after wave of conquest emanated from Cuzco, the Navel of the
World, in an ever-widening pattern of golden ripples cast from the Stone in
the Center. Without was barbarism, death; within lay the possibility for
peace. The power of the Sun-King operated ceaselessly at the frontiers of
danger, subsuming ever greater territories in a vast drive toward equipoise.
It was no different above. The borders of the Fifth Sun had to be established,
secured, and defended.

To say that the Incas "symbolized" their boundaries in a solar idiom is
to miss the almost hallucinogenic quality of the thought-form. When Huayna Capac had golden spikes hammered along the shores of the river
marking the northern boundary of the Empire (see above, pages 37, 65), it
was as much a message to the Powers Above as a warning to the tribes below.
Every ceremony, every thought, every action that the Incas undertook in
establishing the boundaries of the Empire of the Sun was in defense of the
beleaguered Fifth Sun above.

When a tribe was peacefully assimilated into the Empire, the Inca ex-
changed the feathers of a hawk with the local warrior chieftain.[17] As we have
seen, the mythical significance of the raptorial birds is their ability to soar
or dive—like the sun—to the limits of the world of the living, that is, to
the gates of heaven itself, or to the boundaries of the land of the dead.
These birds represented messengers to the boundaries of the Domain of the
Sun, once called kay pacha (the "celestial earth") and now conceptualized as
the kingdom of the Fifth Sun in space-time. In the reciprocal exchange of
hawk feathers with local warlords, the Inca had reinforced the boundaries of
the Empire of the Sun, and the new tribe had pledged fealty to it. "Thy will
be done, on earth as it is in heaven."

A second Inca ceremony for the stabilization of boundaries involved a
game with elements of skill and luck.

Here the aim was to bring down with bolas a large "serpent" made of
wool, which was thrown aloft. The winner was the one who could wrap the
cords of the bola the most times around the serpent. According to Albornoz,
the Inca won many provinces this way. It was understood by the other
contestants—local nobles—that they were to let the Inca win; when they
did so, they were generously recompensed with fields, livestock, and "other
services."[18]

Here one encounters a familiar image. In the tales of Huarochirí, it was the newborn war god Pariacaca who, hurling his "staff of gold," transfixed and froze a great, menacing serpent, establishing once and for all who had the right to "rule." The serpent was symbolic of tectonic upheaval on earth and "uranic" upheaval in the domain of the "celestial earth," the region of the celestial sphere between the tropics. This region, which takes its shape from the extremes of the sun's positions on the celestial sphere, was the celestial analogue or model of the Empire of the Sun on earth. In playing the game of the serpent, the Inca wielded bolas, called *liviac*, which was also a name for lightning. As with Pariacaca and, more to the point, as with Wiraqocha, who invoked cosmic fire by raising his staff, the axis of the celestial sphere doubled as lightning sent from the highest heaven, and he who possessed it was the legitimate ruler of the age. In mastering the mobility of the serpent, the Inca mastered the borders of the Empire. By intentional analogy, he was also mastering the space-time border of the Fifth Sun by mastering the motion of the stars.

The imagery of the hurled weapon "binding" the snake is distinctly martial, and this too was intentional, for it was meant to reflect the cosmic reality of a state of war between the sun and the stars, a conflict expressed in another Inca legend. Here Pachakuti Inca, in desperate battle with a fierce tribe of the eastern forest, saw his army set upon by a gigantic serpent. Pachakuti raised his eyes to heaven in supplication, and immediately a great eagle swooped down, picked up the serpent, and smashed it to death on the rocks below.[19] If, at this juncture, it is disconcerting to note that the glyphic emblem of the Aztec capital, Mexico-Tenochtitlan, was a furious eagle astride a *nopal* cactus, and carrying a serpent in its beak, it is no less challenging to confront the significance of the image itself. For with this picture of the solar eagle defeating the collective power of the stars—the "serpent," which, as with the serpent in the myth of the Fall of Fox, is the natural "leader" of all the (star) animals, once they've "gotten in an uproar"—we move toward the esoteric center of the Inca vision.

A state of war existed between the Sun and the stars.

The Fifth Sun was under attack from the remorseless habit of the stars to weaken its "moorings." So heedless were these stars that they threatened to "nibble the bones of the ancestors" and annihilate those on earth who both worshiped and were descended from them. Those on earth were no better. They too threatened their own religious heritage with their overbreeding and their stiff-necked refusal to stanch the folly. Only the power of the Sun could put things right.

In this formulation we encounter the logical outcome of a process begun when the warriors "bounced" a few new ideas off the celestial sphere. In

projecting a hierarchy of dominance and submission onto the heavens, they
had laid the seeds of disaster both above and below. For in promoting the
fiction that this language was literally true, they had cut the technical language of myth loose from its moorings in the natural pattern by removing
the constraints of metaphorical understanding from the human dialogue with
the Higher. Thus, like the Fifth Sun, the language itself was adrift. As below,
so above. Warfare on earth conformed to a higher pattern, a pattern that, in
the Inca view, now represented a sort of "cosmic authorization" for the
establishment of the Empire; not less than the sons of the Sun, the Sun itself
was under siege. The enemy—above and below—was of a kind, the stars
and their offspring. It was time to act and to prevail, time to save the Sun,
and with it the entirety of Andean civilization.

Pachakuti Inca was no Prufrock. If he paused to ask the question "Do I
dare / Disturb the universe?" the answer was not long in coming. Yes! Yes,
he would "reorganize" the wakas. Anything less would mean capitulation to
his father's fatalism. Pachakuti Inca would not, could not, stand idly by while
the very portals of sacred tradition creaked toward closure on the hinge of
history. As the stars nibbled relentlessly at the bones of the ancestors, they
threatened the Death of the Fifth Sun. The time for hand-wringing had run
out. The moment had arrived for a declaration of war against Time.

V

THE INCA EMPIRE was the outward manifestation of an experiment in sympathetic magic,[20] an experiment without known precedent in the annals of
human history. As the drama of Andean history built toward its foreordained
inundation of sorrows, the only glimmer of salvation lay with the guttering
flame of the Fifth Sun. This, at least, was the Inca perspective. No force in
Andean life beyond the vision of Pachakuti Inca, the "Overturner of Space
and Time," stood between two millennia of Andean high civilization and
cataclysm. Evidence of the gathering storm was written on the vault of
heaven no less than on the deforested hillsides of innumerable highland
hamlets. When it hit, there would be no quarter asked or given. Every wrong
turn, every mistake, every gesture of spite or malice in the unfolding of
Andean civilization was there, present, weighing heavily in the balance of
the god of Justice and Retribution, the Old God, the Father of Time. In this
moment, suspended between heartbeats outside the domain of time itself,
an Inca King determined to restore the seat of Justice to its throne in the
Center. If Time was merciless, then it must be stopped.

To reach the celestial realm, Pachakuti Inca would work through the earthly descendants of the Powers Above. In reorganizing Andean existence through the exercise of measured warfare, he would effect at a distance the coronation of the Fifth Sun on the throne of heaven, bring the stars to heel, and redirect the duties of the planets, the "measurers," the instruments of time.

This was no game. The immensity of the undertaking was dwarfed only by the magnitude of the risk. From the outset, the Incas risked everything. They revealed themselves as the children of the Fifth Sun, stated their intention to restore order to Andean life, and defied every tribe in the known world to deny them their destiny. They were electric with purpose—now fearless, now shrewd, now generous. As the armies of Cuzco set forth from the Center to the four quarters of the earth, they marched under the imperial banner of the rainbow, the face of the Sun dissolving the reign of disorder. The pageantry of imperial Cuzco had a mesmerizing effect on the Andean peoples, bottled up as they had been for generations within enclaves at war with surrounding communities. It mattered not whether the Incas were met with hatred or joy. It was all the same to them, and they were relentless. If the god of retribution, the owner of the Mill, demanded justice, he would have it in abundance.

Every ten men in the Empire had a local representative of the Inca to whom they could appeal for justice. Every ten of those representatives reported to an official of higher rank, and so on up to the Inca himself. If the chain of information was broken—through apathy, venality, or any other cause that left a wrong unrighted—the weak link was executed. Period.

The Inca position was not a pose. It is not possible to understand the Incas without understanding that they were not hypocrites. They tendered every debt, in advance, on the dime, providing not merely the form of justice but its substance as well. The wealth of the Empire was divided by threes: one third for the people, one third for the Inca, and one third for the Sun. The "discretionary income" of the Incas—their third—was redistributed as "strokes" to tame the warriors. The portion of the Sun was lavished everywhere upon the people during the numerous annual festivals. The remainder could be shipped at a moment's notice anywhere threatened by hunger.

The Incas put their power at the disposal of justice. In the endeavor to restore harmony in microcosm and macrocosm alike, they understood that their own interests were indivisible from their responsibilities. Thus, for example, they could not remain content to redivide a static "pie." Among their duties was the restoration of bounty.

I have lost count of the number of times over the years when, in responding to the questions of friends about my interest in the Incas, the name of the Maya has suddenly entered the conversation unbidden. The Maya, it seems, live in imagination because we have at hand vivid pictures for contemplation in the mind's eye: Tikal, Palenque, the Caracól, and so on. With the exception of Macchu Picchu, no such images of the Inca exist. It is not that the Spanish destroyed the great architectural treasures of the Andes, although they destroyed many buildings. The true monuments of Inca civilization exist in a context too humble for ready transmission to modern sensibilities. The Incas were arguably the world's finest stonemasons, but they did not lavish their skill on ornate temple complexes. Instead they built soil.

In the Andes, where the basis of wealth was land and the currency labor, a substantial portion of the labor of the people—their taxes—was converted into soil through the construction of agricultural terrace walls. To this day, at such places as Pisac and Chincheru, tier upon tier of massive stone terraces wrought of exquisite Inca masonry grace the hillsides. These walls were built to create land for the Sun, land that the Incas chose to create rather than to requisition from the people, land that produced the surpluses used to thwart famine. Behind these walls the soils were carefully laid in layers to ensure drainage and promote friability and aeration. The masonry itself, a mosaic of interlocking, irregular polygons, represents tens of thousands of man-hours of labor.

Although at first glance this enterprise may appear quintessentially "earthly," far removed from arcane, celestial preoccupations, Inca terrace-building in fact reveals the Inca passion for confronting the challenge of Time. Over the centuries, these walls have proved invulnerable to earthquake, which is to say triumphant over the S-wave, or Serpent, moving beneath the earth. In an earthquake, the ashlars of Inca terrace walls lock into each other, allowing the whole wall simultaneously to flex and cohere. Inca agricultural terraces were constructed in defiance of the Serpent Time, for a future that never came.

Meanwhile, at virtually the same moment, the War against Time broke out in Mexico as well, for although the Inca experiment was unprecedented, it was not unparalleled. The Aztecs were anything but subtle in maintaining that a state of war existed between the Sun and the stars. The Aztec god of war, Huitzilopochtli, who was identified with the sun,[21] was born fighting against his brothers, the "four hundred stars of the south," who sought in vain to slay him.[22] We have already seen the complicity of the "jealous stars" in thwarting Quetzalcoatl's mission of ascending to the land of the gods with the bones of the dead. In another myth from the Quetzalcoatl cycle, also taken down in Nahuatl, we learn that the death of the Fourth Sun (preceding the Fifth Sun, which the Aztecs labored to keep alive) came at the hands of the stars. This myth, a reworking of some older (and probably destroyed) version, has an exact counterpart in the Andes, the myth of the llama and the flood.[23] For the Aztecs, the stars were the enemies of the Sun, the Fifth Sun.

Again, as with the Incas, the Aztecs sought to reconfigure all previous versions of the mythic past within a shroud of secrecy.

> They preserved an account of their history,
> but later it was burned,
> during the reign of Itzcoatl.
> The lords of Mexico decreed it,
> the lords of Mexico declared it,
> "It is not fitting that our people
> should know these pictures.
> Our people, our subjects will be lost
> and our land destroyed,
> for these pictures are full of lies. . . ."[24]

The reasons for this practice are not hard to understand. The critical change to the technical language of myth in both Mexico and Peru involved the substitution of the term "Sun" for "world-age," and upon acceptance of the authoritative significance of the term "Sun" hung the outcome of the whole enterprise. Miguel León-Portilla moves very close to the heart of the matter when he observes,

> With a dialectic rhythm which attempted in vain to harmonize the
> dynamism of opposing forces, the various Suns appeared and vanished.
> The Aztecs moved to stop this process: they conceived the ambitious
> project of impeding, or at least postponing the cataclysm which was to
> put an end to their Sun, the fifth of the series. This idea became
> an obsession which stimulated and made powerful the inhabitants of
> Tenochtitlan.[25]

The only elements missing in this picture are the reasons why the Aztecs felt the Fifth Sun to be in immediate jeopardy, and the basis of their hope for success. If it must remain "clear" that contact between the Incas and the Aztecs is a chimera of historical imagination, and that all similarities between them are "morphological" only, then, in the case of the Aztecs, perhaps those questions will never be answered. As for the Incas, they had reasons for a measure of optimism.

What train of thought, then, did the Incas entertain that led them to think that no less a task than stopping time itself would be accomplished? One clue lies in language itself, and involves the words for a world-ending cataclysm, *pachakuti*, and a synonym listed by Holguín, *pachaticra*.[26] The word *kuti* means variously "to return, or turn back, whence one came" (*volver alla el que vino*), "to make a half turn" (*dar media vuelta*), or "to go backwards" (*retroceder*).[27] *Ticray* means "to turn over, as a leaf, to turn the other way from how it was" (*volver . . . al reves de lo que estaba*), "to tip over" (*volcar*), or "to put something facing the other way" (*colocar de revés o contra su cara principal una cosa*).[28] The point is that nowhere does one find in the language describing precessional motion a concept of true, continuous rotary motion. Rather the words for this phenomenon give the sense of *reciprocal* motion, of turning and returning.

Not coincidentally, reciprocal motion inheres to those technologies that appear in mythical contexts related to the language of precessional imagery. The Andean rocker mill that gives its name to Tonapa Wiraqocha, bearer of the axis of the celestial sphere, worked on the principle of reciprocal motion —rocking back and forth—and the verb "to grind with a stone," *kut-ay*,[29] even shares its radical with the verb *kut-iy*. Likewise, the firedrill used in rituals in the Temple of the Sun[30] operated by reciprocal motion, as it mimicked—like the Aztec firedrill—the "lighting of fire" along the whole length of the galaxy when, at the dawning of the Age of Wiraqocha, the ancient god of fire and mill-bearer brought the solstice suns into the Milky Way.

It therefore appears that the dominant theory as regards the nature of precessional motion among the Incas was that it was reciprocating, rather than continuously rotary. Those ideas were also held in the Old World, as for example among the Hindus (see figure 10.1), where the axis of the celestial sphere—pictured as a great churn roiling the River of Milk—was conceived as having an oscillating, back-and-forth motion.[31] And why not? Human awareness of the precession apparently did not stretch even as far back as half a cycle, while the technologies available for contemplation suggested that the "hand" of the Mill's owner might at any moment start the great apparatus back in the opposite direction. First and foremost, as far as the Incas were concerned, it was essential to stop the onward motion of precessional time in order to forestall cataclysm. If later it should prove possible to turn back in the direction of the Golden Age, then so much the better. Embedded in their mythical terminology was reason for hope that this outcome was at least possible. What was necessary was that the Powers Above be persuaded to "downshift" immediately.

Persuasion, in fact, was everything. It was with this thought in mind that the Incas waged war, and it was this thought that shaped the manner in which they waged it. The second clue to how the Incas intended to win the war against precessional time is found in Murúa's account of how Pachakuti Inca decided to reorganize the *wakas* and, with them, Andean religious practice. This decision was in direct response to the ominous vision of Wiraqocha above Cuzco, which made clear the imminence of yet another "flood." The first step in reorganizing the *wakas* was to *capture* them, either through war or the threat of it. Again, not coincidentally, it was Murúa's informants who explained this ritual aspect of Inca warfare:

> When the Inca conquered a new Province or pueblo, *the first thing that he did was to seize the principal* [i.e., lineage] *Huaca of that Province or pueblo and take it to Cuzco* thus to hold that people in complete subjection so that they would not rebel. . . . *He put the Huaca in the temple of the sun, called Curicancha*, where there were many altars . . . or else he put these Huacas in other different parts [of the temple], *or in the roads, belonging to the direction of the province of origin*. . . .[32] [Emphasis added.]

The suggestion that the "capture" by the sons of the Sun of the Andean lineage *wakas*, the earthly images of the stars, was an act of sympathetic magic in service of the Fifth Sun is fully corroborated by the Anonymous Chronicler, who informs us precisely how these *wakas* were treated after being brought to Cuzco. Speaking of the Temple of the Sun, the chronicler states:

> There was in Cuzco a temple, which was like the Pantheon in Rome, where were collected all the idols [i.e., *wakas*] of all the nations and pueblos subjected to the Inca, each idol on its altar with its insignia, *but with a chain on its feet*, to denote the subjection and vassalage of its people.[33] [Emphasis added.]

There, in the Temple of the Sun, the *wakas* lay chained beneath the Sun. They were not chained by the hands or by the neck, or even tethered by a single foot. The *wakas* were chained by both feet, because, like the stars they represented, their habit of *motion* in relation to the Sun had at all costs to be arrested, if the Fifth Sun was to survive. So the *wakas* were arrested.

Once again, as with the *intihuatana* and the *seque* system of Cuzco, the dominant image of Inca thought, binding the stars to the destiny of the Sun, comes straight to the fore. Still, a healthy skepticism might weather even this explicit imagery. After all, as the Anonymous Chronicler said, the chaining of the *wakas* was meant "to denote the subjection and vassalage of the people." If behind this image lay nothing more than the Inca ambition, by means of some vague cosmological mumbo-jumbo, to hoodwink the people of the Andes into submission, then the Incas must rank among history's greatest rascals. In turning now to the final phase of Pachakuti Inca's plan to "reorganize" the *wakas*, it is for the reader, in whom the judgment of history ultimately resides, to decide whether the Incas were hypocrites; for one measure of a people's sincerity lies in what they are willing to sacrifice.

VI

ACCORDING TO MURÚA, Pachakuti Inca, having confronted Wiraqocha above Cuzco and having won a reprieve from imminent cataclysm, immediately took two steps: first, he ordered a new mode of worship of the *wakas*; second, he commanded that the year begin on December solstice. Other sources corroborate this information, as for example Betanzos who states that Pachakuti Inca invented the rites of Capac Raymi,[34] the Inca festival that culminated on the December solstice. It was, as mentioned earlier, during this festival that both the feasting of the ancestors and the arming of the young warriors took place. With the gates to the land of the dead threatened by *mama mircuc*, and the imperial practice of "arresting" the lineage *wakas* under way, the affinity of these two aspects of Capac Raymi is clear enough.

Along with the arming of the warriors and the feasting of the ancestors, Pachakuti mandated that a third ritual—called the *capacocha*—also be performed at the December solstice. The *capacocha* was a complex rite involving the sacrifice of animals, foodstuffs, textiles, precious metals, and of human children of both sexes to all the *wakas*—that is, every sacred place and object, including, but not exclusively, the lineage *wakas*—of the Empire.[35] This ritual represented the core of Pachakuti Inca's plan to reorganize the *wakas*, the final stage of War against Time, and, quite literally, the secret of the Incas.

While some sources state that the *capacocha* was performed only occasionally,[36] others assert that it was an annual event, and that it took place at the time of the December solstice.[37] The Andeanist Pierre Duviols credits both traditions, that is, the existence of an annual *capacocha*, with the possibility of performing the rite under extraordinary circumstances.[38]

During the *capacocha*, the Incas sacrificed thousands of llamas. That phase of the annual *capacocha* involving animal sacrifice—specifically the sacrifice of llamas[39]—took place at December solstice, when the status of the struggle of the celestial Llama to hold back the "flood" could be observed directly. Having completed the sacrifice of the llamas, Inca priests then placed the blood of the animals in tiny clay vessels, which must have numbered in the tens of thousands, to be distributed throughout the Empire. This holocaust was one of the central thematic images of the *capacocha*.[40] It was the duty of every able-bodied man in the Empire to place his allotment of these vessels, sanctified in the Temple of the Sun, not only at every minor shrine in the vicinity, but also to hurl them, by sling if necessary, to the top of every hill, cliff, and mountain in the Empire.[41] Apparently, Pachakuti Inca had strong opinions about the relationship between the welfare of the celestial Llama and that of the Fifth Sun. He was prepared to carry all the way to heaven's gates—via every topographical eminence along the entire spine of the Andes—the struggle to keep the Fifth Sun alive.

Duviols has characterized the *capacocha* as "one of the most original institutions" of the Inca Empire.[42] Indeed, virtually every aspect of the rite was the creation of Pachakuti Inca, and every aspect, beginning with the meaning of the word itself, represented a comprehensive response to the Inca prophecy and, as such, an integral component of the War against Time.

Some of the early sources thought the term was *capac qocha*,[43] which would mean either "sea of the king" (or "sea of the measurer") or else "royal sea." None of these renderings carry much information, and they are syntactically suspect in the bargain. If the term was used to refer to a sacrifice to a god, as for example Wiraqocha, it would have been expressed, as were the terms *cuzco capac* and *ticci capac*, as *qocha capac*, "(the sacrifice to) he who measures the (celestial) sea." On the other hand, in the most authoritative texts, those of Pachakuti Yamqui and of the informants of Avila, the term is rendered *capac hucha*.[44]

The word *hucha* has several meanings, one of which is "sin," preferred by Duviols, another "business," as in "affairs," preferred by Zuidema.[45] Ascribing the former meaning to the term—"royal sin" or "the sin of the king"—seems, to my mind, quite impossible on the face of it, since the Incas were concerned with enhancing their power, not tarnishing their mystique. Zuidema's interpretation is closer to my understanding of the term. As he points out, both Guamán Poma and Holguín list terms for imperial secretaries: *Hatun hucha Quipoc* ("*Quipu*-keeper of the great accounts")[46] and *hucha yachak* ("he

who knows the business [hucha] of the Inca").[47] Reference to the entirety of
Holguín's information is helpful:

Hucha, or cama. Sin, or business, or plea. Runaphuchan. Sin.
Dios Hucha. The business of God.
Runa hucha. Plea without the genitive.
Huchacta camacta yachak, or hucha yachak. The secretary of the Inca, or coun-
   selor in his affairs or secrets [secretos] to whom [the Inca] discloses his
   decisions that their resolution may be carried out.[48]

   Hucha, then, means "sin, business (or affair), or plea." According to Holguín, the translation "sin of the king" must be ruled out as a translation for
capac hucha because, as the lexicographer took pains to point out, hucha only
means "sin" when preceded by a noun in the genitive case, such as runaphuchan, meaning "a man's sin." Next, when referring to "God" or to kings, hucha
means "business" not in the sense of commerce, but in the sense of "affairs
and secrets," and Holguín specifically mentions that the Inca shared secrets
with his advisers. Following Holguín, then, the sacrifice of the capac hucha
could mean "a plea" (pleyto) or some "secret business" of the Inca. As we shall
now see, it meant both.
   The capacocha was a rite of staggering inclusiveness. It began with solemn
ritual caravans of tribute pouring into Cuzco from every corner of the
Empire—gold, silver, textiles, llamas, and, "from each lineage or tribe, one
or two male and female children aged about ten years."[49] Duviols has written,

   We can imagine the brilliantly colored processions of porters, dignitar-
   ies, and children setting forth from the villages; their stately and majestic advance which, like tributaries flowing into great rivers, met and
   joined together diverse groups in the district centers, until they formed
   the enormous yet disciplined retinue which proceeded solemnly to
   enter the capital.[50]

   All the emissaries and tribute were then gathered in the Aucaypata, the
great square of Cuzco, where the warriors were armed during the Capac
Raymi ceremonies of December solstice. Priests surrounded the assembly
with a gigantic chain of gold—also a fixture of rites of December solstice[51]
—which encompassed the entire plaza.[52] According to Gutiérrez de Santa
Clara, this chain rested upon "many pillars of silver the size of a man." One
wonders if there were not forty such pillars. In any event, thus cradled in

the imagery of the all-encompassing sun, those who had gathered for the *capacocha* began the solemn ceremonies. These do not make for easy reading.

The entire retinue circled slowly around the statues of Wiraqocha, the Sun, the Moon, and the god of thunder. Next, priests divided the enormous tribute in four, one portion for each of the four *suyus* of the Empire. At this point the priests sacrificed a number of children.[53] According to Betanzos's account of the first *capacocha*, undertaken by Pachakuti upon the inauguration of the Temple of the Sun, children were buried in the foundations, and then the priests painted their own faces and the walls of the Temple in "rays" of llama blood.[54] In Molina's account (probably of the fully developed ritual established after the expansion of the Empire[55]), Inca priests strangled some of the children, and removed the hearts of others, "while still alive." The blood of the children was painted on the faces of their lineage *wakas*.[56]

A solemn procession then made its way to the top of a hill called Chuquicancha, "golden enclosure," where the remains of the "unblemished" children were buried. This hill, to the northeast of the Temple of the Sun, was used for reciprocal observations of the rise and set of the June and December solstice suns respectively.[57] In other words, the children died for the benefit of the solstitial colure, the Sun-Moon axis of the Fifth Sun. Other sources speak of human sacrifices at Mount Pachatusan,[58] "the support pillar of the world-age," marking the equinox sunrise as seen from the Temple of the Sun. Later, more children were killed on a hill to the southeast, Huanacauri,[59] dedicated to the god of war, the "brother" of Manco Capac, Ayar Cachi, Mars. "Afterwards sacrifices were performed at all the fountains, hills and other places in Cuzco that were held to be sacred; but no child was killed for these sacrifices."[60] Sacrifices of gold, silver, and textiles were offered to the 328 *wakas*, or shrines, of the *seque* system, fanning out toward the horizon like so many knots on a forty-stringed *quipu*.

This concluded the initial sequence of the *capacocha*. Thousands of llamas had been slaughtered in anticipation of their blood being distributed to every topographical eminence of the Empire. The tribute, now to be redistributed to every shrine throughout the Empire, had been collected, and children had been sacrificed to the major gods and to particularly important places on the horizon of Cuzco. Now the entire symbolism would be recreated on a scale as vast as the Empire itself. The legations would set forth in return to their points of origin, to carry the *capacocha* to the farthest reaches of the known world, and to tie every people in it directly to the Sun. Molina wrote,

As soon as they had concluded the sacrificial ceremonies in Cuzco, the Priests brought out those who had to be sent to other parts . . . the order of marching with the sacrifices was that all the people who went with the *Capacocha*, also called *Cachahuaca*, took ways apart from each other. They did not follow the royal road, *but traversed the ravines and hills in a straight line, until each reached the places where the sacrifices were to be made.*[61] [Emphasis added.]

In other words, the returning host fanned out on their homeward journey, following the lines of the *seque* system. Zuidema has noted,

The reason why the *capac hucha* walked in a straight direction was probably because they had to follow a specific *ceque* [*seque.*] Since the *ceques* were considered to go out from the Temple of the Sun and since specific *huacas* also had a function in terms of astronomical observation, we may assume that the *ceques* were used as lines of sight for the observation of solar, lunar, and stellar risings and settings.[62]

As Molina's description unfolds, we find the unfolding of the Secret of the Incas: the undertaking of human sacrifice to persuade the Powers Above to stop Time. The *seque* system of Cuzco was a microcosmic model of the Empire of the Sun, which in turn was a model of the relationship of the Fifth Sun to the stars. The 328 *wakas* of the *seque* system were a schematic of the tribes of the Empire. Each *waka* was assigned a relationship to a different day of the year. Each tribe of the Empire was required to keep a priest in Cuzco who would care for that *waka* and propitiate it on the appropriate day. Each *waka* was placed on a *seque*, or ray, that emanated toward the direction of the homeland of its assigned tribe. Further, each *seque* had an astronomical value, in relation to the stars that rose at the given azimuth toward which the *seque* pointed. Likewise, from ancient times, each tribe was understood to descend, ideally, from a different star or constellation. So, as the legations from all over the Empire set out simultaneously on their return homeward, each walked in an undeviating line in the direction of its homeland and assigned star.

The legations contained children yet to be sacrificed, and as they fanned out toward their destinations, they commenced to replicate on the scale of the entire Empire the array of the *seque* system of Cuzco. They stopped at every provincial center on the way, there to sacrifice the preselected local child. Meanwhile, every minor shrine was given its share of the other tribute,

and the blood of the llamas sanctified in Cuzco distributed for hurling to
the mountain peaks. Every legation was accompanied by an Inca priest who
kept an exact accounting, ensuring that every minor holy place of local
veneration was included in the offerings.

The spellbinding resonance established between these twin poles of
horror and beauty was reflected in the solemnity of the occasion through
the minutiae of conduct to which participants and bystanders alike were
enjoined to adhere. Molina wrote,

> [W]hen those who were making the journey over uninhabited tracts
> with the sacrifices met other travellers, they did not raise their eyes to
> look at them, and the travellers prostrated themselves on the ground
> until the sacrifice-bearers had passed. When those bearing sacrifices
> passed through a village, the inhabitants did not come out of their
> homes, but remained, with deep humility and reverence, until the said
> Capac-cocha had passed onwards.[63]

Murúa noted that the eyes of the priests never left the ground, and that
death awaited anyone so foolish as to disregard the rules of conduct.[64]

Onward and onward the legations continued:

> And in this way they travelled throughout the territories which the
> Inca had conquered, to the four quarters of the Empire; and they did
> so making the said sacrifices, until they reached the furthest limits,
> where the Inca had placed boundary markers.[65]

Like the chain of gold, supported on "many" posts in the Aucaypata of
Cuzco, the great circle of the boundaries of the Empire of the Sun—the
geomantic equivalent of the ecliptic—once again encircled all the offerings
of the *capacocha*.

Here, the last of the children reached the end of the line. They were
sacrificed at the boundaries of the Empire of the Sun, thereby establishing
the true "horizon" of Cuzco from the point of view of the Fifth Sun at the
Center, whence all these tragic trajectories emanated, and to which the
lineages of these children were now bound.

And lest there be any doubt as to the significance of the rite, Molina
delivers the crucial datum concerning the sacrifices undertaken by the returning processions: "It is worthy of remark that children were not sacrificed
at all the *huacas*, but only at the chief *huaca* of each lineage or province."[66] In
other words, these children were sacrificed in the name of their tribal *wakas*,

whose identity and ultimate abode lay in the stars. These children were going home.

Here, far from the battlefield and the blare of martial music, lay the most critical front in the War against Time. And herein lay all the keys to both the tragic splendor and the inconceivable vulnerability of the Inca Empire. In the last analysis, the Inca Emperors understood that no heroic measures could ever redeem the Fifth Sun. In the end, only a "plea" might prevail. The *capac hucha*, was indeed a plea, and in this plea lay the secret of the Incas. The Incas did not, like the Aztecs, sacrifice human lives to "feed" the Sun; instead they dispatched emissaries to the stars, emissaries bearing a desperate message.

This is not fancy, for both the name of the messenger and the message itself have been preserved. Molina, among others, noted another name for the practice of human sacrifice: *cachahuaca*, literally "messenger to the *wakas*."[67] The same word *cacha*, "message," also forms the root of the word *cachaui*, which is a synonym for *seque*.[68] The very conception of straight lines to the horizon—*seques*—subsumed an attempt at communication. The Incas, desperate to make peace with the stars on behalf of the Fifth Sun and all who dwelt beneath it, had conceived the means to plead humanity's case at heaven's bar.

For the judge was no less than the Creator himself, Wiraqocha, the god of Time, who, in the end, would make the ultimate disposition. The children of the *wakas* were sent to make the case, but they could not do so directly. In Andean religion, as we have seen, one addressed Wiraqocha through the intercession of one's lineage *waka*. It was those *wakas*, and not humanity itself, that Wiraqocha had created above Titicaca all those Worlds ago. Thus, the children sacrificed were dispatched to their respective *waka* homelands in the stars, bearing the *capac hucha*, that is to say the "royal plea." For then, and only then, might the very stars of heaven, so persuaded by their charges, and speaking as if with one voice, conspire to reach the ear of Wiraqocha, the awesome bearer of the Mill, and plead the case for their earthly children.

A picture of this event, or rather the picture that must have inspired the Inca imagination, exists to this day, at Tiahuanaco, on the Gateway of the Sun itself. Flanking the image of Wiraqocha are three rows of what have been referred to as "angels." (See figure 10.2.) There are forty-eight of these entities, portrayed either as bird-headed men or as human-headed birds, all on bended knee, in supplication to the Creator. In the course of this book there have been numerous examples from Peru, Mesoamerica, and Siberia where the stars are likened to birds, perching on the branches of the world tree. In the myth of the fall of Fox, it was Fox, Puma, and "birds of every kind" that caused all the trouble. Among the Cañari, the lineage *waka* was the macaw. And there, on the Gateway of the Sun at Tiahuanaco is a representation of the Andean creation myth expressed in the symbolism of bird-people: the lineage *wakas* of all the tribes (of the Tiahuanaco ecumene), kneeling in prayer to their Creator, the creator of the sun, the moon, and the stars. How could Wiraqocha, thus reverently approached on bended knee by all the stars of the firmament, fail to sense the justice in their plea?

The lintel of the Gateway at Tiahuanaco reveals the ancient logic that inspired the *capacocha*, now enlisted in desperate urgency for the sole purpose of getting a message through, before Time ran out. Again, not surprisingly, it was Murúa who was told the contents of the message. The message was indeed in the form of a plea, a mantra really, because it was repeated over and over again during the weeks it must have taken for the stately processions of the *capacocha* to reach the limits of the Empire. As the priests walked "four by four," eyes downcast, they paused every few hundred yards ("the distance of an arcabus [arquebus] shot") and repeated these words, words that represent the distillation of two millennia of Andean thought: "May the Sun remain a young man and the Moon a young maiden; may the world not turn over; let there be peace."[69]

This, then, was the plea that the Incas directed to Wiraqocha. When a god got old, as had happened to Wiraqocha himself, the end of his reign was nigh, and the time to leave the earth at hand. So the Incas prayed that Sun and Moon, the Fifth Sun and Moon, remain young. If the lowly Mocoví knew, then surely also did the Incas, that the Sun would "die" when "time [had] sapped its strength." But the Fifth Sun, like the children sacrificed in its behalf, had been born with prospects for a youthful death. So the plea of the Incas reminded the One whose hand rested on the Mill that He, and only He, had the power to forestall the imminent: "may the world not turn over," *Ama pachakuti*. "Let there be peace," because, in the final analysis, the outcome of the War against Time was in the hands of Tonapa Wiraqocha.

So the Incas harbored their prophecy, and labored for reprieve. As Emperor after Emperor succeeded Pachakuti, restlessly expanding the boundaries of the Empire in the attempt to attain "peace," did they also stand shoulder to shoulder with their priests to scan the night skies for any sign of hope? Or were the Incas hypocrites?

Huayna Capac, born to the knowledge that he was meant to be the last Inca, showed signs of the strain. The great Inca conquest machine had previously succeeded as much by guile as by force. The mystique was everything, and wars were not undertaken that could not be won. But Huayna

Capac battled his way relentlessly north, far to the north, in order to secure his heart's desire, a capital at Quito. Over and over again he fought determined foes—the Cañaris and the Chachapoyas—and did not shrink from massacres to achieve his aims. Is it possible that he felt that the last hope of attaining the elusive equipoise—the forestalling of the Mill—lay in securing a place in the sun at the center of the world, at Quito, which lies upon the equator?[70]

It is unlikely that this question will ever be answered. But the answer to the *capac hucha*, the secret entreaty of the Inca Emperors, is known, and it was a terrible one. The Incas pleaded for peace, for the survival of the Fifth Sun, for Wiraqocha to hold back the deluge. To all the world, the Inca Empire appeared to be at its zenith. But as Huayna Capac lay dying, and the bridge to an ancestral world already lost sank beneath the waters of time, Wiraqocha sent his reply. He sent the Spanish.

VII

THE FIRST COMMUNICATION from any European to reach the ears of an educated citizen of one of America's Sun kingdoms was this: "The Spaniards are troubled with a disease of the heart for which gold is the specific remedy."[71] This sentiment, uttered in jocular coldbloodedness by Cortés to an emissary of the Aztec king Moctezuma, was the death knell of the Fifth Sun in Mexico.[72] Eight years later, it would be the same in Peru. The War against Time was lost.

Despite the outward similarities in the collapse of the Sun Kingdoms of the Americas, the Incas and the Aztecs had little in common beyond access to a way of thinking. The Aztecs neither aspired to nor attained true Empire. Theirs had been a history of solitary wandering, of cruel rejection, and of self-reliance in an environment whose human and natural faces were equally pitiless. This experience is reflected in the ghastly simplicity of their political ambition, which was to create a domain based on the principles of domination and submission, a polity whose entire logic was subservient to a single premise: the Sun must be fed. As the children of the Sun, the Aztecs would initiate and sustain eternal warfare in defense of the Fifth Sun.

> And this war should be of such a nature that we do not endeavour to destroy the others totally. War must always continue, so that each time and whenever we wish our gods to eat and feast, we may go there [neighboring cities] as one who goes to the market to buy something

to eat . . . organized to obtain victims to offer our god Huitzilopochtli [the Sun]. . . .[73]

Uninterested in administering conquered territories, the Aztecs viewed other people as raw materials, and other cultures as "markets" where they might browse for the thousands upon thousands of sacrificial victims they required each year:

Rather, let a convenient market be sought where our god may go with his army to buy victims and people to eat as if he were to go to a nearby place to buy tortillas . . . whenever he wishes or feels like it. . . . Our god will feed himself with them as though he were eating warm tortillas, soft and tasty, straight out of the oven.[74]

By contrast, the Incas did not take history personally, for the Andean past was a communal affair. The only "outsiders" in Andean history, the only people truly diminished in memory, were the Lords of Wari. As the Huarochirí myths stated it, "We don't know the origins of the people of those days, nor where it was they emerged from." The Inca Empire was an attempt to set things right, to return to the Andean peoples their birthright of unity in diversity. If it took a certain arrogance to declare themselves the executors of the divine will, the Incas nonetheless attempted to materialize a vision that was self-consciously tempered with historical maturity. Thus, at the moment of the mythical founding of Cuzco in a valley that had known the imprint of both Tiahuanaco and Wari, Manco Capac, along with his brothers and sisters, "walled up" their dangerous brother Ayar Cachi/Mars. The Incas were not interested in compounding the misery unleashed by Wari. Their planetary affinity was with Jupiter, the wise and powerful king, the god of summer and of bounty. The Inca Emperors had no purpose greater than the revivification of the legacy of Tiahuanaco. In this sense they labored from the outset under self-imposed constraints.

While both the Aztecs and Incas endeavored to save the Fifth Sun, the Aztecs fell into the deepest hell of black magic, where every metaphor is literal truth and every dangerous human trait is an aspect of the godhead. The Aztec perspective gestated during a historical incubation period of great suffering and fear. Called *chichimeca*, "descendants of dogs," by the older populations of the Valley of Mexico who had moved in to fill the void left by the collapse of the Toltecs, the Aztecs had wandered for more than a century and a half before finally taking refuge about 1325 on the only land permitted them, a miserable island in the middle of a swamp. Like the serpent-devouring hawk upon a *nopal* cactus, which legend says they found there, the Aztecs would ascend to dominance over their tormentors, and transform their precarious perch into a metropolitan center of splendor and might.

It was as if the Aztecs, long consigned to the dry, cold margins of the Mexican north, had now become bewitched as, basket by basket, they dredged from their swamp the mud to build up their island and create its canals. In a manner eerily mimetic of the teaching of Carlos Castañeda's Don Juan (or any decent depth psychologist), the Aztecs strove to create an island of consciousness, the *tonal*, the Aztec word for "sun" and "light," in the midst of the black waters of the unconscious, the *nahual*, the unseen spirit world. Their mental constructs, embodied in the towering white pyramids of their tribal god Huitzilopochtli, now identified with the (Fifth) Sun, had been redeemed from waters alien to the accustomed elements of their no-madic past. The Aztecs were a people surrounded by enemies, reviled as barbarians, a people who had hungrily absorbed the heroic Toltec heritage, and found in it the cosmic drama of their own situation. The truth was that the Aztecs, like the Fifth Sun, were entirely encircled by enemies, enemies as numerous as the stars. Tenochtitlán became the materialization of the Aztec *tonal*, an island fortress of consciousness eternally under siege from the monsters of the deep.

And so, in the same way that the psyche's first defense against fear is rage, the Aztecs created an Empire of Rage, and Tenochtitlán was its caul-dron. It bubbled with the fire struck in the thoracic cavity of its dis-hearted victims, and was replicated ten thousand times over in the cookpots of the victorious warriors, who devoured the choicest cuts of those sacrificed to "keep the Sun alive." The sudden extrapolation from the ancient database of native American myth of prototypes for such behavior was a leap precisely as preposterous as the suggestion of some modern anthropologists that Aztec human sacrifice was a response to a protein deficiency in the diet of the Valley of Mexico. But then, the extremes of unreconstructed materialism and fanatical mysticism converge upon the same lonely promontory, isolated in the dark, under a cold, hard sky.

This volume will not solve the riddle of how the War against Time was conceived and executed—albeit in radically different styles—simultane-ously by peoples thought to have had little historic contact. For the time being, at least, any answer would be premature. There are too many sources to absorb, and too few scholars who even suspect the existence of a technical language of myth.

Nonetheless, it seems appropriate at this point to hazard an observation.

When Fox and Quetzalcoatl both fall, unable to link the solstitial colure through the Milky Way, both thwarted by the upstart quail, with its peculiar habit of nibbling the bones of the dead, the time has come to look to method and to common sense. So long as the impasse created by the conventions of comparative method prevails, the true scope and drama of the historic cataclysm known as the Spanish Conquest of the New World will remain unexplored.

This observation is not intended as an invitation to oversimplification. For all that they were heirs to the same ancient thought-form as the Aztecs, the Incas could not have responded more differently to intimations of a gathering catastrophe.

Inca civilization was wed to an ancient sorrow, witness through its myths to very great cycles of creation and loss. Along with so many other tribes, the Incas had suffered the legacy of warfare and the memory of better days. This "suffering with" lent the Incas a degree of compassion, evident both in the even-handed administration of their Empire and the legacy of beauty, much of it destroyed, which they left behind them. The Inca endeavor mirrored a psychological truth: that if one withstands the rage that fear inevitably conjures, one encounters sorrow, and with it the abandonment of the heroic quest. This insight into human nature is beautifully captured in the words of the storyteller Michael Meade: "The price of the gifts of nature involves giving up the heroic eye and accepting the cycles of birth and death. The beauty in nature is married to sorrow, and no heroics can remove the sorrow without destroying the beauty."[75]

The Incas are the more remarkable for rising above the temptation to indulge in the easy tribal hatreds of their time. In struggling with a terrible vision of the future, the Incas drew upon the waters of sorrow, rather than rage, to fashion an empire in the image of a prayer. And if this plea, carried on high by the souls of slain children, displayed flawed powers of faith, it also revealed the most terrible sorrow of all: a sense that the Creator might abandon his creation. Like the compulsive gambler who searches, griefstricken, for divine recognition in the perfect winning streak, the Incas risked everything for a sign in the sky.

For the Incas, gold was the symbolic expression of this sorrow, called by them "the tears of the Sun," tears shed at the spectacle of human folly. Gold—and silver as well, the tears of the Moon—were metals so sacred that no object fashioned from them and brought to Cuzco could ever be removed, under pain of death.[76] In a land with no monetary system, gold's value lay in its inherent beauty, a beauty that the Incas used to express the imperishable wonder of the living world.

The first Spanish outriders to reach Cuzco were overwhelmed by the golden garden in the outer courtyard of the Temple of the Sun. It contained life-size effigies of maize and other food plants, of flowers, of golden llamas. By a font of gold stood enormous gold and silver urns overflowing with maize and other sacrificial offerings. The interior walls were clad in gold, and facing the rising sun was an image of the Sun encrusted in emeralds and other precious stones. Countless golden vessels bore the images of every living thing—bird, snakes, crayfish, and caterpillars.[77] For the Incas, too, were "troubled with a disease of the heart for which gold [was] the specific remedy." Surely, if Sun and Moon shed such tears, there must be mercy at the heart of creation.

All unburied Inca gold is gone now, melted into the ingots[78] that financed Christendom's repulsion of the Ottoman Empire. Perhaps the most unforgettable irony of Andean history lies in this concentration of gold. Had the Incas never conceived the ambition of redeeming the humbler cycles of birth and death from the jaws of a greater Ruin, the Spanish might have ascended the Andes to find a desolate hellhole of impoverished, warring tribes. Instead they found, in the tears of the Fifth Sun, that "specific remedy" which would fulfill the prophecy of Wiraqocha Inca.

For the Incas there was always and only a single lake, Titicaca. Still and otherworldly, Titicaca remains to this day forbidding, for it contains too much of the past, a lake of losses, at the heart of the Empire of Sorrow. I think anyone who ventures that far, especially in these troubled times, would make a great mistake not to go to the Island of the Sun, there to contemplate the singular perfection of its Inca shrine, eternally recycling the waters of the deep. And while there, perhaps it would not go amiss, if not to utter a prayer, at least to remember, for both the Incas and ourselves, the enduring lesson of our common heritage: "This, too, shall pass away."

THE PATTERN
OF THE PAST

Heaven within the mountain points to hidden treasures. In the words and deeds of the past there lies hidden a treasure that men may use to strengthen and elevate their own characters. The way to study the past is not to confine oneself to mere knowledge of history but, through application of this knowledge, to give actuality to the past.[1]

—RICHARD WILHELM

I

A CONTEMPORARY BLACK OPS cadre could not have concocted a scenario more certain to unhinge the mind of the last Inca, Huayna Capac, than the events and conditions that bedeviled his final days. Having secured the northern boundary of the Empire, and for the moment uninhibited by the formal responsibilities of the court at Cuzco, Huayna Capac celebrated a rare opportunity to be himself. He liked women and drink, yet possessed a nature so magnanimous that this interlude in the kingdom of Quito was remembered with all the fondness of a Shakespearean revel. Into the midst of this golden moment, messengers came from the coast, announcing the arrival of strangers, come in floating houses, strangers so fierce that they frightened the jaguars of the royal zoological gardens.

"Fearful and melancholy,"[2] Huayna Capac retired and, like his ancestors before him, undertook a rigorous fast in quest of a vision. After some time

Huayna Capac began, apparently, to hallucinate.[3] A vision of three dwarfs declaring, "We came to call you," roused the Emperor to shout for servants. By the time they rushed to the Inca's chamber, the apparition had dissolved. It was then that Huayna Capac knew beyond doubt that he would die, and said so.[4] Only then did smallpox strike the court. Nor was this previously unknown plague attributable to Pizarro and his men.[5] It came from a different direction, down through what is modern-day Colombia from the Caribbean. If the tradition that Huayna Capac commanded that the Empire be divided between his sons Huascar and Atahuallpa is to be credited, then this means that the Emperor also lived to see his beloved son and chosen successor, Ninan Cuychi, die the same terrible death that awaited Huayna Capac himself. In any event, Huayna Capac died, according to several accounts, with the terms of the Inca prophecy on his lips.

With an aura of Magic Realism worthy of Borges or García Márquez, the fell events in Ecuador would be remembered in tales like this:

> At the dinner hour, a messenger arrived, dressed in a black cape. He kissed the Inca with reverence, then gave him a closed box with a key. The Inca ordered the messenger to open the box, but he declined respectfully, saying that the Creator [Wiraqocha] had ordered that the Inca alone must open it. Seeing the logic of the situation, the Inca opened the little box from which flew butterflies or fluttered little pieces of paper, which disappeared. This was the smallpox, and within two days the general Mihacnacamayta along with many captains died, their faces covered with scabs. When the Inca saw all this, he ordered a stone building erected in which to hide himself away. And thus hidden, encased in stone, he too died. At the end of eight days they took his half-rotted body out of there, enbalmed it, and took it to Cuzco. . . .[6]

It was the shaman-priests of Huarochirí who would to leave to history the epitaph for the Incas. Neither so close to the Inca court as to be dominated by political motives, nor so distant from the common fate of all the Andean peoples to be indifferent to these events, the mythographers of Huarochirí left behind what might arguably be called the last myth of the Imperial Americas. This story, a unique treasure of the human heritage formulated even as the hammer of secular materialism began to fall, must be considered one of the last products of the purely archaic mind, as yet undisturbed by an utterly alien mode of thought.

Next, we'll speak about one of Cuni Raya Vira Cocha's feats.

Just before the appearance of the Spaniards, it's said, Cuni Raya [Wiraqocha] headed toward Cuzco.

There he conversed with the Inca Huayna Capac. "Come, son, let's go to Titi Caca. There I will reveal to you who I am," he said.

And there he told him, "Inca, mobilize your people, so that we may send magicians and all sorts of shamans to Ura Ticsi, the world's lower foundations." As soon as he said this, the Inca promptly gave the order.

"I am condor shaman!" some men answered.

"I am falcon shaman!" said others.

"I am one who flies in the form of a swift!" replied still others.

He instructed them, "Go to the world's lower foundations. Then tell my father, 'Your son sent me here. Send me back, bearing one of his sisters.'"

The man who was the swift's shaman, together with the other shamans, set out intending to return within five days.

The swift's shaman was the first to arrive there.

When he arrived and delivered his message, he was given something in a small chest and warned, "You mustn't open this. Lord Huayna Capac himself must be the first to open it."

While the man was bringing it, when he'd almost delivered it to Cuzco, he thought, "No! I'll take a look inside. What could it be?" And he opened it. Inside there appeared a very stately and beautiful lady. Her hair was like curly gold and she wore a majestic costume, and in her whole aspect she looked very tiny.

The moment he saw her, the lady disappeared.

And so, deeply abashed, he arrived at the place called Titi Caca in Cuzco.

Huayna Capac said, "If it weren't for your being the swift's shaman, I'd have you executed right this instant! Get out! Go back by yourself!"

The swift's shaman returned and brought the woman back. When he was bringing her back along the road, dying for something to eat and drink, he had only to speak and a set table would instantly be there. It was just the same when he needed to sleep.

He delivered her exactly on the fifth day.

When he handed her over to them, Cuni Raya and the Inca received her overjoyed.

But before opening the chest, Cuni Raya said, "Inca! Let's draw a line across this world. I'll go into this space, and you go into this other space with my sister. You and I mustn't see each other anymore!" he said as he divided the world.

And he began to open the box. At the moment he opened it, the world lit up with lightning.

The Inca Huayna Capac said, "I'll never again return from here. I'll stay right here with my princess, with my queen." To one man, a kinsman of his, he said, "You go in my stead. Return to Cuzco and say, 'I'm Huayna Capac!'"

At that very moment, then and there, the Inca disappeared forever with that lady of his, and Cuni Raya did the same.

Later on, after Huayna Capac had died, people scrambled for political power, each saying to the others,

"Me first!"

"Me first!"

It was while they were carrying on this way that the Spanish Vira Cochas appeared in Caxa Marca.[7]

Part of the charm of this tale lies in its adherence to the irrepressibly buoyant style of all the Huarochirí myths. Free from the claustrophobic intimation of doom that permeated Inca thought, its power comes from the fact that, more clearly than any other story that has come down to the present, it permits an unobstructed view of the thought processes of the "classical" school of native Andean mythography.

II

THE FIRST TIME I read this story, at the outset of my research into Andean myth, I didn't know what to make of it. Later, when the planetary aspect of the Andean gods began to come into focus, I thought now and again of this myth, but lacked the means to investigate it further. Using a planetarium was out of the question. A planetarium is an analogue machine. Unlike the experiments involving sun-star (precessional) correspondences, where the planetarium is simply tilted to a given year, a question involving the precise placement of the planets at a remote date requires that the machine turn backwards physically through *each day* between the present and the past date in question. A problem like this would tie up a planetarium for upwards of a month. The Planetary Tables give planetary positions only at five-day intervals, and hence are not up to the complexity of this story, which describes a number of planetary interactions over a ten-day period.

While the final chapters of this book were being written, a series of coincidences put me on the phone to a colleague who, for reasons unrelated to this myth, made it clear I needed to look at a piece of computer software called Skyglobe. With the inertia of the barely computer-literate, I had to be talked out of my objections. Yes, it would run on my machine. No, it was not astronomically expensive; it was shareware, twenty dollars. Yes, it took precession into account.

When I understood what this program could do, I thought almost immediately of this story, which I have called "The Epitaph for the Incas." Here, at the eleventh hour, a final means of testing all the basic hypotheses of this book had quite suddenly intervened. If, thus far, the research had been even approximately valid, then the myth at hand was describing a conjunction of Saturn and Jupiter (Wiraqocha and Huayna Capac), followed shortly by the entrance of Venus ("the star with disheveled hair") into the grouping, and finally with Mars (aucayoc, "he with enemies," the planetary ruler of war) either in or near this triple group. Two further conditions also had to be met. First, such a series of events must have occurred at or near the death of Huayna Capac. Second, with all of the above conditions met, the tail of the Western Scorpius must at this time have lain at inferior conjunction, at its lowest (and invisible) point, crossing the north-south meridian beneath the horizon, or at "the world's lower foundation," to use the Andean term. I would be lying if I didn't admit to having been just a bit intimidated by this last minute "opportunity."

At this point I would like to ask the reader to take the time to go back and reread the above myth, and ask a few questions. Is there any way to "read" the astronomy of this myth (assuming for the moment the validity of the previous chapters), other than the way in which I have described? If its characters are understood as planets, is not, in fact, this myth very precise as to its meaning: first Saturn and Jupiter, then a flash of Venus, then the meeting of the three, then their disappearance, then the reign of Mars? If the actions of the mythical characters should correspond identically, line by line, with the motions of *four* planets at a known historical date, what are the chances that this is a meaningless coincidence?

Huayna Capac died somewhere between late 1525 and 1527. The date of 1525 comes from Vasco Nuñez de Balboa, "discoverer" of the Pacific Ocean and the first European ever to hear of the existence of the Inca Empire. Later in his life, he would visit Quito, where Huayna Capac died, and listen to firsthand testimony suggesting a date of 1525. The early chroni-

cler Velasco did likewise, and concluded likewise.[8] Later reports differ somewhat, placing the event in 1527. These details are important because the
myth from Huarochirí describes the death of Huayna Capac in terms of
celestial events that occurred early in the year 1524.

Before turning to an examination of this curious fact, and the entire
"report" of Skyglobe, a few general comments are in order concerning "The
Epitaph for the Incas." When Wiraqocha arrives, he suggests to Huayna
Capac that they go to a place in Cuzco called "Titi Caca." As mentioned
elsewhere, it was, and remains, a common practice in the Andes to set aside
some local bit of land with the name Titicaca, which was associated with
the ancestors and the underworld. Given this association, and given the
importance attached by the priest-astronomers of the Andes to the fate of
the entrance to the underworld in the years immediately preceding the
Conquest, it is not, therefore, surprising to learn that the purpose of Wiraqocha's visit is to encourage the Inca to send "all sorts of shamans" to the
entrance to the underworld. The name given this locus in the story is *ura
ticsi*, literally the world's "lower foundations." As has been noted, the word
ura, or *urin*, was used in the Andes to designate the "lower" moieties. Cuzco
itself was divided by the east-west baseline into "upper" and "lower" halves,
hurin Cuzco lying to the south of this line.

When Wiraqocha and the Inca divide the world in half by drawing a
line, this is probably, as Salomon and Urioste suggest, a reference both to
the ideal east-west baseline dividing Cuzco and to the division of the Empire, which transpired upon the death of Huayna Capac, between his surviving sons Atahuallpa and Huascar.[9] Yet there is a third, purely astronomical,
valence for this reference, as will be noted presently.

A third point, made possible of testing because of the Skyglobe program,
concerns the astronomical identity of the "three shamans." According to the
myth, the three shamans took the form of birds—condor, falcon, and swift.
That fact led me to an initial assumption, that the three birds are stars, since
"birds," as we have seen, is a sort of generic mythic term for stars. This
premise is further supported by chapter 29 of the Huarochirí myths, the one
that includes most of the work's explicit astronomical information. Here a
number of objects other than the llama itself are described. The *lluthu*, or
partridge, is mentioned as the southern end of the celestial Llama. Then the
narrator brings attention back to the hind flanks of the llama to describe her
suckling calf. The next sentences read, "Also we know there are three stars in
a straight line. They called these the Condor, the Vulture and the Falcon."[10]

Here, then, is described a constellation composed of three stars in a line,
representing three species of birds, two of which are identical to the species

specified as the "bird shamans" dispatched by Huayna Capac to the under-world. It is known that Avila drew on the information of several informants, and therefore it is quite possible that the "three stars in a straight line," like the three shamans, were understood as a grouping of birds, whose species might be remembered slightly differently by different informants.

I had for a long time harbored a suspicion concerning the identity of these three stars.[11] Placed as they were, apparently in relation to the hind flanks of the Llama, they appeared to me likely to represent three stars in Scorpius, the same three that form the crosspiece of *cruz calvario*, that is, epsilon Scorpius and the visibly double stars 1 and 2 mu Scorpius and 1 and 2 zeta Scorpius. (See figure 2.2.) (Interestingly, the myth specifies that "men," in the plural, represented each bird, but when referring to the activity of the *swift's* shaman, the language reverts to the singular, suggesting that epsilon Scorpius represented the swift, and the other, paired stars the other shamans.) The reason for this suspicion, beyond the fact that they lie in a straight line at the hind flanks of the llama, is that the three "bird-shamans" of our myth are associated with the land of the dead, by their being dis-patched to the underworld. The three stars in question lie at the entrance to the land of the dead, just at the area of crossing of the Milky Way and the ecliptic in the area of December solstice.

In chapter 29 of Huarochirí, where they are identified as "birds," two of the three birds—condor and turkey vulture[12]—are eaters of carrion, and as such are associated with death. Further, the renaming of them after the Conquest as *cruz calvario*, for purposes of "guerrilla syncretism," makes sense, since Mount Calvary stands in the same relation to ideas of death and rebirth in Christian thought as does the notion in Andean thought of high-flying raptorial "bird shamans" capable of reaching the land of the dead. During the three days of Christ's entombment between Good Friday and Easter Sunday, He is said to have journeyed to the underworld (Hell) to liberate the dead. This same connection is repeated in the myth of Huayna Capac, when he chooses the "bird shamans," condor, falcon, and swift, to journey to the "lower foundations" of the world.

It therefore occurred to me to look for the location of these three stars at the time suggested by the myth in question. The same principles of analysis I had used throughout this study suggested February 1, 1524, as the date to which the myth refers. A meeting of Wiraqocha and an Inca Emperor should signify a conjunction of Saturn and Jupiter. Further, such a conjunc-tion, one would expect, must have occurred on or near the year of death of Huayna Capac. According to the Planetary Tables, such an event took place on February 1, 1524.

At this point I turned my life's work over to Skyglobe, to see what would happen. As I pecked away at the keyboard, calling up that long-ago sky, I remembered another night when, as I trudged beneath a gibbous moon at 3:30 A.M. toward a meeting with an old campesino who had some stars to show me, a howling pack of black dogs had poured down an embankment to snap at my heels. I had to decide there and then whether to turn back. Half an hour later, the old man was showing me *cruz calvario*, cutting through the black-cloud Fox, at the entrance to the underworld. Now, as Skyglobe resolved the image of February 1, 1524, I once again tasted the joy of survival at the gates of the land of the dead.

Figure 11.1 shows the southern horizon shortly after sunset, at 6:52 P.M., on this date. At this time, with the sun depressed nine degrees beneath the western horizon, objects of the magnitude of Saturn and Jupiter, low in the western sky, would first become visible in the twilight. The three bird shamans were precisely where the myth said they should be. As the figure shows, the "three shamans," epsilon Scorpius, 1 and 2 mu Scorpius, and 1 and 2 zeta Scorpius, lie beneath the horizon, plummeting straight down and touching "the world's lower foundation," that is, the southern tropic, at the entrance to the underworld. In astronomical terminology the three stars lie at inferior conjunction; they also happen to mark the crossing point in the stars of the ecliptic and the galaxy, as well as the location in the stars visible rising at December solstice. This result was intriguing, but it was only the tip of an iceberg. As I played the successive nights described in the myth across the computer screen, the planetary events were simply spectacular.

III

FIGURE 11.2A SHOWS the evening sky of February 1, 1524, the day of closest conjunction of Saturn and Jupiter. Wiraqocha has come to visit Huayna Capac, and as we have seen, the bird shamans are plummeting into the underworld, "intending to return within five days." On the way back from the underworld, the swift's shaman makes the mistake of opening the box given him. For a brief instant he sees a beautiful woman with "curly" golden hair, very "tiny," who "disappears" instantly.

Figure 11.2b shows the evening sky, also thirty-six minutes after sunset on February 5—that is, four nights later—during the swift shaman's promised return "within five days." On that evening *chasca coyllur*, the planet Venus, identified in the Spanish Chronicles as a beautiful woman with curly hair, makes its first reappearance from behind the sun after about eight weeks of invisibility. As the figure shows, Venus, with the sun depressed nine degrees, just flashes for an instant on the horizon, disappearing almost instantly in its first reappearance as evening star. Further, just as the myth specifies, Venus, at this point in its orbit, appears at its "tiniest" because of its distance from the earth.[13] On successive evenings, Venus will linger longer in the western sky.

Then the myth says that the swift's shaman was ordered by an angry Emperor[14] to return to the underworld in search of the beautiful woman, and that "exactly" five days later, he presented her to the Inca. Exactly five evenings later, as figure 11.2c demonstrates, on February 10, Venus came into conjunction with Saturn and Jupiter.

Finally, just before Huayna Capac "disappears," he turns to a "kinsman" whom he instructs to return to Cuzco in his stead. In the same way that the myth specifies that the beautiful woman is a "sister" of Wiraqocha, the "kinsman" of Jupiter's regent, Huayna Capac, must also be a planet. And there, a few discreet "paces" away from Huayna Capac's joyful meeting with his consort, stands the planet Mars. Moments later (figure 11.2d), as promised, Jupiter, Saturn, and Venus "disappear." The only player left on the stage is the "kinsman" Mars, now returned to Cuzco to preside over civil war and the Spanish Conquest.

This corroboration had about it a kind of finality, as if the collective spirit of the Andean priesthood, now focused in the eye of history, stared back with unwavering gaze to ask, "Well?" I wanted to be able to say to them that this last communication to humanity from the pre-Columbian Andes would be valued, but I couldn't be sure. For an instant, I think, I touched some portion of the vast sorrow that had engulfed the Andean world. "We wish to be people, not Indians."

How much character does it take, when your world is crashing down around you, to continue to do your job, make your observations, and preserve them for a future that may already have been destroyed? How much love for those as yet unborn does it take to create so sweet a story, designed not to call attention to its guile, but solely to mesh with the apparatus of human memory—a story replete with magic boxes, beautiful maidens, temperamental kings, and bumbling servants—facing all the while the painful likelihood that it will fall on deaf ears?

When the informants of the extirpator-priest Avila sat down with his trained scribe to pour from their hearts and into print the essence of their way of life, they surely knew that they were bidding farewell to their past. Why else would they have spoken? It is entirely possible that the men who spoke to Avila did not fully understand the meaning of the stories they conveyed. These stories had been constructed by specialists for dissemination into the common memory, for safekeeping in the minds and hearts of their people. In times past, these stories, left to bubble at the frontier between consciousness and intuition, might have conjured candidates for shaman. A chance remark by an elder about those three bird-stars—falcon, condor, and vulture—might have set the mind of some young person ablaze with the staggering thought that all the stories heard since childhood spoke of a world incomparably greater than he had ever before imagined.

In times past, such a youth might have approached the priest-astronomer, nearly too embarrassed to voice his thought, passionate with a longing he could barely comprehend. But that was before the Conquest. Now the shaman-astronomer was a hunted animal, by far the most dangerous man to haunt the imagination of the Conquistadores.[15] The Andean shaman was rooted out, tortured, mutilated, beaten to death, dismembered, burned alive. The great river of knowledge that had flowed through the heart of the Andes since before the birth of Christ was reduced to a trickle, and then to dust. The extirpators groomed informers, little men with little grudges, or frightened men who gathered at the priests' black skirts. The most trivial indiscretion might blossom into a sentence of death. As the voice of the Andes fell silent, it left its epitaph.

For me, at least, the issue was settled: the astronomy of Andean myth had existed. I had never in my wildest dreams expected to get so close to the thought processes that had produced Andean myth. "The Epitaph for the Incas" is a very important document of the world's literature for what it tells us about the attitude of the archaic mind. Before turning to this unexpected windfall, it might be useful to sum up the reasons why this myth, considered in relation to the sky, independently corroborates every single major point elucidated in the foregoing chapters concerning astronomical cosmology and practice in the pre-Columbian Andes.

The three "bird shamans" in Scorpius that marked the entrance to the underworld were invisible beneath the horizon. In order to know where they were, the astronomer-priests must have used reference to some other stars. At the moment of inferior conjunction of the three shamans, the western edge of the Milky Way in Gemini was at superior conjunction (i.e., crossing the prime meridian, or north-south line drawn through the sky). (See figure 11.3.) As we saw in chapter 2 and elsewhere, it was common practice in the Andes to keep track simultaneously of both solstice points in the stars. Here these solstice points lie at superior and inferior conjunction, *independent of the horizon.* Because this story refers to a stellar position not visible to the observer, it justifies the conclusion, suggested by each passing myth analyzed in the previous chapters, that the Andean mythographers kept in mind and recorded in myth multiple relations within the sphere of fixed stars, particularly those stars involved in the observation of the solstices. This last fact should put to rest, once and for all, weakly argued claims that Andean peoples did not, and therefore could not, engage in "star to star" observation "totally detached from the locale of the observer."[16] The Andean peoples knew where the stars were even when they couldn't see them.

Next, as figure 11.1 makes clear, the location of "the world's lower foundation" lies precisely where suggested in chapter 3, on the southern tropic, confirming the general thesis that topographic reference is an analogue of positions on the celestial sphere, and the particular point that the lower extremity of "this world," *kay pacha*, extends as far as the southern tropic, where the land of the dead commences. In other words, the language of this myth makes clear that the priest-astronomers of Huarochirí thought in terms of a "celestial earth," bounded by the solstice points. (Compare figure 11.1a and figures 3.13 and 3.14.)

Third, the consistent use in the myth of kinship terms—"father," "son," "sister," "kinsman"—between the planetary deities, and the characterization of the "bird-shaman/stars" assembled by the Inca as royal subjects corroborates the material of chapters 6, 7, and 8, namely that descent systems in the Andes were reckoned in terms of astronomical entities, and that a relationship of ruler to ruled was conceptualized as the replication on earth of the relationship of planets to stars.

Moreover, because the myth relates the passing of the last great Inca to the position of the gates to the underworld at inferior conjunction—"the world's lower foundation"—the myth corroborates in yet another manner the central thesis of chapters 9 and 10 that the primary astrological concern of the Inca Empire was with the "fate" of this location in the stars.

Finally, this myth and its comparison with the night sky corrects the mistaken notion that planets were not named or closely watched in the pre-Columbian Andes, and confirms the findings of chapters 4, 5, and 8 concerning the celestial identity of the "players." This is a myth that mandates interpretation as a very specific night-sky array, which stands up to testing in the minutest detail, and which was formulated "under the guns" of a known historical date. If there are those who wish to maintain that the cosmology described in this book never existed in pre-Columbian Andean civilization, and was not a potent force in its history, then let them explain clearly the reasons why the relationship between figures 11.1 and 11.2a–d, and "The Epitaph for the Incas" represents a meaningless coincidence.

It would be, in my opinion, a senseless waste of the opportunity provided by this unique set of conditions to ignore the implications of this myth. The libraries of the world are bulging with ethnographic information on countless peoples, information that is consulted primarily for the purpose of formulating "laws of culture development." If the great cosmological schema that this book has attempted, however inadequately, to describe, did exist in the Andes, then where might it not also appear? If contact between Old World and New is unacceptable as an explanation for why, in the Andes, the planet Saturn was conceived of as the ancient mill-bearer, Jupiter as the king who hurls, Venus as a beautiful woman with curly hair, and Mars as the ruler over warfare, then the time has come for those who reject this explanation to step up and provide a plausible alternative. The most important implication of this study is a simple one: in deference to an imperfect methodology, we are leaving nothing less than a history of the human race, unsuspected and unimagined, to gather dust on dark shelves.

This history is especially important to our own time, because it is above all testimony to humanity's enduring search for the aim and significance of human life on earth. In this Age of Science, where life is understood as a chance arising, many are led to conclude that such a search is an anachronism. But, before writing off as misguided the labors of those who have gone before us, it might perhaps be of some use to examine one final aspect of "The Epitaph for the Incas" and its relationship to emerging modes of modern scientific thought. That aspect has to do with the curious fact that the myth describes astronomical events that took place *before* the physical death of Huayna Capac. This fact reveals a world of thought whose accessibility to examination in our time represents a very nearly miraculous survival.

IV

SINCE THE EARLIEST credible date (Balboa's) for the death of Huayna Capac was late in the year 1525, the first and most obvious fact revealed by "The Epitaph for the Incas" is that the celestial events of February 1524 must have lain within some mnemonic device for at least a year and a half before being formulated into myth. The simplest explanation of how this was done would be that the priest-astronomers of Huarochirí remembered all the details through a feat of memory. Although possible, this seems unlikely, because the celestial events described were not assigned specific significance until later. If simple memorization of phenomena, undertaken for the purpose of retrospective analysis, was a standard procedure, this would imply a routine memorization of hundreds of observations for possible future use. More likely, the priest-astronomers used some sort of *aide-memoire* such as a tally stick or a *quipu*, the latter being the most probable.[17]

Although it smacks somewhat of condescension to point out that the Skyglobe program "proves" the reliability of the observational and mnemonic capabilities of the Andean priest-astronomers, this much of a concession to modern-day sensibilities seems unavoidable. Science works on the principle of the replicable experiment, not on trust. It is clear, in any case, that the existence of a class of professional, trained astronomers in the pre-Columbian Andes cannot be laid at the door of romantic imagination. For such a tale as this to exist, there must also have existed a series of conventions: systematic observation, very accurate record-keeping, and, finally, the formulation of myths for the long-term preservation of celestial events perceived as significant. People who stayed up all night to watch the skies on behalf of the community cannot have been required to work all day in the fields as well.

This fact in turn discloses the fundamental reason for the authoritative nature and role of Andean myth in Andean life: as members of a professional guild, the priest-astronomers of the Andes were trained to keep accurate records. The training that they underwent, and the feats of observation and recording that they were capable of producing, were the result of a direct and continuous transmission of know-how from the distant past. Trained in such a tradition, the Andean priest-astronomers therefore trusted the mythic database implicitly because they understood how it had been formed, and the meticulousness of their own labors became the measure of their respect for their predecessors.

What, then, was the purpose of this tradition of careful, ongoing celestial observation of which we get a glimpse in the tale of Huayna Capac's last days? This story cannot be labeled astrology, at least not in the popular sense of the word, because it is not a prediction of earthly events. In our day, one has to be phenomenally bored to read last Saturday's horoscope. Yet that is precisely the approach—creation of a database for retrospective study—that appears to have generated the tale from Huarochirí.

Herein lies evidence of the archaic mind at work in the field of *pattern*, where all phenomena become sign and signature of one another. This myth is like a work in progress, a sketch of the possible connection between two events that took place close together in time, but on different scales. In this worldview, the act of divination, whether by means of the heavens or through other Andean techniques, such as examining the random pattern of coca leaves or the viscera of llamas, was an attempt to ascertain a locus for the contemplation of meaningful pattern.

Perhaps the discussion most accessible to the Western mind of this mode of thought is Jung's famous foreword to the *I Ching*.[18] Here Jung discussed the phenomenon of synchronicity, or "meaningful coincidence," of which the *I Ching*, the Chinese *Book of Changes*, ranks among the world's most sophisticated exemplars. An event familiar from Western tradition in which synchronicity was said to have played a decisive role was the journey of the Magi. When they saw "the star in the east"—the triple conjunction[19] of Saturn and Jupiter in Pisces of 6 B.C.—they did not "predict" the birth of Christ, nor did they see this celestial event as "cause," but as something more like the signature of another long-awaited event.[20]

Similarly, according to the Chinese view of acausal connection (synchronicity, or meaningful coincidence), there are, so to speak, "holes" in time. Events fall simultaneously into these "holes" without discernible causal relationship. When one casts the yarrow stalks or the coins in order to construct the elements of the *I Ching*'s hexagrams, what happens, according to the Chinese view, is that the apparent randomness of the act in fact replicates the complexity of the moment. One is in the dark about something, and the oracle illuminates the blind spot by displaying a meaningful pattern, the pattern of the moment. In other words, the *I Ching* does not tell the future; it tells the present. This same point of view is manifest in "The Epitaph for the Incas."

The Andean mythical "database," then, was a history of synchronous events. Its astronomical observations, although demonstrably precise, were not, therefore, "scientific observations" in any sense that we understand the term. Andean astronomical observation—aside from the practical application of keeping the calendar—was undertaken not to find out *how things work*, but to find out *what things mean*.

The archaic perspective on the natural world was that it was a carrier of patterns that operated simultaneously on different scales, and that those patterns represented a manifestation of a higher order of intelligence at work. By observing the celestial dance, one might catch a glimpse of the Choreographer's intentions. By understanding the "message" of pattern, unfolding through time, humankind might find its proper role in the dance. Modern science, by contrast, does not "presume" meaning in the natural order, and has in fact gone rather far in suggesting that the natural order is intrinsically meaningless.

In the archaic view, the question was not whether meaning existed, but how to find it. Therefore it was not conceivable to separate meticulous observation of the natural world from metaphysical inquiry. The functional aspect of the material world was simply of less interest to Andean thought than its potential as a feedback loop concerning the state of the union between mankind and the Powers that Be. Divination of the pattern of forces at work in the present might suggest appropriate ways of meeting the future. The time-depth of the database, stretching back as it did at least seventeen centuries, offered—like the spectrum of hexagrams in the *I Ching*—a wealth of comparative situations against which to measure the significance of present conditions. The portfolio of the Andean *capacas* was the welfare of the people. They did not have time to dabble in science.

And like the counsel of the *I Ching*, the celestial patterns that the Andean priest-astronomers observed represented opportunities for understanding how the people might best serve the greater harmony. In 200 B.C., with the bridges between worlds open, the message was to participate in a moment of great opportunity. The constellation of events in A.D. 650 spoke, on the other hand, of constraints owing to disharmony across scale. The peasants in the myths of the flood, having become lax in respect to the sacred nature of life, and having turned a deaf ear to their own *paqos*, suddenly wake up to an impending disaster, and take measures to *endure*, by recommitting themselves to the old ways. The historical evidence of this course is found in the moiety system. The peasantry did survive, did avoid catastrophe in the aftermath of Wari by *sharing* land (in the spirit of reciprocity), and did maintain autonomous rights to choose their own leaders and modes of worship.

The events commencing in A.D. 650 appear to have ushered in an era of mechanistic astrology in which, to "those in the know," interpreting celestial pattern became "easy." The image of an ever more wrathful god grew stronger in proportion to the projection of human self-will onto the heavens. A perception of inevitability replaced the weighing of alternatives in reading the sky. Mechanistic astrology, the art of prediction, replaced the practice of trying to understand the significance of the present. As the original constraints placed upon the uses of celestial observation were eroded, control rather than adaptation became the overriding concern of the priesthood of the warriors. This change culminated with the Incas, who, in finding celestial patterns not to their liking, decided to try to change the patterns themselves.

Nonetheless, it should not be overlooked that the Incas *did predict* an event on the scale of the Conquest, and that the priest-astronomers of

Huarochirí were also well aware of the imminent opening of this "hole in time." In fact, the reasoning that led to the Inca prophecy was the product of a rather awe-inspiring pattern that, for lack of a better word, might be termed "objective," in the sense that it did actually occur. The major period dates of Andean archaeology, as determined by radiocarbon dating and ceramic stratigraphy, correspond with great precision to the moments of the world-ending cataclysms—*pachakutis*—that Andean myth chronicles. More-over, Andean myth and the archaeological record are in accord as to the substantive content of these pivotal moments and their ensuing ages, with the notable exception that, in many cases, Andean myth offers more insight concerning the dynamics involved than archaeology is able to provide. This comparison makes it possible to formulate a curious statement of fact, based on the archaeological record alone, but one of which the Incas were equally aware from their own mythical database: beginning about 200 B.C., Andean society underwent fundamental transformations each time the solstice suns entered or left the Milky Way. In addition, the eight-hundred-year periodic-ity of the conjunctions of Saturn and Jupiter also took place against the background of the Milky Way at the same time that the major social trans-formations occurred on earth.

To the Western mind, unaccustomed to searching for such patterns running alongside history, this is all coincidence. To the priest-astronomers of the Andes, it was evidence of synchronicity, the playing out of significant pattern on different scales at the same time. By an effort of imagination, we contemporary people might generate a modicum of sympathy for a people "lost" in metaphysical speculation. We might even be able to experience a minor jolt at the realization that the eight-hundred-year periodicity of the Saturn-Jupiter conjunction "returned" in 1444 to reinforce the perception of Pachakuti Inca and the priest-astronomers that the Andean world was poised, once again, on the brink of cataclysm. We might further wonder at the peculiar celestial synchronicity that seemed to shadow the Incas, by noting that the celestial events described alongside the death of the Sun-King in "The Epitaph for the Incas," by yet another coincidence, happened to commence on the eve of the zenith passage of the sun above Cuzco, at a moment when the Inca Empire was likewise poised at the zenith, its power already destined to wane.[21] The ability and will at the heart of Andean myth to observe and remember, across a span of two millennia, a repeating triple conjunction of planetary, precessional, and historical events is impressive. But was this activity evidence of an unusual spiritual perception, or of human suggestibility before a sport of history? To discount the Inca prophecy as

"self-fulfilling" may undervalue the perceptive powers of the Andean shamans, and certainly underestimates the determination of the Europeans to
conquer new worlds.

For me, the single most fascinating question raised by this study is not
how the technical language of myth reached the Andes, or even where and
how it was first developed, but rather *why this system of thought was so readily
accepted by peoples all around the world*. Acceptance is the sincerest form of
endorsement. What, then, was so compelling in this worldview that it motivated so many of the earth's people at one time to align their destiny with
the stars and their fate with the wanderings of planetary deities, each with
the same assigned powers and characteristics? If there was not *something* about
this system of thought that carried a genuine spiritual perception of the
phenomenal world, then why, even after its demise, do we find respectful
reference to it in all later religious traditions from Judaism to Buddhism, and
from Christianity to Islam to Hinduism?

"The Epitaph for the Incas" prompts vivid images—a priest-astronomer,
or perhaps several, alone, high in the cold mountains, watching the dance
of planetary pattern over a series of nights, recording, studying, pondering.
Why? Were these dull and superstitious people, engaged in manufacturing
another of the past's famous "mistakes"? Or did the participation of the
Andean priest-astronomers in this ancient and astonishingly widespread tradition suggest that they possessed access to a mode of perception that
made the practice of celestial observation a useful way of recognizing and
understanding significant pattern?

V

THIS IS NOT the time to launch an apology for astrology, nor could I. There
are, however, certain facts about the technical language of myth that can be
stated without appeals to faith. To begin with, the very complexity of the
language means that the teaching did not serve only, or even primarily,
"practical" ends, such as calendar formation. To do so would be like using a
boat for a paperweight. Furthermore, this was a tradition that—by virtue of
its dependence on a very particular meta-language employing idiosyncratic
conceits—required *transmission*. The student-teacher relationship is written
all over this tradition. In turn, this logic suggests that there must have been
an element of inner training in the transmission of these ideas, an element
concerned with the education of perception. Sensitivity to pattern in the
natural world requires an eye that looks both inward and outward at the same

time. The paintings of Rembrandt maintain a spellbinding power precisely because they depict an inner perception of the outer world. Did Andean myth, and indeed all myth concerned with celestial events, represent an analogous "processing" of phenomenal data through some trained inner eye?

By way of example, one might ask of the Australian aborigines—who, insofar as is known, were *not* exposed historically to the technical language of myth—how it is that they came to the well-documented conclusion that Mars was a very troublesome fellow indeed. If the aborigines independently identified the presence of Mars as somehow disruptive, then there appears at least the possibility of some perceptive mechanism at work by which humans were able to "connect" with planets.[22]

A second aspect of this teaching is one that I have not until now emphasized, although its existence is implicit in everything that has been said. This is the notion of *scale*. The entirety of Andean cosmology, linking the dead, the living, and the gods, represented a scale of a particular kind. As such, it participated in an archaic theory of scale that is deceptively simple.

There is a Chinese saying that "the calendar and the pitch pipes have such a close fit that you could not slip a hair between them."[23] Here is a thought with which Kepler or Pythagoras would have been at home: the notion of laws operative on different scales and in different media, laws equally expressible with the numerical rigor of astronomy or through the vibrations of sound. Like the Chinese pipes, the Andean panpipe is tuned to a pentatonic scale. Andean thought is shot through with "quint-essence": five Suns, five steps on the pyramid, five pairs of mummified Emperors in the Temple of the Sun, five notes in the scale.[24]

Scale. The word comes from the Latin for "ladder" or "stairs," expressing the ascending stages of musical transport as effortlessly as the stairway to the stars. In Peru, where "scale" was expressed sometimes as a ladder, though more often as a bridge, the stairway had five steps. The final "step" that transported Wiraqocha across the Milky Way in Gemini, and into the land of the immortals, appears unmodified in Dante's *Divine Comedy* (fourteenth century), here as a *scala* or ladder that Dante ascended in order to move from the heaven of Saturn to the sphere of the fixed stars in Gemini.[25] Dante's patron was Can Grande della Scala, literally "the Great Dog of the Ladder," a reference to Sirius, the Dog Star beneath Gemini, along the great ladder of the galaxy.[26] Dante and his circle were members of the "old school."

Although the sources of this teaching may stretch even farther back in time than anyone yet suspects, its traces can still be found in medieval musicology as well. Here we find the notations for what today is the standard

Western seven-tone musical scale—do, re, mi, fa, sol, la, si, do. These names were Latin mnemonics for components of the "scale" of the organization of the cosmos, a scheme already ancient in Dante's time.

DO	DOminus	"The Lord, God"
RE	REgina caelum	"The Queen of Heaven" (the moon)
MI	MIcrocosmos	"The Microcosm" (Earth)
FA	FAta	"Planets/Fates"
SOL	SOL	"The Sun"
LA	via LActea	"The Milky Way"
SI	SIdera	"[All] Stars"
DO	DOminus	"The Lord, God"

This "scale" conforms in most respects to modern Western notions of the organization of the cosmos. It begins with the absolute, absolute nothing, God in the Buddhist conception. It moves to the satellites of planets, or moons. Next comes our own planet, that is, the point of view of the observer, the home of life which makes observation possible. Next there are planets in the aggregate, or the solar system. Then comes the jump to an entirely higher level of organization, the sun itself. After that, the scale moves to the aggregate grouping of suns into galaxies, again in accord with contemporary thought. Next comes the realm of all visible celestial objects, the siderium, or fixed sphere of stars. And finally there is the return to the absolute, God beyond all form.

Implicit in this teaching has always been the concept of *consciousness*. In this view, ascending orders of cosmic organization correspond to ascending levels of the organization of intelligence. This ancient idea has recently received wide currency in the so-called "Gaia hypothesis" of geochemist James Lovelock. Lovelock has postulated that the Earth's biosphere is a form of self-regulating intelligence. Thus, while archaic notions of scale may appear almost pointlessly simple—like a child stacking blocks—they have always implied a unified theory of knowledge wherein the same laws that govern the universe, the vibrations of sound, or the possibilities of human cognition (to name but a few possible "sets") obey the same laws.

Before stating one simple fact about the archaic theory of astronomical scale which requires no affinity with mysticism to appreciate, it might be useful to say a few words about how certain trends in scientific thought, connected to the radical shift in scientific perspective in the last hundred years, now appear quite "archaic" in their appreciation of scale.

The direction of modern science took a dramatic turn in our century with the entry of the principle of uncertainty. The appearance of uncertainty raised the stakes in science by calling into question the very foundations of scientific knowledge. One such challenge was to measurement itself, the *sine qua non* of the replicable experiment. Heisenberg's uncertainty principle stated that the measurement of one of two related quantities, such as the location and momentum of a subatomic particle, necessarily created uncertainty in the measurement of the other.

Equally revolutionary was the apparent evaporation of the predictability of behavior in the material world, when viewed at the subatomic level. Beginning with Newton and carrying through the Victorian era up until Einstein's theory of relativity (1904), it had been assumed that by means of sufficiently precise measurements the behavior of any physical process could be predicted. This worldview encompassed a kind of security that man could master the physical environment by being privy to the law-conformable thought processes of the Creator. It came as a shock, therefore, to learn, from work such as that of the Curies, that uncertainty appeared to lie at the very heart of material processes. Investigating the radioactive decay of radium into lead, the Curies concluded that the moment when a particular atom of radium would transform could not be predicted within 500,000 years. In this subatomic Wonderland, the laws of cause and effect were thrown out of court.

A way of surmounting the apparent loss of "control" over principles of order in the material world was provided by Planck's theory of quantum mechanics, which substituted for predictability the principle of statistical probability. Taken in large enough quantities, the proportion of, say, radium that would transform in a given time could be ascertained statistically, even though the behavior of any given atom was impossible to predict. Thus the presence of unpredictability at the heart of the material world could be worked around, since statistical probability was sufficient for technological applications.

In the realm of theoretical physics, however, the pace of discovery slackened. A unified field theory, integrating all the discoveries of subatomic physics, proved elusive. These conditions began to produce a growing discontent among some scientists, who sensed a kind of theoretical gridlock looming. The art of subatomic physics lies in creating great experiments, experiments that strip away as many variables as possible in order to focus on a single phenomenon. As this way of doing science appeared to reach its limit, so, therefore, hope appeared to recede of ever addressing problems in the "real" world—that is, such problems as forecasting weather, in which the number of variables is formidable.

At first it was thought that the data-crunching capabilities of giant digital computers might make it possible to solve such problems as weather prediction. In fact, computers began to reveal undreamed of unpredictability in the material world, behavior that paradoxically appeared to resolve into *patterns* of complexity. These and like discoveries began to coalesce into a new science called Chaos. "It turns out that an eerie type of chaos can lurk just behind a façade of order—and yet, deep inside the chaos lurks an even eerier type of order."[27]

> The modern study of chaos began with the creeping realization in the 1960s that quite simple mathematical equations could model systems every bit as violent as a waterfall. Tiny differences in input could quickly become overwhelming differences in output—a phenomenon given the name "sensitive dependence on initial conditions." In weather, for example, this translates into what is only half-jokingly known as the Butterfly Effect—the notion that a butterfly stirring the air today in Peking can transform storm systems next month in New York.[28]

Or a butterfly emerging from a box one day in Quito could spell the destruction of Cuzco a few years hence.

Contemporary chaos theory depends on mathematical modeling to demonstrate theoretically ideas that the *I Ching* embodies intuitively: that the literally immeasurable richness of interacting phenomena participates in a greater order of discernible pattern. This order exists apart from predictability or predetermination, more like a dance than an equation, yet more like the signature of intelligence than the scribblings of random idiocy.

One of the most potent findings of chaos theory is that the traditional scientific notion that "different systems behave differently"[29] no longer appears to hold true. Chaos theory creates a world where the solution to an ecologist's intractable difficulties in modeling fluctuations in insect populations is suggested by reading an article "about chemical chaos in a complicated laboratory experiment."[30] In other words, the apparently random behavior of nature, whether in living systems or chemical systems—that is, in systems operating on radically different scales—appears to participate in patterns of a universal nature. This is an ancient idea.

"The first chaos theorists, the scientists who set the discipline in motion, shared certain sensibilities. They had an eye for pattern, *especially pattern that appeared on different scales at the same time.*"[31] [My emphasis.] The priest-astronomers of the Andes also searched for pattern across scale. Like modern chaos theorists, the Andean priest-astronomers looked to the "systems behavior" of the heavens for a sense of pattern, a way of calibrating the significance of "holes" in time when, to use the language of chaos theory, whole systems pass from one kind of equilibrium to another through the medium of chaos.

It would perhaps be as great a mistake to make too little of this comparison as to make too much of it.

On the one hand, the human perception of an irreducible unpredictability in the world has been as little assuaged by scientific method as by astrological prediction. No one can tell the future. On the other hand, both archaic notions of scale and modern notions of chaos intuit a form of intelligence at work that, by dint of its paradoxically unpredictable "pattern-resolving" powers, suggests the possibility of a science of right intervention. In the past, this pursuit has gone under many names, among them the Dharma and the Tao.

Before turning to look briefly at what that might imply in our own era, it is time to make one final point regarding the archaic notions of scale as expressed in astronomical cosmology. In the Andes, where the "ladder" to the supernatural worlds was arranged across a pentatonic scale, one element in common with the Western seven-tone scale is noteworthy. This is the transcendent role assigned in both systems to the Milky Way in transactions between this world and the next.

As it happens, the plane of the ecliptic, corresponding roughly to the equator of the sun, cuts across the plane of our galaxy in two places, the area marked by Scorpius and Sagittarius and that marked by Gemini and Taurus. Also, as it happens, those two areas mark the direction of the center of our galaxy and its nearest (to us) outer rim respectively. It may be coincidence that in Andean cosmology (and archaic cosmologies worldwide), the dead "return" through the bridge at Scorpius, the center of the galaxy, while the immortals, like Buddhists escaping the "wheel of karma," "leave" this mortal "coil" via the shortest route—beyond Gemini—to the highest heaven, beyond our galaxy. This "belief" could be explained as the result of associating Gemini with the "prestige" direction of north, and assigning to nobility this location for "crossing the great river."

What is not so easy to explain, however, is the clear assignment to our galaxy, the Milky Way, in cosmologies around the world, of its "proper" (to the Western scientific viewpoint) position in cosmic scale. *La*, that is the Via Lactea, or Milky Way, is the last stop before *si*, the entire expanse of the visible universe. In "crossing the great river," one leaves behind our solar system, and our galaxy itself, to reach the "other side" at *si*, the domain of all the stars—or lineage *wakas*—the highest heaven but one, the last being *do*, the seat of the supreme deity, beyond all form and substance. The reason that the existence of this ancient, persistent notion—placing the Milky Way in its scientifically accurate position in cosmic scale between the sun (individual stars) and all the stars in aggregate—is not so easy to explain is that, *insofar as Western scientific tradition is concerned, the component of cosmic scale known as "galaxy" (from the Greek for "milk") was not discovered, and did not enter the scientific lexicon, until 1924.*[32] Among the later Greeks, to whom we are said owe the "foundations" of Western scientific method, the application of reason to the question of the nature of the galactic band produced Aristotle's assertion that the Milky Way was a concentration of swamp gas.[33]

VI

ON SEPTEMBER 8, 1940, as the battle in the skies over Britain entered its climactic week, a small dog named Robot disappeared into a hole on the grounds of an estate overlooking the French village of Montignac-sur-Vézère. The animal's master, a young apprentice mechanic, and three friends rescued the dog and, in widening the hole, uncovered a vertical shaft down through bedrock. Equal to the adventure before them, they wiggled twenty feet to a cave floor and, with a crude lamp, cast light upon painted walls and ceilings that had lain in darkness for about seventeen thousand years. That beam of light, in the darkest hour of our century, at once reclaimed for posterity the Lascaux Caves, and held out the flicker of a promise that the central question of our unsettling times—"What is our human nature?"—might yield some answers.

Whether this "opening of ways" to our common ancestral heritage accomplished by a little dog named Robot—in the same manner as the jackal-headed god Anubis in Egypt or Fox in the Andes—is a case of life imitating myth is a question unlikely to be asked by modern science. It remains an article of faith[34] of scientific positivism that consciousness arises from matter, a by-product of innumerable synaptic arcings, refined into a survival strategy by Our Lady of Natural Selection. It is under this myth, and in this world, that the word *myth* has become a synonym for *misconception*, and wisdom is understood as the codification of material laws. This worldview is dangerous in a time of crisis, because it suggests to ordinary people that our own inner resources, our consciousness, is a hall of mirrors. If theorists such as James Lovelock are correct in arguing the existence of great fields of intelligence within which human consciousness also participates, then scientific determinism is promoting—albeit unconsciously—a supremely misguided and dangerous fall-back position: that in the end, because consciousness arises from chance events in matter, consciousness itself is not significant, and we are alone. This is an invitation to the Big Sleep.

For this reason the question of whether our common mythical heritage represents human perception or human projection is of more than antiquarian interest. For this question goes directly to the heart of the matter: Who are we, and what are we here for? This is a question that science not only does not ask, but also maintains is intrinsically pointless. There are no bridges, no reciprocal obligations, no beyond. The universe is a heat sink.

It is in the field of tension between myth and science that modern humankind struggles to forge its soul. Science seeks to subdue the powers of darkness through the light of reason. Heroic as this endeavor may be, the ever-present danger of science is to mistake the limits of knowledge for the limits of responsibility. At that moment, as the living of this century know in their bones, the powers of darkness are very near indeed. Myth, on the other hand, using the language of nature, seeks to establish a dialogue with consciousness in order to ask the Big Questions about the nature and extent of human responsibility. The risk of myth is that, like Gilgamesh, we may struggle past the limits of beyond, only to return empty-handed.

Yet myth endures because it is not simply *about* creation, but is itself creativity, that quicksilver energy transformed in the crucible of human experience into a miraculous vessel, set loose upon the vast sea of time. "In the beginning was the Word, and the Word was with God, and the Word was God." The Vedas have it that the material world is Brahma's dream, a crystallization into form of pure consciousness. No less reverent, but more doughty, the Quechua Indians would state that it was the great god Wiraqocha who created the sun, the moon, the stars, the people, plants and animals, and the laws of human interaction and worship, by which they simply meant that understanding of such matters came from above, not below.

Because modern scientific culture conditions our view of the nature of consciousness, it conditions our view of the past as well. Science, for good or ill, has become synonymous with the limits of the knowable. Its great strength is the principle of verification, the replicable experiment. Its great weakness lies in the limitations of its means of measurement. What cannot be measured cannot, as yet, be known. Hence, beyond credibility in the Age of Science are ways of knowing that cannot be quantified—"the numinous," "the Secret of the Golden Flower," "the wisdom of the heart"—and hence also the history of that quest, which is myth. Such pursuits belong to enterprises as agreeably marginal to the cultural mainstream as comparative religion and parapsychology.

History, likewise, has fallen on hard times. At present the dynamics of human nature are increasingly understood as a problem for biologists to sort out, the product of genes and the fluctuations of blood chemistry. In a world where human nature is biologically determined, history is irrelevant. If the past is no more than the serial detonation of genetic impulses, then its content is of value only as archival material for social engineers. Heroism is just testosterone talking, and so on. This is uncomfortable to think about, because it leads toward the thought that the present, as well, might be "a tale told by an idiot. . . ."

The compromise we have reached with history, thus reduced to a chronicle of "behaviors," goes something like this: "People in the past were no different from us, except that we know more now than they did then; and we need to know a little history in order to avoid repeating the mistakes of the past." This sounds like the speech parents deliver before spooning up a dose of castor oil.

If history is to have a future, it lies in helping to reanimate the contemporary understanding of human nature. With the exception of depth psychology, no other secular discipline seems interested in the job. History is *story*. Genetic determinism, or any other interpretation laid on human nature by modern positivism, makes for a lousy story. It doesn't have a second act, which is to say a venue where character meets conflict and the stage for significant action is set. Yet story is precisely what humanity has contrived to create from the moment of its arising, some forty thousand years ago, as Marshack's investigation into Ice Age mobilary so persuasively argues. The whole constellation of Ice Age human activities—cave art, tally sticks, solemn burial, and the rest—was suspended in a field of "storied meaning."

Stories are always about significant choices made in the face of uncertainty—good choices, bad choices, choices avoided. What makes choice both possible and significant is the presence of *hazard*.[35] It is this aspect of life which story addresses, and in so doing affirms the existence of free will and the reality of decision. In that sense, myth expresses a view of our human nature, and the nature of the world, at odds with the perspective of deterministic science. When the *paqo* speaks to the peasant, the peasant is free to beat him anew with yet another ear of the sacred maize. Instead the peasant chooses to listen, and then to respond so that a way of life, plainly at risk, survives the storm.

The stories examined in this book identify moments of maximum hazard —moments whose outcomes would be significant but in which the uncertainty of the outcome was high. Their peculiar perspective is to present "simulcasts" of events occurring on different scales. They are the stories of the choices of a people, choices formulated with an awareness of patterns occurring simultaneously in different spheres. They are stories precisely because they represent *choices* made before hazard. In this sense the technical language of myth might be said to represent a language designed to permit the study of hazard in the unfolding of human history. This is a long-winded way of saying what myth says simply: every so often the world is destroyed and a new one created. In the language of modern science, the astronomical level of myth is concerned with how whole systems across scale pass from one kind of equilibrium to another through the medium of chaos.

The notion of a Creation with hazard woven into its very fabric is an ancient one, whose implications have been understood, and lost, and may perhaps be understood again. In the words of the *Rig-Veda* (ca. 2000 B.C.),

> *Who verily knows, and who can here declare it,*
> *whence it was born and whence comes this creation?*
> *The gods are later than this world's production; who*
> *knows then when it first came into being? He, the*
> *First Source of this creation, whether He formed it*
> *all, or did not form it, He who surveys it in the highest*
> *heaven, He alone knows and even He may not know.*[36]

Although the stories of all the world's people demonstrate humanity's intimacy with hazard, the idea of a God with his sleeves rolled up, a God who labors unceasingly for the redemption of a universe shot through with uncertainty, is an idea that has not, historically speaking, had great staying power. The recognition of the cosmic nature of hazard is a knowledge that

disappears from time to time because there is something in man that is both terribly attracted to hazard and at the same time terrified of it. We are driven to seek ways of denying the reality of hazard and of looking beyond chance to something that is free from chance. Man has always tended to project onto his conceptions of God the notion of a being that is beyond hazard, a supreme power that is secure from the chance and the uncertainty that we see in this world.[37]

The Incas came very close to facing the implications of cosmic uncertainty. The god upon whom they projected their perception of hazard was the Sun. Various chroniclers noted how the Incas viewed the Sun as a working God. The legendary Inca Rocca is said to have laughed at the idea that the Inca, like the Sun, reposed in luxurious splendor. He was said to reply that the Sun never rested from its labors. Inca Pachakuti expressed similar sentiments.[38] But in the end the Incas hedged their bets, drawn to pursue the chimera of control, "lobbying" a creator exempt from the laws of his own creation.

The attraction/repulsion experienced by mankind in contemplation of hazard lies at the very roots of Western tradition. In Greek myth, Prometheus was punished for stealing "fire" from the gods. This strange formulation —in which humankind's assuming of its birthright of creative power, a.k.a. "fire," caused fury among the gods—is a reflection of Western humanity's deep ambivalence toward its own powers of perception. For it was Prometheus—the *pra mantha,* or firedrill/axis of the celestial sphere—who represented man's introduction to creative insight via the contemplation of the sky. The message in the sky spoke to hazard. The question for man has always been how to live in right relation to this knowledge.

Likewise, in the foundation myth of Judeo-Christian thought, the story of Adam and Eve, lies this same terrible test of human character. As in native American myths of the era before agriculture, Adam and Eve inhabit a garden, eating fruits from the trees. They are forbidden only one thing—to partake of the fruit of the tree of the knowledge of good and evil—which, of course, they promptly do. The result? They are cast out of Eden, a state of blissful ignorance, and consigned to a life of agricultural toil.

Although the original Hebrew texts of Genesis do not clearly identify this curious fruit, Western tradition has always held that it was an apple. Why an apple? That is one of those questions I had long ago consigned to the "utterly unanswerable" bin, until, as my father had done for me, and perhaps fathers have since Adam, I showed my son the "star" in the apple. If you cut an apple through its "equator," instead of stem-to-bottom along its "poles," you find a five-pointed star. Remember?

So there it is, the same "original sin" as Prometheus. The apple carries the universal Western symbol for the stars in the sky. The five points of the star symbolize what in Western alchemical tradition was called "quintessence," the power to see the true significance of things. (See chapter 2, note 21.)

In these strange stories of Prometheus and of Adam and Eve, their "original sin" is meaningless unless understood as a sin *in potentiam*. These stories are a statement of almost unbearable nostalgia for some never-to-be-recovered golden age when we were one with nature. This possibility was lost forever when Time began, when humanity grasped the cosmic dimensions of hazard as expressed by precession, and with it the fruit of the tree of the knowledge of good and evil. Such a fruit had to be of an ambivalent nature; it all depended on what one did with it. No wonder the gods were in an uproar. Since Eden and Prometheus, the *original* sin that humanity has now and again perpetrated is the attempt to take an active position in relation to the Choreographer, the attempt to "fix" the law of hazard. "Original sin" arose not because, through disobedience, we inhabit our essential creative nature, but because we are—and this is the unrelenting lesson of the last six thousand years of human history—terribly drawn to use our powers wrongly, powers that blossomed in Eden when Time began. At least that is the message of myth.[39]

If there is a cautionary lesson in the Inca tragedy, it lies in recognizing the illusion of control. If you want to make God laugh, tell Him your plans. What myth, or the scientific recognition of universal uncertainty, implies is that it is not necessary to undertake ventures on an enormous scale to have a real effect on the world. Hazard doesn't work that way; it works through sensitive dependence on initial conditions. Nothing is predetermined, so *everything* is important. Like a good story, hazard affirms the existence and importance of free will.

The illusion of control, the confusion of scale, and the potential for cataclysmic loss are not unfamiliar aspects of our own time. One area where these symptoms abound is Western medicine. The language of contemporary medical care—"fighting" disease, "declaring war" on AIDS, "killing" bacteria, looking for the "magic bullet"—does not speak of being well, but of controlling disease through combat. At the same time, medical insurance companies will not reimburse complementary treatment modalities, such as homeopathy, which seek to strengthen the immune system rather than to "fight" disease. Homeopathy cannot be "controlled" scientifically, because nobody knows just how it works—only that it does.[40] Not coincidentally, such medical strategies require the active participation of the "patient."

It is now well understood that many new and virulent strains of organisms thought to have been "eradicated" have in fact been created (caused to mutate) by the indiscriminate use of drugs designed to "kill" them. In this sense, Western medicine has strengthened the immune systems of pathogens rather than those of people. In recent years, despite the lack of reimbursement from medical insurance, many people have responded to this impasse by seeking alternative medical attention. The increasing hazards of pathogens in a degraded environment make "being healthy" a sounder strategy than "fighting" disease. These apparently unorganized actions, undertaken by individual people and on a small scale, may in the end prove to be the most significant medical development of the late twentieth century. Perhaps it really is true that an apple a day—cut for contemplation along its equator —keeps the doctor away.

VII

WE LIVE IN a time when the greatest form of courage is to act as if our lives made a difference. Myth wants to tell us that, of the marvelous powers of humanity to open to the wisdom of the cosmos: if we knock, it shall be opened. It does so, in the end, by leaving us with the universal myth of the ancient ones, the wise elders of old, steeped in knowledge of the ancient treasure. Whatever knowledge the ancients may have possessed, now lost and now gained again in the successive worlds of human ascent toward the light, it may be that the particular nature of this knowledge is less important than the existence of the myth itself. The myth speaks to an archetype, buried within each of us, of some unbroken chain of transmission energized by love of kind. It is a myth that encourages us to live up to the present. It is a story that beckons us back to ourselves, back to our present moment, back to the realization that myth time is now.

We are an ancient race. We have contrived, in the face of the darker angels of our own nature, not only to survive, but to outwit time itself by preserving at least parts of the epic story. It is not always easy to remember this story, and often harder still to believe it. Yet it has survived, perhaps because we people cannot survive without our stories. And so it seems only fitting to close with a story, the story of a book and a saint, a story about the ancient ones in the midst of our own time, and of a transmission of ideas that may stretch back to the last Ice Age.

The book in question, called *The Arctic Homeland in the Vedas* (1903), was written from a prison cell of the British Raj by B. G. Tilak, later a colleague of Mahatma Gandhi. In this book, Tilak, who was an accomplished Sanskrit scholar, analyzed descriptions of the movements of the heavens as recorded in the earliest Vedic texts and concluded that such observations could only have been made within the Arctic Circle. Although anyone who should leaf through this rare book might find some merit in its arguments, and although more-modern geophysical and archaeological knowledge can, at the very least, not rule out Tilak's hypothesis, the book remains virtually unknown, another undigested "curiosity."

The saint, known as the Shivapuri Baba, was born, with his twin sister, in 1826 in Kerala, India, of Brahmin lineage. His grandfather, upon viewing the infants, declared that the purpose of the family lineage was now fulfilled and was therefore at an end. The baby girl, like her brother, was destined to take a vow of poverty and retire from the world as a *sannyasin*. At the age of five the boy began his formal training, mastering recitation of the Vedas by the age of twelve. At eighteen he retired into the forest, and, some years later, after the death of his grandfather, disappeared into the depths of the Narbada forest to follow the path of Absolute Realization of God Beyond All Forms and Images. He would not see another human being for twenty-five years. When this part of his task was complete, he emerged from the forest, in 1875, and, following his grandfather's instruction, dug up a treasure in diamonds set aside for generations by his family for the purpose of financing a pilgrimage.

Normally this meant a pilgrimage throughout the holy places of India, but in this case, as his grandfather had made clear, the Shivapuri Baba was to travel on foot and by boat around the world. He walked east through Persia, was admitted to Mecca, went on through Jerusalem and Rome, and, when he reached England, was summoned by Queen Victoria. Although the record of her eighteen meetings with the Shivapuri Baba were later excised from her diaries by the Princess Beatrice, it is known that Queen Victoria requested (that is, did not command) the Shivapuri Baba to remain in England until her death. He therefore remained four years in England, resuming his pilgrimage in 1901, walking throughout the Americas, visiting the islands of the Pacific, and at last returning in 1915, after forty years, to India, having walked throughout China and Southeast Asia.

Finally, after fulfilling the obligations of his pilgrimage in India, he retired to the Himalayas, to live out his days in a bamboo hut on a small preserve provided by the Nepali government. Here, a wild leopard emerged regularly from the forest to lie at his feet.

Shortly before his death in 1963, during a discussion about his memories of the political upheavals in India during the initial stages of his long pilgrimage, he was asked if he had known one of the participants in those events, B. G. Tilak. The Shivapuri Baba replied that, yes, he knew Tilak and had once "taught him some astronomy."[41]

THE INTENTIONAL FLOODING OF CUZCO

One corner of the hologram involves a relatively minor ritual, when the Incas intentionally flooded Cuzco. As described in the Spanish chronicles, this event appears to have nothing whatsoever to do with astronomy. In the month of January, according to Molina, the people of Cuzco gathered food, spices, coca, clothing, shoes, ornaments, flowers, gold, and silver, and threw them all into the water behind a dam above the city. At sunset they opened the flood-gates and let a torrent of water rush through the streets of Cuzco. As the floodwaters scoured the streets, they washed along the ashes of all the burnt offerings—placed at curbside—from the previous year. Runners waited at the bottom of the city, at the point where the Tullumayu and Huatanay rivers converged, and swept the offerings into the Vilcamayu River. As the flood approached them, the runners began a race of more than thirty miles along the banks of the Vilcamayu, all the way to Ollantaytambo, where the river begins to drop off steeply toward confluence with the Amazon.

Here, others waited at a bridge spanning the river and threw a final offering of coca into the torrent. Throughout the night, innumerable torch-bearers, stationed along the riverbank, lit the the runners' way. All the offerings were destined for "the northern sea," said to be the abode of the creator, Wiraqocha. The river, then, was meant to carry the offerings right out of this world. When the race to Ollantaytambo was completed, the runners returned to Cuzco, bearing objects symbolic of their order of finish. To the fastest were given effigies of lances and of falcons cast in salt, while the laggards made do with little saline toads.[1]

According to Molina, this event began at sunset in the month of January, that is, when the southeast/northwest branch of the Milky Way was up and moving toward the zenith. During this night the celestial river constelled the same pattern as events below, where the banks of the Vilcamayu—flowing northwestward—lay ablaze in light.

This was not the only time in the year that the Vilcamayu, "the River of the Sun," took on all the trappings of the Milky Way. As mentioned, the pilgrimage route of the Inca priests at June solstice followed the course of the Vilcamayu southeast all the way to its headwaters at the base of the towering peak Vilcanota, "the Place of the Sun." Urton's comment on this rite along the Vilcamayu is to the point: "I suggest that the route traveled by the priests from Cuzco to the southeast was thought of as more than a terrestrial pilgrimage; it was equivalent to a walk along the Milky Way. . . ."[2]

The celestial analogues of the salt effigies borne back to Cuzco by the racers during the rites of January confirm this insight into the Vilcamayu's cosmic role. The slowest runners had to carry toads, whose celestial prototype, *hanp'atu,* is another dark cloud of interstellar dust, not far from the Southern Cross.[3] (See figure 3.5.) As for the falcon, Avila's informants in Huarochirí spoke of "three stars in a straight line," including falcon and condor.[4] Urton's informants placed the celestial condor "above the llama," that is, somewhere on the western side of the Milky Way.[5] As was discussed at greater length in chapter 11, there are good reasons to think that the Falcon was one of three stars in the tail of Scorpius. (See figure 11.1.) These three are the same stars found in the crosspiece of the post-Conquest constellation *cruz calvario.*

As for the "lance of salt" awarded the swiftest runners, the Quechua word for "war lance" is *llaca.*[6] Like the word *paqo, llaca* is a nickname for the male llama,[7] whose celestial counterpart, Lyra/*Urcuchillay,* with the first-magnitude star Vega, also lies near the western "bank" of the Milky Way, deep in the northern sky. During the time of the Incas, the heliacal rise of Vega (figure 3.15) fell in mid-January, when this ritual was performed. As figure 3.15 shows, Falcon and Toad "trailed" Vega, constellating the same order of "finish" as the racers—strung out along the Vilcamayu— in the gathering dawn. And, once again, the prestige direction is north, as shown by the award to the swiftest of a symbol of Vega in the northern heavens.

If the entire ritual on the banks of the Vilcamayu represented a "race along the Milky Way," the Incas were not the only native people to share in the thought-form. In the *Popol Vuh,* the myth cycle of the Quiché-Maya of Guatemala, we read that the Grandmother of the hero-twins Hunahpú and Ixbalamqué (Sun and Moon), desperate to send them a message of warning, enlists Flea, who is swallowed by Toad, who is swallowed by Snake, who is swallowed by Hawk, who reaches the twins. Girard comments that

> to show the relative velocity of the animals in question, the allegory unquestionably objectifies an astronomic episode, the animals sym-
> bolizing celestial bodies whose importance has the same relation as
> that of their relative speed. First, the bird of prey representing the
> sun; next the white snake, which in Chortí mythology represents the

Milky Way; thereafter the *chac* (toad) or god of rain, projected in
the star [?] . . .

It is of interest to point out that for the first time mention is made
of the Milky Way, whose movements were perfectly well known to the
Maya, and which still plays a principal role in Chortí astronomy. . . .[8]

As with the *Popol Vuh*, the Inca idea of "racing along the Milky Way"
constituted a form of "tech talk."

And if the outer form of the ritual conformed to celestial geometry—
racing along a northwest-flowing river beneath its celestial analogue above,
and finishing with triumphant reference to the Vega in the northeast as the
other branch of the celestial river began to rise—its inner content reflected
the "spiritual geometry" implicit in these natural phenomena.

On the morning of this reenactment of the "flood," the Inca and all the
people assembled at the Huacaypata, Cuzco's central plaza, and "brought
out all the *huacas* and embalmed bodies of the dead, where they paid
their customary respects to them."[9] That evening the floodwaters were
loosed. This prelude to the flooding took place about two weeks after the
most important festival of the year, the Capac Raymi at December solstice, when the ancestors of all the tribes of the Empire, as represented by
the mummified remains of the Inca kings and the lineage *wakas* of all the
tribes, were considered actually to have been present. This notion was,
as shown in chapter 3, connected to the fact that the Milky Way rose
heliacally at December solstice, laying open the entrance to the land of
the dead.

Two weeks later, the Incas staged a "race along the Milky Way." The
ritual began in Cuzco, the southeast terminus of the event, with southeast
standing for the direction of the annual return of the dead across the Milky
Way at sunrise on December solstice. Upon the floodwaters roaring northwest out of Cuzco were tossed the innumerable offerings to Wiraqocha—
northwest representing the direction for crossing the Milky Way in order to
reach the land of the gods. By strict "geometrical" reasoning, this entrance
—to *hanaq pacha*, "the world above"—lay open, as shown in chapter 3, at
the "other end" of the southeast/northwest axis of the solstice cross, that is
at sunset on June solstice. In accord with this reasoning, the final act of the
ritual took place on a bridge above the Vilcamayu, which stood for the
bridge spanning the Milky Way connecting *kay pacha*, "this world," and *hanaq
pacha*, "the world above," the domain of the gods, whence all the offerings
were being dispatched. The invocation of the celestial imagery of the Milky
Way by means of a race along its terrestrial counterpart constituted the

paradigmatic action of Andean civilization: to maintain connection between the domains of the dead, the living, and the gods. And, as shown in chapter 2, this ritual shares the convention found also in myth of simultaneous reference to *both* solstice points in the stars. This little "chip" of the hologram recapitulates in microcosm the entirety of Andean astronomical cosmology.

THE HORIZON-ZENITH
PARADIGM

The use of polar and equatorial coordinates is not supposed to have existed in the Andes, and to propose such knowledge constitutes a flat contradiction of the most influential model of how Native American peoples living in tropical latitudes, from Mexico to Bolivia, conceptualized celestial motions. This paradigm, developed by Anthony Aveni (1981), asserts that, since the motions of celestial bodies appear more symmetrical in mid-latitudes, the fundamental reference system for observation will be the circle of the horizon and the vertical axis formed by the sun's passage through the zenith, a phenomenon that occurs only in tropical latitudes.

Aveni's theory rests upon two assumptions. The first is that peoples everywhere will develop their own astronomies. The second is that those who live between the tropics will look to the horizon and the zenith, while those in temperate latitudes will look up into the sky without much interest in where celestial objects rise and set. "[B]ecause of the remarkable differences in the arrangement and motion of celestial bodies as viewed from the tropical and temperate zones, we must expect that different systems of astronomy might develop in these zones."[1]

According to Aveni, these differences in terrestrial vantage point led to different ways of seeing the sky:

[N]early all tropical cultures that developed indigenous astronomical systems, regardless of whether the motive was largely practical or religious, gravitated toward a reference system consisting of zenith and nadir as poles and the horizon as a fundamental reference circle. Such an arrangement stands in remarkable contrast to the celestial pole-equator (or ecliptic) systems developed by ancient civilizations of the temperate zone.[2]

Again according to Aveni, astronomers in northern latitudes practiced "star to star" observations, that is, observations of the night sky unconnected to the horizon. He cites cuneiform tablet entries such as "Venus in Gemini" and "sun three degrees east of beta Scorpii" as examples of how such observations are "totally detached from the locale of the observer. They are not viewed in a local frame of reference, but, rather they are abstracted to a universal one."[3]

Recent work by Freidel, Schele, and Parker (1993) among the Maya has called such distinctions into question, distinctions that have troubled other scholars as well:

> Schele's arguments do confirm what Barbara Tedlock has been suggesting for some time: that the Maya weren't limited to "horizon-based astronomy"—calculations of celestial motions dependent on the horizon—but had fully mastered star to star astronomy, or "relational astronomy" as it is technically known.[4]

Despite such inconsistencies, Aveni's theory remains the primary lens through which most scholars view pre-Columbian native astronomy. The fundamental difficulty with this hypothesis is that it must accommodate the huge number of exceptions found in both tropical- and temperate-latitude astronomies, exceptions that Aveni was the first to point out:

> Still, there is danger in expressing too rigidly generalizations about the influence of geography on developing astronomies. . . . Of course we can find cultures in the higher latitudes that use horizon references in their practice of astronomy. We need look no further than Stonehenge . . . an excellent counterexample to my thesis. Certain examples from the study of North American archaeoastronomy also demonstrate that it would be erroneous to conclude that all nontropical cultures will shun a horizon reference frame. [Here Aveni cites Eddy's work on North American Medicine Wheels.] . . . Conversely the ecliptic and equator are found to surface as astronomical concepts utilized among tropical people. Indeed pages 23 and 24 of the Paris Codex, a book of ancient Maya writing, have been interpreted as a zodiac consisting of thirteen constellations. . . . Rather than searching out similarities between tropical and temperate-zone astronomies, I have chosen to emphasize simple differences that may be profound. If the modern western scientist shares any common ground with the ancient astronomers of the tropics, it is perhaps that both seek the simplest formalism dictated by the observations.[5]

In 1981, Aveni organized a conference titled "Ethnoastronomy and Archaeoastronomy in the Tropics," to explore his thesis further. The conference papers did not resolve the problems involved in Aveni's approach.

Owen Gingerich, who was asked to write the conference's summary document, said:

> This conference on archaeoastronomy and ethnoastronomy of the tropics was organized under the principle that there exist *two* essentially different archaeoastronomies. One, the Megalithic astronomy of high latitudes, records the carousel-like motions of the heavens around the observer: up, around, down. In this northern archaeoastronomy of the British Isles, and possibly the Medicine Wheels of North America, the obvious calendarial moments are related to motions along the horizon. The other is the archaeoastronomy of the tropics, where the motions are up, over, down and under. When the sun can pass directly overhead, that moment takes on a prime calendrical significance, and while horizon markers may be present, they will tend to record events associated with the solar zenith passage.
>
> So much for the hypothesis that has given the conference its rationale and framework. Has it been demonstrated? Has it successfully supplied the thematic glue to hold the conference together? In my opinion the answer is no! From the point of view of a central thesis, the conference was a shambles.[6]

JAGUAR MYTHS OF THE
EASTERN SLOPES OF THE ANDES

It is clear from the myths of Twins menaced by jaguars as told on the eastern slopes of the Andes that knowledge of the technical language of myth was not confined to the highlands. In each of the versions of the myth, a pregnant woman is devoured by a jaguar or jaguars, while the Twins in her womb escape and eventually end up living in considerable danger in the "little house" of the Grandmother of the jaguars. In the end, the Twins avenge their mother, killing almost all the jaguars and escaping across a river or road or by a chain of arrows to the sky. For the sake of simplicity, let me focus on the Amuesha version.

In this version a young woman is magically impregnated by lightning. Because she is unmarried, suspicion falls on her brother, but he is exonerated when the wisest elder of the tribe, composed of jaguars and lizards, confirms the paternity of lightning. One day the girl is accosted at a spring by Grandmother Jaguar, who eats her. The Twins in her womb, Sun and Moon, escape and hide at the bottom of a river. Grandmother Jaguar says that she is obligated to raise the Twins, because she killed their mother. Soon, Grandmother Jaguar tires of the pair and, preparing to eat them, boils water in a large pot (*olla*). The Twins cause her to fall asleep, dismember her, and put her in the *olla*. When the other jaguars—relatives of the Grandmother —arrive to eat, the Twins hide in the roof of the little house (*choza*), and when the jaguars become suspicious, the Twins set fire to the house and escape across the river, cutting a "bridge" behind them, whereby nearly all the jaguars plunge to their death.

In all three myths the old jaguar is Grandmother, called Patonille in the Amuesha version, and Lari in the Guarani tale. Further, in both the Amuesha and Jívaro versions, the old woman is visibly associated with a large pot, or *olla*. In the Jívaro version she puts the Twins in the *olla* for safekeeping, and as the Twins grow, they are placed in larger and larger *ollas*. As in the Amuesha version, Grandmother meets her fate in her own boiling *olla*. The possibility that the larger and larger *ollas* suggest the (waxing) moon is corroborated and explained by reference to the *Popol Vuh*, in Girard's analysis of a scene where the Twins Hunahpú (Sun) and Ixbalamqué (Moon) divert their grandmother's attention by asking her to draw some water from the river. Grandmother (whose zoological *nahual* was, as noted, the jaguar) wastes much time trying to close a hole "in the face of her water jar." Says Girard,

> We have emphasized Ixmucané's [i.e., Grandmother's] expression re-
> garding the "face of her water jar" because in it we find the genesis of
> the glyph for the moon, shown as a large, narrow-mouthed pitcher
> (cantaro) which is the symbol for Ixmucané, the old water goddess and
> Lunar deity. The "face of her water jar" is similar to the very face of the
> goddess, i.e., her starry form seen in the sky, inasmuch as the Indian
> conceived the moon as a giant pitcher that pours water from the sky.
> The use of this globe-shaped receptacle, which goes back to the matri-
> archal[sic]-horticultural period, is typical of people such as the Taoajka
> who preserve the culture of that time and continue making such pitch-
> ers even now.[1]

That the presence of the *olla* in these tales is meant, as in the Quiché example, to indicate the moon, is also demonstrable by means of analysis of the topographical referents for the jaguars in all three versions. In the Amuesha version the fateful meeting between the young mother and Grand-mother Jaguar takes place at a spring. In the Jívaro version the house of the Grandmother lies at the base of a towering cliff. In the Guarani tale, the house was a cave (*gruta*) at the base of the same towering cliff. We have seen in Andean myth how all such terrestrial low points—caves, springs, and so on—represent the point of interface with the underworld, whose celestial analogue lies at the December-solstice point in the stars. In the case of the Andes, this location in the stars was styled *choqquechinchay*, that is the celestial jaguar, and was associated with the ideal position of the moon at December solstice.

In the *Popol Vub*, as well, we find the proposition that the ideal position of the moon is in the stars of December solstice in the episode where Hunahpú and Ixbalamqué take up their positions on the ball court: "Hu-nahpú and Ixbalamqué, playing alone for a long time on opposite sides of the court, represent the position of the sun and moon at opposing solstices, just as continues to be depicted on Chortí altars."[2]

As for references to the sun at June solstice in the three South American tales at hand, they are abundant. In the Amuesha version the Twins, after killing the Grandmother and putting her in the pot, hide in the roof thatch to await the other jaguars. As we have seen, in the architectonic image of the celestial sphere, the roof of the house stands for June solstice. Next, the Twins set fire to the whole house—suggesting the entry of the June-solstice sun into the Milky Way, a view corroborated by the fact that the Twins escape by fleeing across a "river." Earlier, when Grandmother Jaguar savages the pregnant mother of the Twins, so much amniotic fluid is released that it creates a rushing river, which sweeps the Twins to safety, and they hide at the bottom (*en el fondo*) of the river.

This image suggests in another manner (than that of striking fire) the entry of the sun and moon, representing opposing solstices, into the Milky Way. If one takes the image at face value, namely that the sun (and moon, representing the other solstice) are "at the bottom of the river," the image suggests the *heliacal rise* of the Milky Way, when the "river" is visible rising, with the sun beneath the horizon, at the "bottom" of the celestial river. The era of the heliacal rise of the Milky Way at June solstice, that is, with the "river" in visible contact with the horizon, began about 200 B.C. (See figure 6.2.)

The June-solstice imagery employed in the Jívaro and Guarani tales is that of the towering precipice, comparable to the cliff at Titicaca and the myths of the flood at June Solstice Mountain. It is here that the jaguars are said to range when hunting, a formulation comparable to the Andean convention of telling both solstice points in the stars by referring simultaneously to the December-solstice animals, including Puma, Fox, and so on, taking refuge on the mountain. In both stories the Twins take their revenge on the jaguars by leading them a merry chase from their cave, up the "cliff," and across a "bridge," which the Twins sabotage, causing most, but not all, of the jaguars to fall to their deaths, in one version drowning in a river.

One further example of concordance between Mesoamerican, South American forest tribes, and Andean sources demonstrates the holographic nature of even the most apparently minor reference in myth. In the Guarani version—even though, in nature, the jaguar is omnivorous in its choice of game animals—the meat of choice is specified as venison (*venado*). Given that the jaguars range to the mountaintop to hunt, this situation suggests that the deer is associated with June solstice. This "prediction," in a sense inevitable if one takes seriously the logic of the technical language of myth, is borne out fully by the *Popol Vuh*.

Here Hunahpú and Ixbalamqué, in their roles as instigators and protectors of agriculture, roust marauding animals out of the fields or *milpas*. Girard explains the episode: "[T]he deer and rabbit ran with their tails between their legs (a sign of fear) and their pursuers seized them. But the tails broke off and Hunahpú and Ixbalamqué were left holding only the ends. From that time rabbits and deer have stubby tails."[3]

As to the substitution of rabbit for jaguar as lunar symbol, Girard notes elsewhere that the "intimate cooperation between Lunar goddess (Ixba-lamqué) and the rabbit is most clearly expressed in the lunar hieroglyph . . . [which] shows a large, narrow-mouthed pitcher—symbol of the moon—inside of which is a rabbit."[4]

Similarly, Linda Schele has studied the glyphic representations of deer and rabbit at Palenque and has concluded that the glyph for "rabbit" is always associated with the moon, and the "deer" glyph with the *kin* or sun sign. Furthermore, she cites the ethnographic evidence that Mesoamerican people saw in the moon—where we see the "old man"—a rabbit: "The shape of the rabbit is very obvious even to western eyes in the dark area of the moon."[5]

Since the "rabbit in the moon" is completely visible only at full moon, and since, as we have seen, the ideal relation of Hunahpú and Ixbalamqué is at opposing solstices, we find, in this picaresque "tale of the tails" from the *Popol Vuh*, the association of deer not simply with the sun (it was Hunahpú/sun who pulled deer's tail), but with the sun at June solstice. And, just as the South American jaguar myths suggest—by the terrestrial opposition of hunter and hunted, jaguar and deer—the celestial opposition of the stars rising at opposing solstices, Kelley has noted that the Mesoamerican celestial deer appears to lie 180 degrees from the tail of Scorpius, termed "lasso" or "snare" for catching deer.[6] In the Andes, as we have seen, the tail of Scorpius is identified sometimes as a jaguar and sometimes as a "sling of stars."

This reading is further corroborated by Lamb's work in colonial-period lexicons of the Yucatec Maya language, where he found the following commentary when looking up the word for star, *ek*: "spots like those of the tigers and deer when small," and "spots that are on the body of the deer." Lamb also adds, "The Maya symbolized stars with jaguar's spots and the night sky with its skin."[7] In this information we encounter what might be called a psychological convention of the technical language of myth, where vivid mental images of great beauty are used to express complex relationships, here those of sun/day/deer/June solstice and moon/night/jaguar/December solstice: the jaguar's spots are seen by moonlight, while those of the deer, if one's eyes are sharp enough, are picked up among sun-dappled spots in shady bowers, camouflage for the young.

While this story from the *Popol Vuh* makes clear why the Guarani jaguars had to "go up onto the mountain" in search of deer, it also opens a window onto an ancient, seminal moment in the development of civilization in the Americas. Deer and rabbit lose their tails, according to myth, at the precise moment of the advent of agricultural civilization. In both Mayan and Andean thought, it was at this moment that the stars "awoke." Whereas, previously, those areas of the sky rising around the solstices were vaguely related to stars like spots of jaguar and deer, they are now precisely located by the means of sun and moon at opposing solstices—a reference to the refinement of the agricultural calendar—and these luminaries are symbolized now by the white, docked tails of the deer and rabbit.[8] Further, it appears that with the advent of the Twins, Sun and Moon, we find memorialized the discovery of the obliquity of the ecliptic in the formulation of sun and moon at opposing solstices. Finally, it should be noted in passing that deer and rabbit fulfill the same taxonomic requirements as Andean animals in marking the boundaries between the three worlds, as the deer ranges up on the "mountain" in search of food, while the rabbit lives in a "hole" in the ground.[9]

As for the Andes, it is sufficient to note the name of a constellation, Topaturka, mentioned by Acosta, Cobo, and Polo, and defined by Polo's editor Urteaga as "a contraction of *Tupac taruka*," meaning "royal deer,"[10] or possibly "reed deer," if glossed as *topa taruka*. This constellation has never been identified. I think the reason for this, as with the vagueness of identification for the Jaguar constellation in the Andes, is explained by the same context as the Maya vagueness about stars being like spots on deer and jaguars. Mythic formulations involving the opposition of hunter and hunted had become culturally obsolete artifacts in the age of agriculture, and hence were dropped in favor of constellation names more relevant to an agricultural society.

The cultural significance of the deer was well remembered in the Andes (see chapter 7), but its celestial identity, perhaps never fully correlated with any particular stars but rather with the idea of June solstice, was forgotten in the face of the necessities—both practical and religious—of creating the sun, moon, and stars that would beam down upon the agricultural terraces of the Andes. This view finds eerie parallels in the iconography of Palenque, where the glyphic representation of both deer and rabbit show them as skeletons—icons of a defunct age.[11]

THE COSMOLOGY OF TIAHUANACO'S MONUMENTS

Descriptions of the ceremonial core of Tiahuanaco have only recently come into print. The entire ceremonial complex of Tiahuanaco is surrounded by a moat whose purpose, to use Alan Kolata's words, "was to evoke the image of the city core as an island" to separate the ordinary, everyday world from "the space and time of the sacred."[1] Eliade has documented this same symbolic usage in the Old World, as with the Roman *mundus* ("world"), or circular moat, which "constituted the point where the lower regions and the terrestrial world meet."[2] The purpose of such enclosures was to create the sacred space within which the temple, or model of the cosmos, might be constructed, "the zone where the upper (divine) terrestrial and subterranean worlds intersected."[3] As we have seen Eliade recount, the central symbolism of such temple structures was that of the cosmic mountain, standing for the navel of the earth connecting the three regions.

The dominant structure of Tiahuanaco's sacred center was the Akapana, a truncated pyramid over fifty feet in height, called by Kolata "the sacred mountain of Tiwanaku."

The Akapana pyramid rose in seven levels. The number seven, as already discussed, is associated with "father sky," which is to say the use of polar and equatorial coordinates, expressed by reference to the cardinal directions. The ancient Aymara system of orientation involved seven directions, employing the four cardinal directions along with zenith, center, and nadir. The Akapana is oriented to the cardinal directions.[4]

The same inference is found in the relationship between the adjacent complex of structures called the Semisubterranean Temple and the Kalasaya. They are laid out along a due east-west axis, speaking for the rise and set points of the sun at the equinoxes, when the sun crosses the celestial equator.[5] Stairs leading upward and westward from the Semisubterranean Temple to ground level lead directly to a second stairway rising into the aboveground-level precincts of the Kalasaya, where the monolithic statue of a god (the so-called Ponce Stela) faced due east, back toward the Semisubterranean Temple.

This conceptual modeling of the equinox line in terms of stairways at once brings to mind the Andean constellation *chacana* ("stairway"), the three stars of Orion's Belt, which lie upon the celestial equator.

These axially related structures also offer good evidence of the religious cosmology associated with the Titicaca emergence myth. As we have already seen, in the architectonic symbolism of the celestial sphere, the floor of the house, standing for the southern tropic, ought, strictly speaking, to be below ground level, thereby allowing ground level to stand for the celestial equator. As noted, the Hopi kiva most precisely fits these demands. As we saw in the myth of the House of the False God, this problem was solved by finding a "hole" beneath the grindstone allowing "visual access" to the toad, deep "underneath" the "earth." In ritual practice, the same statement was and continues to be made in the Andes by burying a llama fetus (remember, the celestial Llama's suckling lies right at the crossing of the Milky Way and the ecliptic at the southern tropic) beneath the foundations of the house.

As its name implies, the Semisubterranean Temple was constructed about six feet below ground level, open to the air. Therefore, again strictly speaking, the floor of the Semisubterranean Temple ought to stand for the southern tropic and access to the land of the dead. (In the same way, the sunken floor of the Quiché ball court was said to rest upon the roof of the house of the lords of the underworld.) Consistent with this interpretation is the fact that the lineage *wakas* of the agricultural tribes participating in the Tiahuanacan sphere of influence were found implanted in the floor of the Semisubterranean Temple.[6] In the midst of this array a second Stela, called the Bennett Stela, encrypted with complex calendric information regarding the agricultural year, stared due west (the celestial direction associated with the moon, night, rain, and the dead) back at the Ponce Stela on the raised precincts of the Kalasaya. Conversely, the Ponce Stela, above in the Kalasaya, commanded a view of the eastern horizon.

A second, smaller sunken courtyard was placed atop the seventh level of the Akapana pyramid. As with the Old World pattern, in which the top of the sacred temple mountain represents the "navel of the earth," the Akapana's sunken courtyard, symbolically speaking, was an *omphalos*. This sunken courtyard was laid out in the form of a square sumperimposed over a Greek cross (figure 8.5). The cross, standing for (and oriented to) the cardinal directions (and hence referencing polar and equatorial coordinates), represents the celestial realm, or Father Sky. The square, as we have already found in the form of the quadrangular *maras*, or "female" grindstone (which takes its name from the Aymara word for "year") delineates, by its corners, the intercardinal points representing the rising and setting loci of the solstice suns, that is, the parameters of the "celestial earth" as determined by the ecliptic plane. Connect the corners by making the diagonals, and X marks the spot, the center, the navel of the earth goddess. This symbolism is, as already noted, found in the standard, or *unanacha*, of Wiraqocha in Pachakuti Yamqui's diagram, placed as it is above the intercardinal female-designated cross below; and, also as mentioned in chapter 6, precisely this same symbolism is found among the Quiché, where the God-Seven, glyphically represented as Ursa Major and Orion, is laid out on the navel of the earth goddess.

A second, unique feature of the Akapana's sunken courtyard has only recently been unearthed. This courtyard served as a catchment for rainwater, and was connected to a system of drains that alternately poured water out of the vertical facing walls of each level, took the water back underground horizontally beneath the standing surface of each tier, and then brought it forth, again and again, cascading down all the levels of the pyramid.[7]

So the builders of Tiahuanaco constructed a "mountain full of water" in sight of a lake and an island called Titicaca, or "Lion Cliff," where water gushed forth from a cliff, and whose glyphic analogue in Mexico—a mountain with fangs and a cave at the base—represented the village, *alteptl*, literally "mountain full of water." And like any true cosmic mountain, the Akapana recycled as well the waters of spiritual life, whose headwaters arose at the top of the cosmic mountain, at June solstice in the precincts of the Milky Way.

PALEOLITHIC ORIGINS OF
THE CONCEPT *WAKA*

Worldwide notions of extreme antiquity relate animals to a celestial proto-type in the stars. Marshack has discussed animal images on Upper Paleolithic mobilary (i.e, "portable") art in their relation to seasonal phenomena.[1] He has shown how animals, alternatively calving or in rut, are depicted within a wider context of simultaneous seasonal events, such as the spawning runs of the salmon, followed upriver by seals, while plants flower, and so on. One particular image, that of the ibex, and its consistent placement in composi-tions with references to early spring, around the vernal equinox, have led Marshack to suspect a seasonal ritual of ibex-sacrifice at the time of calving, around vernal equinox.[2] Of particular interest is an engraved horn from Cueto de la Mina dating from the Upper Magedelanian (ca. 14,000–12,000 B.P.) depicting not only an ibex associated with the advent of spring, but surrounded by day notations organized around lunar phases over a period of about nine months. Marshack remarks:

> The technique of running a series of day-units (or month- or year-units)
> horizontally along an edge, with symbols juxtaposed above the days . . .
> to indicate moments of significant rite, myth, observation, or seasonal
> change, appears in the historic Greco-Roman calendars, the Scandina-
> vian calendar rune stick, the English Clogg almanac, the Siberian Yakut
> calendar, and on certain American Indian record sticks. . . . On this
> bone from the site of Cueto de la Mina we seem to have an example
> indicating the integrated beginnings of arithmetic, astronomy, writing,
> abstracted symbolism, and notation. There is also the implication that
> these cultural skills were related to the economic and ritual-religious
> life of the hunting groups.[3]

In turn, Dechend has sought that point in the ethnographic record where peoples of Upper Paleolithic culture horizon have left a record of their ideas concerning the seasonal habits of animals that they hunt. At this point she encountered star lore: how and why, for example, the African Bushmen—just as in the Peruvian Andes—found in the stars, the guardians of the various species:

In the mythology the stars are held to have once been animals or people of the Early Race. . . . Many of the stars and constellations, as Dr. Bleek points out, bear names which they apparently owe only to the fact that *they are seen at certain times when the animals or other objects whose names they bear come into season or are most abundant.*[4] [Emphasis added.]

The practice of naming of stars after animals whose seasonal activities corresponded with the appearance of the given star, arose not only from practical considerations, but also because the conscience of the hunter sought out a mode of conveying respect to the life taken. The Bushmen took great care never to damage the bones of game because the soul of the animal, upon returning to its appointed star, is revived and reanimated through the bones. If the bones were damaged, then, according to the Bushmen, "the light of the starry sky would vanish."[5] Copious materials collected by Dechend describe customs of (1) carefully preserving the bones of game animals; (2) treating the kill with respect; and (3) taking ritual measures to ensure that the soul of the animal will return to be hunted again. "Animals properly propitiated return 'home' and they tell in the sky how well they had been treated."[6]

If one moves to the culture horizon of mesolithic peoples, such as the Naskapi of Labrador, ideas associating the origin of people and the starry realm begin to appear. According to the Naskapi of Labrador, the souls of the living originated in the sky, where they "rest in the firmament until they become reincarnated."[7] Likewise, in Siberia, "The Goldi, the Dolgan, and the Tungus say that before birth, the souls of children perch like little birds on the branches of the Cosmic Tree [the uranic realm] and the shamans go there to find them."[8] In South America, among the Puelche of Patagonia, it is held that there was a time when "stars were people," while these same people "today are animals."[9]

These data demonstrate that stars were originally named by hunters who associated the seasonal activities of animals with the seasonal "activities" of stars. This simple hypothesis, based on reliable ethnographic and archaeological material, not only brings alive Ice Age artifacts, but tells us why, throughout the world, most constellations are named after animals and why so few constellations look anything like the animals they are meant to represent. Noting that certain groups of stars rose at critical times, because they marked the seasonal activities of important game animals, the hunters named those stars after the animal in question. Thus astro-nomy, the naming of stars, became an important mnemonic device for teaching and remembering when, and when not, to take different species of game. Over time, these named constellations came to be viewed as the "game lords," or spirit-world guardians of the species that bore their names, allowing humankind a "storied backdrop" upon which to project philosophical notions concerning the nature of death and birth. Finally, this logic explains why the stars of the ecliptic plane, that is, those stars toward which attention would most naturally be drawn in the gathering dawn, were called, in ancient Western tradition, "zodiac," or "dial of animals."

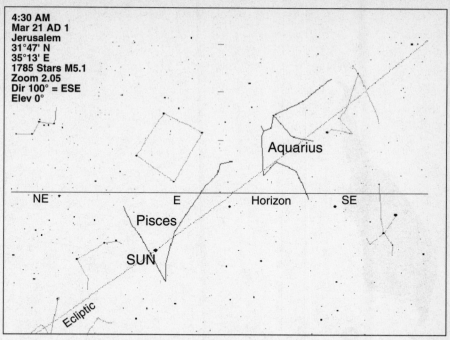

FIGURE 1.1A. The heliacal rise of Pisces
at spring equinox in the era of the birth of Christ.

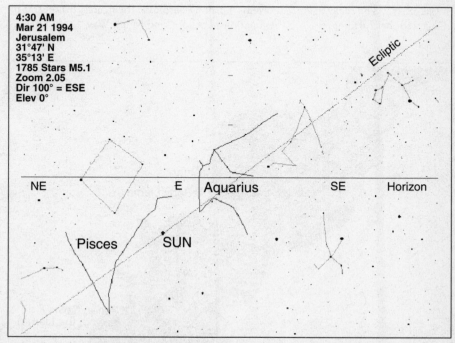

FIGURE 1.1B. Nearly two millennia later, on the same day, the constellation Pisces
has been "replaced," owing to precession, by Aquarius "descending."

Baby Llama

FIGURE 2.1. The celestial Llama with her suckling.

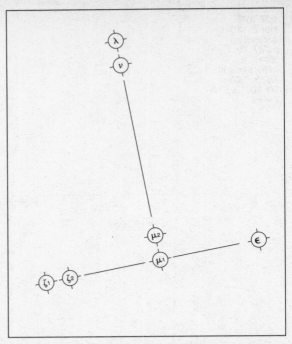

FIGURE 2.2. The Quechua constellation *cruz calvario*, composed of stars in the tail of the Western Scorpius: lambda, upsilon, zeta 1 and 2, mu 1 and 2, and epsilon Scorpius. Epsilon Scorpius is the nearest bright star to the junction of ecliptic and Milky Way.

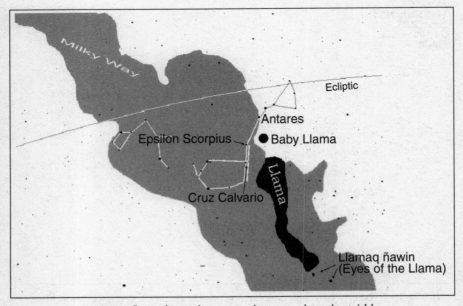

FIGURE 2.3. *Cruz calvario* shown in relation to the celestial Llama.

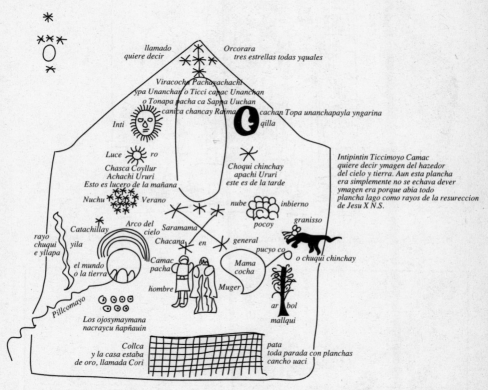

FIGURE 2.4. The cosmological diagram of Juan de Santacruz Pachakuti Yamqui Salcamaygua.

FIGURE 2.5. Guamán Poma's depiction of the typical house type of the Third Age.

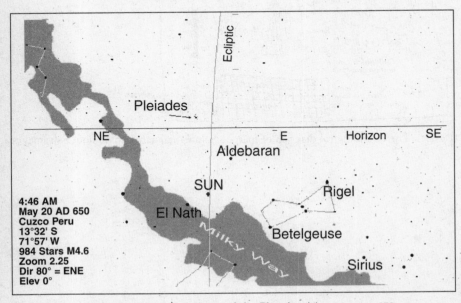

FIGURE 2.6A. The heliacal rise of the Pleiades, May 20, A.D. 650,
one month before the "flood."

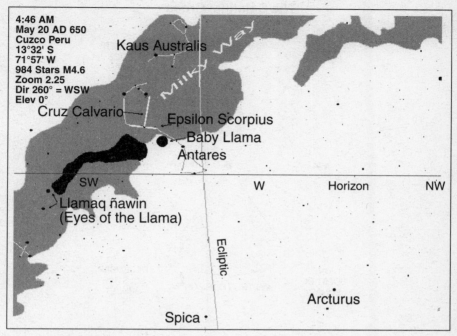

FIGURE 2.6B. Simultaneous set of the celestial Llama, May 20, A.D. 650.

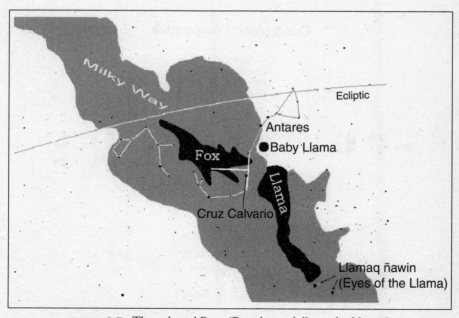

FIGURE 2.7. The celestial Fox. "Fox always follows the Llama."

The Solstitial Cross

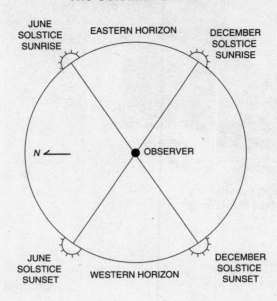

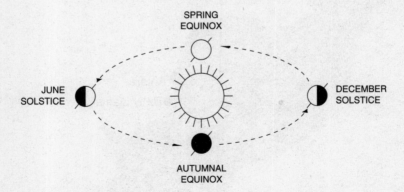

FIGURE 2.8. The ideal relationship of the intercardinal cross to the rising and setting points of the solstice suns.

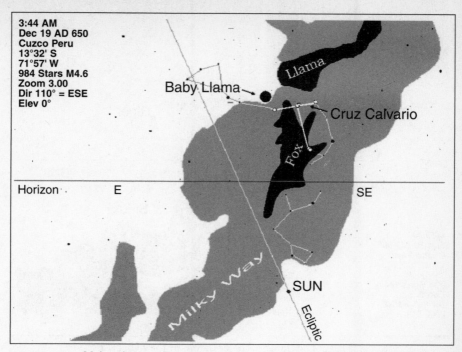

3:44 AM
Dec 19 AD 650
Cuzco Peru
13°32' S
71°57' W
984 Stars M4.6
Zoom 3.00
Dir 110° = ESE
Elev 0°

Baby Llama

Llama

Cruz Calvario

Fox

Horizon   E

SE

Milky Way

SUN

Ecliptic

FIGURE 2.9A. Heliacal rise at December solstice A.D. 650, or "Why Fox's Tail Is Black."

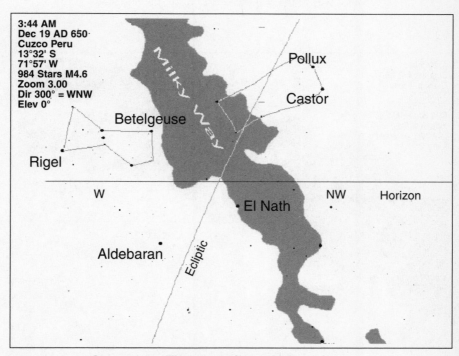

3:44 AM
Dec 19 AD 650
Cuzco Peru
13°32' S
71°57' W
984 Stars M4.6
Zoom 3.00
Dir 300° = WNW
Elev 0°

Milky Way

Pollux

Castor

Betelgeuse

Rigel

W

NW   Horizon

El Nath

Aldebaran

Ecliptic

FIGURE 2.9B. The view to the northwest at the same
moment as Fox's "mishap" (Figure 2.9A).

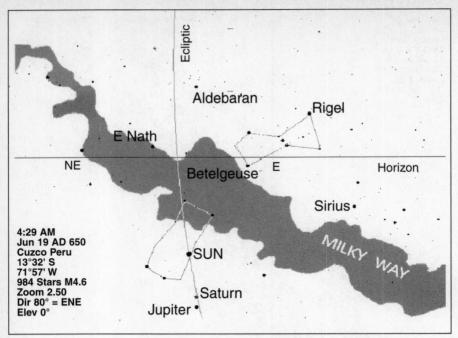

FIGURE 2.10A. The "flood": The cessation of the heliacal rise of
the Milky Way at June solstice, A.D. 650. The sun is no longer in the
Milky Way at the point where it crosses the horizon.

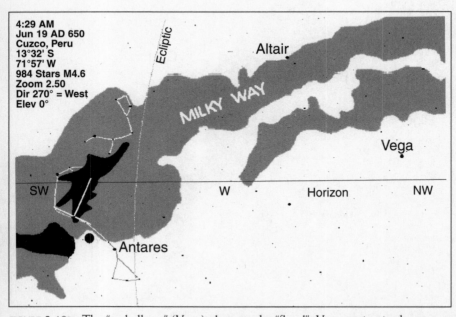

FIGURE 2.10B. The "male llama" (Vega) observes the "flood": Vega setting in the west at
the moment of heliacal rise (figure 2.10A), June solstice, A.D. 650.

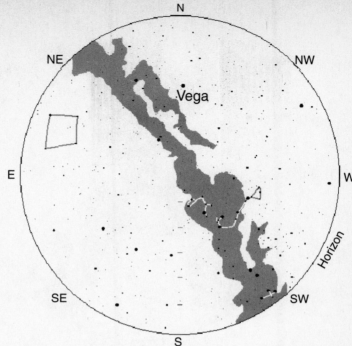

11:45 PM
Jun 19 AD 650
Cuzco Peru
13°32' S
71°57' W
984 Stars M4.6
Zoom 1.05
Dir 180° = South
Elev 90°

FIGURE 3.1A. The northeast/southwest branch of the Milky Way passing overhead, June solstice, A.D. 650.

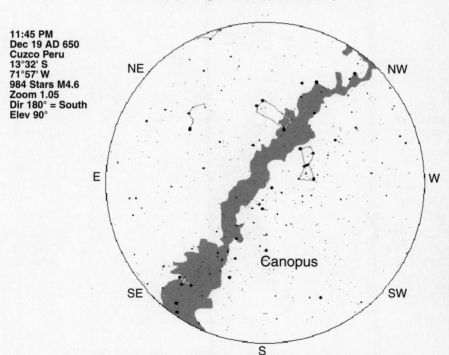

11:45 PM
Dec 19 AD 650
Cuzco Peru
13°32' S
71°57' W
984 Stars M4.6
Zoom 1.05
Dir 180° = South
Elev 90°

FIGURE 3.1B. The northwest/southeast branch of the Milky Way passing overhead, December solstice, A.D. 650.

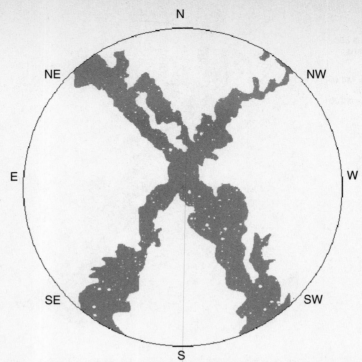

FIGURE 3.2. The imagined crossing of the two branches of the Milky Way, creating the quadripartition of celestial space.

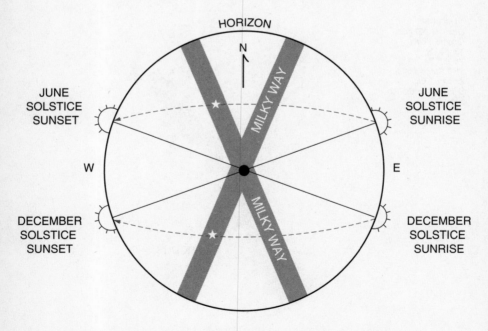

FIGURE 3.3. The ideal configuration of solstices and the Milky Way: each solstice heliacal-rise event (marked by a star) "nested" in the Milky Way. This ideal configuration ended in about A.D. 650.

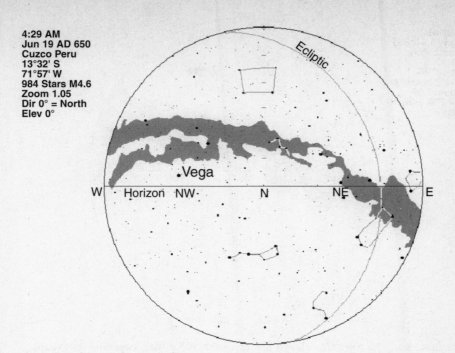

4:29 AM
Jun 19 AD 650
Cuzco Peru
13°32' S
71°57' W
984 Stars M4.6
Zoom 1.05
Dir 0° = North
Elev 0°

FIGURE 3.4A. The "headwaters" of the Milky Way
in the northern sky at heliacal rise, June solstice, A.D. 650.

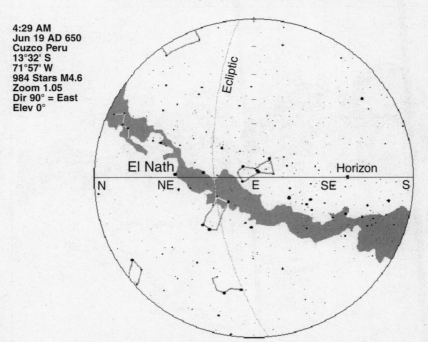

4:29 AM
Jun 19 AD 650
Cuzco Peru
13°32' S
71°57' W
984 Stars M4.6
Zoom 1.05
Dir 90° = East
Elev 0°

FIGURE 3.4B. Northwest/southeast branch of the Milky Way, sweeping
southward beneath the eastern horizon at heliacal rise, June solstice, A.D. 650.

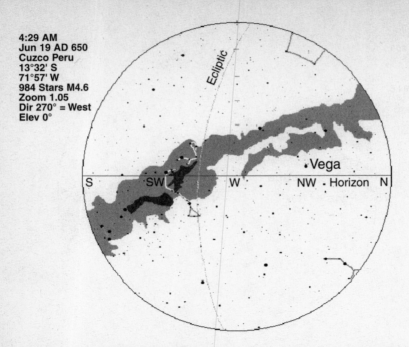

Ecliptic

Vega

S   SW   W   NW · Horizon   N

FIGURE 3.4C. Northeast/southwest branch of the Milky Way, sweeping southward beneath the western horizon at heliacal rise, June solstice, A.D. 650.

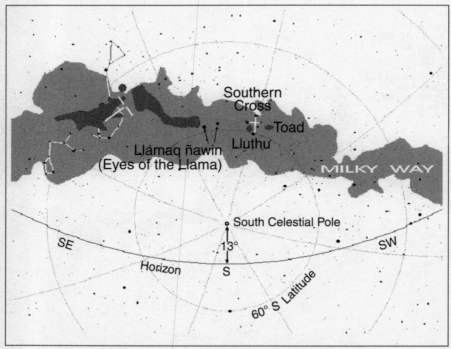

Southern
Cross

Toad

Lluthu

Llámaq ñawin
(Eyes of the Llama)

MILKY WAY

South Celestial Pole

13°

60° S Latitude

SE

SW

Horizon   S

FIGURE 3.5. The southern, near-circumpolar constellations, including the Southern Cross, *llamaq ñawin* (alpha and beta Centaurus), Toad, and *lluthu* (partridge).

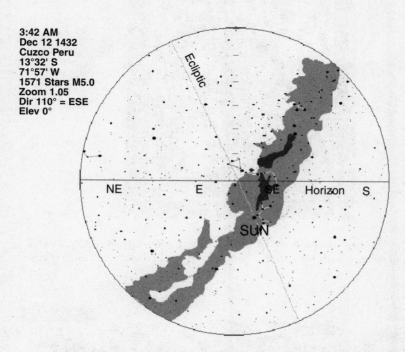

FIGURE 3.6. The "opening" of the land of the dead: the eastern horizon at heliacal rise on December solstice during the era of the Incas.

FIGURE 3.7. The sarcophagus lid of Lord Shield-Pacal, showing a vertically stacked, three-tiered cosmos, with the entrance to the lower world flanked by conch shells.

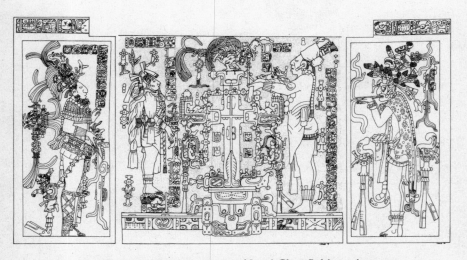

FIGURE 3.8. The accession monument of Lord Chan Bahlum, demonstrating the same three-tiered cosmos and conch shells as in figure 3.7.

FIGURE 3.9. A Zapotec genealogical register, with conch
shells flanking the "Jaws of the Underworld."

FIGURE 3.10. Pattern from a Conquest-era drinking cup depicting
"the birth of the sun" at the "headwaters" of two rivers.

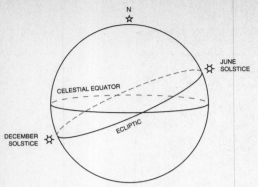

FIGURE 3.11A. The celestial sphere in relation to the earth's orientation (= "north") with the positions of the solstice suns along the ecliptic. In mythical terminology, the relationship of ecliptic to celestial equator was termed "the separation of the world parents."

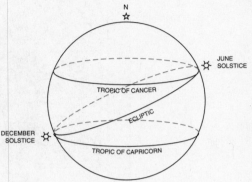

FIGURE 3.11B. The celestial sphere with tropics.

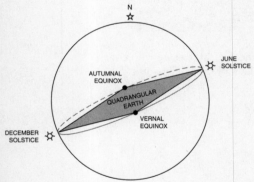

FIGURE 3.12A. The quadrangular earth, or square made by linking the points in the stars marking heliacal rise at the solstices and equinoxes.

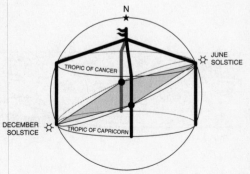

FIGURE 3.12B. The "World House" supported by the four pillars at the four "corners" of the quadrangular earth.

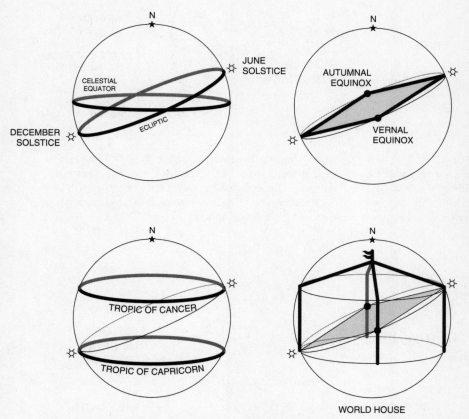

FIGURE 3.12C. From the observation of the two distinct planes of ecliptic and equator (top left) arises the idea of the "quadrangular earth" (top right), leading in turn to the establishment of the boundaries of the "celestial earth" (bottom left), or, in alternative imagery, the structure of the "world house" (bottom right).

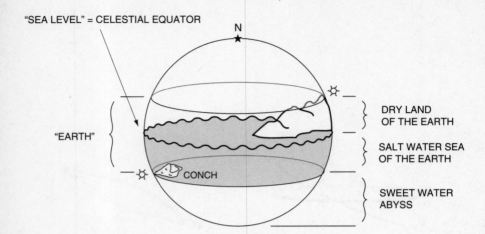

FIGURE 3.13. The "celestial earth," showing the location of the "highest mountain" at June solstice, and the conch shell at the "bottom of the sea," or December. "Sea level," dividing "dry land" and "sea" represents the celestial equator. The "celestial earth" and the "world house" (see figure 3.12B) were different terminological conventions for describing events on the same area of the celestial sphere.

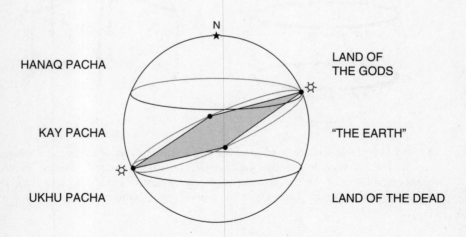

FIGURE 3.14. The three "worlds" on the celestial sphere.

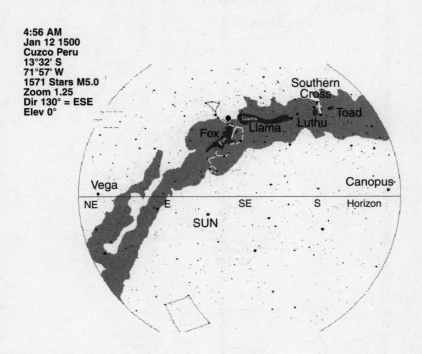

FIGURE 3.15. The heliacal rise of Vega at the time of the intentional flooding of Cuzco by the Incas. (See Appendix 1.)

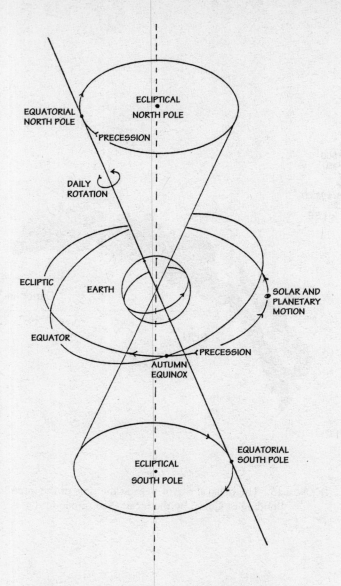

FIGURE 4.1. The precession of the equinoxes.

FIGURE 4.2. The Gateway God of Tiahuanaco.

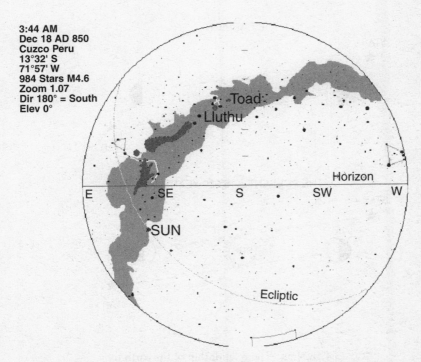

3:44 AM
Dec 18 AD 850
Cuzco Peru
13°32' S
71°57' W
984 Stars M4.6
Zoom 1.07
Dir 180° = South
Elev 0°

Toad

Lluthu

Horizon

E   SE   S   SW   W

SUN

Ecliptic

FIGURE 4.3. The southern horizon at heliacal rise on December solstice, A.D. 850.

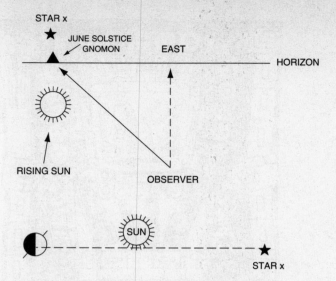

FIGURE 4.4. The heliacal rise of star x at June solstice, as seen by the naked eye (above), and from the Copernican perspective (below).

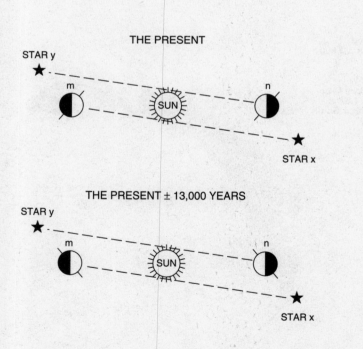

FIGURES 4.5A, 4.5B. The relationship of the earth to the heliacal rise of stars x and y through precessional time.

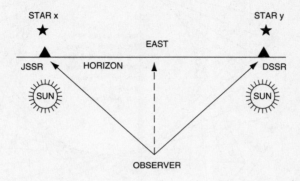

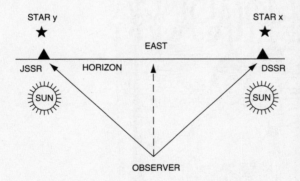

FIGURES 4.6A, 4.6B. The same event as in
Figures 4.5A and B from the naked-eye perspective.

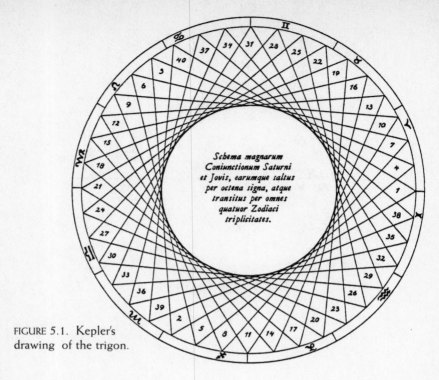

Schema magnarum
Coniunctionum Saturni
et Jovis, earumque saltus
per octena signa, atque
transitus per omnes
quatuor Zodiaci
triplicitates.

FIGURE 5.1. Kepler's
drawing of the trigon.

DE INGAS

MANGO CAPAG

ukynga raynojabeclung acamacta

FIGURE 5.2. Manco Capac
wielding the *tupayauri*.

SATURN · JUPITER · MARS · SUN · MOON · VENUS · MERCURY

650

	SATURN LONG.	SATURN LAT.	JUPITER LONG.	JUPITER LAT.	MARS LONG.	MARS LAT.	SUN LONG.	JULIAN 16.00U	MOON LONG.	MOON LAT.	VENUS LONG.	VENUS LAT.	MERCURY LONG.	MERCURY LAT.
(prev.)									255.7	-4.5	331.59	-1.02	270.24	-0.71
1	94.62	-0.26	86.62	0.14	49.17	2.26	293.62	JA 5	326.9 29.8	1.2 5.1	337.37 343.07	-0.71 -0.37	277.74 285.56	-1.23 -1.64
2	93.91	-0.24	85.67	0.16	51.94	2.23	303.75	10JA15	89.6 153.7	3.7 -1.8	348.70 355.23	0.00 0.41	293.70 302.20	-1.92 -2.06
3	93.32	-0.22	84.99	0.17	55.38	2.18	311.83	20JA25	222.8 293.8	-5.3 -1.8	359.66 4.96	0.85 1.31	311.08 320.35	-2.02 -1.78
4	92.88	-0.20	84.63	0.19	59.35	2.13	323.87	30//4	0.8 61.4	3.8 5.0	10.11 15.09	1.79 2.29	329.93 339.58	-1.29 -0.55
5	92.61	-0.17	84.59	0.21	63.73	2.07	333.85	9FE14	122.6 190.9	1.0 -4.6	19.88 24.43	2.80 3.31	348.77 356.63	0.41 1.50
6	92.52	-0.15	84.87	0.22	68.43	2.00	343.78	19FE24	262.3 330.3	-4.1 1.5	28.70 32.63	3.82 4.32	2.21 4.88	2.52 3.24
7	92.62	-0.13	85.46	0.24	73.39	1.93	353.65	1MR 6	33.5 93.2	5.1 3.3	36.16 39.21	4.80 5.24	4.50 1.72	3.44 2.98
8	92.90	-0.10	86.33	0.25	78.56	1.87	3.46	11MR16	157.2 229.7	-2.1 -5.1	41.66 43.40	5.62 5.92	357.97 354.96	1.93 0.59
9	93.35	-0.10	87.45	0.26	83.90	1.80	13.21	21MR26	300.6 5.1	-1.0 4.1	44.22 44.28	6.10 6.12	353.74 354.57	-0.71 -1.76
10	93.96	-0.08	88.80	0.27	89.37	1.73	22.91	31//5	65.8 125.8	4.6 0.5	43.24 41.23	5.93 5.47	357.26 1.49	-2.49 -2.91
11	94.71	-0.06	90.34	0.28	94.97	1.66	32.56	10AP15	193.8 268.7	-4.6 -3.3	38.47 35.35	4.73 3.75	7.00 13.60	-3.03 -2.87
12	95.60	-0.05	92.05	0.29	100.67	1.59	42.17	20AP25	337.0 38.7	2.4 5.0	32.36 29.95	2.61 1.43	21.20 29.76	-2.67 -1.85
13	96.59	-0.03	93.89	0.30	106.46	1.51	51.75	MY 5	98.1 160.2	2.5 -2.7	28.41 27.87	0.32 -0.67	39.25 49.58	-1.06 -0.17
14	97.68	-0.01	95.85	0.31	112.33	1.44	61.30	10MY15	232.2 306.5	-4.9 0.0	28.29 29.58	-1.50 -2.17	60.45 71.37	0.70 1.40
15	98.85	0.00	97.90	0.33	118.28	1.37	70.83	20MY25	11.6 71.4	4.6 4.2	31.63 34.29	-2.69 -3.08	81.82 91.51	1.84 1.98
16	100.07	0.02	100.03	0.34	124.30	1.29	80.36	30//4	136.7 196.7	-0.5 -4.9	37.48 41.09	-3.35 -3.51	100.31 108.26	1.84 1.44
17 ↑	101.13	0.03	102.20	0.35	130.37	1.22	89.88	9JN14	271.0 342.5	-2.9 3.2	45.06 49.32	-3.59 -3.60	115.27 121.29	0.83 0.03
18	102.62	0.04	104.40	0.37	136.55	1.14	99.42	19JN24	44.7 104.2	5.2 1.8	53.82 58.53	-3.54 -3.42	126.19 129.71	-0.92 -1.98
19	103.92	0.06	106.61	0.38	142.78	1.06	108.97	JL 4	166.3 235.2	-3.5 -4.9	63.42 68.46	-3.25 -3.04	131.55 131.35	-3.06 -4.03
20	105.20	0.07	108.82	0.40	149.08	0.98	118.56	9JL14	309.0 16.6	0.4 5.0	73.62 78.91	-2.79 -2.52	129.00 125.07	-4.65 -4.64
21	106.46	0.09	111.00	0.42	155.45	0.90	128.17	19JL24	76.8 137.6	3.9 -1.2	84.29 89.77	-2.22 -1.91	121.14 119.15	-3.88 -2.55
22	107.67	0.11	113.13	0.44	161.89	0.82	137.83	29//3	203.5 274.3	-5.2 -2.7	95.33 100.96	-1.59 -1.26	120.32 124.81	-1.06 -0.26
23	108.81	0.12	115.19	0.46	168.41	0.73	147.54	8AU13	345.3 49.2	3.4 5.0	106.66 112.43	-0.93 -0.60	131.92 140.59	1.19 1.70
24	109.87	0.14	117.17	0.48	175.01	0.64	157.30	18AU23	108.8	1.4	118.25	-0.28	149.85	1.83

FIGURE 5.3. The Tuckerman Tables for June solstice, A.D. 650.

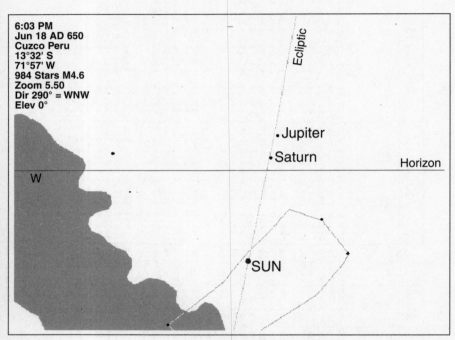

FIGURE 5.4. The conjunction of Saturn and Jupiter at June solstice eve, A.D. 650.

FIGURE 6.1. The Second Age house type, according to Guamán Poma.

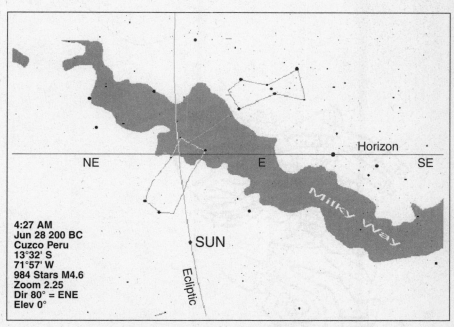

FIGURE 6.2. The "coming to earth" of the Milky Way.
The eastern horizon at heliacal rise on June solstice, 200 B.C.

FIGURE 8.1. Portrait of a
Wari ruler, from a ceramic
offering at Conchopata.

FIGURE 8.2. The "sacrificer" of Pucara.

FIGURE 8.3. The ritual sacrifice of a llama, according to Guamán Poma.

FIGURE 8.4. The hilltop fortress, house type of the Fourth Age, according to Guamán Poma.

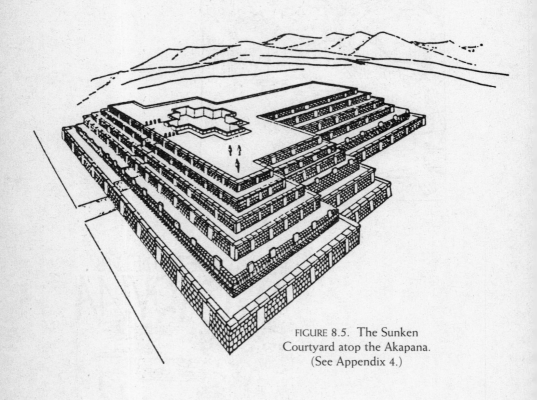

FIGURE 8.5. The Sunken
Courtyard atop the Akapana.
(See Appendix 4.)

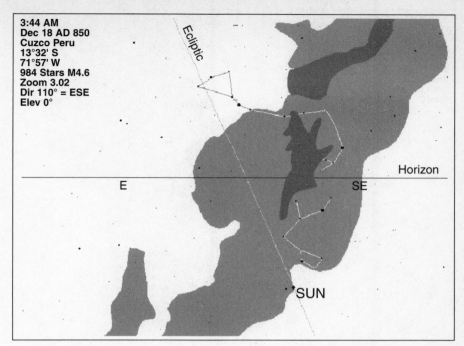

FIGURE 9.1. Fox slips. Heliacal rise at December solstice, A.D. 850.

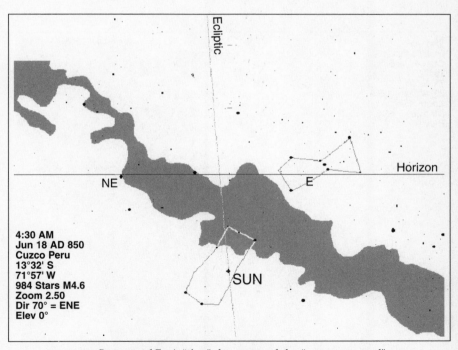

FIGURE 9.2. Because of Fox's "slip," the origin of the "irrigation canal" is now "lower down" on the "mountain." Heliacal rise at June solstice, A.D. 850. (Compare with figure 2.10A.)

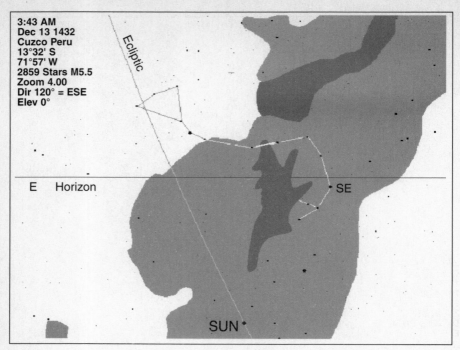

3:43 AM
Dec 13 1432
Cuzco Peru
13°32' S
71°57' W
2859 Stars M5.5
Zoom 4.00
Dir 120° = ESE
Elev 0°

FIGURE 9.3A. Heliacal rise at December solstice, A.D. 1432.

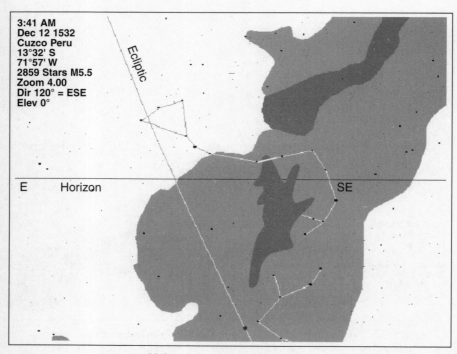

3:41 AM
Dec 12 1532
Cuzco Peru
13°32' S
71°57' W
2859 Stars M5.5
Zoom 4.00
Dir 120° = ESE
Elev 0°

FIGURE 9.3B. Heliacal rise at December solstice, A.D. 1532.

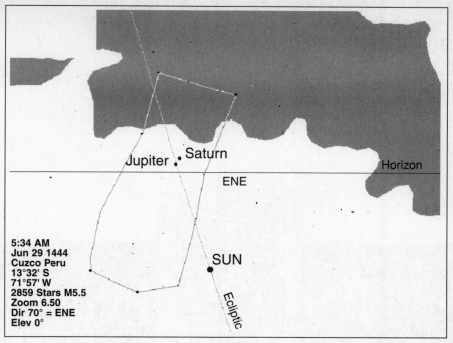

FIGURE 9.4. Conjunction of Saturn and Jupiter, A.D. 1444.

FIGURE 10.1. Hindu Titans at
the Mill. Note the technology
of reciprocating motion.

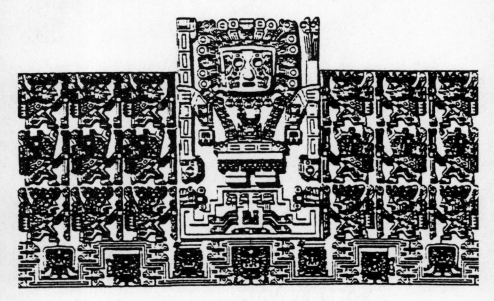

FIGURE 10.2. Gateway God Frieze.

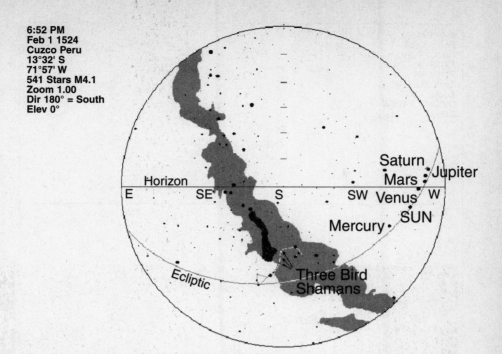

FIGURE 11.1. The three bird shamans en route to the underworld.

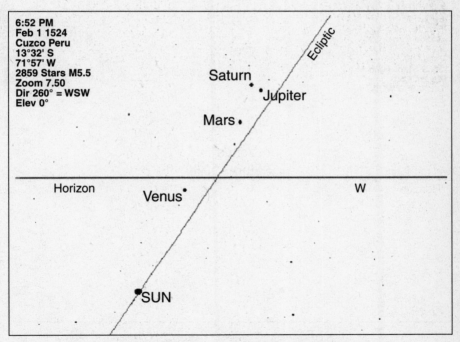

FIGURE 11.2A. February 1, 1524. Wiraqocha meets
Huayna Capac, the conjunction of Saturn and Jupiter.

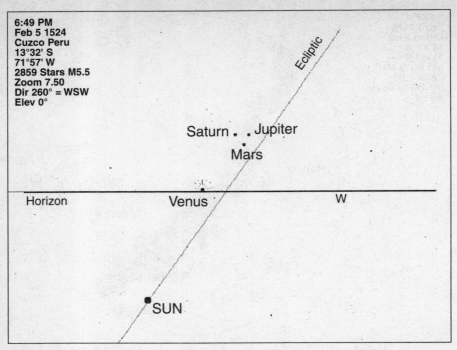

FIGURE 11.2B. February 5, 1524. The overcurious bird shaman opens the box and sees a "tiny" woman who disappears; Venus makes its first reappearance as evening star.

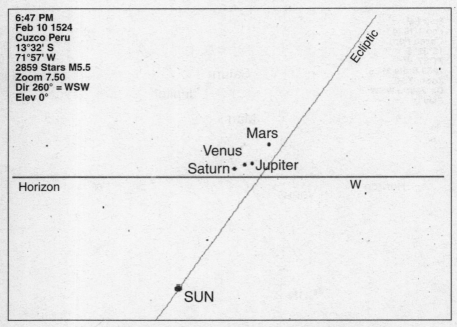

FIGURE 11.2C. February 10, 1524. "Exactly five days later," the shaman delivers the gift to Huayna Capac and Wiraqocha; Venus, Jupiter, Saturn conjunct, with Mars a few degrees apart.

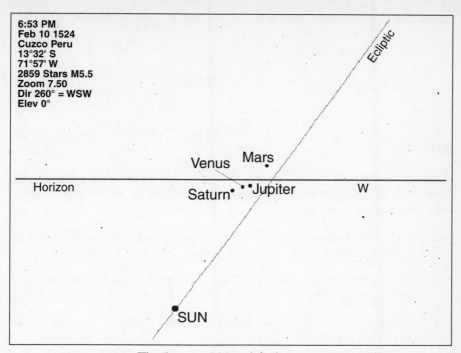

FIGURE 11.2D. The "kinsman," Mars, left alone to oversee civil war and the Spanish Conquest.

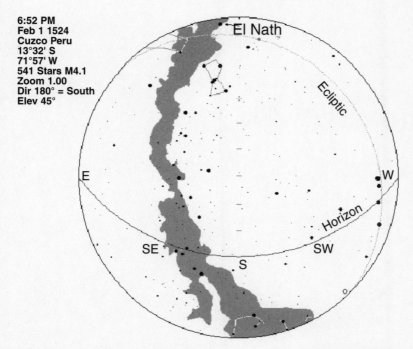

FIGURE 11.3. Milky Way in Gemini at superior conjunction at the same time the bird shamans visit the underworld.

Grateful acknowledgment is made to the following for permission to reproduce previously published illustrations:

FIGURES 8.1 and 8.2, Dr. Anita Cook: from *Wari y tiwanaku: entre el estilo y la imagen* by Dr. Anita Cook. (Fondo Editorial, Pontificia Universidad Catoloca del Peru, Lima, 1994). Used by permission of the author.

FIGURE 8.5, Instituto Nacional de Arqueologia, La Paz: drawing of "Idealized Reconstruction of the Arkapana Pyramid" by Aro. Javier Escalante M. Used by permission.

FIGURES 3.7 and 3.8, University of Texas Press: from *Native American Astronomy* by Anthony Aveni. Copyright © 1977 by Anthony Aveni. Drawing by Linda Schele.

The star maps in the preceding pages were created with *Skyglobe* v. 3.6 from KlassM SoftWare, © 1989–93 Mark A. Haney.

NOTES

CHAPTER 1. THE MYTH OF PREHISTORY

1. Hemming 1972, 347–51, 349n.
2. As recounted by Prescott (1851: 202–425), and especially in the superb narrative of Hemming 1972, 23–45.
3. Marshack 1972, 23.
4. Muller 1878.
5. Usually reticent, Marshack was moved to comment (1972, 24, 25) on the resistance he foresaw to the implications of his research into prehistory, research that led him to the working assumption that *Homo sapiens sapiens*, "before history and in the Ice Age was not much different from what he is now":

Having made these assumptions, I had to make others, until finally I was questioning, in one way or another, many of the accepted basic theories concerning man's intelligence, instincts and activities—his magic, fertility rites, rites of initiation, rites of sacrifice, his art, symbols and even the meaning of religion itself.

It was not that ancient man did not participate in these activities, but that science had given these activities labels at a distance that tended to be classificatory, clinical or even derogatory as though they were essentially early and, therefore, "primitive" manifestations. Yet, as activities of the same brain we have today, they could not have been much different from the activities that the brain conducts today.

6. The Andean *quipu*, a cluster of knotted cords used, so far as is known, for keeping records of commodities and even perhaps for astronomical observations, apparently required that the user understand the context of a given piece, in order to be able to decipher it. Cord, color, knot size, spacing, and so on changed with context, and so a given *quipu* could not be read without access to other, spoken information.
7. Sullivan 1979.
8. Pucher 1948; Urton 1978a, 1978b, 1979, 1980, 1981a, 1981b; Zuidema 1973c, 1976; Zuidema and Urton 1976.
9. Molina 1873 [1573], 9–10.
10. Avila 1966 [1598?], 31.

11. Anonymous Chronicler 1950 [1585–89], 151. I recently learned that the late Robert Randall saw the same connection (1987, 74).

CHAPTER 2. WHY FOX'S TAIL IS BLACK

1. Pucher 1948, 4 (see also Ibarra Grasso and Lewis 1986: 13); Urton 1978b; also 1981, 169–91, 207–9; Zuidema and Urton 1976, 59 ff.; Sullivan 1979: 15–30. See figure 3.5 for identification of most of these objects.
2. Murra 1972, 430.
3. Molina 1873 [1573], 4.
4. Cieza de León 1883 [1551], 6; see also Sarmiento de Gamboa 1942 [1572], 49; Pachakuti Yamqui 1927 [ca. 1613], 132.
5. Arriaga 1920 [1621], 21–22.
6. Alan Kolata, personal communication.
7. Kolata 1993, 181–205; see also National Research Council 1990, 6–7.
8. Avila 1966 [1598?], 22–23.
9. Arguedas y Pineda 1973, 227.
10. It is noteworthy that the only other New World civilization with a tradition of five worlds was the Aztecs'. The Maya and Hopi, on the other hand, hold that their ascent from ignorance to civilization transpired across four ages, the last of which continues to this day. Today, in Central America and the southwest United States, descendants of the Maya and the Hopi dandle children on their knees and go to town for salt and tea. But the Incas and the Aztecs are gone.
     Fivefoldness, it seems, involves certain inherent dangers. Five is a dangerous number to bring public, a heralding of what is by nature esoteric, namely the power to see the true significance of things. The word *quintessence*, literally "five-essence," is a term from medieval alchemy signifying arrival at the Faustian crossroads, where the secrets of heaven and earth lie exposed before the initiate, and the initiate, in turn, lies exposed to all the weaknesses of his own character. Access to quintessence is an inherently unstable position because, in the field of tension between the pull of one's lower nature to exploit the power of such knowledge, and the aspiration of one's higher na-

ture to surrender to the Author of such glory, no person stands indefinitely. Even Christ on the mountain hurried the process along, saying, "Get thee behind me, Satan." A sacrifice is required, either of the lower or the higher.

Leonardo da Vinci's famous drawing of man as pentagram—feet firmly on the ground, head erect, arms upraised—expressed the optimism of his time that humankind was at last free to inhabit its essential nature, but the Renaissance did not last very long. The obverse of this figure, the "black" pentagram with a single point touching the earth, expressed other possibilities, taking from heaven and directing the power toward earthly gain. Thinking in number stems, in Western tradition, from Pythagoras, whose famous maxim "numbers are things" neatly masked the activities of this most esoteric of schools. Such traditions still survive, as with the Naqshbandi dervishes, charged with the preservation of the knowledge of number and symbol.

Four-term systems, as for example expressed by the Greek cross (+), are inherently stable. Fourfoldness, a favored symbol of most North American Indians as well as the Maya and the Andean peasantry, represents the maintenance of right life. The vertical axis stands as between ground and goal—that is, between a clear-eyed appraisal of the limits and possibilities of human nature on the one hand, and man's duty to higher powers on the other. The horizontal axis takes into account the material world, mediating between agency and means, i.e., between forms of tribal organization such as descent systems, settlement patterns, food-getting strategies on the one hand, and the needs of the natural environment on the other. When a symmetrical balance among these four elements is struck—demanding neither too much nor too little, either of human nature or of the earth—a system of great stability is born, able to maintain itself indefinitely, as the Maya and the Hopi can attest. In Western astrology, the Greek cross inside a circle stands for the earth.

11. Guamán Poma 1956 [1584–1614], 35–58.
12. Murúa, cited in Ossio 1973, 188. If the reader is surprised at finding a schema based on the same principles of earth, air, fire, and water as found, for example, in ancient Greece, so was Seler as well, when he found it in Mexico: "These four distinct prehistoric or precosmic ages of the Mexicans, each one oriented towards a different direction of the heavens, are astonishingly related to the four elements water, earth, wind, and fire, known to classical antiquity and which even now constitute the way that the civilized peoples of East Asia look upon nature." (Cited in León-Portilla 1978, 46.)

13. León-Portilla 1978, 36.
14. Pachakuti Yamqui 1927 [ca. 1613], 131.
15. Holguín 1952 [1608], 268.
16. Ibid., 57.
17. The full majesty of this terminology was not lost upon the first clearly historical Inca king, Tupac Inca Yupanqui, who took this word as his name. Henceforth known as Pachakuti Inca—"the overturner of space-time"—this warrior king wrapped around his person the numinous mantle of the Andean mythical heritage and proceeded to conquer the known world.
18. Holguín 1952 [1608], 270.
19.

> Ah Uiracochanticcicapac . . .
> Maypin Canqui . . .
> Hanancochamantarayac
> Hurincocha
> Tiyancayca

> Ah, Wiraqocha, Prime Measurer . . .
> Where are you? . . .
> From the sea above us
> To the sea beneath,
> All this is your throne.

(Pachakuti Yamqui 1927 [ca. 1613], 148–49. Emphasis added.)
20. The pitfalls of insisting that myth be earthbound, and all waterways terrestrial, are illustrated by Santillana and Dechend's recounting of some modern interpretations of the voyages of Jason's Argo, a constellation afloat on the southern "celestial sea" near Canopus:

Apollonius of Rhodes, in recounting the heroic travels of the Argonauts, carefully preserved the double level of meaning, for the adventures are set in an earthly context, yet they make, geographically speaking, no sense at all. The explorers do sail up the Po, where they are confronted, as was said, with the stench of Phaethon's remains—but those might be located higher up in a waterfall in the Alps, near Dammastock, as one distinguished scholar would like to suggest. For the Argo moves from the Po into Lake Geneva and the Rhone, goes down it to the sea again and sails out following the same longitude; then, by a considerable feat of portage crosses the Sahara all the way to the coast of West Africa, and reaches Fernando Po. This is at least how those who understand the text as geography read it without blinking. (Santillana and Dechend 1969, 254–55.)

21. Urton 1981, 185–88; Zuidema and Urton 1976; Sullivan 1979, 27–30.
22. Avila 1966 [1598?], 161.
23. Garcilaso 1869, 183.
24. For a discussion of the importance of heliacal-

rise phenomena in Old World astronomy, see Hartner 1968, 231–32.

25. It is not as easy as one might imagine to make the solstice observation. A Zuni story recounts the travails of the first sun priest, Pekwin, when he endeavored to determine the date of the December solstice:

The man who went to the sun was made Pekwin. The sun told him, "When you get home, you will be Pekwin, and I will be your father. Make meal offerings to me. Come to the edge of the town every morning and pray to me. Every evening go to the shrine at Matsaki and pray. At the end of the year, when I come to the south, watch me closely; and in the middle of the year in the same month, when I reach the furthest point on the right hand, watch me closely." "All right." He came home and learned for three years, and he was made Pekwin. The first year, at the last month of the year, he watched the sun closely, but his calculations were early by thirteen days. Next year he was early by twenty days. He studied again. The next year his calculations were two days late. In eight years, he was able to time the turning of the sun exactly. The people made prayer sticks and held ceremonies in the winter and in the summer, at just the time of the turning of the sun. (Cited in Williamson 1984, 91.)

We do not learn the secret of the Pekwin's eventual success, but we do learn how failure to make the solstice observation is a virtual certainty for the neophyte. After eight years he has learned a few tricks, almost certainly to do with the heliacal-rise of stars.

26. Zuidema and Urton 1976, 102.

27. Ibid., 98.

28. Sullivan 1979, 35–42. This location in the sky, discussed at length in chapter 3, is loaded with cosmological meaning in Quechua astronomy, marking as it does the crossroads of the ecliptic plane, i.e., the apparent annual path of the sun through the stars we call the zodiac, and the westernmost edge of the Milky Way.

29. Arriaga 1920 [1621], 14, 152.

30. During fieldwork for a master's degree, I learned that Quechua-speakers in Bolivia referred to the Pleiades as *coto*. The explanation was that this bright cluster of stars looked like a little pile of seeds. There, and in the Department of Cuzco, the relative clarity of the individual stars is observed as a means for divining the proper time to plant. In the Department of Cuzco, the term for the Pleiades is *collca*, meaning "granary," and this term was used at the time of the Conquest. The reason why the term *coto* should be used to the north of Cuzco, in Huarochirí, is probably explained by its association with the word *vilca*, which is not a Quechua word, but rather Aymara,

the language of the Lake Titicaca region and the language associated with Tiahuanaco, and the religion of Wiraqocha. *Coto* is also an Aymara word (Bertonio 1879, 53), meaning the same as the Quechua, and it may be that *coto* is an Aymara loan word to Quechua. This might explain why *coto* is used by Quechua speakers in Bolivia, where Aymara language influence is strong. Whatever the case, the term *vilcacoto*, literally "Sun-Pleiades" is but the first of a very large number of pure Aymara terms used, at the time of the Conquest, to denote ideas of high religious import among the Incas and their subjects.

31. Among the Maya, the Pleiades are called "a handful of seeds." (Freidel, Schele, and Parker 1993, 96.)

32. Urton 1981, 118–22, 200; Sullivan 1979, 31–35.

33. "Bilcanota is a mountain which, according to the opinion of the people is in the highest place in Peru." (Acosta, cited in Larrea 1960, 214, n. 3.) A fuller discussion of the astronomical significance of this complex ritual follows in the next chapter.

34. Broda 1989, 143.

35. *"Marca. El soberado, o los altos de la cassa . . . Ancas. Lo azul."* (Holguín 1952 [1608], 231, 25.)

36. Zuidema 1979, 233.

37. "Five days" are specified in the version from Huarochirí. This time span, mentioned a number of times in the Huarochirí tales, is mythical shorthand for periods of time charged with a numinous sense of apprehension, in anticipation of a transformation of state. For example, in chapter 28 it is specified that the dead return to earth five days after expiring (Avila 1966, 156–57). In chapter 14, emissaries from the Inca to the underworld are warned that they must return within five days (Avila 1966, 90–91). Or, again, in the first chapter, it is stated, with questionable botanical accuracy, that the period of germination for seeds in general is five days (Avila 1966, 20–21). This datum brings to mind Girard's observation that the notion expressed in the *Popol Vuh*, that maize requires five days to germinate, was true for the hot lowlands where maize was first cultivated, but not for the historic homeland of the Quiché-Maya, where about ten days are required (Girard 1979, 206–7). In the Andes, at least twelve days are required for the germination of maize. It may be from the first observation of this central mystery of Amerindian culture that the period of five days originally took on its numinous significance. In any case, this number became ubiquitously synonymous with processes of transformation not visible to ordinary perception. The Aztecs characterized the five intercalary days after December solstice *nemontemi*, as

days of danger in the passage from one year to the next (Soustelle, 1972, 247).

38. See Zuidema 1979, 226. The sidereal lunar month is the amount of time it takes for the moon to return to the same place in the stars (27⅓ days). The synodic lunar month, or month of phases, is the number of days from, say full moon to full moon (29½ days). The Quechua terminology for lunar phases, that is, the synodic month, is expressed in terms of the word *killa* (Urton 1981, 82–85).

39. Aveni 1980, 109–17; Hartner 1968, 233.

40. Because, as the earth turns, the sun appears to move through fifteen degrees an hour, or 360 degrees in twenty-four hours, one degree of distance equals four minutes of time.

41. Aveni 1980, 111.

42. Hartner 1968, 236, 233.

43. At this point the reader may wish to understand some of the arcana involved in dating astronomical phenomena. The calendar that we now use is called the Gregorian Calendar, after reforms instituted by Pope Gregory XIII and put into effect in Europe in the 1580s. These reforms made up for shortcomings in the Julian calendar (after Julius Caesar) wherein calendar and solar dates had drifted apart. For example, when the Gregorian calendar went into effect, the June solstice occurred on Julian date June 11, but on Gregorian date June 22. Most astronomical tables—including the Planetary Tables used in this volume, as well as the Skyglobe program—follow a convention of using the older, *Julian* dates for astronomical events before the 1580s. The idea was to help historians (of the West) align astronomical phenomena described in literature with the calendar then in use. Obviously this convention is of no particular value for the Andes, but in reading the tables, one must make the adjustments. Thus, in A.D. 650, the June solstice took place on June 19, Julian date. The heliacal rise of the Pleiades occurred on May 20, Julian date, thirty days before the solstice. The diagrams of particular astronomical events described in this book are presented, according to the convention, in Julian dates. The solar significance of the date, e.g., solstices, is stated in the text.

44. This guess would prove to have been a good one. I later learned that the Andean astronomers had named epsilon Scorpius as one of the "bird-shamans" that plummeted to the underworld. (See chapter 11, section II.)

45. Stars *setting* heliacally are less affected by the rising sun than are those on the eastern horizon. With the sun depressed eighteen degrees in the east, a third-magnitude star setting in the west might be visible for about ten minutes before extinction. Professor Gingerich thought epsilon Scorpius would therefore have been a poor choice for keeping track of the Llama.

46. Arnold and Yapita Moya 1992, 22.

47. Cited in Urton 1981, 188.

48. See figure 2.7 for Fox. See also chapter 6, section I, for feline identifications in the tail of Scorpius.

49. Urton 1981, 45, 65, 201. One says "ideally" because villages are sited for considerations other than astronomical observation, which is conducted higher up in the mountains. See also Girard 1979, 28–29, for evidence of the same schema among the Quiché-Maya.

50. Urton 1981, 70–71.

51. Ibid., 116–17.

52. The dimmest visible stars can be seen at heliacal rise with the sun depressed twenty degrees. At the same time, the dimmer the star, the greater the obscuring effect of haze at the horizon (Aveni 1980, 107). I explained to Professor Gingerich that the myths appeared to me to indicate an interest in seeing the "black cloud" objects against the background glow of the Milky Way and the relation of such objects to the horizon. He felt that, because of the extreme clarity of the Andean air, such observations could have been made, given that the sun be depressed a further four degrees. In other words, the minimum distance between the sun and the Milky Way would have to be twenty-four degrees for an observer to be able to detect Fox against the background glow of the Milky Way.

Throughout this study, all figures showing the heliacal rise of the Milky Way in different eras have held to the same convention, i.e., sun depressed twenty-four degrees.

53. See note 52, above.

54. See note 43, above.

55. Figure 2.10b also depicts the southwest terminus at the horizon of the northeast-southwest axis of the solstitial cross, where one gets a dramatic view of just how useful the solstice cross was in calibrating the "parameters" of a world-age, as marked out in the stars: poor Fox's tail flutters like a pennant in the gathering dawn. In other words, at dawn on June solstice, a look southwest shows what is happening to Fox at December solstice in the same era. (Compare with figure 2.9a.) Likewise, a glance between figures 2.9a and 2.9b shows how, at the moment of heliacal rise of Fox at December solstice, the view northwestward along the other (southeast-northwest) intercardinal axis reveals or, as it were, reprises, the fateful relationship of the Milky Way to the horizon in the area of

June solstice. (Compare figure 2.9b to figure 2.10a.) These "looks" demonstrate the usefulness of the intercardinal cross in making simultaneous, real-time observations relevant to the heliacal rise of objects at *both* solstices.

CHAPTER 3. THE THREE WORLDS

1. Bierhorst 1972, 100. The Wintu are a small tribe of Northern California.
2. Davidson 1979, 23.
3. Holguín 1952 [1608], 145. ("*Caypachapim hanac-pacha llactanchicmanta hahuanchananchic.*")
4. Bierhorst 1972, 12. The Tewa are a Pueblo people of northern New Mexico.
5. Blake 1993, 1.
6. Cobo 1956 [1653], 368.
7. Urton 1981, 56–65; Sullivan 1979, 25, 67.
8. Cobo 1956 [1653], 347; Molina 1943 [1573], 17.
9. Allen 1963, 477.
10. Speck 1938, 15, 50, 65.
11. Zuidema and Urton 1976.
12. In 1530, the year in which Pizarro set forth from Panama toward a rendezvous with destiny, Copernicus published his *Commentariolus*, a first exposition of his heliocentric hypothesis.
13. Urton 1981, 54–65.
14. See also Urton 1981, figures 19, 21, 22. This configuration may be pictured like the stitching or piping dividing the dome of a baseball cap into four quadrants. The button atop the cap is analogous to the crossing point of the two branches of the Milky Way.
15. Urton 1981, 60–65.
16. Ibid., 59.
17. Bierhorst 1974, xvi; see also xiv.
18. Holguín 1952 [1608], 145, 350.
19. Bertonio 1879 [1612], 242.
20. Santillán cited in Lastres 1953, 69.
21. See, for example, Casaverde Rojas 1970, 204–5.
22. Cobo 1892, 342–43.
23. Krickeberg (1969, 131) notes: "It is uncertain to what extent the survival myth recounted by our Spanish sources [in which the fate of the individual soul is determined by ethical criteria] is a product of Christian influence. According to this interpretation the righteous go to a solar paradise in the sky, 'the upper world,' *Hanaq Pacha*, and the unrighteous go to the underworld, *Ukhu Pacha*, in the bowels of the earth, there to suffer torments of cold and hunger, with nothing to eat but stones. The use of specific native terms for the upper and nether world suggests that these are indigenous

concepts; but it may well be that the division originally was made on the basis of status rather than virtue. Support for this supposition is provided by an alternative—and clearly older—version in which the aristocracy passes automatically into the upper world, the kingdom of the sun god, while the common people live on in the depths of the earth. . . ."
24. The "River Jordan" in Western tradition is associated with the mythical celestial river Eridanus, which is sometimes identified as the other, seasonal branch of the Milky Way on whose banks lie Orion's dogs. The reason why the identification of Eridanus with this branch of the Milky Way is only provisional is itself a precessional problem, since, as times shifted the relation of sun to stars, new "tributaries" had to be carved out in order for the original thought-forms still to function. (These necessities did not, however, prevent the Hindus, for example, from continuing to refer to the Milky Way as "the bed of the Ganges" [Allen 1963 (1899), 475].) In the Andes, the problem is compounded by the collapse at the time of the Conquest of the indigenous nobility, who had "exclusive rights" to the "northern bridge" around June solstice. Perhaps the peasantry had all along remembered the time before the establishment of a class system (ca. A.D. 650—see chapter 8) and considered either branch viable. This was the case with the classless Mangaian Islanders, who state that spirits of the dead can enter heaven at either solstice, those from the northern part of the island in June, those from the south in December (Santillana and Dechend 1969, 242–43). The point, at present, is that, historically speaking, the Quechua peasantry had been restricted to use of the "southern bridgehead."
25. Brinton said, referring to his own work, ". . . among the universally interesting questions which I attempt to solve in this book are: What are man's earliest ideas of his own origin and destiny? Why do we find certain myths, such as of a creation, a flood, an after-world; certain symbols, as the bird, the serpent, the cross; certain numbers as the three, the four, the seven—intimately associated with these ideas by every race?" (Cited in Paul M. Allen's introduction to Brinton 1976 [1868], viii-ix.)
26. In warming to this particular subject, Brinton was moved to remark, "Those who have complained of the hopeless confusion of [native] American religions have but proven the insufficiency of their own means of analyzing them." (Brinton 1976 [1868], 261.)
27. Swanton 1946, 772.
28. Kroeber 1925, 682.

29. Lehmann-Nitsche 1924b, 76.

30. Jones 1939, 21.

31. Zuidema and Quispe 1973; Marzal 1971, 84–85; Oscar Núñez del Prado 1952, 2–3; Juan Núñez del Prado 1970, 109–15; Casaverde Rojas 1970, 202–11. Compare Zuidema and Quispe's transcription of the account of the near-death experience of an Andean woman who had to pass by the realm of the "four-eyed dogs, tawañawi" (1973, 359), with the Rig-Veda, where the afterlife journey to the celestial realm of Yama, King of the Dead (a.k.a. Saturn), required the soul's passage by Yama's four-eyed dogs (Eliade 1974, 417).

32. Marzal 1971, 84; Casaverde Rojas 1970, 202; Juan Núñez del Prado 1970, 110.

33. See note 24, above.

34. Arriaga 1920 [1621], 69–70.

35. Zuidema and Quispe 1973, 367.

36. Arriaga 1920 [1621], 70. Compare with the sacrifice of a "steel-colored" dog by the Yakuts of Siberia, made to the "prince of the shamans," a denizen of the underworld and the western sky. The entrance to the underworld is guarded by dogs, in the view of Siberian shamanism (Eliade 1974, 188, 248, 251, 295, 466).

37. Brinton 1976 [1868], 265–66.

38. Urton 1981, 63.

39. Juan Núñez del Prado 1974, 239.

40. Roca Wallparimachi 1966, 42, 57–59.

41. See Appendix 1 and chapter 11.

42. According to Zuidema and Urton, Capac Raymi began on November 30 (Gregorian date) and lasted twenty-three days until December 22 (Zuidema and Urton 1976, 89, 93, 102). This accords with Molina's description of Capac Raymi as a festival of twenty-three days (Molina 1943 [1573], 48–60). Molina called this month "November" because it began on November 18 of the Julian calendar. Murúa reveals the importance of the December solstice in Inca thinking by noting that they marked the end of the year by this day (Murúa 1922 [1613], 59–60).

43. Molina 1943 [1573], 61.

44. According to Molina, it was two days before the solstice that, for the first time "all the wakas," that is, not just the mummies of the Inca royalty and the statues representing the sun and moon, but the statues of all the lineage wakas of the entire tribal citizenry of the Empire, were brought forth from their various shrines (Molina 1943, [1573], 59–61).

45. Molina 1943 [1573], 61.

46. Cobo 1893 [1653], 117.

47. Avila 1966 [1608], 157.

48. Cobo (1893, 98) mentions the blowing of the

trumpet during Capac Raymi. Avila (1966, 143) states that during the festival conducted in Huarochirí in December, the conch was blown to mark the time for separating the flocks of llamas for purposes of shearing and breeding. Molina (1943, 60) fixes the date of this same ceremony in Inca Cuzco as the day before the toasting of the ancestors.

49. Zuidema 1973c, 17.

50. Arriaga 1920 [1621], 70.

51. Santillana and Dechend 1969, 63.

52. Foerstmann 1904, 423–30.

53. Dechend 1979, 135–37.

54. Eliade 1974, 179.

55. Bierhorst 1974, 18.

56. Polo de Ondegardo 1916 [1571], 109–10.

57. Schele 1977, 43–52.

58. Ibid., 49.

59. Marcus 1980, 61.

60. One could continue indefinitely in producing such allusions. The Chumash of California engaged a California energy company in an extensive legal battle during the 1980s. The company wanted to build a port for LNG (liquefied natural gas) tankers at Point Concepción on the California coast. As it happened, Point Concepción was the most sacred piece of real estate in the Chumash universe, because it was from here, so said the Chumash, that the souls of the dead departed this earth at sunset on December solstice to cross the Milky Way and achieve access to the land of the dead. In fact, the souls of the dead "stage" here, waiting most of a year, depending on individual dates of death, for the only moment when the "western gate" swings open. The company won the early rounds despite the arguments of Chumash lawyers that Point Concepción was the most seismically active bit of coastline in California, and had by far the worst storms. They pointed to the consequent danger of the rupture of an LNG tanker and/or its attendant pipeline. Since the release of supercooled gas into the atmosphere would create, by heat inversion, a spreading cloud of flammable gas that would hug the ground, it was pointed out that, given "favorable" winds, Los Angeles might one day be granted the opportunity to mimic Dresden. Not being vindictive people, the Chumash simply heaved a sigh of relief when someone in the company apparently looked at some maps. In any event, the western gate is still presumably operative.

61. Marcus 1980, 51.

62. Hemming 1972, 127–28.

63. Cieza de León 1973 [1551], 243–44.

64. Cieza de León 1883 [1551], 223, n. 1.

65. McIntyre 1984, 18, 19, 113.

66. Holguín 1952 [1608], 25.

67. Eliade 1974, 128 n. 52.

68. Arnold and Yapita 1992, 12, 13.

69. Garcilaso 1871 [1609], 457–58.

70. Urton 1981, 201–2.

71. Bertonio 1879 [1612], 386; Lara 1971, 295; Holguín, 1952 [1608], 31.

72. Molina 1943 [1573], 11. Those versions recording the tradition that the god's point of departure was Manta in Ecuador are Sarmiento de Gamboa 1942 [1572], 55, and Betanzos 1924 [1551], 89.

73. Pachakuti Yamqui 1927 [1613], 137.

74. This is because the earth, as it executes its precessional wobble, maintains a constant inclination of about twenty-three and a half degrees to the ecliptic plane.

75. Santillana and Dechend 1969, 242.

76. Davidson 1979, 37–38, 193, 234, 227, 236.

77. Brinton 1976 [1868], 265.

78. Holguín, 1952 [1608], 89; Bertonio 1879 [1612], 67.

79. Holguín, 1952 [1608], 90.

80. Urton 1981, 138–39. See also Urton 1980.

81. By definition, the sun crosses the celestial equator at the equinoxes and, regardless of one's latitude, rises due east and sets due west on those days.

82. Anthony Aveni, communication.

83. Urton 1980, 87–110; Urton 1981, 129–50; Zuidema and Urton 1976, 62–64.

84. Avila 1966 [1608], 161.

85. Urton 1981, 59.

86. Santillana and Dechend 1969, 62.

87. Because Santillana and Dechend were reluctant to oversimplify the rich literature about the topography of, for example, the underworld, they were less explicit about its location than they were about the location of the "celestial earth." This reluctance probably involves a very sensible assessment of the difficulty of expressing in words the visualization involved in understanding that, for example, any present day's equinox stars—destined to be tomorrow's solstice stars—will necessarily carry with them, in their respective ascent to June solstice and descent to December solstice, whole constellations that, though now firmly between the tropics, are destined for residence—for a time—in either the land of the gods or the land of the dead. Among the truly "permanent residents" of "other worlds" are those stars that lie within the circle described in the stars by the precessing axis of the earth, that is, a circle of about forty-seven degrees (twice twenty-three and a half). Thus the different levels of hell, and "steps" to the highest heavens of heaven.

88. The dark-cloud serpent, *machacuay*, according to Urton (1981, 103, 170–71), is a "large S-shaped dark streak between Adhara and the Southern Cross."

89. Arnold and Yapita 1992.

90. In Western taxonomy, foxes belong to the genus *vulpes* of the dog family.

91. Arnold and Yapita 1992, 14, and 13, fig. 1.

92. Compare Fox's role as psychopomp, placed between Scorpius and Sagittarius, with Boll's observation that while the Gilgamesh epic places "scorpion men," at the entrance to the underworld, Virgil and Dante have it that the gates to the underworld are guarded by centaurs, standing for Sagittarius. Cited in Santillana and Dechend 1969, 293, 296.

93. Zuidema and Urton 1976, 86–87; Holguín 1952 [1608], 206 ("Llaca chuqui *Lança de guerra enplumada.*"), 122 ("Llacachuqui. *La lança con borlas de pluma*).

94. Juan Núñez del Prado, personal communication.

95. Zuidema and Quispe 1973, 369.

96. Ibid., 368.

97. Aveni 1981.

CHAPTER 4. WIRAQOCHA

1. Eliade 1974a, 259.

2. Ibid., 269 and ch.8, passim.

3. Ibid., 266–67.

4. Ibid., 261.

5. Ibid., 234, 278.

6. Girard 1979, 168.

7. Eliade 1974, 270.

8. Waters 1976, 30.

9. Santillana and Dechend 1969, 137.

10. Ibid., 89–90.

11. Ibid., 141.

12. Eliade 1974b, 15–16.

13. Eliade 1974a, 264.

14. Ibid., 506.

15. Santillana and Dechend 1969, 121–25.

16. See, for example, Lehmann-Nitsche's survey of suggested etymologies for Wiraqocha (1928, 85–103).

17. As espoused by Aveni (1981, 161–71). See also Appendix 2.

18. Garcilaso 1869 [1609], 176, 275; Anonymous Chronicler 1950 [ca. 1585–89], 136; Holguín 1952 [1608], 98.

19. Holguín 1952 [1608], 98.

20. Velikovsky 1973, 174.

21. According to the present-day ethnoastronomical literature, planets—again with the exception

of Venus—do not appear to have names, but rather are recognized, as "morning star" or "evening star" or "zenith star," by dint of their happening to occupy such positions in the sky. (Urton 1981, 166–67.)

22. Velikovsky 1973, 174–75.

23. Santillana and Dechend 1969, 355–56.

24. Ramsdell 1973, 836. Note also the name of the delicate maidenhair fern, *Adiantum capillus venerus*, "Venus's-hair." As an inner planet, between the earth and sun, Venus has phases, that is, it appears now brighter, now dimmer to the naked eye. When the planet's radiance, from the point of view of the observer, is confined to the "bottom" portion of the planet, Venus may also appear to have a "beard"—she was described as possessing this surprising attribute by the Chaldeans, for example. Venus, resplendent at full phase, could be described as having disheveled—or what today is called "important"—hair.

25. Lara 1971, 93.

26. Now identified as Blas Valera.

27. Anonymous Chronicler 1950 [ca. 1585–59], 138.

28. Ibid., 136–37.

29. The German Andeanist J. J. von Tschudi wrote as clearly on the matter as anyone:

The anonymous Jesuit speaks of the worship of the planets, which so much resembles that of the Old World as to leave perfectly ample room to doubt that his affirmations correspond to reality, the more so since they are not confirmed in any way by any trustworthy earlier chronicler. . . . The attributes of Mars, Mercury and Jupiter are, without doubt, the product of his own imagination, or, perhaps, the fantasy of some predecessor of his, whose manuscript he had at hand and reproduced. (Tschudi 1918, 115).

30. Avila 1966 [1608], 162–63.

31. Holguín 1952 [1608], 284.

32. Thanks to Washington Irving, every child in upper New York State knows that the sound of thunder is caused by Henry Hudson's men bowling in the sky.

33. The following entries are, first, Quechua, then Aymara:

"Qhon—onomatopoeiac expression for the sound of ripping thunder." (Lara 1971, 238.)

"Qhon—One of the names of the god Wiraqocha in the Inca Empire." (Ibid.)

Qhona—"Spherical stone used for grinding." (Ibid.)

"Cunununu. The great sound of thunder or of a building or mountain which falls, or earthquake." (Holguín 1952 [1608], 55.)

"Ccuna—Grinding stones." (Bertonio 1879 [1612], 62.)

34. Cusihuaman 1976b, 232.

35. See note 24, above.

36. Santillana and Dechend 1969, 373–76.

37. Ibid., 133.

38. Ibid., 222.

39. Ibid., 136.

40. Ibid., 140, 250–62.

41. Cornford 1975, 105ff.

42. Santillana and Dechend 1969, 134–35.

43. Ibid., 133.

44. For a description of the Paleolithic origins of the logic by which stars were originally named, see Appendix 5.

45. Santillana and Dechend 1969, 135.

46. What follows is a discussion of how the practice of making observations of the heliacal rise of stars (figure 4.4) could lead to observing the precession of the equinoxes.

The precession of the equinoxes is produced by a wobble of the earth's axis, caused by the gravitational pull of sun and moon, whereby the earth's axis describes, at each pole, a circle about forty-seven degrees in diameter (see figure 4.1). One such revolution requires approximately 26,000 years to complete. As the earth's axis wobbles, the orientation of the earth within the sphere of stars necessarily changes. Thus the Pole Star (in the northern hemisphere) or the polar locus (in the southern hemisphere) changes. So also do the stars constituting the celestial equator.

On the other hand, the earth/sun relationship remains unchanged. If one likens the precessing earth to a top, spinning like the earth on its axis, with special attention to the top's habit of tilting in relation to the table and wobbling lazily in a circle, even as it spins rapidly on its axis, one can grasp the essential kinetics of precession. The top tilts in relation to the table in the same way that the earth is tilted at about 23.5 degrees to the path it follows around the sun (the ecliptic). So long as the earth's angle of tilt remains constant to the ecliptic (and it does), *its precessional wobble has no effect on the horizon point marking, for example, June-solstice sunrise. Were it not for the stars rising heliacally, there would be no way in a system of naked-eye astronomy of knowing that precession was occurring.* To put this another way, suppose our entire solar system were like a birdcage. Given the earth's tilt to its orbital path, it would precess. But if, each night, some celestial "keeper" put a night hood over the cage—that is, blocked the view of the fixed sphere of stars—none of us "birds" would have, by means of naked-eye observation, any way of recognizing the existence of precessional motion.

Moreover, unless one lived in a culture where the observation of the heliacal rise of stars at given solar dates was made *and recorded*, the observation of precession, as a practical matter, would not occur. You would never know it was happening. Figures 4.4, 4.5, and 4.6 are designed to help visualize these ideas.

Figures 4.5a and 4.5b contrast the earth's present orientation within the celestial sphere with its position halfway through a precessional cycle, when its axis of rotation has moved halfway around a circle of forty-seven degrees in diameter. In 4.5a, the earth, at position *m*, is experiencing June solstice, with star *x* rising heliacally. (Remember, the definition of June solstice has nothing to do with the stars. It is strictly a sun-earth relationship, transpiring within the "birdcage," the moment when the northern end of the earth's axis of rotation points directly toward the sun [figure 4.4].) Six months later, with the earth at position *n* of figure 4.5a, and the northern end of its axis pointed directly *away* from the sun, it is December solstice, with star *y* rising heliacally. But in 4.5b, thirteen thousand years later (or earlier), the earth at position *m* is experiencing *December* solstice, again a phenomenon of the relationship of tilted earth to sun. The stars of summer have become the stars of winter, and vice versa.

Now, from the point of view of a horizon-based, naked-eye astronomy, the horizon locations of the solstitial sunrises would have been *completely unaffected* throughout these thirteen thousand years, their position being entirely dependent on the constancy of the angle of the earth's tilt in relation to the ecliptic plane. Figures 4.6a and 4.6b relate the fixed quality of the solstice sunrise positions on the horizon to the precessional changes expressed in figures 4.5a and 4.5b. In 4.5a, June solstice occurs with the earth at point *m*. In 4.5b, June solstice occurs with the earth at position *n*. Only the fixed backdrop of the stars can provide "feedback" about precessional motion. To reiterate, these diagrams demonstrate two important concepts regarding the naked-eye perception of the effects of precession: (1) precession does not affect the horizon points at which the sun rises at a given solar date, as for example the solstices; this is because, while precessing, the earth maintains (with very small, cyclical variations) its 23.5-degree tilt to the ecliptic; but (2) precession does change the stars rising heliacally at a given solar date. Thus, just that effort required to fine-tune a solar calendar, by means of the observation of the heliacal rise of stars, could produce a database that would eventually reveal the effects of precessional motion.

As a practical matter, then, what are some of the observable effects of precession from the point of view of a naked-eye observer? In the first place, the term "observable effect" is misleading because it implies that a man could observe precessional shift over time. This might be true if a man lived to be two hundred or so years old, but since a given star will change its day of heliacal rise only every seventy-two years, i.e., a shift of one degree every 72 years (72 years times 360 degrees giving the number of years in the precessional cycle), it would require more than a human lifetime to get any clear idea of the nature of the precession. In societies without writing, some sort of mnemonic system—as for example, myth—would be required to build up a database sufficient for making comparisons of heliacal-rise data over time. Along with the slow displacement of the Pole Star or its opposite spot, this phenomenology, the stubborn habit of the stars over time to "arrive late" is the most easily observable effect of precession.

47. Bierhorst 1974, 190–91.
48. Santillana and Dechend 1969, 147.
49. Just as the loom mills behind the scenes in Euripides, and elsewhere, weaving fate fashioned from yarns spun about the planetary shuttlings.
50. Santillana and Dechend 1969, 134.
51. Ibid., 136.
52. Ibid., 283; see also 239.
53. Krupp 1979, 211.
54. Santillana and Dechend 1969, 272–73.
55. Ibid., 270.
56. Ibid., 268–73.
57. Ibid., 271.
58. Pachakuti Yamqui 1927 [1613], 132.
59. Betanzos 1924 [1551], 87; Sarmiento de Gamboa 1942 [1572], 54; Pachakuti Yamqui 1927 [1613], 132.
60. Holguín 1952 [1608], 340.
61. Pachakuti Yamqui 1927 [1613], 143; Sarmiento de Gamboa 1942 [1572], 52; Garcilaso 1919 [1609], vol. 2.), 102.
62. Cieza de León 1973 [1551], 19; Pachakuti Yamqui 1927 [1613], 132; Sarmiento de Gamboa 1942 [1572], 49.
63. Sarmiento de Gamboa 1907 [1572], 35–36; see also Cieza de León 1973 [1551], 19–20; Pachakuti Yamqui 1927 [1613], 134; Betanzos 1924 [1551], 86–88.
64. Garcilaso 1871 [1609], 69–70; Larrea 1960, 213–19.
65. McIntyre 1984, 27.
66. Molina 1943 [1573], 27.
67. Middendorf, cited in Larrea 1960, 215.
68. Garcilaso 1871 [1609], 69.
69. Cited in Larrea 1960, 221 (my translation).

70. As described in Appendix 1.
71. Ramos Gavilán, cited in Larrea 1960, 217.
72. Guamán Poma de Ayala 1956 [1584], vol. 1, 345.
73. Molina 1943 [1573], 39.
74. Holguín 1952 [1608], 174.
75. Pachakuti Yamqui 1927 [1613], 164–65, 148.
76. Zuidema and Quispe (1973, 263–65) have noted that this arrangement mirrors the descent systems reckoned for the Inca kings in incestuous marriage to their sisters.
77. See chapter 6.
78. Bertonio 1879 [1612], 379 (my translation).
79. Zuidema and Urton 1976, 64–69.
80. Holguín 1952 [1608], 57.
81. Ibid., 231.
82. Cusihuaman 1976, 86.
83. Santillana and Dechend 1969, 389.
84. Holguín 1952 [1608], 357; Bertonio 1879 [1612], 239.
85. Bertonio 1879 [1612], 378.
86. Cited in Lehmann-Nitsche 1928, 104.
87. Lanning 1967, 162.
88. Bertonio 1879 [1612], 364.
89. Holguín 1952 [1608], 347.
90. Valcárcel 1945, 14.
91. Holguín 1952 [1608], 57.
92. See chapter 8, pp. 221–22.
93. Holguín 1952 [1608], 355.
94. Zuidema 1973c, 25; see also Lehmann-Nitsche 1928, 79; Zuidema and Urton 1976, 64–65.
95. Bertonio 1879 [1612], 116.
96. Kelley and Moran 1969, 151–52 and passim.
97. Urton 1981, 79.
98. Lehmann-Nitsche 1928, 82.
99. See Cusihuaman 1976b, 229–31.
100. Cieza de León 1883 [1551], 8–9.
101. Holguín 1952 [1608], 353.
102. Ibid., 291.
103. Garcilaso 1871 [1609], 66–67.
104. Collapiña, Supno, y otros Quipucamayos, 1974, 38.
105. Lehmann-Nitsche (1928, 92) does note the existence of this dictionary entry, but is in such a rush to dismiss it that he offers an incomplete rendering of Bertonio's entry, noting only that *uira* means "ground."
106. Bertonio 1879 [1612], 388.
107. Ibid., 141.
108. Molina 1943 [1573], 27.
109. Larrea 1960, 219–20.
110. Bertonio 1879 [1612], 374.
111. Urton 1981, 201.
112. Lara 1971, 126.

113. Avila 1966 [1598?], 34–39.
114. Roca Wallparimachi 1966, 42.
115. This image, incidentally, demonstrates the fluidity of the technical language of myth in adapting to narrative necessity. A nobleman would not live in a structure with a central support pillar, but in a proper house. It was understood that if any part of the "frame" of the cosmos moved, all "parts," that is heliacal-rise dates of stars, also moved. Therefore, the "four pillars" or corners of the world house, like the "quadrangular earth" represented by the *maray*, were vulnerable to the "hopping" of a single tiny toad. Such refinements were not lost upon the Incas, who did *not* name their equinox mountain "Pachatunu," after the *central* support pillar, but Pachatusan, *tusan* referring to the support posts in the walls of quadrangular houses.
116. Santillana and Dechend 1969, 278–79.
117. From the *Florentine Codex*, cited in León-Portilla 1980, 201–2.
118. León-Portilla 1980, 35.
119. Molina 1873 [1573], 28.
120. Soustelle 1972, 129–30.
121. Garcilaso 1871 [1609], 70.
122. Santillana and Dechend 1969, 221.
123. Ibid., 135.
124. Bertonio 1879 [1612], 353, 43; see also Sarmiento de Gamboa 1942 [1572], 52; Garcilaso 1879 [1609], 228.

CHAPTER 5. PASSING THE STANDARD

1. Pachakuti Yamqui 1927, 148; following Metraux 1973, 128.
2. Anonymous Chronicler 1950 [ca.1585–89], 136–37.
3. Pachakuti Yamqui 1927 [1613], 175, 121 n.
4. Garcilaso 1918 [1609], 54, 109; Lara 1971, 223; Tschudi 1853, 130.
5. Eliade 1974, 269.
6. Santillana and Dechend 1969, 219.
7. Pachakuti Yamqui 1873 [1613], 76.
8. Cobo 1893 [1653], 65.
9. Bertonio 1879 [1612], 340, 32.
10. Holguín 1952 [1608], 135.
11. Bertonio 1879 [1612], 42.
12. Betanzos 1924 [1551], 180–82.
13. Holguín 1952 [1608], 134.
14. Bertonio 1879 [1612], 36.
15. The dimensions of the historical questions raised by the use of the palm measure, *capa*, by the Andean god/Saturn are not limited to the astronomy of myth. *Capa* has all the earmarks of a loan-

word: "Kaph . . . the eleventh letter of the Hebrew alphabet . . . meaning 'hand,' 'palm of the hand,' 'hollow of the hand,' 'a measure,' 'a handful,' . . . 'a pan,' . . . Assyrian *kappu* (resembling the Greek *kappa*), 'hand,' 'a pan'; *kappatu*, 'hollow'; Aramaic 'hand,' 'palm.' " (Moran and Kelley 1969, 88.)

16. Lewis 1979, 242–43.

17. León-Portilla 1978, 27–28, 20–21.

18. ("*el brazo derecho alto con la mano casi cerrada, y los dedos pulgar y índice altos, come persona que está mandando*") Murúa 1922 [1613], 217; see also Molina 1943 [1573], 20.

19. Santillana and Dechend 1969, 268.

20. Ibid., 134.

21. Ibid.

22. Zuidema 1973b, 736–40; Zuidema 1964.

23. Zuidema 1973b, 740.

24. Ibid., 746.

25. Ibid., 746–49.

26. Holguín 1952 [1608], 287; Bertonio 1879 [1612], 167.

27. Lehmann-Nitsche 1928, 194; Quiroga 1901, 182.

28. Holguín 1952, 287 (listed under *pirhua*)

29. Cited in Lehmann-Nitsche 1928, 194, n. 1.

30. Arriaga 1920 [1621], 29; Acosta 1880 [1590], 374.

31. Cieza de León 1973 [1551], 118–19; Betanzos 1924 [1551], 139; Pachakuti Yamqui 1927 [1613], 141–42.

32. Considerations of space make the search for the celestial identity of Manco's seven "siblings" a luxury. Suffice it to say that the ruse of the other brothers and sisters to dispose of the unruly brother, Ayar Cachi (later worshiped as the god of war) by inducing him to retrace the steps of the journey to the "place of origin" of the Incas in order to retrieve some sacred items, is an apparent description of the retrograde motion of Mars. (Sarmiento de Gamboa 1942 [1572], 65 ff.; Cieza de León 1973 [1551], 26–29; Tuckerman 1964, 343.)

33. Sarmiento de Gamboa 1942 [1572], 64–65, 68; Garcilaso 1869 [1609], 64–65.

34. It is interesting to note that in the case of both the words "Wiraqocha" and "Manco Capac," Garcilaso refers their significance to a "lost" court language. This language has been sought, among other places, in a dialect of Puquina spoken by the healers to the Inca court, the Callaway of Bolivia, who also knew, and know, Aymara. The unremitting presence of Aymara loan words at every crucial cosmological juncture of Inca thought suggests that the "court dialect" of the Incas may have drawn heavily on Aymara.

35. Holguín 1952 [1608], 228–29.

36. Bertonio 1879 [1612], 213.

37. Ibid., 215.

38. Pachakuti Yamqui 1873 [1613], 71, 73, 74, 75–76.

39. Holguín 1952 [1608], 347.

40. Ibid.

41. Bertonio 1879 [1612], 395.

42. Pachakuti Yamqui 1927 [1613], 177–78.

43. Holguín 1952 [1608], 347.

44. "Thupatha. To brush, rasp, or polish." "Tupu. Measure." (Bertonio 1879 [1612], 368, 365.)

45. Krupp 1983, 56.

46. Hall 1990.

47. *Hun*, "one" or "unity"; *na'ab*, the width of the palm with fist doubled, *ku*, "temple" or "house." Girard 1979, 87, 92; Harleston 1984, 4.

48. Zuidema 1979, 236–37.

CHAPTER 6. THE SEARCH FOR FATHER

1. Rowe 1946, 295; Willey 1971, 175–76; Bankes 1977, 148–49.

2. See Demarest 1981, 61.

3. Ibid., 61–62.

4. Bankes 1977, 148–49.

5. The same associations survive to the present. Mishkin (1946, 464) cites contemporary renderings of the hail-feline *ccoa*, "seen with hail running out of his [*sic*] eyes."

6. Zuidema 1976, 206, 214, 216. For a more complete discussion of these apparent contradictions, see Sullivan 1988, 307–15.

7. Lehmann-Nitsche 1928, 180.

8. Urton 1981, 85, 122.

9. Molina 1943, 29–30.

10. Mishkin 1946, 464.

11. Ricardo, cited in Zuidema and Urton 1976, 63.

12. Lehmann-Nitsche 1928, 162.

13. Pachakuti Yamqui 1927 [ca. 1613], 185.

14. La Barre 1948, 201.

15. Urton 1981, 114.

16. Grzimek 1975, 343.

17. Girard 1979, 245–46. Girard compares this testimony of the *Popol Vuh* to the *Chilam Balam of Chumayal*, a colonial Maya book of omens that confirms that at the commencement of the Fourth Age, "the stars awoke and from that moment the world began."

18. Ibid., 338–39.

19. Ibid., 88–89. It is also noteworthy in this context that the ancient Aymara (Lake Titicaca region) system of orientation also involved seven directions in three dimensions: the four cardinal directions, through the intersection of which ran a

line connecting the zenith to the nadir. (Kricke-berg et al. 1968, 142.)

20. Girard 1979, 341–42.

21. Girard 1979, 28. This is exactly the same pro-cess as found in the Andes, where "earth" has also an esoteric meaning, the area of the stars circum-scribed by the annual path of the sun through the stars, and represented by the solstitial cross. This figure for the solstitial cross, $\times$, was the Maya glyph—*kin*—for the sun. The Maya glyphic rep-resentation of the marriage of heaven and earth—which, of course, presupposes the separation of the world parents—consists of the (polar-equatorial) "god-Seven upon the umbilicus of the earth." (Girard 1979, 37.)

22. Ibid., 37.

23. Ibid., 68. The sense of the "one-leggedness" of the god Hunrakán/Ursa Major resides in the ki-netic "behavior" of this constellation, that is, its continuous turning around the Pole Star, Polaris, as if on one leg. This imagery is incorporated in the Turning of the Mevlevi ("Whirling") Dervishes of Turkey, whose ritual dance involves continuous turning in place on the left leg in a counterclock-wise direction, the same direction as the earth turning within the sphere of fixed stars. Amid this motion, the Dervish seeks not ecstatic frenzy but the stillness at the Center. The word *Hunrakán* has given us the English word "hurricane." The defin-ing experience of a hurricane is to stand for a mo-ment within the "eye" of the storm, there to behold, within the eerie calm of the center, the great counterclockwise whirl of the storm.

24. Girard 1979, 141, 185, 187, 338–39.

25. Ibid., 87.

26. Ibid., 131.

27. The word *migration* is Girard's usage, by which he renders the sense of incremental expansion into new territories ever farther afield, owing to the logic of slash-and-burn agriculture. By this term he does not mean long, wholesale treks of whole peoples across vast spaces, necessitated by dis-placement by invasion or other disaster. The sense in which Girard uses the term is usually expressed in archaeology as *fission:* "Fission is particularly characteristic of tropical swidden cultivators but occurs among most cultivators residing in an area of abundant land. . . . By the process of fission gradual expansion of a cultural system over a large territory may ultimately occur." (Sanders and Ma-rino 1970, 108.)

28. For the Amuesha version see Tello 1923, 128 ff.; for the Jívaro version, Tello 1923, 124 ff.; for the Guarani version, Tello 1923, 115 ff.

29. Steward and Métraux 1948, 535.

30. Métraux 1948, 75.

31. Girard 1979, 246.

32. Ibid., 64.

33. Betanzos 1924 [1521], 82.

34. Ibid., 83.

35. Sarmiento 1907 [1572], 32–33.

36. Girard 1979, 161.

37. Ibid., 158.

38. Ibid., 125–32.

39. Ibid., 127–31.

40. Ibid., 127.

41. Cited in ibid., 55.

42. Ibid.

43. Ibid., 156.

44. Lowie 1920, 189.

45. "Although the concept of a matriarchy is sup-portive of a wide range of social ideologies, is use-ful in presenting diverse points of view, and so neatly fills the gaps in our knowledge of the past, it simply does not have any scientific validity. It is pure speculation, apparently congenial to every-thing but fact." (Hammond and Jablow 1976, 4.)

46. Lowie 1920, 191; Fox 1977, 95–96.

47. "To the so much feared tiger of the East, he [the jaguar] is equal in fierceness; and it is owing, perhaps, to his being nocturnal in his habits to a great extent, that he seldom issues from the deep swamps or the almost impenetrable thickets or jungles of thorny shrubs, vines and tangled vegeta-tion which compose the chaparrals of Texas and Mexico, or the dense and untracked forests of cen-tral and south America, to attack man. From his haunts in such nearly unapproachable localities, the Jaguar roams forth towards the close of the day, and during the hours of darkness seizes on his prey. During the whole night he is abroad, but is most frequently met with in moonlight. . . ." (Au-dubon and Bachmann 1967, 258.)

48. Lewis 1976, 269–70.

49. Fox 1977, 99.

50. Girard 1979, 118.

51. Cited in ibid., 57.

52. Cited in ibid., 246.

53. Grzimek 1972, 344.

54. Ibid.

55. Girard 1979, 187.

56. Silverblatt 1976, 326–327.

57. Zuidema 1973b, 17; see also Lounsbury 1964.

58. La Barre 1948, 143.

59. Ossio 1977, 108.

60. Ossio 1977, 107.

61. Pachakuti Yamqui 1927 [1613], 134.

62. Lanning 1967, 25.

63. Sarmiento de Gamboa 1942 [1572], 52. This motif of the "dulling of the moon" is widespread in South America, as among the Witoto, Zaparo, and Cuna. It is interesting that here, Moon is a nosy

brother who, in true matrilineal fashion, pokes his nose into his sister's boudoir to determine the identity of her lover, and gets a faceful of *genipa* juice (made from the fruit of a tropical tree) for his trouble. (Métraux 1946, 119.) It matters not a whit that Moon is a male; what matters is that "lunar" descent systems are matrilineal, with all the strains thus placed on marital ties by the mother's brother.

64. Girard 1979, 160–61.

65. Avila 1966 [1598?], 23.

66. The sense of both the Quechua word for husband and the Mayan view of the matter correspond precisely in emotional pitch and significance to the English word, whose Teutonic roots render the meaning as literally "housebound."

67. Alan Kolata, personal communication. According to Kolata, the earthworks around Titicaca could not, "for ecological reasons," have been operative much before 500 B.C., 600 B.C. being the most remote feasible date.

68. Lanning 1967, 109; Willey 1977, 154.

69. Tello 1923; 186–87.

70. Bertonio 1879 [1612], 151.

71. Ibid.

72. Girard 1979, 251–52.

73. Bertonio 1879 [1612], 191.

74. Ibid.

75. Ibid., 364.

76. At this point, the notion crossed my mind that I had never considered the position of the moon during the events of June-solstice eve A.D. 650. I returned to the Tuckerman Tables (figures 5.3), which, as one can see, make clear that there was a full moon that night, the moon being at 271 degrees, that is, 180 degrees around the earth from the sun. But this, alas, is what is known as anecdotal evidence, and although it only further convinced me that the llama/flood myths recorded a combination of celestial events so rare as to constitute one of the baseline events in Andean "sacred history," this pregnant coincidence had no real probative value.

CHAPTER 7. A BOLT FROM THE BLUE

1. Griaule 1965, 137. The Dogon are a tribal people from Mali.

2. Kelley 1971, 60.

3. Ibid.

4. Ibid., 65.

5. Stein 1967, 355.

6. Zuidema 1973c; Silverblatt 1976; see also Lounsbury 1964.

7. Silverblatt 1976, 321.

8. Bankes 1977, 144.

9. Kolata 1993, 148.

10. Cobo 1892 [1653], 331.

11. Fox 1977, 81–82; 92–95.

12. Ibid., 93.

13. Kolata 1993, 59–63.

14. Browman, cited in ibid., 222–23.

15. Kolata 1993, 222–23.

16. Avila 1991 [1598?], 80–81, 324 n.

17. Ibid., 127; see also ibid., 66.

18. Arriaga 1920 [1621], 20.

19. Bertonio 1879 [1612], 195.

20. Flores Ochoa 1977; Browman 1974a, 1974b.

21. Isbell 1994, 1031.

22. Browman 1974b.

23. In other myths told by peoples with a pastoral heritage, there are references to their places of emergence, their *pacarinas*. As we have seen, the notion of the *wakas* and *pacarinas* is integral to the Titicaca creation myth, suggesting that the pastoralists at one time embraced the teaching of Wiraqocha. The *wakas*, being androgynous, allowed for tracing descent through both lines, again suggesting that pastoralists who acknowleged— through reference to a *pacarina*—the spiritual teaching of Titicaca may have adopted a system of double descent as well as greater agricultural undertakings. This in fact is a complex argument, because these same pastoralists—the Yauyos and Huancas—would later trace descent unmistakably through the *male* line. Nonetheless, in the case of the Yauyos, it is clear that their mythical male ancestor "came into being" about A.D. 850, during the collapse of the Wari state. So it is possible, though there is no way to proving the case one way or the other, that virtually all pastoralists of the Andes at one time adopted the double-descent system, later to revert to patrilineal descent as a means of claiming land. The logic behind these ideas is fully explored in chapter 8.

24. Kolata 1993, 232.

25. Lira n.d., 89; Lara 1971, 102.

26. Cobo 1892 [1653], 333.

27. Holguín 1952 [1608], 55, 142; Bertonio 1879 [1612], 62; Lara 1971, 238.

28. See ch. 4, n. 27.

29. Found in Avila's preface to his book of bilingual sermons, cited in Avila 1992, 86–87, n. 366.

30. See also Flores Ochoa 1977, 211.

31. Arriaga 1920 [1621], 27. As with Arriaga's description, a second definition of the word *illa* makes clear the atavistic power of the thunderstone: "Whatever is ancient, guarded for many years." (Holguín 1952 [1608], 367.)

32. Arriaga 1920 [1621], 28.

33. Eliade 1974, 139.

34. Girard 1979, 31.
35. Ibid.
36. Ibid.
37. As noted, *llamaq ñawin,* or alpha and beta Centaurus, are the "eyes of the llama." A diamond-shaped motif, repeated on a large percentage of Andean weavings, is the "solar eye," *intip ñawin.*
38. Girard 1979, 31.
39. In this regard, it is interesting to take note of the work of Ray White at Macchu Picchu. White found, carved on the base of the Intihuatana stone, depictions of the four constellations ruling the four *suyus,* or quarters, of the Empire. He was then able to find three of four outlying stones with the same asterisms carved upon them, and to propose a way to find the missing *usñu* at Macchu Picchu, which should lie at the intersection of the (four) outlying stones. (Personal communication.) The relation of this work to the notion of the "eyes of heaven" is that the constellations represented—the Southern Cross, the Summer Triangle, the Pleiades, and the Eyes of the Llama—were represented as if *projected* onto the stone from "above" or "behind the stars." In other words, the perspective of these images is suggestive of some entity "beyond" the stars looking down upon our world through the stars of the celestial sphere, or *ojos imaimana* ("eyes of every kind"), to use the phrase of Pachakuti Yamqui's drawing.

For Old World examples of the "view from the other side," see Eliade 1974, 260, where, for example, we learn that among the Turko-Tartars the sky is a tent where "the Milky Way is the 'seam,' the stars the 'holes' for light. According to the Yakut, the stars are the 'windows of the world.'"

40. Arriaga 1920 [1621], 14.
41. Métraux 1946, 116–17.
42. Arriaga 1920 [1621], 57.
43. Ibid., 56–58; Avila 1966 [1598?], 186–93.
44. Harris 1913, xix.
45. See Avila 1991 [1598?], 145.
46. Arriaga 1920 [1621], 57.
47. Mariscotti de Gorlitz 1978, 366.
48. See Avila 1991 [1598?] (Salomon and Urioste translation), 148, n. 855.
49. Avila 1991 [1598?], 146, n. 840.
50. Bierhorst 1974, 265. Another parallel regarding the sin of lasciviousness in both areas: The *Popol Vuh* identifies lascivious behavior with the horticultural cycle, specifically unbridled, riotous merrymaking typified by dancing (Girard 1979, 143), while, in the Andes, Arriaga noted, male twins were referred to as *Taqui Huahua,* "children of dancing." (Arriaga 1920 [1621], 56.)
51. Bierhorst 1974, 240.

52. Bertonio 1879 [1612], 338–39.
53. Ibid., 339.
54. Guamán Poma 1956 [1584–1614], 35–38.
55. Lara 1971, 102; Holguín 1952 [1608], 366.
56. Arriaga 1920 [1621], 27.
57. Molina 1873 [1573], 4.
58. Broda 1989, 143.
59. Ibid., 142–43.
60. Following the terminology of animal husbandry, as in, "That ewe always throws twins."
61. Allen 1963, 222 ff.; see also Harris 1913, xxi.
62. Allen 1963, 225–26.
63. Ibid., 227, 229.
64. Harris 1913, xv.
65. Holguín 1952 [1608], 366.
66. Kelley 1960, 331.
67. Lara 1971, 102; see also Holguín 1952 [1608], 17, under *ahua.*
68. Bertonio 1879 [1612], 173.
69. Lara 1971, 103; see also Lira n.d., 89.
70. Lara 1971, 103.
71. Anonymous Chronicler 1950, 137.
72. See Mariscotti de Gorlitz 1978, 366, citing also Trimborn and Kelm.
73. Arriaga 1920 [1621], 28–29.
74. Holguín 1952 [1608], 41.
75. Brinton 1976, 125.
76. Molina 1943 [1573], 13–14.
77. Santillana and Dechend 1969, 133, 139.
78. This latest alternative metaphor for the pole recalls a comment of David Kelley's regarding the nature of archaic tech-talk: "They [mythographers] seem often to use two or three different analogies in order to underscore the point that these *are* analogies, but few people seem to recognize this fact."
79. Allen 1963, 229.
80. Davidson 1979, 169.
81. Sahagún 1953, 60; see also Simeon 1977, 253.
82. Aveni, for example, (1980, 35), opts for the belt and sword of Orion because "The firedrill constellation must be formed out of two rows of stars, meeting at an acute angle."
83. See, for example, "Derekey and Derevuy," among the Tupi-Guarani, and the Amuesha "Yatash and Yachur." (Tello 1923, 115–17, 128–30; Harris 1913, 9 ff.)
84. Soustelle 1972, 128.
85. Ibid., 134.
86. Kelley 1980, S22.
87. Soustelle 1972, 79 ff.
88. Kornfield 1993, 315.
89. Molina 1943 [1573], 15–16; Cobo 1892 [1653], 312–14; Sarmiento de Gamboa 1942 [1572], 50–51.

90. Cobo 1892 [1653], 314.

91. Guamán Poma 1956 [1584–1614], vol. 1, 43; Holguín 1952 [1608], 167; Anonymous Chronicler 1950 [ca. 1585–89], 138.

92. Girard 1979, 102–3, 109.

93. Cobo 1892 [1653], 314.

94. Holguín 1952 [1608], 17. "*Ahhua. Guacamaya papagayo grande.*"

95. Molina 1873 [1573], 8.

96. Precession moves about one degree each seventy-two years. Figure 6.2 shows the advent of the heliacal rise of the Milky Way at June solstice ca. 200 B.C., while Figure 2.10a shows the cessation of this phenomenon in A.D. 650 some 850 years later (850 divided by 72 equals 11.8).

97. Sarmiento de Gamboa 1907 [1572], 30–31.

98. Kolata 1993, 232.

99. Holguín 1952 [1608], 321–22.

100. Holguín 1952 [1608], 36. ("*Atau o ataucay. La ventura en guerras, o honores como Sami. La ventura en juegos, o ganancia, y cussi. La ventura en obras, o succesos temporales . . .*")

101. Lorenzo Huertas Vallejos reports a tantalizing datum from the records of the extirpators of the Cajatambo region in the northern sierra: ". . . twins were considered the children of the stars called Chuchu Coillor [= Quechua 'twin stars']" (Huertas Vallejos 1981, 88). Alas, the extirpators neglected to ask the identity of those stars.

102. Rowe 1960, 411.

103. Ibid., 410–11.

104. Ibid., 410.

105. Rowe 1966, 339.

106. Lyon 1978, 121.

107. For the following lessons into the history of the development of the comparative method, I am indebted to the unpublished lecture notes of Hertha von Dechend (1979).

108. Robert Heine-Geldern (1966, 292) points out that between the years 1775 and 1885, twenty Japanese junks were carried to involuntary landfall on the Pacific Coast of the Americas by northwest Pacific currents, an average of one every five years.

109. Hemming 1972, 449, citing Ocampo and Murúa.

110. Hemming 1972, 449.

111. Arriaga 1920 [1621], 58.

112. Stein 1967, 163.

113. Smith 1975, 97; Bertonio 1879 [1612], 185. ("*Laccampu hauira, la via lactea, o el que llaman camino de Santiago.*")

114. Harris 1913, 9 ff.

115. Isbell 1991, 310. Archaeologists peg the end of the Early Horizon and the beginning of the Early Intermediate Period at 200 B.C.

116. See Burger 1988, 141–43.

CHAPTER 8. THE AGE OF THE WARRIORS

1. Isbell 1978, 270.

2. The archaeological chronologies developed for the Andean highlands are based on ceramic stratigraphies with approximate absolute dates supplied by means of radiocarbon measurements. The Early Intermediate Period (ca. 200 B.C.–ca. A.D. 600) preceded the advent of warfare. The so-called Middle Horizon—marking the rise of Wari and an intense period of political and ideological interchange up and down the Andes—began somewhere between A.D. 550 and 600. Moseley and Lanning, for example, prefer A.D. 600 (Moseley 1992, 161; Lanning 1967, 25), while others follow Menzel's preference of A.D. 550. For the sake of clarity, I have eliminated the use of archaeological period names in the text and have instead followed the chronology of Menzel (1977, 88–89) as interpreted in terms of absolute dates by Anita Cook (1994, 330, fig. 10) whenever the text of particular articles speaks of archaeological periods—or else I have used absolute dates offered by authors of particular articles. Following this convention, then, a reference in a particular article to the "end of Middle Horizon 1B" (A.D. 625–650), is simply written as "A.D. 650." Not every archaeologist will agree with every absolute date, but it is also my understanding that no archaeologist would seriously challenge any date referenced in this chapter, given that I have not violated the sense of the ceramic stratigraphies and that such stratigraphies are referenced in the archaeological literature with an implicit plus-or-minus factor of about fifty years.

3. Isbell 1987, 84–89; Isbell 1988, 173–82.

4. Isbell 1988, 176–77.

5. 200 B.C.–ca. A.D. 600.

6. Isbell 1991, 308.

7. Moseley 1992, 218.

8. Ibid., 209.

9. Isbell 1987, 90. Likewise, Martha Anders has seen evidence of an ecological crisis at the heart of the turbulent events surrounding the rise of Wari:

We do have striking ritual behaviour between 600 and 700 A.D. in the series of offering deposits of elite/ceremonial pottery which was smashed and thrown into pits. . . . I have suspected that they are . . . responses to environmental stress of some kind. Since the icons—felines, birds, snakes—show an overwhelming emphasis on fertility and regeneration, I suspect these offerings are elaborate pagapu or ritual payments to the wamani or mountain deities who assure fertility of crops and herds. (Personal communication.)

10. Isbell 1991, 309–10.

11. According to Isbell (1991, 309), Cerro Baul is

the "earliest Hauri provincial administrative center yet identified."

12. Kolata 1993, 246; Parsons and Hastings 1988, 223.

13. Kolata 1993, 256. Kolata's view of the nature of rulership in Tiahuanaco has points in common with structuralist analysis, which understands religious ideology as a strategy employed by elites for gaining control of resources. My own opinion is that it is unclear, on the basis of archaeological evidence alone, whether the relationship of Tiahuanaco with a far-flung resource network is evidence of calculated "control," or of what archaeologists call "adaptive evolution." In other words, Tiahuanaco's influence may equally well constitute evidence that it had good ideas and techniques that others willingly copied. As we have seen, the ethnohistorical/mythical testimony of indigenous highland communities strongly indicates that right up until the "flood" of A.D. 650, the agricultural communities of the Andes viewed Tiahuanaco as *the* enabling force in establishing free, independent, and prosperous peoples up and down the Andes.

An analogy may help make the point. During the Depression of the 1930s, the federal government of the United States undertook rural electrification in the Tennessee River Valley. There is famous newsreel footage of the night the lights were turned on. Hundreds of farmers emphatically hurled their kerosene lanterns onto a giant bonfire: adaptive evolution. One could speak just as validly in Marxist terms of the creation of a new "captive market," but, at least on that night, the last people to consider themselves "victimized" were the farmers of the Tennessee Valley.

Suffice it to say that Tiahuanaco appears never to have maintained a standing army. Even within the Tiahuanaco heartland, the use of military force was rare. As a rule of thumb, the further from the Titicaca basin that Tiahuanaco influence extended, the less likely it was to have been enforced by arms. Tiahuanaco's influence was as strong as its ideas.

14. I.e., early in the seventh century (Kolata 1993, 127). Carbon date: 610 B.C. ± eighty years. (Kolata 1993, 124.)

15. Ibid., 121–23.

16. Ibid., 124.

17. See note 9 above.

18. Kolata 1993, 135.

19. ". . . apart from a few exceptions, the expansion of Tiahuanaco was not the product of a militaristic grand strategy worked out self-consciously by the lords of Tiwanaku and implemented through force of arms . . . nor was its expansion

primarily the work of warrior-kings with huge, standing armies ready at an instant to conquer, intimidate, and oppress local populations." (Kolata 1993, 243.)

20. Carbon date A.D. 580 ± 60 years. (Isbell 1988, 181.)

21. Isbell 1988, 181–82; Isbell 1991, 303–6.

22. Isbell 1991, 306.

23. Ibid., 309.

24. See Cook 1994, 183–205, and fig. 52.

25. Isbell 1988, 182; Isbell, Brewster-Wray, and Spickard 1991, 32.

26. McEwan 1991, 111.

27. Ibid., 99.

28. John R. Topic 1991, 142–44; Theresa Topic 1991, 242–43.

29. Theresa Topic 1991, 244; Moseley 1992, 219, 221.

30. Isbell 1991, 310.

31. Cook 1994, 180.

32. Expert in astronomy, the *capacas* controlled a calendar integrating resource use and ritual activity throughout the Titicaca basin. In this sense they earned their keep, with leadership flowing toward expertise. Further, the archaeological evidence suggests that they did not surround themselves with luxury or the trappings of power. In A.D. 650, their quarters in the so-called Putuni complex were modest. (Kolata 1993, 153.)

33. Speaking of the Wari complex at Pikillacta, McEwan (1991, 98) observes: "The net effect of this settlement pattern is that of a strategically chosen, purposefully designed entity, well adapted and oriented . . . to a society in which administrative and economic processes took precedence over ritual concerns." Isbell and McEwan (1991, 14) find "little evidence for large civic rituals" in Wari constructions. Conklin (1991, 290) notes: "In Huari architecture, no iconographic images at all have been discovered yet in the vast sites that have been investigated. The complete absence of carved stone images or murals could reasonably be interpreted as some form of prohibition." John Topic (1991, 162) mentions the relatively "low ideological content" of Wari ceramics. Isbell (1991, 310) suggests that the victory of Wari at Moquegua "contributed to the reorientation of Huari society toward a more militarisitic and secular government."

34. Isbell 1988, 182. See also ibid., 187.

35. Isbell, Brewster-Wray, and Spickard 1991, 20; John R. Topic 1991, 161, 163; Schreiber 1991, 211.

36. Schreiber 1991, 211; Browman 1974, 195.

37. McEwan 1991, 117.

38. John R. Topic 1991, 162.

39. Theresa Topic 1991, 243; Lanning 1967, 135.

40. Valcarcél's (1959) early, perceptive term.

41. Cook 1994, 187 ff.

42. Chávez 1975.

43. Cook 1994, 190–95.

44. Kolata 1993, 141.

45. This commitment at Tiahuanaco is manifest not only in the systematic spread of agricultural colonies supported by llama caravans emanating from the Titicaca basin, but also by the fact that at the same time the leaders of Tiahuanaco turned the Akapana over to the cult of the warriors, they began construction on a new earth shrine—the Puma Punku ("Lion Gate")—to replace it. A four-tiered platform pyramid, with its own system of cascading water, and exquisite, stone-carved architraves, the Puma Punku has been called "one of the most beautiful and architecturally complex structures ever created in the ancient Andean world." (Kolata 1993, 99.) It was above the main entrance to this structure that the figure of the Gateway God—whose significance to agricultural civilization has already been discussed at length—originally rested. It was mistakenly replaced above the entrance to the Kalasaya at a time, and by persons, unknown.

46. Obsidian points have always been found in association with Wari's trophy-head cult. Spectrographic analysis of the finely worked obsidian points at Cerro Amaru show an origin in the valley of Cuzco. (Theresa Topic 1991, 243.) Likewise, five hundred miles to the south, in the valley of Cuzco at Pikillacta, archaeologists have found "an apparent offering of ten human skulls . . . a standard form of Huari ceremonial behaviour." (McEwan 1991, 117.)

47. See Miller 1977.

48. Isbell and McEwan 1991, 14.

49. Isbell 1991, 302.

50. Conklin 1991, 281 ff.

51. Ibid., 289–90.

52. Isbell 1991, 302.

53. Ibid., 298 ff.; Conklin 286 ff.

54. Isbell 1991, 298.

55. McEwan 1991, 116.

56. Conklin 1991, 287.

57. McEwan 1991, 112.

58. See Lanning 1967, 186.

59. Conklin 1991, 287.

60. Parsons and Hastings 1988, 202, 218, 224, 227.

61. Ibid., 208.

62. Ibid., 227.

63. Kolata 1993, 284–98.

64. Parsons and Hastings 1988, 219, 226.

65. Lanning 1967, 140, 150.

66. Ibid., 155.

67. Arriaga 1920 [1621], 138; Zuidema 1973c, 17.

68. Arriaga 1920 [1621], 138.

69. Zuidema 1973c, 17.

70. Silverblatt 1976, 301.

71. Zuidema 1973c, 17.

72. Silverblatt 1976, 302.

73. Kolata (1993, 129) suggests that the placement (ca. A.D. 650) of the Puma Punku, the earth shrine of the agricultural viewpoint in Tiahuanaco, to the south of the Akapana, now under the control of the warriors, may represent the first spatial formalization of ideas about moiety divisions. At this time, Kolata argues (1993, 134), warrior-priests dominated Tiahuanaco. As I have stated, I believe the evidence can also be interpreted as bespeaking a tripartite division, very much like ancient Vedic society, into priests (Brahmins), warriors (Rajputs), and farmers (Dhungis).

74. Duviols 1973.

75. Huertas Vallejos 1981, 95–96, 14–15.

76. One aspect of this tradition was the attempt by some indigenous chroniclers to reconcile bibilical and Andean tradition. With varying degrees of caution, scholars now agree that this post-Conquest effort may have drawn on some earlier source of historical perspective. Salomon calls this period a "renaissance" pointing particularly to Pachakuti Yamqui and Guamán Poma, but qualifies this remark, surmising that the ideas they presented were a "reconceptualization" of the past, based upon Guamán Poma's expressed intention of reconciling bibilical and Andean chronologies. (Salomon cites, but is apparently somewhat skeptical of, Turner's [1988] argument that such works as the Huarochirí myths have structural similarities in common with the Bible as the result of similar structural historical conditions. [Salomon 1991, 3].) On the other hand, as regards Guamán Poma (whom even the most exacting of scholars has termed "dotty" [Hemming 1972, 18]), Monica Barnes has recently shown that a series of portraits of Inca kings, painted, without apparent reference to Guamán Poma, by an unknown artist in the mid-eighteenth century

contains a royal genealogy until now believed to be unique to Guamán Poma's idiosyncratic account finished in 1615 . . . both Guamán Poma de Ayala and the Gilcrease painter . . . [appear to have been] . . . drawing upon a common historical tradition. . . . The startling similarity between the historical philosophy underlying both the Gilcrease portraits and Guamán Poma's Inca genealogy make the latter chronicler seem less a uniquely creative, eccentric individual unconstrained by western logic, and more an exponent of an alternate historical tradition that he may not have invented himself. (Barnes 1994, 235–36.)

My own opinion is that such writers as Guamán Poma drew on Andean mythical tradition, which, according to the arguments set forth in this book, had far more in common with bibilical tradition than simple "structure."

77. Isbell 1991, 310. See also chapter 7 of the present work.

78. "The editor's original intent seems to have been to treat ancient matters earlier in the text. . . ." (Salomon 1993, 5.)

79. Avila 1991 [1598?], 88.

80. Ibid., 46.

81. Flores Ochoa 1977, 227.

82. Girard 1979, 70.

83. ". . . *seis hijos e hijas* . . ." (Molina 1943 [1573], 16.)

84. Avila 1991 [1598?], 53.

85. Avila 1991, 53, n. 81.

86. "Chapter 3, telling the myth of the deluge, and chapter 4, telling of the Sun's disappearance, end the section dedicated to remote antiquity." (Salomon 1991, 5–6.)

87. Avila 1991 [1598?], 41.

88. Avila 1966 [1598?], 105.

89. Rostworowski de Canseco 1978, 31–47.

90. Salomon 1991, 6.

91. Bonavía 1984, 5.

92. Menzel 1977, 53; Lanning 1967, 135–37.

93. Netherly 1988, 264. One suspects this culti-gen also produced a superior high.

94. Rostworowski de Canseco 1977, 26, 27, 28.

95. Netherly 1988, 262 ff.

96. This theme is raised in the first chapter of the Huarochirí myths, and elaborated upon later in chapter 27.

97. Avila 1991 [1598?], 129.

98. Ibid., 44.

99. The word *caru*, found in the name of Huallallo Caruincho, is Quechua for "very distant," and means "foreigner" when applied to people. (Holguín 1952 [1608], 50–51.)

100. Avila 1966 [1598?], 81.

101. Ibid., 109.

102. Ibid., 63.

103. Ibid., 54.

104. Ibid.

105. Ibid., 46.

106. Ibid., 54. A point driven home by the man's name, meaning "baked potato gleaner," "a mark of poverty." (Avila 1991 [1598?], 55, n. 94.)

107. The reader may recall, from chapter 2 of this book, that the priest-astronomers of the Incas

dressed in a rough cloak, fasted, and lived alone in the mountains, in the same manner as the male llama of the flood myth. In my opinion this tradition must go back to Tiahuanaco, and in another manner indicates the essentially humble outward demaneanor of the *capacas* of the Titicaca basin, reflected in their equally humble quarters at Tiahuanaco. (See note 32, above.)

108. See Avila 1991 [1598?], 55 and nn. 100–101.

109. The son-in-law is driven to the *antis*, traditionally associated with the "savagery" of Amazonian tribes of the eastern slopes and lower. Antisuyu—running to the borders of deep Amazonia—was the Inca name for the eastern quarter of the Empire. Salomon (1991, 44, n. 25) points out that the word *antis* may also mean the lower and lusher areas of the *chaupiyunga* to the west, toward the Pacific, but in the case of the son-in-law, he is driven *up*, which, in Huarochirí, is to the east.

110. Avila 1966 [1598?], 37.

111. Ibid., 35.

112. Ibid.

113. It is also very likely that the word *yupay*, "to count," found in this mythical context (specifying the ability to raise a large labor force as a manifestation of great political power) explains the origin of the Inca dynastic title *yupanqui*—literally, "you will count"—assumed by no less a personage than Pachakuti Inca himself.

114. Avila 1966 [1598?], 45.

115. Avila 1991 [1598?], 62.

116. See note 99, above.

117. Avila 1991 [1598?], 68.

118. Ibid., 70.

119. Ibid., 70, n. 216. This claim has the ring of truth. The Huancas had very close ties with Wari. Wari presence in Huanca territory is evident on two counts. First, the distinctive Wari pattern of high-altitude terracing of formerly pastoral lands appears intrusively in the Huanca region at about A.D. 650. Browman believes this represents the enforced reduction of Huanca villages at Wari's command, whereas Moseley suspects "adaptive evolution." Whatever the case, one of the most important shrines in the Wari sphere of influence was the spring, known as Wariwillka, from which the Huanca claimed to have emerged. If my suggestion that Wari worked by empowering pastoralists is correct, Wari influence in the Huanca region—which, up until A.D. 650, supported the single greatest concentration of llama herds outside the Titicaca basin—may have been the result of cutting the Huancas in on the prestige trade in coca and Pachacamac wares. In turn, this would

explain the ancient enmity between the Yauyos —themselves masters of llama caravans—and the Huancas, working with Wari to extend its influence to the central Pacific coasts, and bringing their own llama caravans into the midst of a trade network previously serviced by the Yauyos.

120. See note 119, above.

121. Avila 1991 [1598?], 61.

122. Ibid.

123. Huertas Vallejos (1981, 99–100) has published ethnohistorical documents from Cajatambo in which the speaker, a member of the area's local warrior moiety, which worshiped Libiac ("lightning"), expresses the same theme. After dispatching a boy to a village of huaris (autocthonous folk), they learn that these villagers have killed the boy. The village is then destroyed by black snow and hail sent by Libiac. Likewise, centuries later, the Incas would employ the same mythical strategy in justifying their own conquests. According to Guamán Poma, in the time of Pachakuti Inca, "God" in the form of a poor old man seeking charity—food and clothing—would enter the public squares of villages celebrating festivals. If he was ignored, the village in question would be destroyed by "Pachacamac Ticze Cailla-Uiracocha." (Guamán Poma 1956, 207.) Of course, in the time of Pachakuti Inca (ca. 1445), it was the Incas who were obliged to do Wiraqocha's bidding.

124. Avila 1966 [1598?], 20–21.

125. Avila 1991 [1598?], 88.

126. Ibid., 91.

127. Avila 1966 [1598?], 96–97.

128. Holguín 1952 [1608], 339.

129. Avila 1991 [1598], 93, n. 399.

130. Hocquenghem 1987, 212.

131. From the Greek "to turn over."

132. Cited in Duviols 1976, 45.

133. ". . . Mars . . . was chiefly invoked by the later Romans as a warlike deity, and a bundle of spears, his magical weapon, was kept in the Temple of Mars in Rome and consulted for omens in times of trouble." (Michell 1975, 148.)

134. Cieza de León 1973 [1551], 26; Betanzos 1924 [1551], 92; Sarmiento de Gamboa 1942 [1572], 66.

135. Sarmiento de Gamboa 1942 [1572], 66.

136. Cieza de León 1883 [1551], 16.

137. Paria is a bright red quartzlike crystal—cinnabar—pulverized for the extraction of quicksilver. Caca means "rock" or "cliff." See Arriaga 1920 [1621], 47.

138. Stein 1967, 1007.

139. Molina 1873 [1573], 4.

140. Arriaga 1920 [1621], 22; Cobo 1892 [1653], 312; Molina 1943, 9.

141. Urton 1981, 70–71, 188–90.

142. Zuidema and Urton 1976.

143. Acosta 1954 [1590], 143.

144. Cobo 1892 [1653], 330.

145. Anonymous Chronicler 1950 [1585–89], 137.

146. Cobo 1892 [1653], 351.

147. Avila 1966 [1598], 133.

148. Arriaga 1920 [1621], 50.

149. Avila 1991 [1598], 16.

150. Girard 1979, 109.

151. Avila 1991 [1598], 73–74.

152. Anonymous Chronicler 1950 [1585–89], 152.

153. Garcilaso 1918 [1609], 91.

154. Holguín 1952 [1608], 165.

155. Bertonio 1879 [1612], 150.

156. Lehmann-Nitsche 1924b, 66, 71.

157. Holguín 1952 [1608], 18.

158. Lehmann-Nitsche 1924b, 97–98, 100.

159. Arriaga 1920 [1621], 70.

160. Anonymous Chronicler 1950 [1585–89], 136–37.

161. Avila 1966 [1598], 63.

162. Arriaga 1920 [1621], 138.

163. Unfortunately, the word for "god" in the original text is the Spanish "dios," hence short-circuiting any further investigation into the precise significance of the claim.

164. Holguín 1952 [1608], 207.

165. Bertonio 1879 [1612], 242.

166. Lao-Tze 1974, 100.

CHAPTER 9. THE INCA PROPHECY

1. Garcilaso 1869 [1609], 183.

2. Ibarra Grasso 1965, 161.

3. Conklin 1991, 287.

4. Valcárcel 1933.

5. Avila 1991, 67–68, 116.

6. Parsons and Hastings 1988, 223–24.

7. Hemmings 1972, 581, n. 245.

8. Garcilaso 1871 [1609], 89–90.

9. Garcilaso 1919 [1609], 44.

10. Cieza de León 1973 [1551], 242; Murúa 1922 [1613], 30.

11. Prescott 1851, vol. 1, 334–36.

12. Garcilaso 1919 [1609], 44.

13. Collapiña et al. 1974 [1542–44], 38, 42–43.

14. Garcilaso 1871 [1609], 464–65.

15. McIntyre 1975, 52.

16. Garcilaso 1919 [1609], 112–28; Murúa 1922

[1613], 22; Cieza de León 1973 [1551], 139 ff.;
Montessinos 1930 [1630], 99–116.

17. Pachakuti Yamqui 1927 [ca. 1613], 179, 185–
86; Sarmiento de Gamboa 1942 [1572], 95, 97–
98.

18. Collapiña et al. 1974 [1542–44], 36 ff.

19. Anonymous Chronicler 1950 [ca. 1585–89],
162.

20. Betanzos 1924 [1551], 191–92.

21. Pachakuti Yamqui 1927 [ca. 1613], 185–86.

22. Cieza de León 1973 [1551], 145.

23. Zuidema 1962, 110.

24. Demarest 1981, 46.

25. Zuidema 1962.

26. Ibid.

27. Sarmiento de Gamboa 1907 [1572], 42.

28. Garcilaso 1919 [1609], 48; Sarmiento de
Gamboa 1942 [1572], 92.

29. Murúa 1922 [1613], 22.

30. Guamán Poma 1956 [1584–1614], 79; Cieza
de León 1973 [1551], 139; Murúa 1922 [1613], 21.

31. Guamán Poma 1956 [1584–1614], 79.

32. Cieza de León 1973 [1551], 139 ff.

33. Sarmiento de Gamboa 1942 [1572], 96; see
also Hemming 1972, 298.

34. Cited in Métraux 1973, 63.

35. Cieza de León 1973 [1551], 15–16.

36. Parsons and Hastings 1988.

37. Zuidema 1973b, 747.

38. Anonymous Chronicler 1950 [ca. 1585–89],
162.

39. Ibid., 150.

40. Garcilaso 1918 [1609], 45; Cieza de León
1973 [1551], 15.

41. Guamán Poma 1956 [1584–1614], vol. 1, 227;
Cieza de León 1973 [1551], 24–25.

42. Guamán Poma 1956 [1584–1614], vol. 1, 80–
82; Pachakuti Yamqui 1927 [ca. 1613], 191.

43. Sarmiento de Gamboa 1942 [1572], 106.

44. Mason 1968, 115.

45. Cieza de León 1973 [1551], 163.

46. Ibid., 124–25.

47. Guamán Poma 1956 [1584–1614], vol. 1, 51;
Cieza de León 1973 [1551], 143.

48. Guamán Poma 1956 [1584–1614], vol. 1, 79.

49. Pachakuti Yamqui 1927 [ca. 1613], 185–86.

50. Mason 1968, 121–22.

51. Silverblatt 1976, 319.

52. Polo de Ondegardo 1916 [1571], 54.

53. Mason 1968, 122.

54. Ibid., 202.

55. See, for example, Cieza de León 1973 [1551],
194–95.

56. Guamán Poma 1956 [1584–1616], 50.

57. Polo de Ondegardo 1916 [1571], 5; Cobo
1892 [1653], 330.

58. Holguín 1952 [1608], 225.

59. Ibid., 242.

60. Zuidema 1973c, 25.

61. Lira 1946, 18.

62. Urton 1981, 118–21; Sullivan 1979, 31–35.

63. Sullivan 1979, 18–19, 69–70.

64. Avila 1966 [1598?], 50–51.

65. A similar interest in the azimuth (of set) of
the Southern Cross is found in the archaeological
record of Mesoamerica as well. The peculiar pen-
tagonal shape of Building J at Monte Alban, and
possibly also Building O at Caballito Blanco, contains a marked point, like the back of home plate
on a baseball diamond. At Monte Alban this angle
points to the azimuth of set of the Southern Cross
in the era of the building's construction. (Aveni
1980, 251–53; Aveni 1972, 529–30.)

66. Bierhorst 1974, 8.

67. León-Portilla 1978, 107.

68. Bierhorst 1974, 5.

69. The version used here is Bierhorst's translation
(1974, 17–21); see also León-Portilla 1978, 107–9
ff.

70. Bierhorst 1974, 69, n. 7.

71. León-Portilla 1978, 45.

72. Bierhorst 1974, 75. Here Bierhorst speaks of
the portion of the *Annals of Cuauhtitlan*, a document
in the Nahuatl language, which treats of the Quetzalcoatl myth. The *Legends of the Sun*, which contains the "Fall of Quetzalcoatl," itself offers no
date. Instead, we learn that the Fifth Sun was "the
Sun of our Lord Quetzalcoatl in Tula." (León-
Portilla 1978, 39.)

73. Bierhorst 1974, 69, n. 6.

74. Ibid., 207.

75. Ibid., 251.

76. Wertime and Schuster 1993, 30.

77. Bierhorst 1972, 251.

78. Avila 1991 [1609], 132–33.

79. Hemming 1972, 18.

80. Urton 1990.

81. Murúa 1922 [1613], 59–60.

82. Pachakuti Yamqui 1873 [1613], 97.

83. Guamán Poma 1956 [1584–1614], 80.

84. Betanzos 1924 [1551], 114–15, 141.

85. Molina 1943 [1573], 64.

86. León-Portilla 1978, 109.

87. Ibid., 32.

88. Kelley 1980, S22.

89. Mason 1968, 121; Lanning 1967, 157.

CHAPTER 10. THE SECRET

1. Guamán Poma 1956 [1584–1614], 180–81.

2. Garcilaso 1869 [1609], 336.

3. Cited in Santillana and Dechend 1969, 310–11.

4. Ibid., 53–54.

5. Garcilaso 1919 [1609], vol. 3, 19–22.

6. Garcilaso 1869 [1609], 125.

7. Murúa 1922 [1613], 208.

8. Lehmann-Nitsche 1924b, 68–69.

9. Krupp 1983, 47–48.

10. Holguín 1952 [1608], 186.

11. Dechend 1979, 51–55.

12. Ibid., 52.

13. Forty is the number offered by Cobo. The investigations of Zuidema (1979, 233) suggest there may have been forty-one.

14. In fact it is the forty-first conjunction that brings the planets once again to the same point in the stars. (See note 13 above.) The first conjunction in a series counts as zero; twenty years later comes the "first" conjunction, and so on until, after eight hundred years (793) the trigon has turned one third of the way through the ecliptic.

15. In this sense the horizon was assimilated to the ecliptic in the same way that north was assimilated to "up." This reading is supported by a fact mentioned earlier (see page 33), that the number 328 was related directly to the days of invisibility of the Pleiades, which lie squarely on the ecliptic. The Pleiades—along with sun, moon, and planets, all "ecliptic-dwellers"—were venerated in the Temple of the Sun.

16. Guamán Poma 1956 [1584–1614], 180–81; Garcilaso 1869 [1609], 101.

17. Zuidema 1967, 49.

18. Ibid., 41.

19. Pachakuti Yamqui 1873 [ca. 1613], 96.

20. "*sympathetic magic*, magic predicated on the belief that one thing or event can affect another at a distance as a consequence of a sympathetic connection between them." (Stein 1967, 1441.)

21. León-Portilla 1980, 220 ff., 191 n. 3, 220 n. 77.

22. Ibid., 221; León-Portilla 1978, 50.

23. The myth in question is one of four fragments —Fragment B, "The Ceremonial Fire"—of the myth of Quetzalcoatl translated by Bierhorst from the Nahuatl (Bierhorst 1974, 21–24). The hero of this story, Ce Acatl, or Venus, reaches manhood and joins his father, the Sun, in order to make war against Ce Acatl's uncles, the four hundred Mimixcoa (Bierhorst 1974, 71, n. 14; 72, n. 17). The four hundred Mimixcoa, identified by Seler as stars (Bierhorst, citing Seler, 1974, 72, n. 15), kill Ce Acatl's father, the Sun, and bury him in sand. Ce Acatl retrieves the corpse and buries it at Cloud Serpent Mountain.

The image of the mountain suggests that the myth of the death of the Fourth Sun devolves around events at June solstice. Bierhorst notes that the image of the reburial of the Sun-father at "Cloud Serpent Mountain" recalls the "actual custom of interring a king in the manmade 'mountain' or pyramid temple dedicated to a god he had served." The identity of the "god" served by the defunct Fourth Sun is rendered in the mountain's name, *mixcoatl,* literally "cloud serpent," the Aztec name for the Milky Way. (Bierhorst 1974, 72, n. 17.)

So the Fourth Sun, which "served" in the Milky Way, must have perished at the cessation of heliacal rise of the Milky Way at June solstice, buried in the sands of time. The date for this event in Andean myth was marked from A.D. 650. In this Aztec version (of some older, and probably destroyed, Toltec version) the event dates from a particular year, Reed 1 of the Aztec fifty-two-year count. According to Bierhorst, "The manuscript *Annals of Cuauhtitlan,* from which this myth has been extracted, incorporates a count of years beginning with the year 1 Reed (A.D. 641) and continuing for the better part of a millennium—with every year named in order." (Bierhorst 1974, 74–75, n. 25.)

Finally, the particular way of naming the stars —the "four hundred uncles"—adds a decisive dimension to the tale. In the myth of the "Fall of Quetzalcoatl" the innumerable stars of the underworld were described simply as "Holy Ones" or "subjects" of the underworld god. Here they are specified as the "four hundred." In the Quiché-Maya tradition, the Pleiades are most frequently referred to as the "four hundred boys." (Girard 1979, 77, 237.) In projecting the sense of menace to the life of the Sun, embodied in the "warlike" activities of the fixed sphere of stars, the Aztec myth makes specific allusion to the role of the Pleiades in the death of the Fourth Sun. Taken as a purely technical statement, this formulation is *identical* with the Andean myth of the llamas predicting the flood. In the Andean case, the "flood" of A.D. 650 was remembered in myth as occurring exactly one month after the day of heliacal rise of the Pleiades.

24. From the *Codice Matritense,* cited in León-Portilla 1962, xx.

25. León-Portilla 1978, 36.

26. Holguín 1952 [1608], 270.

27. Ibid., 57; Lara 1971, 136; Lira n.d., 120–21.

28. Holguín 1952 [1608], 341; Lara 1971, 277; Lira n.d., 372–73.

29. Holguín 1952 [1608], 57.

30. Prescott 1851, vol. 1, 107.

31. Santillana and Dechend 1969, 163–64.

32. Murúa 1922 [1613], 218.

33. Anonymous Chronicler 1950 [ca. 1585–89], 145.

34. Betanzos 1924 [1551], 172.

35. Collapiña et al. 1974 [1542–44], 39; Molina 1943 [1573], 69 ff.; see also Duviols 1976.

36. Betanzos 1924 [1551], 192–93.

37. Cieza de León 1973 [1551], 32, 110, 111. (Cieza notes that at the time of the *capacocha*, the Incas brought out a great chain of gold. This chain appears during the Capac Raymi ceremony. He also said that one of the purposes of the *capacocha* was to divine how the coming year would be, suggesting that this event took place at December solstice, the beginning of the year.) Guamán Poma 1956 [1584–1614], 181, 172–73. (Guamán Poma said that the *capacocha* was performed at the June solstice as well as the December solstice, but he is the only source so to state.) Sarmiento de Gamboa 1942 [1572], 70. (Sarmiento says that the *capacocha* took place at the same time as the "arming of the knights," i.e. Capac Raymi at December solstice.)

38. Duviols 1976, 12.

39. Cieza de León 1973 [1551], 108.

40. Duviols 1976.

41. Murúa 1922 [1613], 221.

42. Duviols 1976, 11.

43. See Duviols 1976, 39 ff., for a review of the orthographic variations for this term in the original manuscripts.

44. Duviols 1976, 38.

45. Zuidema 1979, 231.

46. Guamán Poma 1956 [1584–1614], 270.

47. Holguín 1952 [1608], 199.

48. Ibid.

49. Molina 1873 [1573], 54.

50. Duviols 1976, 13.

51. Cieza de León, cited in Zuidema 1976, 208.

52. Cieza de León 1973 [1551], 110–11.

53. Molina 1873 [1573], 54. Duviols (1976, 13) has speculated, given the descriptions of tribute pouring in from every area, no matter how remote, that "the number of human victims is far greater than generally believed." Few estimates are to be found in the original sources. Guamán Poma (1956 [1584–1614], 180–81), no friend of the Incas, estimated five hundred children annually. Whatever the true number, it was a function of the number of distinct lineages, not of imperial whim or bloodlust, and would not have fluctuated wildly from year to year. For now, five hundred deaths appears the best available estimate.

54. Cited in Duviols 1976, 14.

55. In this opinion Duviols (1976, 15) concurs.

56. Molina 1873 [1573], 55.

57. Zuidema 1979, 256; ibid. 1976, 212, 223–24.

58. Pachakuti Yamqui 1927 [1613], 201.

59. Molina 1873 [1573], 57.

60. Ibid.

61. Ibid.

62. Zuidema 1979, 233.

63. Molina 1873 [1573], 59.

64. Murúa 1922 [1613], 220.

65. Molina 1943 [1573], 76.

66. Molina 1873 [1573], 58.

67. Ibid., 59.

68. See Duviols 1976, 16–17.

69. Murúa 1922 [1613], 220.

70. See Zuidema 1973a, 151 ff.

71. Wolf 1959, 161.

72. Paralyzed with anxiety, the Aztec Emperor Moctezuma saw, in the reports of the "floating mountains" spotted in the Bay of Campeche, which were the ships of Cortés, the fulfillment of the prophecy of the return from the east of Quetzalcoatl, the just god-king of Tula. "We will be judged and punished," he lamented. "And however it may be, and whenever it may be, we can do nothing but wait." (Sahagún, cited in León-Portilla 1966, 55.) Moctezuma roused himself long enough to send a legation to the "floating mountains" with gifts, the finery of the god Quetzalcoatl —inlaid masks, collars, breastplates, greaves, mirrors, and sandals, fashioned variously from gold and turquoise, silver, emeralds, jade, mother of pearl, jaguar skin, and quetzal feathers. When the ambassadors came aboard Cortés's ship, they kissed the deck before his feet, then dressed him in the treasure. Cortés responded, "Is this all?" (Sahagún, cited in León-Portilla 1966, 22–26.)

73. León-Portilla 1978, 163–64.

74. Ibid., 163.

75. Meade 1993, 163. I am indebted to this writer's understanding of the emotional level of meaning just under the surface of various lakes in Old World folk tales.

76. Cieza de León 1883 [1551], 40.

77. Hemming 1972, 132.

78. The gold paid as part of Atahuallpa's ransom is known, from the meticulous records made at Cajamarca, to have been melted down into ingots of 22.5-carat gold weighing 13,431.2 pounds. This estimate is, if anything, conservative because the Spanish King's portion was to be one fifth, making any underestimation of benefit to those in Peru dividing the spoils. Further, the estimate does not include the gold that disappeared en route to Cajamarca when word of Atahuallpa's murder went out. Nor does it include the far greater treasure taken in the sack of Cuzco. At current bullion rates (ca. $380 per ounce), the gold in Atahuallpa's ransom alone would be worth well in excess of $80,000,000, yet this estimate fails to express the

gold's true purchasing power in Europe at the time. (Hemming 1972, 72–74, 72–74 n., 131–32.) Had these objects been preserved, their current value would run to multiple billions.

CHAPTER 11. THE PATTERN OF THE PAST

1. Wilhelm's commentary on the *I Ching*. (Wilhelm 1976, 105.)
2. Cobo 1983 [1653], 160.
3. Such fasts included strict abstention from salt. As with the native North Americans' sweat lodges, which remove salts from the blood, such practices alter the electrolyte balance of the blood—a practice considered dangerous by modern sports physicians and the manufacturers of such electrolyte enhancers as Gatorade—and are implicated in the production of altered states of consciousness.
4. Cobo 1983 [1653], 160 ff.
5. Hemming 1972, 547, n. 28.
6. Pachakuti Yamqui 1927 [ca. 1613], 216.
7. Avila 1991 [1598?], 88–90.
8. Prescott 1851, vol. 1, 338, n. 6.
9. Avila 1991 [1598?], 89, n. 382.
10. Ibid., 133.
11. ". . . to the north of the llama on the western edge of the Milky Way." (Sullivan 1988, 279.)
12. Avila 1991 [1598?], 133, n. 723.
13. Aveni 1980, 85.
14. Note that Mars has now entered the picture.
15. See, for example, Arriaga 1920 [1621], 112 ff.
16. See Appendix 2.
17. Since it has been assumed heretofore that the Andean peoples had not differentiated between planets, students of the *quipu* have not searched for evidence of planetary record-keeping. An observation such as the one at hand would have required identification of each planet, perhaps by knots of a specific color, indication of conjunction, perhaps by proximity, and a record of the passage of nights, perhaps by knots of some neutral "background" color. The *quipus* have yet to yield their secrets, as Garcilaso implied (1871, 209) when he noted a statement attributed to Pachakuta Inca: "He who attempts to count the stars, not even knowing how to count the marks and knots of the *quipus* ought to be held in derision."
18. Wilhelm 1976, xxi-xxxix.
19. When outer planets such as Saturn and Jupiter lie 180 degrees from the sun, they will undergo "retrograde motion," that is, they will appear to move backwards through the stars as the earth "catches up" and passes them. When a conjunction of Saturn and Jupiter takes place 180 degrees from the sun, the planets will perform a "triple conjunc-

tion," appearing to separate and come together three times.
20. Santillana and Dechend 1969, 244–45. Among the reasons for the assumed importance of this conjunction was that as the vernal equinox moved into the constellation Pisces, the solstices "regained" a seat in the Milky Way, once more to "open the gates" to the worlds beyond. As with Andean thought, a conjunction of Saturn and Jupiter at a location in the stars involved in a significant precessional shift was considered a "synchronous" event, that is, a significant coincidence. As Santillana and Dechend (1969, 244–45) point out, Virgil earned a special place in Dante's *Divine Comedy* for proclaiming, "*Iam redit Virgo*," "Now the Virgin returns." He was speaking of the "return" of the constellation Virgo to a fiducial point—the autumnal equinox. She had "returned" to an important location for the first time since she had occupied the June solstice position some six thousand years earlier—one might add, during the era of the neolithic Great Mother cultures of Anatolia and Mesopotamia.
21. Julian date February 1, on which the events described in the myth commenced, corresponds to Gregorian date February 12, the eve of the zenith passage of the sun above Cuzco, one of two days in the year when, at this latitude, the sun casts no shadow at noon.
22. This observation in no way contradicts the conclusion that diffusion seems the most likely vehicle for the transmission of the technical language of myth around the world. It is the use of distinctive *language*—"mills," "conch shells," consistent use of topographical references, and so on that render this language identifiable as a cultural artifact rather than as a system of thinking (or perceiving) susceptible to independent realization.
23. Cited in Santillana and Dechend 1969, 4.
24. See chapter 2, note 10.
25. "I saw a ladder raised aloft so far / It soared beyond the compass of my sight. / Thereon I saw descend from bar to bar / Splendors so numerous I thought the sky / Had poured from heaven the light of every star." (Dante xxi, 29–33, Sayers and Reynolds, eds.)
26. Santillana and Dechend 1969, 279.
27. Douglas Hofstadter, cited in Gleick 1987, endpiece.
28. Gleick 1987, 8.
29. Ibid., 303.
30. Ibid., 316–17.
31. Ibid., 5.
32. "It remained for E. P. Hubble to establish in 1924 the status of the hitherto mysterious spiral structures and other extragalactic nebula. . . .

These were galaxies beyond our own." (Baker 1973, 651.)

33. As noted by Urton 1981, 198 and n. 214–15.

34. The word *faith* is used advisedly, since a number of recent scientific conferences, convoked for the express purpose of eliciting a definition of consciousness, have failed to make any headway, concluding rather that the existence of consciousness cannot be measured quantitatively. Hence, from a strictly scientific perspective, consciousness, at present, does not exist.

35. From the Akkadian *zar*, meaning "die" (as in the singular of "dice"), and expressing through the ancient game of backgammon the principle of chance or uncertainty entering all complex processes. See Bennett 1991, 16 ff.

36. Cited in Bennett 1991, 88.

37. Bennett 1991, 16.

38. Cobo 1983 [1653], 134.

39. The great powerhouse in which these lessons lie—like Arthur, asleep for a thousand years—is the mythical doctrine of the Ages of the World. If versions of this teaching found in Central and South America differ in any significant respect from Old World versions, it is in the Native American idea that the advent of these teachings was wholly good. This may have to do with the way in which they were transmitted to the New World. If so, the absence of the Promethean "warning" may be a clue to the identity of the transmitting culture.

40. A large, double-blind study on the effectiveness of homeopathy was recently completed in Great Britain. A physician once highly skeptical of homeopathy, who had been involved in the study, delivered the results to a professional audience, concluding that the study showed one of two things: either homeopathy was an extremely inexpensive and effective treatment modality, or else there was some basic flaw in Western scientific method. The report was shelved and never implemented.

41. Bennett 1975, 21.

APPENDIX 1. THE INTENTIONAL FLOODING OF CUZCO

1. Molina 1943 [1573], 65–66; see also Acosta 1880 [1590], 373–74.

2. Urton 1981, 201.

3. Ibid., 102, 208–9; Sullivan 1979, 22–23.

4. Avila 1966 [1608], 160–61.

5. Urton 1981, 136.

6. Holguín 1952 [1608], 206.

7. Zuidema and Urton 1976, 86–87.

8. Girard 1979, 170.

9. Molina (*el cuzqueño*) 1943 [1573], 64.

APPENDIX 2. THE HORIZON-ZENITH PARADIGM

1. Aveni 1981, 161.

2. Ibid.

3. Ibid., 164.

4. Wertime and Schuster 1993, 32.

5. Aveni 1981, 171.

6. Gingerich 1982, 333.

APPENDIX 3. JAGUAR MYTHS OF THE EASTERN SLOPES OF THE ANDES

1. Girard 1979, 167.

2. Ibid., 168.

3. Ibid., 164.

4. Ibid., 202.

5. Schele 1977, 54, 52–55.

6. Kelley 1960, 322; Kelley 1957, 20, 101–2.

7. Lamb 1979, 2.

8. One might ask why the myths specify the moment of the advent of agriculture (with its sophisticated astronomical knowledge) as the time when deer and rabbit lose their tails. In Old World myth, the convention of telling precessional time by reference to both solstitial (or equinoctial) points in the stars simultaneously was also employed. Here, a third referent, the location of the celestial pole of rotation in the stars, was also included, just as it is implicit in the *Popul Vuh* by the fact that the *nahual* of Hunahpú/Sun is Ursa Major. The great circle connecting both solstices (or both equinoxes) through the pole is called the "celestial colure." The word *colure*, as noted elsewhere, comes from the Greek. It means "docked tail," descriptive of that portion of the celestial colure permanently invisible, or "docked," by the southern horizon.

9. All these propositions are eloquently recapitulated in a fragment of the Mixtec myth of origin, referring to what, in the Andes, was termed the end of "darkness" by the "creation of the sun, moon and stars."

> In the year and in the day
> of obscurity and utter darkness,
> before there were days and years,
> the world being in deep obscurity,
> when all was chaos and confusion,
> the earth was covered with water,
> there was only mud and slime

on the surface of the earth.
At that time . . .
there became visible
a god who had the name 1-Deer
and the surname Snake of the Lion
and a goddess, very genteel and beautiful,
whose name was also 1-Deer
and whose surname was Snake of the Tiger.
These two gods are said to have been the beginning
of all the other gods. . . .
[Cited in León-Portilla 1980, 145.]

"Before there were days and years," there were nights and moons.
10. Polo 1916, 5, n. 6.
11. Schele 1977, 55.

APPENDIX 4. THE COSMOLOGY OF
TIAHUANACO'S MONUMENTS

1. Kolata 1993, 90–91. But see also Isbell 1994, 1031. Note also that the Aymara word for "island," *buatta* (Bertonio 1879 [1612], 152), has a possible

Quechua cognate, *buata*, meaning "year" (Holguín 1952 [1608], 185).
2. Eliade 1974b, 15–16. See also Eliade 1959, 46–47.
3. Eliade 1974b, 16.
4. Kolata 1993, 96.
5. Ibid., 143.
6. Ibid., 141–42.
7. Ibid., 111.

APPENDIX 5. PALEOLITHIC ORIGINS OF THE
CONCEPT *WAKA*

1. Marshack 1972, 169–234.
2. Ibid., 179, 218.
3. Ibid., 218.
4. Schapera 1930, 174 ff., citing work by Wilhelm Bleek published in *Cape Monthly Magazine*, February 1874, 101 ff., all as cited in Dechend's unpublished lecture notes.
5. Froebenius 1933, 130.
6. Dechend 1979, 11, 7–12.
7. Speck 1935, 50.
8. Eliade 1974, 272.
9. Lehmann-Nitsche 1919, 183–84.

BIBLIOGRAPHY

Acosta, José de 1880. *The Natural and Moral History of the Indies* [1590]. Edited by Clements R. Markham, translated by Edward Grimston. Works issued by the Hakluyt Society, 1st series, no. 61. New York: Burt Franklin.

——— 1954. *Historia natural y moral de las Indias* [1590]. In Biblioteca de autores españoles, vol. 74, 3–247.

Allen, Richard Hinckley 1963. *Star Names: Their Lore and Meaning.* New York: Dover Publications.

Anonymous Chronicler [Blas Valera] 1950. *Relación de las costumbres antiguas de los naturales del Perú* [ca. 1585–89]. Edited by J. Jimenez de la Espada. In *Tres relaciones de antiguedades peruanas.* 135–203. Lima: Editorial Guaranía

Arguedas, José María, and Josafat Roel Pineda 1973. "Tres Versiones del Mito de Inkarri." *In Ideologia Mesiánica del Mundo Andino,* edited by Juan Ossio, 219–36. Lima: Edición de Ignacio Prado Pastor.

Arnold, Denise Y., and Juan de Dios Yapita Moya 1992. " 'Fox Talk': Addressing the Wild Beasts in the Southern Andes." *Latin American Indian Literatures Journal,* 8, no.1. Pennsylvania State University.

Arriaga, Pablo José de 1920. *La extirpación de la idolatría en el Perú* [1621]. In Colección de Libros y Documentos Referentes a la Historia del Perú, 2nd series, vol.1, edited by Horacio H. Urteaga. Lima.

Audubon, John J., and John Bachmann 1967. *The Imperial Collection of Audubon Animals.* Edited by Victor H. Cahalane. Maplewood, New Jersey: Hammond.

Aveni, Anthony F. 1972. "Mount J, Monte Albán: Possible Astronomical Alignment," *American Antiquity* 37, no. 4, 528–31.

——— 1980. *Skywatchers of Ancient Mexico.* Austin: University of Texas Press.

——— 1981. "Tropical Archaeoastronomy," *Science* 213, no. 4504, 161–71.

Avila, Francisco de 1966. *Dioses y hombres de Huarochirí* [1598?]. Translated by J. M. Arguedas. Lima: Instituto de Estudios Peruanos.

——— 1991. *The Huarochirí Manuscript* [1598?]. Translated by Frank Salomon and George L. Urioste. Austin: University of Texas Press.

Baker, Robert Horace 1973. "Astronomy." In Encyclopedia Britannica, vol.2, 643–51. Chicago: William Benton.

Bankes, George 1977. *Peru Before Pizarro.* Oxford: Phaidon Press.

Bennett, John Godolphin 1975. *The Long Pilgrimage.* San Francisco: Rainbow Bridge.

——— 1991. *Hazard.* Santa Fe: Bennett Books.

Bennett, Wendell C. 1953. *Excavations at Huari, Ayacucho, Peru.* Yale University Publications in Anthropology II. New Haven: Yale University Press.

Bertonio, Ludovico 1879. *Vocabulario de la lengua Aymara* [1612]. Edición facsimilaria. Leipzig: B. G. Teubner.

Betanzos, Juan Diez de 1924. *Suma y narración de los Incas* [1551]. In Colección de Libros y Documentos Referentes a la Historia del Perú, edited by Horacio H. Urteaga, 2nd series, vol. 8, 79–208.

Bierhorst, John, ed. 1972. *In the Trail of the Wind: American Indian Poems and Ritual Orations.* New York: Farrar, Strauss, and Giroux.

——— 1974. *Four Masterworks of American Indian Literature.* New York: Farrar, Strauss, and Giroux.

Blake, A. G. E. 1993. "A New Time." *The Dramatic University: The UniS Journal* 4, no. 4, (November 1993), 1–6.

Bonavía, Duccio, Fabiola León Velarde, Carlos Monge, María Inés Sanchez-Griñán, and José Whittembury 1984. "Tras las Huellas de Acosta 300 años después: Consideraciones sobre su descripción del 'mal de altura.' " *Historica* 8, no.1, 1–31. Lima: Pontifica Universidad Católica del Perú.

Brinton, Daniel G. 1976. *Myths of the Americas: Symbolism and Mythology of the Indians of the Americas.* Blauvelt, N.Y. Multimedia Publishing Corp.

Broda, Johanna 1989. "Geography, Climate and Observation of Nature in Prehispanic Mesoamerica." *In The Imagination of Matter: Religion and Ecology in Mesoamerican Traditions,* edited by David Carrasco. Oxford: BAR International series 515.

Browman, David L. 1974a. "Pastoral Nomadism in the Andes." *Current Anthropology* 15, no. 2, 188–96.

——— 1974b. "Trade patterns in the Central Highlands of Peru in the first millenium B.C." World Archeaology 6, 322–29.

Burger Richard L. 1988. "Unity and Heterogeneity in the Chavín Horizon." In Peruvian Prehistory, edited by Richard W. Keatinge. Cambridge: Cambridge University Press.

Casaverde Rojas, Juvenal 1970. "El mundo sobrenatural en una Comunidad." In Allpanchis Phuturinqa 2, 121–243. Cuzco: Instituto de Pastoral Andino.

Chávez, Sergio 1975. "The Arapa and Thunderbolt Stela: a case of stylistic identity with implications for Pucara influence in the area of Tiahuanaco." Ñawpa Pacha 13, 3–25. Berkeley.

Cieza de León, Pedro 1883. The Second Part of the Chronicle of Peru [1551]. Translated by Clements R. Markham. Works issued by the Hakluyt Society. 1st series, no. 68. New York: Burt Franklin.

——— 1973. El Señorio de los Incas [1551]. Lima: Editorial Universo S.A.

Cobo, Bernabé 1892. Historia del Nuevo Mundo [1653], vol. 3. Edited by D. Marcos Jiménez de la Espada. Seville: Sociedad Bibliófilos Andaluces.

——— 1893. Historia del Nuevo Mundo [1653], vol. 4. Edited by D. Marcos Jiménez de la Espada. Seville: Sociedad Bibliófilos Andaluces

Collapiña, Supno, y otros Quipucamayos 1974. Relación de la descendencia, gobierno y conquista de los Incas [1542–44]. Lima: Ediciones de la Biblioteca Universitaria.

Conklin, William J. 1991. "Tiahuanaco and Huari: Architectural Comparisons and Interpretations," In Huari Administrative Structure: Prehistoric Monumental Architecture and State Government, edited by William H. Isbell and Gordon F. McEwan, 141–64. Washington, D.C.: Dumbarton Oaks Research Library and Collection.

Cook, Anita G. 1983. "Aspects of State Ideology in Huari and Tiwanaku Iconography: The Central Deity and the Sacrificer." In Investigations of the Andean Past edited by Daniel H. Sandweiss, 161–85. Ithaca, N.Y.: Latin American Studies Program, Cornell University.

——— 1994. Wari y Tiwanaku: entre el estilo y la imagen. Lima: Pontificia Universidad Católica del Perú.

Cornford, Francis MacDonald 1975. Plato's Cosmology: The Timaeus of Plato. Indianapolis: Bobbs-Merrill.

Cusihuaman G., Antonio 1976a. Diccionario quechua: Cuzco-Collao. Lima: Ministerio de Educación.

——— 1976b. Gramatica quechua: Cuzco-Collao. Lima: Ministerio de Educación.

Davidson, H. R. Ellis 1979. Gods and Men of Northern Europe. Harmondsworth, Middlesex, England: Penguin Books.

Dechend, Hertha von 1979. "Ages of the World." Unpublished lecture notes, 24 October 1979, Massachusetts Institute of Technology, Syllabus 21.965 J = STS 630 J.

Demarest, Arthur A. 1981 Viracocha: The Nature and Antiquity of the Andean High God. Cambridge; Mass.: Peabody Museum Monographs.

Duviols, Pierre 1973. "Huari y Llacuaz. Agricultores y pastores un dualismo prehispánico de oposición y complementaridad." In Revista del Museo Nacional (Lima) 39, 153–91.

——— 1976 "La Capacocha." Allpanchis Phuturinqa 9, 11–57. Cuzco.

Eliade, Mircea 1959. The Sacred and the Profane. New York: Harcourt Brace & World.

——— 1974a. Shamanism: Archaic Techniques of Ecstasy. New York: Princeton University Press, Bollingen Series 76.

——— 1974b. The Myth of the Eternal Return. New York: Princeton University Press, Bollingen Series 66.

Eyzaguirre S., Delfín 1956. "Astronomía Aymara." Khana: Revista municipal de artes y letras 3, nos. 19–20, 82–96.

Flores Ochoa, Jorge A. 1977. Pastores de Puna. Edited by Jorge A. Flores Ochoa. Lima: Instituto de Estudios Peruanos.

Forstemann, Ernst 1904. "Tortoise and Snail in Maya Literature." Bulletin of the Bureau of American Ethnology 28, 423–430. Washington, D.C.: U.S. Government Printing Office.

Fox, Robin 1977. Kinship and Marriage. Harmondsworth, Middlesex, England: Penguin.

Freidel, David, Linda Schele, and Joy Parker 1993. Maya Cosmos. New York: William Morrow.

Froebenius, Leo 1933. Kulturgeschicte Afrikas; Prologomena zu einer historischen Gestaltlehre. Zurich: Phaidon-Verlag.

Garcilaso de la Vega, El Inca 1869. The Royal Commentaries of the Incas:Volume I [1609]. Translated by Clements R. Markham. Works issued by the Hakluyt Society, first series, no. 41. New York: Burt Franklin.

——— 1871. The Royal Commentaries of the Incas: Volume II [1609]. Translated by Clements R. Markham. Works issued by the Hakluyt Society, first series, no. 45. New York: Burt Franklin.

——— 1918. Los Commentarios Reales de los Incas [1609], vol. 1. Edited by Horacio H. Urteaga.

Colección de Historiadores Clasicos del Perú. Lima: Imprenta y Librería Sanmarti y Ca.

——— 1919. *Los Commentarios Reales de los Incas* [1609], vol. 2, 3. Edited by Horacio H. Urteaga. Colección de Historiadores Clasicos del Perú. Lima: Imprenta y Librería Sanmarti y Ca.

——— 1920. *Los Commentarios Reales de los Incas* [1609] vol. 4. Edited by Horacio H. Urteaga. Colección de Historiadores Clasicos del Perú. Lima: Imprenta y Librería Sanmarti y Ca.

Gingerich, Owen 1982. "Summary: Archaeoastronomy in the Tropics." In *Ethnoastronomy and Archaeoastronomy in the American Tropics*, edited by Anthony F. Aveni and Gary Urton, 333–36. New York: New York Academy of Sciences.

Girard, Raphael 1979. *Esotericism of the Popol Vuh*. Translated from the Spanish by Blair A. Moffett. Pasadena: Theosophical University Press.

Griaule, Marcel 1965. *Conversations with Ogotommêli*. Oxford, England: Oxford University Press.

Grzimek, Bernard, ed. 1972. *Grzimek's Animal Life Encyclopedia, vol. 12. Mammals III*. New York: Van Nostrand Reinhold.

Guamán Poma de Ayala, Felipe 1956. *El primer nueva crónica y buen gobierno* [1584–1614]. 3 vols., edited by Luis F. Bustios Galvez. Lima: Editorial Cultura.

Halifax, Joan 1982. *Shaman: The Wounded Healer*. New York: Crossroad.

Hall, Robert 1990. "Some Implications of the Astronomical Associations of the La Mojarra Stela 1 and Tuxtla Statuette Long Dates." Paper prepared for the Third International Conference on Archaeoastronomy, University of St. Andrews, Scotland, 10–14 September.

Hammond, Dorothy, and Alta Jablow 1976. *Women in Cultures of the World*. Menlo Park, Calif.: Cummings Publishing Co.

Harleston, Hugh Jr. 1984 *The Keystone: A Search for Understanding: A New Guide to the Pyramids of Mexico Book I: The First Dimension*. Limited edition.

Harris, J. Rendel 1913. *Boanerges*. Cambridge: Cambridge University Press.

Hartner, Willy 1968. *Oriens-Occidens: Ausgewahlte Schriften zur Wissenschaftsund Kulturgeschichte*. Festschrift zum 60. Geburtstag. Hildesheim: Collecteana 3.

Heine-Geldern, Robert 1966. "The Problem of Trans-Pacific Influences in Mesoamerica." In *The Handbook of Central American Indians*, vol. 4, 277–345. Austin: University of Texas Press.

Hemming, John 1972. *The Conquest of the Incas*. New York: Abacus.

Hocquenghem, Anne Marie 1987. *Iconografía Mochica*. Lima: Pontificia Universidad Catolica del Perú, Fondo Editorial.

Holguín, Diego González 1952. *Vocabulario de la lengua general de todo el Perú llamada lengua Quichua o del Inca* [1608]. Lima: Instituto de Historia, Universidad Nacional Mayor de San Marcos.

Huertas Vallejos, Lorenzo 1981. *La religion en un sociedad rural andina (siglo XVII)*. Ayacucho, Peru: Universidad Nacional de San Cristobal de Humanaga.

Ibarra Grasso, Dick Edgar 1965. *Prehistoria de Bolivia*. La Paz: Editorial Amigos del Libro.

Ibarra Grasso, Dick Edgar, and Roy Querejazu Lewis 1986. *30,000 Años de Prehistoria en Bolivia*. La Paz: Enciclopedia Boliviana: Editorial Amigos del Libro.

Isbell, William H. 1978. "Cosmological Order Expressed in Prehistoric Ceremonial Centers." In *Actes de 42nd Congrès International des Americanistes* (Paris), vol. 4, 269–97.

——— 1983. "Shared Ideology and Parallel Political Development: Huari and Tiwanaku." In *Investigations of the Andean Past*, edited by Daniel H. Sandweiss, 86–208. Ithaca, N.Y.: Latin American Studies Program, Cornell University.

——— 1987. "State origins in the Ayacucho Valley, central highlands, Peru." In *The Origins and Development of the Andean State*, edited by Jonathan Haas, Shelia Pozorski, and Thomas Pozorski, 83–90 Cambridge: Cambridge University Press.

——— 1988. "City and State in Middle Horizon Wari." In *Peruvian Prehistory*, edited by Richard W. Keatinge, 164–89. Cambridge: Cambridge University Press.

——— 1991. "Huari Administration and the Orthogonal Cellular Architecture Horizon." In *Huari Administrative Structure: Prehistoric Monumental Architecture and State Government*, edited by William H. Isbell and Gordon F. McEwan, 293–315. Washington, D.C.: Dumbarton Oaks Research Library and Collection.

——— 1994. "Review" of Kolata's *The Tiwanaku*. *American Anthropologist* 96 (December 1994) 1030–31.

Isbell, William H., Christine Brewster-Wray, and Lynda E. Spickard 1991. "Architecture and Spatial Organization at Huari." In *Huari Administrative Structure: Prehistoric Monumental Architecture and State Government*, edited by William H. Isbell and Gordon F. McEwan, 19–53. Washington, D.C.: Dumbarton Oaks Research Library and Collection.

Isbell, William H., and Gordon F. McEwan, eds. 1991. *Huari Administrative Structure: Prehistoric Monumental Architecture and State Government*. Washington, D.C.: Dumbarton Oaks Research Library and Collection.

Jeremias, Alfred 1929. *Handbuch der Altorienta-lischen Geisteskultur.* 2nd edition, revised. Berlin-Leipzig.

Jones, William 1939. *Ethnography of the Fox Indians.* Smithsonian Institution, Bureau of American Ethnology Bulletin 125. Washington, D.C.: U. S. Government Printing Office.

Keatinge, Richard W. 1988. "A summary view of Peruvian prehistory." In *Peruvian Prehistory,* edited by Richard W. Keatinge, 164–89. Cambridge: Cambridge University Press.

Kelley, David H. 1960. "Calendar Animals and Deities." *Southwestern Journal of Anthropology* 16, no. 3, 317–37.

——— 1971. "Diffusion: Evidence and Process." In *Man Across the Sea,* edited by Carrol L. Riley, J. Charles Kelley, et al., 60–65. Austin: University of Texas Press.

——— 1980. "Astronomical Identities of Mesoamerican Gods." *Contributions to Mesoamerican Anthropology.* Publication no. 2. Miami: Miami Institute of Maya Studies.

Kolata, Alan Lewis 1992. *The Tiwanaku: Portrait of an Andean Civilization.* The Peoples of America. New York: Blackwell.

Kornfield, Jack 1993. *A Path with Heart.* New York: Bantam.

Krickeberg, Walter, Hermann Trimborn, et al. 1969. In *Pre-Columbian American Religions,* translated by Stanley Davis. New York: Holt, Rinehart, and Winston.

Kroeber, Alfred 1925. *Handbook of the Indians of California.* Smithsonian Institution Bureau of American Ethnology, Bulletin 78. Washington, D.C.: U.S. Government Printing Office.

Krupp, E. C. 1979. *In Search of Ancient Astronomies.* New York: McGraw-Hill.

——— 1983. *Echoes of the Ancient Skies.* New York: Harper & Row.

La Barre, Weston 1948. *The Aymara Indians of the Lake Titicaca Plateau, Bolivia.* Memoirs of the American Anthropological Association, no. 68. Menasha, Wisconsin.

Lamb, Weldon 1979. "Overlooked Yucatecan Maya Star Lore." Santa Fe Conference paper. St. John's College, 12 June 1979.

Lanning, Edward P. 1967. *Peru Before the Incas.* Englewood Cliffs, N.J.: Prentice-Hall.

Lao-tze 1974. *The Canon of Reason and Virtue.* Translated by D. T. Suzuki and Paul Carus. La Salle, Ill.: Open Court.

Lara, Jesus 1971. *Diccionario qheshwa-castellano, castellano-qheshwa.* La Paz: Editorial "Los Amigos del Libro."

Larrea, Juan 1960. *Corona Incaica.* Buenos Aires: Imprenta Lopez.

Lastres, Juan B. 1953. "El Culto de los Muertos entre los Aborigenes Peruanos." *Perú Indigena* (Lima) 4, no. 10, 63–74.

Lehmann-Nitsche, Robert 1919. "Mitología Sudamericana II: La Cosmogonía según los Puelche de Patagonia." In *Revista del Museo de la Plata,* vol. 24, part 2, 188–205. Buenos Aires: Imprenta y Casa Editora «Coni».

——— 1924a. "La Astronomía de los Chiriguanos." *Revista del Museo de la Plata,* vol. 28, 80–102. Buenos Aires: Imprenta y Casa Editora «Coni».

——— 1924b. "La Astronomía de los Mocovi." *Revista del Museo de la Plata,* vol. 28, 66–79. Buenos Aires: Imprenta y Casa Editora «Coni».

——— 1925. "La Astronomía de los Tobas." *Revista del Museo de la Plata.* vol. 28, 181–209. Buenos Aires: Imprenta y Casa Editora «Coni».

——— 1928. "Coricancha." *Revista del Museo de la Plata* 7, series 3, 1–256.

León-Portilla, Miguel 1966. *The Broken Spears: The Aztec Account of the Conquest of Mexico.* Boston: Beacon Press.

——— 1978. *Aztec Thought and Culture.* Translated by Jack Emory Davis. Norman: University of Oklahoma Press.

———, ed. 1980. *Native American Spirituality.* New York: Paulist Press.

Lewis, David 1979. *We, the Navigators.* Honolulu: The University Press of Hawaii.

Lewis, I. M. 1976. *Social Anthropology in Perspective.* Harmondsworth, Middlesex, England: Penguin.

Lira, Jorge 1946. *Farmicopea tradicional indígena y prácticas rituales.* Lima: Talleres Graficos "el Condor."

——— n.d. *Breve Diccionario Kkechuwa Espanol.* Cuzco. Edición Popular.

Lounsbury, Floyd 1964. "Some Aspects of the Inca Kinship System." Trabajo presentado al Congreso Internacional de Americanistas, Barcelona.

Lowie, Robert 1920. *Primitive Society.* New York: Liveright.

Lyon, Patricia J. 1978. "Female Supernaturals in Ancient Peru." *Nawpa Pacha* 16, 95–137. Berkeley: University of California.

Marcus, Joyce 1980. "Zapotec Writing." *Scientific American* 242, no. 2 (February 1980), 50–64.

Mariscotti de Gorlitz, Ana Maria 1978. "Los Curi y el Rayo." *Actes du 42nd Congres International des Américanistes: Congres du Centenaire,* vol. 4, 365–76. Paris: Fondation Singer-Polignac.

Marshack, Alexander 1972. *The Roots of Civilization.* New York: McGraw-Hill.

Marzal, Manuel, S.J. 1971. *El Mundo Religioso de Urcos.* Cuzco: Instituto Pastoral Andino.

Mason, J. Alden 1968. *The Ancient Civilizations of Peru* (revised edition). New York: Penguin.

McEwan, Gordon F. 1991. "A Provincial Huari Center in the Valley of Cuzco." In *Huari Administrative Structure: Prehistoric Monumental Architecture and State Government*, edited by William H. Isbell and Gordon F. McEwan, 93–119. Washington, D.C.: Dumbarton Oaks Research Library and Collection.

McIntyre, Loren 1984. *The Incredible Incas and Their Timeless Land.* Washington, D.C.: The National Geographic Society.

Meade, Michael 1993. *Men and the Water of Life.* San Francisco: Harper Collins.

Menzel, Dorothy 1964. "Style and Time in the Middle Horizon." *Nawpa Pacha* 2, 1–106. Berkeley: Institute of Andean Studies.

Métraux, Alfred 1946. "Twin Heroes in South American Indian Mythology." *Journal of American Folklore* 59, 114–23.

——— 1948. "The Guarani." *Handbook of South American Indians, vol. 3, Tropical Forest Tribes*, 69–94. Bureau of American Ethnology, Bulletin 143. Washington, D.C.: Smithsonian Institution.

——— 1973. *The History of the Incas.* New York: Schocken Books.

Michell, John 1975. *The View over Atlantis.* London: Abacus.

Miller, George R. 1977. "Sacrificio y beneficio de camélidos en el sur del Perú." In *Pastores de puna*, edited by Jorge A. Flores Ochoa, 193–210. Lima: Instituto de Estudios Peruanos.

Mishkin, Bernard 1940. "Cosmological Ideas among the Indians of the Southern Andes." *Journal of American Folklore* 53, 225–41.

——— 1946. "The Contemporary Quechua." In *Handbook of South American Indians*, edited by Julian Steward, vol. 2, 411–70. Bureau of American Ethnology, Bulletin 143. Washington D.C.: Smithsonian Institution.

Mitchell, William P. 1977. "Irrigation Farming in the Andes: Evolutionary Implications." In *Peasant Livelihood: Studies in Economic Anthropology and Cultural Ecology*, edited by Rhoda Halperin and James Dow, 36–59. New York: St. Martin's Press.

Molina (el Cuzqueño), Cristóbal de 1873. *Narrative of the Rites and Laws of the Incas* [1573]. Translated by Clements R. Markham. Works issued by the Hakluyt Society, 1st series, no. 48. New York: Burt Franklin.

——— 1943. *Fábulas y ritos de los Incas.* Edited by Francisco A. Loayza. Lima: Los Pequeños Grandes Libros de Historia Americana, series 1, vol. 4, 1–84.

Moran, Hugh A., and David H. Kelley 1969. *The Alphabet and the Ancient Calendar Signs.* Palo Alto: Daily Press.

Moseley, Michael E. 1992. *The Incas and Their Ancestors: The Archaeology of Peru.* New York: Thames and Hudson.

Müller, F. Max 1878. *Lectures on the Origin and Growth of Religion, as Illustrated by the Religions of India.* Oxford: Longmans, Green & Co.

Murra, John V. 1972. "El 'control vertical' de un máximo de pisos ecológicos en la economía de las sociedades andinas." In *Visita de la provincia de León de Huánuco [1562], Iñigo Ortiz de Zùñiga Visitador*, 429–76. Huánuco, Peru: Universidad Nacional Hermilio Valdizán.

Murúa ("Morua"), Fray Martín de 1922. *Historia de los Incas: Reyes del Perú* [1613]. Colección de Libros y Documentos Referentes a la Historia del Perú, edited by Horacio H. Urteaga. 2nd series, vol. 4. Lima.

National Research Council Panel on Lost Crops of the Incas 1990. "Lost Crops of the Incas." Reprinted in *Arnoldia* 50, no. 4 (1990), 2–15.

Netherly, Patricia J. 1988. "From event to process: the recovery of Late Andean organizational structure by means of Spanish colonial written records." In *Peruvian Prehistory*, edited by Richard W. Keatinge, 164–89. Cambridge: Cambridge University Press.

Núñez del Prado, Juan 1970. "El mundo sobrenatural del los Quechuas del sur del Perú a través de la comunidad de Qotobamba." *Allpanchis Phuturinqa* 2, 57–119. Cuzco: Instituto de Pastoral Andino.

——— 1974. "The Supernatural World of the Quechua of Southern Peru as Seen from the Community of Qotobamba." In *Native South Americans*, edited by Patricia Lyons, 238–51, Boston: Little, Brown.

Núñez del Prado, Oscar 1952. *La Vida y la Muerte en Chinchero.* Cuzco: Universidad Nacional del Cuzco.

Onions, C. T. ed. 1955. *The Oxford Universal Dictionary on Historical Principles*, 3rd edition. Oxford: Oxford University Press.

Ossio A., Juan M. 1973. "Guamán Poma: Nueva Crónica o Carta al Rey. Un Intento de Aproximación a las Categorías del Pensamiento del Mundo Andino." In *Ideología Mesiánica del Mundo Andino*, edited by Juan M. Ossio, 153–213. Lima: Edición de Ignacio Prado Pastor.

——— 1977. "Los mitos de origen en la Comunidad de Andamarca." *Allpanchis Phuturinqa* 10, 105–113.

Pachakuti Yamqui Salcamaygua, Juan de Santa Cruz 1873. *Narratives of the Rites and Laws of the Incas* [ca. 1613]. Translated by Clements R.

Markham. Works issued by the Hakluyt Society, 1st. series, no. 48. New York: Burt Franklin.

———— 1927. *Relación de antiguedades deste reyno del Perú* [ca. 1613]. Colección de Libros y Documentos Referentes a la Historia del Perú, edited by Horacio H. Urteaga, 2nd series, vol. 9. Lima.

Parsons, Jeffrey R., and Charles M. Hastings 1988. "The Late Intermediate Period." In *Peruvian Prehistory*, edited by Richard W. Keatinge. Cambridge: Cambridge University Press.

Polo de Ondegardo, Juan 1916. *Los errores y supersticiones de los indios sacados del tratado y averiguación que hizo Licenciado Polo* [1571]. Colección de Libros y Documentos Referentes a la Historia del Perú, vol. 3. Lima: Imprenta y Librería San Marti y Ca.

Prescott, William H. 1851. *History of the Conquest of Peru*. 2 vol. New York: Harper and Brothers.

Pucher, Leo 1948. "El zodiaco americano," *La Razon* (La Paz), 7 March 1948, 4.

Quiroga, Adan 1965. *La Cruz en America*. Buenos Aires: Imprenta "La Buenos Aires."

Ramsdell, Lewis S. 1973. "Rutile." In *Encyclopedia Britannica*, vol. 19, 836. Chicago: William Benton.

Randall, Robert 1987. "Del tiempo y del rió: El ciclo de la historia y la energía en la cosmología incaica." *Boletin de Lima* 54 (November 1987), 69–95.

Raymond, J. Scott 1988. "A View from the Tropical Forest." In *Peruvian Prehistory*, edited by Richard W. Keatinge, 279–300. Cambridge: Cambridge University Press.

Recinos, Adrian, Delia Goetz, and Sylvanus Morley 1950. *Popol Vuh, The Sacred Book of the Ancient Quiché Maya*. Norman, Okla.: University of Oklahoma Press.

Riley, Carroll L. et al., eds. 1971. *Man Across the Seas: Problems of Pre-Columbian Contacts*. Austin: University of Texas Press.

Roca Wallparimachi, Demetrio 1966. "El sapo, la culebra, y la rana en el folklore actual de la pampa de Anta." *Folklore, Revista de Cultura Tradicional* 1, no. 1, 41–66.

Rostworowski de Canseco, María 1977. *Etnía Sociedad: Costa Peruana Prehispánica*. Lima: Instituto de Estudios Peruanos.

———— 1978. *"Señorios indigenas de Lima y Canta*. Lima: Instituto de Estudios Peruanos.

Rowe, John Howland 1946. "Inca Culture at the Time of the Spanish Conquest." In *Handbook of South American Indians*, edited by Julian Steward, vol. 2, 183–330. Bureau of American Ethnology, Bulletin 143. Washington, D.C.: Smithsonian Institution.

———— 1960. "The Origins of Creator Worship Among the Incas." In *Culture in History: Essays in Honor of Paul Radin*, edited by Stanley Diamond, 408–29. New York: Columbia University Press.

———— 1966. "Diffusionism and Archaeology." *American Antiquity* 31, 334–39.

Sahagún, Fray Bernardino de 1953. *Florentine Codex: General history of the things of New Spain. Book 7: The sun, moon and stars and the binding of the years*. Translated from the Nahuatl by Arthur J. O. Anderson and Charles E. Dibble. School of American Research, Archaeological Institute of America Monograph 14, part 8, book 7. Ogden: University of Utah Press.

Salomon, Frank 1991. "Introductory Essay: The Huarochirí Manuscript." In *The Huarochirí Manuscript* [1598?], translated by Frank Salomon and George L. Urioste. Austin: University of Texas Press.

Sanders, William T., and Joseph Marino 1970. *New World Prehistory*. Englewood Cliffs, N.J.: Prentice-Hall.

Santillana, Giorgio de, and Hertha von Dechend 1969. *Hamlet's Mill: An Essay on Myth and the Frame of Time*. Boston: Gambit.

Sarmiento de Gamboa, Pedro 1907. *History of the Incas* [1572]. Translated by Clements Markham. Works issued by the Hakluyt Society, 2nd series, no. 22. Cambridge: University Press.

———— 1942. *Historia de los Incas*. Buenos Aires: Emece editores.

Schapera, I. 1930. *The Khoisan Peoples of South Africa*. London: G. Routledge and Sons.

Schele, Linda 1979. "Palenque: The House of the Dying Sun." In *Native American Astronomy*, edited by Anthony F. Aveni, 42–56. Austin: University of Texas Press.

Schreiber, Katharina J. 1987. "From state to empire: the expansion of Wari outside the Ayacucho Basin." In *The Origins and Development of the Andean State*, edited by Jonathan Haas, Shelia Pozorski, and Thomas Pozorski, 97–110. Cambridge: Cambridge University Press.

Silverblatt, Irene 1976. "La organización femenina en el Tawantinsuyu." *Revista del Museo Nacional* (Lima), vol. 42, 299–340.

Simeon, Remi 1977. *Diccionario de la Lengua Nahuatl o Mexican*. [1885]. Mexico City: Siglo Ventiuno Editores, sa.

Soustelle, Jacques 1972. *Daily Life of the Aztecs*. Translated by Patrick O'Brien. Harmondsworth, Middlesex, England: Penguin Books.

Speck, Frank G. 1935. *Naskapi: The Savage Hunters of the Labrador Peninsula*. Norman: University of Oklahoma Press.

Stein, Jess, ed. 1967. *The Random House Dictionary of the English Language: The Unabridged Edition*. New York: Random House.

Steward, Julian H., and Alfred Métraux 1948. "Tribes of the Peruvian and Ecuadorian Montana." In *Handbook of South American Indians*, vol. 3, 535–56. Bureau of American Ethnology, Bulletin 143. Washington, D.C.: Smithsonian Institution.

Stuart, Gene S. 1985. *The Mighty Aztecs*. Washington, D.C.: National Geographic Society.

Sullivan, William 1979. "Quechua Star Names." Dissertation submitted for the degree of M. Litt., University of St. Andrews, Scotland.

——— 1988. *The Astronomy of Andean Mythology: The History of a Cosmology*. Doctoral dissertation, University of St. Andrews, Scotland. Ann Arbor: UMI.

——— 1992. "Andean Gods as Planets." In *Ancient Thoughts, Ancient Images: The Archaeology of Ideology Proceedings of the 23rd Annual Chacmool Conference*. Calgary, Alberta: Archaeological Association of Calgary.

Swanton, John 1946. *The Indians of the Southeastern United States*. Smithsonian Institution, Bureau of American Ethnology, Bulletin 137. Washington D.C.: Smithsonian Institution.

Tello, Julius 1923. "Wira Kocha." *Inca: Revista Trimestral de Estudios Antropológicos Organo de Arqueología de la Universidad Mayor de San Marcos*, vol. 1. Lima.

Tilak, Bal Gangadhar 1903. *The Arctic Home in the Vedas*.

Topic, John R. 1991. "Huari and Huamachuco." In *Huari Administrative Structure: Prehistoric Monumental Architecture and State Government*, edited by William H. Isbell and Gordon F. McEwan, 141–64. Washington, D.C.: Dumbarton Oaks Research Library and Collection.

Topic, Theresa L. 1991. "The Middle Horizon in Northern Peru." In *Huari Administrative Structure: Prehistoric Monumental Architecture and State Government*, edited by William H. Isbell and Gordon F. McEwan, 233–46. Washington, D.C.: Dumbarton Oaks Research Library and Collection.

Tschopik, Harry Jr. 1946. "The Aymara." In *Handbook of South American Indians*, edited by Julian Steward, vol. 2, 501–73. Bureau of American Ethnology, Bulletin 143. Washington, D.C.: Smithsonian Institution.

Tschudi, J. J. von 1853. *Die Kechua-Sprache*. Vienna: Kaiserlich-Koniglichen Hof- und Staatdruckerei.

——— 1918. *Contribuciones a la Historia, Civilización y Lingüística del Perú Antiguo*, vol. 2. Translated by German Torres Calderon. Colleción de Libros y Documentos Referentes a la Historia del Perú, vol. 10, edited by Horacio H. Urteaga. Lima: Imprenta y Librería Sanmarti y Ca.

Tuckerman, Bryant 1964. *Planetary, Lunar, and Solar Positions A.D. 2 to A.D. 1649 at Five-Day and Ten-Day Intervals*. Philadelphia: The American Philosophical Society.

Turner, Terrence 1988. "Ethno-ethnohistory: Myth and History in Native South American Representations of Contact with Western Society." In *Rethinking History and Myth: Indigenous South American Perspectives in the Past*, edited by Jonathan D. Hill, 235–81. Urbana: University of Illinois Press.

Urton, Gary 1978a. "Orientation in Quechua and Incaic Astronomy." *Ethnology* 17, no. 2, 157–67.

——— 1978b. "Beasts and Geometry: Some Constellations of the Peruvian Quechuas." *Anthropos* 73, 32–40.

——— 1979. "The Astronomical System of a Community in the Peruvian Andes." Ph.D. dissertation, University of Illinois, Urbana-Champaign.

——— 1980. "Celestial Crosses: The Cruciform in Quechua Astronomy." *Journal of Latin American Lore* 6, no. 1, 87–110.

——— 1981a. *At the Crossroads of Earth and Sky*. Austin: University of Texas Press.

——— 1981b. "Animals and Astronomy in the Quechua Universe." *Proceedings of the American Philosophical Society* 125, no. 2, 110–27.

——— 1990. *The History of a Myth: Pacariqtambo and the Origins of the Incas*. Austin: University of Texas Press.

Valcárcel, Luis E. 1933. "Esculturas de Pikillajta." In *Revista del Museo Nacional* (Lima) 2, no. 2, 19–48.

——— 1945. "El Diluvio." *El Aillu: Revista de Antropología, Etnología, Folklor, Linguistica, Historia* 1, no. 1, 13–14.

——— 1959. "Simbolos mágicos religiosos en la cultura andina." *Revista del Museo Nacional* (Lima), vol. 27, 3–18.

Velikovsky, Immanuel 1973. *Worlds in Collision*. New York: Dell.

Waters, Frank 1976. *The Book of the Hopi*. New York: Ballantine.

Wertime, Richard A., and Angela M. H. Schuster 1993. "Written in the Stars: Celestial Origin of the Maya Creation Myth." *Archaeology* 46, no. 4 (July/August 1993), 26–32.

White, Raymond E. Jr. 1985. "Recent Results in the Archaeoastronomy of the Citadel at Macchu

Picchu." *Newsletter of the Astronomical Society of New York* 2, no. 8, 5–17.

Wilhelm, Richard, tr. 1976. *The I Ching.* Princeton: Princeton University Press/Bollingen Series 19.

Willey, Gordon R. 1971. *An Introduction to American Archaeology,* vol. 2 (South America). Englewood Cliffs, N.J.: Prentice-Hall.

Williamson, Ray A. 1984. *Living the Sky.* Boston: Houghton Mifflin.

Wolf, Eric 1959. *Sons of the Shaking Earth.* Chicago: University of Chicago Press.

Zuidema, R. Tom 1964. *The Ceque System of Cuzco.* Leiden: E. J. Brill.

——— 1966. "El calendario inca." *Congreso Internacional de Americanistas, Actas y Memorias* 2, 24–30 (Seville).

——— 1967. "El juego de los ayllus y el amaru." *Journal de la Société des Américanistes* 56, 41–51.

——— 1973a. "La quadrature du cercle dans l'ancien perou." *Signes y Langages des Ameriques: Recherches Amerindiennes au Quebec* 3(1,2), 147–65.

——— 1973b. "The Origin of the Inca Empire." *Receuils de la Société Jean Bodin pour L'histoire Comparative des Institutions, no. 31: Les Grand Empires,* 733–57. Brussels: Ed. de la Libraire Encyclopedique.

——— 1973c. "Kinship and Ancestorcult in Three Peruvian Communities. Hernández Príncipe's Account of 1622." *Bulletin de l'Institut Francais d'Etudes Andines* 2, no. 1, 16–33.

——— 1976. "La imagen del Sol y la huaca Susurpuquio en el sistema astronómica de los Incas en el Cuzco." *Journal de la Société des Americanistes* (Paris) 63, 199–230.

——— 1979. "The Inca Calendar." In *Native American Astronomy,* edited by Anthony F. Aveni, 219–59. Austin: University of Texas Press.

——— 1983. "Llama sacrifices and computation: the roots of the Inca calendar in Huari-Tiahuanaco culture." *Acts of the Congress on Ethnoastronomy.* Washington, D.C. (in press).

Zuidema, R. Tom, and U. Quispe 1973. "A Visit to God: The Account and Interpretation of a Religious Experience in the Peruvian Community of Choque-Huarcaya." In *People and Cultures of Native South America,* edited by Daniel K. Gross, 358–74. Garden City, N.Y.: Natural History Press.

Zuidema, R. Tom, and Gary Urton 1976. "La constelación de la Llama en los Andes peruanos." *Allpanchis Phuturinqa* 9, 59–119.

INDEX